# It's Not Over

## Learning From the Socialist Experiment

# It's Not Over

## Learning From the Socialist Experiment

Pete Dolack

Winchester, UK
Washington, USA

First published by Zero Books, 2016
Zero Books is an imprint of John Hunt Publishing Ltd., Laurel House, Station Approach,
Alresford, Hants, SO24 9JH, UK
office1@jhpbooks.net
www.johnhuntpublishing.com
www.zero-books.net

For distributor details and how to order please visit the 'Ordering' section on our website.



ISBN: 978 1 78535 049 8
Library of Congress Control Number: 2015935817



A CIP catalogue record for this book is available from the British Library.

Design: Stuart Davies

Printed and bound in the USA by Edwards Brothers Malloy

# CONTENTS

For Fran, with whom I have been fortunate to share a decade's worth of adventure and struggle

# Preface

This is a book about the future in which the first five of the six chapters are about the past. As enriching as studying history for its own sake can be, the book in your hands proposes to study history for the purpose of drawing lessons that can be applied not only to an understanding of today's world but toward finding a path to a better world tomorrow.

An understanding of today and finding a path to the future is impossible without an understanding of the past: Erasing the past is erasing the future.

The history presented in this book is a study of some of the attempts to create societies organized on a basis other than capitalism. Although other alternatives will be examined, the focus of attention must be given to the Soviet Union, the most powerful challenger to capitalism during the twentieth century. The Soviet Union did not prove to be an enduring alternative, and although such a system will not be replicated in the future that does not mean there is nothing to learn from a study of it.

Two decades have passed since the crumbling of the Soviet bloc—surely enough time has passed to allow a sober study, based on the historical record, of the twentieth century's socialist experiments. That history has been distorted by a feverish ideological campaign that has slackened only minimally since the Berlin Wall fell and capitalism was restored in the Soviet Union.

Shrill denunciations of "evil" will not provide us with an understanding of this history, and readers who expect yet another book of mockery and/or one-sided indictments can already find all the material they could want. Enough forests have been felled in the service of those agendas. But nor can we be satisfied with the no less unreflective idea that everything would have been fine but for the CIA, or MI6, destroying it. Even if it were true that Western interference had brought down the Soviet Union, we would still be confronted with asking what were the weaknesses that put it in such a state that it could be destroyed from outside. There is no way to avoid an unsparing look at the Soviet system—one that examines its foundation, its historical trajectory and its final years. And because it is more useful to examine multiple examples with disparate starting points, rather than a single example, similar examinations of the internal workings of Czechoslovakia and Nicaragua will be presented.

Nonetheless, we should not go so far as to suggest that there is no connection between the capitalist world and the world that called itself socialist. The larger capitalist countries had a profound effect on those countries attempting socialist experiments: Capitalist hands did try to strangle many a socialist baby in the crib, attempts at destruction that can't be disentangled from the complex of factors that deformed more than one revolution. The economic and cultural backwardness that Russia inherited from the Romanov dictatorship and Nicaragua inherited from the Somoza dictatorship would have been difficult enough to overcome without outside interference.

Socialism, in all its forms, is a direct response to the problems of capitalism. Any study of the 20th century's experiments in supplanting capitalism is inextricably intertwined with the continual interrelationship among capitalist states, anti-capitalist movements and post-capitalist states. Inevitably, then, this is also a book about capitalism.

Separate, but at the same time connected, sets of psychological explanations have been invoked to explain the different outcomes of capitalist systems and systems that called themselves socialist. Perhaps the most frequently invoked is that of acquisitiveness. Simply put, an ideological underpinning of capitalism is that money and profit are the dominant, perhaps only, source of human motivation. But such an assertion, once we examine it a bit, is simply absurd: Does anyone expect a profit from having children? Humanity regularly does so nonetheless. Men, women and young people volunteer for unpaid work of all kinds, without which no society could function. Social volunteers give valuable time in countless ways, and nothing would change without the efforts of political activists, who generally also work without pay. Human beings possess a range of characteristics; although these characteristics are distributed quite unevenly, solidarity and cooperation are at least as much natural instincts as competition. Humanity wouldn't exist today without cooperation, the basis of the hunter-gatherer stage that is by far the longest segment of human history; nor would modern-day production be possible without workplace cooperation.

On balance, it is perhaps not going out on a limb to suggest that feelings of having a place in society, of believing you have a place in a state that works for your community, lead to greater social participation. Extremely rare is the state that does not claim to exist for all its citizens, but no state in practice has yet achieved that—all states have been governed on behalf of one or another social group. The creation of a state that would be a state of all citizens was a central goal of the revolutions studied in this book. An abstraction such as the "state" contains no inherent goodness or badness; it cannot be intrinsically sublime or evil. What type of states exist, the purpose for which states exist, who controls states, who is able to wield decisive influence in states and what reforms are or are not possible in states are fundamental questions that underlie any serious exploration of social, economic and political organization.

The set of questions in the preceding paragraph are central to the history studied in this book. A history that was shaped by flesh-and-blood human beings—leaders of movements and uncounted men and women in the streets and in the workplaces motivated by a desire to create a better world. That the results of uprisings as diverse as the October Revolution, the Prague

Spring and the Sandinista Revolution did not meet the revolutionaries' expectations is a tragedy that requires explanation, but does not require us to deem those revolutionaries as failures.

This book's study of socialist experiments will focus on the men and women who made these revolutions by analyzing their words and actions—why they acted the way they did, under what theories, guided by the speeches and writings they made at the time and in reflection later. Not simply the revolutions themselves, but the conditions that created those revolutions and the concrete results of those revolutions under the impact of internal and external pressures. These results cannot be limited to the decisions made by those thrust into leading political positions nor the personal fates of those leaders, but must include the everyday experiences of the millions of people who put new revolutionary ideas into practice and simultaneously were buffeted by the enormous internal and external forces acting upon them.

Such a study naturally has a focus on the experience of the Soviet Union, the full history of which must be understood before the question of why it collapsed so dramatically can be answered. Nonetheless, it might seem odd to begin this study in 1871, with the Paris Commune in France. The study begins there because the Paris Commune was the first, albeit short-lived, attempt at constructing a socialist society. The bloody suppression of the Commune profoundly affected the development of Marxist theory for decades afterward, not excepting the movement's strongest branch before World War I, the Social Democratic Party of Germany. The failure of the revolution in Germany helped seal the fate of the October Revolution. The formative years of the Soviet Union cannot be understood outside an international context.

The first chapter of this book will examine the growth of the Marxist movements of Germany and Russia, the different fates of the revolutions of the two countries, the connections between the two revolutions, and the potential for revolutions across Europe as empires and régimes collapsed at the end of World War I. Russians staked their revolution on the success of revolutions across Europe, and the absence of successful revolutions left the October Revolution isolated—an isolation with enormous consequences and all the more devastating due to Russia's backwardness.

The second chapter examines the socio-economic forces that shaped the gradual rise to absolute power of Josef Stalin during the 1920s and the consolidation of his dictatorship in the 1930s. There was nothing preordained about the Stalin dictatorship—nor was its creation a simple process. A myriad of internal and external social forces helped to push the Soviet Union along the path to centralization, compounded by the hasty improvisations made in the face of continual crises. Successive internal oppositions realized a little too late on what path the revolution was traveling, but found themselves hamstrung by the rules that they had used to defeat previous oppositions.

For the sake of comparison, the third and fourth chapters examine two very different attempts at forging a post-capitalist society. One of these two attempts took place in Czechoslovakia, one of the world's most industrialized countries in 1968, when the inappropriate Soviet-style system imposed on it had led to a political, economic and cultural crisis. History has concentrated on the tragedy of the political leaders, but much of the innovation of Prague Spring came at the grassroots level, where self-organized workers began to devise the beginnings of a system of social control over industry free of bureaucratic shackles. Grassroots creativity propelled forward a Spring begun by leaders of a monopoly party who believed that the full democratic and human potential of socialism had to be allowed to blossom, requiring dramatic changes.

The second of this comparative pair took place in an agricultural country, Nicaragua. The Sandinista Revolution's goal was a mixed economy, not the creation of a socialist system, but although that mixed economy created a new set of problems it also improved the lives of Nicaraguans. Previously blocked from any meaningful participation in society, Nicaraguans began making decisions affecting their lives—a "vanguard" party introduced representative democracy along with experiments in direct democracy. Years of armed attacks severely damaged Nicaragua, but the instabilities resulting from a mixed economy, including an increasing dynamic of providing subsidies to its capitalists, were not without effect. The Sandinistas left economic power in the hands of the country's capitalists, leaving them with the ability to undermine the revolution.

Neither of these experiments could survive heavy external pressures—the Prague Spring was ultimately crushed by the Soviet Union and the Sandinista Revolution was crushed by the United States.

In a very real sense, the preceding four chapters are a prelude to the central question: Why did the Soviet Union collapse? That collapse, unimaginable before the country's final year of existence, is examined in the fifth chapter. The reasons can be found entirely within its borders—the attempts of anti-communists in the United States to take credit for the collapse are not quite at the level of the rooster taking credit for the sunrise, but very little more. Military competition from the United States, and US covert actions, certainly were present, but nonetheless internal factors and actions brought down Soviet communism. The mounting problems of the Soviet Union were not unnoticed within its borders—academic institutions published reports detailing the bottlenecks built into the system and reform plans were drawn up within the government, but mostly were ignored.

The edifice of the Soviet Union was something akin to a statue undermined by water freezing inside it; it appears strong on the outside until the tipping point when the ice suddenly breaks it apart from within. The "ice" here were black marketeers;

networks of people who used connections to obtain supplies for official and illegal operations; and the managers of enterprises who grabbed their operations for themselves. Soviet bureaucrats eventually began to privatize the economy for their own benefit (fulfilling a prediction made by Leon Trotsky half a century earlier); party officials, for all their desire to find a way out of the crisis, lacked firm ideas and direction; and Soviet working people, discouraged by experiencing the reforms as coming at their expense and exhausted by perpetual struggle, were unable to intervene.

Six years of reform with meager positive results in essence caused Mikhail Gorbachev to throw in the towel and begin to introduce elements of capitalism. Gorbachev intended neither to institute capitalism nor bring down the Soviet system, but by introducing those elements of capitalism, the dense network of ties that had bound it together unraveled, hastening the end.

The sixth and final chapter looks to the future, with the benefit of the history just described. There will be no attempt at designing a blueprint, for such a thing cannot exist—different nations will find different paths forward and it is impossible to apply any formula across multiple societies at differing levels of development and possessing divergent cultural traditions.

The reader will not find any definitive answers to the question of what a better, more just, society will look like—merely preliminary sketches and ideas that, it is hoped, will stimulate further discussion and theoretical development. What we can be certain about is that democracy has to mean much more than a narrow political concept; without democracy in the economy for those whose work fuels that economy there can't be a true democratic society, if by that term we mean a society in which all citizens have a real say in how it is run and that it is run for the benefit of everybody, not simply a few who massively benefit from their positions at the highest levels of giant corporate and financial institutions. Dramatic times should inspire dramatic ideas, so in that spirit this book will propose something that should be classified as common sense but instead is a radical concept: Those who do the work should earn the rewards.

The repeated crises of capitalism provide us with an urgency to tackle these enormous problems, problems we ignore at our collective peril. The ongoing global economic crisis has caused people around the world to ask if capitalism is reaching its end. As these words are written, it is impossible to know—and even if the terminal crisis of capitalism truly has begun, the disintegration will take decades to unfold. A far more common belief is that capitalism is forever: As others have written, it is easier to imagine the end of the world than the end of capitalism. Hollywood reinforces this inculcated triumphalist mindset with a steady diet of movies depicting apocalyptic end times in which small numbers of people grimly struggle in wars of all against all—the end of the world, indeed. Moreover, such media images subtly reinforce capitalism: Ruthless competition among all people is the only conceivable relationship and without the veneer of civilization imparted by capitalist institutions, we'd quickly descend into barbarism, literally instead of figuratively killing to survive. So the institutions of the capitalist world tell us in endless ways.

There is no need to suffer from a dearth of imagination. Thinking about the basic contours of a better world is a prerequisite to becoming effective in bringing about a better world. The march forward of human history is not a gift from gods above nor presents handed us from benevolent rulers, governments, institutions or markets; it is the product of collective human struggle on the ground. Humanity does not have to suffer from stagnation or collapse. We can do better. But not by mere wishful thinking. "If there is no struggle, there is no progress," Frederick Douglass wrote in words as true today as when he wrote them. "Power concedes nothing without a demand. It never did and never will."

There are concrete reasons for why Soviet-style societies have ceased to exist. They are failures in the basic, non-judgmental sense that they no longer exist. But failure simply means the time has come to try again, with something better.

# Acknowledgments

No author of a non-fiction work truly works completely alone, no matter how many nights spent in solitude writing, editing, revising or researching. Feedback and criticism for a work in progress is essential, and in my case I have been fortunate to have several generous colleagues read over various parts of this book. The resulting suggestions have made this a stronger work, although the responsibility for the final contents, including any mistakes, remains with myself.

In particular, thanks must go to Fran Luck, Paul Gilman and John Moran for detailed comments, suggestions and markups. Each took considerable time out of busy schedules to give me sometimes strong critiques—challenging critiques that were needed. Fran, my partner, countless times discussed with me the contents as they took shape, sharpening my thinking and making this a better work. Madeleine Artenberg, Tom Coughlin, Robert Gold, Jean Lehrman, Brant Lyon, Joel Meyers and Julie Weiner each kindly read parts of the work in early drafts and/or offered useful feedback. Thanks also to Immanuel Ness, whose invaluable advice and unflagging optimism helped me get this book to publication. A tip of the hat is also owed to many dedicated activists in New York City and elsewhere with whom I have debated, discussed and analyzed the issues presented in this book, and a myriad of others, during my own years of activism.

Finally, it is only proper to acknowledge the work of dozens of historians, social scientists and activist-writers on whom I have leaned—as even a glance at the footnotes can attest. I have sometimes drawn very different conclusions than the original author whose work I studied; that is the inevitable result of studying books and journal articles with widely diverging perspectives. But this book would not have been possible without the research of those scholars.

# Notes on Style

Maintaining a consistent style throughout a work such as the book in your hands is a difficult task, all the more so because of the shifting contexts that materialize in a complex work. Nonetheless, some consistencies in usage need to be imposed.

One potential source of confusion is the two different primary usages of "right," "center" and "left" in political contexts. To minimize confusion, these three words are capitalized when used to describe positions on the overall political spectrum but are lower-cased when used to describe relative positions within a party or movement. Therefore, the Bolsheviks are a Left party, but the Bolsheviks can have left and right wings: A right Bolshevik is not as radical as other Bolsheviks, but is nonetheless on the Left in comparison to members of other parties.

Another word that requires clarity is "liberal," which means one thing in North America and something different in the rest of the world. Throughout this book, "liberal" is used in its more widely used global meaning—a political term denoting a belief in complete freedom of trade, in minimal government involvement in the economy or social affairs, and in allowing the "market" to determine economic and social outcomes. In North America, such a philosophy is known as "libertarianism." In the nineteenth century, liberalism became a potent political force in concert with the rise of capitalism; continuity with the word's original meaning is the reason why extreme programs in favor of unregulated markets and against social safety nets are known as "neoliberalism" around the world. (In contrast, in the United States, where such a philosophy is inevitably intertwined with militarism and an expansionist foreign policy, it has come to be termed "neoconservatism.")

There is no universally accepted term to describe the guiding ideology of the mature Soviet Union; in the interest of using one reference word, "Soviet orthodoxy" will be used in this context in this book. The term "Stalinism" is often employed as an indiscriminate pejorative and therefore is avoided, except when needed as a reference to the specific characteristics of the Stalin dictatorship. The use of "post-capitalist" rather than "socialist" as a description of the overall systems under study reflects that these were attempts to go beyond capitalism but were not socialist in the strict meaning of that term.

Then there is the matter of transliterations from the Russian. Generally, transliterations in this book are literal equivalents of Russian Cyrillic spellings with a couple of deviations for the sake of clarity. Exceptions are made in the cases of famous people whose names are widely familiar; thus, for example, Leon Trotsky instead of Lev Trotskii. In the case of pre-1918 dates in Russia, when Russia was almost the last country to still use the Julian calendar, then 13 days behind the modern Gregorian calendar, the Gregorian dates are used throughout this work rather than the Julian dates. The Bolsheviks switched calendars soon after the October Revolution, which is why anniversaries of the October Revolution are observed in early November (and why it takes place in November in this book).

Finally, the use of the word "billions" in the text is the North American usage, meaning one thousand million.

## Chapter 1

# Foundation for Isolation: The Revolutionary Period of 1917–21

As 1917 began, the Bolshevik Party of Russia was a small, hounded group with much of its leadership in foreign exile and others banished to remote Siberian villages, cut off from all legal political activity; a party little known outside of Socialist circles and the tsar's ubiquitous secret police. The Social Democratic Party of Germany was the most powerful political group of working people in the world, boasting an organization with its own social institutions, dozens of newspapers, thousands of paid officials and the largest following of any German party despite property restrictions on voting.

Yet it was the Bolsheviks who, before the year was out, carried out a revolution while the German Social Democrats not only failed to bring about the revolution that was central to its program, but its leadership actually suppressed its rank-and-file who believed in their party's program. Revolutions failed or didn't happen across Europe, leaving Russia isolated. Fourteen countries invaded Russia, seeking to crush the October Revolution, and provided material support for the White armies led by the tsar's military officers in a civil war fought without mercy. With the country's industry and infrastructure already in ruins under the impact of World War I, the Civil War further aggravated an already desperate situation.

The October Revolution shouldn't have survived.

### Arc of a movement: Fervent militancy to quiet accommodation

In so many ways, it is difficult for us today to imagine the world of the mid-nineteenth century. Similarly, the men and women who lived when socialist, syndicalist and anarchist movements began to attract millions of followers would find present-day technological advances and the radically changed zeitgeist dizzily disorienting. Yet the economic organization of today would be familiar to them. Friedrich Engels wrote these words about the United States in 1891:

> [E]ach of the two great parties which alternately succeed each other in power is itself controlled by people who make a business of politics, who speculate on seats in the legislative assemblies of the Union as well as of the separate states…[N]evertheless we find here two great gangs of political speculators, who alternately take possession of the state power and exploit it by the most corrupt means and for the most corrupt ends.[1]

The world those millions lived in would seem cruel to today's eyes, but that is not solely the product of evolving social standards—it also due to the fact that the violence used to maintain the privileges of the powerful was then more undisguised than it is today. Seeking to create a better world, some among those millions organized the first experiment in socialist government, the Paris Commune, and, true to their times, there was no ambiguity in the violence that put an end to it.

Russian Bolsheviks and German Social Democrats were both profoundly influenced by the Paris Commune. Although occurring a generation before the October Revolution, in 1871, the cynical and manipulative use of nationalism on the part of German and French social elites, the naked and swift dumping of nationalism when the class interests of social elites in both countries required they unite against the rest of the French nation, and the drowning of the Commune in blood as an exemplary punishment for challenging the elites left a vivid impression on the international social democratic movement.

("Social democratic" was the label, before World War I, for those who believed that working people would one day collectively overthrow capitalism and establish a class-free society. The term "Marxist" did not begin to come into usage until after Marx's death, and until the outbreak of World War I most Marxist parties included "social democratic" or "socialist" in their names.) Popular anger against the Russian elites' inability to govern effectively, as well as their cruelty, created the conditions for Russia's 1917 revolutions, and a similar dynamic had prevailed in Paris a generation earlier.

The chain of events that caused tens of thousands to die in the Franco-Prussian War and culminated in the Paris Commune began with the writing of a brief letter. A letter that was selectively edited before its publication with the express purpose of provoking war. The extraordinarily powerful, and reactionary, Prussian chancellor, Otto von Bismarck, was the editor of the letter written in July 1870 by the king of Prussia, Wilhelm I.

Prussia had steadily expanded by absorbing smaller German states, and neighboring countries' disquiet over Prussia's growing strength was inflamed when the Spanish parliament invited a Prussian prince to become Spain's king. France, fearful of a close alliance between countries on its opposing borders, was particularly displeased. Believing that yielding to French protests would be a prudent move diplomatically, Wilhelm ordered the prince (his nephew) to decline the Spanish offer, but the French ambassador to Prussia followed up by requesting that Wilhelm promise that no member of his dynasty would ever be allowed to sit on the Spanish throne.

Wilhelm refused to make such a promise, and authorized Bismarck, who as chancellor oversaw Wilhelm's government, to make public his written account of the discussion. Bismarck saw the public release of the king's letter as an opportunity to provoke a war between Prussia and France—a war, Bismarck believed, that would spark the unification of the remaining independent German states under Prussian hegemony through the example of a pan-German lightning military victory that would stimulate popular feelings of German nationalism.[2]

Bismarck selectively edited the letter to make it appear that the king had rudely insulted the French and that the French ambassador had made an arrogant demand. For added effect, Bismarck released his edited version the day before Bastille Day, the French national holiday. The chancellor told two of his generals that the letter would provide a "red rag to taunt the Gallic Bull": He needed France to initiate hostilities so that Prussia's alliances with the other German states would be triggered.[3] France did indeed declare war—not for the first or last time had nationalism been used to goad a population into willingly waging war.

Not all were quick to leap, however. As war fever heated, French members of the International Workingmen's Association—a federation of working-class organizations and individuals to which followers of Karl Marx, other socialists and the leaders of various anarchist movements belonged—issued the following statement: "German Brothers! In the name of peace refuse to listen to the hired or servile voices of those who are trying to deceive you concerning the true mind of France. Be deaf to mad provocations, for war between us would be fratricidal…A quarrel between us can only lead, on both sides of the Rhine [River], to the complete triumph of despotism."[4]

The German members of the International responded in similar fashion: "Inspired with fraternal sentiments, we join hands with you…[W]e assure you that there is no trace of national hatred in our hearts, but that we are under the thralldom of force, and that only through compulsion shall we form part of the fighting forces which are about to spread wretchedness and disaster over the peaceful fields of our countries."[5]

These voices were too few in number to have any effect. Although it was the French king, Napoleon III, who declared war, it was Prussia that was far better prepared; its superiority in weaponry, tactics and mobilization quickly led to a rout of France. Napoleon III had wanted a war against Prussia to maintain the image of France as a great power. Leading his army on the battlefield, he ended his adventure by surrendering—ultimately, 375,000 French soldiers were taken prisoner—and abdicating his crown.

The republican opposition to Napoleon III assumed power, forming a "Government of National Defense." Prussia, having crushed the French army, now began a siege of Paris, sealing the city from outside supplies and bombarding it. The people of Paris had already endured mass poverty under Napoleon III and now bore the brunt of the Prussian siege, reduced to eating cats, dogs and rats to survive. Parisians also swelled the ranks of the National Guard, boosting the militia's size to 350,000 and changing its social composition through election of its officers.[6]

The new Government of National Defense proved inept and twice narrowly survived attempts to overthrow it by the people of Paris, actions sparked by rumors that it was about to surrender Paris to the Prussians. Those rumors became reality—after the second overthrow attempt, the Government of National Defense did begin secretly negotiating a surrender. The government's vice president snuck out of Paris, crossing enemy lines to talk with the Prussians because he believed "civil war only a few yards away, famine a few hours."[7]

The Prussian terms of surrender were draconian, but readily agreed to. One of these terms required the Government of National Defense to call a national election to ratify the surrender within eight days. An election was held despite the impossibility of such a vote being organized fairly; the election for a National Assembly returned a substantial majority of reactionary monarchists from the countryside because communications from inside Paris were blocked by the Prussian occupation and throughout the country there was insufficient time for anyone but the aristocracy and priests to organize for the election. The regular French army was to be disarmed, but received permission from the Prussian occupiers to enter Paris to disarm the National Guard, the popular militia that had held off the Prussians for five months and was in no mood to surrender.

On 18 March 1871, the regular French army was sent to confiscate the National Guard's cannons, but when the first cannon was to be taken, Parisian women surrounded it. "This is shameful; what are you doing here?" they demanded,[8] holding firm. Inspired, the National Guard refused to surrender its cannons. The regular army soldiers refused to obey their officers' commands, defecting to the defenders of Paris. Faced with the soldiers' fraternizations with Parisians, army officers fled or were arrested. The Government of National Defense, headed by Adolphe Thiers (who had given the order to disarm the National Guard), fled Paris.

An arch-opportunist, Thiers had helped crush popular rebellions against the monarchy in the 1830s and 1840s, and in 1870 he had agitated for war against Prussia before switching to opposing the war once it became apparent that France would lose. Such maneuvering enabled Thiers to be elected president by the newly elected National Assembly. Ultimately, much of Thiers' maneuvering throughout his long career was on behalf of France's capitalists despite the sometimes populist-sounding statements he made during his periods out of office. Thiers was summed up succinctly by Charles Beslay, an engineer who once was the proprietor of a machine foundry and a former parliamentary colleague of Thiers who was elected to the Paris Commune: "The enslavement of labor by capital has always been the cornerstone of your policy, and from the very day you saw the Republic of Labor installed at [Paris City Hall], you have never ceased to cry out to France: 'These are criminals!'"[9]

Following Thiers' flight from Paris, the city was briefly governed by the elected central committee of the National Guard, until, on 26 March, the citizens of Paris elected a municipal council—the Commune—as the new government. This was the first election in French history with universal male suffrage; despite the initiative of the revolutionary women who were the first to resist confiscation of the National Guard cannons, the vote was not given to them. The Paris Commune enacted several progressive laws—banning exploitative night work for bakers, suspending the collection of debts incurred during the siege, separating church from state, providing free education for all children, handing over abandoned workshops to cooperatives of workers who would restart production, and abolishing conscription into the army. Commune officials were subject to instant recall by voters and were paid the average wage of a worker (an example that would one day be emulated by the organizers of Russia's soviets).

The elected communards represented a mix of occupations and ages: Workmen were a minority while professionals, journalists and others from the middle class were larger in number.[10] The significant turnout for the Commune elections and the fact that a crowd of 200,000 people turned out to watch the peaceful handover of power did not prevent Thiers from menacingly responding in this fashion: "No, France will not let wretches triumph who would drown her in blood."[11]

Blood was on the mind of Thiers and his government. France's capitalists, now amply represented by the monarchists who dominated the National Assembly, had whipped up nationalism to compel the working people of France to fight against Prussia. They now turned to the very same Prussia for help in crushing those same working people.

By early April, Thiers had secured the release of French prisoners of war held by Prussia to rebuild his army and began his own siege of Paris, complete with bombardments—the very acts for which the French leaders had, weeks earlier, condemned the Prussian army. Prussian commanders also allowed the reconstituted French army to pass through their areas of control, despite that being forbidden under the terms of surrender. After weeks of attacks, French soldiers entered the city on 21 May, taking eight days to gain control and crush the Commune, drowning in blood the popular experiment in self-government. Simultaneous attempts to create communes in cities across France were also defeated.

What mistakes had the Commune made that contributed to its demise? These mistakes were both tactical and a result of simple human kindness, and flowed out of a lack of political organization. The buildup of authority in the National Guard and the subsequent Commune was spontaneous, and what political ideas the Communards had generally flowed from two anarchist tendencies. A majority, influenced by Louie-Auguste Blanqui, who believed that a small group of conspirators could stage an insurrection to change society, sought to make a radical leap without having any concrete political or economic program; others were influenced by Pierre-Joseph Proudhon, who believed that society could be changed through organizing workplace cooperatives while "ignoring" the state.[12]

The concrete result of those ideologies was a failure to disperse the French army and government as they left Paris in late March, allowing them to regroup freely at Versailles; failing to seize the gold still held in the central bank vaults in Paris, which would have cut off all funds to Thiers and his Versailles government; failing to prepare a military defense or to attack Versailles before Thiers' forces could regroup; and failing to organize a proper defense of the city, under the assumption that the Prussians would not allow the French army to pass.[13] A National Guard commander freed captured French army officers in a spirit of "comradeship," to the point where a top army commander was let go in exchange for a promise that the commander would henceforth be neutral—a promise that was swiftly broken.[14]

The Communards' magnanimity was repaid with a horrific bloodbath. An estimated 30,000 Parisians were massacred by the marauding French army in one week,[15] executed on sight in the streets or after 30-second "trials." Another 40,000 were held in prisons, and many of these were exiled to a remote South Pacific island where they became forced laborers on starvation diets, eventually barred from fishing in the sea or foraging for food,[16] and routinely subjected to torture.[17] The restored government exerted itself to deny any political or moral content to the Communards' actions, instead treating them as the worst common criminals as part of what developed into a de facto "social cleansing" of Paris; the French official overseeing the deportations, in his public statements, directly linked socialist politics with chronic petty crime.[18]

A leading newspaper of French capital, *Le Figaro*, echoed the restorationist desires of France's capitalists and aristocracy who were eager to reassert the upper hand, when it declared: "Never has such an opportunity presented itself for curing Paris of the moral gangrene that has been consuming it for the past 25 years."[19] The general who oversaw the massacre of Parisians had meekly surrendered to Prussia alongside Napoleon III. There was no mercy now, as gruesomely described in a contemporary account of one of the places of execution: "There were so many victims that the soldiers, tired out, were obliged to rest their guns actually against the sufferers. The wall of the terrace was covered with brains; the executioners waded through pools of blood."[20] This was not the first such lesson administered: The revolutions of 1848, popular uprisings that had swept Europe, had also ended in bloodbaths in France and elsewhere.

*The Communist Manifesto*, the pamphlet written by Karl Marx and Engels, was one of the products of those 1848 attempts at liberation. Writing a new preface for an 1872 German edition of the Manifesto, the two, summing up the Paris Commune, wrote: "One thing especially was proved by the Commune, that 'the working class cannot simply lay hold of the ready-made state machinery and wield it for their own purposes.'"[21] The people of France had been hit sufficiently hard that it would be years before significant social unrest would materialize there again, but the lessons of the Commune were taken note of elsewhere—during the next three decades, in no place more so than Germany. Bismarck's dream of a united Germany did come true as a result of Prussia's lightning victory against France; soon afterward the progressive organizations of the new country themselves united, forming the Social Democratic Party of Germany (SPD).

The new party did not shrink from distilling the lessons of the Commune into a political program. Bismarck, who became chancellor of the united Germany under Wilhelm I, soon banned the SPD, further inculcating among social democrats the belief that working people could not achieve liberation and freedom without an overthrow of the existing capitalist orders. Karl Kautsky, a talented writer still in his twenties but already an important voice in the SPD, laid out the case for a seizure of power in plain terms in 1881, a time when all socialist activities were banned in Germany:

"The Social Democratic workers' party has always emphasized that it is a revolutionary party in the sense that it recognizes that it is impossible to resolve the social question within the existing society," Kautsky wrote.

> Even today, *we would prefer*, if it were possible, to realize the social revolution *through the peaceful road*...But if we still harbor this hope today, we have nonetheless ceased to emphasize it, for every one of us knows *that it is a utopia*...Today we all know that the popular socialist state can be erected only through a violent overthrow and that it is our duty to uphold consciousness of this among ever broader layers of the people.[22]

The insurrection necessary to do away with the repressive capitalist state can be only a popular undertaking with widespread support, he said.

> No, the revolution cannot be the work of a party but must come from the people. No party can provoke it, and still less a secret sect. It must be the consequence of conditions which are necessarily born of the organization of the state and society...Revolutions always arise from the *mass* of the people...Our task is not to organize the revolution, but to organize ourselves *for* the revolution.[23]

Marxists believed that the growing inequalities, mass poverty, horrendous working conditions and bruisingly long work hours imposed by capitalism, leading to deeper crises, economic upheavals and recurrent wars of conquest, would create the conditions for widespread dissatisfaction leading to revolutionary uprisings; the organization of the economy into larger units of production and gigantic trusts would create the socialization necessary for working people to organize among themselves and would also create the material means to produce enough to satisfy the needs of the entire population.

Many within the Marxist movement came to believe that this process was unstoppable, and the repeated bloody crushings of popular attempts at easing repression throughout Europe and the banning of socialist activity in Germany and elsewhere reinforced the belief that true democracy—society being organized to benefit everyone instead of a minuscule privileged minority and providing the opportunity for everyone to participate in societal decision-making—is not possible under capitalism.

Germany had an additional barrier to popular participation in its backward institutions. The newly united Germany, born as a world power with imposing military might and rapidly developing modern industries, nonetheless did not have a modern political system. Although the German states, in particular Prussia, had industrialized rapidly from the mid-nineteenth century—and this trend accelerated after unification—the capitalist elite did not dominate politically. Rather, it was the landed aristocracy of Prussia who had the upper hand. This aristocracy, the "Junkers," owned vast plantations spanning tens of square kilometers on which the rural population at their mercy lived in feudal conditions. Bismarck and the officers of the Prussian (now German) army came from the Junkers and it was on their behalf that Bismarck ruled with his iron fist, although the unification of Germany, through eliminating borders that impeded trade, benefited capitalists.

In Prussia (which constituted more than half of the united Germany), voting was distorted by property restrictions that divided people into three categories, further concentrating power in the hands of Junkers and, to a lesser extent, capitalists and small property owners. That the capitalist class (the "bourgeoisie") had so failed to modernize German institutions gave working people an additional reason to believe it would be their historical task to take power and create a democratic state.

Under the impetus of all the above factors, the SPD grew rapidly despite Bismarck's anti-socialist laws, becoming the leading party of social democracy; Marxists across Europe looked to the SPD for leadership. Following Wilhelm I's death in 1888, his grandson, Wilhelm II, became German kaiser and two years later dismissed Bismarck. (Bismarck had possessed vast powers, but only at the pleasure of the kaiser. Germany, after all, was a monarchy and no chancellor under Wilhelm II would wield anywhere near the powers that Wilhelm I had ceded to Bismarck.)

The anti-socialist laws were repealed after Bismarck's removal, allowing SPD leaders to return from foreign exile and party bureaucrats to enjoy all the perks of holding seats in

Germany's parliament, the Reichstag. Wilhelm II's policies gave German capitalists more say in the running of the state (although the Reichstag remained an impotent body with little ability to affect the government) and an aggressive foreign policy bringing home booty from imperialism compensated the capitalists for having to share political power with the Junkers.

The relaxation of the internal political atmosphere, increasing vote totals for the SPD and steady growth in union membership led some party leaders to begin to think of growing their way into power, and a fear of a return of the anti-socialist laws led to the party shrinking from discussing in public the methodology of taking power, instead speaking of it in an abstract manner. The party was now groping toward an idea that the revolution would "come" all on its own. As early as 1891, longtime SPD leader August Bebel said to a party conference: "Bourgeois society is working so effectively towards its own downfall that we need merely wait for the moment to pick up the power dropping from its hands."[24]

From such seeds grew "revisionism"—the idea that the SPD would steadily increase its Reichstag vote total until it could simply assume power and implement a socialist government, and that the capitalists and Junkers would simply stand by and allow this to happen. Therefore, revisionists argued, struggle and revolution were no longer necessary to bring into being a better world. The seeds of this trend began to grow soon after the revocation of the anti-socialist laws as party leaders began to grow comfortable in their legislative seats and official posts.

Revisionism was given form as a theory by party veteran Eduard Bernstein. Among the founders of the SPD, Bernstein was close enough to Engels while in exile during the years of Bismarck's anti-socialist laws to be chosen as Engels' literary executor. But despite Engels' radicalizing influence on him while Engels was alive, Bernstein, a bank clerk turned journalist, was decisively influenced by English reformers during his years in

London. He gradually adopted the belief that Marx's formulations on the development of capitalism were erroneous, causing him to advocate revisions in the movement's tactics.

Taking note of the fact that the conditions of Germans at the end of the 1890s were better than they had been in the past, Bernstein drew the conclusion that "there can be no more doubt today than formerly of the hopefulness of the position of the worker."[25] Moreover, evolutionary improvements were preferable to revolutionary ones because legislation represented "intellect" as opposed to the "emotion" of revolution—"legislation works as a systematic force," Bernstein wrote.[26] But the pigeonholing of his schema grew not only out of the creation of an artificial unbreachable wall between legislative and revolutionary actions, but from a lack of confidence in his party's rank-and-file. "We cannot demand from a class, the great majority of whose members live under crowded conditions, are badly educated, and have an uncertain and insufficient income, the high intellectual and moral standard which the organization and existence of a socialist community presupposes," Bernstein wrote. "We will, therefore, not ascribe it to them by way of fiction."[27]

More than a little paternalism, and more than a small contradiction, is revealed here. If Bernstein's description of the poor state of the SPD rank-and-file were accepted, it would directly contradict the belief that they had enjoyed steady, significant improvements. The material conditions of Germans had improved in the years since unification, but the current poor conditions described by Bernstein would therefore represent such a slow pace of improvement that the date on which the SPD could assume the running of the state would recede far into the distant future. And that is the kernel that is revealed in Bernstein's infamous conclusion: "The final goal is nothing; the movement is everything." Bernstein, speaking on behalf of an increasing number of SPD officials, drew the conclusion that the

SPD could bring about a never-ending series of reforms that would gradually evolve into socialism, and that there would never be any reversals or attempts by Germany's rulers to take back the reforms.

Taking up the opposition to Bernstein's revisionism was a young revolutionary, new to the movement, named Rosa Luxemburg. She had escaped from the Russian-occupied portion of Poland at age 18, just ahead of an arrest that would have led to her banishment in Siberia. Fresh from obtaining a doctorate in Zürich, she arrived in Berlin determined to participate fully in the life of the SPD, and quickly gained a reputation as an outstanding orator and writer. Her contributions to the debate about revisionism would propel Luxemburg into the ranks of the leading social democratic theorists.

Luxemburg argued that trade union bargaining over wages and working conditions is necessary, but is ultimately a defensive measure that cannot lead to social change. Such negotiations do not touch the question of ownership and therefore are "not a threat to capitalist exploitation, but simply the regulation of this exploitation. When Bernstein asks if there is more or less of socialism in a labor protective law, we can assure him that, in the best of labor protective laws, there is no more 'socialism' than in a municipal ordinance regulating the cleaning of streets or the lighting of street lamps,"[28] Luxemburg wrote. "It is not true that socialism will arise automatically from the daily struggle of the working class. Socialism will be the consequence of (1) the growing contradictions of capitalist economy and (2) the comprehension by the working class of the unavoidability of the suppression of these contradictions through a social transformation."[29]

She argued that capitalist exploitation can't be legislated away through reforms because such exploitation is not codified in any law. "Poverty, the lack of [possessing] means of production" compels submission to the yoke of capitalism, and the "level of wages is not fixed by legislation, but by economic factors. The phenomenon of capitalist exploitation does not rest on a legal deposition, but on the purely economic fact that labor power plays...the role of merchandise possessing, among other characteristics, the agreeable quality of producing value—*more* than the value it consumes in the form of the laborer's means of subsistence,"[30] Luxemburg wrote. Capitalists' immense wealth derives from paying employees wages that are far less than the value of what their work creates, and only ending capitalism can end that exploitation—reforms cannot touch it. Bernstein, Luxemburg wrote, "began by abandoning the *final aim* and supposedly keeping the movement. But as there can be no socialist movement without a socialist aim, he ends by renouncing the *movement*."[31]

Three distinct currents of opinion developed within the SPD:

- A party right wing that backed revisionism and sought to adapt to the capitalist state and which implied backing German militarism.
- A self-described "Marxist center" that opposed revisionism in speeches and writings but whose actions increasingly aligned with the revisionists.
- A left wing that firmly believed that all evidence pointed to the necessity of revolution.

The SPD deputies from the right and center factions had also grown comfortable in legislative and party posts; and this careerism assisted the process of the party leadership seeing the attainment of socialism recede into the distant, hazy future.

The leadership of the trade unions proved to be another conservative influence. An outbreak of strikes across Germany and in Russia and Italy in 1905 heralded an upswing in militancy, leading to a debate on the use of general strikes for political purposes within the SPD. The party was divided on the question but the trade union leadership was uniformly opposed to general strikes. A major strike during this wave of militancy was a walkout by Ruhr miners, who were joined by workers in other industries. This strike ended in something of a tie—the Prussian authorities were afraid to use force against it, a development that demonstrated to the strikers the power of organized action, but the strikers went back to work after six weeks without winning any substantial concessions.[32] The lesson that the union leadership chose to take was that mass strikes were not effective, and therefore their use presented too great a risk to workers to use the tactic to press political demands.[33]

The trade union leadership, headed by Karl Legien, who would prove to be a consistent conservative brake on the social democratic movement, wanted union work to focus exclusively on narrow economic demands, and pressed the SPD to agree to this conception. The SPD and union leadership held a secret meeting at which the SPD capitulated to the demands of union leaders that no strikes would be called without the union apparatus' approval. The unions had a larger membership than the SPD and they could withhold their electoral support for the SPD if the party didn't knuckle under. At a subsequent party congress, Bebel declared that mass strikes were too risky and that without "the adherence of the leaders and members of the unions, the feasibility of a mass strike is unthinkable."[34] A recent trade union congress had put forth the slogan "The trade unions need peace and quiet above all!"[35] The leadership that produced such a slogan was now in a position to dictate to the SPD.

Despite those resolutions, a series of Sunday demonstrations broke out across Prussia during February and March 1910 to back demands for electoral reform at a time when 200,000 building workers achieved a victory after enduring a three-month lockout by their employers.[36] But the SPD bureaucracy seemed to become afraid of the militancy the rank-and-file were showing. In a dramatic show of strength, grassroots organizers at the last minute switched the site of a demonstration that had been banned by Berlin police, with the result that a hundred thousand appeared at the new site while the police were sealing off the previously announced location.[37]

This demonstration of what amounted to a disciplined show of force did not fail to attract attention, but a renewed discussion on the use of the mass strike as a tactic was discouraged, and both the central SPD newspaper, *Vorwärts*, and the party's leading theoretical organ, *Die Neue Zeit* (edited by Kautsky), refused to publish an article by Luxemburg that advocated mass strikes.[38] Kautsky, on behalf of the SPD center faction, joined the revisionists in arguing that the SPD's political activity should be concentrated in the Reichstag and state legislatures, and further mass actions should be discouraged.

Meanwhile, the threat of war was slowly growing more serious. The SPD continued to pass resolutions opposing war and continued to participate in Socialist International conferences in which the world's social democratic and labor parties vowed to coordinate with each other so as to do everything possible to prevent the outbreak of war. Yet the SPD's actions did not square with its stated vows. Bebel, the party leader, declared that he would personally take up arms in the event of war against Russia, a contrast to his party's official viewpoint of opposing all militarism. The anti-militarism platform, however, was becoming increasingly rickety. Reichstag elections in 1912 gave the SPD its biggest vote total yet, but in the second round of voting, the party leadership would not leverage its new strength, instead choosing to "tone down" its campaign in a compromise with a Centrist liberal party.[39] Militarism and imperialism had gained support in Germany, and the SPD leadership was accommodating itself to them.

The next year, the SPD crossed still another line when it voted for a massive arms buildup. The party's Reichstag delegation had always voted against the government budget as a matter of principle: "For this system, not one man nor one penny" had been one of its slogans. The prominent army leader Erich Ludendorff (who would become de facto military dictator of Germany during World War I) sought a massive increase in military arms. Although far short of constituting a majority, the SPD was now the largest single party in the Reichstag and would cast the deciding votes. The government told SPD officials that the arms buildup would be funded by a direct property tax, a tax that would be borne by the rich and therefore a significant step toward a progressive taxation system, which the party favored. This choice, however, was not so simple—the party could vote against the desired tax system because those taxes would be used for a purpose that it had opposed, or it could abandon opposition to militarism.

For the left wing of the party, this was no choice: "[T]he second choice is the greater evil for Social Democrats from any angle," Luxemburg told a party congress. Otherwise, "you put yourselves in a position when war breaks out and we can no longer stop it, where you will face the question of whether to cover military expenses through direct or indirect taxes, and you will find yourselves voting for war credits."[40] The SPD right wing, already openly backing German militarism, was in favor of voting yes. That the center faction had moved decisively toward the right was given confirmation by Kautsky, whose tortured logic was reduced to an oxymoron. He wrote that the party must wage a struggle against chauvinism developing among the masses because "in the epoch of general military service, no great war can be waged without chauvinist agitation," yet he denounced the left wing's "adventurism" and support for mass actions, fearing the strength of the ruling classes and the violence the ruling classes could potentially unleash against the people.[41]

It is true that potential violent reactions by the powerful must be taken into consideration when determining tactics, but how can chauvinism and militarism be combatted if there is no public effort to combat them? Kautsky's circular argument illustrated that the path the SPD was traveling was leading further away from its theoretical program. Luxemburg's prediction on war credits would become true less than a year later.

## Acceleration in retrograde: Social democracy marches off to war

When leaders of Europe's socialist parties gathered for an emergency conference in Brussels, days after the Austro-Hungarian Empire's ultimatum had been rejected by Serbia and with Russia already beginning to mobilize, they brought with them a mood of despair. Despite their years of vowing international solidarity in opposition to war, most of those gathered either wrung their hands or threw up their hands in defeat. The words of the leader of the Austrian Social Democrats, Viktor Adler, were particularly dispiriting. This was not only because of the content of what he had to say at this conference, but because he was one of the most important leaders in the movement and because a firm stand would be needed from his party due to Austria-Hungary's determination to start a war against much smaller Serbia in revenge for a Serbian nationalist's assassination of the heir to the Austrian throne—a war certain to engulf the entire continent because of treaty obligations.

"Up to now we have fought against war as well as we could," Adler said. "The workers also did their utmost against the war intrigues. But don't expect any further action from us. We are in a state of war. Our press is censored. We have a state of emergency and martial law as a backdrop. I did not come here to address a public meeting, but to tell you the truth, that when hundreds of thousands are already marching to the borders and martial law holds sway at home, no action is possible here."[42]

Adler's dispiriting words did not occur in a vacuum. The French socialist leaders had traveled the same path as the German revisionists; the words of French leaders such as Jean

Juarès had sounded the same themes as those of the right wing of the Social Democratic Party of Germany (SPD).

Far from linking hands across borders, the parties that constituted the membership of the Socialist International were preparing to support the capitalists of their respective countries in a war of conquest, a war triggered by an imperialist scramble for colonies, expanded markets and new territories. Europe's governments, for the most part unaccountable to their populations and long accustomed to intrigue, for decades had formed and reformed a series of alliances in a never-ending scramble to gain an advantage over their neighbors and rivals. The jockeying had become particularly intense in the past few years against a widespread expectation that war would soon break out. Austria-Hungary's ultimatum to Serbia following the heir's assassination would have stripped Serbia of its sovereignty; the list of demands was so harsh it seemed devised to be rejected. The German government fully supported Austria-Hungary's ultimatum, Russia would join the fighting in support of Serbia, and a web of obligations would draw in Europe's other large countries.

Each of the leaderships of the Socialist International parties attempted to convince itself that its country was fighting a defensive war—but how could every country be on the defensive?

A day after the socialists' emergency conference in Brussels, full mobilizations were under way among the countries of both European treaty alliances, and Germany was poised to open hostilities. An SPD leader, Hermann Müller, traveled to Paris in a last-minute attempt to coordinate a response by French and German socialists, but Juarès was assassinated by a French nationalist that night.[43] Müller told the French leaders that the SPD deputies in the Reichstag would probably vote against war credits, but the French socialists replied that, because they believed France to be on the defensive, they would vote in their parliament to support the war.[44]

The SPD now had to make its decision. The day before the Reichstag's vote on war credits (4 August 1914), the SPD's Reichstag members gathered to decide what to do. Most of the parliamentarians argued in favor of voting for war credits. As a compromise, the party decided it would publicly state that its support was conditioned on Germany being on the defensive and that it would withdraw support in the event that Germany turned the war into one of conquest—but this statement was deleted at the request of the chancellor, Theobold von Bethmann-Hollweg.[45] Fourteen of the party's 92 Reichstag members were opposed to voting for war credits, but each submitted to party discipline. The SPD delegation thus voted unanimously for war, and the SPD's status as the leading party of the Socialist International made it easier for other countries' socialists to go along with the war.

International solidarity, and the Socialist International with it, had collapsed. There were varying motivations for Europe's social democratic parties to support their country's war efforts despite the many solemn declarations that the impending war would be met by a wall of opposition. The SPD latched onto the excuse that Russian reaction would overrun everything the SPD had built up since German unification; the French socialists wished to oppose Prussian militarism; the Social Democratic Party of Austria wanted to keep the multinational Austro-Hungarian Empire intact and feared Russian tsardom; and the British Labour Party saw the war as a struggle between democracy and autocracy. All the social democratic parties received ample support for their new-found pro-war positions from union federations, which were generally even more enthusiastic for war. Old-fashioned nationalism for the moment proved much stronger than international class solidarity, and this was undeniably so among rank-and-file working people.

One member of the German Reichstag wrote of the influence

of conversations he had before the vote on war credits:

> Some socialist reservists I knew said to me: "We are going to go to the front with an easy mind, because we know the party will look after us if we are wounded, and that the party will take care of our families if we don't come home." Just before the train started for Berlin, a group of reservists at the station said to me: "König, you're going to Berlin, to the Reichstag; think of us there. See to it that we have all we need; don't be stingy in voting money." I told [Wilhelm] Dittmann what a deep impression all this had made on me. Dittmann confessed that things had happened to him, too, which affected him in the same way.[46]

Undoubtedly, these kinds of encounters played a role in changing the minds of some SPD Reichstag members—it is understandable that SPD delegates would not want to see themselves as abandoning their supporters. But the party leaders had done much to set up such encounters with their ever deeper flirtations with Germany's industrialists and Junkers, and with the militarism that the country's powerful pursued—Germany had already conducted brutal conquests in China and Africa, and sought to gain further overseas colonies at the expense of other European countries. And before the vote on war credits, the trade union federation, headed by Karl Legien (who had in past years asserted veto power over the SPD), halted all strike-support payments and negotiated a ban on strikes for the duration of the war.[47]

Nor did the SPD leadership stop to consider the trustworthiness of the men whom the party had sought to replace, whether by electoral or revolutionary means, at the helm of the state. The German government declared war on Russia and opened World War I by invading neutral Belgium, simultaneously imposing press censorship and declaring martial law.

Sensational (and untrue) government reports of bombings, frontier breaches and water poisonings went unchallenged,[48] and the SPD leadership chose to uncritically accept these reports.

The SPD's vote for war credits—joining all other Reichstag parties—came mere hours after Germany ruthlessly, and unilaterally, invaded Belgium. The kaiser, Wilhelm II, responded with a speech in which he said he no longer knew parties, only Germans. Thus was born the "Burgfrieden," or civic peace. But because the chancellor and the government ministers were appointed by the kaiser and answerable only to him, the SPD now shared responsibility for the war without having any say in policy. And as the war went on, the kaiser gradually withdrew and the German government became a military dictatorship—the SPD continued to share a burden of responsibility without any decision-making power, although the party's Reichstag leadership could at least talk to the decision-makers. These parliamentarians were no longer despised by Germany's rulers.

"They had now become socially acceptable, they frequented the government offices, even at [army] General Headquarters they were occasionally received and politely listened to," noted Sebastian Haffner in his outstanding account of the German revolution of 1918–19, *Failure of a Revolution*. "It was an unusual experience for them and the new politeness and accessibility of the mighty could not help but give them a warm and pleasant feeling."[49] An amazing turnaround considering that, days before the vote on war credits, the party funds had been moved to Switzerland in the expectation that the leadership might be jailed. The new-found respectability was only for the leaders of the SPD's political side, its Reichstag deputies; for the SPD rank-and-file, harsh discipline in the trenches and food shortages at home would become unendurable. Thus, a yawning gap widened between the party's political leadership and the membership.

The SPD's behavior was not unique; similar arrangements occurred in France and the Netherlands. The French socialists had on occasion provided parliamentary support for Centrist governments and readily joined the "Union Sacrée," or sacred union, when this new government coalition was formed three weeks after the German invasion. The conservative French president, Raymond Poincaré, had called for such a unity government on the day that the war broke out. The French sacred union, like the German civic peace, contained a good number of contradictions as the parties of the Right, Center and Left had sometimes very different reasons for accepting their national unity government.

Socialists in other countries joined wartime governments, although not as part of a formal national unity body. In the United Kingdom, the Labour Party leaders Arthur Anderson and J.H. Thomas joined David Lloyd George's cabinet,[50] and right socialist Emile Vandervelde joined the Belgian cabinet. Although the Netherlands remained neutral, Peter Troelstra, leader of the Social Democratic Workers Party, declared "the national idea is greater than the national differences."[51] And in the Austro-Hungarian Empire, the socialists supported their war-making government throughout the war. Some of the Social Democratic Party of Austria's top leaders, such as Karl Renner, outdid their international counterparts by opposing the efforts of Austria-Hungary's captive minority nations to free themselves from the empire's tight grip,[52] thereby adding imperialism to nationalism as previously verboten policies now supported. The Austrian socialist leadership maintained its support for the war even though parliament there, rather than merely ignored as in most other belligerent countries, was dismissed for three years.

What had happened? Socialists on the right wings of their parties were for war—having easily convinced themselves that their country was on the defensive, they needed to make no excuses. But some did so anyway. Philipp Scheidemann, who would become the second-ranking person in the SPD at the conclusion of World War I, declared at the war's start, "We are defending the fatherland in order to conquer it."[53] Such self-deceptions were not possible for socialist center factions—their capitulations went against their stated opposition to war, however soft and equivocal that opposition had become in the years leading up to the war. Karl Kautsky, the leader of the SPD's "Marxist center," took up this challenge.

Kautsky had enjoyed years of enormous respect from the movement as Marxism's leading theorist, although his increasing accommodation of revisionism began to make him the target of heated opposition. Son of a Czech father, Kautsky credited the contempt he received from Germans while growing up in Vienna for creating a rebellious attitude, which was channeled into socialism upon being inspired by the Paris Commune. Joining social democracy as a university student, he was soon contributing to movement journals. He became editor of *Die Neue Zeit* in 1883, and the prestige of the movement's most prominent theoretical journal accrued to him. Kautsky assumed his mantle when Karl Marx's lifelong collaborator, Friedrich Engels, died in 1895. (Marx had died in 1883.) Kautsky had spent five years working with Engels while in exile during the period of the German anti-socialist laws and wrote the SPD's official program after those laws were rescinded.

Although a prolific writer and analyst, Kautsky increasingly contented himself with wrestling with abstract theory, a consequence of his steady drift toward the view that the revolution would not occur until the distant future and therefore parliamentary work should be substituted for mass actions. Kautsky's abstract theorizing had increasingly become divorced from day-to-day tactical considerations, the evolving conditions under which social democracy operated and the increasing militancy of rank-and-file working people in the wake of successful mass demonstrations. Kautsky, to summarize, did not possess the ability to connect theory with the actual practical experiences of the movement.

The Russian revolutionary Leon Trotsky, as early as 1907, found that "[h]is mind was too angular and dry, too lacking in nimbleness and psychological insight."[54] Kautsky's militant-sounding 1881 call for the seizure of power, quoted earlier, in retrospect contained a kernel that signaled his later recoil from anything that so much as held the potential to be a first step toward a revolutionary upsurge by working people. That 1881 call had declared that social democrats had no need to organize a revolution, but rather merely needed to "organize ourselves *for* the revolution." Kautsky had not ceased to hold this last belief, but the consequences of applying it as an abstract theory disconnected from events on the ground was to provide intellectual justification for the belief that revolution would "come" and the SPD need only wait for the future to unfold. Because that future was far from imminent, working for incremental reforms had to become the focal point of movement activity, and any actions beyond that were deemed senseless adventures.

Kautsky, as also noted earlier, additionally opposed mass actions because he feared the strength and potential violence of Germany's ruling classes. Kautsky's fear of the capitalist state's likely violent reaction also demonstrated the hollowness of his and other SPD theorists' insistence on the inevitability of the gradual takeover of the state for socialism. If German working people had made so much progress toward supplanting the industrialists and Junkers, how could it be that they had so much to fear from challenging the same industrialists and Junkers? With no way to escape this insoluble dilemma, his arguments, in the last years before the war, became increasingly convoluted, and he outdid himself in attempting to explain away—actually, deny—the collapse of the Socialist International and its helplessness at the outbreak of war.

Kautsky first tried to claim that it was an impossible task to analyze the validity of voting for war credits because "valid historical research" into the outbreak of hostilities could only be done "after the war," but then declared that German and French socialists voted for war credits because both sought to provide the means of defense for their country.[55] Kautsky later argued that "The outbreak of the war signifies not the *bankruptcy* but on the contrary the *confirmation* of our theoretical conceptions…We have no regrets, nothing to revise."[56] Finally, Kautsky dismissed the entire movement as irrelevant in times of war: "It [the Socialist International] is not an effective weapon in wartime; it is essentially an instrument of peace. Namely peace in a twofold sense: the struggle for peace, and the class struggle in peacetime!"[57]

The movement's left wing tore apart such arguments. We again turn to Rosa Luxemburg for the counterargument. "This [is a] theory of a voluntarily assumed eunuch role, which says that socialism's virtue can be upheld only if, at the crucial moments, it is eliminated as a factor in world history," she wrote.[58] "The global historical appeal of the *Communist Manifesto* undergoes a fundamental revision and, as amended by Kautsky, now reads: proletarians of all countries, unite in peacetime and cut each other's throats in war!"[59] She argued that unity can't be limited to peacetime because exploitation increases during periods of war, and the movement defeats itself by supporting militarism. "[W]ars originate in the competitive interests of groups of capitalists and in capitalism's need to expand," Luxemburg wrote. "Both motives, however, are operative not only while the cannons are roaring, but also during peacetime, which means they prepare and make inevitable further outbreaks of war."[60]

Trotsky, a participant in the Socialist International's August 1914 emergency meeting in Brussels, saw that the collapse of the International was a direct result of the policies of the years leading up to the war. "Condemned for decades to a policy of opportunist waiting, the [SPD] took up the cult of organization as an end in itself," Trotsky wrote. "And there can be no doubt that the question of the preservation of the organizations, treasuries,

People's Houses and printing presses played a mighty important part in the position taken by the [SPD deputies] in the Reichstag towards the War. 'Had we done anything else we would have brought ruin upon our organization and our presses,' was the first argument I heard from a leading German comrade."[61]

Europe's soldiers marched off to war full of patriotism and with a willingness to sacrifice in the name of national defense, but the rulers had much different motivations for rushing to war. Russia was fighting to acquire Constantinople, the straits between the Black and Aegean seas, and Galicia; the United Kingdom sought Persia, Egypt and large parts of the Ottoman Empire; and France sought other Ottoman territories, Alsace-Lorraine and the west bank of the Rhine River—each agreed to allow its allies a "free hand" in setting borders with Germany.[62]

These agreements were codified in secret treaties; not even the parliaments knew of them. They saw the light of day only when Trotsky, upon becoming Russian foreign minister in 1917, promptly published the secret pacts. The government of Italy even negotiated with both sides in an effort to see which side would grant it the most territory in the event of victory,[63] although Italy's historic rivalry with Austria-Hungary and its desire to acquire South Tyrol and Trieste, both Austrian territories, made it more or less inevitable that Italy would join on the side of the Entente, which it did in 1915. Germany sought to reduce Belgium to a vassal state and expand to the east.

Not everyone on the Left joined their capitalist rulers in the rush to war. Both the German and Austrian social democrats had minorities that opposed voting for war credits but voted with the majorities in favor of the credits due to party discipline. The Italian Socialist Party, the Bulgarian Tesnyaki (the most pro-Bolshevik party outside of Russia), the internationalist wing of British Labour, Serbian socialists and the United States Socialist Party all opposed participation in the war. So too did the Russian Bolsheviks and the left wings of Russia's Mensheviks and

Socialist Revolutionaries.

There were divisions in each of the parties, and as the war dragged on, three currents developed within socialism that corresponded closely (although not identically) with the three pre-war groupings of German social democracy:

- A left wing that opposed the war or wanted to turn the war into a revolutionary class war.
- A center that opposed the war on a pacifist basis but did not wish to act on that opposition out of deference to the front-line soldiers.
- A right wing that fully supported war efforts.

As the war dragged on, and support for it waned among the soldiers and sailors, and among those toiling in factories and on farms away from the front, these divisions became irreconcilable and led to splits in socialist parties across Europe and North America.

## The paths of experience: Rebellions and schisms as nationalism fades

During times of national emergencies, both real and manufactured, struggles are dropped and public opinion can profoundly shift, especially under manipulation by a government outside popular control. Europe in the first years of the twentieth century was mostly governed by monarchies, autocratic dictatorships and assorted ancien régimes. With industrialization and modernization increasingly taking hold across the continent, more people were being educated, and the old methods of autocratic rule had become creaky. Although new levels of education provided more scope for mass-media manipulations, there was also less willingness to cede all decision-making to elites. And once the shock of the mobilization for World War I wore off, and the realization that, far from the promised fast-moving war of brief duration, a long war of attrition more horrible than anyone could have imagined had become the reality, opinions began shifting. No amount of courts-martial, capital punishments or draconian discipline could stop this change in people's minds, no matter what generals thought.

Even if a bit of a cliché, it is true that generals start fighting a war using the tactics of the previous war. This seemed all the more so for World War I, except that military minds seemed wholly unable to grasp that motorized vehicles and machine guns called for new tactics. Instead, frontal assaults across fields with no protection were ordered against positions defended with machine guns—suicide missions that left millions slaughtered.

Humanity had never seen death on such a mass scale. At the start of the war, the French army suffered more than 300,000 casualties in less than two weeks in a failed counteroffensive against the initial German attack.[64] More than one million soldiers died in each of two 1916 battles, Verdun and the Somme. At the end of the battle of the Somme, the British lines had moved forward 10 kilometers after five months.[65] Yet millions of soldiers continued to be ordered to fling themselves at opposing lines no matter how well fortified—human flesh continued to meet the fate expected when thrown against steel. After two years of trench warfare, a historian of the war noted, "German machine gunners watched in amazement as the British walked toward them."[66]

It was not until the war was well into its third year that military minds were able to develop a new tactic. The new French commander, Robert Nivelle, in April 1917, designed a plan whereby an offensive thrust was to break through German lines within 48 hours or be called off. The "Nivelle Offensive" failed to meet its goal, but the attack was not called off. As it dragged into its second month, the first mutinies began. Soldiers refused to take part in any further offensive actions or to even return to the front; an estimated 35,000 soldiers were involved in "collective indiscipline."[67] Nivelle was removed from command, replaced by Philippe Pétain, who called off the offensive.

The independent thinking of the soldiers, however, could not be tolerated by military commanders. Force and compulsion were possessed in abundance—wielding them the very point of the military—and pitilessly aimed at the enlisted personnel through exemplary punishments. Pétain court-martialed 3400 soldiers and sentenced 450 to death.[68] By June 1917, reports of "collective indiscipline" involved two-thirds of the divisions of the French army.[69] Another 68 French soldiers were executed in July.[70]

Unwillingness to continue to be human sacrifices was by no means limited to the French army. Rebellions broke out at a British base camp; the Italian army suffered mass desertions; Flemish soldiers created clandestine organizations that circulated newspapers and pamphlets, set up demonstrations and organized strikes; German army desertion rates reached 10 percent by spring 1918; and mutinies and rebellions spread across most of the navies.[71]

Attempts by Italian authorities to punish civilian revolts backfired by culminating in Italy's worst defeat of the war, at Caporetto in October 1917. German divisions had been sent to the Italian Alps to augment the weakening Austro-Hungarian troops. The subsequent German-led offensive was a bigger success than its commanders could have predicted—200,000 Italian soldiers surrendered. A young German captain, the future "Desert Fox" of World War II, Erwin Rommel, invited the Italians to surrender, later recording the scene: "Suddenly, the mass began to move and, in the ensuing panic, swept its resisting officers along downhill. Most of the soldiers threw their weapons away and hundreds hurried to me…For the Italians on Mrzli peak the war was over. They shouted with joy."[72]

The surrendering units had included thousands of munitions workers who had participated in a revolt in Turin and were then sent to the front lines as punishment—the punished workers promptly agitated among the other soldiers, helping to crystallize dissent. Some officers of these units locked themselves into their quarters at night, so afraid were they of their own troops, according to the chief of the British Red Cross in Italy.[73]

Resistance to the war had begun to take shape earlier away from the front, particularly among socialists who dissented from their parties' pro-war stands. Left socialists from several European countries on both sides and from neutral countries gathered for a 1915 conference in Switzerland, and although this gathering had no immediate practical effect, the example of people from opposite sides of the front lines shaking hands provided a potent symbol. More practical work began taking shape at the start of 1916 in Germany, when a group of Social Democratic Party (SPD) left-wingers, including Rosa Luxemburg, Karl Liebknecht, Klara Zetkin, Franz Mehring and Leo Jogiches, organized themselves into the Spartacus League. This was not a split from the party, but rather an organized faction within it that sharply criticized the SPD's official pro-war line and the stifling of dissent within the party. Two months later, a minority of the SPD's Reichstag delegation, including Liebknecht, voted against war credits in the latest of a series of such votes. The majority promptly voted to expel the anti-war voters from the SPD Reichstag caucus.[74] The expelled then formed a delegation independent of any party—they remained as formal members of the SPD but were independent now in their capacity as Reichstag members.

Many who decided to join the Spartacus League believed that the situation in the SPD had become too intolerable to stay. "These comrades pressed for a new and completely independent party, but Rosa was resolutely opposed to this," one of Luxemburg's closest followers, Paul Frölich, wrote of this time in his biography of Luxemburg. "She granted their aim should be to form a revolutionary party eventually, but as long as it was still possible for them to work within the old party without abandoning their principles they should do so; under no circumstances should they voluntarily leave the rank-and-file membership in the hands of apostate leaders."[75]

That attitude did not preclude street actions, however. On May Day 1916, a demonstration in Berlin was to feature an anti-war speech by Liebknecht. He had time only to utter the words "Down with the war!" before being grabbed by police and hustled off. Ignoring the fact that Liebknecht possessed parliamentary immunity, Liebknecht was sentenced to two and a half years of hard labor (later extended to four years). More than 50,000 went on strike in Berlin on the day of his sentencing. Liebknecht's act of bravery and the public support for him was answered with the arrests of hundreds of Spartacus members and the conscription into the army as punishment for thousands of factory workers.[76] Luxemburg and Mehring were soon arrested, too—Luxemburg was never charged, but was imprisoned for the rest of the war in "protective custody."

Opposition to the war was rapidly growing, as confirmed by Karl Kautsky in a letter he wrote to Austrian social democratic leader Viktor Adler following Liebknecht's trial: "The danger from the 'Spartacus' group is great. Its radicalism corresponds to the immediate needs of the broad, undisciplined masses. Liebknecht is now the most popular man in the trenches. This is universally confirmed by all those returning from the front."[77] Kautsky added that the right wing of the SPD and the trade unions wanted the Spartacists to leave the party "before it becomes the majority."[78]

The Spartacist leaders, men and women with decades of struggle behind them, believed that as long as the masses remained with the SPD, they needed to remain in it. None believed that more than Jogiches, a behind-the-scenes organizer highly skilled at clandestine work who assumed the faction's leadership after the jailing of other leaders. That is why, in January 1917, when not only the Spartacist League but also the party centrists opposed to the war who by this time had become less unwilling to act on their opposition were both expelled from the SPD, the Spartacists joined with the centrists in forming a new party, the Independent Social Democratic Party of Germany, or USPD.

The Spartacists and the centrists had held a joint conference to respond to the administrative punishments and expulsions of dissident members that the SPD leadership, primarily from the party's right wing, had increasingly imposed. The SPD leadership swiftly responded to the conference by voting for the mass expulsions.[79] The USPD was born as a party that would be too heterogeneous to survive in the long term—its members included Eduard Bernstein, the theorist of revisionism, Spartacists and every shade of opinion in between. The only commonality among them was opposition to the war. The USPD's first manifesto did hail the February Revolution in Russia, which swept the tsar from his throne weeks after the USPD's formation, contrasting the support for a democratic republic by Russia's socialist parties with the SPD's continued acceptance of monarchy.[80]

The February 1917 Revolution in Russia represented the single most dramatic event since the outbreak of World War I. Russia's socialist leaders were in exile in Europe or the United States, or in internal exile in Siberia, thousands of miles from the capital. Practical work had been extraordinarily difficult because of unrelenting repression—those who stayed in the Russian cities were repeatedly imprisoned or sent to Siberia; those who left Russia could only smuggle their newspapers and books back home.

Russia's social democrats were split into two parties, the Bolsheviks and the Mensheviks, and there was continual fighting not only between those two parties, but among the factions within each as well. So fierce had the divisions become among Russia's social democrats that much of their funds were controlled by three trustees from the SPD—Kautsky, Mehring and Zetkin—who were forced to attempt to referee continual disputes over the funds.[81] Although the Russian Social Democratic Workers' Party had split into Bolsheviks and Mensheviks in 1903, they did not formally become separate parties until shortly before World War I. The two parties and their factions held sometimes sharply different views on organization and tactics, but a much larger percentage of Russian socialists opposed the war than socialists in the other large countries.

That opposition came to be popular as none of the belligerent states was in worse shape than Russia. Its soldiers were subjected to routine floggings and executions, and suffered casualties by the millions (in excess of any other country) thanks to being badly under-equipped and the incompetence of tsarist officers. The resulting mutinies and wholesale defections of soldiers and sailors to the side of the workers and peasants played a decisive role in the February and October revolutions.

Unrest was not limited to Germany and Russia. A series of strikes broke out in France in 1917 and 1918; mass strikes broke out across ethnic-German areas of Austria, as well as in Budapest, in January 1918;[82] and a January 1918 general strike in Berlin saw 400,000 workers walk out.[83]

Food shortages and other deprivations, particularly in Germany and Austria-Hungary, and resentment against war profiteering steadily stirred dissension. The August 1917 uprising of munitions workers in Turin was sparked in part by a visiting delegation from the Petrograd Soviet, a leading Russian revolutionary organization, for whom 40,000 socialists and metalworkers turned out, greeting the delegation with shouts of "Long live the Russian revolution, long live Lenin!"[84] Protests over bread shortages quickly escalated into strikes with political demands; the Italian police put them down in brutal fashion by machine-gunning crowds, killing 50 and wounding hundreds.[85]

In June 1917, a socialist conference in Leeds, England, called for the establishment of workers' and soldiers' councils.[86] Taking a more direct approach, syndicalist trade unions and the unemployed staged an attack on the stock exchange in Copenhagen in February 1918 to protest the high cost of living.

Russia's February Revolution quickened the pace of events.

## Preparing the spark: Russia's long decades of struggle

Russians had accepted their country's participation in World War I the same as the peoples of other countries, but the complete lack of even the rudiments of democracy and the lethally inept management of Russia's war effort made them the first to rise in rebellion. Nonetheless, the February Revolution in Russia came as a surprise to all political factions, whose leaderships played no direct role in the event. Nor could they have, so thorough was the tsarist régime in its repression, although members of those parties participated and it was the tireless work of those parties that laid the foundation.

There was sufficient unrest in the Russian capital city, Petrograd (as St Petersburg was then called), in the weeks leading up to the revolution that a police report found the state of the city

> on the edge of despair…The slightest explosion, however trivial its pretext, will lead to uncontrollable riots…The inability to buy goods, the frustrations of queuing, the rising death rate owing to poor living conditions, and the cold and damp produced by a lack of coal…have all created a situation where most of the workers are ready to embark on the savage excesses of a food riot.[87]

The city's working people were prepared to do more than simply riot.

Labor unrest had increased sharply during the preceding few months, but economic and political unrest had flared up for many years, defying the unrelenting brutality of tsarist absolutism. Attempts at forging mass movements had begun in the 1870s, when thousands of intellectuals—a group collectively known as the "Narodniks," a word that can be loosely translated as "populists"—went out into the countryside to explain to the peasants the necessity of overthrowing the tsar.

The tsar of that time, Aleksandr II, had freed Russia's serfs in 1861, but their emancipation had earned them meager gains. They no longer were obligated to work the estate owners' land for no pay while being legally bound to their lord, but now had to pay for the small strip of land they had been allotted to grow their own food. The required payments were far beyond the ability of subsistence farmers to meet, causing them to fall deep into debt.

The estate owners retained most of the land, and the best land, regardless of whether it was worked, and also retained the meadows for pasturing and the only source of fuel, the forests. The ex-serfs would have to pay to have access to those, incurring further debt. And they remained tied to the land, because all the ex-serfs of an estate were required to join a "commune," which made all decisions and collected taxes for the state. Peasants could not withdraw from the commune without paying all outstanding debts, an impossibility given their impoverishment, nor could they leave without the commune granting them a passport. The land they were allowed to buy was often a smaller plot than what they had been allotted as serfs, leaving them on the brink of starvation in the absence of a strong harvest.

The tsar had doled out a tiny drop of freedom and balked at anything more. Chafing against the lack of any meaningful reform, the Narodniks became influenced by the revolutionary ideas gaining hold across Europe. There was no organization that provided a guiding hand to this movement, but the writings of a Russian mathematician and artillery officer turned exiled philosopher, P.L. Lavrov, was the dominant influence. Lavrov wrote that Russia's educated owed what they had to the illiterate and toiling masses, and they therefore had a duty to repay that debt by enlightening the peasants.[88]

But when the Narodniks went to live among the peasants to explain to them why they were still so badly off, the peasants were not interested despite their anger at being cheated out of the land they believed belonged to them. The peasants, deeply superstitious and without schooling, believed that the tsar was chosen by God to rule over them and that Aleksandr II in particular was their "liberator." The aristocracy had bitterly opposed the abolition of serfdom, but Aleksandr believed it was better to abolish serfdom from above rather than have it overturned from below. The vast majority of Russians were now simply held under a more modern form of subjugation, and the tsar's secret police made short work of the Narodniks, sentencing them to hard labor in Siberian exile or executing them.

By the 1880s, two Narodnik offshoots grew: the "People's Will" and the nucleus of what would become the Russian Social Democratic Workers' Party. The program of the former, although an indigenous set of beliefs and not directly taken from the anarchist Louis-Auguste Blanqui, nonetheless bore some resemblance to Blanqui's thesis that a small self-selected "elite," acting secretly, could carry out an insurrection—the People's Will believed that a tiny group of terrorists could inspire the populace to rise up in revolt through the example of assassinations. This was a tiny group, but before they were crushed they did succeed in assassinating Aleksandr II in 1881. The Narodniks and People's Will believed that the peasants were the revolutionary class, and that Russia could skip capitalism altogether, leaping from feudalism to an agrarian socialism that would be based on village communes cleansed of their repressive components.

From this intellectual soil would later arise the Socialist Revolutionary Party.

The other Narodnik offshoot abandoned mystical beliefs in the holiness of the peasantry and came to be influenced by Marxism. The leading philosopher of this grouping was Grigorii Plekhanov, who would become known as the "father of Russian Marxism." Plekhanov dropped out of university to devote himself to revolutionary work, joining the People's Will. But he soon came to abhor terrorism, leaving the People's Will and instead turning to Marxism because of the latter's philosophical underpinning of emancipation through mass action—the oppressed will liberate themselves through their own struggle. Industrialization began to take hold in Russia in the 1890s, and although it remained an overwhelmingly agrarian country, there could no longer be illusions that capitalism would not establish itself. Despite the massive exertion of the tsarist security apparatus, the outside world could not be kept entirely outside the borders.

"Russia will continue to proceed along the path of capitalist development, not because there exists some external force, some mysterious law pushing it along that path, but because there is no effective internal force capable of pushing it from that path,"[89] Plekhanov wrote in 1895. The poverty and overpopulation of the countryside had begun to create a flow of people into the cities to work in the new factories, and the more advanced capitalism elsewhere in Europe could not be willed out of existence—vast Russia represented an untapped territory for the expansion of foreign capital.

As a potentially rich source of new profits, some of the Russian aristocracy would naturally try their hand at manufacturing or trading; it was already too late to stop this process. "Perhaps the village community is *not* breaking up?" Plekhanov asked his "utopian" challengers. "Perhaps the expropriation of the people from the land is *not* in fact taking place?...It is the capitalist prose that exists, and we are asking ourselves, how can this prose be fought, how can we put the people in a situation even somewhat approaching the 'ideal'?"[90]

Plekhanov had already earned a reputation for the high quality of his writing, particularly on philosophical topics, having spent 15 years in exile at the time he wrote the above words. He was a decisive influence in the development of Russia's social democratic leaders, Vladimir Lenin not excepted. Two decades after going abroad, Plekhanov gained acceptance for his viewpoints that the future revolution would have to face the necessity of restricting the civil liberties of those who would be overthrown and of closing any parliamentary body that refused to accept the revolution's program. But Plekhanov was more than a little arrogant, and was unable to update his theories as conditions and experiences required, nor to successfully use theory as a guide to understand what adjustments the actual socialist movement needed to effect in response to concrete conditions. As a result, he gradually lost his authority. He grew more conservative, to the point of enthusiastically supporting Russia's participation in World War I, and when the revolution came and did exactly what he had once instructed it to do, he bitterly opposed it.

Plekhanov, a highly influential figure similar to Karl Kautsky, traveled a similar path. Plekhanov interpreted Marxism in a mechanical fashion, believing that a "law" of history dictated a fixed sequence of development from feudalism to capitalism to socialism. He, too, believed that socialist revolution was far in the future, and that tsarist monarchy could be succeeded only by capitalism; therefore socialists must support liberals in their building of capitalism until the day in the hazy future when conditions would become ripe for socialism.

The first attempt to gather this Marxist-oriented movement into a formal party came in 1898, when a handful of activists not in exile met in Minsk in the first congress of the Russian Social

Democratic Workers' Party. All participants were promptly arrested. The nascent party's platform was certainly an ambitious one:

> The further east one goes in Europe, the weaker, the more cowardly, and the meaner in political relations becomes the bourgeoisie and the greater are the cultural and political tasks that fall to the lot of the proletariat. On its strong shoulders, the Russian working class must and will carry the work of winning political liberty. This is a necessary step, but only the first, toward accomplishing the great historical mission of the proletariat—the creation of a social structure in which there will be no place for the exploitation of man by man.[91]

That concept, very much the product of Plekhanov's thinking, was very similar to the program of the Social Democracy Party of Germany. But how could such a program be implemented? The German party's debate, in the form of the controversy over "revisionism," had just begun; similar divisions, although on different grounds, ripped apart the Russian party from its beginnings. A more serious attempt at building a formal party structure took place in 1903, outside Russia this time so that the exiles in Europe (where most of the movement's leaders were forced to live) could attend. Instead, the party's second congress resulted in a split between two factions, Bolshevik and Menshevik.

The leading figures of the movement, including Plekhanov, Yulii Martov and Leon Trotsky, went with the Mensheviks; the one exception among the party's leaders was Lenin. The split had to do with the structure of the party—a fundamental issue for an organization that had to operate under extreme repression and which was riddled with informants working for the tsar's secret police, which operated inside and outside Russia.

The Mensheviks believed that the party should be open to all who wished to join and should attempt to operate strictly in the open under whatever openings tsarist law would allow. The Bolsheviks believed that the party had to operate in multiple ways: It should have a legal wing but also a clandestine wing to conduct underground work that could evade tsarist censorship and repression to the extent possible, and that, because of the sensitive nature of clandestine work, party membership should be restricted to those whose work earned the trust of the membership.

The Bolsheviks won a majority of the congress for their views—their name derives from the Russian-language word for "majority," *bolshe*. Initially, Plekhanov sided with Lenin. But when the Mensheviks threatened to boycott the newly elected party Central Committee and the movement's newspaper, *Iskra*, which had acted as the movement's de facto organizing center, Plekhanov demanded that the results of the congress be reversed. Plekhanov's desire for unity at all costs was sufficiently strong that he was willing to disregard the vote. Lenin rejected this demand; nobody had the right to reverse the majority decision of a democratic body.[92] Plekhanov then defected to the Mensheviks, who carried out their boycott and formed a separate, shadow central committee. Henceforth, repeated attempts at the reunification of the two factions would all falter.

The split would not prevent a revolutionary situation from developing inside Russia in 1905. Similar to the revolutions of 1917, the 1905 revolution was triggered by a war that Russia was unequipped to wage. Rivalry between Russia and Japan concerning the ongoing partition of China led to Japan attacking the Russian naval base at Port Arthur, China, and the ensuing war consisted of an unbroken chain of Japanese victories over Russian forces until a September 1905 ceasefire. Unrest spread, most notably after "Bloody Sunday," a massacre of thousands in January 1905 when the tsar ordered Cossack guards to open fire on a procession led by an Orthodox priest, and in June, when the sailors of the battleship *Potemkin* revolted when officers ordered sailors shot for complaining about having to eat meat riddled with worms.[93] But the unrest was unorganized and sporadic until October, a month after the ceasefire with Japan.

Railroad employees went on strike that month, and workers in Moscow, St Petersburg and elsewhere joined them in what quickly blossomed into a general strike with political demands, including the creation of a parliament, political amnesty and an eight-hour workday.[94] The tsar then proclaimed his "October Manifesto" promising a parliament and civil liberties. The manifesto divided the movement in the streets, as intended: Liberals now advocated against any further agitation, taking the tsar at his word and fearing that continuing to voice demands would bring down renewed repression, while the more militant forged ahead by organizing "soviets" in St. Petersburg and Moscow.

*Soviet* is the Russian-language word for "council," and these soviets were representative bodies created by working people during the latest outburst of strikes and unrest. They were intended to be a new form of popular organization. Trotsky was elected as chair of the St Petersburg Soviet, giving a speech in which he said, "Our strength is in ourselves. With sword in hand we must defend freedom. The tsar's manifesto, however…is only a scrap of paper. Today it has been given to us and tomorrow it will be taken away and torn into pieces as I am now tearing it into pieces."[95]

But there had not been sufficient time to organize properly, and the army, full of peasants from the countryside where the revolution had not taken hold, remained loyal to the tsar. Nor were the police wavering, and soon arrests and official threats to "restore order" with violence drew attention to the revolution's weakness. The St Petersburg Soviet was arrested en masse in December. The dénouement came in Moscow, where police and the army entered the last neighborhood to hold out, burning homes to the ground and killing or wounding more than 1000.[96] That was only the beginning, as from 1906 to 1908 at least 60,000 political detainees were exiled, sentenced to hard labor or executed without trial under the tsar's new hard-line prime minister, Petr Stolypin.[97] The promised reforms were swiftly taken back, except for the newly created parliament, the Duma, but that was a farce—the Duma was elected under rules that heavily favored large property owners and was little more than a debating society.

Militancy died down until 1912, when army troops opened fire on striking workers at the Lena gold mine, inflicting 500 casualties. The tsar's interior minister summed up the massacre succinctly: "So it has been, and so it will be in the future."[98] A flurry of sympathy strikes followed, only to be greeted by another harsh wave of repression—30 rounds of arrests by the secret police were carried out in Moscow alone from 1912 to 1916[99] and waves of arrests crushed organizations in St Petersburg and many other Russian cities. All socialist organizations were decimated during these years; the Bolsheviks and Mensheviks lost more than 90 percent of their membership from 1907 to 1910.[100]

In the countryside, Stolypin, fearing the communes could hold the potential to organize peasants despite their repressive setup, attempted to weaken them by allowing members to withdraw, demand a consolidation of their holdings and fence off the consolidated lands. Fear of rural unrest was underlined by a 1905 police report on the state of the peasantry: "Very often the peasants do not have enough allotment land, and during the year cannot feed themselves, clothe themselves, heat their homes, keep their tools and livestock, secure seed for sowing and, lastly, discharge all their taxes and obligations to the state."[101] A small number withdrew from the communes, and, taking advantage of favorable loan terms, a small class of big farmers, or kulaks, was able to emerge, separate from the big estate owners, leaving most peasants with land of less quality.[102]

Still, there was little organized unrest in rural areas, and neither the Bolsheviks nor the Mensheviks could make inroads in the countryside, where they had few organizers. They had a dwindling number in the cities as their cadres who stayed inside Russia were repeatedly arrested, imprisoned and shipped to Siberia. The émigrés outside Russia had become fissiparous with their links to Russia becoming tenuous. Those who had gone back home in late 1905 had to again escape the country. The Bolsheviks of these years bore very little resemblance to the stereotyped image of an unwavering band marching shoulder to shoulder to the revolution.

Lenin was now the leader of a faction of Bolshevism, adhering to the program that had initially carried the majority at the 1903 congress and insisting that the party participate in elections to the Duma, no matter how farcical the body, because getting even one deputy elected would give social democracy a valuable platform—the speeches of a Duma deputy would be virtually the only legal, above-ground activity the party could engage in. But there were two other strong trends within Bolshevism, syndicalism and "god-building." These two trends were not discrete tendencies, but largely overlapped.

The god-builders argued that the peasants weren't ready for socialism and, therefore, the Bolsheviks should appeal to them through religion and spiritualism.[103] Anatolii Lunacharskii and Maksim Gorkii developed this tendency, which gained a following as the result of the deep pessimism that had set in following the onset of the post-1905 repression. Lunacharskii sought a higher belief: "The faith of an active human being is a faith in mankind of the future; his religion is a combination of the feelings and thoughts which make him a participant in the life of mankind and a link in that chain which extends up…to a perfected organism," he wrote. "If the essence of any life is self-preservation, then a life of beauty, goodness, and truth is self-realization."[104] Gorkii believed that socialism should be turned into a cult because "its basic core—man's consciousness of his connection with the masses—only grows stronger."[105]

That sort of elevation of collectivity into a mythologized higher spiritual state dovetailed with syndicalism, a growing European movement with particularly strong roots in France and Italy, and which now captured the minds of many Bolsheviks. Syndicalism rejected political parties and parliaments. Instead, its adherents preached "direct action," in which workers would organize within their workplaces, gradually becoming strong enough to expropriate the means of production from the owners—industrial organization and general strikes, supplemented by the violence of a militant minority, would lead to the overthrow of capitalism and its state.

Although through their emphasis on direct action syndicalists did not plan to wait for power to "come" to working people through some automatic, unfolding "law," syndicalism did have in common with Marxist revisionism a tacit underlying belief that the capitalist ruling class would simply sit back and allow a long-term weakening and ultimate overturning of its order to take place. Bolshevik syndicalism, therefore, was anathema not only to Lenin's faction but to the Mensheviks, and the syndicalists' loud demands to withdraw from any Duma participation were firmly rejected both by the Bolsheviks who remained with Lenin and by the Mensheviks.

Because Stolypin had closed the Duma, arrested and exiled the social democratic deputies to Siberia, then convened a new Duma with even more restrictive rules designed to keep all but the rich from being represented, the syndicalists were gaining support among émigrés and among Bolsheviks working underground inside Russia. Seeing the general strike as the tactic to be pursued, Aleksandr Bogdanov, writing on behalf of the Bolshevik syndicalist faction, declared that "A partial strike even when prolonged sometimes simply wastes energy, when a general strike would quickly attain success"—this was something of a shortcut as Bogdanov saw the general strike as providing part of the experience necessary for working people to eventually take over the state.[106]

But the conditions for a general strike did not at this time exist in Russia; even "partial" strikes had become far less frequent. Despairing from the period of reaction that had hardened inside Russia and frustrated with the ongoing factional fighting, the leaders of god-building and syndicalism gradually withdrew from active work, drifted back toward a more orthodox Bolshevism or joined, with many ex-Mensheviks, an independent social democratic group called the Interdistrict Organization. The Interdistrict Organization, including future Bolshevik leaders such as Leon Trotsky, Aleksandra Kollontai and Lunacharskii, was formed in 1913 and stayed aloof from both the Bolsheviks and Mensheviks before merging into the Bolsheviks in 1917.

Inside Russia, labor militancy began to rise again in July 1914, a development that was quickly cut off by the outbreak of World War I in the following month; strikes in Russia virtually stopped until August 1915 as a wave of patriotism swept the country as it had elsewhere in Europe. The working people of Russia, however, did not benefit from their new attitude—the average wage in Moscow's largest metal factory, for instance, was cut 30 percent by March 1915.[107] Hyperinflation raged through 1915 and 1916, but wage increases did not keep up, and food shortages also contributed to further deteriorating living standards. From August 1915 through the end of 1916, dozens of strikes involving tens of thousands of people took place every month in Petrograd alone.[108] Petrograd was the new name for St Petersburg—at the outbreak of the war, the capital's name was changed because St Petersburg sounded "too German."

The war meant big profits for Russia's capitalists. Between 1914 and 1917, industrial output in Petrograd doubled thanks to war orders; in the metalworking industry, by far the city's largest, nearly all the workforce worked on war orders.[109] But Russia's creaky infrastructure was coming apart under the strain of this frenzied activity. The war cut off foreign supplies of raw materials and Russia's fragile railroad system was unable to transport sufficient domestic supplies; one-quarter of the engines in use were more than 25 years old.[110] Special government committees that year and the next were organized to oversee distribution and set prices of critical materials; suppliers then attempted to conceal their stock, adding to the inflationary pressures.[111] The massive growth of the army took skilled workers out of the factories, further hurting productivity, and took away nearly half of the able-bodied male population of the countryside, leading to severe personnel shortages on the farms and therefore adding to agricultural difficulties.[112]

Conditions only became worse as the war dragged on. Wages for Moscow metalworkers, adjusted for inflation, in March 1917 were half of what they had been four years earlier, simultaneous with factory profits increasing fourfold.[113] Workplace conditions were horrific and conditions on the front inhumane—Russia's war effort was so disorganized (despite the converting of almost all industry to the war effort) that some soldiers were sent to the front unarmed.

The tsarist government was inept in almost every way with one notable exception—the secret police. The secret police, known as the "Okhrana," operated across Europe, and inside Russia successfully planted its agents in high-ranking posts within all the socialist parties. The Okhrana was particularly skilled at breaking up socialist organizations through mass arrests, jailings, deportations to Siberia and killings, continually disrupting attempts at creating stable organizations. Ultimately, efficient secret police proved to not be a substitute for a functioning government and economy—by no means the last time this lesson would be imposed. Tsarist state terror had prevented sustained organized resistance within Russia, but that ability crumbled during the first two months of 1917.

More than 300,000 Petrograd workers took part in strikes during the seven weeks immediately preceding the February Revolution, during which time three major demonstrations were planned, and mutinies spread throughout the army—the fruits of organized agitation in the military by left Socialist Revolutionaries, Bolsheviks and the Interdistrict Organization[114] that spoke to the concrete conditions of soldiers and sailors. The tsarist régime responded with lockouts of factory workers, mass shootings of strikers by the police and army, and mass arrests.[115] City and city-district organizations of the left socialist groups had been destroyed by the Okhrana during 1916, followed by still more arrests in the first weeks of 1917—although no organized leadership was left, the factory cells of the left socialist groups were active and functioning as unrest continued on the eve of what would become the February Revolution.[116]

The city "on the edge of despair," as the police report called Petrograd, seemed to have reached the limits of patience. But it can never be known in advance when or where the spark will ignite. Russia's socialists had tirelessly laid the groundwork, and although the tsar's secret police had decimated their ranks and so many had paid with exile, banishment, hard labor, jail and execution, the ideas could not be stamped out. The memory of 1905 may have lain dormant, but those memories still existed and could be revived. The talks of the socialist agitators, the words of the socialist newspapers, pamphlets and fliers, resonated with the experiences of Russians—not only in the cities, but in the countryside and in the army and navy. It was this practical work, carried out over many years, that provided the people of Russia with the tools necessary to understand, and then change, their conditions.

One more strike, one additional action following hundreds of actions, one action that on the day it began did not seem noticeably different from previous actions, put the revolution in motion. Why this one? It is impossible to say. Perhaps all that can be said is that on that particular day, enough Russians, or at least enough Petrograd women and men, were sufficiently exasperated to do something about it. The February Revolution is an excellent example of the necessity of continuing to struggle: It is usually impossible to predict which spark will be the one to catch fire. The revolutionaries were surprised by the revolution, and perhaps that could not have been otherwise. But the revolution would not have happened without their work.

## Russia can't sit still: February's thaw brings October's storms

Angered by shortages of bread, tens of thousands of women textile workers in Petrograd walked out on International Women's Day, 8 March (23 February in the old-style Julian calendar still in use in Russia), lighting the spark that started the revolution. The women walked to nearby metal factories, told the men there to join them on strike, and both groups inspired workers in other factories to walk out. More struck the next day. By 10 March, a general strike was under way in Petrograd, with demonstrators shouting anti-war and anti-monarchy slogans.

That day, Tsar Nicholas II ordered his Petrograd military commander to forcibly put down the demonstrations, and police and military units fired machine guns on Nevsky Prospekt, the main street of central Petrograd, and mounted cavalry attacks. But one military battalion rebelled, opening fire on the police. A crowd stormed the main arsenal, taking control of it, and other military units began switching to the side of the people—the soldiers were peasants and urban working people drafted into the army who did not see why they should fire on people like themselves. The huge Kronstadt naval base, which would be crucial in the October Revolution, was taken over by rebelling sailors while soldiers began taking over rail stations outside of Petrograd. In Moscow, Russia's other major city, production was brought to a halt as hundreds of thousands marched on the Kremlin and disarmed the police.

Preparations were made for the taking of Petrograd's largest military garrison, the Peter and Paul Fortress, but before any plan could be carried out, the fortress's commandant resigned, whereupon the staff promptly surrendered.[117] The Winter Palace was ordered evacuated by Grand Duke Mikhail, brother of the tsar, and the revolutionaries were in charge of the capital.[118] All that was left was for the tsar to abdicate.

On 15 March, several generals sent telegrams asking the tsar to step down in the name of Russia, the salvation of the dynasty and the war effort.[119] These telegrams make for amusing reading, each mostly consisting of obsequious and groveling references to the tsar's greatness and begging forgiveness for asking, usually obliquely, for him to step down. In a typical example, a general wrote, "Make the sign of the cross and transmit to him your legacy. There is no other solution."[120] This general evidently believed Nicholas II sat on his throne through providence, when in fact the tsars got their start as tax collectors for the Mongol empire in medieval times, when the khans allowed them to use any means, no matter how brutal, so long as they extracted the taxes from the peasants. The plan to save the monarchy centered on Nicholas II abdicating in favor of his brother, which he did that day, but Mikhail wisely decided to avoid the dubious honor and promptly surrendered his authority to the Duma, the rubber-stamp parliament that had met only at the pleasure of the crown and which was heavily weighted toward factory owners and the aristocracy.

At this point, a brief discussion of the political forces in Russia is appropriate. Three of the four largest parties were considered socialist, although not all shades of opinion within two of those parties were necessarily socialist.

- The Bolsheviks, one of the two parties born out of Russian social democracy, constituted Russia's Left-most party. Bolshevik agitators had been the most militant in the factories, and they had participated in and organized strikes and other workplace actions, but because of this their ranks were decimated and they represented only a minority of Russians, even in Petrograd and Moscow, at this time. The Bolsheviks stood for socialist revolution, although they were divided in their attitude toward the February Revolution and therefore in how far and fast to push the revolution forward. The party had put considerable effort into organizing Russia's soldiers and sailors, and had an increasing following among them.

- The Mensheviks, the more moderate side of Russian social democracy, believed that socialism would come into being gradually, and that Russia, because of its lack of development, could have only a capitalist revolution, putting the date of any socialist revolution far into the future. They therefore sought to participate in coalition governments with the capitalist parties. The Menshevik party contained a wide range of opinion. Its left wing, the Internationalists, headed by Yulii Martov, overlapped with the right wing of the Bolsheviks in advocating a government coalition comprised of all socialist parties. The Mensheviks had a strong following in Petrograd immediately following the February Revolution.
- In addition to the two main social democratic parties, there was also the "Interdistrict Organization" that tried to straddle the difference between the Bolsheviks and Mensheviks. This group included several brilliant figures, among them Leon Trotsky, who had either moved away from the Mensheviks or had been part of the pre-war Bolshevik opposition factions. In the summer of 1917, the organization's members would join the Bolsheviks. Many who belonged to the Interdistrict Organization previously

hoped for a unification of the Bolsheviks and Mensheviks, but the last illusions that the unification of two groups with such wide differences remained possible had disappeared. Its base was in Petrograd.

- The third socialist party, the Socialist Revolutionary (SR) Party, was the party of the peasants, and was a direct descendant of the nineteenth-century Narodnik and the People's Will movements. The SRs contained an even wider span of opinion than the Mensheviks, and that People's Will ancestry was reflected in the small terrorist cells within its ranks. The left wing of the SRs, which included anarchist influences, would formally split and form the Left SR Party in October, joining the Bolsheviks in a coalition government. The rest of the party, which would become known as the Right SRs, tended to form a bloc with the Mensheviks—they, too, sought to form coalitions with the capitalist parties and also sought to hold back the peasants from doing anything to change land ownership and relations in the countryside. The then-singleton SRs had a significant following in Moscow immediately after the February Revolution, and the party's left wing had also organized among the military's enlisted personnel. The SRs officially stood for distributing land to the peasants, but had wide disagreements on how any redistribution of land should be accomplished.
- Moving further toward the Right, a much smaller party was the "Populist Socialists," into which the Labor Group, a small Duma party whose elected members were SRs running under this label, merged in 1917. The leader of the Labor Group was Provisional Government minister Aleksandr Kerensky. Despite their name, Populist Socialists were not at all socialist; their base were groups like shopkeepers and conservative peasants. This party was created by a right-wing split from the SRs after the

1905 revolution had cooled.

- The fourth major party, in addition to the three socialist ones (Bolsheviks, Mensheviks, SRs), was the Constitutional Democrats, whose name was usually shortened to "Kadets." This was the main liberal party, a conservative group with some Centrist tendencies representing primarily the upper-middle and upper classes. The Kadets wanted to retain Russia's monarchy, but in a constitutional manner such as that of the United Kingdom. On the political spectrum, the left end of the Kadets bumped up against the right end of the Mensheviks and SRs. The Kadets sought to put a stop to any attempt to go beyond the immediate results of the February Revolution, believing it had already gone too far, and sought to continue to fight World War I. The Kadets favored the removal of Nicholas II because they believed they could fight the war more effectively.
- Furthest to the Right was the Octobrist Party, monarchists who wanted a powerful tsar restored to the throne, although not necessarily with the same absolute powers. This group tended to evaporate over the course of 1917 due to the immense unpopularity of this opinion; Octobrists, who openly sought a dictatorship of the Right but with more political power for big capitalists than they had possessed under the tsar, tended to drift to the Kadets, who gradually moved further Right as the year progressed.

Soviets were formed in the opening days of the revolution—the February Revolution started where the events of 1905 had left off, then quickly moved beyond. The same day that the tsar and grand duke abdicated, two governments were set up—leading members of the Duma organized a Provisional Government and right Mensheviks and right SRs sitting in the Petrograd Soviet brought into being an Executive Committee. The members of the Duma had been elected on a very limited franchise in 1912, and the government they organized unilaterally reflected those limitations—an aristocrat who was the leading representative of Russia's rural nobles, Prince Georgii Lvov, was named prime minister; Pavel Miliukov, the pro-war head of the Kadets, was named foreign minister; and Aleksandr Guchkov, an industrialist and founder of the Octobrist Party, was named the minister of war.

In contrast to the self-appointed Provisional Government, the Petrograd Soviet was a more representative body, with direct elections to it from workplaces and military units; the soviet in turn elected its Executive Committee. Similar soviets sprang up in other cities, in army and navy units and, more slowly, in rural regions across Russia. The soviets were seen as more democratic than parliaments because soviet delegates weren't elected to fixed terms but could be recalled at any time. Thus the soviets saw rapid changes in composition; by September the Bolsheviks would hold a solid majority in Petrograd and Moscow, Russia's two main cities.

In theory, the Petrograd Soviet Executive Committee was the representative of working people, soldiers and sailors, but in practice this was not so clear-cut because the executive was dominated by right Mensheviks and right SRs who hoped to dampen the revolutionary excitement. The right socialists spent the first two days vainly attempting to prevent the strikes; failing totally at that task, they switched to calling for soviets in an effort to outflank the left socialists. A Menshevik described the right socialists' position this way: "Holding that the immediate successors to the autocratic régime were the bourgeois elements of the country, we expended all energies in order to force the propertied classes to take power into their own hands."[121]

Nonetheless, in the wake of the February Revolution, the soviets, by virtue of their popular nature, had much more credibility in the streets than did the Provisional Government, which had the upper-class composition that the right socialists sought in government. Thus the two bodies had different constituencies, not a surprising development in light of the deep class divides of Russia. Both bodies proclaimed they would firmly defend their respective followers, but in reality the two groups amicably set up a "dual" government.

The Provisional Government was given that name because it was to govern until a Constituent Assembly could be convened to decide all constitutional issues; its members assumed that the soviets would not last, certainly not beyond the Constituent Assembly, but for now they were necessary to quiet the masses. The right Mensheviks and right SRs who dominated the soviet didn't want the soviets to exist in the long term, either, and didn't possess sufficient confidence to govern, so the Provisional Government met their needs, too.

Both governments, in fact, hoped most of all to contain the masses who had just overthrown the tsar and were beginning to upset the previous order in the factories as well. Not at all an untypical attitude was expressed by a conservative monarchist who was one of the leaders of the Duma, Vasilii Shulgin, who wrote this in his diary about the crowds outside the Tauride Palace, seat of the Duma:

> [N]o matter how many of them there were—they had one face: vile—animal—stupid...or wicked...Machine guns! Machine guns—I wanted them. For I felt that only the language of machine guns would be understood by the street crowds and that only lead would be able to drive this terrible escaped beast back into his den...That which we so dreaded, that which we wanted to avoid was already a fact. The revolution had begun.[122]

A member of the Petrograd Soviet's military commission, Sergei

Mstislavskii, a left-wing SR who would be sent to formally arrest Nicholas II days later to prevent the Provisional Government from sneaking the deposed monarch off to England, was in the Tauride Palace as the dual government was being put into place, and with a clear eye discerned the rationales for those forming the two governments. "[N]ot only did they have no intention of capsizing one another, but they frantically grasped at any and all grounds for agreement. And this was both inevitable and natural, for despite all the apparent differences...[they] were united from the first hours of the revolution by one single characteristic which determined all else: this was their fear of the masses."[123]

Of the Petrograd Soviet Executive Committee, Mstislavskii wrote, "they feared government no less than they feared the workers and soldiers...They would be hard put to know exactly what they were fighting for, in the event of a final break with the bourgeois elements in the Duma cabinet. Under these conditions, they naturally could not commit themselves to 'taking power.'"[124] The Provisional Government, on the other hand, "would never have deigned to associate with 'people of a certain sort' (the words of the blue-blooded [Duma President Mikhail] Rodzianko)...had it not been for that same fear of the masses...[T]he socialists were the lightning conductor they needed."[125]

The Executive Committee formally consented to the formation of the Provisional Government on the condition that it submit to an Executive Committee "watchdog" commission to monitor its performance.[126]

The composition of the Provisional Government represented a disappointment to the workers, soldiers, sailors and others who overthrew the tsar—nobody who played any role of any kind in the revolution was in it. Worse still, Miliukov, the new foreign minister, made it quite clear he intended to continue the war, vowing to wage it more effectively; a vow strongly in the face of popular opinion. With one exception, the remainder of the cabinet were Kadets or Octobrists. The one "socialist" was Kerensky, although at this time Kerensky did possess credibility because of his energetic work as a lawyer defending revolutionaries in the tsarist courts. A leading right Menshevik, Nikolai Chkheidze, was invited to join the Provisional Government cabinet, but declined, and emerged as the chair of the Petrograd Soviet.

The day that Nicholas II abdicated, the Petrograd Soviet issued its Order Number One, endorsing committees of elected soldiers and sailors that would negotiate with their officers, and declaring that no Provisional Government order that conflicted with the soviet should be obeyed. The Mensheviks and SRs who dominated the soviet did not necessarily want to go any further, or at most move very cautiously from here; and the first Bolshevik party leaders arriving from Siberian exile, freed by the revolution, such as Lev Kamenev and Josef Stalin, were of similar mind, despite the opposition to such cautious tactics among the Bolshevik rank-and-file. The Bolsheviks followed a policy of tacit support of the Provisional Government until Vladimir Lenin arrived from Switzerland the next month, issuing a call to develop the revolution into a more radical, socialist stage.

Already, the people of Petrograd, Moscow and elsewhere were developing the revolution. Employees immediately began forming and electing factory committees; these were to be bodies to supervise management but when necessary took direct responsibility for production. This was particularly true in state-run factories—in some cases, workers wanted to ensure that production for the war would continue, but in other cases it was a combination of wanting to implement deep reforms in how industry operated and/or having to assume management because, in many factories under direct military control, the officers in charge fled during the revolution.[127] In factories across Petrograd, employees "fired" their managers by placing them in wheelbarrows, carting them out and dumping them—dozens were given this treatment in some large plants.[128] Workers quickly imposed an eight-hour day and, given the revolutionary mood, the organization representing the owners of Petrograd's biggest businesses agreed to the eight-hour workday and to recognize the factory committees less than two weeks after the fall of the tsar.[129] Moscow workers also imposed an eight-hour day, backed by the Moscow Soviet, and factory owners there, too, albeit with grumbles, accepted the more humane workday.[130]

Understanding the mood in the streets and analyzing a political climate in which yawning gaps would only grow wider, Lenin, on his arrival from Switzerland, argued in his "April theses" that the period of "bourgeois government" would be short, and that either a second, fully socialist revolution would take place, or the only alternative would be monarchists, military officers and other reactionaries reinstalling the tsar. Lenin argued that no support should be given to the Provisional Government; instead all power should be transferred to the soviets.

Bolshevik political leaders were stunned at this dramatic proclamation, and Lenin met considerable initial resistance to his thunderbolt from the party's Central Committee. The Bolsheviks' newspaper, *Pravda,* published Lenin's "April theses" with a disclaimer that they represented a personal opinion and were not endorsed by the Central Committee.[131] But the popular masses did want the revolution to go forward and did want the war to end, goals impossible to achieve under the Provisional Government.

At this point, even the Bolsheviks trailed public opinion, so strongly toward the Left had it moved. The other parties were still further behind events, and it was the Bolsheviks' ability to represent popular moods—most concretely in their "Peace, bread, land" and "All power to the soviets" slogans—that enabled them eventually to enjoy the support of a significant majority of urban working people. Lenin did begin winning converts to his theses later in April, but the party's right wing would continue to moderate Bolshevik policy. (The old pre-war divisions had been superseded, but although the party was now united, new differences emerged over tactics and tempo.)

In the meantime, Miliukov issued a note to Russia's war allies assuring them that Russia would fight to the end and not seek a separate peace. This prompted more demonstrations, forcing Miliukov to resign. A May Provisional Government shuffle brought five right socialists into the cabinet, but the Kadets held a majority and government policy continued unchanged. The Provisional Government continued to postpone the Constituent Assembly because the Kadets were afraid of socialists gaining control of it. The impatience of workers, soldiers and sailors mounted, and the Bolsheviks decided to call a demonstration in Petrograd to coincide with a national congress of soviets there in June—the soviets had been uncoordinated local bodies and this decentralized nature was one reason for opposition to them as the basis of a new government.

The congress, a meeting of representatives of soviets from across Russia designed to create a national structure for them, passed a resolution supporting the Provisional Government, and decided to ban the Bolshevik march. Under heavy pressure, the Bolsheviks called off their demonstration.[132] The congress then decided to call a demonstration of its own, in part to defuse tension in the capital. The plan backfired, however, when the 500,000 who marched overwhelmingly carried banners bearing Bolshevik slogans.[133]

Throughout the spring, employee rebellions assumed a more organized character, becoming more oriented toward preventing lockouts and plant closures as opposed to lashing out against individual managers. Efforts to deepen and institutionalize "workers' control" flowed from this development, with several factories in Petrograd and Moscow putting managers on salaries under the supervision of the workers.[134] In many Petrograd factories, factory committees had to send delegations on searches for fuel, sometimes to other regions.[135] Party politics played a role in workplace struggles as more people paid attention to the various programs—the timidity of the Mensheviks and the disorganization and wide internal divergences of the Socialist Revolutionaries (SRs) as contrasted to the more militant stands of the Bolsheviks fueled extensive shifts in the strengths of the parties. An already tepid proposal on factory committees put forth by the Petrograd Soviet was further watered down before being passed by the Provisional Government on 6 May; under this law, the factory committees were to confine themselves to representing workers in pay disputes and engaging in educational work.[136] But the factory committees were already taking on much more responsible tasks than these and so the new law was ignored by them.

Although the Mensheviks and SRs continued to control the soviets in June, the massive show of support for the Bolsheviks at the soviet congress-sponsored demonstration was not a fluke. The first citywide conference of Petrograd factory committees in early June and the ensuing central council of factory committees had large Bolshevik majorities.[137] The Bolsheviks also became the largest bloc in the Petrograd Council of Trade Unions, although they needed the votes of the Menshevik left wing, the Internationalists, to form a stable majority.[138] At Kronstadt, the crucial naval base in the waters leading to Petrograd, the Bolsheviks had a strong following among the sailors, who took control of the base in June.[139] The factory owners were not remaining quiet, however, as industrialists in Moscow and southern Russia coordinated lockouts in June and the Provisional Government's labor minister, a Menshevik, sided with mine owners' demands to curtail their workers' demands.[140]

Unrest in the countryside was on the upswing as well—open seizures of land by peasants steadily increased through the spring.[141] The Provisional Government, backed by most of the SR leadership, postponed all discussion of land reform until the convening of the Constituent Assembly. This implied a ban on any rural changes. The government did indeed prohibit all land seizures and instituted a freeze on land relationships, thereby preventing peasants from obtaining legal title to land they already owned, but allowed the big estate owners to buy and sell land on the basis that freezing their land might hurt their property values—a set of policies bitterly opposed by peasants, who saw them as one-sided against them.[142]

In Petrograd, rank-and-file Bolsheviks continued to agitate, calling for the immediate overthrow of the Provisional Government. Lenin and the party leadership worked to hold back this sentiment, believing that a show of arms was premature, but the dramatic increase in the party's membership reflected increasing societal militancy. Local Bolshevik bodies, most importantly the party's Military Organization (soldiers and sailors who organized among their ranks) and the party organization for the Vyborg District of Petrograd (a neighborhood of many large factories with militant workforces), went forward with preparations for a 16 July armed demonstration without the authorization of the party's Central Committee. "Workers' militias" organized by the capital city's factory committees and sailors from the Kronstadt naval base agitated for an armed demonstration, and some of these agitators wanted to go further and stage an uprising. This was in part reflective of the general pull away from the center that periods of intense political ferment generate—Miliukov in his Kadet newspaper was now calling for the arrest of Lenin and Trotsky for "subversive activity," while anarchists chided the Bolsheviks for timidity.[143]

The workers' militias were also angered because the Petrograd city legislature, a pre-revolutionary holdover now loyal to the Provisional Government, had been trying to force them to disband in favor of the "official" civil militia; both militias had sprung up after the police were dispersed by the revolution and the police stations burned.[144] Bolshevik leaders attempted to call off the armed demonstration without success; in contrast to the previous month, militancy had become too strong to hold back. Part of the crowd besieged the Tauride Palace, headquarters of the Petrograd Soviet, demanding that the right socialists break their coalition with the Kadets. After two days of occupying the streets of Petrograd, the demonstrators' energy ran out and, as word went around that detachments of troops from the front loyal to the Provisional Government were being sent to confront the demonstrators and as Bolsheviks leaders continued to ask the demonstrators to disperse, the action came to an end.

The Provisional Government used the indecisive outcome of the demonstration, which became known as the "July Days," to disband the workers' militias by prohibiting militia members from receiving their regular factory salary when serving in the militias—this hostility directed against them further radicalized the militia members against the Provisional Government and the right socialists.[145] But the backlash that now set in went far beyond the reining in of the militias: Lenin was absurdly accused of being a German agent; arrest warrants were issued for Bolshevik leaders; and Bolshevik offices and printing facilities were destroyed by rampaging police and Right-wing street gangs. The newspapers of non-Bolshevik groups began printing a barrage of white-hot denunciations and wild, obviously false accusations. Lenin and his closest associate, Grigorii Zinoviev, fled to Finland; other Bolsheviks found themselves in the notorious Kresty prison.

Trotsky's biographer, Isaac Deutscher, painted a grim picture of Kresty's conditions:

> The conditions inside the prison were even worse now [than under the tsar]. The cells were extremely overcrowded: the rounding up of suspects continued, and large batches were brought in daily. Criminal and political offenders were herded

> together, whereas under the old régime the political offenders had enjoyed the privilege of separation. All were kept on a near-starvation diet. The criminals were incited against the "German agents," robbed of their food and manhandled. Prosecutors, examiners and jailers were the same as under the Tsar. The contrast between the pretensions of the new rulers and the inside aspect of the judicial machinery was striking and, as Trotsky watched it, he reflected that Lenin was not so mistaken when he decided to take refuge.[146]

Ironically, despite the gain in strength enjoyed by the Provisional Government from these roundups, its second cabinet dissolved. Kerensky replaced Lvov as prime minister but needed three weeks to form a new cabinet of right socialists and Kadets. The right socialists still wanted a coalition with the Kadets, and the sudden explosion of anger directed at the Bolsheviks must have made it easier for them to do so. The reaction against the Bolsheviks became so furious that Lenin, by now hiding out in a barn well outside of Petrograd, fell into a temporary mood of despair in which he expected to be hanged and said the party should go underground "seriously and for a good long time."[147] Kerensky was lifted by a crowd onto their shoulders at a well-attended memorial for seven Cossacks who had died during the July Days.[148] But the pendulum would suddenly swing just as sharply the other way in less than two months. Despite surface appearances to the contrary, militancy had not disappeared—a citywide meeting of Petrograd union leaders soon after the July Days voted to authorize a general strike and condemn government persecution of Bolsheviks before deciding to accept an arbitration settlement of a new contract.[149]

Seeking to capitalize on the new mood, monarchists and conservatives began agitating not only for the disbanding of the soviets, which had always been anathema to them, but also against the Provisional Government. General Lavr Kornilov, whom Kerensky had appointed commander-in-chief, started moving military units in and around Petrograd without informing the government amid rumors of a possible coup attempt. On 9 September, Kornilov issued a public statement that he was seizing power, and troops were already marching toward Petrograd under his orders.

Kerensky would not be able to defend himself and his government without Bolshevik help. The government hastily began arming Red Guards and using the Bolshevik Military Organization to train volunteers in the use of arms. Menshevik, SR and Bolshevik unions and organizations pledged to defend the revolution; soldiers opposed to Kornilov vowed to fight his coup attempt; sailors passed a resolution declaring Kornilov a traitor and calling for all power to be transferred to the soviets; and railway workers were given orders to stop Kornilov's advance, by ripping up railroad tracks if necessary. The Kornilov coup was defeated virtually without a shot. Agitators met many detachments and converted the soldiers on the spot; in at least one case soldiers then arrested their commanding officer.

Soon, later in September, the Bolsheviks had obtained a majority in the soviets of Moscow, Petrograd, Kiev, Odessa and other cities. One measure of the rapid shift in public opinion is the voting for the Moscow city legislature. In June 1917, SRs won a majority of seats, with the Bolsheviks winning only 11 of 98 seats; in September, the Bolsheviks won half the seats, 47, with the Menshevik total dropping from 12 to 4.[150] Popular opinion was now decisively for an all-socialist government, but the right Mensheviks and SRs still refused to break with the Kadets even though the Kadets had asked Kerensky to step down during Kornilov's coup attempt and suggested a Kornilov-aligned general as the new prime minister. Further, one reason for the continued Provisional Government refusal to call for an election to a Constituent Assembly was to appease the Kadets, still fearing a socialist-dominated body.

With their support rapidly dwindling in the soviets, the Mensheviks and SRs attempted to buy some more time for themselves by creating a "Democratic State Conference" that would be tasked with providing guidance on Russia's future form of government and electing members from its ranks to a "pre-parliament" that would in turn prepare for the Constituent Assembly, still somewhere in the unspecified future. The Democratic Conference was not only a delaying tactic; it was also set up to give extra weight to peasant soviets and rural nonpolitical organizations and less representation to workers', soldiers' and sailors' soviets and other urban institutions. In sum, it was stacked to give right Mensheviks and right SRs a comfortable majority, and did so. Even this relatively conservative body denounced Kerensky over the Kornilov coup attempt and, despite containing a majority in favor of forming a new coalition Provisional Government, it voted against any continued coalition with the Kadets. Yet Kerensky formed another new cabinet with Kadets.

Pressure for an all-socialist government continued to grow from below and now, with soviet majorities, Lenin agitated within his party for taking power from the Provisional Government, without any other socialist parties if need be. Failure to do so, he believed, would result in another, much stronger, coup attempt by Kornilov and Kornilov's reactionary allies, which next time might well succeed. The party was deeply split on this question, with Lenin's long-time associates, Kamenev and Zinoviev, the most forceful opponents of Lenin's plan for taking power.

The Bolsheviks remained a divided party; their rapidly growing support coupled with the ineptitude of other parties, each even less unified than the Bolsheviks, were critical factors in the events of October.

## The elusiveness of power and fragmentation of the parties: The crisis of October

During the rare moments when a country is at a revolutionary moment, state power has become unmoored. Prior to the February Revolution, power in Russia had been held by an absolute monarchy, an anachronistic arrangement. The aristocracy and the industrialists supported the downfall of the tsar only to the extent that state power would fall into their hands; without the disaster that World War I inflicted on Russia, they might have remained content with tsarism since the practical effect of Tsar Nicholas II's government policies was the maintenance of the interests of the aristocracy and the industrialists, backed by unlimited force. But as capitalism develops, it becomes unnatural for industrialists and financiers (the capitalist class classically known as the "bourgeoisie") to not wrest state power for themselves.

The months following the February Revolution had seen industrialists and aristocrats attempt to bend the state to their whims; that the industrialists' political representatives, the liberal Kadets, had steadily moved Right was a signal that they believed force was the only way to overcome the refusal of working people to cooperate with the taking of power that the capitalists saw as their natural right. The masses, and the left socialists, had struggled to place state power into the hands of working people.

In the peculiar "dual government" of Russia, this duel was expressed in the ongoing push and pull between the Provisional Government and the soviets. Now that the left socialists had been voted into the majority in the soviets, the question of state power would have to be decided soon. The two groups that dominated the soviets for much of 1917, the right Mensheviks and right Socialist Revolutionaries, treated power as a hot potato, and kept trying to hand it to the liberals. The Provisional Government was discredited in the eyes of the popular masses; the aristocrat/liberal coalition cabinet of its first lineup, featuring

Kadet leader Pavel Miliukov's vow to prosecute the war to a victorious conclusion, was a bitter disappointment to many, and subsequent cabinets had not been looked upon with any more favor.

The Provisional Government had an existence because the Petrograd Soviet endorsed it; the government derived what popular legitimacy it had from the right Mensheviks' and SRs' willingness to accept cabinet portfolios. These two leaderships would not have looked upon the dissolution of the soviets with sadness. Through most of the year, the Bolsheviks had raised the call, "All power to the soviets," which the Mensheviks and SRs adamantly opposed although it would have meant that they would take power. Both party leaderships believed that governing without the liberals would be impossible and, in any event, undesirable, which meant negotiating a succession of coalition cabinets with much watered-down policies and a body too divided and too out of sync with popular opinion to be able to govern. The Kadets, behind Miliukov, abandoned any pretense to democracy, instead openly seeking a Right-wing dictatorship, whether with Kornilov or another military commander. It was no longer politically possible for right socialists to link with the Kadets, but, in their political myopia, they refused to see that.

Miliukov saw Russia as incapable of democracy at this time; given that dictatorship would be its only salvation, a Right-wing dictatorship was the only acceptable version. Miliukov convinced himself that installing a monarchist general deeply hostile to any increment or form of democracy—from this pool were the only candidates to lead a dictatorship of the Right—would someday eventually lead to a democratic opening.[151] But the candidates for a Right dictatorship, such as Kornilov or other high-ranking military officers, despised the Kadets; there would have been no room in such a dictatorship even for liberals who had become pseudo-monarchists.

Miliukov put his anti-democratic views on display during a 31 October speech: "The German successes [on the battlefield] are directly proportionate to the successes of those who call themselves the revolutionary democracy. I do not wish to say 'to the successes of the revolution,' because I believe that the defeats of the revolutionary democracy are victories for the revolution."[152] In so many words, Miliukov said a revolution made for democracy can only be a success when democracy is defeated.

The views of monarchists were well summed up by Mikhail Rodzianko in a widely publicized speech in late October: "Petrograd appears threatened...I say, to hell with Petrograd...People fear our central institutions in Petrograd will be destroyed. To this, let me say that I should be glad if these institutions are destroyed because they have brought Russia nothing but grief."[153] And that outburst was in response to rumors that Provisional Government head Aleksandr Kerensky was about to surrender the capital to the Germans in order to throttle the revolution. Rodzianko had been the leader of the Duma before the fall of the tsar, and he had done everything he could to keep Nicholas II on the throne; in response to one of Rodzianko's warnings just before his fall imploring the tsar to act to save his throne, Nicholas II responded by saying, "Again that fat-bellied Rodzianko has written me a lot of nonsense which I won't even bother to answer."[154]

Rodzianko was unusual only in voicing such sentiments in so public a fashion. One major Russian capitalist declared revolution "a sickness," adding that "sooner or later the foreign powers must intervene here...Starvation and defeat may bring the Russian people to their senses."[155] Other Right figures admitted that the breakdown of the economy was "part of a campaign to discredit the Revolution," efforts that included flooding mines, sabotaging machinery and crippling locomotives.[156]

All socialists condemned such nihilistic destruction, but nonetheless had widening divisions among themselves. One manifestation of these divisions was that the Socialist Revolutionaries were now splitting into two parties. An unwieldy group covering many shades of opinion, the SRs were also undergoing some shifting to the Left under the impacts of accelerating events, and the peasants' widespread taking of land from the big estates. Although the SRs were the party of the peasants, the party leadership in the Provisional Government, drawn from its right wing, continued to advocate a freeze in the countryside despite ongoing peasant seizures of land and timber, rendering themselves irrelevant.

The Right SRs continued to be preoccupied with the pre-parliament. Nikolai Avksentiev, one of the party's leaders, who had been president of the executive committee of the peasants' soviets since March and Provisional Government interior minister since July, became the pre-parliament's president. Avksentiev tried to assemble a coalition of right socialists and big capitalists—the same basic lineup as the Provisional Government. Nothing came out of this body, which was riven by divisions; the only thing members could agree on was that they hated the Bolsheviks. "A unitary institution had been created for the democrats and bourgeoisie, but there was no unity in it," Avksentiev later wrote. "The contradictions remained just as potent."[157]

The Left SRs agreed with the Bolsheviks (and the Menshevik Internationalists) that Russia needed an all-socialist government. But in contrast to Bolshevik thinking, the Left SRs believed there was no need for any sort of uprising, because the Provisional Government no longer had any credibility. "The March government was finished…the power, unified and undivided, had to go to the Soviets," wrote Sergei Mstislavskii, a party leader. "We were so sure of the inability of the Provisional Government to offer any resistance to the transfer of power…we stepped forward in unambiguous and absolute opposition to Lenin's doctrine of revolt. Revolt—an appearance, a highly visible violent takeover—seemed from our point of view to complicate the situation needlessly" by rupturing ties with all other groups.[158]

Mstislavskii believed that such a rupture would lead to a strong government by necessity, and that such a government would have to be built on existing institutions. "Since a radical uprooting of the whole system was beyond our means—owing to political and military considerations—we were inevitably drawn back into the charmed circle of using the old government apparatus which we had, in words at least, rejected."[159] Such a development would make the soviets unrealistic as a new form of permanent government.

> To persist on this course would be tantamount to suicide. For the dirty work of this "transitional period"...it was necessary, or so we thought, to make use of the right Socialist parties, whose activities would be fuelled by the unremitting pressure of the revolutionary masses led by the Bolsheviks and Left Socialist Revolutionaries. They would perish [politically], eventually, while performing this service, and on their bones would arise a new and real (and I emphasize this word) Soviet political order.[160]

Mstislavskii's Left SR colleague, Boris Kamkov, offered a similar retrospective in a November speech:

> [The Bolshevik] course seemed to us both dangerous and senseless. After coalition had so bankrupted itself, after it had become an empty shell and the very word coalition had become a term of abuse in worker and soldier circles, and when among workers and peasants it was impossible to find a single solid group which would defend coalition government,

> it seemed to us that it would be possible to rid ourselves painlessly of this skeleton by action of the All-Russian Congress of Soviets. At the same time, we believed that if this were done another way, say by means of the seizure of power…before the Congress, this might appear to be adventurist…[making] it impossible to avoid civil war.[161]

The Bolshevik overthrow of the Provisional Government was planned for the day that the Second All-Russian Congress of Soviets, a national assembly of soviets, was to take place: 7 November (25 October in the old-style Julian calendar still in use in Russia). The congress would elect a new Central Executive Committee, a standing federal executive, which would be responsible for setting policy for the soviets. The executive had contained a majority of Mensheviks and SRs since the first congress in June, and the rapid changes in the composition of soviets across the country would now be reflected in the new executive. Once seated, the Bolsheviks would command a majority on their own. The Bolsheviks wanted to present a fait accompli.

Kamkov said the Left SRs wanted the congress to organize a new government, and had agitated for armed support of the congress, but a few days before the convening, "it became clear to those of us working in factories and barracks that the Bolsheviks were mobilizing their forces not simply to defend the government [that would be] established by the congress, but rather to seize power in advance of the congress."[162] Mstislavskii, in a 26 October Left SR newspaper editorial, said an early armed uprising "would be a monstrous crime."[163]

The Mensheviks also ranged widely in their opinions, although they would hold together; not even its left wing, the Internationalists led by Yulii Martov, would split the party or join a post-overthrow coalition government, as the Left SRs did. Fedor Dan, a right Menshevik, opposed any transfer of power in almost apocalyptic terms. "The masses are sick and exhausted. They have no interest in the revolution. If the Bolsheviki start anything, that will be the end of the revolution…The counter-revolutionaries are waiting with the Bolsheviki to begin riots and massacres," Dan said at a meeting of the Central Executive Committee the day before the Second All-Russian Congress of Soviets was to open its session, which was to elect the new committee. "All power to the Soviets—that means death! Robbers and thieves are waiting for the moment to loot and burn!…Those who are urging this are committing a crime!"[164]

Dan brought a thunder of jeers upon himself for this speech. For it would seem odd to consistently oppose handing power to a representative of the only bodies freely elected and on which you sit.

Martov, for the left Mensheviks (although the Internationalists were decidedly a minority within their party), said at that same meeting: "The Internationalists are not opposed to the transmission of power to the democracy [the soviets], but they disapprove of the methods of the Bolsheviki. This is not the moment to seize power."[165]

Kerensky, feeling boxed in and undoubtedly feeling the end was near, one way or another, sought the means to suppress the Left. At a pre-parliament session on 6 November, Kerensky asserted that the Bolsheviks were assisting the German ruling class, not the German proletariat. After reading from a circular issued by left socialists, Kerensky exclaimed, "This is an attempt to incite the rabble against the existing order!" and vowed that "those groups and those parties which have dared to raise a hand against the free will of the Russian people, threatening at the same time to expose the front to Germany, are subject to immediate, decisive and total liquidation."[166] Kerensky sought a free hand to repress his many opponents, but he was not going to get it, among other reasons because there was no force willing to back him.

A long break followed Kerensky's angry speech, and when the meeting resumed, Kamkov was the first to speak. He asked, "Is there anybody at all who would trust this government? It does not have the support of the revolutionary army, or the proletariat, and coming out against it is not the rabble but precisely the most politically conscious elements of the proletarian democracy. If we are seriously interested in eliminating the soil in which the horrors of civil war are maturing, we must openly declare that the only way out of the present predicament is through the creation of a homogeneous, revolutionary, democratic government in which there will be no elements who organize demonstrations of homage to Kornilov."[167]

Martov spoke next, offering similar views: "The language of the prime minister, who permitted himself to speak of a rabble movement when what is at hand is a movement of a significant portion of the proletariat and the army, even if directed toward mistaken objectives, is a provocation for civil war...Repression can not be substituted for satisfaction of the needs of the revolution. An announcement must be made immediately that Russia is pursuing a policy of immediate peace, that land committees will have control over alienated lands awaiting settlement, and that democratization of the army will not be stopped."[168]

Dan, after roundly criticizing the Bolsheviks, then urged similar steps: "If you want to remove the soil in which Bolsheviks are growing like rotten mushrooms, we must turn to political measures. What is necessary is the clear enunciation by the government and the [pre-parliament] of a platform in which the people will see their just interests supported by the government and the [pre-parliament] and not the Bolsheviks."[169]

These last three statements, however, were aimed at the Provisional Government, which continued to resist any meaningful reform.

The pre-parliament then adopted a resolution put forth by the

Left and endorsed by more conservative figures such as Dan that criticized the Provisional Government's delays in putting forth reforms and called for a "land and peace" program.[170] Kerensky was furious, declaring to a delegation of right socialists that his government had "no need for admonitions and instructions and would cope with the rebellion by itself."[171]

The Bolsheviks had their own divisions. Vladimir Lenin, in hiding in Finland, wanted an immediate insurrection, without any other parties. Leon Trotsky and others wanted the uprising to be an act of the Second All-Russian Congress of Soviets, timed to that congress, and not simply of one party. Lev Kamenev and Grigorii Zinoviev, close associates of Lenin since the 1903 split with the Mensheviks, took a position very close to those of the Left SRs and Menshevik Internationalists. The two believed that an uprising was a suicidal adventure: "Before history, before the international proletariat, before the Russian revolution and the Russian working class, we have no right to stake the whole future on the card of an armed uprising...There are historical situations when an oppressed class must recognize that it is better to go forward to defeat than to give up without a battle. Does the Russian working class find itself in such a situation? No, and a thousand times, no!"[172]

Kamenev and Zinoviev wanted an all-socialist government, with the Bolsheviks sharing power with the Mensheviks and SRs. The two did not see European revolution as imminent, which would leave the Russian revolution fatally isolated. "If we should come to the conclusion...that it is necessary to wage a revolutionary war, the masses of the soldiers will run away from us." To the argument that the majority of the world's workers were already with the Bolsheviks, Kamenev and Zinoviev replied, "Unfortunately, this is not so."[173]

Most of the rest of the Bolshevik leadership felt confident that a Russian socialist revolution would be a prelude to, and perhaps the spark for, similar revolutions across Europe. This viewpoint embodied Trotsky's "theory of the permanent revolution." Under this theory, revolutions break out in one country after another, and only then can socialism be established because a successful string of revolutions would create a bloc of countries that could support and assist one another and have enough resources to withstand the inevitable attacks from the remaining capitalist states. So firmly did many Bolsheviks believe in the imminence of European revolution, they simply dismissed the question of what would happen if no other revolutions occurred, although they had absolutely no illusions that Russia was ready for any sort of socialism on its own. A single undeveloped country like Russia, standing alone as a socialist state, would be bound to go under, an event that would be followed by a furious counter-revolution mad with revenge. Believing that Russia would likely become isolated, Kamenev and Zinoviev wanted the Bolsheviks to avoid that fate.

Trotsky felt no such doubts. While in New York, still in exile, at the beginning of 1917, he was asked at a public meeting what would happen if no rising occurred in Germany. Trotsky dismissed such thoughts as "altogether improbable" and, when pressed on the point, replied, "Really we need not rack our brains over so implausible a supposition."[174] Trotsky certainly hadn't changed his mind now.

Nikolai Bukharin, who would lead the party's right opposition in the 1920s but at this time was a firebrand for the left of the party, saw the same solution to the question of how a backward, primarily peasant country like Russia could possibly be ripe for a socialist revolution. "There is no doubt whatsoever that the Russian revolution will spread to the old capitalist countries and that sooner or later it will lead to the victory of the European proletariat," he wrote shortly after the fall of the tsar.[175] Bukharin later elaborated: "A lasting victory of the Russian proletariat is...inconceivable without the support of the Western European proletariat."[176] Lenin expressed no doubts, repeatedly writing in the weeks leading up to the October Revolution that European revolution was around the corner, and seeing the sporadic mutinies in the German navy as a harbinger.

Those revolutions, as it turned out, weren't coming, which would seem to vindicate Kamenev, Zinoviev, Kamkov, Mstislavskii and Martov. Conventional wisdom holds that Lenin, Trotsky and the rest of the pro-insurrection Bolsheviks were unrealistic dreamers. That seems too harsh a judgment, even with the benefit of hindsight. The answer to the question of whether European revolution was a realistic possibility is much more ambiguous. Uprisings, often with explicitly socialist demands, did happen across Europe, including in Germany. (A survey of which will be taken up later in this chapter.)

Regardless of developments elsewhere in Europe, Russia could no longer be governed as it had been since February. Conditions in the city and country continued to deteriorate—the Provisional Government not only was more and more out of sync with the country's moods but had shown itself unable to cope with Russia's myriad of problems. Working people in the city viewed it with hostility, seeing it as arrayed against themselves and in favor of the big capitalists; Rightists within the cities loathed the Provisional Government for not displaying sufficient vigor in putting a halt to the revolution; and peasants across the countryside simply ignored it.

Russia's infrastructure was collapsing—industrial production had fallen by as much as 40 percent from February to September, goods shipments drastically declined and more than one-quarter of the engines serving an already poorly built and inadequate railroad system were out of service.[177] Living standards declined drastically during this time, ravaged by inflation and food shortages. The Provisional Government did not help its credibility when, in the midst of the September Kornilov coup attempt, the Menshevik minister of labor issued two circulars undercutting the factory committees and asserting the rights of owners to return to pre-February conditions.[178] Oil barons in the Caspian Sea city of Baku refused to honor a negotiated contract with their workforce,[179] igniting a general strike there,[180] and industrialists in the Ural Mountains region threatened to shut down all of the region's factories to stop even minimal attempts at instituting workers' control.[181]

By September, authorities had reduced the daily bread ration in Moscow to less than one-quarter of a kilogram per day, and in response to shortages groups of residents seized stockpiles of sugar and coffee found in warehouses and residences, turning them over to neighborhood food supply committees.[182] In the six weeks before the October Revolution, an estimated 1.5 million Russians went on strike.[183] Conditions were no calmer outside the cities. The Provisional Government had instituted a grain monopoly, but by August peasants widely refused to sell at the monopoly price; sometimes they simply refused to send grain to the cities or to the army, and when the government attempted to requisition it, resisted with arms.[184] The countryside was in dramatic upheaval—land-hungry peasants had not only continued to seize land from the estate owners, they began seizing estate owners' crops and blocking the transport of grain from outside their local areas.[185] Food shortages began occurring even in rural areas and, in response, peasants in these areas seized grain being transported through their areas for their own use or to sell on the black market.[186]

But the political debate went beyond questions of land ownership in the countryside or what would constitute "workers' control" in the cities—the core of the debate was what sort of state Russia would be. An irony is that it was the Mensheviks, and not the Bolsheviks, as is frequently asserted, who were the inflexible dogmatists. The Mensheviks believed that a long period of development from feudalism to capitalism to socialism could not be avoided; therefore, because Russia was underdeveloped, the country had no choice but to carry through a capitalist revolution and then go through a long period of capitalist development before it would be ripe for any socialist revolution. Although Russian Marxist pioneer turned pro-war nationalist Grigorii Plekhanov had ceased to have any influence even among Mensheviks, it was nonetheless his overly mechanical formulation to which Mensheviks clung.

The February Revolution had been a capitalist revolution, even if those who had made the revolution wanted it to go further, but implicit in the Mensheviks' ideology was that the revolution had to be frozen at February. The Mensheviks wanted to institute a stable parliamentary form of government and allow the new industrialists a free hand to build up industry, thereby eventually creating the large working class needed for an eventual transition to socialism.

The Menshevik viewpoint tacitly assumed Russian society had reached stability, with a broad social agreement on a new liberal state. There was no such stability or agreement. The Bolshevik right, Left SRs and Menshevik Internationalists, with some nuances of difference among them, saw that the liberal forces, now ironically only represented by the right socialists, were spent, incapable of governing and with a base that was rapidly vanishing. The Kadets, who should have been a logical political home for liberals, moderately conservative middle-class people and those industrialists who were relatively more moderate, instead had joined monarchists in lusting for a military dictatorship of the extreme Right. Such a dictatorship could have easily led to the reinstitution of tsardom; it could not be imposed without bloody tsarist-style crackdowns on behalf of Russia's industrialists and aristocracy.

The Mensheviks now represented liberal opinion, but the Mensheviks' vote totals vanished with that base; they were now trailing all the other major parties, polling only minuscule minorities. Urban blue-collar workers were overwhelmingly socialist; their support went to left socialists, primarily the

Bolsheviks. Portions of the middle class were doing the same and the progressive intelligentsia were increasingly backing the Bolsheviks and Left SRs. Excepting the dwindling numbers who still held to a liberal outlook, the rest of urban society was now backing the forces of the Right—the Kadets, monarchists and others who simply wanted a strong hand to restore "order."

Therefore, in the view of the Bolshevik right, Left SRs and Menshevik Internationalists, only an all-socialist government could withdraw Russia from the war, cope with the immense problems of rebuilding the country and enjoy the support of most Russians. Peasants in large majorities still backed the SRs, but the Left SRs had become a separate party in all but name by autumn and they sanctioned the peasants' taking of land from the rural elite's estates, which was happening regardless, and would enjoy at least the passive support of the peasantry. And since soldiers and sailors, as militantly socialist as any segment of Russia, were primarily peasants, much of the Left spirit was being exported to the countryside as desertions continued.

The center and left Bolsheviks, while differing on tactics, believed that a seizure of power was the only way a socialist government could be brought into power. Because the present situation was unstable, either Russia would go forward with a socialist revolution, and then receive badly needed helping hands from the newly socialized industrial countries of Europe that were about to come into existence, or it would fall back into a punishing reaction, with a military dictatorship or a reinstalled tsar not only ending all democracy and reinstituting the harshness of the ancien régime, but ruthlessly drowning the revolution in blood with massacres that could easily total hundreds of thousands or millions. That Right dictatorship would also keep Russia in the war and keep it yoked to Entente demands; as late as October, the French and British governments were demanding a new offensive from Kerensky. Since it was faced with two, and only two, choices, Russia had no choice, and the sooner the takeover, the better, in the view of these Bolsheviks.

The Bolsheviks drew confidence in their viewpoints from the tidal wave of votes going their way. By mid-September, 126 soviets passed resolutions asking the national-level Central Executive Committee to take power from the Provisional Government.[187] The Second All-Russia Congress of Soviets, which would elect a new Central Executive Committee, had been scheduled for September; congresses were supposed to be convened every three months. But the right Mensheviks and right SRs in control of the executive elected in June had refused to convene the congress.[188] This was another delaying tactic just as their creation of the Democratic State Conference and pre-parliament was intended to delay the convening of a Constituent Assembly. When the congress finally did convene, 507 out of 670 elected delegates voted in support of "all power to the soviets."[189]

In mid-October, Kerensky was preparing a reshuffling of troops on the excuse that he was strengthening the front; in reality, he intended to transfer regiments loyal to the Bolsheviks out of the capital in anticipation of a showdown with the soviets. The Petrograd Soviet began discussing if it should veto the order, which it had the authority to do under its Order Number One issued in March. On 22 October, the Petrograd Soviet created a Military Revolutionary Committee to help organize the defense of the capital; this body, which included Bolsheviks and Left SRs, would become the general staff of the revolution. Overwhelming backing by the representatives of factory and barracks soviets carried the motion.

On 23 October, 12 of the 21 members of the Bolshevik Central Committee met in the apartment of a party activist; to ensure the secrecy of the meeting she had asked her husband, a Menshevik Internationalist, to promise to not come home that night because of bad weather. The vote was 10–2 in favor of insurrection, and for the first time the Bolsheviks had made a decision on an uprising. But the two dissenters, Kamenev and Zinoviev, then appealed to lower levels of the party.

Six days later, on the 29th, the regiments of the Petrograd garrisons declared they would ignore Kerensky and stay where they were. The garrison did follow an order by Trotsky, on the authority of the Military Revolutionary Committee, to provide 5000 rifles to Red Guards. That same day, the Bolshevik Central Committee met again to confirm its 23 October decision. It did, but not without differences of opinion.

Nikolai Krylenko, head of the party's Military Organization, said only a minority of the organization's leaders favored insurrection, and then only on initiative of the soviets, not the party, because they feared the revolutionary ardor of the soldiers was waning. Grigorii Sokolnikov, a prominent party leader who oversaw the party's newspapers and who was a popular speaker at mass meetings, argued for the uprising to happen after the Congress of Soviets was convened, because of the widespread view of the soviets as Russia's legitimate authority. Kamenev and Zinoviev renewed their arguments against any insurrection. Lenin again argued for the fastest possible insurrection in the name of the party, but ultimately agreed to a compromise resolution stating that the Bolshevik Central Committee and the soviets should jointly set the date, implicitly tying any uprising to the congress. The day tentatively chosen was 2 November (20 October old style), the eve of the expected opening of the congress.[190] That opening date coincidentally was quickly pushed back a few days by the soviets' Central Executive Committee, still under the control of the Mensheviks and Right SRs until the congress opened.

But dissent among the Bolsheviks had not been spent; this time, Kamenev and Zinoviev made their objections public, publishing them in an independent newspaper. This led to a new debate on what to do about what any political organization would consider a serious breach. Lenin immediately demanded his two old associates be expelled; others wanted to accept the resignation that Kamenev now tendered but not expel either; Josef Stalin was for both continuing to hold seats on the Central Committee, but Stalin came under attack for an "ambiguous" attitude displayed in the party's press; Yakov Sverdlov strongly condemned Kamenev and Zinoviev but opposed expulsion. Nobody backed Lenin's expulsion demand.[191] Kamenev and Zinoviev, however, stood with the party when the revolution began, and would hold responsible posts until after Lenin's death in 1924.

The Petrograd Soviet instructed the garrison to carry out only orders signed by the Revolutionary Military Committee, which was conveyed to them by Trotsky on 3 November and agreed to with a declaration calling for the All-Russia Congress of Soviets to assume all power. The last military outpost for which loyalty was in doubt was the Peter and Paul Fortress, and its loyalty to the soviets was secured on 5 November. The next day, Kerensky ordered the arrest and prosecution of the entire Revolutionary Military Committee, the Petrograd Soviet and the Bolshevik leadership.

Both sides were now in frenzied preparation; the uprising had to proceed within a day, before the Provisional Government could strike against it. The night of 6 November, a meeting of delegates assembling for the next day's Congress of Soviets was called; it was at this meeting that Dan made his speech equating "all power to the soviets" with "death." Dan then called for immediate peace negotiations and land reform, bringing upon himself derisive laughter and shouts of "too late"—he had just endorsed what the left socialists had called for all along and he and the right socialists had consistently opposed. It was a sign of how far public opinion had moved.

Overnight, Red Guards and regular military regiments began occupying key buildings throughout the city and a six-ship Baltic flotilla began steaming to Petrograd, as did trains full of sailors and soldiers. Finally, only the Winter Palace, where the Provisional Government ministers were holed up, remained out of the insurgents' hands. Kerensky fled in a United States embassy car just before the palace was encircled; he had no other means to leave Petrograd. The remainder of the cabinet, in the palace, morosely debated what to do, then decided to name a dictator with "unlimited power" and spent two hours deciding who the dictator should be as the armed units who were to have defended them began leaving the building.[192]

Finally, after an ultimatum, the naval ship *Aurora* began firing blanks at the Winter Palace. Sometime around 2 a.m., when it had become apparent most of the armed defenders had left, a detachment led by Vladimir Antonov-Ovseenko, one of the leaders of the Military Revolutionary Committee, made its way into the palace, found the cabinet ministers and arrested them. It had been an extraordinarily peaceful revolution—six people had died in Petrograd as compared to 1400 during the February Revolution.

## Taking power: Coalition or the dustbin?

Peace was not immediately at hand. In a more ominous sign, several hundred died during eight days of fighting in Moscow. Mensheviks and Right SRs who sat on the Moscow city legislature organized a "Committee of Public Safety" to counter the Moscow Soviet's declaration of support for the Bolshevik government in Petrograd. The district military commander, on behalf of the committee, surrounded the Kremlin, trapping Red Guards inside. Although the Red Guard leader agreed to surrender, the military academy officer candidates who mostly made up the commander's forces shot many of the Red Guards after they laid down their arms.[193] A second massacre, of arsenal workers in another part of the Kremlin, followed.[194] Reinforcements eventually tipped the scales in favor of the revolutionary forces—but when the Committee of Public Safety's military surrendered, they were merely disarmed and allowed to go free.[195]

In Petrograd, as the waiting for the dénouement at the Winter Palace dragged on, the Congress of Soviets finally convened, faced with the fact of the overthrow of the Provisional Government. The Bolsheviks held nearly two-thirds of the seats; they, the Left SRs (now formally a separate party) and Menshevik Internationalists proposed that the seats on the new Central Executive Committee be proportional to the vote. The new executive consisted of 14 Bolsheviks, 7 SRs, 3 Mensheviks and 1 Menshevik International; the Mensheviks declined to take their entitled seats.

Yulii Martov then proposed immediate negotiations for a unified socialist government. Sergei Mstislavskii agreed for the Left SRs and Anatolii Lunacharskii, speaking for the Bolsheviks, also agreed; the proposal passed unanimously. But then a succession of right socialists denounced the Bolsheviks and announced they were walking out of the congress, which they did to screams of "deserters" and "good riddance."[196]

Martov still sought to effect a compromise, and again presented a proposal for negotiations. This time, though, the proposal contained a reference to a "coup d'etat [that] threatens to bring about bloodshed, civil war and the triumph of counter-revolution" before calling for "a peaceful settlement" and "negotiations with other democratic organs and all the socialist parties."[197] Instead, all the bitterness, all the tension of the past weeks and months burst forth. The soldiers, sailors, working people and others who had just made the revolution couldn't help but see the "coup d'etat" reference as anything other than a provocation. And although Martov was not affiliated with the right factions that had left, it made his unity plea seem a little hollow.

Leon Trotsky replied with a harsh, unyielding speech well remembered by history: "A rising of the masses needs no justification," he began. "What has happened is an insurrection, and not a conspiracy...And now we are told: Renounce your victory, make concessions, compromise. With whom? With those wretched groups who have left us or who are making this proposal?...No one in Russia is with them any longer." Trotsky concluded: "You are miserable bankrupts, your role is played out. Go where you ought to go, into the dustbin of history!"

Martov and his Menshevik Internationalists did leave, leaving only the Left SRs, who stayed, and who would join the Bolsheviks in a coalition government later in the year. But that last exchange perhaps encapsulates the contradictions of the October Revolution. The revolution really did need unity among the socialist parties, yet the right socialists refused to unify; the Bolsheviks represented the true feelings of a large majority of Russians, directly in the cities and indirectly in the countryside through their willingness to endorse the actions of the peasants although they commanded only a small fraction of rural votes, yet they had little willingness to try to effect some sort of compromise with broader segments of socialists; the dangers of one party going alone were on display on the first day of the revolution, yet the other parties stubbornly continued to refuse to acknowledge the pace of the revolution or to genuinely seek any kind of compromise with socialists to their left.

How different might history have been if all three socialist parties, or least broad majorities in each, had grasped what was happening, and willingly dismissed Aleksandr Kerensky and the Provisional Government while forming a new all-socialist government based on the All-Russian Congress of Soviets? Such a government need not have been based permanently on the soviets, but there was no other realistic basis for any government at the moment. An agreement on the basis of a government in which each of the parties would agree to participate would have given the revolution a broader base, and possibly it would have had an easier time, in part because there would have been less political space for the counter-revolution. But the same internal foes, and the same bitter hostility of the capitalist countries, would have been there just the same, so it is difficult to say just how much easier the next years might have been.

Despite all the bitterness that exploded that night, there was a final attempt at creating a coalition. On 11 November, after a final armed march on Petrograd organized by Kerensky was defeated, the Bolshevik Central Committee, in the absence of Vladimir Lenin and Trotsky, voted to reopen negotiations. The right Bolsheviks were still anxious to create a socialist coalition government and railway workers threatened a strike if a coalition was not formed. The Mensheviks and Right SRs countered with their demands for agreeing to a coalition: Any new government would be responsible to undefined "broad democratic circles" rather than to the soviets, the Red Guards would be disarmed, and Lenin and Trotsky would be barred from the government.[198]

No party could agree to such unrealistic conditions; no party that had just successfully led a revolution could immediately throw overboard its two top leaders to placate other parties. To agree to this set of demands would mean annulling the revolution that had just happened, and the masses who had just made it would not have stood for that. The Bolsheviks countered that any party that recognized the authority of the soviets would be invited to join a coalition government. The Mensheviks and Right SRs refused to recognize soviet authority on the ground that would constitute recognition of the Bolshevik takeover of power.[199] That they could not do.

Despite the conditions laid down by the Mensheviks and Right SRs, which meant negating the revolution and allowing opposition parties to dictate its leadership, the Bolshevik Central Committee discussed them, and the party's right voted to accept the conditions. But outvoted, the right, including five ministers in the new Bolshevik government, resigned all posts. Soon enough, they returned, and all was forgiven again, although not all regained important posts. The Bolsheviks nonetheless kept Central Executive Committee seats open for the other parties in proportion to their elected strength, should they decide to recognize the soviets.[200]

The final right socialist bid to annul the October Revolution came in January, when the Constituent Assembly at last convened—among the Bolsheviks' first acts was to schedule a vote for it. After eight months of refusal to convoke the Assembly, the Provisional Government parties suddenly put great stock in it. Voting was conducted at the end of November, and socialist parties won about 76 percent of the vote.[201] But even that impressive vote total doesn't measure the strength of the Left because the Left SRs had formally split to form a separate party too late to avoid running on a unified SR ticket instead of appearing on ballots as the separate party they had become.

The Kadets, with whom the right socialists were so desperate to create a permanent coalition, won all of 5 percent of the vote; the Mensheviks polled 3 percent.[202] The Bolsheviks did well in the cities—in Petrograd, they took almost half the vote in a 19-party field, nearly twice the votes of the second-place Kadets and more than 20 times more votes than the Mensheviks.[203] But the countryside voted for the single SR slate, which easily won the most seats. The single SR list had been drawn up months earlier, during the repeated postponements of the vote, and contained mostly Right SR members who had previously made up much of the party leadership and had sought to freeze the revolution at February.

The most thorough study of the Assembly has been conducted by the historian Oliver Radkey, who concluded:

> The election, therefore, does not measure the strength of [Left SRs]. The lists were drawn up long before the [SR] schism occurred; they were top-heavy with older party workers whose radicalism had abated by 1917. The people voted indis-

> criminately for the SR label...[T]he leftward current was doubtless stronger everywhere on November [25] than when the lists had been drawn up.[204]

The Right SRs benefited from the goodwill earned by the Left SRs, who supported the peasants' unilateral land reform, and also from good will earned by local officials who also backed the peasants. Rural soviets were primarily organized by SRs, and it was local-level party members who were responsive to the moods in the villages that induced peasants to vote for the SR ticket, not the national party that had disillusioned them.[205] But it was national party leaders who dominated the list of names on that ticket.

A possible measure of the relative strength of the two SR parties are two Congresses of Peasant Soviets that convened during a five-week period starting in late November. In the first, Left SR delegates outnumbered Right SRs by a 3-to-1 ratio and in the second they were roughly equal.[206] If we split the difference and apply a 2-to-1 ratio to the SR results for the Constituent Assembly, then the Bolshevik/Left SR coalition would have won roughly half the vote. Given the heterogeneous fragmentation of the remainder of the vote among numerous small groups, many of whom were nationalist parties representing Ukraine and other non-ethnic Russian areas, the Bolshevik/Left SR coalition likely would have been able to assemble a majority, and would have simply endorsed government by the soviets. The Constituent Assembly would then have become a footnote, and therefore would have played no more of a role in the events of the revolution than it actually did.

Mythology surrounding the Constituent Assembly claims that it was "forcibly dispersed" by the Bolsheviks. It is closer to the truth to argue that it simply expired from irrelevancy. But, before the body could convene, Right SR activists organized a demonstration that was intended to be turned into a coup, with planned attempts to kidnap or assassinate Lenin and Trotsky.[207] The Right SR leadership refused to sanction the plot, and also refused to organize any defense for themselves on the basis that they were the people's elected representatives.[208]

Perhaps the madhouse inside the Constituent Assembly before it started is fitting. The Central Executive Committee of the soviets designated Yakov Sverdlov, a highly capable Bolshevik organizer who was Stalin's predecessor as general secretary (although the formal position did not yet exist), to open the meeting, symbolically putting the Assembly under the authority of the soviets. Before Sverdlov could get to the podium, the Right SRs sent their oldest member to the podium to start the session, a move intended to symbolize their belief that the Assembly authorized itself. The Bolsheviks and Left SRs drowned out the Right SR on the podium in a wave of yelling and screaming, and the Right SRs responded with a torrent of applause for their representative. Both sides rushed the podium, but Sverdlov finally appeared to restore some measure of order and officially start the session. Speeches then commenced, interrupted by yelling on all sides. This chaos was not altogether surprising, at least according to the left socialists.

"We knew those 'representatives of the people' would discuss matters 'among themselves,' would make some 'decisions,' would cast some votes. And then they would disperse, embarrassed by the own uselessness," wrote the Left SR Mstislavskii, who was a spectator at the Assembly. "That was the program as sketched out by history ahead of time. And that is why we were getting ready for the Assembly as we would for a stage performance: we knew that this day there would be no action, as such—only spectacle. And we were not disappointed."[209] The Bolsheviks didn't expect to stay long, either. They planned to introduce a "declaration of the rights of working people" for adoption, which would have the effect of endorsing soviet government. If it were voted down, which they expected, they would walk out.

The Assembly, reflecting its majority, voted to take up a proposal to discuss Right SR proposals on peace, land and immunity for Assembly members instead of the Bolshevik proposal. The parties went into a recess. The Bolsheviks decided to leave without returning to the hall, designating one of their delegates, F.F. Raskolnikov, to read a statement announcing their walkout. "There was only one item on the [Bolshevik recess] agenda: what was to be done with the Constituent Assembly after our fraction's departure from it," Raskolnikov later wrote. "Vladimir Illyich [Lenin] proposed that the Assembly not be dispersed, but allowed to spend the night in talk for as long as they liked. Then the members should be allowed freely to go home. But when morning came, nobody should be allowed back into the Tauride Palace," the Assembly meeting place.[210]

That left the Left SRs to decide when they would walk out. After a numbing list of speakers droned on, Vladimir Karelin stood up and announced the Left SR walkout: "We are withdrawing because we have no wish to cover up, by our presence, that crime which in our view is being committed against the people, against the workers' and peasants' revolution, by the Constituent Assembly."[211]

The meeting dragged on. Viktor Chernov, a Right SR elected as the Assembly chair after the session officially opened, endlessly discussed a land-reform bill that took no account of the complete rural upheaval effected by the Russian peasantry nor that the ad hoc redistribution of land had already been approved by the revolutionary government. The Right SRs still acted as if Russia were in the first days of the February Revolution. They had repeatedly called for a freeze on any change in land relations while sitting in the Provisional Government so that the Constituent Assembly could decide all questions. Now that day had happily arrived for them, but it was far too late—it could no longer be seen as relevant. In fact, Chernov had overseen that policy of a freeze in land relations as the Provisional Government's agricultural minister, bowing to party discipline despite personally favoring allowing some reform to go forward, and his execution of that policy stripped him of credibility.

Chernov, however, suddenly had company on the podium. As Raskolnikov recounted the story, he was in a side room long after his speech when a fellow Bolshevik came in to tell him what had just happened while "choking with laughter": "The sailor [Anatolii] Zheleznyakov had just gone up to the chairman of the Assembly, placed his broad hand on the shoulder of a Chernov numb with astonishment and said to him in a peremptory tone, 'The guards are tired. I propose that you close the meeting and let everyone go home.'"[212]

Zheleznyakov, an anarchist and Kronstadt sailor who would be killed in action in the Civil War, was the head of the guard assigned to protect the Assembly. (His post was something of an irony because anarchists bitterly opposed the Assembly.) It was 4:30 in the morning. Chernov still wanted to finish the discussion of the land-reform bill. Breaking the mood of boredom, wrote Mstislavskii, who had remained in the gallery, one of the sailors nearby suddenly yelled, "That's enough!" In a flash, the entire group of sailors—almost everyone else in the gallery had long ago left—joined in, chanting, "That's enough! That's enough!" Chernov finally declared the session closed.[213]

The next day, the Right SRs organized a march on the Tauride Palace, but by the time a detachment led by Vladimir Antonov-Ovseenko arrived, the demonstration was over. "The adherents of the Assembly had come, had made a glorious noise and had disappeared…There had been no more than 5,000 demonstrators in all," Antonov-Ovseenko wrote.[214]

That was it for the Constituent Assembly. Even the Kadets had no use for it, declaring it was "neither necessary nor advisable" to restore it as it was incapable of discharging its duties or restoring order.[215] Another observer, the United States journalist Louise Bryant, summed up the end of the Assembly: "It happened because the people were with the Soviets and the bayonets were in the hands of the people; there was no force to oppose the Soviets."[216]

A version of the Bolsheviks' working peoples' declaration was adopted five days after the Constituent Assembly, at the Third All-Russia Congress of Soviets. The declaration promised to establish "workers' control" and the "right to self-determination" but also to "crush exploiters mercilessly."[217]

Defining the "exploiters" would prove to be not as easy as the Bolsheviks had thought.

## The German revolution: Fueled from below but guided from above

Frederich Ebert hated revolution "like sin." As 1918 was drawing to a close, he was determined to put a stop to the revolution that was sweeping Germany, a country stunned by its sudden defeat but also unable to endure any longer its rigid class hierarchy and militaristic top-down institutions. Ebert, naturally, was not the only German who did not wish to see any sort of revolution. But what was unusual about Ebert was that at this time he was the head of the Social Democratic Party of Germany (SPD) and the revolution was being driven primarily by members of his party.

As World War I drew to a close, Germany made a virtually overnight transition from military dictatorship (the military High Command, in the person of General Erich Ludendorff, had been given effective control of the government by the kaiser, Wilhelm II) to a democratic republic. This happened in such a quick fashion because it was a "revolution from above." Prior to this overnight change, Germany possessed some forms of a modern democracy, but in reality bore more than a little resemblance to a Prussian police state. This was due in part to the manner of German unification, which was mostly effected by Prussia overrunning or absorbing the other German states, except

Austria, which was kept out of a united Germany because it lost an 1866 war to Prussia that decided which was to finally dominate "middle Europe."

A majority of the population of Germany lived in the Prussian portion of the country, where the franchise was severely limited by property restrictions. There was an elected national legislature, the Reichstag, but it was more an advisory body than a true parliament; the head of the government, the chancellor, was appointed by the kaiser and responsible only to the kaiser. The cabinet was also appointed, with ministers not necessarily holding seats in the Reichstag as they do in any normal parliamentary system.

Power, ordinarily, was held by the kaiser, who could dismiss any government, any chancellor, at will. But Wilhelm II had gradually withdrawn from actively running the state during World War I, ceding control to his generals. In 1916, Paul von Hindenburg became field marshal, or the chief of the High Command, and appointed Ludendorff his second in command. Hindenburg was a national hero through his battlefield victories and the person who received the attention. It was Ludendorff, however, who was the effective dictator—he had a far more dynamic personality but was content to remain in the background, and sought approval for all his plans from Hindenburg.

By all accounts a tireless worker, Ludendorff had a fast rise through the ranks as a staff officer, earning distinction within the army for his acumen in organization and planning. An aggressive commander, Ludendorff pushed through the German policy of unrestricted submarine warfare against neutral as well as Entente shipping; the admirals had wanted this policy but the chancellor, Theobold von Bethmann Hollweg, had opposed it, fearing it would lead to the United States entering the war. Bethmann Hollweg was soon pushed out of office by Ludendorff.

The High Command had consistently given upbeat reports about the progress of the war; Germans widely expected victory until the very end. The reality had become very different. Ludendorff's spring 1918 offensive had failed, costing Germany almost one million casualties, and now Entente counterattacks were pressing the German army. By August, German soldiers were deserting or giving themselves up; a month later, Germany's allies Austria-Hungary and Bulgaria were collapsing. Suddenly all seemed lost for Germany. The censorship that had suppressed all bad news could no longer be sustained in the face of a collapse on the western and Balkan fronts.

What to do? Ludendorff sprang two surprises, to put it mildly—he declared to the chancellor that the government must ask for an armistice within 24 hours because of the army's decomposition and that a new parliamentary government needed to be implemented.

Just like that, Ludendorff handed over his power. Because the SPD was the largest party in the Reichstag, that meant an SPD leader would become chancellor at the head of a coalition government. On 28 September, Ludendorff presented his plan to Hindenburg, who agreed; the next day, Ludendorff saw the kaiser, the chancellor and the foreign minister, who also agreed. The chancellor at this time, the aristocrat Count Georg Hertling, a monarchist, did not want to see a parliamentary government and resigned. A relatively moderate aristocrat, Prince Max von Baden, was named chancellor for what would prove to be a brief transition period.

Why did Ludendorff suddenly decide to do this? (It is also a sign of the weakness of German institutions at this time that the general could impose his will so readily.) This was not an act of benevolence; it was an effort to hand off to democratic parties the responsibility for defeat in the war. After Ebert and the SPD leadership halted the revolution and the country stabilized, Ludendorff began to speak publicly of an SPD "stab in the back."

The general would go on to participate in a 1920 military coup that attempted to overthrow the parliamentary government and by 1923 had become one of Hitler's most prominent supporters, taking part in Hitler's Munich beer hall putsch.

What allowed the myth of the "stab in the back" to flourish was that the handover of power to a parliamentary government was done entirely in secret—it was simply presented to the public after the decisions had been made. Some SPD leaders recognized they might be grasping a poisoned chalice and weren't in favor of taking power; Philipp Scheidemann, the party's second-ranking official, opposed rescuing a "bankrupt concern."[218] Ebert, who had just learned in a briefing the true state of the army, countered that the party should not avoid its "patriotic duty."[219]

Ebert later gave a Reichstag speech explaining his position:

> "Certainly, it would have been more comfortable for us to stand aside and wash our hands in innocence. But in the German people's hour of destiny, such a policy could never be justified before history, before the nation and before the German working class. We joined the government because what is at stake today is the whole nation, its future, its existence or non-existence."[220]

This is not so different from the rationales Ebert and the rest of the SPD leadership had put forth four years earlier to justify their full-throated support of German participation in World War I, which, in reality, was support for the expansionist imperialism of Germany's big capitalists and ultra-nationalists in direct conflict with the party's supposed program. Now the SPD would pass from support to governing on behalf of these same industrialists and the militarism that propped up the industrialists. The logic of the SPD's actions of the past four years compelled the party's leadership to do this, and in doing so they had put themselves on a path from which they would no longer be able to deviate.

The government formed was a coalition of the SPD; the Catholic Centre Party (forerunner of the present-day Christian Democratic Union), a party whose followers voted for it based more on shared membership in the Catholic Church than any coherent political program and which overlapped the middle of the political spectrum; and the Progressive Party, a Center-Right liberal group that favored the creation of a republic. The two main Right parties, both fervently pro-war to the end, were excluded.

Because leaders of the Entente powers, particularly United States President Woodrow Wilson, now claimed to be fighting to save the world from German autocracy, it was hoped that the change to a democratic form of government would lead to leniency on the part of the Entente. But Entente leaders believed the kaiser was still in charge and saw the new government as a sham; Wilson continued to issue harsh conditions to agree to end the war. But the change proved to be real. As Wilson's conditions grew harsher, Ludendorff, without notification to the government, issued an order of the day to the army saying the latest note from Wilson "could only be a challenge for us soldiers to continue resistance with our utmost strength."[221] For a government seeking the fastest possible end to the war, such an order could only be seen as insubordination. No longer irreplaceable, Ludendorff offered his resignation to the kaiser, and this time the kaiser called his bluff, accepting the resignation. Military rule was no longer possible.

The kaiser himself would soon be swept out of power. Discontent was building across Germany, the army was disintegrating and the navy continued to have mutinies. Wilhelm II, now holed up at Military General Headquarters in Spa, Belgium, did not understand how widespread the wish for his abdication had become; he was completely out of touch with his country. Von Baden and Ebert both wished to save the monarchy and believed that Wilhelm II's abdication was the only way to save it—similar to the Russian generals and monarchists who saw Nicholas II's abdication as the only way to save their crown.

Sick of the war, starving from a lack of food and in an increasingly militant mood, the German people wanted the kaiser to step down. Military officers and the upper classes from which most officers came wanted desperately to forestall an uprising. Although the kaiser could not be persuaded to abdicate, it was the naval command that sparked Germany's November Revolution. As in so many revolutions, the spark came suddenly and unexpectedly.

Naval commanders issued, on 28 October, a surprising order to the fleet at the ports of Kiel and Wilhelmshaven to put to sea for a battle against the British Navy despite the common knowledge that the war was about to end. Moreover, the German government had ordered an end to submarine warfare a week earlier. The command issued its order to put to sea in defiance of government policy and in secret. The official reason given was to provide relief for the western-front army, but that excuse could easily be seen through as a naval engagement could have no effect on ground conditions so rapidly was Germany's position deteriorating. The real reason was to uphold the military command's anachronistic sense of "honor"—that fighting must continue even after a situation has become hopeless.

Ludendorff, who, after his resignation had been accepted, snuck out of the country on a false passport to Sweden, put this sense of "honor" in these words on 31 October:

> Certainly, our situation was no longer capable of improvement...For a few months, we could have kept the War going. A fortress which surrenders before making a last-ditch stand is cursed with dishonor. A people which accepts humiliations and submits to conditions destructive of its existence, without having pitted its last strength, is courting

> its final downfall. If it submits to a similar fate after making a last supreme effort, it will live.[222]

To the sailors, this officers' honor was simply suicide. They refused to sail. Two days after the original order, on 30 October, the order was reissued and again ignored. The next day, more than 1000 sailors were arrested and faced execution. Some ships had not mutinied, but moods were evolving quickly. On 3 November in Kiel, finding a union meeting hall locked and under armed guard, sailors held their meeting outside, where they were joined by local workers, who then joined in a march. The march was intercepted by an officers' patrol, which opened fire, killing nine and injuring 29. As the marchers dispersed, an armed sailor shot dead the lieutenant who ordered the patrol to open fire.

The next day, sailors organized councils (replicating the soviets of Russia), disarmed their officers, ran up red flags on the ships, converted to their side army troops dispatched to put down the mutiny and occupied the military prison, freeing the imprisoned sailors. Dock workers called for a general strike. Kiel was in full revolt. The November Revolution had begun.

The revolution had not necessarily begun as an explicitly political movement, but it would have to become one, for if the Kiel revolt did not expand, it would be drowned in its participants' blood. But mixed in with demands for better treatment from the officers and liberation of political prisoners, including the mutineers, were calls for the abdication of the kaiser, abolition of martial law, and equal suffrage for men and women throughout Germany. As with the previous year's "bread riots" in Petrograd, the naval mutiny of Kiel quickly became a political revolution expressing the hopes of the popular masses.

The evening of the first day of the revolt, 4 November, two representatives of the government, Gustav Noske of the SPD and Conrad Haussman of the Progressive Party, arrived in Kiel. Although some in Kiel followed the SPD and others followed the

Independent Social Democratic Party of Germany (USPD), a group to the left of the SPD created when its leaders were expelled from the SPD, Noske, as an SPD person, was seen as "their man" and a sailors' council proclaimed Noske "governor" of Kiel. Except for the kaiser's abdication, Noske "accepted" their demands. By doing so, Noske was able to re-establish order and even talked the sailors into returning to their normal duties. Within two months, Noske would begin performing the service of stopping revolutions in cities across Germany, but with deadly force; on this one occasion the man who would become known as the "hangman of the revolution" did so with talk, a service of "rolling back" much appreciated by von Baden.

The spark of Kiel, however, ignited nearly all of Germany. Revolts spread across Germany like a wave; by 6 November, rebels had taken over in the northwest bastions of the Left, Hamburg and Bremen, among other cities; by 9 November, the wave of revolution had reached most corners of Germany, including the capital, Berlin. Although aware of the revolutionary moods that had taken root, Left political leaders had nonetheless been taken by surprise by the start of the uprisings. Hugo Haase, a leader of the USPD, confided in a 4 November letter, "We had heard nothing of unrest in the fleet."[223]

At this point, a survey of the political forces in Germany is in order.

- The SPD continued to remain the party of most working people after the wartime expulsion of its anti-war advocates. Despite its support for World War I, the SPD officially remained committed to a goal of socialism by evolution. The SPD leadership wanted a parliamentary party that would not dream of acting outside parliamentary bounds, but many of its followers still clung to the idea that it was a revolutionary party.
- To the left of the SPD was the USPD, an unstable heteroge-

neous hodgepodge united only in opposition to the war. This party included revisionists who first articulated the theory of long-term evolution into a future socialist state as some sort of automatic process, such as Eduard Bernstein; pacifists from the center of socialist opinion, such as German social democracy's most prominent pre-war theorist, Karl Kautsky; and a left wing that opposed the war for political reasons, without apologies. The USPD's left included the "Spartakusbund," or Spartacist League, a group that maintained its own central committee and institutions and included most of the movement's best theorists and leaders, among them Rosa Luxemburg, Leo Jogiches and Karl Liebknecht. The openly revolutionary Spartacus League would form the nucleus of the German Communist Party at the end of the year.

- Another significant group of the Left was the "Obleute," or Revolutionary Shop Stewards, a group of Berlin factory workers that had formed during the previous January's mass strikes; they had the factory workers of Berlin behind them. A much smaller group was the Bremen Left, a group of revolutionary Leftists influenced by the Bolshevik Revolution and linked with Karl Radek, a highly capable organizer who worked in Germany and Russia; Radek became a leader of the Bolsheviks and in the Communist International. But this group was mostly confined to Bremen and the nearby city of Hamburg.
- To the right of the SPD, occupying the Center and Center-Right, were the "Zentrum," or Catholic Centre Party, and the Progressive Party, which would soon rename itself the German Democratic Party. As previously noted, these two parties formed a coalition with the SPD when Ludendorff handed power to the Reichstag and the chancellery. These were Germany's liberal parties; both were pro-republic. The Democratic Party was led by moderate industrialists

and aspired to be the party followed by the middle class. The Centre also had a large following among farmers.
- The two main parties of the Right were the National Liberals, who would rename themselves the "German People's Party" in light of the popular mood, and the Conservatives, who would rename themselves the "German National People's Party." The People's and National parties were strongly nationalistic and were pro-monarchist until the crown was swept away but remained hostile to any democratic republic—these were the parties of large industrialists, Junkers (owners of massive landholdings measured in square kilometers; feudalism had not ended for the workers on these estates) and reactionary nationalists. The People's Party was the relatively more moderate of the two; the National Party would play a leading role in a 1920 right-wing coup against the government.

Now that the revolutionary wave had reached Berlin, the fate of the country would be settled on 9 and 10 November. Ebert and others in the SPD leadership wanted to halt the revolution before it could go any further; the USPD was split but contained a strong left wing that wished to proceed to the overthrow of the capitalist order, opinions that were not limited to the Spartacists; and the Revolutionary Shop Stewards were already planning an uprising for 11 November.

All were overtaken by events. The SPD had told von Baden that it could no longer stay in the government unless the kaiser abdicated; von Baden, joined by the High Command on the morning of the 9th, tried without success to get the kaiser to step down. Hindenburg and Ludendorff's successor, General Wilhelm Gröner, were no longer sure of the army's loyalty, and therefore of its willingness to put down opposition forcibly.

An example of the new mood of the soldiers is illustrated by a unit that had been marched into Berlin to put down demonstrations. The morning of 9 November, a delegation of soldiers arrived at the office of the lead SPD newspaper and asked someone to accompany them back to their barracks to explain to them what was happening in Berlin. They didn't understand who, or why, they were supposed to fight. Otto Wels—who would earn a footnote in history 15 years in the future by making the last speech opposing Hitler in the Reichstag as it was handing Hitler absolute power—went with the soldiers. He told the soldiers, "It is our duty to prevent civil war! I call upon you to cheer the people's free state!" The soldiers cheered him, and other units as well would no longer follow orders to put down the revolution.[224]

Across Germany and in field armies still in Belgium and elsewhere, soldiers' councils were already being set up, with the councils working on an equal basis with their officers on demobilizations and other matters.[225] By 10 a.m., unaware of the conversions, carrying signs saying "Brothers, no shooting!," hundreds of thousands of workers began streaming out of the factories, marching toward the center of Berlin.

Wilhelm II continued to dither; it was now too late to head off unrest. The Revolutionary Shop Stewards had largely laid the groundwork for the mass strike that had begun; they and the USPD appeared best positioned to assume the leadership of the uprising, which the SPD had opposed. Von Baden, at noon, tired of waiting, unilaterally issued a statement to the press that the kaiser had resigned. It was a last-ditch effort to stop the revolution; von Baden had already decided he himself would step down, seeing Ebert as the person who could bring a halt to the mounting unrest. The two agreed that the chancellery would be handed to Ebert effective immediately.

There was no constitutional basis for this, for no chancellor could hand power to a hand-picked successor, but attention to legal details was far from uppermost on their minds just now—

von Baden, a staunch supporter of the monarchy, had just announced the kaiser's abdication before the kaiser had decided anything. Von Baden's last move was to issue an order that shots not be fired except to defend government buildings, but this, too, was too late; the troops were already fraternizing with Berlin's citizens in the streets. Ebert's first move was to announce that everybody should leave the streets, which was ignored.

Liebknecht now intended to proclaim a socialist republic; partly to pre-empt that move, Scheidemann, the SPD's second-ranking official, went to a balcony of the Reichstag and proclaimed Germany a republic to a huge crowd outside. Ebert, invariably described as "purple with rage" in accounts describing this exchange, berated Scheidemann for making such a declaration, fuming that only a constituent assembly could decide Germany's new form of government. Ebert also likely acted as he did because he retained hopes of salvaging the crown.

Not to be undone, Liebknecht, two hours later, proclaimed Germany a socialist republic from the royal palace, on which a red flag was now flying. Hundreds of thousands still held the streets of Berlin. The SPD, USPD, Revolutionary Shop Stewards and Spartacists all wished to decisively influence events. It would be Ebert—who had proclaimed to von Baden, "I hate revolution like sin"—who would prove to be able to master events.

Ebert's vision was that of the right wing of the SPD: gaining a parliamentary majority to bring about evolutionary gains. His main preoccupation was with order in the party's affairs; it is perhaps not surprising that he so desperately wished order in affairs of the state. Sebastian Haffner, in his classic study of the German revolution, *Failure of a Revolution*, described Ebert:

> [A] typical German artisan: solid, conscientious, a man of limited outlook but within his limitations a man of skill;

> quietly dignified in his treatment of important customers, laconic and bossy in his own workshop. The SPD officials tended to shake in their boots in his presence like journeymen or apprentices in the presence of a strict master. He was not particularly popular in the Party but he enjoyed enormous respect. He had played no big part in the great discussions which shook the Party before the War—about revolution or reform, mass action or parliamentarianism—but when he was elected to the Party Executive he had at once installed telephones and typewriters and a decent filing system in the Party offices. Ebert could be relied on to be systematic.[226]

If the revolution could not be stopped, then Ebert would place himself at the head of it. The SPD placed itself at the head of the revolution so that it could slam on the brakes.

The first order of business was to form a new government. Ebert was pleased to be the new chancellor, but needed to bring the USPD into the new government to bring the situation under control. The USPD was divided, and much of its leadership was initially in the middle, not subscribing to the party's right or left wings, and it was unable to make a decision when Ebert offered it three seats in a new cabinet. Finally, early on 10 November, the USPD agreed to join the government on condition that the government be all-socialist and that the cabinet consist of six "People's Commissars."

At the insistence of the USPD negotiators, the new government would be answerable to the workers' and soldiers' councils already being formed and a constituent assembly to decide the permanent form of government would not be convened until the revolution had consolidated itself.[227] But these were general principles, open to interpretation, and not codified with any specificity.

This new government consisted of three SPD members, Ebert, Scheidemann and Otto Landsberg, and three USPD members,

Hugo Haase, Wilhelm Dittmann and Emil Barth. Barth was also a Shop Steward leader and was the only true left socialist of the six; he was a replacement for Liebknecht, who refused to sit in any government that included the SPD.

As negotiations, mostly within the party delegations rather than between the parties, had dragged on during 9 November, all signs of the old order's power had vanished in the face of the enormous number of people in the streets, who started the day not knowing if they would be mowed down by the army and police and now seemingly were the victorious conquerors of Berlin, taking over public buildings at will. Could it really be that easy? A Shop Steward leader, Richard Müller, marveled at how the day had enfolded:

> The characteristic feature of this rising lay in the elemental force with which it broke out, in its wide range, and its uniform, almost methodical activity in all parts of the enormous area of Greater Berlin. The rising did not develop from partial actions into one big action, it began as a single entity…It was as though the millions of workers and soldiers had been guided from a single spot. But there was no direction of that kind.[228]

The Revolutionary Shop Stewards did attempt to provide leadership to the uprising, but failed; they simply weren't a mass group. They had a large following among Berlin-area workers, but not among soldiers, or in the rest of the country. Of the two mass parties of the Left, the SPD was determined to stop the revolution and the USPD was too divided and unorganized to provide effective leadership. The rest of the Left consisted of small groups with local or small followings. All but the SPD had to contend with strong desires, particularly among the soldiers, for socialist unity—this was an advantage the SPD exploited. A mass party capable of action would have had a good chance at establishing a socialist government; there was not yet such a party. Nor had the Left carried out systematic agitation in the army and navy as the Bolsheviks, Left Socialist Revolutionaries and Interdistrict Organization had done in Russia—German soldiers had simply gone home without organizing themselves or disarming their officers. Instead, the reactionary officers' corps had been left untouched.

The Shop Stewards tried to move the revolution forward by calling for a meeting of council representatives, at which a parallel government would be set up, further replicating the model of Russian soviets. The evening of 9 November, the Shop Stewards, in the midst of continual commotion, occupied the Reichstag chamber, began a session on their own initiative and passed a resolution stating that all factories and barracks should elect councilors and that the councilors should meet the next day at the Busch Circus, a large Berlin meeting hall, to elect a government.

This body was to be the equivalent of the Executive Committee of the Petrograd Soviet by virtue of being an executive body for the councils but also because this would be an executive representing the capital city—only Berlin councilors could attend the organizing meeting on such short notice. (A national congress to represent councils from across Germany would be organized in the next month.) Upon hearing this news, Ebert, still in the chancellery, resolved to gain control of this council government, which would be in direct competition with the government he headed as chancellor with his five fellow People's Commissars.

The next morning (10 November) workers, soldiers and sailors did gather at their workplaces and barracks to elect their councils. The Revolutionary Shop Stewards had won a big round, or so it seemed; they organized furiously for a body that was to theoretically have control over the chancellor and the cabinet, a body that would exist because of their agitation. But the SPD also organized furiously, and its well-read main newspaper led with a headline calling for unity. Wels continued his agitation among the soldiers; the SPD earned a particularly strong vote total in the barracks. The soldiers wanted unity and many did not care about the differences among the parties; the SPD agitation skillfully played to this by telling them the only way to have a socialist government was to put the SPD in power.

The Shop Stewards planned to have a council executive elected by the delegates in the Busch Circus that would be filled entirely by themselves. But Ebert's speech calling for unity was loudly cheered; thanks in part to the commanding victory the SPD won in the barracks it had a clear majority among the 3000 delegates. Liebknecht's speech denouncing the SPD was met with the soldiers' chants of "unity, unity." Barth, the Revolutionary Shop Steward and a leader within the USPD, made a speech calling for an executive excluding the SPD. Again, the soldiers interrupted, calling for unity and executive parity. An executive evenly split between SPD and USPD representatives was elected, and each party's lineup was in turn to be evenly split between workplaces and barracks.

The meeting of council representatives ended with an endorsement of the People's Commissars—Ebert now had the backing of the councils, the representative of the revolutionary working people in the streets, as well as the backers of the capitalist state on whose behalf von Baden had handed him power the day before. That the latter was what mattered to Ebert was dramatized that night, following the meeting of the council representatives at Busch Circus. Ebert received a call from Gröner, Ludendorff's successor on the High Command, reminding him of the need to fight radicalism and bring about a return to "order." Ebert needed no prompting. Gröner and Ebert would now coordinate government responses to the popular movements. The general later wrote of this first telephone talk: "Ebert agreed to my suggestion of a pact. From then on, we consulted with each other every evening about the necessary measures, using a secret line between the Chancellery and the High Command. The pact proved itself."[229]

Ebert had weathered the storm; as early as 11 November he told a Dutch news agency that the revolution was over.[230] That was not true yet, but the old state institutions (and the imperial bureaucrats who staffed the government) remained in place and the councils intended to supervise their work disappeared over the course of 1919. Hindenburg, on 12 November, told the military that he was now commander-in-chief in place of the kaiser, who had left for the Netherlands, tacitly vacating the throne although he never formally abdicated. Gröner asked Ebert if the government would uphold the officers' full power of command and discipline; Ebert confirmed that was so.

All three USPD People's Commissars agreed to this demand under the theory that only the retention of the traditional command would enable the speedy evacuation of the army that had to be completed within 15 days under the conditions of the armistice that had just been signed.[231] But such a huge concession to the High Command was unnecessary—Germany's troops were already demobilizing, thanks in part to the soldiers' councils, and demobilization in Austria was occurring speedily with few of the feared problems despite a much greater decomposition of the army there and widespread abandonment of duty by officers.[232]

Gröner later was quite clear about his intentions at this time: "We hoped, through our actions, to secure for the army and the officer corps part of the power in the new state; if we succeeded in this, then the best and strongest elements of the old Prussia were saved for the new Germany, in spite of the revolution."[233] The Prussian officer corps had been mostly drawn from the upper classes, and when middle-class officers were needed in the expanded army in the 1860s, they quickly assimilated the outlooks of the noblemen; the army's loyalty, moreover, was to the monarch rather than the state.[234] This Prussian ethos carried over into the military of the unified German state, including independence from parliamentary oversight.

In the meantime, the new government of the People's Commissars did provide concrete advances—on 12 November, it abolished martial law and censorship, amnestied the political prisoners not already released by the uprisings, decreed universal suffrage for men and women aged 20 or older, provided unemployment relief, and decreed an eight-hour working day. But if the revolution did not consolidate itself, begin to bring the military command under control and begin to put socialists in positions of authority throughout the vast machinery of the state, then it would not only not be able to hold on to its new gains, it would inevitably succumb to a backlash. The dizzying success of November came about in no small part due to the upper classes' loss of confidence; as the demands of Hindenburg and Gröner signaled, those industrialists and Junkers were beginning to regain their confidence.

The executive elected by the councils, despite its even split in composition, did attempt to assert the supervisory duties it claimed for itself, but as Ebert controlled a 5–1 majority among the People's Commissars (and even the dissident, Barth, often voted with the majority) that included USPD votes, it gained the upper hand in the power struggle that inevitably developed between the two bodies.

Like in Russia, a "dual government" could not stand for long, but unlike in Russia, it was the cabinet rather than the councils that steadily gained the upper hand. One important reason for this was that, in Germany, the SPD backed the People's Commissars whereas in Russia the Bolsheviks backed the soviets. In Germany, the political development of the soldiers lagged well behind that of their Russian counterparts and so simple calls for "unity" were highly persuasive; political education and agitation in the military had been a priority among left socialists in Russia, but there had been no equivalent effort in Germany. Another factor was that the Executive Council was a Berlin body; it was not representative of Germany as a whole.

Hamburg provides an example of the pressure put on the councils by the old rulers, and the councils' steady retreat. Heinrich Laufenberg, a local left USPD leader, had become chairman of the Hamburg Workers' and Soldiers' Council, and at a 12 November meeting of the council's executive body pushed through his motion to dissolve the legislature (Hamburg is a city-state); the council took over city hall and flew a red flag over it as the old legislature moved out. Four days later, the city's leading bankers and financiers, led by Max Warburg, head of one of Germany's most powerful financial houses, paid Laufenberg a visit. Warburg told Laufenberg that Hamburg's credit was at grave risk because of the revolutionary upheaval, whereas the financiers' credit was still good. The financiers agreed to provide funds, but demanded a say in government and the reconstitution of the legislature, arguing that legislators asking for funds would look much more respectable than council members. The council promptly decreed the legislature back into existence, theoretically under its control.[235]

The old government departments had continued their work uninterrupted, and power slipped away from the councils. "There can be no doubt that, in fact, much of the real governing power in Hamburg resided exactly where it had always resided—in the hands of the leaders of business, finance and the state bureaucracy,"[236] noted a historian of city history.

More than one method was used to assert this governing power. An anti-labor retired army officer reached a pact with a Hamburg state senator to bring the council under control. The retired officer got himself put on the soldiers' council and, with the help of money from a local banker, managed to pack the council with more pliable men from the SPD right.[237] Things went further on 6 December, when a plot by a group of military officers to arrest and imprison the executive of the Workers' and Soldiers' Council was uncovered.[238]

In Berlin, a new move by the High Command to assert control came in early December, when ten armed divisions were marched into the capital. Gröner, at a hearing years later, testified that the intention was "the disarming of Berlin, clearing Berlin of Spartacists."[239] By "Spartacists," Gröner meant all socialists to the left of the SPD's right wing and anybody who supported the councils; the typical military officer saw a "Spartacist" as any socialist, no matter how reformist. An army order issued at the time was even more draconian: "Whoever is found to be in possession of arms without a license is to be shot. Whoever keeps war material, including motor vehicles, will be summarily convicted…Whoever assumes an official function without authorization is to be shot."[240] But almost all the men of the ten divisions dispersed and went home after marching into Berlin—Gröner and Ebert did not factor in soldiers' desire to be done with military service. The soldiers simply went home for the holidays.

Another military unit did arrest members of the Executive Council and another fired machine guns into a Spartacist march without warning, on orders by Wels, killing 16.[241] Wels had been named by Ebert as the commander of soldiers stationed within the city of Berlin. No longer the SPD representative who won over the soldiers weeks earlier with a speech hailing the revolution, Wels was now actively engaged in putting down the revolution with force on behalf of the SPD as the Berlin commandant. Posters violently attacking the Spartacists with lines such as "Strike its leaders dead!" and "Kill Liebknecht!" were put up, and Wels organized a Right-wing mercenary gang to hunt down Liebknecht and Luxemburg, who had to sleep in a different location each night.[242]

Shortly thereafter those threatening developments, the first national congress of councils opened in Berlin on 16 December.

The congress's SPD majority backed Ebert and voted for an early convocation of a constituent assembly, which would decide on a permanent form of government for Germany. With that, the councils handed their power back to Ebert and the People's Commissars, effectively ending dual government. But the congress also, with almost no dissent, approved a proposal to drastically curtail military officers.

Known as the "Hamburg Points," the proposal called for command of the military to be taken from the High Command and given to the People's Commissars, abolishing all ranks, placing military discipline into the hands of soldiers' councils and providing for the election of officers. There was widespread agreement to these reforms, and some of the demands had been implemented by the soldiers' and sailors' councils at the start of the revolution in November. The High Command, and other ranking military officers, were already attempting to enforce their version of "order" and vehemently opposed the Hamburg Points, making their opposition known to Ebert in no uncertain terms.

Here the contradictions of the revolution show themselves again—the revolutionary proclamations in the Hamburg Points would have, if implemented, represented a stunning deepening of the social movement, while at the same time the congress ensured that no such development would happen by handing all power to the most conservative elements of the movement, which saw its mission as stopping the revolution and was now working closely with the High Command. Actions contradicted words.

A much more immediate issue sparked the next incident, on 24 December. About 1000 sailors were stationed in the royal palace and were becoming restless. Known as the People's Naval Division, some of these sailors had taken part in the Kiel mutiny and arrived in Berlin with the first wave of the November Revolution—they had removed their officers and elected one of their fellow sailors as the new commander. Wels, in his capacity as the Berlin city commandant, had tried unsuccessfully to disband the unit, and he withheld their pay in an effort to disperse them. (Most of the sailors in the division had been summoned by Wels and in mid-November Wels had stationed them in the palace to put a stop to looting of it.[243]) Finally, the government agreed to give them their pay if they evacuated the palace. Agreeing to do so, the sailors went to the chancellery with the palace keys, but Wels refused to accept them, claiming he needed Ebert's permission and that Ebert could not be found.

The sailors then sealed the chancellery, not allowing anyone out and cutting the phone lines, except for the secret line between Ebert and the High Command, which the sailors would not have known about. By now, it became known that a detachment of soldiers was being sent to Berlin to "suppress the Spartacists."[244] Barth asked Ebert if this was true, but Ebert, still dissembling, denied any knowledge of troop movements. Frustrated, the sailors grabbed Wels, and took him back to the palace as a hostage.

Army troops did arrive, surrounding the palace, that night; the military's commanders were pleased to have been given an excuse to intervene in Berlin with force. At an emergency meeting of the People's Commissars, Ebert again kept the three USPD members in the dark. Overnight, he ordered the assembled army units to attack the palace in the morning. The stated reason was to rescue Wels, but attacking a place where hostages are held generally makes it much more likely that the hostages will be harmed. Moreover, the sailors, before dawn, agreed to release Wels.[245]

Nonetheless, the army units began bombarding the palace early in the morning with artillery and machine guns; ultimately, 30 people were killed. The sounds of heavy gunfire drew a crowd, which sided with the sailors. So did a detachment from the Berlin police, who were commanded by the city police chief, Emil Eichhorn, a USPD member placed in his position by the councils. The soldiers, fraternizing with the crowd, ceased fighting. The battle ended with an agreement that the sailors would leave the palace, but the division was not dissolved as Wels had wanted.[246]

The High Command had been defeated by this episode; its conclusion was that the regular army could no longer be trusted. The solution: form new, independent units. These units, the "Freikorps," or Free Corps, were mainly comprised of military officers and reactionary enlisted soldiers unable to adjust to civilian life. It was the Free Corps that would soon be mercilessly unleashed on city after city by Noske, drowning in blood the aspirations of Germans for a better world. Noske had the chance to do this in part because of a blunder by the USPD.

By now the USPD was straining against its internal centrifugal forces. The party's right wing, embodied by people like Kautsky and Bernstein, who joined the party out of pacifism, had much in common with the SPD, particularly now that the war, their main point of disagreement, was over; its center-right, exemplified by Dittmann and Haase, opposed the SPD tactics and wanted the revolution to go forward, but were committed to staying within the bounds of the constitutional structures and wanted the councils to have merely consultative status; its center-left, exemplified by Barth, strongly opposed the SPD and wanted sharper tactics than many in the party would have liked, and wanted a strong role for the councils, envisioning them as a legislature; and its left wing, composed of Spartacists, Revolutionary Shop Stewards and others, were rapidly moving toward insurrectionary frames of mind and already agitating for all power to be exercised through a system of councils.

As Kautsky, who saw no role for the councils, put it,

> Our party presented a grotesque appearance, as perhaps no other party has done in the history of the world. Its right wing was in the government, and its left wing worked for the

> downfall of that very government...What kept it together was no longer a common program, a common tactic, but only a common hatred of the majority socialists [the SPD] which had been inherited from wartime.[247]

Those divisions remained, but no longer was the USPD in government. The party's first mistake had been at the national congress of councils earlier in the month, when it boycotted the election to the Central Council, an executive for the councils that was being created by the congress. The USPD put forth a proposal that the Central Council approve or reject all legislative bills that was rejected by the SPD majority in favor of a vague, undefined "parliamentary supervision."[248] The party then refused to participate in the elections to the Central Council, leaving it with an all-SPD membership. Then, after the Christmas battle with the People's Naval Division, the three USPD People's Commissars confronted Ebert and the other two SPD commissars, but with no backing from the Central Council they had no way force Ebert to step down.

Barth, Dittmann and Haase resigned from the government; they were replaced by two SPD members, Noske and Rudolf Wissell. The government was now completely in SPD hands, controlled by Ebert without checks, and including Noske, soon to assume his role as the revolution's hangman, as defense minister.

This relinquishing of government posts was followed by the Spartacists formally splitting from the USPD and forming the new Communist Party of Germany (KPD) in a merger with the Bremen Left. But some of the USPD's left remained; the Revolutionary Shop Stewards disliked the Spartacists' tactics of continual street demonstrations, seeing them as amateurish, even "putschist." The Shop Stewards would seem to have been a much better fit with the new KPD than with the parliamentary USPD, but refused to link with the Spartacists and Bremen Left because, unlike them, it wanted to remain in the trade unions and participate in elections.

The Shop Stewards were radical trade unionists and had grown in the workplaces—their entire following was there, so it would have been suicidal for them to leave the unions. The majority of the KPD wanted to boycott, so the Shop Stewards stayed with the USPD. The KPD saw the unions as bastions of counter-revolution and wanted nothing to do with them; the trade union leaderships had shown themselves as more conservative than the SPD leadership. But that would seem to be another reason not to leave organized workers in the hands of conservative union leaders without the strong counter-balance the Revolutionary Shop Stewards already represented.

Regardless of these debates, the mood in the streets was becoming more militant. A long procession at the funeral of the People's Naval Division sailors who were killed in the battle at the royal palace featured many mourners holding signs calling Ebert and other SPD leaders the sailors' killers and calling for "Violence against Violence!" and chanting "Down with the traitors!"[249] That anger would burst in just a week.

## Impatience and reaction: Disorganization in German streets is countered by organized force

Events were now moving so quickly in Germany that an attempt to overthrow the Social Democratic Party (SPD) government was ignited in part by members of a party that had been in formal existence for less than a week; primary leadership for this uprising came from another group that had reproached the first for its "putschist" street tactics. The uprising of 5–12 January 1919 quickly went into history as "Spartacist Week," and although much of its rank-and-file eagerly took part, the Spartacist leadership was almost unanimously opposed. This was an uprising in which the government would have fallen with a single well-aimed push, but the push never came; it ended with the government unleashing pitiless massacres and the murder of the most able Spartacist leaders.

By mid-December 1918, it had become impossible for the Spartacists to remain in the Independent Social Democratic Party (USPD). The growing left wing of the USPD had increasingly chafed at the party leadership's tactics, unsuccessfully demanding the convening of a party conference, and also believed a stronger organization was needed to carry the revolution forward—the Spartacist League was a loose organization at the time of the November Revolution and its ranks swelled with students and others who were becoming more militant.[250]

Signaling the likelihood of their becoming an independent party, the Spartacists proclaimed their program in a manifesto written by Rosa Luxemburg. It called for all power to reside in the councils; disarming all police, military officers and "non-proletarian soldiers" (the mercenary Free Corps); arming all adult men for a self-defense militia; expropriation of large and midsize agricultural concerns; and annulling state and other public debts. The Spartacists sought the creation of a socialist society based on the "great majority" of workers taking power in a very broad-based revolution.

"Mere decrees on socialization issued by high revolutionary authorities are of no more value than empty sounds. Only the working class, by its own efforts, can change these sounds into actuality," the manifesto stated. "The emancipation of the working class must be the work of the workers themselves."[251] The Spartacists vowed they would not join any SPD government, but also said they would not assume power without a firm mandate:

> The Spartacist League will also refuse to take over the power of government merely because the Scheidemann-Ebert element have completely discredited themselves, and the

> Independent Socialist party, through cooperation with them, has reached a blind alley. The Spartacist League will never take over the power of government otherwise than by a clear manifestation of the unquestionable will of the great majority of the proletariat mass of Germany [and with] conscious approval by the mass of workers of the principles, aims, and tactics of the Spartacist League.[252]

This platform also stressed the long-term nature of this project.

From 30 December to 1 January, the Spartacists and the smaller Bremen Left formally created the Communist Party of Germany. The two main questions at the foundation conference were the decision to found the party and whether the new party should contest elections to the constituent assembly. Although the vote to create the new party was nearly unanimous, it was not without misgivings—Leo Jogiches had previously argued that a Spartacist split from the USPD "must by necessity lead to the separation of a minute circle of the best comrades from the party and must condemn those comrades to complete impotence. Such tactics we consider dangerous, even fatal."[253]

Luxemburg also had misgivings, and throughout the war had argued for the Spartacists to remain first in the SPD, then, after their 1917 expulsion, in the USPD. She believed the Spartacists could better influence those in the USPD who were increasingly disenchanted with its leadership by remaining within, although she now backed leaving the USPD. Contained within the second question was a more serious hint of internal problems—almost all of the most experienced leaders wanted to participate in the constituent assembly to use it as a platform to propagate their views; the rank-and-file delegates were mostly opposed, wishing instead for immediate direct action.

Paul Frölich, present at the foundation conference, later wrote of those so eager to adopt only the most radical tactics:

> [T]he great majority of the delegates to the conference and the members they represented regarded it as a contradiction to reject the [constituent assembly] on principle and yet to participate in elections to it. They had the Russian example all too clearly in mind, but they saw only the final October victory and not the long period of preparation involving careful and often very complicated maneuvering. This majority was so certain of the victory of the German Revolution that participation in parliamentary elections appeared as a highly doubtful detour—or even worse.[254]

The Spartacists' following had been in the cities of Germany and the Bremen Left's in two cities, Bremen and Hamburg. The SPD still retained a strong following in most of those cities and the revolution had barely touched the countryside; much work remained to be done. Luxemburg argued that a "long revolution" was in its early stages and rejected a crude choice of "guns or parliament."[255]

Rejecting comparisons with Russia's October Revolution, Luxemburg told the delegates, "Comrades, you make it too easy for yourselves with your radicalism. We must not…abandon the necessary seriousness and calm reflection…Your activism may seem simpler and easier, [but] our tactics envision a longer road."[256] Paul Levi, speaking on behalf of the new party's central committee, argued that the constituent assembly would provide a platform to put forth their views.[257] Both were coolly received and Levi frequently interrupted; delegates from the floor shouted that "ten men on the street are worth more than a thousand votes."[258] The conference delegates, mostly younger, less experienced activists, voted by a 3-to-1 ratio to boycott the assembly.

Simultaneous with the first day of that foundation conference, a quite different meeting took place—Chancellor Frederich Ebert, the SPD leader, met with Gustav Noske, newly installed as defense minister and as a People's Commissar, and with the High Command, a meeting at which Ebert directed Noske to use force against the revolution.[259] Agents provocateurs in place and a provocation were necessary to enable a violent blow to be struck against the revolution, and the provocation came quickly.

The government of Prussia, an all-SPD body similar to the federal government because the USPD had also resigned from it, moved to dismiss Emil Eichhorn as Berlin police chief. Eichhorn, a left USPD member who had remained with the party, was falsely accused of embezzlement and was not allowed to defend himself against the charges. Eichhorn refused to step down, arguing that the executive of the Berlin councils had placed him in his position and only it could dismiss him.

The USPD and the Revolutionary Shop Stewards called for a mass demonstration for 5 January and the newly formed Communist Party of Germany (KPD) threw its support behind the action. As many as 700,000 people turned out, not only from the three radical organizations but SPD rank-and-filers as well. There was no plan or organization for this demonstration, and agents provocateur were able to lead groups into occupying various newspaper offices, including that of the leading SPD paper, *Vorwärts*, providing the SPD government with an excuse to launch a crackdown.[260] Other groups took over railway stations and other points without resistance.

Intoxicated by the sight of the enormous crowds filling the streets, the Revolutionary Shop Stewards, who had condemned the Spartacists/KPD for alleged "putschist tactics," now decided to outdo them. That evening, a group of 86 people gathered at the Berlin police headquarters. Seventy were Shop Stewards, 10 were from the Berlin branch of the USPD, 2 were delegates from the KPD (one of whom was Karl Liebknecht), and there were also 2 soldiers, 1 sailor and Eichhorn. What to do next? No one had a clear idea. The sailor in attendance, Heinrich Dorrenbach, the leader of the People's Naval Division, declared that his unit and other Berlin regiments were ready to overthrow the SPD government.

The two soldiers expressed serious doubts that their colleagues were prepared to intervene, but Dorrenbach had kindled the others' hopes: By a nearly unanimous vote, the group declared itself a "revolutionary committee," proclaimed the overthrow of the government and issued a proclamation declaring a general strike the next day, a Monday, for the seizure of power. The committee chairs who formally issued the proclamation were Paul Scholze for the Revolutionary Shop Stewards; Georg Ledebour for the USPD, who had no authority for any such action by his national party; and Liebknecht for the KPD, who also had no such authority, signing without any consultation with his party and in fact completely contradicting the KPD program.

The people of Berlin responded, turning out in the streets of the center of the city in the same gigantic numbers as the day before. A few public buildings were taken over, but there was no attempt to storm the seats of government. The massive crowds waited for leadership; there was none. The army units promised by Dorrenbach did not materialize and even his People's Naval Division declared neutrality. That the effort to overthrow the government was rather less than resolute was embodied in a delegation of 300 armed men who were sent to occupy the war ministry—a lieutenant on duty at the ministry refused to recognize an announcement of the overthrow of the government because the paper it was written on was not signed, whereupon the delegation's leader left to obtain signatures.[261] No attempts were made to seize any other government office.

The revolutionary committee continued to deliberate, unable to come to any decisions. The hundreds of thousands participating in the general strike spent the day in the streets, then, cold and hungry, began dispersing as night fell. The government likely would have fallen in the face of such a demonstration if there had been any leadership. The People's Commissars, now an all-SPD body, met inside the chancellery building, surrounded by a hostile crowd, themselves unable to decide what to do. Noske later wrote in his memoirs, "If these crowds, instead of being led by prattlers, had possessed resolute leaders, conscious of where they were going, they would have been masters of Berlin before midday."[262]

Would that have been a good idea? The KPD, under Luxemburg's guidance, had declared it wouldn't assume power just because the SPD could no longer govern. Karl Radek, the éminence grise behind the Bremen Left, opposed any attempt at seizing power and then urged the demonstrations to be wrapped up as quickly as possible. Luxemburg, Jogiches and other KPD leaders who had formed the Spartacist leadership opposed the switch to offensive tactics and saw that the street actions had become pointless. The KPD leadership even considered a formal disavowal of Liebknecht's signing of the proclamation. But not wanting to abandon the workers in the midst of an uprising, Luxemburg and the rest of the leadership decided to support the rising publicly. Ledebour, the USPD's chair on the revolutionary committee, later said he and others on the committee believed that the occupation of the newspaper offices had presented them with a fait accompli, forcing them to go forward.[263]

This was a no-win situation. Klara Zetkin, an activist with decades of organizing behind her, summed up the situation this way, based in part on a letter from Jogiches:

> The aim of the struggle could only be a forceful defense against the blow of the counter-revolution. Thus: reinstatement of Eichhorn in his office; removal of the troops…arming of the workers, and transfer of military power to military-political representatives of the proletarians…[The KPD] could not make the objective…"overthrow of the

> government" its own; it had to reject it, but at the same time it could not lose touch with the masses who had become engaged in the struggle...For this purpose, the Communist Party had to show its own face...without damaging the proletarian, revolutionary solidarity which it owed to the fighters. Thus its role in the struggle had to be simultaneously negative-critical and positive-encouraging.[264]

If the government was initially equally unsure of what to do, it was able to rally due to the one steady hand it possessed at this time: Noske. As the government met that night, 6 January, Noske declared his readiness to use force. General Max Hoffman was proposed as commander-in-chief, but it was pointed out that the hard-line Hoffman was widely despised—he had been the commander of the eastern front during World War I and oversaw a brutal occupation of Ukraine. Noske continued to insist that action had to be taken. "Somebody said: 'Perhaps you'll do the job yourself,'" Noske later wrote in his memoirs. "To this, I replied, briefly and resolutely, 'I don't mind, somebody's got to be the bloodhound! I'm not afraid of the responsibility.' It was decided forthwith that the government would grant me extraordinary powers for the purpose of re-establishing order in Berlin."[265]

Noske set out to finish preparations for the taking of the city by the Free Corps, slipping unnoticed past the crowds still filling the center of Berlin after he left the chancellery. Although what remained of the army would not come to the aid of the uprising, neither could it be depended on to defend the government. Therefore, Noske would unleash the "freelance" bands organized by the High Command, removed from all legal constraints, which had already been gathering on Berlin's outskirts.

By now, the national leadership of the USPD, including the former People's Commissars, offered to mediate, and both sides accepted. Ebert demanded the *Vorwärts* building, still occupied, be evacuated, but the occupiers refused to leave. On the night of 10 January, Free Corps mercenaries stormed the *Vorwärts* building, retaking it. Prior to the storming, as a Free Corps unit was bombarding the building, six men from inside went out holding white flags to negotiate; one was sent back inside with a demand for unconditional surrender and the other five were summarily shot. After the retaking of the *Vorwärts* building, several more were shot and others beaten. From 9 to 12 January, the Free Corps fought in the center of Berlin, finishing off the uprising on the 12th.

Hundreds of thousands had poured into the streets, first to defend Eichhorn from being sacked as police chief and then rallying behind an explicit call for taking power, because they felt cheated by a revolution that seemed to be not a revolution after all. The vast ranks of the old imperialist bureaucracy remained in place, as did government officials at all levels and the commanders of the military. The People's Commissars had been placed above the bureaucracy, but that had little more than cosmetic effect—the old machinery of the state still moved under its own power. And now that lesson had been bloodily reinforced.

No matter how justified the anger at the meager results of the November Revolution, the rising was a senseless adventure—not only did the lack of leadership and absence of planning prove fatal, but there was nowhere near the "great majority" of working people necessary for a successful overthrow of capitalism called for in the Spartacist program. "Spartacist Week" bore considerable similarity to the "July Days" in Petrograd between Russia's February and October Revolutions, but proved far more disastrous. Although the Bolshevik party's ability to control its local branches and its rank-and-file members was limited, it had enough cohesiveness to be able to extricate its followers from the precarious position they put themselves in and bring an end to the street actions before any serious violence could be unleashed by the government. The Bolsheviks by then arguably had the largest backing of any party in the capital, already holding majorities in Petrograd's unions and factory committees.

Neither the Spartacists, nor any other Left group, possessed the ability to prevent street actions from developing into leaderless adventures that gave the government a pretext for raining down violence, nor did these groups command a majority in any German city. The massive crowds in Berlin responding to the calls for a general strike would have been far smaller without the followers of the SPD participating. That they would answer a call put forth by parties more to the Left demonstrated a latent potential for a revolution, but these participants nonetheless still maintained a loyalty to the SPD, the leadership of which was hostile to the revolution and had already sanctioned violence against it. Because Germany's military structure had been left intact, there was ample force available to defeat insufficiently organized demonstrators.

As Jogiches, Levi and Luxemburg had warned, the revolution was in its early stages, and this state was demonstrated in the vote for the constituent assembly. The contradictions of the revolution revealed themselves again—one week SPD members took the streets in force, in effect against their own government, then the next week voted to give the SPD a plurality in the assembly. That vote amply confirmed KPD leaders in their view that any revolt would be premature.

The SPD won the most seats for the constituent assembly, 163; another 22 went to the USPD. That combined total represented only 45 percent of the vote—the two Center/Center-Right parties, the Catholic Centre and the Democrats, won another 163 seats. The nationalist Right won only a tiny minority of votes. But this vote was not necessarily fully representative—the KPD and others on the Left boycotted and as the Free Corps continued to maraud across Germany some SPD support eroded in favor of the USPD. A vote held a couple of months later likely would have had different results.

The SPD formed a coalition government with the Catholic Centre and the Democrats, and Germany now had a "new" government that was the same as the "old" government. The millions across the country who wanted a new start felt cheated; a movement to reanimate the councils began, and further strikes took place across the country, but Noske unleashed the Free Corps, who methodically occupied city after city with ruthless force and declarations of martial law.

SPD founder and long-time leader August Bebel, years earlier, had declared that power would land at the party's feet and it would merely need to pick it up. Power did not simply "come" but rather could be grabbed because a revolutionary moment arose due to widespread refusals to continue to accept dominance by the upper classes. The party did pick up the power laid at its feet, only to promptly hand it back to Germany's industrialists and Junkers.

In their final articles, Liebknecht and Luxemburg remained defiant. Liebknecht declared, "We haven't fled; we are not beaten! And even if you put us in chains, we are here, and we shall stay here!"[266] Luxemburg, in a more measured analysis, wrote,

> [T]he masses of soldiers who, even now, are still letting themselves be misused by their officers for hostile, counter-revolutionary purposes—is alone already proof that a lasting victory of the revolution was not possible in this encounter. On the other hand, this immaturity of the military is itself but a symptom of the general immaturity of the German revolution.[267]

Not sparing her party, she concluded,

> The leadership failed. But the leadership can and must be

> created anew by the masses and out of the masses. The masses are the crucial factor; they are the rock on which the ultimate victory of the revolution will be built. The masses were up to the task. They fashioned this "defeat" into a part of those historical defeats which constitute the pride and power of international socialism. And that is why this "defeat" is the seed of future triumph.[268]

The next day, both leaders would be dead, cruelly murdered by a Free Corps unit. Others were killed as well and the influential theorist Franz Mehring, 72 years old and in ill health, died soon afterward, crushed by the weight of the tragic reverse. Jogiches would be murdered two months later. The KPD's best leaders were wiped out. Liebknecht and Luxemburg had their heads bashed in with rifle butts, then were shot; Luxemburg's body was thrown in a canal, washing ashore four months later. This was not spontaneous butchery; fliers calling for Spartacists to be beaten to death had circulated for weeks and the SPD government had assigned military officers to shadow their movements. Once Berlin—although not yet the workers' districts of the city's north and east—was under control, Free Corps units moved across Germany to suppress unrest, put down strikes or simply depose elected local governments with declarations of martial law, beatings and summary executions.

One of the first cities to be invaded was Bremen. Local Leftists briefly proclaimed a "dictatorship of the proletariat," simultaneous with the uprising in Berlin, but dissolved it when it became apparent the uprising had failed. Despite the restoration of the previous régime, Bremen was occupied in a bloody battle. In Hamburg, a nearby city, socialists feared they would be next. Although the SPD was firmly in control there, the Hamburg council executive voted to send a regiment to Bremen to join the city's defenders and sent Noske a telegram threatening intervention. Noske responded curtly that, if they did so, "all those involved will be held strictly to account."[269] The Hamburg SPD backed down.

As the wave of counter-revolution methodically advanced from city to city, in contrast to the rapid revolutionary advances of November, the final showdown in Berlin came in March. At least 1200 were killed by Free Corps units, crushing a general strike. A typical episode was the fate of the People's Naval Division, which was summoned to receive discharge papers. Arriving unarmed, 30 of the sailors were taken into a courtyard and executed on the spot.

The final stand was, strangely, Bavaria. Perhaps the most conservative area of Germany, populated at the time mostly by Catholic peasants, it nonetheless was the site of a brief "soviet republic." It was as if a socialist government in the United States had been proclaimed only in Texas or a Canadian socialist government had taken root in Alberta. A network of peasants' councils, more extensive than anywhere else in Germany, existed in Bavaria, but there was limited cooperation between them and workers' councils, a friction that contributed to peasants withholding food supplies and was reflective of the Bavarian countryside's hostility to the revolution.[270] A group of local leftists took power on their own after months of chaos, proclaiming the soviet republic on 6 April. Bavarian communists opposed this as a hopeless adventure. On 13 April, a right-wing coup to overturn it failed, and, with renewed chaos, the local communists, led by Eugene Leviné, reversed themselves and seized power, proclaiming a second soviet republic.

These two republics, however, didn't extend outside Munich, the Bavarian capital; farmers resisted and the provincial premier, who had moved his government outside Munich, organized a blockade.[271] On 1 May, Noske's troops entered Munich and quickly gained control with unrestrained terror. Shootings went on continually for a week; a conservative, noting the frequency with which people were dragged out of buildings or trains to be killed, wrote "we have got quite used to the constant shooting."[272] A week of massacres was punctuated when 21 members of a Catholic association, opponents of the councils, had their meeting raided by their Free Corps "liberators" and were all summarily shot as "Spartacists."[273]

The verdict on the Munich councils was harsh. Richard Müller, the USPD leader, wrote, "The declaration of the soviet republic [on 6 April] was nothing but miserable and unscrupulous play acting at revolution by political pushers and coffee house scribblers, who became intoxicated by their own words."[274] Paul Levi, who had assumed the KPD leadership, declared the soviet republics "a nothing" and "an absurdity."[275]

"Socialism in one country" (although the term would not be invented for another few years) would prove to be an impossibility in the Soviet Union—"socialism in one city," which is what the Bavarian soviet republic amounted to, is worse than an illusion. But the events served to tip the Bavarian political spectrum further to the Right; already the nucleus of the Nazi Party was forming in Munich.

## Blind to its right: Social democracy gives the counter-revolution a free hand

This one-sided "civil war" had its effects. The Communist Party of Germany (KPD) became a small, semilegal group harassed by police with its leading newspaper banned and widely discredited among socialists for its tactics, including its refusal to contest elections and its bitter hostility toward labor unions. Paul Levi, a follower of Rosa Luxemburg who had reluctantly become party head after Leo Jogiches was murdered, decided that the KPD had to become a mass party and could only do so by purging its adventurist left wing, which he accomplished by announcing that the party would now reverse its attitude toward elections and unions, and those who disagreed must leave. This resulted in an immediate shrinking of the membership by half, but Levi, unlike Luxemburg, was willing to split the party in the belief that, in the longer run, this was the only way in which it could become an effective mass party.

The divisions within the Independent Social Democratic Party (USPD) continued to deepen, with the party's right wanting to rejoin the Social Democratic Party (SPD) and its left wing increasingly flirting with the KPD, its bitterness toward the SPD becoming as hot as that of the KPD. By the end of 1919, the left was gaining the upper hand within the USPD. Dissent grew within the SPD, with many of its members queasy from Gustav Noske's use of the Free Corps; some began to switch to the USPD. The USPD in turn was under attack—several hundred of its leaders were rounded up in January 1920 and its meetings banned.

The SPD leadership continued to see the only threat as coming from the Left, while the Right, through the medium of the Free Corps, was becoming increasingly emboldened. Heinrich Ströbel, former editor of the SPD's leading newspaper *Vorwärts* but now a right USPD figure, put the country's attitude this way in November 1919:

> Except for a handful of political careerists and a stately swarm of profiteers…the whole country feels greatly depressed by the course and results of the revolution…Today, as the first anniversary of the birth of the republic approaches, not only are the Junkers and upper bourgeoisie simply itching to give it a mortal blow at the first opportunity, but…the small man and the peasant…and even the proletarian…considers democracy simply the façade behind which capitalist exploitation and bureaucratic-military despotism are carrying on exactly as they carried on under the monarchy and the undisguised dictatorship of the sword.[276]

Rudolf Wissell, the former People's Commissar and now a

minister for the SPD, acknowledged, "The government has not lived up to the expectations of the people. We have, indeed, constructed a formal political democracy, but fundamentally we have done no more than continue the program initiated by the imperial government of Prince Max of Baden."[277]

Rumors of a Right-wing coup had become rampant, and the Free Corps didn't try very hard to disguise their attitude. They hated the SPD, hated the republic, and because the government had shown itself so weak, quite naturally the Free Corps drew the conclusion that they should take power for themselves. The government had become wholly dependent on the Free Corps—its ability to govern depended on the Rightist thugs thanks to its destruction of all other potential sources of support. But the Free Corps saw the SPD as a temporary expedient to be dispensed with at the earliest opportunity.

A Free Corps lieutenant colonel, early in 1919, declared: "This state, born of revolt, will always be our enemy…For the Reich! For the people! Fight against the government! Death to the Democratic Republic!"[278] Another Free Corps leader, Peter von Heydebreck, who would go on to become a high-ranking member of Hitler's stormtroops, said, "War against the state of Weimar and Versailles! War every day and with every means! As I love Germany, so I hate the Republic of November 9!"[279]

Some Free Corps units were now flying the swastika as their insignia and Right nationalist groups were springing up, with anti-Semitism prominently on display. The Pan-German League, a reactionary mass group with members from across the country founded in the 1890s, declared in its statutes "the oppressive and disintegrating influence of Jewry [is] the main cause of the collapse, and the elimination of this influence [is] the precondition of political and economic reconstruction and the saving of German culture."[280] A leader of the National Party, one of the two main Right parties in the Reichstag and in the constituent assembly, later wrote of 1919: "From my experience, the cry of 'Jew' would come from the audience at almost all political meetings when criticism was expressed of political circumstances. Besides, I was often able to notice that a sleepy meeting would wake up and the house applaud as soon as I started on the subject of the Jews."[281]

In July 1919, the Versailles Treaty was signed and, although Paul von Hindenburg and Wilhelm Gröner resigned, their extreme Right political outlooks, widely shared by the officers' corps, remained within the military. When in January 1920 Germany was bound by the treaty to reduce its army to 100,000 soldiers, this meant disbanding the Free Corps. By now the army was composed mostly of Free Corps units and had 400,000 under arms. The generals refused to disperse their units. Noske ordered the disbanding of an elite brigade on the last day of February 1920; the top army commander, Walther von Lüttwitz, responded by marching the brigade, wearing swastikas on helmets, on a parade and flatly declaring it would not stand down.

Lüttwitz had already been demanding the prohibition of strikes and the abolition of unemployment benefits, and the generals were demanding the dissolving of parliament and the calling of new elections. On 10 March, Frederich Ebert demanded Lüttwitz's resignation, but Lüttwitz instead conferred with other generals and decided to overthrow the government. Thus was the "Kapp Putsch" born.

Rumors of an imminent coup, substantial enough to be printed in that evening's newspapers, swirled through Berlin on 12 March. Orders for the arrest of the coup leaders were issued, but the city police, now firmly a reactionary bastion with the successful removal of Eichhorn, instead tipped off those they were supposed to arrest. The chief of the military High Command, General Hans von Seeckt, declared that no army units would defend the government. About 10 p.m., brigades began marching on Berlin from the city's outskirts; government ministers were given until 7 a.m. to capitulate or be arrested.

Noske called a 1 a.m. meeting with military commanders, including von Seeckt, where Noske was informed that any orders by him to defend the government would be ignored. Noske then rushed to an overnight meeting of the cabinet, which decided to flee Berlin.

The SPD cabinet members, after 16 months of putting down strikes and street demonstrations, now decided that a general strike was their only salvation. They issued a proclamation, then fled for Stuttgart, in the southwest corner of Germany, far from Berlin. Their government coalition partners, the Catholic Centre and Democratic parties, refused to sign the general-strike proclamation, which did not mince words:

> Workers! Comrades! We did not make the revolution in order to submit now to a régime of bloody mercenaries...Down tools! Strike! Cut the ground from under the feet of this reactionary clique!...There is only one weapon against the dictatorship of Wilhelm II: to paralyze the entire economy! Don't lift a finger! No proletarian must help the military dictatorship! A general strike all along the line![282]

The Free Corps marched unopposed into the center of Berlin, and proclaimed a dictatorship headed by Wolfgang Kapp, a prominent figure in ultranationalist circles, as the new chancellor, and Lüttwitz as defense minister. Kapp, owner of an East Prussian estate and longtime head of a Junker-dominated agricultural organization, had sought an open military dictatorship during World War I and had continued to actively seek the overthrow of the republican government after the war. Joining the march on its final steps was none other than Erich Ludendorff, who had handed the reins of government to the SPD to escape the responsibility of losing World War I, now back from Sweden.

The Left was not immediately impressed by the SPD's sudden

change of heart. A USPD leader, the moderate Arthur Crispien, told Berlin union leaders, "The SPD has treated us like dogs. They cannot now ask us to forget everything."[283] With its head, Levi, in jail, the acting KPD leadership refused to support the general strike, demanding that workers "not lift a finger for the democratic republic" and, in an editorial in its lead newspaper, declared, "The situation is crystal clear. The watchword is evident: All revolutionary workers must rally around the red flag of the proletarian dictatorship."[284]

This "advice," wildly out of step with popular feelings, was flatly ignored. The trade unions quickly endorsed the call of the general strike, and so thoroughly had the dormant militancy of Germans been brought back to life that the conservative union leader Karl Legien, who had made a career of collaborating with industrialists and holding back the SPD for three decades, assumed leadership of the strike.

Berlin was brought to a standstill. Blue- and white-collar workers and civil servants, from all parties, ceased work—so thorough was the strike that water, gas and electricity were cut off. After the first full day of the strike, the KPD, seeing its rank-and-file join the strike, reversed itself and endorsed the action. The USPD leadership did the same. The strike spread across Germany, and in one region grew into an armed rebellion against the Kapp Putsch. Local army commanders attempted to arrest strikers in the Ruhr Valley, Germany's industrial heartland, and in response, working people formed themselves into a "red army" for their mutual self-defense. By 19 March, this "red army" was in control of the region.

In the meantime, the coup leaders began looking for a way out. The putsch was supported by Junkers and the National Party—Kapp was on the party's ruling committee and other Nationals were among Kapp's accomplices. Germany's industrialists remained "neutral" during the putsch; they didn't support it because they thought it unnecessarily disrupted the economy.[285] That ambiguity was reflected in the industrialists' People's Party, the somewhat less extreme of the two anti-republican parties of the Right, who were initially fellow travelers. But the People's Party, as well as the Democratic Party, a junior member of the government coalition, decided that the Kapp Putsch leaders would have to be persuaded to resign. The Democratic leader, Vice Chancellor Eugen Schiffer, said the coup could not be undone by the general strike because that would lead to "Bolshevism."[286]

The People's Party leader, industrialist Gustav Stresemann, took it upon himself to initiate negotiations for the Kapp putschists to step down.[287] Four-party talks among the two junior members of the government (Democratic and Catholic Centre) and the two Right opposition parties (People's and National)—with SPD officials giving approval from an adjoining room—reached an agreement that, in exchange for the resignation of the putschists, new elections would be called and an amnesty would be granted to all coup participants.[288]

Leading the negotiations for the coup leaders was Captain Waldemar Pabst, who had headed the Free Corps unit that murdered Karl Liebknecht and Luxemburg. "Schiffer even offered false passports and money for [Pabst and Lüttwitz], which Pabst declined with thanks. The insurrectionists had already procured false passports from their friends at Police Headquarters," a study of the putsch later reported.[289]

Out on the streets, a very different outcome was proposed. Legien, the union leader, refused to call off the general strike, even after the Kapp putschists resigned, until the reinstated coalition government accepted an eight-point plan. Legien demanded punishment of the coup leaders, the democratization of local government, the disbanding of counter-revolutionary army units and the removal of food distribution from the hands of profiteers. The demands were agreed to when the SPD ministers returned to Berlin, but never implemented. But with the resignation of Noske, among others, from the cabinet, a new government had to be formed as the promised new elections were three months off.

Legien approached the USPD leadership and asked if they would form an all-socialist coalition government with the SPD and himself as chancellor. The right wing of the USPD wanted to do so, on condition it be given a majority of the cabinet posts. Legien agreed.[290] Separately, two followers of Levi, who was furious at his party's initial opposition to the anti-Kapp general strike, reached an agreement that the KPD would constitute a "loyal opposition" as long as such a government stayed true to its program. But the left wing of the USPD balked at joining with the SPD. The USPD left saw the SPD as traitors, and saw no reason why such a coalition would not again end in disaster as it had at the end of 1918.[291] And SPD repression of their party was fresh in their minds. The USPD left threatened to split the party if the coalition offer was accepted, and the party said no to Legien.

In the absence of any partner to its Left, the SPD formed another government with the Centre and Democratic parties; a right SPD figure, Herman Müller, was appointed chancellor (Ebert by now had become president) and a Democrat became Noske's replacement as defense minister. The army continued to have a free hand under the new minister. After all the turmoil and the dramatic undoing of the coup, this amounted to nothing more than a reshuffling of cabinet posts.

Was the USPD decision an act of suicide by the German Left? With hindsight, refusing to enter the government when it would have been the senior partner, albeit with Legien as chancellor, appears to be a mistake. The country had swung Left, and a new government that began to make good on popular expectations would have had an electrifying effect. Legien drastically moved from his earlier positions by calling for a program of nationalizing the mines, improved social legislation and agrarian reform against the powerful Junkers of Germany's east.

These proposals did not represent a revolutionary program, but as the premature uncoordinated uprisings of January 1919 had demonstrated, the country was not yet prepared for an all-out revolution nor was there was a party capable of providing revolutionary leadership. Given the concrete situation, there is a strong argument that the better course for the USPD would have been to join the government, move it to the Left by use of its majority, arm the Ruhr Valley red army and others willing to defend the gains of the November Revolution, and begin long-term preparations to move the country toward permanent popular control.

On the other hand, the USPD left wing had ample reasons for its lack of trust in the SPD—the SPD had suppressed its own revolution; had given the murderous Free Corps a license to unleash terror against working people; had consistently lied to its USPD junior partners in 1918 and to the country as a whole; and remained in awe of the old ruling classes. To put all that aside would have required swallowing very hard indeed. It is entirely comprehensible why so many in the USPD could not bring themselves to trust the SPD. But politics requires a thick skin; the verdict must be that the decision was wrong, especially given that socialists could only defend themselves against the resurgent nationalist Right by some measure of mutual self-defense. A USPD government that made good on principles previously unfulfilled by the SPD potentially could have led to a collapse of the SPD with an accompanying movement to the Left by voters.

The decision having been made, the "new" SPD-Centre-Democratic coalition government, unchecked by the Left, moved to put down the Ruhr uprisings and allow the Kapp putschists to freely leave Berlin. The strikes over, the remaining holdouts were too isolated to continue. In Chemnitz, future KPD leader Heinrich Brandler negotiated a peaceful end. But to put down the industrial workers and miners in the Ruhr, the Social

Democrats sent in the very Free Corps units that had just attempted to overthrow them.

It was more difficult to reach an agreement here as the uprising was larger and contained several elements (KPD, USPD, SPD, anarcho-syndicalists and others unaffiliated) some of whom wanted to hold out no matter the situation. It didn't help that the army, itching for revenge, made difficult demands, creating the impression that the military did not want a peaceful solution.

The Free Corps, again given a free hand by an SPD leadership seemingly unable to learn even the most elementary of lessons, used maximum brutality to regain control of the Ruhr. Here is how one member of a Free Corps unit described what happened, in a letter:

> Yesterday morning I got to my company and at 1 p.m. we made the first assault. If I were to write you everything, you would say they are lies. No mercy is shown. We shoot even the wounded. The enthusiasm is marvelous, almost incredible. Our battalion has two dead, the reds 200 to 300...[W]e also shot dead instantly ten red-cross nurses, each of whom was carrying a pistol. We shot at these abominations with joy, and how they cried and pleaded with us for their lives! Nothing doing! Whoever is found carrying arms is our enemy and gets done. We were much more humane against the French in the field.[292]

The Free Corps also made sure to leave a calling card in Berlin. The elite brigade that had refused to disband, triggering the sequence of events that led to the Kapp Putsch, was still intact and allowed to leave Berlin untouched. As the brigade marched on their way out of the city, a spectator, a boy, began to laugh. "Two [Free Corps] soldiers broke ranks, knocked the youth down with their rifle butts and kicked him where he lay in the gutter," one account reported.

> The crowd began to hiss its hatred. In response, an officer shouted an order and a rank...at once raised their rifles and, at point-blank range, fired a volley into the crowd. Then they turned about, the order to march was given, and the brigade tramped off to the west...Before they disappeared down the Charlottenstrasse, individual troopers broke ranks, ran to the sidewalk and beat lone civilians, using their potato-masher hand grenades as clubs. It was their final gesture to the people of Berlin.[293]

Twelve were killed and 30 injured by the brigade on its march.[294]

The moment of a mobilization containing the potential of a permanent shift in German institutional structures had passed. The latest bloodbaths inflicted by the Free Corps grimly illustrated that the pendulum had instead swung decisively to the Right thanks to the demoralizing dénouement of the general strike. The SPD paid for its repeated double-crosses in the new parliamentary elections, held in June—promises made to the Kapp putschists were kept. The SPD vote total fell to less than half of its vote total in the last election; it barely won more votes than the USPD, which increased its Reichstag seat total to 81 from 22. The KPD also entered the Reichstag for the first time. But the Right also gained as the Catholic Centre Party lost some support and the Democratic vote total also fell by more than half.

The SPD was asked to form a government as it still had more seats than any other party but only about one-quarter of the Reichstag; again they approached Crispien for a coalition with the USPD, this time in a four-party grouping with the Democratic and Centre parties.

The Ebert-Müller government had completely failed to fulfill its promises, had once again unleashed the Free Corps and failed to bring a single putschist to justice. It had become impossible for the USPD to join such a government, especially as its drastically increased following voted for it on the basis of its post-Kapp socialist program. Instead, a minority government of the Centre, Democrat and the People's parties was formed. These three parties did not constitute a majority and could form a government and remain in power only by virtue of the SPD "tolerating" it by refusing to vote it out of power.

The SPD long expected that, doing nothing, it would automatically gain an ever larger following and thereby would be able to continue to introduce incremental changes that at some point in the hazy, distant future would culminate in a socialist society. Instead, it was now in opposition to a capitalist government of the Right and physically menaced by the extreme Right. Germany's industrialists had not only recovered their confidence, they now had a stronger grip on the country than ever before.

Inflation became a problem by the latter part of 1922 and the government could not meet its expenditure requirements because industrialists and bankers refused to pay taxes or agree to currency controls.[295] Ebert (who remained as president because he was elected separately from the Reichstag) appointed a prominent industrialist, Wilhelm Cuno, as chancellor, at a time when business leaders sought an end to the eight-hour day and a rollback of trade union recognition and unemployment benefits.[296] Cuno's government responded by unleashing hyperinflation through massive printing of new money—by making the German currency worthless, industrialists and Junkers were relieved of their debt obligations, while the resources of labor organizations were destroyed.[297]

The High Command and the industrialists had also begun a secret program of rearmament that was hidden from the SPD (by setting up factories to build aircraft and submarines in Russia, Spain, Sweden and Switzerland), and when a new, stable currency was introduced to bring an end to the period of hyperinflation, the industrialists, having reduced their debt obligations to virtually nothing, had more money to finance the secret rearmament, spread nationalist propaganda and subsidize the

Nazis.[298]

The SPD would sit in opposition for most of the next 12 years, until Hindenburg, Ebert's successor as president thanks to SPD support, simply appointed Hitler chancellor. Hindenburg possessed the unilateral power to do so under the SPD-written Weimar constitution.

Ebert's reward for his many services to the old ruling classes and appeasement of reactionary nationalists was to be hounded as a "November criminal," the nationalists' term of abuse for anyone seen as responsible for the creation of the republic, the same people the Right blamed for supposedly losing the world war. So furious was the Right's campaign against him that Ebert died shortly after his health was broken in the wake of a 1924 court decision that upheld politically inspired accusations of high treason against him.

"Political murder organizations" inspired by the Free Corps began to kill others branded as "November criminals" by the Right—even Matthias Erzberger, the long-time leader of the Catholic Centre Party who was a supporter of Wilhelm II and German militarism, was among the hundreds assassinated in this way.[299] Of the 705 persons officially listed as involved in the Kapp Putsch, only one, Kapp, received a prison sentence and only because he returned from Sweden.[300] Ludendorff remained untouched in Bavaria. No one was ever prosecuted for the murders of Liebknecht, Luxemburg, Jogiches or the tens of thousands of others during 1918 to 1920.

Ebert, Noske and the SPD leadership opened the road for Hitler.

## Revolution in Europe: Wishful thinking or a near miss?

Soldiers who returned from the battlefields of World War I would say it was impossible to understand what conditions were like unless you experienced them first-hand. No argument. It is not much easier to comprehend the scale of carnage; the lives sacrificed to an imperialist scramble for expanded territories, new colonies and expanded markets. Tens of millions condemned to the agony of living in open trenches, facing death from poison gas or the next order to be cannon fodder in the latest offensive using the same hopeless tactics, so that big business could fatten profits through expansion and the officers of the militaries that made the expansion possible could cover themselves with self-created glory.

Nationalism and a military arms race had set the stage; nascent popular culture glorifying war reflected dominant elite attitudes. Nonetheless, enthusiasm was far from universal—all belligerent countries instituted a draft to ensure they could fight. Numbers are faceless, especially when so large, but to give some sense as to why drafts and patriotic exhortations were so necessary: nine million deaths and seven million permanent invalids among 30 million battle casualties.

Perhaps more comprehensible, if we are trying to understand the casual cruelty of the war's military commanders and national rulers, the sheer contempt for the lives of the ordinary soldier and sailor, are the casualties at the very end. German negotiator Matthias Erzberger asked the Entente supreme commander, Marshal Ferdinand Foch of France, for a ceasefire on 8 November 1918, while negotiations were under way. Foch refused, although it was a foregone conclusion the war was over. The armistice was finally signed at 5 a.m. on 11 November, and it had been decided during the negotiations that the war would end at 11:11 a.m. on 11/11.

Despite knowing the armistice had been signed, commanders from all belligerents continued to order attacks that morning, right to the final minutes and in some cases even afterward. Nothing could be gained or lost; Germany would be given two weeks to evacuate from all territories outside its borders.

On that final day, 11 November, there were almost 11,000

casualties, including 2738 deaths—more casualties than on D-Day in 1944.[301] For what? General Erich Ludendorff, in his memoirs, approvingly quoted one of his predecessors: "Eternal peace is a dream—and not even a beautiful one. War is part of God's world order. Within it unfold the noblest virtues of men, courage and renunciation, loyalty to duty and readiness for sacrifice—at the hazard of one's life. Without war the world would sink into a swamp of materialism."[302] Of course, Ludendorff and the aristocrats who primarily formed the officer corps didn't have to climb out of gas-filled trenches to face machine guns on open fields themselves; they possessed enormous privilege and thus occupied positions in which they ordered farmers, factory workers, clerks and others without privilege to do it for them and then claim this constituted "honor."

These sorts of experiences opened millions of eyes on more than one front. No amount of propaganda could erase this bitter truth, although military commanders tried. Again, Ludendorff provides an example although, again, by no means a unique one. Germany's de facto dictator issued a 1917 order requiring that 60 minutes each day be dedicated to "patriotic instruction" in which officers denounced peace proposals.[303] The British, Italian and other militaries did the same. This didn't stop mutinies and other actions from happening, as we saw earlier in this chapter. Inevitably, these experiences would continue to shape the combatants' societies once the soldiers and sailors returned home.

Concomitant with the appeals to patriotism was the demonization of the enemy. Entente propaganda regularly raised the specter of bestial Huns destroying civilization and routinely invoked the carnage in Belgium. To be sure, the German invasion and occupation of Belgium was extraordinarily ruthless—hundreds of thousands of troops passed through, leaving behind a scorched earth of destroyed cities and executed civilians.

Germany's occupation forces expropriated food and material so severely that the civilian population faced starvation, and Germany intended for Belgium to be reduced to a "vassal state."

Yet there was no commotion over Belgium's more brutal occupation of Congo. Entente countries had maintained silence as Belgium King Leopold II's relentless drive for profit turned Congo into a vast slave labor camp where eight to ten million people were killed. Africans were tortured, had hands severed, were killed or had family members taken hostage for failing to meet their assigned rubber-gathering quota. The Belgian king, and the corporations to whom he granted concessions, amassed gigantic fortunes and massive public works were built across Belgium on the backs of those Africans—the entire present-day Democratic Republic of Congo was Leopold II's personal property on the force of his own declaration.

So too did Entente propagandists come to declare the war a campaign to bring democracy to Germany. Yet Germany, albeit under the impetus of an internal revolution, allowed all adults to vote, including women, by the end of 1918; women did not receive the vote in the United States until 1920, and not until 1928 in the United Kingdom and 1944 in France—long after almost all other European countries. In the United Kingdom, only 7.5 million adults out of 45 million were eligible to vote in 1911, a much lower percentage than in Germany. In the years before World War I, British women who campaigned for the right to vote were frequently imprisoned; when imprisoned women resorted to a hunger strike, they were force-fed.[304]

German opponents of the war landed in jailed or were drafted into the army, but US repression could be more severe, and did not end with the conclusion of the war. The US entry into the war was soon followed by the passage of the Espionage Act, making it a crime to oppose the war, and the rapid formation of national vigilante groups that, with official imprimatur, worked to silence all opposition. About 900 were sent to prison under the

Espionage Act, with several hit with 20-year sentences. Socialist Party leader Eugene V. Debs was given ten years for making a speech; he was not pardoned until December 1921, more than three years after the war he opposed had ended. In the two years following the end of the war, at least 16,000 people were arrested in a series of highly publicized mass arrests that became known as the Palmer Raids, for President Woodrow Wilson's attorney general, Mitchell Palmer. (Palmer was ably assisted by a 24-year-old aide, J. Edgar Hoover, who in future decades would go on to create an unaccountable secret police force within the Federal Bureau of Investigation.) About 250 men and women, including Emma Goldman, were placed on a ship and forcibly deported to Russia. A man in Connecticut was thrown in jail for six months for pointing to a picture of Lenin and calling him a "brainy man."[305]

Such were the democratic paradises that millions found as they left the trenches and shipyards behind.

It is commonplace to believe the Bolsheviks were dreamers when they staked the Russian Revolution on socialist revolution in Europe. The reason for this verdict is simple—there were no successful revolutions in Europe. But is this reductionist reasoning accurate? The answer is not so simple.

The French socialist party, the SFIO, had eagerly signed on as part of Raymond Poincaré's "sacred union" at the outset of World War I, but this cross-class unity government was breaking down by 1918. Strikes and mutinies occurred with increasing frequency, and Russia's October Revolution began to be seen by many as an example. The "old words" used by traditional elitist leaders were "cancelled out," observed D.H. Lawrence.[306] Mounted on top of the lies of political leaders that had become too obvious to ignore, the French government carried out demobilization at a snail's pace. By March 1919, United Kingdom Prime Minister David Lloyd George warned Georges Clemenceau, the French prime minister, that "The whole of

Europe is filled with the spirit of revolution. There is a deep sense not only of discontent, but of anger and revolt among the workmen against prewar conditions. The whole existing order, in its political, social, and economic aspects is questioned by the masses of the population from one end of Europe to the other."[307]

Councils were created in Paris and an influx of radicalized people swelled the ranks of the SFIO and the reformist French trade union umbrella, the General Confederation of Labor (CGT), which, like its union counterparts across Europe, had assisted the local socialists in subsuming the movement to the war effort. The SFIO and CGT had assumed there would be rewards for their working-class memberships after the war, but none seemed forthcoming.

Part of the reason for this inertia was the elitism that pervaded French institutions. "The typical member of the elite had passed through the Paris Law Faculty and Bar, the École Libre des Sciences Politiques, which had a near monopoly on recruitment to senior positions in the administration and ministerial cabinets, before acceding to parliament and a ministerial portfolio,"[308] is the summation of one historian of this period. These elites kept the franchise limited, excluding all women and immigrants, so that only a minority of adults were eligible to vote, and the elites wanted only those from a very narrow pool to actually govern. But these elites were deeply divided, along with the electorate—there were cleavages among monarchical and Catholic Rightists; liberal republicans of the Right and Center-Right who were less influenced by the clergy; the Radical Party, a Centrist party of shopkeepers and white-collar workers that was not at all radical despite its name; and the SFIO on the Left.

Many on the Right responded to this instability by yearning for an authoritarian state, which would be another recruitment point for the Left. By the end of the war, Clemenceau ruled over all of this with near dictatorial powers on behalf of France's Right despite being a former Radical. Inflation was destroying living standards—prices increased fivefold from 1914 to 1920 and the franc lost half its value in the first half of 1919.[309] Further sapping any recovery was massive government debt, which increased by more than sevenfold during the war as the more economically advantaged were reluctant to pay taxes.[310] Wages badly fell behind price increases, triggering unrest—500 strikes with 180,000 participants in 1918, and 2200 strikes with 1.16 million participants in 1919.[311] Most strikes featured denunciations of war profiteers.

The pace of events began to quicken. In late March 1919, the assassin of Jean Jaurès, the SFIO founder, was acquitted, with 100,000 demonstrating against the judicial outrage. Mutinies occurred in the French fleet on the Black Sea as sailors refused to participate in the invasion of revolutionary Russia; commanders were forced to bring the fleet home. The national legislature had just voted funds for the imperialist adventure, a decision that brought on more strikes. Hoping to head off a massive May Day march called by the CGT, Clemenceau promised Léon Jouhaux, the CGT's reformist leader, he would have an eight-hour workday put into law, granting a key demand. The new law was passed and Clemenceau simultaneously banned all May Day marches. Despite the ban, large crowds came out in Paris, resulting in numerous clashes between demonstrators and police. Hundreds were injured. Hundreds of thousands joined strikes in May and June alone, but union leaders were now getting cold feet and began selling out their rank-and-file.

One of these sellouts triggered a strike of metalworkers in June. The metalworkers' union leadership agreed to a contract that did not codify the shortened eight-hour day, but did include requirements for increased productivity in exchange for any reduction in the length of the workday.[312] In response, metalworkers walked out, and transport and chemical workers in Paris went on strike in sympathy. The striking metalworkers also explicitly went out against their union's chief, Alphonse

Merrheim, whom they accused of being "sold out to the bosses, to the government."[313] The strike's original leaders were supplanted by an ad hoc action committee that took charge, calling for a general strike as a precursor for a revolution that would hand power to the CGT.[314] That demand was a reflection of the strong syndicalist sentiment in France, a variety of anarchism that strongly competed with more Marxist-oriented political tendencies.

The metalworkers' strike eventually failed; Merrheim helped bring it to an end because he wanted to create a larger union that he believed would be more capable of bargaining with the bosses. "Those who believe that one can consume more and produce less deceive the working masses and prepare them for a future of unspeakable suffering," Merrheim said, adding he did not want to be "dragged along by the unorganized masses, by the unchained crowd."[315]

A July strike, supported, perhaps reluctantly, by the CGT and SFIO, was called to show solidarity with Russia and Hungary, now also a soviet republic, in coordination with a strike in Italy and a demonstration in Great Britain. Clemenceau called a meeting with CGT leaders and promised a speeding up of demobilization, a partial amnesty and a strong effort to contain inflation. The CGT agreed to call off the strike.[316]

That outcome reflected the growing cleavages in the CGT as well as the SFIO; both now had the familiar pattern of right, center and left factions. One line of fracture was attitudes toward Russia's October Revolution and other international developments. The left wing wanted to link up with the Bolsheviks and other revolutionary movements, which were forming a Communist International to coordinate revolutionary groups; the right wing preferred to stay with the Socialist International that had collapsed at the outbreak of World War I. The center tried to steer a middle course between those two wings; this group saw the Independent Social Democratic Party of Germany (USPD) as a logical ally.

Overlaid over the above basic division were the differences in political tendencies. In contrast to most other European countries, France had a very strong syndicalist tradition—syndicalists believed that workplace organizing would be the route to revolution, rejected political parties and parliaments, and believed in the general strike as the mechanism to overthrow the capitalist state. Followers of Pierre-Joseph Proudhon, the proponent of organizing through workplace cooperatives while "ignoring" the state whose ideas had influenced the Paris Commune in 1871, played a significant role in the founding of the CGT in the 1890s. The syndicalist belief in "direct action" remained a strong tendency within the union federation in the years before World War I,[317] but CGT leaders joined the war effort and union ranks were decimated by callups into the army.

Syndicalists existed in large numbers in the SFIO. The French Left was still gathered in one political party, whereas in Russia, Germany and many other countries two or more parties already existed. The SFIO rank-and-file was moving left, partly because of the militants joining in large numbers, eager to overthrow the government that had brought such misery upon them. Despite that influx, the center gained the upper hand at the SFIO's April 1919 conference, adopting a cautious program written by Léon Blum, a leader of the center faction, that warned against "premature movements and impulsive demonstrations" yet contradictorily declared the party "would not run away from any opportunities presented it."[318]

Fernand Loriot, for the left faction, condemned the program for being reformist in a revolutionary time. Loriot later wrote that he didn't believe reforms were useless, but that the program was an "anachronism" trying to "perfect" the existing order when a revolutionary moment had arrived.[319] Despite this feeling, groups on the left wing of the socialist movement decided to keep their organizations within the mass groups, the

SFIO and CGT.

Separate from this ferment, the first post-war elections were held in November 1919. The SFIO fared badly. Under the new rules, blocs could be elected rather than single parties; this encouraged parties to form blocs, but the SFIO, not having a compatible partner, ran on its own. Multiple seats were selected from each parliamentary district on a proportional basis, but if a single party or bloc gained a majority of votes, that party or bloc would win all the seats in the district. Thus the socialists won 23 percent of the vote but 11 percent of the seats, losing seats despite increasing their vote total. The parties of the Right did create blocs and won a majority of the seats on an explicitly anti-Bolshevik and nationalist platform, making promises based on extravagant claims of riches to be had from German reparations.

A backlash had set in. One sign of this backlash was the failure to grant women the vote when success seemed at hand. Here it was Radical Party senators from rural districts who blocked female suffrage: Their spokesman said nature had given women a different role from men and that their hands were for kissing, not for ballots.[320]

Although the SFIO had adopted the cause of female suffrage, it did not show signs that it was serious about the cause. Men in each of the party's factions tended to believe that women's liberation could only come about through socialism, thereby relieving themselves of the duty to do anything about the subordinate status of women at the present time. French socialist men also resisted the formation of autonomous women's sections for anti-feminist reasons,[321] and the very fact that there was not a single prominent woman leader speaks volumes about the lack of seriousness. The French Left's failure to take up the cause of women led to reactionary results—abortion and birth control were made illegal in 1920, and even advocacy of either was illegal. Women were gradually pushed out of the workplace and did not secure the vote until after the overthrow of the World War

II Pétain régime.

The three factions continued to battle within the SFIO; a February 1920 party conference again backed the center when it voted to join the German USPD in leaving the Socialist International but not join the Communist International on the basis that more study was needed. But as the debates raged, the revolutionary potential of the past two years was subsiding. Railway workers went on strike, joined by miners in two regions. Too little support and solidarity was offered, allowing the government to react with force and arrests while employers hired scabs. Jouhaux, the CGT leader, then stepped forward and surprisingly called for a general strike beginning on 1 May. There was not a strong response, and the CGT "was forced into a humiliating climbdown."[322] More than 15,000 workers were fired after the strike ended. Clemenceau's successor as prime minister, a former socialist appointed to his office by a conservative president, felt emboldened enough to attempt to ban the CGT.[323]

The tensions within the SFIO caused by these reverses forced the party to split in December 1920. The centrist Blum made an impassioned speech for the majority to stay in the SFIO; veteran German revolutionary Klara Zetkin, who snuck across the border, delivered an electrifying speech asking for adherence to the Communist International.[324] By a 2-to-1 margin, delegates voted to form the French Communist Party; the minority remained in the SFIO. France now had a revolutionary party, a mass group, but the potential for revolution had already passed.

Italy, too, had a period of revolutionary upheaval hobbled by a lack of leadership. Similar to the French, the Italian Socialist Party (PSI) was split into right, center and left wings, with some wings containing more than one faction. The party, and the PSI-aligned Confederation of Labor, one of Italy's two national union umbrella organizations, grew rapidly after the war; the PSI emerged with the largest numbers of seats in the November 1919 parliamentary election, albeit well short of a majority in a deeply divided body. The PSI also enjoyed support by virtue of its consistent opposition to the war, as did the party that emerged as its main rival, the "Popolari," or Italian Popular Party, a heterogeneous Catholic party of peasants, small landlords, shopkeepers and the Centrist middle class. The other main Italian labor confederation was allied with it. The Popular Party tended to a play a negative role, generally opposing all other parties but without ever advancing a program of its own. The remainder of the parliament consisted of a hodgepodge of liberal, republican and conservative parties, with a smattering of small Left groups.

Despite ongoing unrest, frequent strikes and grassroots organizing in workplaces, the Socialists proved inept. As with the Russian Mensheviks and German Social Democrats, the PSI's large right and center wings believed in the inevitability of socialism, thereby relieving themselves of any responsibility because the state would eventually fall into their hands. The Socialists were at the same time fond of issuing strong calls for revolution. A historian of Italy, Denis Mack Smith, delivered a harsh judgment of this era that is difficult to argue against: "The only constant factor among the socialists was their association of violent language with a timid uncertainty in deed, and this was bad tactics as well as self-deception."[325]

Factory councils began springing up, composed of elected workers who would adjudicate local disputes, although unrest had begun with strikes by white-collar workers, many of whom were women.[326] An April 1919 agreement between the metal-workers' union and the Turin employers' federation formalized this structure. Not to be confused with Russia's soviets, which were intended to be government organs, Italy's councils nonetheless provided a nucleus to channel labor unrest.

The unions' attitude to the councils was ambiguous, but left Socialists saw them as a route toward eventual workers' control of industry. Antonio Gramsci, leader of one of two left factions within the PSI, saw traditional unions as large apparatuses that alienated and stifled its members that would be supplanted by the council system. "The Council is the most appropriate organ for mutual education and for fostering the new social spirit that the proletariat has managed to distill out of its fruitful, living experience in the community of labor,"[327] Gramsci wrote. "The existence of Councils gives workers direct responsibility for production; it encourages them to improve their way of working; it introduces a conscious and voluntary discipline and it creates the mentality of the producer, the maker of history."[328]

At an October 1919 PSI conference, the left wing won support for its direct call for revolution, but the right socialist leader Filippo Turati recoiled from what he saw as a gratuitous threat. "Goodbye to parliamentary action and goodbye to the socialist party," would be the result of an inevitable counterattack, Turati said.[329] The PSI did little practical work to back its words, turning Turati's fear-ridden remark into a post-facto prophesy.

The factory council movement continued to grow, although still centered in the northern industrial cities of Turin and Milan. In contrast to the complacent forecasts of the inevitable victory of socialism, which rested on a tacit belief that the capitalist ruling class would sit and watch its power being taken away, factory owners locked out their employees in March 1920, provoking an April mass strike involving hundreds of thousands that explicitly sought to bring industry under political control.

This wave was buoyed by syndicalists who were outside of both the PSI and the two labor confederations. Despite the refusal of the PSI and the PSI-aligned Confederation of Labor to back the strike, it spread to dock workers in Genoa, and to railway workers in Florence and Pisa who refused to transport troops. The Confederation of Labor eventually stepped in, settling the strike by giving in to employers' demands for sharp restrictions on the factory councils.

The PSI's left wing did support the strike, raising its prestige and deepening the party's divisions, although there was as yet no attempt at splitting. Gramsci's group did not hesitate to analyze: "The reason why the worker and peasant forces lack revolutionary co-ordination and concentration is that the leading organs of the Socialist Party have shown themselves utterly lacking in any understanding of the phase of development that we are currently passing through in national and international history...The Socialist Party is watching the course of events like a spectator."[330]

Emboldened by union leaderships undercutting their members and by a lack of vigorous opposition by the Socialist Party, factory owners attempted to cut wages, triggering factory occupations across northern Italy in September 1920. At least 500,000 workers participated, and soon the factories were running again under the workers' self-management. Peasants began seizing land, railway workers again refused to transport troops, and this time government officials and teachers went on strike. But the PSI was again caught by surprise with no plan, and left the initiative to the Confederation of Labor, which had not sanctioned the actions; the Popular Party-based labor confederation refused to join in any way.

The factory owners asked the government to use force to break the impasse, but by now Giovanni Giolitti was once again prime minister. Giolitti, a liberal who was a past master of effecting compromises and playing off factions against one another, had served as prime minister five times since 1892 and was often recalled from retirement when the capitalist parties were unable to solve the latest crisis. Giolitti resolved to find a peaceful end to the factory occupations and quietly brought about negotiations. The factory owners eventually agreed to the councils' participation in management, bringing the strikes to an end. But this agreement was never implemented. Deep disappointment set in, and the revolutionary tide quickly ebbed. Benito Mussolini and his fascist squads had quietly sat on the sidelines, waiting to see which side would win. When it was the owners who won, the fascists began a savage wave of violence. The capitalists were only too happy to see death and destruction meted out to workers and peasants, and tolerated the fascists' myth that they were restoring order against a socialist revolution.

The Italian Left now began a series of splits, mergers and purges, disorganizing itself as the fascist wave of violence, aided by government authorities, met little or no resistance. By the time of the PSI's January 1921 conference, the party was under considerable pressure by the Communist International to split. The International had decreed its 21 conditions for membership, and pressured the left wings of European and North American parties to form "pure" communist parties and split from center and right. The PSI's center faction, the "unitary communists" led by Giacinto Menotti Serrati, accepted the 21 conditions in principle, but argued that all parties should implement them based on their local conditions and refused to endorse an expulsion of the right wing, declaring unity was a necessity for a quicker conquest of power. The PSI right, the "socialist concentration" led by Turati, backed the center and the 21 conditions, but opposed any split and refused to model itself on Russia, arguing that a near-term overthrow of the Italian government was out of the question. The PSI left forced a vote calling for the expulsion of the concentration faction and, when it failed by a 2-to-1 margin, left to form the Communist Party of Italy (PCI). The new PCI had two distinct groups, an anti-parliamentary group led by Amadeo Bordiga, who became party head, and that of Gramsci, which looked to Russia's October Revolution for inspiration.

Because the Communist International was beginning to become accustomed to interfering in the affairs of the national parties, the debate over organization extended beyond Italy. German Communist leader Paul Levi disapproved of a mechanical split that did not occur from the experience of the

Italian party's membership. "[W]e can win over the masses...create a big party...[by] drawing them ever more tightly to us instead of splitting them off," Levi wrote.[331] (Levi, ironically, had begun to realize his genuinely held desire to build a mass communist party by purging his party's left wing.)

In contrast, Karl Radek argued that the split was a necessity because reformers had to be removed and that the centrist Serrati was vacillating instead of being firm. "The question at stake was whether the Communist International would permit the centrist elements who had infiltrated its organization...to sabotage its policies from within by granting them the right to adapt, meaning in reality to invalidate, the resolutions of congresses to the 'conditions of a country,'" Radek wrote.[332] In other words, there would be much less space for opposition in Communist International-affiliated parties than had been the case in the Socialist International—the looseness of the latter was seen as a factor in its helplessness in the face of the outbreak of war.

Italian rank-and-file socialists didn't understand the split. Serrati had sat on the presidium of the Communist International's second world congress months earlier—how could he suddenly be a traitor? Later that year, the International dumped its policy of splitting parties in favor of a united-front policy of cooperation, having come to the reasonable conclusion that revolutions, with the cooling of the post-war unrest, could no longer be considered imminent—it now pressed the PCI to fuse with the PSI, which had become a centrist group after Turati's right faction was expelled after the communists split. Bordiga opposed this, but the PCI eventually agreed to the merger over his objections. The rump PSI then split again, with only the left-most members joining the PCI, Serrati among them. While this endless factional fighting went on, the fascists, unchecked, were fomenting bloody violence, cutting the Left movement to pieces on behalf of Italian big business.

In the crumbling Austria-Hungary Empire, a multitude of

different revolutions were taking place. The energies of the oppressed subject nationalities—all others apart from the Germans and Hungarians—were channeled into traditional national movements. Desires for independence greatly outweighed other considerations. The Poles, who had been split among the Austrian, German and Russian empires, united to recreate Poland; the Czechs and Slovaks formed the new country of Czechoslovakia; the Slovenes, Croats and Bosnian Muslims joined Serbs, Montenegrins and Macedonians to found what would become Yugoslavia; the South Tyrol region joined Italy; and Transylvania reunited with Romania. With the war ending, these new countries found it simple to create new armies since many units were organized on national lines, and declared independence with the knowledge that it would be difficult for the empire's ethnic Germans and Hungarians to counter them militarily and knowing they had the backing of the victorious Entente powers. Despite strong social democratic parties, there were no attempts at social revolution in any of the newly created countries, except for the brief, nearly forgotten, Slovak Socialist Republic.

Austria, like Germany, had a long Social Democratic tradition, although almost all of its leaders were ethnic Germans based in or near Vienna. The provisional government founded at the formation of "German Austria" when the empire dissolved at the end of World War I consisted of the Austrian Social Democratic Party (SPÖ) and the conservative Christian Socials. The SPÖ held the chancellorship and the most important ministerial posts.

Simultaneous with the downfall of their counterparts in Germany, the Hapsburg monarchy, which had ruled since the thirteenth century, was declared null and void, a republic was proclaimed and a constituent assembly election was scheduled for February 1919. There was little support for a socialist revolution, and the SPÖ leadership was unified in opposing any upheaval.

Otto Bauer, a prominent party leader, believed that the peasants would oppose any revolution and would cut off food to the cities, and that Austria, now a rump of its former self, could not survive without its remaining farmland. "It is not the case that the German workers alone could build the German-Austria Republic," Bauer said in a speech. "The great difference between our situation and that in Russia is above all that the Russian peasant—socially, culturally, economically and legally—is quite different from our peasant here." Russian peasants had a stake in their country's revolution by virtue of their taking land from the great estates, but in Austria, Bauer argued, peasants felt as though they were landowners and opposed the working class, leaving any takeover attempt as representative of only a minority. "Eight days after the attempt such a government would be bound to collapse through famine, because from the day such an attempt was made we would not receive any food from the peasants. The use of force against the peasants would only be possible in the neighborhood of industrial towns; but little food could be collected that way and it would cause a bloody civil war."[333]

The SPÖ never swerved from this path, and easily stopped two attempts at communist takeovers that amounted to putsch attempts by a small minority. As in Germany, workers' and soldiers' councils sprang up; the SPÖ easily controlled these and the councils never threatened to become any sort of dual government.

Naturally, not all agreed, and the Communist Party of Austria (KPÖ) was founded on 9 February 1919. The KPÖ refused to participate in the constituent assembly or parliament, instead seeking control of the councils, which were being formed in all provinces of Austria. But the SPÖ never lost its council majority. The KPÖ tried to storm parliament on 17 April, but was repulsed by units of the new People's Militia that was now Austria's army.

The militia, too, remained loyal to the SPÖ. The communists had become excited by the proclamation of a soviet government in Hungary; the Hungarian leader, Béla Kun, promised food, money and assistance after a successful revolt. But Kun did not have a strong grasp of reality, a trait he would repeatedly show as he had the habit of popping into history during the next few years.

In the meantime, Kun had sent out an urgent call for help. The Austrian Social Democrats argued that they might like to help Hungary, but the Entente, on which it was dependent, would surely cut off food supplies if it did and Hungary could not make up the difference. Kun was now determined to force the pace of action. He sent a wealthy emissary, Ernst Bettelheim, to Vienna to organize another revolt. The KPÖ issued a 14 June call for an uprising the next day, declaring, "Every member of the People's Militia has the duty to participate in this demonstration with weapon in hand."[334] The Vienna workers' council responded by saying workers should follow only its directives: "Do not let yourselves be used for an attempted putsch!...Remain aloof from the unscrupulous demonstrations of the communists!"[335]

To make sure the uprising would falter, 115 KPÖ leaders were arrested that night, and the action went nowhere the next day. The action was a ridiculous adventure, and by no means had unanimous support from Austrian communists. Radek sharply condemned Bettelheim's putsch as having no authorization from any body, certainly not the Communist International, and against all communist principles that working classes could only liberate themselves—no outside "liberator" could do it for them. Instead, the KPÖ should have concentrated on organizing instead of following a "pseudo-messiah,"[336] Radek wrote.

This attempt to "force" a revolution spelled the end of any real role for Austrian communists. But the SPÖ now lost its way. Its tepid attempts at nationalization were resisted, and it found itself running the machinery of a capitalist government on behalf of capitalists. In 1920, the SPÖ used the opportunity of a disagreement to leave the coalition government. But it would not regain a chance to govern and with the Left having spent itself in uprisings with no chance of success, it no longer formed an adequate counterweight, allowing Austria's politics to move to the Right.

Hungary, like all the countries of the Central Powers, ended World War I exhausted; a general strike in June 1918 shutting down Budapest was one sign of ferment. Hungary had been ruled by a super-chauvinistic aristocracy that featured concentration of land in few hands in Hungary proper and a harsh subjugation of its subject peoples. Power fell into the hands of a liberal count, Michael Károlyi, at the end of the war, more or less by default, but he was unable to govern with any effectiveness. His government collapsed in April 1919 and, in the ensuing vacuum, a soviet republic was declared under the rule of a fused social democrat/communist party with Kun, who became a communist while held as a prisoner of war in Russia, at the head.

Although a communist was the head of the government, it was the larger social democrats that had the upper hand. The soviet government started out with welcome reforms, and brought medical care and education to many who had not had access to them, but with so many inexperienced leaders (because all but the aristocracy had been completely shut out of all positions of authority it could not be otherwise) serious mistakes were made. One mistake was to declare a complete nationalization. Done in an abrupt manner, industrial production was hurt, creating opposition in the cities. The nationalization of the large estates was handled poorly, with the estates turned into "collectives" controlled by the local gentry, sparking bitterness from the peasants. A new currency was issued that was not accepted by peasants, causing food distribution to the cities to decline; this led to episodes of armed requisitions of food. Faced with unrest, the government created a "commission to maintain order" and put in charge a zealot, Tibor Szamuely, who proceeded to use terror, including death sentences, in the countryside and against strikers before he was countermanded.

Regardless of internal problems, Hungary was far too small to survive any length of time as a socialist state on its own. Kun counted on support from Russia and a successful revolution in Austria, and realistically needed a socialist Germany as well. The latter two were not forthcoming, and Russia had to deal with its civil war and could provide no help at that time. The capitalist Entente powers were also extremely hostile to a soviet Hungary, and that alone would have been enough to doom Kun's régime. Faced with encirclement, a Hungarian red army was created, which first invaded Slovakia before being thrown back, then invaded Romania, before this turned into a Romanian advance on Budapest. On 1 August, the soviet government resigned.

Kun, in his final speech, was bitter: "No one will succeed in governing this country. The proletariat, which was discontented under our rule, which was shouting…'Down with the dictatorship!,' this proletariat will be much more discontented with all other governments."[337] A Right government soon came to power, unleashing a vengeful terror while restoring the nearly feudal social structure that had previously existed. Despite Kun and others fleeing, some socialists stayed in their posts in an effort to maintain some semblance of order; their reward was to be arrested, with many of them tortured to death. A fascistic government under Admiral Miklós Horthy would be the ultimate result.

The invasion of Slovakia, while perhaps well-intentioned, represented a towering lack of perspective. Slovakia has just liberated itself from a thousand years of Hungarian rule; in the last decades, Hungarian triumphalism had reached grotesque proportions. The Hungarian crown denied the existence of the Slovak people, tried to call Slovakia "Upper Hungary," banned the Slovak language, closed all schools there and used continual repression to enforce its rule and to keep Slovakia undeveloped. Even under a red banner, this just-concluded history was not going to be forgotten. Adding insult, the first Hungarian post-war government under Károlyi dismantled factories in Slovakia and sent them to Hungary on rail lines Hungary still controlled.[338]

The spark for the Hungarian soviet republic's invasion was an incursion by a Czech army after a series of armed moves by both sides. Hungary announced a counter-offensive on grounds of self-defense, and quickly occupied two-thirds of Slovakia. On 16 June 1919, the Slovak soviet republic was proclaimed by Czech and Slovak social democrats. The new government issued decrees nationalizing banks, large estates and other property; released small farmers from debt; instituted universal suffrage; and proclaimed full rights for all languages.[339]

All this, however, was dependent on the Hungarian red army, which was seen by most Slovaks as invaders. On 22 June, Clemenceau, the French prime minister, demanded an immediate Hungarian withdrawal. The social democrats who formed the majority of the Hungarian government wanted peace, the Czech social democrats asked for a withdrawal and the Entente countries were in position to invade Hungary to back Clemenceau's demand.[340] The red army withdrew, restoring a unitary Czechoslovak state.

Many other countries saw upheavals, most notably in Finland. Although not yet independent of Russia, an election was held for a post-war parliament in Finland, with the social democrats gaining a majority. The parliament convened itself after the February 1917 Revolution in Russia, but the Provisional Government of Aleksandr Kerensky found it intolerable and demanded a new election. That was done, this time with the Social Democrats in the minority. This result, blocking all reforms, along with widespread unemployment and the growing militancy in Russia, led to the formation of Finnish Red Guards.

Counter-revolutionary White Guards also formed.

After the October Revolution, Finland declared its independence, which Lenin's government immediately recognized. Left Socialists and Red Guards gained control of the more industrial south of Finland, where socialist support was strong; the Whites, commanded by a Baltic baron, Gustaf Mannerheim, controlled the north. The Whites were to win a short but savage civil war, augmented by 15,000 German soldiers, Swedish volunteers[341] and a large line of credit and material from Sweden.[342] Mannerheim disarmed and sent home Russian garrisons, then used his superior forces, also boosted by forced conscription, to defeat the Red Guards, who were almost entirely comprised of ordinary civilians, in three months. The Red Guards executed about 1600, while the White Guards executed 8300 and allowed another 13,000 to die of starvation in their prison camps.[343] Another 7000 died in battle; overall, Finland lost about 1 percent of its total population. German troops proceeded to occupy the country, until the armistice forced their withdrawal.

The continent-wide unrest had its effects in other countries as well. In the Netherlands, the capitalist parties were worried enough to push through major economic and political reforms, including universal suffrage, a pension system and an eight-hour workday. A threatened general strike in Denmark in 1920 enabled electoral reforms to go through, defeating Danish industrialists who threatened a mass lockout to counter wage demands.[344] Swedish reforms, too, came after a general strike was threatened.

The United Kingdom saw 1600 strikes involving 1.9 million people in 1920; the UK government used the trade unions to put the brakes on labor militancy: a government minister commented that "the trade union organization was the only thing between us and anarchy."[345] The government of Spain was compelled to institute an eight-hour workday after a 1919 general strike in Barcelona—Spanish authorities jailed union leaders, declared martial law and tried to induct strikers into the army, but had to back down and free the prisoners when the general strike began.[346]

Although outside of Europe the possibility of socialist revolution did not exist, there was significant unrest by urban workers. In the central Canadian city of Winnipeg, a general strike in May 1919 shut down city services before armed forced was used against it. Sympathy strikes broke out in cities across western Canada; authorities in Winnipeg responded by arresting strike leaders, deporting legal immigrants, broadening legal definitions of "sedition" and issuing orders to return to work under pain of dismissal. After five weeks, mounted police, army units with machine guns and mercenary "deputized police" armed with bats supplied by local merchants used force to intimidate leaders into ending the strike.[347]

Not even the United States was immune—1919 saw a general strike in Seattle (ended before massed force could be used against it), more than 350,000 strike in the Pittsburgh region and 150,000 textile workers walk out in New England and New Jersey,[348] among other actions. A long series of revolts had begun in Mexico in 1911, but the country was constrained by US domination that sharply limited its development.

Ferment was also beginning in East Asia. One of the delegates at the founding of the French Communist Party was Ho Chi Minh, future leader of Vietnam, and Marxism began making favorable impressions on Chinese by 1920. Continuing unrest swept China from the last days of the Qing dynasty, but the development of Chinese communism was stunted for years by Josef Stalin's order for an alliance with Chiang Kai-Shek's nationalists; this alliance ended when Chiang aligned with Shanghai's capitalists and organized-crime leaders to carry out massacres of communists, unionists and students in 1927.

## Fight to the finish: The Civil War in Russia

Mao Zedong famously said that "revolution is not a tea party." Civil wars are even less so. The US Civil War provides a good example: 620,000 combatants died, scored-earth tactics laid waste to vast areas, prisoners of war were treated extraordinarily inhumanely even by the standards of the day (perhaps 30,000 Confederates died in Union prisons), and President Abraham Lincoln suspended habeas corpus and forcibly dispersed the state legislature of Maryland.

By no standard was the Civil War that ravaged Russia following the October Revolution a tea party. Issues of class and power were bound up inextricably; the revolution was seen as a bad example by rulers in more powerful countries; Russia's rulers were accustomed to using extreme violence to maintain their positions; the ruled had endured centuries of brutality and little education; and the modern world was forcing its way into an intellectually stunted land mutilated by feudal despotism. Ways of life were under direct challenge: The privileged were prepared to use maximum force to maintain their positions; the vast mass of the ruled seethed, craving revenge against their cruel oppressors and ready to answer the untold amounts of their spilled blood with the blood of those who would finally be brought down.

There will never be a fully accurate summing up of the toll of the Russian Civil War. The Red Terror, of course, is amply cataloged and trotted out to show the Bolsheviks' supposed bloodlust, but rarely is there an attempt to document the White Terror, far crueler and with much higher body counts. In part this is due to the fact that the Bolsheviks didn't hide their terror—on the contrary, they proclaimed it and attempted to provide a justification. The counter-revolutionary White armies, aided by the armed forces and material support of 14 countries, tended to cloak their activities nor did they keep records of their terror.

But the much more important reason for the disparity in how the two sides are treated is ideological: If the Reds are unspeakable barbarians, then the Whites fighting them must be honorable souls, and since the Whites represent military officers, the rich and the powerful, they must automatically be just and wonderful since it is the perspective of these people through which the media and publishing houses of the capitalist countries view the world.

That so much unleashed fury found such horrific outlet is not surprising, however much better it would have been not to have occurred. What is surprising is the extent to which Bolshevik leaders at first refused to indulge this fury, holding back their own supporters, even at their own risk. In part this was because they saw the continual violence used to enforce tsarist rule as endemic to the rule of a numerically minuscule class and thought the working class better than that, but also because they were highly conscious of the slippery slope the Jacobins had slid down during the French Revolution and they were anxious not to repeat that example.

A good example of those beliefs in action is provided by Vladimir Antonov-Ovseenko, who led the taking of the Winter Palace in the October Revolution. Antonov had been an officer in the tsarist army until he ended his career when he could no longer act as an agent of tsarist repression, was sentenced to death for his rebellion, escaped from prison and joined the socialist struggle for liberation. Four days after the fall of the Provisional Government, in a last-ditch effort to reverse the October Revolution, a group of military academy officer candidates occupied the Petrograd telephone agency, a key spot that held the main communications switchboards, and imprisoned several Bolsheviks, Antonov among them. (Officer candidates in Russia, who were the sons of Russia's minuscule elite, were known as "yunkers.") The yunkers, under the supervision of a French officer, set up barricades to fortify their position, taking this action despite being released from detention after being captured in the taking of the Winter Palace upon their promise to not participate further in any fighting.[349]

The yunkers, however, found themselves surrounded by a Red Guard detachment. Albert Rhys Williams, a US minister turned journalist was present, getting inside the telephone agency building when he accepted a ride from a group of tsarist military officers who drove through the Red Guard detachments surrounding the building by posing as Red Cross volunteers. Finding themselves in a bad situation—they were surrounded with no escape route or reinforcements—the officers tore off their insignias and scrambled to find civilian clothes, abandoning the yunkers. The yunkers begged Williams for help, suggesting he talk to Antonov.

Suddenly freed, in an instant going from condemned to commander, Antonov agreed to spare the lives of the yunkers and officers. A mob outside had no such thoughts. When Antonov escorted the yunker prisoners outside, they were greeted by yells of "Death to the yunkers!" and "Wipe out the butchers!" Facing the crowd alone, Antonov announced that the yunkers had surrendered and were now prisoners. The crowd demanded they be killed.[350]

Williams recorded the scene:

> Antonov faced the tornado. Drawing a big revolver, he waved it aloft, crying out, "I have given the yunkers my word for their safety. You understand! I will back up my words with this." The crowd gasped. This was incredible. "What's this? What do you mean," they demanded. Clutching his revolver, finger on the trigger, Antonov repeated his warning: "I promised them their lives. I will back that promise with this."

The angry crowd was stunned when Antonov said he would shoot whoever attempted to interfere. Williams continued:

> "What do you mean?" they yelled. "To save these officers, counter-revolutionists, you kill us workmen-revolutionists?" Retorted Antonov, derisively, "Revolutionists! Where do I see revolutionists? You dare call yourself revolutionists? You, who think of killing helpless men and prisoners!" His taunt went home. The crowd winced as though struck by a whip. "Listen," he went on. "Do you know what you are doing? Do you realize where this madness leads? When you kill a captive White Guard, you are not killing the counter-revolution, you are killing the revolution. For this revolution, I gave twenty years of my life in exile and in prison."…"But if they had us there, there would be no quarter," bellowed a peasant, "they would kill us." "True, they would kill us," answered Antonov. "What of that? They are not revolutionists. They belong to the old order, to the tsar, to the [whip], to murder and death. But *we* belong to the revolution. And the revolution means something better. It means life and liberty for all. That's why you give it your life and blood."[351]

Having calmed the crowd, Antonov led them in a pledge to safeguard the prisoners' lives, and escorted the prisoners away. According to Williams, the yunkers were released from a prison a few days later and immediately joined another White Guard unit, breaking their solemn promises to not resume fighting for the second time in a week.[352]

Earlier in the year, as tensions were about to explode into the July Days, Leon Trotsky single-handedly saved Viktor Chernov, a right Socialist Revolutionary who at the time was minister of agriculture in the Provisional Government. A hostile crowd, angry at the Provisional Government's holding back of the revolution, had trapped Chernov in the back seat of a car, surrounding the vehicle and seemingly intent on lynching him. Trotsky arrived, and attempted to calm the crowd, at first without success. Trotsky then asked those who wanted violence to be done to Chernov to raise their hands. When no hands were raised, Trotsky took Chernov by the arm and led him into the Tauride Palace.[353] The interior minister, a member of Chernov's party, jailed Trotsky days later.

When General Petr Krasnov, one of the tsarist army's highest-ranking commanders, answered Kerensky's summons and marched a detachment of Cossacks on Petrograd within a week of the October Revolution and was captured, he was set free in exchange for his "word of honor" not to resume fighting. He immediately broke his word, becoming a chief organizer of the White armies.[354] Krasnov left for Germany, eventually aligning with the Nazis and organizing military units for them during World War II.

Additionally, Trotsky released the Provisional Government ministers after briefly holding them under house arrest; he did so after the Menshevik Yulii Martov, a day after leaving the Congress of the Soviets as Trotsky shouted at him to "go to the dustbin of history," interceded with Trotsky on the ministers' behalf.[355]

Similar to striking employees in other ministries, Ministry of Public Welfare bureaucrats hid the keys to the safe; when the keys were finally delivered it was discovered that the former minister, Countess Panina, had taken all the ministry's money, intended for orphans and wounded veterans. Panina was brought before a revolutionary tribunal—and was ordered to return the money and then be freed to face public censure.[356]

Not in all cases were the Bolsheviks able to hold back popular anger, and in the case of Tsar Nicholas II it would have been very difficult to do so. The Ural Mountains region was a hotbed of Bolshevik support,[357] and although the tsar and his family were temporarily sent there, far to the east of the capital, the new government had already begun preparations to put the ex-monarch on trial. The tsar and his family were to be sent to Moscow, but the Urals Regional Soviet used armed force to intercept the train transporting them and held them in Yekaterinburg—Moscow had no control over the soviet.[358]

A combination of a rapidly advancing White army a few days from overrunning Yekaterinburg and baiting from local anarchists, Left Socialist Revolutionaries and their own rank-and-file for softness toward the ex-monarch caused the Bolshevik leaders of the regional soviet to disobey orders and hurriedly order the execution of the entire family. Yakov Sverdlov, chair of the Central Executive Committee (the standing national body of the soviets), had told the local military commander no permission would be given for an execution, and Vladimir Lenin insisted that the tsar and his family be evacuated west to keep them from falling into the hands of the Whites.[359]

At public meetings, demands for the immediate execution of "Nicholas the Bloody" were repeatedly made, backed by threats by the speakers to kill him themselves and overthrow the soviets if the Bolsheviks didn't do the job.[360] Although refusal to sanction any execution had been recently reiterated to them, with communications cut because of the advancing White armies, the Urals Soviet executed the family, doing so incompetently and harshly in the basement of the mansion in which they had been held. Two members of the soviet later separately wrote that they disobeyed orders, deciding on the executions themselves.[361] They then sought an ex post facto approval. Sverdlov did send a telegraph approving the decision after the fact (evidently unaware that the family had also been executed), but nonetheless the chair of the Urals Soviet was fearful that Lenin would charge him with insubordination.[362]

But why did they wreak revenge against the entire family? Unfortunately for the royals, the system of dynastic succession came into play—any son or daughter of the tsar would have made a potent banner for the White armies. The murderous Nicholas II—thoroughly incompetent, blindly arrogant and numbly indifferent to any human being not in his immediate family—had sat on his throne through that principle, and now pitiless logic turned that principle against his family. The tsars' savagery had kept Russia a backward state, and that backwardness exacted its revenge in the manner of the end of the Romanov monarchy.

By the time of the tsar's execution, the Civil War was well under way. As early as November 1917, tsarist generals were already organizing White armies and openly calling for the restoration of the tsar. The government banned the Kadets (the "Constitutional Democrats" who openly backed a monarchist restoration or a military dictatorship) on 11 December because of accusations that the Kadets were organizing the White armies and had attempted to break into the Tauride Palace with the intention of declaring themselves the Constituent Assembly.[363]

But as post-revolutionary repression began, Trotsky was still mindful of history: "We have made a modest beginning," he said. "At the time of the French Revolution, more honest men than the Kadets were guillotined by the Jacobins for opposing the people. We have not executed anyone and do not intend to do so, but there are moments when the fury of the people is hard to control. The Kadets had better take warning."[364] Lenin noted at this time that "[w]e are arresting, but we are not resorting to terror."[365] Lenin, however, had unrealistic expectations about how the revolution would unfold the previous summer when he remarked that it would be sufficient to "arrest 50 or 100 magnates of banking capital for a few weeks…and to place the banks, the syndicate of bankers, and the businessmen 'working' for the state under the control of workers."[366]

A not untypical attitude of Russia's rich comes to us from Louise Bryant, a journalist from the United States. One evening, Bryant's host in Russia complained that her cook had left. The cook, a young woman, had complained to her employer that her shoes wore out from having to stand long hours in bread lines on the employer's behalf all day, wearing out her shoes, and that one pair of shoes cost her the equivalent of seven and a half months' salary. Bryant wrote, "My hostess thought the girl was extremely unreasonable. 'She ought to be beaten with a knout,' she said." (A knout is a hardened whip that was frequently used in Tsarist Russia to administer severe, and sometimes fatal, floggings.) After the host and her family said they hoped the Germans would come in so that "dogs of peasants" would have to run for their lives, Bryant expressed sympathy for the Bolsheviks. In response to Bryant's suggestion that the Bolsheviks were the only party with the "backbone" to give the people what they wanted, her host "sat up straight in her chair. 'Why, my dear,' she said, sincerely shocked, 'you don't know at all what you are talking about. Why, my servants are Bolsheviki!'"[367]

Although that upper-class woman hosting Bryant might have provided a bit of unintended comic relief, there was nothing funny about the White armies who intended to back those sentiments with force. General Lavr Kornilov, northern commander of the White armies, declared "the greater the terror, the greater our victories," saying this before the formation of the Red Army. He later said, "We must save Russia…even if we have to set fire to half the country and shed the blood of three-fourths all of the Russians."[368] The White commander in Siberia, Admiral Aleksandr Kolchak, soon to be the self-styled "supreme ruler of Russia," ordered a general "to follow the example of the Japanese, who, in the Amur region [near the Pacific Ocean], had exterminated the local population."[369] At the beginning of the Civil War, territory had to be parceled out among the tsarist generals as they found it difficult to reach agreements—Kadets and monarchists such as Pavel Miliukov and Mikhail Rodzianko pushed White military commanders to reach an agreement among themselves so as to appear more presentable to outside governments.

As battles between Reds and Whites began in December, economic sabotage continued in the cities and food was being hoarded by speculators, the Bolsheviks created the Extraordinary Commission for Struggle Against the Counter-Revolution, or "Cheka." Another factor behind the creation of the Cheka was the breakdown in the judiciary system, and the Cheka was seen as a temporary expedient that would also deal with ordinary criminal matters. The Polish revolutionary Feliks Dzerzhinsky was placed in charge; Dzerzhinsky was something of a fanatic but also personally completely honest. Although the Cheka's later incarnations, particularly when the secret police were known as the GPU and then the NKVD under Josef Stalin, became havens for sadists, at the Cheka's beginning only the most honest revolutionaries were seen as fit for duty in it—breaches of trust by its agents were punished severely.

The Cheka was charged with liquidating "all attempts and acts of counter-revolution and sabotage," to "hand over for trial by revolutionary tribunals all saboteurs and counter-revolutionaries; and to work out a means to combat them." The means to do this were "confiscation, expulsion from domicile, deprivation of ration cards, publication of lists of enemies of the people, etc."[370] Left Socialist Revolutionaries as well as Bolsheviks became Chekists as the two parties joined in a coalition government. The Cheka, however, gradually usurped more power until it took upon itself the powers of judge and jury in addition to investigation and arrest.

Still more problems beset the new government. The Bolsheviks, immediately after taking power, asked Germany for a peace settlement, but even if the Bolsheviks had wanted to continue the war they couldn't as the army had disintegrated. The conundrum was that Russia wanted a peace without annexations but the German High Command was determined to expand into as much territory as it could, and the Germans still had a functioning army whereas Russia did not. Trotsky, as the new foreign minister, first sounded out the other Entente powers about a peace offer, but was ignored by diplomats as "illegitimate." Trotsky then proposed peace talks to the Germans, who accepted.

The peace talks at Brest-Litovsk deeply split the Bolshevik leadership, and the Bolsheviks from their Left Socialist Revolutionary coalition partners. There was a division between the two major Central Powers, Germany and Austria-Hungary, because Austria's ability to go on fighting was nearing its end, but the German military was determined to gain as much as it could and Russia was too weak to seriously parry them. This was a series of meetings that dramatically highlighted the stark social divisions that were explosively coming to the surface: On one side were aristocratic generals and diplomats, while on the other were revolutionaries unknown to the world weeks earlier, people who had endured prison and exile, often at the hands of the same sort of aristocrats.

The Bolsheviks dragged out negotiations, until Germany gave its final terms in February 1918, which included vast annexations. Not wishing to sanction what had become an inevitable outcome, the Bolsheviks formulated a policy of "neither war nor peace." Trotsky declared that Russia was withdrawing from the war (it had stopped fighting months earlier) but would not sign any such peace agreement. Trotsky concluded his speech with an uncategorical declaration: "We refuse to endorse terms which German and Austro-Hungarian imperialism is writing with the sword on the flesh of living nations. We cannot put the signature of the Russian Revolution under a peace treaty which brings oppression, woe and misfortune to millions of human beings."[371] The Germans responded that withdrawing from the war was of no consequence and, because the treaty was not signed, its army would launch new offensives. Which it promptly did.

The Bolshevik Central Committee was almost evenly split on the question of how to respond to the renewed aggression. The peace faction, which included Lenin, argued that any German offensive would lead to even greater losses, and Russia would eventually have to sign a much worse treaty because, he believed, there was no way Russia could mount any defense. By a one-vote majority, with Trotsky joining the peace faction, the Central Committee voted to sue for peace. The terms were now indeed worse—Germany demanded that Russia completely demobilize and cede Ukraine, Finland, Latvia and Estonia; it was already grabbing Poland and western Ukraine. And Germany granted 48 hours for a reply and three days for negotiation.

The Bolshevik Central Committee debated "war or peace" anew. The peace faction renewed its arguments, and Lenin now also argued that Russia needed a respite no matter how bitter the terms; he was additionally gambling that either Germany would undergo a revolution, which would annul the treaty, or that Germany would lose the war and have to give up its new territory. The war faction argued that Germany would not allow Russia to have a respite and that giving up the farmlands and coal basins of Ukraine would cripple Russia's ability to get its economy back on its feet. The war proponents also denied that Russia was incapable of fighting; they believed that the population would rise up in self-defense against an invader intent on destroying the revolution.

Nikolai Bukharin, one of the youngest among the Bolshevik leadership but already a prominent leader and theorist, cited European revolution for why there was no alternative to fighting Germany: "The Russian revolution will either be saved by the international proletariat or it will perish under the blows of international capital."[372] Bukharin drew optimism from the strikes that had broken out in Berlin, Budapest and Vienna, and believed that a fighting Russia would be an example that the European masses would follow. He believed that, regardless, the capitalist powers on both sides would inevitably link up to crush Russia—the only antidote would be European revolution. "We always said…that sooner or later the Russian Revolution would have to clash with international capital. That moment has now come."[373]

The two sides were as they had been earlier in the Central Committee, except Trotsky was wavering. He now leaned toward the war faction, and would cast the deciding vote. Lenin was so sure peace was the only possible position that he said he would resign from the Central Committee and the government, and go into opposition if he lost this vote.[374] Could that happen? Bukharin, though he thought Lenin's policy "fatal," did not contemplate pushing Lenin out as leader. "Am I of sufficient stature to become leader of a party and to declare war on Lenin and the Bolshevik Party? No, don't let us deceive ourselves."[375] Dzerzhinsky, however, did believe the party could carry on without Lenin, but then had second thoughts and abstained in the final vote.[376]

Trotsky, at this time, would have been the only possible successor as he and Lenin were seen as the revolution's co-leaders. But Trotsky believed that, if the war faction prevailed and Lenin did resign, Lenin would be so formidable in opposition that, under the extreme stress of fighting Germany and coping with Russia's internal problems, the Central Committee might have to arrest Lenin, perhaps would even have to resort to using force against him. Trotsky could not take responsibility for such a development and abstained with the waverers in the war faction, allowing Lenin and the peace faction to win the vote.[377] With an uneasy conscience, the Bolsheviks had their respite, which might prove illusory, and sacrificed Ukraine, the country's breadbasket, in the process.

The Bolsheviks held about 65 percent of the seats for the Fourth All-Russia Congress of Soviets, scheduled for mid-March, and thanks to party discipline it was a foregone conclusion that the national soviet congress would ratify the Brest-Litovsk Treaty with Germany, despite the opposition of all other parties. The signing was too much sacrifice of principle for the Left Socialist Revolutionaries, who were bitterly opposed to any such peace treaty, and left the government.

Although the Left SRs who headed ministries resigned, the party remained in the soviets and in other posts—in essence, they became a "loyal opposition" in the parliamentary sense, although not necessarily for long. Left SR leaders Boris Kamkov and Maria Spiridonova loudly demanded a revolutionary war. At the Fifth All-Russia Congress of Soviets in July, Spiridonova accused Lenin and Trotsky of treason and declared, "I shall grasp in my hand the revolver and the bomb, as I once used to do."[378]

Spiridonova may have been a physically frail person, but she was one of astounding courage—and quite capable of carrying out a terror campaign. Bryant left a vivid portrait of her:

> Her early history as a revolutionist is exceptional even in the minds of the Russians, and they have grown used to great martyrs. She was nineteen when she killed Lupjenovsky, Governor of Tambov. Lupjenovsky had as dark a record as any official ever possessed. He went from village to village taking an insane, diabolical delight in torturing people. When peasants were unable to pay their taxes or offended him in any way at all, he made them stand in line many hours in the cold and ordered them publicly flogged. He arrested anyone who dared hold a different political view from his own; he invited the Cossacks to commit all sorts of outrages against the peasants, especially against the women…One afternoon, [Spiridonova] met him in the railway station. The first shot she fired over his head to clear the crowd, the next she aimed straight at his heart… First the Cossacks beat her and threw her quite naked into a cold cell. Later they came back and commanded her to tell the names of her comrades and accomplices. Spiridonova refused to speak, so bunches of her long, beautiful hair were pulled out and she was burned all over with cigarettes. For two nights she was passed around among the Cossacks and gendarmes. But there is an end to all things;

> Spiridonova fell violently ill. When they sentenced her to death she did not know about it, and when they changed the sentence to life imprisonment [after an international campaign on her behalf] she did not know. She was deported to Siberia in a half-conscious condition. None of her friends ever expected to see her again.[379]

Spiridonova survived her exile and was released from a Siberian prison camp 11 years later in the wake of the February Revolution. She also had a practical side: When the Right SRs complained that the Bolsheviks were "stealing" their land program, she "only laughed. 'What difference does it make,' she wanted to know, 'who gives the peasants their land—the principal thing is that they get it.'"[380]

The Left SRs were not going to content themselves with mere talk. The Left SR Central Committee on 24 June had already voted to launch a terror strike against German officials, and Spiridonova began to organize an assassination attempt against the German ambassador to Russia, Count Wilhelm Mirbach.[381] The Left SR leadership, at this meeting, vowed that "extreme measures [would] make the toiling peasantry and the working class take part in the uprising and actively support the party in its proceedings," but added, "We regard our policy as an attack on the present policy of the government, not as an attack on the Bolsheviks themselves."[382]

The Left SRs hoped that either the Germans would become so enraged so as to get them to renew the war, thereby forcing Russia to take up a revolutionary war and negating the Brest-Litovsk treaty, or to spark a guerrilla war against the German occupiers.

The day after Spiridonova's threat to grasp the revolver and the bomb at the July soviet congress, a member of her party, Yakov Blumkin, assassinated Mirbach. Simultaneously, Left SRs staged an unorganized uprising, taking Dzerzhinsky hostage, and occupying several buildings, including the telegraph office. But as the conspirators had no plan, the Bolsheviks were able to restore order within a day without bloodshed. Thirteen members of the Cheka who participated in the uprising were executed for abusing their positions, but all others were soon amnestied, including Spiridonova. Blumkin escaped capture, although he later repented for his act of terror, joined the Bolsheviks and was allowed back into the Cheka.

In August, the Left SRs struck again, this time more seriously and directly against the Bolsheviks. The Bolshevik chair of the Petrograd Cheka was assassinated, and Lenin was seriously wounded by another assassin, narrowly avoiding death. A full-voiced vow of revenge now thundered from all Bolshevik points. The party's newspapers threatened massive payback and the Central Executive Committee (the standing executive body elected by the congresses of the soviets to which the government was responsible) declared that "White terror" would be countered by "a Red terror against the bourgeoisie and its agents," promising that "individuals involved in counter-revolutionary plots will be destroyed and crushed by the heavy hammer of the revolutionary proletariat."[383] The Bolsheviks made good on this, executing several hundred in the ensuing weeks, although it seems that most of the executions were of the old ruling class rather than Socialist Revolutionaries.[384]

Ironically, the Petrograd Cheka chair had been a restraining influence who blocked his subordinates from carrying out repressive actions, but with his assassination, the chair of the Petrograd Soviet, Grigorii Zinoviev, took charge. Zinoviev, prone to panic, unleashed far more harsh measures than were carried out in other cities—similar to his descent into despair after the setbacks of the July Days leading to his opposition to the October Revolution, he again panicked in the face of what he saw as defeat for the revolution.[385]

If the White generals had been able to organize more quickly, or if the capitalist powers had intervened more seriously at this early point, the Bolsheviks would have been toppled. Soon enough, the Whites would be organized enough to start a full-blown civil war. But by then Trotsky had begun building the Red Army, and although the fronts went back and forth considerably for two years, the Bolsheviks were able to prevail. The resistance of workers, soldiers and sailors in Canada, France and the United Kingdom hindered those governments' intervention efforts, and vacillation on the part of the United States, where not all officials seemed to have the same policy, also helped. The ultimate factor, however, was the reality of the Whites' restorationist governments—as more people experienced it, more rallied to the Red banner. Even SRs and Mensheviks reluctantly joined the Bolsheviks because the alternative was worse, and because the White generals didn't differentiate among any of the socialist parties or factions.

This was a civil war without mercy, a war where the combatants felt their only choice was to kill or be killed. The White armies, led by parts of the old ruling class, intended to physically exterminate their enemies, eliminate anyone who represented an alternative to their rule, and through the use of violence cow peasants and working people into returning to their former places. The Red Army had to fight on this basis, whether or not the Bolsheviks and their followers wished to do so.

The Civil War was fought on three main fronts and the Whites at times controlled huge swatches of land. Kolchak, the self-styled "supreme ruler of Russia," was the dictator of Siberia, controlling much of that vast region, but at times also the Ural Mountains and regions west of the Urals. General Anton Denikin was the commander in the southwest, controlling much of Ukraine and areas extending well north and east of the Black Sea. These areas also featured peasant and/or anarchist movements (representing third, "Green" forces). Nestor Makhno was perhaps the best known of these leaders, although none were able to hold their ground for long periods of time. Ukrainian nationalist armies represented a fourth grouping. General Nikolai Yudenich commanded in the northwest, and at one point his White forces reached the outskirts of Petrograd.

There were also foreign interventions in numerous locations, among them Britons who landed at the northern ports of Murmansk and Archangel, French in the Black Sea and Caucasus region, Czechs and Slovaks who took control of the critical Trans-Siberia Railroad, Americans in Siberia and Japanese in eastern Siberia and at the Pacific port of Vladivostock. Until the armistice forced them out, the Germans ruled cruelly over much of Ukraine.

History has left a much larger record of Kolchak's rule than of the other White dictatorships. Born into a military family and groomed for a naval career from early childhood, Kolchak had a meteoric rise in the ranks of the Russian navy, holding a series of commands before attaining the rank of admiral at the extraordinarily young age of 42. When he was commander of the Black Sea fleet in June 1917, a mutiny of sailors demanded all officers be disarmed. Kolchak declared this demand an insult, took his sword and threw it overboard, ending his career.

After the October Revolution, he telegraphed the British military, offering his services. Kolchak became dictator from the Whites' base in the western Siberian city of Omsk. Shortly thereafter, the governments of France, Italy, Japan, the United Kingdom and the United States notified Kolchak that they would assist him with munitions, supplies and food to establish his régime as the government of Russia.[386] (This notification was later brought to light by Major General William S. Graves, a US army officer who spent this period in Siberia under instructions to assist a US ambassador, and later wrote a book detailing what he saw.)

Kolchak's rule was marked by countless atrocities, widespread opposition in the areas he and his generals controlled, and in the end he had also so alienated the Czechoslovak Legion that the legion captured him as he was traveling on a section of the railroad it controlled, and turned him over to Red Army representatives in Irkutsk, who executed him and threw his corpse into a hole in the ice of a river.

Kolchak became dictator by overthrowing a previous government that itself was the merger of a military régime based in Omsk and a provisional government set up to the west by Right SRs from the disbanded Constituent Assembly who were backed by the Czechoslovak Legion. Kolchak seized power with the assistance of General Alfred Knox, the British military attaché to Russia. Knox, on the eve of the October Revolution, proposed a simple solution to the millions of Russians rising up: "These people need a whip. A dictatorship's the thing…We [should] shoot them."[387]

One month after Kolchak declared himself "supreme ruler," an uprising occurred in Omsk, which succeeded in freeing 200 from prison, most of whom were political prisoners, including the Right SR members of the Constituent Assembly who were no longer needed after the institution of Kolchak's whip. Kolchak's local military commander ordered all escapees to return to jail and said anyone who didn't would be shot on sight. All the Right SRs, and other political prisoners, voluntarily returned to jail. That night, they were taken out and shot.[388]

Perhaps the worst of Kolchak's commanders was General Sergei Semenov. One of Semenov's inner circle was quoted as saying that Semenov would boast "he could not sleep peacefully at night unless he had killed someone that day."[389] In one three-day period, he killed 1000 people, varying the method by day, including burning victims alive. A US observer called Semenov "tolerably severe" and US President Woodrow Wilson ordered assistance to be provided to him.[390]

Another of Kolchak's generals, S.N. Rozanov, issued this order in March 1919:

> In occupying the villages which have been occupied before by bandits (partisans) to insist upon getting the leaders of the movement, and where you can not get the leaders, but have sufficient evidence of the presence of such leaders, then shoot one out of every ten of the people. If, when the troops go through a town, and the population will not inform the troops, after having a chance to do so, of the presence of the enemy, a monetary contribution should be demanded from all, unsparingly. The villages where the population meet our troops with arms should be burned down and all the full grown male population should be shot; property, homes, carts, etc. should be taken for the use of the Army.[391]

In areas of Kolchak's control, Cossack bands rode into villages, looting, beating, abducting, torturing and murdering villagers.[392] Another feature were "trains of death" in which thousands of people were sealed inside bare railroad cars and left to die.[393]

Conditions weren't much different in areas under Denikin's control, where many pogroms occurred. Particularly brutal was the treatment meted out in the Donetsk basin, the main coal-mining region of Ukraine. Working conditions for miners were feudal. Pay was low and during World War I, pay was kept down by threats of being sent to the front; adjusted for wartime inflation, wages decreased by 30 to 50 percent during the war.[394] A detailed code of rules was backed by a system of fines that deprived miners of 10 to 25 percent of their wages.[395] Workers could be fired for refusing to pay a bribe, and when strikers were arrested, they were flogged in public.[396] Quite naturally, miners and other workers flocked to the socialist parties. But because the mines were such a crucial resource, fighting between Reds and Whites was particularly fierce here, resulting in savage reprisals.

In one town, Whites under General Aleksei Kaledin, in

December 1917, dissolved the workers' soviet, killed 20 and dumped their bodies into cesspools and dung piles; in another town, Cossacks plucked out the eyes of arrested workers and slit their throats; elsewhere workers were shot or thrown alive down mine shafts.[397] In April 1918, the Donetsk basin was occupied by Germans and Austrians, who installed a puppet government that restored the old managers, increased working hours, cut wages, banned strikes and shut down unions.[398] When a town or mine came back under Red control, workers would beat up managers and technicians in revenge, and sometimes shoot them.[399] In areas under White control, one of every ten workers were shot if coal production fell, and some were shot for being workers under the slogan, "Death to callused hands."[400] Denikin routinely either shot or pressed into his service captured prisoners.[401] Nor was brutality limited to the main combatants—the short-lived Right SR government west of Omsk, faced with desertions, publicly flogged and hanged peasant leaders, took hostages to force deserters out of hiding and burned villages.[402]

The more brutal of the two main peasant army leaders, Nikofer Grigorev (who at times was aligned with Ukrainian nationalists), regularly massacred Jews in pogroms,[403] while the other, the anarchist Makhno, frequently destroyed buildings, including libraries, as part of a macabre "city-hatred."[404] Pogroms against Jews were a regular feature of White, anarchist/peasant and Ukrainian nationalist armies. From 1918 to 1921, more than 2000 pogroms took place: Children were smashed against walls; men killed by various tortures, including being buried up to their necks and trampled by horses; and women raped. The toll from these pogroms is estimated at 150,000 killed and 500,000 left homeless.[405]

The attitude of the Russian Orthodox Church, unswerving absolute backer of the tsars and supporter of the White armies in their "holy war," was typified by a church leader who ordered that the message "Bless yourselves, beat the Jews, overthrow the people's commissars" be read to all parishioners.[406]

Wherever they conquered, the Whites quickly annulled all progressive changes that had been made in an attempt to reinstall the ancien régime. Many Whites even began circulating the *Protocols of the Elders of Zion*, the virulent anti-Semitic document concocted by the tsar's secret police, the Okhrana.[407] The Whites represented everything that so many in Russia, in urban and rural areas, had decisively rejected. Peasants were already working their new land, and when they refused to give it back to the old landlord, their village would be burned down. Crop requisitions and high taxes were imposed. In the cities, striking or organizing work actions was prohibited, and anyone arrested under these laws would be tried by a military court and executed.[408] The more monarchist-minded of the White generals even detested the Kadets, their liberal backers, because they saw them as assisting in the fall of the tsar.

The choices came down to the Reds or the Whites, and so many flocked to the Reds that in the end they had a much bigger army, enabling them to counteract the massive foreign aid given to the Whites and overcome the simultaneous embargo placed on the Bolshevik government. Just in the first few months of 1919, the British sent the Whites 1 million rifles, 15,000 machine guns, 800 million rounds of ammunition, clothing and equipment.[409] Estimates of the number of troops sent by the 14 intervening countries range up to 300,000.

Although the Mensheviks and Right SRs came to defend the Bolshevik government from the Whites, that didn't mean they didn't continue to have criticisms of the Bolsheviks. Both believed that the Bolsheviks needed to alter their policies or go, and that if they would make some compromises with them, conditions would improve. Martov, leader of the Menshevik left, in early 1919 noted that foreign intervention made Russian conditions worse, because "the continuation of hostilities, the need for an army and of active defense were bound to intensify the least desirable qualities of the revolution, whereas an agreement, by lessening the tension, would certainly lead to moderation of the Bolshevik policy."[410]

Arthur Ransome, traveling in Russia in early 1919 under the guise of a sympathizer but in reality an agent for the British foreign spy agency MI6, summarized the difficult position of the Mensheviks as follows: "The Mensheviks would like the reintroduction of capitalists, of course much chastened by experience and properly controlled by themselves."[411] That was a policy unlikely to draw support from the Bolsheviks' supporters or from the capitalists.

The Right SRs, chastened by their fiasco with Kolchak's régime, came around to the viewpoint that there was no alternative to mounting a common defense. V.K. Volsky, a Right SR who had been among the leaders of the Right SR government that preceded Kolchak's seizure of power, predicted far more violence would result from a successful counter-revolution. "If by any chance Kolchak, Denikin & Co. were to win, they would have to kill in tens of thousands where the Bolsheviks have had to kill in hundreds, and the result would be the complete ruin and collapse of Russia in anarchy,"[412] Volsky said.

Then there were the Left SRs, of whom Ransome said, "Not wanting a regular army (a low bourgeois weapon) they would welcome occupation in order that they, with bees in their bonnet and bombs in their hands, might go about revolting against it."[413] The Left SRs still wanted to wage a revolutionary war, opposed the use of officers who had served in the tsarist army (Trotsky employed 30,000 of them to build the Red Army) and opposed the continued employment of technicians and engineers who had held those positions before the revolution, believing that they were automatically untrustworthy. But Russia already was struggling to prevent economic collapse. How could it simply dispense with the services of all these people? Furthermore, of what use is condemning entire groups of people—how could support for a revolution be sustained with mass exclusions for rigid ideological purposes? This attitude was unrealistic, and the Left SRs disappeared in a cloud of futility, the party's more realistic members eventually drifting to the Bolsheviks or dropping out of active political participation.

A serious mistake made by the Bolsheviks, one that would provide an unfortunate signal for the future, involved an ill-thought invasion of Poland. But the mistake did start with a provocation. Jozef Piłsudski, who might be thought of as the Slavic Mussolini (he was a socialist before World War I, became a nationalist and eventually ruled as a quasi-fascist dictator), was now hoping to extend Poland's borders as far east as he could, well beyond the territory in which ethnic Poles lived. Refusing to settle the border, Piłsudski invaded Ukraine in April 1920, sweeping over large areas, including Kiev. Piłsudski's army committed numerous atrocities, but Trotsky, the Red Army commander, issued strict orders against non-humane treatment of Poles and closed down an army newspaper for printing a chauvinistic anti-Polish article.

Piłsudski was supported with loans and materiel by France, partly as an effort to weaken Russia but also because France desired a strong Poland as a counterweight to Germany. By June, the Red Army began pushing Piłsudski back. Chasing the Poles back to Poland, the Bolshevik leadership made the fateful mistake of continuing the chase. The two Poles among the party's leadership, Karl Radek and Dzerzhinsky, both counseled against entering Polish territory, arguing that Poles would see the Red Army not as bearers of liberation from their aristocracy but as their old Russian masters returning to re-conquer. Trotsky vehemently opposed further advance on the ground that only Poles could liberate Poland, not an outside intervening force. Lenin, impressed by the recent actions of Germans in undoing the Kapp Putsch, but also feeling that revolutionary impulses in Europe needed a spark, came to the conclusion that he could "probe Europe with the bayonet of the Red Army."[414]

The army was ordered to enter Poland, pushing to the outskirts of Warsaw before a counter-offensive, buoyed by a resurgence of nationalism, pushed the Red Army out of Polish territory. Ultimately, a compromise was reached that settled the border. By attempting to impose a revolution a bedrock Marxist belief, that working people can only be liberated through their own efforts, had been thrown overboard.

The other White armies now defeated, there remained only Denikin's forces, now commanded by another ex-general, Baron Petr Wrangel. (Denikin had resigned and left the country.) Seeing opportunity because the Red Army was battling Polish troops, Wrangel staged a final offensive from Crimea, but once hostilities with Poland were over, the Red Army could fully concentrate on this last threat, and pushed back. Wrangel was offered amnesty and the right to emigrate, but he refused and was thrown back to the Black Sea; he and much of his army evacuated on a flotilla mostly composed of British and French ships.[415] The Civil War now over, the local population of Crimea took a furious revenge on those Whites unable to evacuate, in part out of fear that the counter-revolutionary movement might yet revive. The toll from this bout of violence is unknown, but the number of executions might have reached thousands.[416]

## Ebb tide: The Communist International orders a revolution and fails

The fiasco in Poland punctuated the fact that the revolutionary period in Europe was now winding down. There were to be two more attempts at revolution in Germany, neither close to successful, and one disastrous attempt in Bulgaria, before the isolation of the Russian Revolution could no longer be denied.

"Denial" is what, to some extent, where communists were already. The ill-conceived Polish counter-offensive was not the last attempt to "force" the pace of events, a tendency much reinforced by the centralization of the Communist International, an organization of revolutionary parties intended to coordinate policies and tactics.

The International had been founded in January 1919 on something of a prayer. Rosa Luxemburg, days before her murder, had sent a representative to Moscow to vote against its formation, on grounds that most parties in Europe were still too weak and that she opposed Vladimir Lenin's centralizing tendencies. Luxemburg believed that a true International could only be a body of equal partners, making collective decisions but leaving each national party with the freedom to run its own affairs based on its knowledge of local conditions. An International in present circumstances would inevitably be dominated by the Russians.

Lenin and the Bolshevik leadership were not certain if the time to found a new International had arrived; the meeting was intended to be something of a sounding-out of parties. Regardless, it wasn't a representative gathering as most European parties were unable to send delegates due to the blockade thrown up against Russia and their governments' refusals to grant passports. Some countries were "represented" by delegates who happened to be in Russia but were not in contact with their parties back home. There was some doubt about what to do, until an Austrian delegate arrived and gave what proved to be an exaggerated account of revolts breaking out across Europe. With the German delegate standing aside, the Communist International was founded.

As time went on, and revolutions failed in Europe, the International, indeed soon dominated by Russians, became accustomed to making decisions for its member parties and eventually imposed leadership changes on them. This would be a grave source of weakness for the movement. As the Stalin faction gradually gained control of the Bolsheviks, it was able to impose its preferred leadership on the other parties as well as dictating wild swings in strategy, gyrations that would come every couple of years and were often badly out of sync with concrete conditions, repeatedly fail to find traction and culminate in repeated lashing out at scapegoats.

But it would be overly simplistic, and inaccurate, to say that this development was imposed on the other parties. The pre-war Socialist International had sought to align the programs of its member parties, and there the Germans had been the "big brother" party. German Social Democrats had taken a role in some parties, including, as we saw earlier, holding in trust Russian money and attempting to referee disputes among the Russian factions. There had not been an agreement to make decisions of the Socialist International binding on member parties, however, and the anti-war socialist left believed that was a factor in the inability to mount any effective resistance to the war. A new International, they believed, had to possess a mechanism capable of coordinating policy across the parties.

As the only party that successfully carried out a revolution, the Bolsheviks naturally felt that they had something to teach to others. But as revolutions failed or did not happen elsewhere, communist leaders elsewhere became inclined to think they did have something to learn, that it was natural for them to look to Moscow for inspiration and even instruction. The two aspects tended to reinforce each other, and so while a youthful Communist Party of Germany (KPD) could make its mistakes all on its own in 1919, by 1923 fiascos in Germany and Bulgaria would come on direct orders from the Communist International.

In 1921, however, that process was still developing, and the blame for the "March Action" in Germany that year could reasonably be assigned to Berlin and Moscow, albeit more to Berlin. The KPD had grown when Paul Levi brought about its merger with the much larger left wing of the Independent Social Democratic Party, initiated participation in Reichstag elections and encouraged working with trade unions. Levi sought to turn the KPD into a mass party. But Levi was also unpopular with many communists—he was seen as a haughty, remote personality, and that he was a wealthy lawyer with sophisticated cultural tastes also was held against him by some party activists.

The opening of the crisis that developed into the March Action occurred in Italy, at the Livorno convention where the communists split from the Italian Socialist Party. The Hungarian Mátyás Rákosi and the Bulgarian Christo Kabakchiev had pushed for the Italian split on behalf of the Communist International, then traveled to Berlin, where they demanded the KPD endorse their actions. Levi had been a critic of their actions in Livorno, believing that the split was mechanical rather than the product of the Italian movement's organic activity—approval of the Italian split implied a condemnation of Levi.

The KPD's highest body, the Zentrale, narrowly voted against Levi, whereupon he, Klara Zetkin and three others resigned from the Zentrale. Levi left on a vacation, and the Communist International sent Béla Kun to guide the KPD on its "offensive" plans, which now had a firm majority in the KPD leadership due to the resignations. Kun and the president of the International, Grigorii Zinoviev, were partisans of the "theory of the offensive," which meant attempting to create an uprising regardless of conditions.

These were two unfortunate personalities to have in charge—"subtlety" and "preparation" were unknown concepts to the impulsive Kun, who always took a maximalist position and was prone to excitability and panic in moments of crisis. Those qualities had contributed to the swift demise of the Hungarian Soviet Republic that he had led. Zinoviev was seemingly still embarrassed over his public opposition to the taking of power in 1917 and was now busying himself with ultraleft phrase-mongering, never missing an opportunity to loudly proclaim that revolution would momentarily sweep all of Europe. (He was now International head as well as chair of the Petrograd Soviet.)

Almost wholly lacking in judgment, arrogant but at the same time quick to avoid any responsibility, the now adventurist Zinoviev had become his political opposite from the time of the October Revolution—except that he was still apt to panic in a difficult situation.

The "theory of the offensive," moreover, did not seem to be well thought out. Rosa Leviné-Meyer, wife of Ernst Meyer, a leading KPD official, and a prominent party activist herself, noted her own confusion over the theory:

> There was no mounting revolutionary tide, no mass movement, only a resolution from the top agreed by the central committee. The propaganda was accordingly vague and abstract and I, for one, did not grasp where it was leading...It did not occur to me that [having to ask Meyer questions] in itself showed up the weakness of the new policy—not every Party member had at his disposal a member of the [Zentrale] for information. I was a good testing ground: if the motives and urgency remained unclear to me, they could not be clear to the workers, either.[417]

Likely aware of the KPD's plans, the Social Democratic governor of the state of Saxony, Otto Hörsing, sent police to occupy the mines around Mansfield to head off disorder under the official excuse of preventing theft of coal. The KPD had planned to launch its offensive after the coming Easter holiday. There was little reaction in Germany when this call came; the response primarily came from miners in Mansfield and chemical workers in Halle who declared a general strike and armed themselves. The KPD furiously agitated for workers across Germany to join, and called for a countrywide general strike, but met with almost no response except in Hamburg.

Leviné-Mayer grimly recalled the ineffective hectoring:

> The Communist press tried to boost the campaign with vile abuse of the "treacherous socialist leaders" and thundering appeals to the workers, commanding furious appeals, more like threats: "The blood of the victims will fall not only on the heads of your leaders but also on your own heads," or by true war declarations: "He who is not with us is against us!" which of course did not improve matters.[418]

The next step was even more incomprehensible—the KPD decided it would force workers out of their workplaces. The party armed the unemployed, forming them into brigades, and had them attempt to force their way into factories to shut them down. These brigades of the unemployed were joined by anarchist bands. The factory workers fought back, often with clubs, and vicious fighting broke out. The workers continued to keep the factories running, but those employed communists who did heed their party's call to walk out were fired.

And yet again did Kun and the KPD leadership cook up a wild scheme—now they would engineer a provocation. Plans to blow up various buildings, mostly their own regional headquarters buildings, were discussed seriously, on the theory that the party could say to its followers that "they destroy your property" and thereby incite uprisings.

In at least two instances, local KPD leaders really did attempt this. "In Breslau, the local committee attempted to blow up part of its own premises and, for some reason about which we can only speculate, chose to begin with the toilet of its office," wrote an ex-Communist International employee, Franz Borkenau, in an account that captures the seriousness and absurdity of the March Action. "The toilet went into the air without any loss of life and without other than ridiculous after-effects."[419] Later, many details of this last phase were published when the leading Social Democratic newspaper, *Vorwärts*, began publishing KPD documents that had been confiscated from Zetkin by border agents when Zetkin was traveling to Moscow for a Communist International discussion of the March Action.

Finally there was no choice but to call off this fiasco. Some 4000 participants drew prison sentences at the hands of special courts,[420] the membership of the KPD was halved as members left in droves, and much of the leadership that had come into the party from the Independent Social Democratic Party, but also some ex-Spartacist leaders, quit. But some among the leadership of the KPD's left wing still approved, and vowed to repeat, such offensives, believing that they would electrify the working class and weaken capitalism. Arkadi Maslow wrote, "If it is asked what is actually new about the March Action, it must be answered: precisely that which our opponents reprove, namely that the party went into struggle without concerning itself about what would follow."[421]

These suicidal tactics would soon be quashed by the Bolsheviks. In the meantime, Levi and Zetkin attempted to start an internal debate about what had just happened, but were rebuffed. The KPD central committee, a larger body to which decisions of the party's top body, the Zentrale, could be appealed, refused to allow Levi to speak at its next meeting. But Zetkin, about to turn 65, an outstanding party leader and labor organizer for decades and Luxemburg's closest collaborator, could not be silenced. She demanded an end to "revolutionary gymnastics" and called for the convening of a special congress to conduct a full public discussion. Unmoved, the central committee voted, 43–6, against Zetkin.[422]

Rebuffed from the inside, Levi wrote a scathing pamphlet exposing the KPD's tactics and giving the party leadership a piece of withering criticism. "The irresponsible play with the existence of the party, and with the lives and fates of its members, must come to an end. It has to be terminated by the action of the members, particularly in view of the fact that those responsible refuse even today to recognize what they wrought," Levi wrote.[423]

Hurling thunderbolts against the KPD leadership and Kun, Levi compared them with Erich Ludendorff, the wartime military dictator who demanded blind obedience, and Mikhail Bakunin, the nineteenth-century anarchist who believed that the "will" of activists is the foundation of social revolution, without regard to material conditions. These were insults sure to hit their mark. Quoting several demands in KPD newspapers demanding that non-communist workers join the action in terms that amounted to threats, Levi wrote, "And in case they are not willing to submit voluntarily to this condition, they are given the alternative: 'He who is not for me is against me!' A declaration of war is made on four-fifths of the German workers at the beginning of an action!"[424]

The KPD responded to Levi's pamphlet by expelling him from the party and demanding he relinquish his Reichstag seat. Zetkin and several others backed Levi, to no avail.

That summer, a discussion on the March Action, conducted behind closed doors, was taken at the Communist International's third world congress in Moscow. German communists on both sides of the controversy expected to win the argument on appeal there, but Lenin and the Russian leadership of the International had already decided everything. Lenin's arguments gained a majority among the Bolshevik leadership: Agreeing with Levi's critique and imposing a change of tactics to align with that analysis, but endorsing the KPD's expulsion of Levi on the basis that his pamphlet, by airing party business outside party channels, constituted a breach of discipline.

Zetkin had a series of conversations with Lenin in which she strongly backed Levi, and in which Lenin told Zetkin what the International's judgment would be. "Can it actually be called a theory?" Lenin asked Zetkin in these conversations, later recorded by Zetkin. Calling the theory of the offensive "an illusion" and "romanticism," Lenin told Zetkin it was "fabricated in the 'land of the poets and thinkers' with the aid of my dear Béla [Kun], who also belongs to a poetically gifted nation and who considers himself obliged to be constantly more left than the left: We cannot afford to write poetry and to dream."[425] Lenin later added, "The congress will throttle this splendid 'theory of the offensive' and decide on a tactic corresponding to your view. In return the congress has to give to the supporters of the 'theory of the offensive' some crumbs of solace."[426]

Lenin added his view that Levi hurt his cause by criticizing so strongly, and after Zetkin energetically defended Levi and his personality, Lenin responded, "I have no argument with you about it. You are a better attorney for Levi than he himself...He certainly will find it very hard. I sympathize with him and I feel genuinely sorry for him. Please do believe me. I cannot save him from this difficult trial period."[427] Levi was given the chance to return to the KPD, but never did, eventually joining the Social Democratic Party, where he became an ineffective critic from the left.

The debate over the March Action dominated the three-week world congress, but the role of the International's executive body, and of Kun, was carefully excluded from discussion and Zinoviev, who ultimately bore responsibility for the International's role, made sure to leave the debating to others. Zetkin resumed her criticism, demanding a full debate and asking why Levi was punished when those responsible for the March Action were not. Ernst Reuter, on behalf of the KPD Zentrale, furiously counterattacked, declaring "we shall talk about these mistakes only with those comrades who fought alongside us."[428]

Once the expulsion of Levi was confirmed, the debate shifted to the March Action itself, and Levi's viewpoints carried the congress. Lenin pointed out that his party "had a majority of the workers' and peasants' councils" and "at least half the army" before the October Revolution, and that none of the European parties had anything like that: "Have you the majority of the army? Show me such a country."[429] The world congress ended by calling for new tactics, ending adventures and preparing for a long period of struggle by patiently winning over others and becoming involved in trade unions, embodied in the slogan "To the masses!"

The most important outcome of the third world congress of the Communist International was one that was implied in the final thesis but not appreciated at the time. The International, dominated by Russians, had arrogated to itself the right to make decisions for other parties and to have the final say in any controversy. There could be such a right because member parties were required to implement all International decisions. This was to have enormous consequences to all parties, but none more so than the Communist Party of Germany.

The KPD, at its foundation, had the benefit of many years of movement experience to draw upon and independent leadership. Rosa Luxemburg, Karl Liebknecht and Leo Jogiches were outstanding, albeit differing, personalities. On Liebknecht, it seems that no two opinions ever agree. Seemingly always in motion, sometimes compulsive, he was a person of action occupied by the day-to-day struggle. On one count, however, there is unanimity—that Liebknecht was courageous, as exemplified by his anti-war speech on May Day 1916 defying martial law in an atmosphere still heated by pro-war and nationalist feelings whipped into a frenzy.

Jogiches is much less known than the other two, but by all accounts was a skilled organizer who preferred to work clandestinely. A highly self-disciplined and self-sacrificing personality, Jogiches made an early decision to be an underground organizer, renouncing the comforts of his wealthy family background. He played a significant part in the creation of theory and tactics outside the limelight. Jogiches and Luxemburg also led the more radical of the two pre-war Polish socialist parties—the two were lovers for many years in a sometimes stormy relationship that was also a political partnership.

Although overshadowed by Liebknecht during their lifetimes, Luxemburg achieved the higher stature in the decades afterward. A highly gifted person, generous, humane and with a wide scope of interests, she has yet to be eclipsed as a theorist by any person in any corner of Marxism. She was a theorist who embodied the oft-discussed, but seldom achieved, goal of synthesizing theory with practice. She stood by her conclusions, even when those conclusions seemed a personal contradiction—she opposed completely all nationalism, to the point of vehemently opposing Polish independence although she was Polish. (A discussion of nationalism will be taken up in more detail in Chapter 4.) This was one of three main areas where she disagreed with Lenin, and to this day Luxemburg's approach is remembered as an "alternative" to Leninism.

Although she is sometimes invoked as some sort of safe alternative, it is important to remember that she criticized Lenin from Lenin's left on two of the three main areas of criticism—on national independence, which Lenin supported, and on encouraging peasants to take over the land as smallholders, which Lenin backed but Luxemburg believed made agriculture less efficient and created a class of small proprietors who would inevitably confront the cities with hostility.

Her third point of departure from Lenin was the most crucial—her belief that over-centralization would be the death of a party and that no revolution could dispense with the creative energy of those making the revolution. But, especially in light of the future development of the Russian Revolution, it is easy to look back and make more of this difference than actually existed. Luxemburg and Jogiches ran the clandestine Polish party more tightly than Lenin ever did the Bolsheviks (due to the extremely repressive conditions under which Poland was occupied by Tsarist Russia) and Lenin by no means had a lack of faith in the creativity of working people (as will be discussed presently in Chapter 2).

After Luxemburg's death, Levi continued her policy vis-à-vis the Communist International, and most of Luxemburg's close followers stayed on this path, with the noteworthy exception of Paul Frölich, who became a partisan of the "theory of the offensive." With the tragic murders of Luxemburg, Liebknecht, Jogiches and others, German communism lost its front-rank leaders. When Levi, Zetkin and their allies were pushed out in 1921, the movement lost its second bench. Less capable, and much less independent, personalities came to the fore, men and woman who were not accustomed to seeing the Russian leaders as equals with whom they could have a free give-and-take.

Perhaps if Levi and Zetkin and their allies had stayed in their posts they might have been able to prevent the March Action from taking place, or at least reduce its excesses. Such a viewpoint, however, must confront the fact that the action did have plenty of support. The KPD's adventurists had not learned sufficient lessons from the tragedy of "Spartacist Week" and the party might nonetheless have torn itself apart over the issue. The German "theory of the offensive" reflected an overly mechanical mindset in which its adherents wanted to follow the path of Russia as if it were some sort of a blueprint—except that they didn't grasp even the basics of the Russian path to revolution, as Lenin pointed out. The "offensive"-minded saw November 1918 as Germany's "February" and sought to immediately create Germany's "October" without thinking about the work that had gone into the October Revolution or the differences between Russia and Germany.

Ironically, this mechanical thinking bore similarities to the pre-war Social Democratic right and center embodied in Eduard Bernstein's revisionism and Karl Kautsky's gradual acceptance of imperialism. Although the theory of the offensive was a doctrine of action and the other two were content to passively wait out developments, all three believed a formula existed that could be followed regardless of concrete conditions, a complete misreading of the writings of Karl Marx and Friedrich Engels, whom each claimed to be following.

Another danger was that German communism, the strongest and most important outside of Russia, began to accept the tutelage of the Bolsheviks. For now, the Bolshevik-dominated Communist International was content to dictate tactics, and debate on a range of topics continued within it, but in two years the seed of passing judgment on a leadership question would blossom into dictating changes in leaderships.

By late 1923, Zinoviev and Josef Stalin were able to impose new leaders on the French, German and Polish parties. In the cases of the German and Polish parties, they were able to do so because the ousted leaderships had become unpopular with the rank-and-file. But Zinoviev and Stalin interfered in each of the three because the leaders they ousted backed Leon Trotsky; Lenin had become incapacitated from a stroke and Zinoviev's and Stalin's struggle against Trotsky had burst to the surface. Stalin would soon gain the upper hand against Zinoviev and reduce the world revolutionary movement to his shadow.

It is very difficult to imagine that later disastrous development happening had a strong German leadership survived.

There were two more brief attempts at revolution—the stillborn "German October" and a Bulgarian uprising, both in 1923. The Bulgarian uprising ended in a complete rout of the communists—they had stood by idly as a relatively progressive peasant-oriented government was overthrown in a Right-wing coup, then belatedly, in drastically worse circumstances, moved against the coup government. The German uprising, with too long a planning period and insufficient popular support, had to be called off at the last minute. These uprisings were ordered in Moscow, but in reality the revolutionary moment in Europe had already ended in early 1921 with the failure of the German March

Action.

The March Action happened almost at the same time as the Kronstadt rebellion in Russia. Continuing shortages of food and fuel, and the increasing inability of industry to function because of ongoing shortages, had caused many Russian city dwellers to leave for the countryside and unrest among those who remained. Strikes broke out in Petrograd in early 1921, followed by a mutiny at Russia's most important naval base, Kronstadt, which was situated on a strategic island in the waters leading to Petrograd. Kronstadt had been the backbone of Bolshevik sailors in 1917—rebellion there represented a potent symbol.

The sailors, echoing demands being made in Petrograd, called for power to be taken out of the hands of the bureaucracy and handed back to the soviets, and that there should be new, free elections to the soviets, a demand that, if fulfilled, likely would have removed the Bolsheviks from power—they surely would have been punished at the polls as the governing party. But there were many competing groups and it was by no means certain that a clear result would have occurred. The Bolsheviks believed they constituted the only party strong enough to defend the revolution and that any alternative to themselves would culminate in the old régime coming back and unleashing a new, unbridled White terror. After all the blood that had been spilled in the Civil War defending the revolution, they had no intention of handing power to those they had just defeated at such staggering cost.

All the frustrations and deprivations of a population immiserated by foreign blockade; the brutal Civil War and the severe policies of the Bolsheviks in coping with it; threats of invasion; the occupation of much industry, farmland and sources of raw materials, cutting them off without replacement; the destruction of mines and factories by Germans and Whites in the areas they had controlled; and the concomitant further collapse of industry and transportation following their deep decline during World

War I under tsarism, had burst to the surface. The Bolsheviks knew they could not go on with their Civil War policies and they had been attempting to work out new policies in late 1920, when Menshevik and Socialist Revolutionary delegates to the Eighth Congress of Soviets called for a replacement of food requisitions with a tax.[430]

The deepest fear of the Bolsheviks was that the Kronstadt rebellion would provide an opening for a White restoration; they did not believe that the sailors were directly manipulated by the White leaders and fundraisers who were still operating abroad.[431] But violent anti-Semitic propaganda echoing that of the Whites on the part of the Kronstadt leaders, the frayed nerves still raw from the just-concluded Civil War, and fear that the ice encasing the naval base would soon melt, which would make an assault against it extremely difficult, fueled the Bolsheviks' desire to suppress the rebellion.[432] Neither side was in a mood to negotiate, and the Bolsheviks launched a series of unsuccessful assaults across the kilometers of ice between the mainland and the well-defended naval base.

The Kronstadt sailors bombarded the advancing government army units with artillery, breaking the ice under the feet of the white-shrouded soldiers and tearing them to pieces with machine-gun fire. Snowstorms and icy thick fog caused frequent stoppages before the carnage and drownings would begin again—there was no place to hide on open fields of ice. But the sailors had counted on a simultaneous uprising in Petrograd—none materialized—and they began to run out of food, fuel and war materiel.[433] So serious was the rebellion taken that 300 delegates from the party's congress left to join the final assault on Kronstadt, including members of the two Bolshevik opposition factions who had been engaging in bitter polemics with Lenin and his backers.

Just in time for the final assault, that party congress voted to put an end to the Civil War policies, replacing compulsory food collections with a tax and granting labor unions more autonomy; these were to be followed by a series of reform measures forming the basis of the "New Economic Policy." This news boosted the army's morale and, coupled with Kronstadt's dwindling food supplies, a reinforced army forcibly subdued the rebellion.[434] But this coda to the Civil War ranked among the bloodiest battles—the Kronstadt sailors suffered 1600 casualties with another 2500 taken prisoner, while the Bolsheviks suffered 10,000 casualties.[435]

The Bolsheviks had decreed nationalization and a host of emergency measures to cope with the crushing problems they had faced, but, as Mensheviks and Right SRs predicted two years earlier, "life itself would compel the Bolsheviks to alter their policy."[436] The "New Economic Policy" was designed to provide what Lenin desperately wanted, breathing space. It was in this spirit that Lenin argued successfully for the Communist International's change of tactics embodied in the new slogan "To the masses!"; the German left communists who wanted to continue their offensives were badly out of step with this new mood.

Having, somewhat miraculously, survived a civil war savage beyond all civilized standards, the Bolsheviks found themselves in charge of a country devastated beyond imagination. More than 17 million people were displaced; Petrograd and Moscow had lost 2 million people (more than half of their populations); 3 million Russians had died in combat; millions of civilians died from typhoid fever, a flu pandemic and a famine that struck due to a 1921 drought (all made much worse by an embargo on medical supplies); agricultural output had slid to a small fraction of its pre-1914 level and industry was even further behind.

The working class that the Bolsheviks saw themselves as representing, and which propelled them into power, had essentially ceased to exist. Much of the working class had died in the Civil War defending the revolution or taken up party or administrative work to fill urgent needs; much of the remainder dispersed to the countryside with industry at a standstill and food scarce in the cities. The Bolsheviks fully supported the peasants' taking of their landlords' estates, but the country was now divided into 25 million individual farms, most of them small and only big enough for the family tilling the land to feed themselves. It would now be more difficult for farmers to produce the food that the cities needed to survive. And with industry destroyed, it would be difficult for years to come to create a sufficient output of products that could be exchanged for food, leaving the farmers with less incentive to produce more food.

Not only had its working-class base largely evaporated, there was no revolution in Europe to provide any help, leaving Russia surrounded by a blockade thrown up by hostile capitalist countries still determined to strangle the revolution. There is no record before this time of any Bolshevik believing Russia could stand alone without revolution taking hold in a significant portion of Europe.

The key to Europe was Germany—a successful revolution in Germany would have been electrifying to Europeans and provided a strong material base for a socialist bloc because of its industrial development; such a revolution might have provided inspiration for nearby countries and a wave of revolutions possibly could have taken root in several countries, creating a large enough bloc to not simply survive but flourish. The rise of Hitler would have been blocked and the development of alternatives to capitalism would have had less stunted social traditions to draw upon. The history of the twentieth century would have been very different.

Speculation, however, can take us only so far: Reality is what the Russian Revolution had to face, bitter as it was. Isolated, faced with having to organize severe scarcity rather than portion out plenty, their social base dispersed, and locked into a cycle of tightening control as they grappled with profound crises, aware of the acute sufferings in town and country, the Bolsheviks somehow had to find a way forward in conditions neither they nor any fellow believers could have foreseen. This isolation would have catastrophic consequences.

## Notes to Chapter 1

1 Friedrich Engels, "20th anniversary of the Paris Commune," introduction to 1891 edition of Karl Marx, *The Civil War in France,* posted on the Marxist Archives website, www.marxists.org

2 Geoffrey Wawro, *The Franco-German War: The German Conquest of France in 1870–1871,* pages 21–4 [Cambridge University Press, 2003]

3 ibid, page 37

4 G.M. Stekloff, *History of the First International,* chapter 12 ("The Franco-German War and the Paris Commune"), posted on the Marxist Archives website

5 ibid

6 Chris Harman, *A People's History of the World,* page 369 [Verso, 2008]

7 ibid, citing Alistair Horne, *The Fall of Paris,* page 53

8 Prosper Olivier Lissagaray, *History of the Commune of 1871* (English translation by Eleanor Marx Aveling), page 79 [Monthly Review Press, 1967]

9 Marx, *The Civil War in France,* chapter 3 ("France Capitulates & the Government of Thiers"), posted on the Marxist Archives website

10 Lissagaray, *History of the Commune,* pages 153–5; Murray Bookchin, *The Third Revolution: Popular Movements in the Revolutionary Era* (Volume 2), pages 228–30 [Cassell, 1998]

11 Lissagaray, *History of the Commune,* page 126–30

12 Bookchin, *The Third Revolution,* pages 228–31; Harman, *A People's History,* pages 372–3; Stekloff, *History of the First International,* chapter 12

13 Harman, *A People's History*, pages 372–3; Stekloff, *History of the First International*, chapter 12
14 Stekloff, *History of the First International*, chapter 12
15 Wawro, *The Franco-German War*, page 301; Alice Bullard, *Exile to Paradise: Savagery and Civilization in Paris and the South Pacific*, 1790–1900, page 67 [Stanford University Press, 2000]
16 Lissagaray, *History of the Commune*, pages 395, 419, 445–8; Bullard, *Exile to Paradise*, page 248
17 Bullard, *Exile to Paradise*, pages 235, 243–52
18 ibid, pages 67, 93–7
19 Harman, *A People's History*, page 373
20 Lissagaray, *History of the Commune*, page 79
21 Marx and Engels, *The Communist Manifesto*, pages 120–1 [Washington Square Press, 1964]
22 Massimo Salvadori, *Karl Kautsky and the Socialist Revolution 1880–1938*, page 20 (emphasis in original) [Verso, 1990]
23 ibid, pages 20–1
24 Sebastian Haffner, *Failure of a Revolution: Germany 1918–1919*, pages 15–16 [Banner Press, 1986]
25 Rosa Luxemburg, *Reform or Revolution*, page 88 [Pathfinder, 2000]
26 ibid, page 94
27 ibid, page 96
28 ibid, page 34
29 ibid, pages 42–3
30 ibid, page 69 (emphasis in original)
31 ibid, page 76 (emphasis in original)
32 Salvadori, *Karl Kautsky and the Socialist Revolution*, page 91
33 ibid, page 92
34 ibid, page 111
35 Paul Frölich, *Rosa Luxemburg: Her Life and Work*, page 130 [Monthly Review Press, 1972]
36 ibid, page 170

37 D.A. Smart, *Pannekoek and Gorter's Marxism*, page 18 [Pluto Press, 1978]

38 ibid

39 Frölich, *Rosa Luxemburg*, page 174

40 Salvadori, *Karl Kautsky and the Socialist Revolution*, pages 179–80

41 ibid, page 180

42 Frölich, *Rosa Luxemburg*, page 200, citing an account by Friedrich Adler, Viktor Adler's son, who was also in attendance

43 ibid, page 203

44 ibid, pages 203–4

45 Salvadori, *Karl Kautsky and the Socialist Revolution*, pages 182–3

46 A.J. Ryder, *The German Revolution of 1918: A Study of German Socialism in War and Revolt*, page 45 [Cambridge University Press, 1967]

47 Smart, *Pannekoek and Gorter's Marxism*, page 22

48 Ryder, *The German Revolution of 1918*, page 41

49 Haffner, *Failure of a Revolution*, page 21

50 Franz Borkenau, *World Communism*, page 72 [University of Michigan Press, 1962]

51 J.C.H. Bloom and E. Lamberts, *History of the Low Countries*, page 422 [Berghahn Books, 1999]

52 Norbert Leser, "Austro-Marxism: A Reappraisal," anthologized in *The Left-Wing Intellectuals between the Wars 1919–1939*, page 119

53 Ryder, *The German Revolution of 1918*, page 47

54 Leon Trotsky, *My Life*, chapter XVI ("My Second Foreign Exile: German Socialism"), posted on the Marxist Archives website

55 Salvadori, *Karl Kautsky and the Socialist Revolution*, page 184

56 ibid, page 185 (emphasis in original)

57 Frölich, *Rosa Luxemburg*, page 207

58 Luxemburg, "Rebuilding the International," anthologized in Paul Le Blanc (ed.), *Rosa Luxemburg: Reflections and Writings*, page 200 [Humanity Books, 1999]

59 ibid, page 204

60 ibid, page 205

61 Trotsky, *The War and the International*, chapter IX ("The Decline of the Revolutionary Spirit"), posted on the Marxist Archives website

62 Arno J. Mayer, *Wilson vs. Lenin: Origins of the New Diplomacy 1917–1918*, pages 18–20, 62, 70–1 [Meridian Books, 1969]; Isaac Deutscher, *The Prophet Armed: Trotsky 1879–1921*, page 289 [Verso, 2003]

63 Dennis Mack Smith, *Italy*, pages 294–8 [University of Michigan Press, 1959]

64 D.E. Showalter, "Manoeuvre Warfare: The Eastern and Western Fronts, 1914–15," anthologized in Hew Strachan (ed.), *The Oxford Illustrated History of the First World War*, page 43 [Oxford University Press, 2000]

65 Megan Trudell, "Prelude to Revolution: Class Consciousness and the First World War," *International Socialism*, September 1997, online version at www.isj.org.uk

66 ibid, quoting E.J. Hobsbawm, *The Age of Extremes*, page 31

67 "Eastern Front and Western Front, 1916–1917," Robin Prior and Trevor Wilson, anthologized in Strachan, *Oxford Illustrated History*, page 188

68 ibid

69 David Englander, "Mutinies and Military Morale," anthologized in Strachan, *Oxford Illustrated History*, page 197

70 ibid

71 ibid

72 Trudell, "Prelude to Revolution," quoting J. Winter and B. Blaggett, 1914–18, page 10

73 G.M. Trevelyan, "Memoirs & Diaries: The Battle of Caporetto," posted on the FirstWorldWar.Com website,

www.firstworldwar.com
74 Salvadori, *Karl Kautsky and the Socialist Revolution*, page 207
75 Frölich, *Rosa Luxemburg*, page 224
76 ibid, page 226
77 Salvadori, *Karl Kautsky and the Socialist Revolution*, page 209
78 ibid
79 ibid, page 210
80 ibid, page 214
81 Robert C. Williams, *The Other Bolsheviks: Lenin and His Critics, 1904–1914*, pages 67, 162–72 [Indiana University Press, 1986]
82 F.L. Carsten, *Revolution in Central Europe 1918–1919*, pages 12–13 [Temple Smith, 1972]
83 Ryder, *The German Revolution of 1918*, page 117
84 John Horne, "Socialism, Peace, and Resolution, 1917–1918," anthologized in Strachan, *Oxford Illustrated History*, page 232
85 Trudell, "Gramsci: the Turin years," *International Socialism*, Spring 2007, online version at www.isj.org.uk
86 Horne, "Socialism, Peace, and Resolution," page 233
87 Trudell, "Prelude to Revolution," citing Marc Ferro, *The Great War 1914–1918*, page 178
88 Edward Crankshaw, *The Shadow of the Winter Palace: Russia's Drift to Revolution 1825–1917*, pages 258–9 [Da Capo Press, 1976]
89 Grigorii Plekhanov, *The Development of the Monist View of History*, page 241 [International Publishers, 1972]
90 ibid, pages 246–7
91 David Joravsky, "Communism in Historical Perspective," *American Historical Review*, June 1994, page 853
92 Hal Draper, "The Myth of Lenin's 'Concept of the Party' or What They Did to What Is To Be Done?", posted on the Center for Socialist History website, csh.gn.apc.org
93 Kenneth F. Mailloux and Heloise P. Mailloux, *Lenin the Exile*

*Returns*, pages 21, 22 [Auerbach, 1971]

94 Kevin Murphy, *Revolution and Counterrevolution: Class Struggle in a Moscow Metal Factory*, page 17 [Haymarket, 2007]

95 Deutscher, *The Prophet Armed*, page 107

96 Williams, *The Other Bolsheviks*, pages 74–5

97 Murphy, *Revolution and Counterrevolution*, page 18

98 ibid, page 19

99 ibid, page 21

100 Williams, *The Other Bolsheviks*, page 83

101 Graeme Gill, *Peasants and Government in the Russian Revolution*, page 11 [Macmillan, 1979]

102 ibid, page 13

103 Michio Kaku, *Hyperspace: A Scientific Odyssey through Parallel Universes, Time Warps and the 10th Dimension*, page 67 [Oxford University Press, 1994]

104 Nina Tumarkin, "Religion, Bolshevism, and the Origin of the Lenin Cult," *Russian Review*, page 42, January 1981

105 Williams, *The Other Bolsheviks*, page 111

106 ibid, page 170

107 Murphy, *Revolution and Counterrevolution*, page 27

108 S.A. Smith, *Red Petrograd: Revolution in the Factories 1917–18*, pages 50–1 [Cambridge University Press, 1985]

109 ibid, page 9

110 Silvana Malle, *The Economic Organization of War Communism*, 1918–1921, page 44 [Cambridge University Press, 1985]

111 ibid

112 Gill, *Peasants and Government in the Russian Revolution*, page 14

113 Murphy, *Revolution and Counterrevolution*, page 36

114 Michael Melancon, *The Socialist Revolutionaries and the Russian Anti-War Movement 1914–1917*, pages 114–31, 198, 217–18, 229 [Ohio State University Press, 1990]

115 ibid, pages 190–1, 206–8

116 ibid, pages 210–12
117 Sergei Mstislavskii, *Five Days Which Transformed Russia*, page 45 [Indiana University Press, 1988]
118 ibid, page 47
119 Vadim Petrov, Igor Lysenko and Georgy Egorov, *The Escape of Alexei, Son of Tsar Nicholas II: What Happened the Night the Romanov Family was Executed*, pages 24–7 [Harry N. Abrams Inc., 1998]
120 ibid, page 25
121 Melancon, *The Socialist Revolutionaries*, page 253
122 Mailloux, *Lenin the Exile Returns*, page 39
123 Mstislavskii, *Five Days*, pages 63–4
124 ibid, page 65
125 ibid, page 66
126 ibid, page 71
127 S.A. Smith, *Red Petrograd*, pages 60–1
128 ibid, pages 54–6
129 Ronald Grigor Suny, "Toward a Social History of the October Revolution," *American Historical Review*, February 1983, page 36
130 William G. Rosenberg and Diane P. Koenker, "Limits of Formal Protest: Worker Activism and Social Polarization in Petrograd and Moscow, March to October, 1917," *American Historical Review*, April 1987, page 301
131 Mailloux, *Lenin the Exile Returns*, page 59
132 Alexander Rabinowitch, *The Bolsheviks Come to Power: The Revolution of 1917 in Petrograd*, page xxx [Haymarket Books and Pluto Press, 2004]
133 ibid, page xxxi; Deutscher, *The Prophet Armed*, page 222
134 Rosenberg & Koenker, "Limits of Formal Protest," page 313
135 S.A. Smith, *Red Petrograd*, page 147
136 ibid, page 79
137 ibid, pages 84, 156
138 ibid, pages 111–12

139 Rosenberg & Koenker, "Limits of Formal Protest," page 314
140 Murphy, *Revolution and Counterrevolution*, page 53
141 Gill, *Peasants and Government in the Russian Revolution*, page 189
142 ibid, pages 64, 89, 93, 110
143 Deutscher, *The Prophet Armed*, pages 219, 223–4
144 S.A. Smith, *Red Petrograd*, pages 98–101
145 ibid, page 102
146 Deutscher, *The Prophet Armed*, page 230
147 Rabinowitch, *The Bolsheviks Come to Power*, page 37
148 ibid, page 41
149 S.A. Smith, *Red Petrograd*, page 126
150 John Reed, *Ten Days That Shook the World*, page 276 [Penguin Books, 1977]
151 Moshe Lewin, *The Soviet Century*, page 280 [Verso, 2005]
152 Reed, *Ten Days*, page 293
153 Rabinowitch, *The Bolsheviks Come to Power*, page 226
154 Mailloux, *Lenin the Exile Returns*, page 39
155 Reed, *Ten Days*, page 34
156 ibid, pages 34–5
157 Lewin, *Soviet Century*, page 284
158 Mstislavskii, *Five Days*, pages 114–15
159 ibid, page 115
160 ibid, page 116
161 Rabinowitch, *The Bolsheviks Come to Power*, pages 213–14
162 ibid, page 213
163 ibid
164 Reed, *Ten Days*, page 84
165 ibid, page 86
166 Rabinowitch, *The Bolsheviks Come to Power*, pages 256–7
167 ibid, page 257
168 ibid, page 258
169 ibid
170 ibid, page 259

171 ibid, page 260
172 Deutscher, *The Prophet Armed*, page 241
173 ibid, page 242
174 ibid, page 203
175 Stephen F. Cohen, *Bukharin and the Bolshevik Revolution: A Political Biography, 1888–1938*, page 55 [Alfred A. Knopf, 1973]
176 ibid, page 56
177 Rosenberg & Koenker, "Limits of Formal Protest," page 322
178 S.A. Smith, *Red Petrograd*, page 180
179 Rosenberg & Koenker, "Limits of Formal Protest," page 318
180 Suny, "Toward a Social History of the October Revolution," page 47
181 Ronald I. Kowalski, *The Bolshevik Party in Conflict: The Left Communist Opposition of 1918*, page 159 [Macmillan, 1991]
182 Rosenberg & Koenker, "Limits of Formal Protest," page 320
183 ibid, page 322
184 Gill, *Peasants and Government in the Russian Revolution*, pages 89, 107
185 ibid, page 106
186 ibid, pages 107–8
187 Murphy, *Revolution and Counterrevolution*, page 58
188 Reed, *Ten Days*, page 43
189 Murphy, *Revolution and Counterrevolution*, page 60
190 Deutscher, *The Prophet Armed*, page 249
191 ibid, pages 462–3 (note), citing official party record of the meeting
192 Rabinowitch, *The Bolsheviks Come to Power*, pages 284–5
193 James Bunyan and Harry H. Fisher, *Bolshevik Revolution, 1917–1918: Documents and Materials*, pages 176–7 [Stanford University Press, 1934]; Bookchin, *The Third Revolution* (Volume 3), page 250; Victor Serge, *Year One of the Russian Revolution*, chapter 2 ("The Insurrection of 25 October 1917"), posted on the Marxist Archives website

194 Serge, *Year One of the Russian Revolution*, chapter 2
195 ibid; Bunyan & Fisher, pages 179–80
196 Rabinowitch, *The Bolsheviks Come to Power*, pages 293–4
197 ibid, page 295
198 Deutscher, *The Prophet Armed*, page 274
199 ibid, page 275
200 ibid, page 279
201 Calculated from tables in Oliver Radkey, *Russia Goes to the Polls: The Election to the All-Russian Constituent Assembly, 1917*, pages 148–60 [Cornell University Press, 1989]
202 ibid
203 Reed, *Ten Days*, page 345 (note)
204 Radkey, *Russia Goes to the Polls*, page 74
205 Gill, *Peasants and Government in the Russian Revolution*, pages 128–9
206 Bunyan & Fisher, pages 210–18
207 Serge, *Year One of the Russian Revolution*, chapter 4 ("The First Flames of the Civil War: The Constituent Assembly"), citing an article written by a Right SR, Boris Sokolov (Sokolov, "In Defense of the Constituent Assembly," Archives of the Russian Revolution, Vol. 3 [Berlin, 1924])
208 ibid (same source)
209 Mstislavskii, *Five Days*, page 137
210 F.F. Raskolnikov, "The Tale of a Lost Day," from *Tales of Sub-Lieutenant Ilyin*, posted on the Marxist Archives website
211 Mstislavskii, *Five Days*, page 150
212 Raskolnikov, "The Tale of a Lost Day"
213 Mstislavskii, *Five Days*, page 153
214 Deutscher, *The Prophet Armed*, page 468 (note)
215 Lewin, *Soviet Century*, page 286
216 Louise Bryant, *Six Red Months in Russia*, page 89 [Arno Press, 1970]
217 Mayer, *The Furies: Violence and Terror in the French and Russian Revolutions*, page 250 [Princeton University Press, 2000]

218 Ryder, *The German Revolution of 1918*, page 123
219 ibid
220 ibid
221 Haffner, *Failure of a Revolution*, pages 43–4
222 ibid, page 49
223 Ryder, *The German Revolution of 1918*, page 141
224 Haffner, *Failure of a Revolution*, pages 70–1
225 Carsten, *Revolution in Central Europe*, pages 56–7
226 Haffner, *Failure of a Revolution*, page 81
227 Carsten, *Revolution in Central Europe*, page 39
228 Ryder, *The German Revolution of 1918*, page 155
229 Haffner, *Failure of a Revolution*, page 100
230 Ryder, *The German Revolution of 1918*, page 159
231 Carsten, *Revolution in Central Europe*, page 58
232 ibid, pages 24–6
233 ibid, page 55, quoting Wilhelm Gröner, *Lebenserinnerungen*, page 468
234 Dennis E. Showalter, "Diplomacy and the Military in France and Prussia, 1870," *Central European History*, December 1971, page 350
235 Richard A. Comfort, *Revolutionary Hamburg: Labor Politics in the Early Weimar Republic*, page 47 [Stanford University Press, 1966]
236 ibid, page 48
237 ibid, page 52
238 ibid
239 Haffner, *Failure of a Revolution*, page 111
240 ibid
241 Frölich, *Rosa Luxemburg*, page 272
242 ibid, page 273
243 Haffner, *Failure of a Revolution*, pages 116–17
244 Ryder, *The German Revolution of 1918*, page 189
245 ibid; Bookchin, *The Third Revolution* (Volume 4), pages 49–51
246 Carsten, *Revolution in Central Europe*, page 64

247 Ryder, *The German Revolution of 1918*, page 183
248 Carsten, *Revolution in Central Europe*, page 134
249 Haffner, *Failure of a Revolution*, page 128
250 Frölich, *Rosa Luxemburg*, pages 279–80
251 "What Does the Spartacus League Want?", originally published in *Die Rote Fahne*, 14 December 1918; anthologized in Helmut Gruber (ed.), *International Communism in the Era of Lenin: A Documentary History*, pages 125–6 [Cornell University Press, 1967]
252 ibid, page 132
253 Carsten, *Revolution in Central Europe*, page 210
254 Frölich, *Rosa Luxemburg*, page 281
255 Dick Howard, *Selected Political Writings of Rosa Luxemburg*, page 362 [Monthly Review Press, 1971]
256 Werner T. Angress, *Stillborn Revolution: The Communist Bid for Power in Germany 1921–23*, page 24 [Kennikat Press, 1972]
257 Howard, *Selected Political Writings of Rosa Luxemburg*, page 362
258 ibid
259 Frölich, *Rosa Luxemburg*, page 285, citing court testimony of Gröner
260 ibid, pages 288–9, citing in part a Prussian Diet commission
261 Carsten, *Revolution in Central Europe*, pages 215–16
262 Serge, *Year One of the Russian Revolution*, chapter 10 ("The German Revolution")
263 Carsten, *Revolution in Central Europe*, page 215
264 Angress, *Stillborn Revolution*, pages 30–1
265 Serge, *Year One of the Russian Revolution*, chapter 10
266 Howard, *Selected Political Writings of Rosa Luxemburg*, page 364
267 ibid, page 411
268 ibid, page 415
269 Comfort, *Revolutionary Hamburg*, page 71
270 Carsten, *Revolution in Central Europe*, pages 188, 194, 204

271 ibid, pages 220–1
272 Haffner, *Failure of a Revolution*, page 175
273 ibid, page 176; Borkenau, *World Communism*, page 151
274 Ryder, *The German Revolution of 1918*, page 214
275 Paul Levi, "The Munich Experience: an Opposing View," anthologized in Gruber, *International Communism in the Era of Lenin*, pages 185–90
276 Ryder, *The German Revolution of 1918*, page 230
277 Geoffrey Barraclough, *The Origins of Modern Germany*, page 444 [W.W. Norton, 1984]
278 Haffner, *Failure of a Revolution*, page 159
279 ibid
280 Carsten, *Revolution in Central Europe*, page 249
281 ibid, page 247
282 Haffner, *Failure of a Revolution*, page 185
283 ibid, page 188
284 Angress, *Stillborn Revolution*, page 45
285 Gerald D. Feldman, "Big Business and the Kapp Putsch," *Central European History*, June 1971, pages 128–9
286 Haffner, *Failure of a Revolution*, page 190
287 Jonathan Wright, *Gustav Stresemann: Weimar Germany's Greatest Statesman*, pages 153–4 [Oxford University Press, 2002]; Feldman, "Big Business and the Kapp Putsch," page 114
288 Wright, *Gustav Stresemann*, pages 154–6
289 Haffner, *Failure of a Revolution*, page 191 (quoting Johannes Erger, *Der Kapp-Lüttwitz-Putsch*, who corroborated the statements with Pabst and Schiffer)
290 Borkenau, *World Communism*, page 155
291 ibid, pages 156–7
292 Haffner, *Failure of a Revolution*, pages 192–3
293 Richard M. Watt, *The Kings Depart: The Tragedy of Germany: Versailles and the German Revolution*, page 507 [Simon & Schuster, 1968]

294 Haffner, *Failure of a Revolution*, page 192
295 Gordon Alexander Craig, *Germany, 1866–1945*, pages 445–7 [Oxford University Press, 1978]
296 ibid; Barraclough, *The Origins of Modern Germany*, page 447
297 Lindley Fraser, *Germany between Two Wars: A Study of Propaganda and War-Guilt*, pages 87–8 [Oxford University Press, 1945]; Barraclough, *The Origins of Modern Germany*, page 447
298 Fraser, *Germany between Two Wars*, pages 81, 88
299 Watt, *The Kings Depart*, page 508
300 Ryder, *The German Revolution of 1918*, page 243
301 Joseph E. Persico, *11th Month 11th Day 11th Hour: Armistice Day, 1918*, page 378 [Random House, 2004]
302 Erich Ludendorff, *On Overcoming the Consequences of the Lost War*, excerpted on H-Net website, www.h-net.org
303 Englander, "Mutinies and Military Morale," page 196
304 Barbara Humphries, "Women and the Suffrage," New Youth website, www.newyouth.com
305 *The Nation*, 17 April 1920
306 Robert Wohl, *French Communism in the Making*, page 115 [Stanford University Press, 1966]
307 ibid, page 116
308 James McMillan, *Modern France*, page 41 [Oxford University Press, 2003]
309 Wohl, *French Communism in the Making*, page 120
310 Herbert Tint, *France Since 1918*, page 11 [Harper & Row, 1970]
311 Wohl, *French Communism in the Making*, page 120
312 Jack Ray, "1895–1921: The CGT, France," posted on the libcom.org website, libcom.org
313 Wohl, *French Communism in the Making*, page 137
314 ibid
315 Donny Gluckstein, "Revolution and the Challenge of Labour," *International Socialism*, Winter 1993, quoting Roger

Magrew, "Paris 1917–1920: Labour Protest and Popular Politics," anthologized in Chris Wrigley (ed.), *Challenges of Labour: Central and Western Europe 1917–1920*, page 137

316 Wohl, *French Communism in the Making*, page 138

317 Ray, "1895–1921: The CGT, France"

318 Wohl, *French Communism in the Making*, page 130

319 ibid, page 133

320 Rod Kedward, *France and the French: A Modern History*, page 100 [Overlook, 2006]

321 McMillan, *Modern France*, page 55

322 Kedward, *France and the French*, page 102

323 Tint, *France Since 1918*, page 14

324 Kedward, *France and the French*, page 103

325 D.M. Smith, *Italy*, page 327

326 Gluckstein, "Revolution and the Challenge of Labour"

327 Antonio Gramsci, "Unions and Councils," *L'Ordine Nuovo*, 11 October 1919, anthologized in *Gramsci: Pre-Prison Writings*, page 118 [Cambridge University Press, 1994]

328 ibid, page 119

329 D.M. Smith, *Italy*, page 328

330 Gramsci, "Towards a Renewal of the Socialist Party," *Pre-Prison Writings*, pages 156–7

331 Levi, "The Beginning of the Crisis in the Communist Party and International," published 24 February 1921, anthologized in Gruber, *International Communism in the Era of Lenin*, page 306

332 Karl Radek, "The Italian Question," anthologized in Gruber, *International Communism in the Era of Lenin*, pages 310–11

333 Carsten, *Revolution in Central Europe*, pages 31–2

334 "Austrian Communist Broadside of June 14, 1919," anthologized in Gruber, *International Communism in the Era of Lenin*, page 199

335 "Declaration of the Viennese Workers' Councilors," anthologized in Gruber, *International Communism in the Era of*

*Lenin*, page 200

336 Radek, "The Lessons of an Attempted Putsch: the Crisis in the German-Austrian Communist Party," anthologized in Gruber, *International Communism in the Era of Lenin*, pages 205–9

337 Carsten, *Revolution in Central Europe*, pages 245–6

338 Peter A. Toma and Dusan Kovác, *Slovakia: From Samo to Dzurinda*, page 67 [Hoover Institute Press, 2001]

339 ibid, page 75

340 ibid, page 77

341 Heikki Ylikangas, "Liberation or Suppression?", *Books From Finland*, second quarter 1998

342 T.K. Derry, *A History of Scandinavia*, page 308 [University of Minnesota Press, 1979]

343 Ylikangas, "Liberation or Suppression?"

344 Derry, *A History of Scandinavia*, page 312

345 Gluckstein, "Revolution and the Challenge of Labour"

346 "1919: La Canadiense and Barcelona General Strike," posted on the libcom.org website

347 Canadian Museum of Civilization, www.civilization.ca

348 Howard Zinn, *A People's History of the United States: 1492–present*, pages 368–72 [HarperCollins, 1995]

349 Albert Rhys Williams, *Through the Russian Revolution*, pages 124–25 [Boni and Liveright, 1921]

350 ibid, pages 139–42

351 ibid, pages 142–3

352 ibid, page 152

353 Deutscher, *The Prophet Armed*, page 225

354 Serge, *Year One of the Russian Revolution*, chapter 3 ("The Urban Middle Class against the Proletariat")

355 Deutscher, *The Prophet Armed*, pages 278–9

356 A. Williams, *Through the Russian Revolution*, pages 161–2; Reed, *Ten Days*, pages 232–3, 334

357 Kowalski, *The Bolshevik Party in Conflict*, pages 158–67

358 Greg King and Penny Wilson, *The Fate of the Romanovs*, pages 81–100 [John Wiley & Sons, 2003]

359 ibid, pages 286–7; Petrov, et al., *The Escape of Alexei*, page 70

360 King & Wilson, *The Fate of the Romanovs*, page 282; Petrov, et al., *The Escape of Alexei*, page 71

361 King & Wilson, *The Fate of the Romanovs*, pages 288–90

362 Petrov, et al., *The Escape of Alexei*, page 76

363 Bunyan & Fisher, *Bolshevik Revolution, 1917–1918*, pages 357–9

364 ibid, page 360 (Trotsky speech published in *Izvestia* on 19 December 1917)

365 Mayer, *Furies*, page 255

366 ibid, citing Kondratieva, *Bolsheviks*, page 57

367 Bryant, *Six Red Months*, page 183 (emphasis in original)

368 Mayer, *Furies*, page 254

369 ibid

370 ibid, pages 256–7

371 Deutscher, *The Prophet Armed*, page 316

372 Cohen, *Bukharin and the Bolshevik Revolution*, page 66

373 ibid, page 67

374 ibid, page 65

375 ibid

376 Deutscher, *The Prophet Armed*, page 325

377 ibid, pages 323–4

378 ibid, page 333

379 Bryant, *Six Red Months*, pages 164–5

380 ibid, pages 166–7

381 Rabinowitch, "Maria Spiridonova's 'Last Testament,'" *The Russian Review*, July 1995, pages 426, 440

382 Lutz Häfner, "The Assassination of Count Mirbach and the 'July Uprising' of the Left Socialist Revolutionaries in Moscow, 1918," *The Russian Review*, July 1991, page 330

383 Mayer, *Furies*, page 279

384 ibid, pages 280–2

385 M.P. Yakubovich, "G. Zinoviev," anthologized in Roy Medvedev (ed.), *Samizdat Register 2: Voices of the Socialist Opposition in the Soviet Union*, pages 90–2 [W.W. Norton & Co., 1981]

386 William S. Graves, *America's Siberian Adventure*, page 223 [Peter Smith, 1941]

387 Maida Castelhun Darton (ed.), *Harper's Pictorial Library of the World War*, Volume IX, pages 108–9 [Harper's & Brothers, 1920]

388 Graves, *America's Siberian Adventure*, page 245; Trudell, "The Russian Civil War: A Marxist Analysis," Reds/Die Roten website, www.marxists.de

389 Fedor Babanine, "From the Sea to the River: Admiral Aleksandr Kolchak and Russian Civil War," WWW Irkutsk website, www.irkutsk.org

390 ibid

391 Graves, *America's Siberian Adventure*, page 214

392 Babanine, "From the Sea to the River"

393 ibid; A. Williams, *Through the Russian Revolution*, pages 288–92

394 Hiroaki Kuromiya, "Donbas Miners, Revolution, and Civil War," anthologized in Lewis H. Siegelbaum and Ronald Grigor Suny (eds), *Making Workers Soviet: Power, Class and Identity*, page 142 [Cornell University Press, 1994]

395 ibid

396 ibid

397 ibid, page 152

398 ibid, pages 152–3

399 ibid, page 155

400 Trudell, "The Russian Civil War," citing O. Figes, *A People's Tragedy*, page 665

401 Mayer, *Furies*, page 266

402 Trudell, "The Russian Civil War," quoting Figes, page 583

403 Mayer, *Furies*, page 381

404 ibid, page 385
405 Zvi Gitelman, *A Century of Ambivalence: The Jews of Russia and the Soviet Union, 1881 to the Present*, page 70 [Indiana University Press, 2001]
406 ibid, page 65
407 Mayer, *Furies*, page 269
408 Babanine, "From the Sea to the River"
409 Trudell, "The Russian Civil War"
410 Arthur Ransome, *Russia in 1919*, page 205 [B.W. Huebsch, 1919]
411 ibid, page 199
412 ibid, page 211
413 ibid, pages 197–8
414 Deutscher, *The Prophet Armed*, pages 383–6
415 Mayer, *Furies*, page 306
416 ibid, page 307
417 Rosa Leviné-Meyer, *Inside German Communism: Memoirs of Party Life in the Weimar Republic*, page 18 [Pluto Press, 1977]
418 ibid
419 Borkenau, *World Communism*, pages 217–18
420 Angress, *Stillborn Revolution*, page 167
421 Arkadi Maslow, *Die Internationale*, page 254 [Berlin, 1921] (quote retrieved from Marxist Archives website)
422 Angress, *Stillborn Revolution*, page 168
423 Levi, *Unser Weg*, anthologized in Gruber, *International Communism in the Era of Lenin*, page 320
424 ibid, page 332
425 Klara Zetkin, Reminiscences of Lenin, excerpted in Gruber, *International Communism in the Era of Lenin*, page 351
426 ibid, page 352
427 ibid, page 354
428 Angress, *Stillborn Revolution*, page 180
429 ibid, pages 185–6
430 Paul Avrich, *Kronstadt 1921*, pages 220–1 [Princeton

University Press, 1970]

431 ibid, pages 132–4

432 ibid, pages 136, 178–81

433 ibid, pages 200–2

434 ibid, pages 198–201, 210

435 ibid, page 211

436 Ransome, *Russia in 1919*, page 211

**Chapter 2**

# The Socio-economic Bases for the Rise of the Stalin Dictatorship

During 1922, in his last months of active life, his health slipping away and sidelined from his duties for long stretches, Vladimir Lenin analyzed the direction of the revolution. In a speech at that year's party congress, Lenin compared the state to a car that would not go in the direction the driver desired, and lamented what he believed to be a refusal to acknowledge that by the administrators put into their posts by the revolutionary government.

The desperate struggle to win the Civil War had done much to distort institutions and to trample on ideals, compounding the massive destruction from seven years of war and the inherited dearth of education. Large numbers of the old tsarist bureaucracy remained in place, unable or unwilling to change their old ways. But these and related factors couldn't account for the entire picture. Lenin sought answers at a more fundamental level, and came to believe that Bolsheviks, and the working people who had formed their base and those who joined their ranks after the revolution, were at a miserably low cultural level.

The cultural level of Tsarist Russia was atrociously low: Among other barriers reinforcing its low level were an unchallengeable class system that institutionalized cruelty and mass illiteracy, top-down institutions that bred inefficiency and corruption, and a rigid resistance to change or scientific developments. These factors helped create a population that, in large numbers, had been woefully unprepared to play meaningful roles in society. Appalling poverty and an unyielding censorship that kept out ideas from abroad had reinforced backwardness and blocked the creation of the material bases needed for any significant improvement.

But as low as the cultural level of the officials of Tsarist Russia had been, it was nonetheless higher than that of the communist cadres now attempting to modernize a desperately backward state; in essence, the "vanquished" state was imposing itself on the new state. The communist administrators, "lacking culture" (in Lenin's words), were unable to perform administrative functions and, worse, were failing to learn how to do so. This sobering picture was Lenin's conclusion as to the underlying reasons for the inability of the revolution to overturn the dead weight of Russia's absolutist heritage and for its tendency to be hamstrung by bureaucratic inertia.

Just what sort of country was Tsarist Russia? A vast sea of illiterate peasants and a growing but still very small and largely undereducated body of industrial workers, where even the minuscule layer of industrialists, landed aristocracy and nobility (the groups that would ordinarily constitute a ruling class) was effectively frozen from any real say in affairs of state despite constituting the tsar's crucial base propping up this system. The vast expanse of the Russian Empire, built through centuries of conquest and containing dozens of captive nations, covering nearly one-sixth of the world's landmass, was ruled by an all-powerful monarch, a tsar, whose every word was indisputable law. The tsar ruled as a direct representative of God, according to a potent belief system continually reinforced by the Russian Orthodox Church—tsar and church provided justification for each other's repression.

A typical Russian in tsarist times had three or four years of schooling if they were fortunate, and would be working on the farm at an early age. In urban areas, factory work would start at age 12 or 13. Workdays could be 17 hours long. Boys could be drafted or press-ganged into the army at age 12, with Jews, who were forced into the army through a system of village quotas, expected to serve for a minimum of 25 years. Poverty was so deep that girls as young as 8 would be sent to work as maids.[1] Despite the overwhelming agrarian nature of Russia, famine and starvation occurred frequently. Peasants typically lived in small cottages with dirt floors and no chimneys, and dung spread on walls was a common insulation.

This backwardness was enforced through unlimited terror; the tsar had at his disposal secret police and military units, which were generously supplemented by "Black Hundreds," reactionary death squads subsidized by the tsar who regularly terrorized the population, killing people who showed any sign of dissent and regularly fomenting pogroms against Jews. A good example of what the tsars thought of any challenge, no matter how benign, is the "Bloody Sunday" of 1905. On that January day, about 200,000 people, led by an Orthodox priest and carrying portraits of the tsar and religious icons, walked to the Winter Palace to petition the tsar for help. Nicholas II ordered his troops to fire on the crowd without warning, killing or wounding 4600.[2]

The city where that massacre happened, St Petersburg, was created on the bones of hundreds of thousands of workers who died constructing it under wretched conditions; even the French architect who helped to design the new city's general plan was beaten to death by Tsar Peter the Great.[3] Peter had dictated that a new city would be built on swampland, ordering peasants from across Russia to build it and transporting them there under armed guard.[4] Russians were ordered to move to the city regardless of their health or finances, then would be ordered to move within the city under threat of demolition.[5] Peter, who involved himself in the minutiae of life to the point of ordering beards trimmed and "modernizing" the Cyrillic alphabet, regularly backed his edicts with whippings, burnings with hot irons, breaking bodies on racks and tearing out tongues.[6]

The tsarist system of prison and massacres was supplemented by exile to Siberia. Prisoners would be lashed with the infamous hardened Russian whip known as the knout; often had an ear, foot, hand or nose mutilated, or could be branded; and then would spend a year in transit to an exile village in eastern Siberia, walking thousands of miles in leg irons to their destination.[7] Later reforms allowed these trips to be made by dogsled, still a journey that took months. Many prisoners, upon reaching their Siberian exile, were put to work in mines as forced laborers, required to wear 5-kilogram fetters and subject to random floggings. Forced laborers had no days off, until an 1885 reform allowed them two days off per month.[8]

## Lenin's goal of a reduced state, and the opposite results

Lenin sketched his vision of post-revolutionary society in one of his best-known works, *The State and Revolution*, completed in the summer of 1917 while in hiding. There is enough material in this compact book to enable a reader to quote whatever Lenin one wishes to find. But on close inspection its reputation for inconsistencies and contradictions is not entirely fair; Lenin does offer a consistent vision, albeit a multi-staged one. In summation, Lenin forecast a short period of the use of force on the part of the working class to secure a socialist revolution by suppressing the old ruling class, followed by a gradual withering away of the state when organized groups of working people would form armed militias, thereby eliminating the need for an army or police, and would begin to manage enterprises and carry out government functions themselves, eliminating bureaucracy. *The State and Revolution* is written in a blistering style, packed with insults against the many critics of Lenin within the broad European socialist movement. But it nonetheless is the best encapsulation of the evolution of Lenin's thinking.

In the book, Lenin quotes Karl Marx's lifelong collaborator, Friedrich Engels, at length to support the concept that the state exists only as a means for one class to dominate other classes—

once classes have been abolished, there will no longer be a need for a state. But, Lenin wrote, the expected "withering away" of the state is a later development; first, the old state has to be overthrown and then a post-revolutionary government is established that puts the working majority of the population into power.

> [A]s soon as it is the majority of the people *itself* which suppresses its oppressors, a "special force" for suppression is *no longer necessary*! In this sense the state *begins to wither away*. Instead of the special institutions of a privileged minority (privileged officialdom, the high command of the standing army), the majority itself can directly undertake [the duties of public safety and government], and the more the functions of state power are undertaken by the people as a whole, the less need is left for such a [formal, elite] power.[9]

This popular control would also occur in the economic sphere as well, Lenin wrote.

> Capitalist culture has *created* large-scale production, factories, railways, the postal service, telephones and so forth, and *on this basis* the great majority of the functions of the old "state power" have become so simplified and can be reduced to such very simple operations of registering, filing and checking that these functions will become entirely accessible to all literate people, that these functions will be entirely performable for an ordinary "workman's wages" and that these functions can (and must) be stripped of every shadow of association with privilege or peremptory command.[10]

But before such a phase of mass participation in governing can be attained, "the socialists demand the *strictest* control by society and *by the state* over the measure of labor and the measure of consumption; but this control must *start* with the expropriation of the capitalists, with control exercised by the workers over the capitalists, and must be exercised not by a state of bureaucrats but by a state of *armed workers*." This will be a "genuinely democratic state, a state of the *Soviets of Workers' and Soldiers' Deputies*."[11] (*Soviet* is the Russian-language word for "council"; the soviets were the basis of government on which the October Revolution was proclaimed.)

Lenin went on to write that

> If really *everyone* takes part in the administration of the state, capitalism simply cannot survive. And the development of capitalism in turn creates the *prerequisites* for everyone really *to be able* to take part in the administration of the state. Among these prerequisites are: universal literacy, which has already been achieved in a number of the most advanced capitalist countries; then the "training and disciplining" of millions of workers by the [capitalist system's] huge, complex, socialized apparatus of the postal services, railways, large-scale factories, large-scale commerce, banking, etc.[12]

The continuation and systematizing of this discipline, however, merely represents a stage: "[T]his 'factory' discipline…[which] will extend to the whole of [post-revolutionary] society, is by no means our ideal or our ultimate goal. Rather it is a *step* for the radical purging of society of all the infamies and abominations of capitalist exploitation *and for further progress*."[13]

Lenin believed that once everybody is involved in the administration of the state and of its enterprises, commonly owned by all, there will no longer be a need for a state and therefore institutions used by some people to repress other people would cease to exist. "So long as a state exists there is no freedom. When there is freedom, there will be no state,"[14] he wrote.

The catch in Lenin's theory is the requirement of a fully

educated, literate population, which Russia most certainly did not possess when he wrote those words. Russia had gone forward with a socialist revolution, but could do so only because revolution in at least some major advanced capitalist European states seemed imminent—revolutions that would lend ample helping hands to backward Russia. Lenin's belief in European revolution, solidified by the upheavals of World War I, had underlain his "April theses" advocating immediately working toward a socialist revolution that had so shocked his Bolshevik colleagues. Russia, despite its underdevelopment, was the first to achieve socialist revolution and therefore had to take the first steps in circumstances far less than ideal.

The most basic question, underlying many of the problems that had to be tackled immediately, was how to give concrete meaning to a revolution of working people. Workers in the cities assumed political power with the success of the October Revolution. But economic power had not changed hands—it still resided in the hands of Russia's industrialists. Working people, thanks to the strong organizations they had forged themselves, were able to impose an eight-hour workday and other reforms on the owners, carted out hated individual bosses in wheelbarrows in some Petrograd factories and formed factory committees to "oversee" management, but those reforms, significant as they were, did not change economic relations. Owners were still owners and employees were still employees.

A functioning government was the first necessity. A council of ministers, initially all Bolsheviks, was announced the day after the revolution, and this new government would be answerable to the soviets, specifically the Central Executive Committee, which served as the standing executive body of the All-Russian congresses of soviets. It was on the basis of the Bolsheviks winning a large majority of seats—and therefore a large majority for taking power—in the Second All-Russian Congress of Soviets that the Provisional Government of Aleksandr Kerensky was deposed. (Strictly speaking, this was a government of "people's commissars," not ministers, and Russia's ministries were now people's commisariats, a name intended to "bear witness to the fact that they were plenipotentiaries of the revolutionary people," according to Lenin's wife, Nadezhda Krupskaya.[15] The council of ministers was known as the "Sovnarkom," a contraction of its name in Russian. Years later, Josef Stalin would reinstate the term "ministry" and, for convenience, the term minister rather than commissar will be used throughout this chapter.)

Among the first decrees put into force by the new government was the Decree on Workers' Control of 27 November 1917, three weeks after the revolution. The decree was intended to institutionalize "workers' control," through the medium of the elected factory committees. These committees would have the right to "control all business correspondence" and the right to inspect all books and accounts of the enterprise.[16] Private ownership of the means of production would continue, and the factory committees were not to become management organs.[17] The decree was followed, on 1 December, by the formation of the Supreme Council of the National Economy, a government body that was to coordinate economic policy by issuing directives.[18]

The creation of the economy council represented an attempt at centralization in a form not necessarily compatible with the local control implied in the concept of factory-level workers' control. But there existed a more fundamental controversy: Just what is "workers' control"?

Broadly speaking, four major points of view crystallized in these early days of the revolution. The focus of the debate centered on the extent to which the factory committees were to supervise management, and this major aspect of the debate was bound up in rivalries between the different ideas of the factory committees and the trade unions.

- The conception of the factory committees was to situate themselves as bodies working toward popular control of the entire economy. Employees would directly supervise management within the enterprise and production would be organized through local bodies based on factory committees that would elect higher-level coordinating bodies.
- The unions foresaw a long transitional period with no immediate changes to economic structures. Workers' control was defined here as vigorous regulation, a regulation that would be more effective carried out by unions organized on national industry lines rather than at the "parochial" individual factory level.
- There was also a school of thought that demanded immediate nationalization of enterprises, demands put forth by the more militant Bolshevik rank-and-filers.
- Still others, particularly anarchists, also demanded the immediate seizure of all enterprises, but agitated to have them turned over to the workforces. Factory committees in this conception were envisioned as the nucleus for the management of society as a whole in conjunction with freely elected and independent soviets, both of which would be organized at the local level, and the abolition of the Sovnarkom.

Separate from the four broad viewpoints just sketched, there were those who resisted workers' control. These tended to be engineers and white-collar technical staff who chafed at the thought of having to account to line workers and other blue-collar co-workers. And quite naturally the enterprise owners were opposed to any workers' control of any sort, frequently threatening to close their factories.

The main debate was between the factory committees and the trade unions. The more radical view of the factory committees was encapsulated in the "instructions" issued in mid-December 1917 by the Petrograd Central Council of Factory Committees, which had been formed in June with an ongoing large elected Bolshevik majority. The central council did not see a contradiction between employee control over individual workplaces and coordination among the workplaces because it believed that both would work toward an eventual popular control of the economy. The central council's instructions declared:

> Workers' control of industry, as an integral part of control over the whole of economic life, must be understood…in the broad sense of intervening in the employer's disposal of capital, stocks, raw materials and finished goods in the factory…[Control must be] closely coordinated with and firmly tied to the general regulation and organization of production, both in the individual enterprise and in the branch of industry as a whole. Control must be seen precisely as a transitional stage toward organizing the whole economic life of the country on social lines.[19]

By contrast, the All-Russian Council of Workers' Control, a short-lived body created after the October Revolution that contained members from several institutions although dominated by trade union officials, developed a much more moderate set of instructions. Under this conception, factory committees (or equivalent control bodies) would remain subordinate to the trade unions and would have limited duties: "Administrative rights to manage the enterprise and its operations and activities remain with the owner. The control commission does not take part in the management of the enterprise and does not bear any responsibility for its operations and activity."[20]

The perspective of trade union officials was perhaps put in more stark form by a Bolshevik trade union leader, A. Lozovskii. The debate on the extent of workers' control of production could not be separated from the question of the nature of the revolution: Could Russia immediately move to socialism? Lozovskii's belief was that Russia could not yet become a socialist country and although this viewpoint was unpopular among many urban Russians, it was consistent with the Bolsheviks' pre-revolutionary belief that Russia was not ripe for socialism without revolution in the advanced capitalist countries of Europe. "If one thinks that Russia can pass to the immediate realization of a socialist system...[o]ne must socialize all enterprises and hand the whole apparatus into the hands of the workers," he wrote in a January 1918 pamphlet.[21]

But, Lozovskii argued, to do so would be unrealistic.

> There can be no doubt that the immediate socialization of the means of production and exchange is not on the agenda of the Russian Revolution...Workers' control is a transitional revolutionary measure [that] does not affect the foundations of the capitalist system. It leaves intact the private property in the means of production and the whole private trading apparatus—not because this is better from the point of view of proletarian interests, but because at the present historical moment the proletariat does not have the power to do more, given its lack of organizational experience, and in the absence of a socialist revolution in the economically advanced countries of Western Europe.[22]

The new government had enough gigantic problems to face without attempting a nationalization of the economy. The Civil War was already starting to flare in December 1917, and during it almost all of Russia's supplies of oil and coal, and its most fertile agricultural areas, would be cut off first by German occupation and then by the White armies. The Entente blockade of Germany quickly morphed into a blockade of Russia after the October Revolution, sealing off imports; Russia had always imported most of its machinery. Continuing shortages of food, a problem since the early days of World War I, led to the formation of a food procurement ministry. The new ministry bartered the government's large supply of agricultural tools and machines in exchange for crop surpluses.[23]

Migration out of the cities to the countryside also began because the formalizing of land reform immediately following the October Revolution (well before the Constituent Assembly convened) induced a migration to the countryside by those who sought to take part in the distribution of land.[24] Simultaneously, large numbers of the most enthusiastic people for revolution were lost to production when the Sovnarkom called for the formation of a "socialist army" in January 1918. By April, more than 200,000 had already volunteered.[25]

In the midst of the immense problems the Bolsheviks inherited from the tsarist régime and the Provisional Government, there had to be resolutions of the debates between factory committees and trade unions, of the split in authority between the Sovnarkom and the soviets' Central Executive Committee, and of the balance between local control and central organization. These questions began to be settled during the course of 1918. By June, the factory committees were merged into the trade unions. Some autonomy for the committees was retained, with trade unions creating a system of "workers' inspectorates" that oversaw safety and health issues.[26] Many of the members of the factory committees would now sit on the management boards that were to supervise enterprises, but these would steadily lose their importance as a push toward traditional styles of top-down enterprise management was already gathering momentum.

It was not only the owners who pushed back against workers' control but the inherited tsarist bureaucracy as well. The State Control Office, a tsarist holdover converted into a Sovnarkom ministry (as were many of the previous government ministries) continued to inspect the books of other government bodies; it defended its prerogatives and, although the highest-ranking officials were replaced, about 90 percent of its personnel were tsarist-era employees well into 1918.[27]

The debate over workers' control could not be separated, in the long term, from ongoing debates over nationalization. The revolutionary government, until a sudden reversal at the end of June 1918 that flowed from the ratification of the Brest-Litovsk Treaty with Germany, consistently opposed nationalizing enterprises. A handful of enterprises were taken over during the first eight months of the revolution, but most of these were spontaneous local takeovers. The Sovnarkom and the Supreme Council of the National Economy declared themselves the only bodies that could lawfully take over an enterprise, and the economy council, to enforce those declarations, was prompted to announce that enterprises nationalized without approval would be denied funds.[28] But these local takeovers were not done for ideological reasons, but rather because of ownership sabotage of production or refusal to implement any measure of workers' control.[29]

These issues were given a full discussion at a congress of the economy council at the end of May, at which the council's executive body would be elected by delegates representing the council itself, the Sovnarkom, trade unions, workers' cooperatives and other institutions. The official proposal of the economy council called for a complete nationalization of the mining and metal industries on the basis that a large number of mines had already been taken over in a series of spontaneous moves, but that nationalization should be gradual in other industries and only after thorough preparatory work.[30]

The Bolshevik left wing, in contrast, called for rapid nationalization, arguing that much of Russia's industry was in foreign hands, with economic initiatives often being dictated by Germany, and that private owners left in place would block the preparatory work envisioned by the official proposal.[31] Additionally, delegates from the Ural Mountains region put forth a proposal to base the economy on a system of workers' management, but one much more decentralized than that proposed by the left Bolsheviks.[32] The official proposal, calling for going slow, was adopted by the congress. Yet within four weeks, the government would effect a sudden reversal.

During World War I, the tsarist government had compelled a forced sale of some foreign-owned property, measures aimed at German capital, and the Brest-Litovsk Treaty required the return of all enterprises and ownership shares except for property taken over directly by the state.[33] Any form of nationalization taking place after 1 July 1918, would have to be fully paid for and indemnified. In anticipation of this deadline, literally overnight a list of the country's large enterprises was created, and a decree announcing the nationalization of everything on the list was published on 29 June, two days before the deadline.[34]

Thus a monumental change in economic relations was effected, dramatically changing prior policy, with virtually no discussion, and going beyond what even the most ardent proponents of nationalization had argued four weeks earlier, simply to keep factories out of the hands of German capitalists. Had that step not been taken, those German capitalists would have gained a significant control over the Russian economy, undermining efforts to harness the economy for the benefit of the people of Russia.

Ironically, the single most dramatic step toward eventual centralization of all economic life was taken because of the weakness of the Bolsheviks, not from a position of strength.

That the nationalization decree was unplanned was embodied in its affirmation that the former owners could retain their enterprises under a free lease from the government and continue to invest in and benefit from their enterprises.[35]

The question of centralization was also implied in the attempt to delineate the prerogatives of the Sovnarkom and the Central Executive Committee. At the outset, the Sovnarkom (the government ministers) were to be answerable to the Central Executive Committee (the standing body of the soviets). The Central Executive Committee was elected by the national congresses of soviets, and the delegates to those congresses were elected by lower levels. More than 90 percent of congressional delegates were elected at the city or city district level,[36] providing for strong local representations. These national congresses met approximately every three months through the end of 1918, a frequency that was designed to effect a rapid turnover in the membership of the Central Executive Committee to quickly reflect changes in popular opinion. But the Sovnarkom, within days of its formation, arrogated to itself the right to promulgate laws.[37]

The withdrawal of the Left Socialist Revolutionaries from the Sovnarkom in March 1918 because of their vehement opposition to the Brest-Litovsk Treaty and the Left SRs' August wave of assassinations against the Bolsheviks, including nearly killing Lenin, left the Sovnarkom and the Central Executive Committee firmly in Bolshevik hands. Harassment of the other parties and the pressures of the Civil War allowed the Bolsheviks to maintain overwhelming majorities in the Central Executive Committee. Despite this majority, the soviets were seen by the Bolsheviks as unable to provide the decisive leadership necessary to survive the Civil War, and the Bolshevik party congress of March 1919 ended the government controversy by placing power squarely in the hands of the Sovnarkom.[38]

But with no meaningful participation by other parties, the soviets would have become superfluous anyway. In the normal course of political life, party members meet ahead of meetings and decide how they will vote. But if one party has decisive control, then the meetings cease to actually decide political questions, since the party will have already decided the outcome ahead of time. Thus, the soviets withered away during the Civil War, disappearing in their original form altogether by 1921.

Debates over governing structures aside, the working people of Russia had been the decisive factor in the two revolutions of 1917, but this dynamism increasingly wound down. Pulling out of World War I paradoxically resulted in short-term economic disruption, and what in less dramatic circumstances would have been a problem soon overcome instead became one of several devastating problems that quickly unraveled the Russian economy. Russian industry had produced almost solely for war materiel, and factories had to retool once war orders stopped. The labor ministry ordered factories closed for a month to enable retooling for civilian production, and plans were drawn up for orderly layoffs and the payment of expenses for laid-off Petrograd workers to move elsewhere.[39] But the resumption of hostilities by the German army before the signing of the Brest-Litovsk Treaty and food shortages resulted in an exodus from Petrograd during the first months of 1918, causing the city's factory workforce to shrink by more than one-half.[40]

Fear of German occupation also caused the Bolsheviks to move the capital to Moscow. But conditions were no better there; factory workers left for the countryside and did not return to their jobs. Fuel shortages aggravated decaying conditions, forcing shutdowns throughout the Civil War period; fuel supplies available for Moscow in 1919 amounted to 4 percent of the pre-war level.[41] Almost all of Russia's sources of oil and gas were unavailable, causing large-scale industry to become less efficient and making the country almost completely dependent on wood for fuel.[42]

Production was also hurt by the lack of food for those who remained in the cities, and all spheres of life suffered from the capitalist countries' embargo on medical supplies. A typhoid epidemic, the outbreak of an extraordinarily virulent flu and a cholera outbreak each exacted severe tolls, with typhoid alone causing 25 deaths a day at one point in Moscow.[43] Under such conditions, workplace solidarity frequently was replaced by a scramble for survival, and theft became a persistent problem, with items stolen from workplaces bartered for food from peasants.[44]

Because of the dire conditions, increasing production was seen as an increasingly urgent task. As early as March 1918, Lenin had written of a need to return to "one-man management," and later stressed the need for better productivity: "The Russian worker is a bad worker in comparison with the advanced nations…To learn to work is the task that the Soviet government must set the people in all of its scope."[45] Both the trade unions and the factory committees also saw a need for increased productivity and during 1918 increasingly oriented themselves toward labor discipline, a policy that did find some support on shop floors among those who retained their political ardor.[46]

But the bulk of the most motivated joined the Red Army, or took up party or administrative posts, and the working class was otherwise decimated by the exodus to the countryside, hunger and illness. The centralization needed to survive and then win the Civil War further eroded grassroots initiative, and the resulting constriction of political life into a one-party system fueled the withering of the soviets, which were to have been the guarantor of democracy. The consolidation of one-party rule was a crucial factor in the process of the merger of party and state.

The pre-revolutionary vision of government based on soviets and administration being the province of working people, with salaries of public officials set at the level of an average worker's wage, was based on the model of the Paris Commune. But the desperate struggle to survive the hostility of the capitalist powers in the Civil War badly eroded that vision. Those pressures and, perhaps more importantly, the dispersal of the working class that negated its ability to enforce workers' control in the enterprises, led to a return of "one-man management" (as the Bolshevik leadership called it) and vertical models of economic organization.

Nor did the successful conclusion of the Civil War break the momentum. "The demobilization of the Red Army [after the Civil War] played no small role in the formation of the bureaucracy," Trotsky later wrote. "The victorious commanders assumed leading posts in the local soviets, in economy, in education, and they persistently introduced everywhere that régime which had insured success in the civil war. Thus on all sides the masses were pushed away gradually from actual participation in the leadership of the country."[47]

The pressure to centralize in order to effectively mobilize scarce resources fueled the steady nationalization of the economy. The paper decree nationalizing larger enterprises was steadily turned into a physical reality through a series of regulations, and the need for rationing and bartering reduced the circulation of money. With less scope for private enterprise to operate, nationalization of enterprises progressed to the point that 90 percent of the labor force worked for nationalized enterprises by the end of 1920.[48]

The system of centralization during the Civil War became known as "war communism." As victory in the Civil War began to come into view, the limitations of war communism became more noticeable. Despite the short-term boost the policies provided for the winning of the war, they couldn't work in the long term. Organizing an economy in the style of the military was not acceptable, even to those who did accept the necessity to order mobilizations for self-defense, and the peasants increasingly resisted food-requisition brigades sent from cities, further aggravating food shortages in the cities.

The party leadership asked Trotsky to devise a plan to make war communism "work." Although he privately thought war communism was a dead end and that more economic freedom should be given to the peasants to encourage them to produce more food,[49] Trotsky devised a plan within the parameters of war communism. Seeing that force was the only way to make such a system continue to work, Trotsky proposed military-style discipline in the workplace, which would convert trade unions into the disciplinarians of their members by stressing production instead of representing the workers' interests. This thesis was presented at a party congress in March 1920, and predictably was vehemently opposed from virtually all quarters.

The party quickly disavowed such ideas, but Trotsky was held responsible for them despite his presenting them on behalf of the party leadership that had asked him to propose new ideas.[50] Trotsky, however, had also threatened a "shakeup" of the unions, separate from the proposal on war communism, and had even removed leaders of one union; these threats against unions would not be forgotten. The picture of Trotsky as an "ogre" generated by this episode would later be used against him in the power struggle following Lenin's death.

The repudiation of conscripted labor didn't mean the contradictions of war communism had somehow faded away. Anarchist agitators, as well as agitators from the defeated socialist parties (the Mensheviks and Social Revolutionaries) increasingly found audiences, strikes broke out across Petrograd and Moscow, and peasant uprisings became more numerous. When the Kronstadt rebellion of sailors erupted, it was no longer possible to ignore that a drastic change of course was necessary.

The March 1921 Bolshevik party congress concluded with the rapid acceptance of Lenin's "New Economic Policy," which reintroduced a measure of capitalism. Under NEP, private trade was again legalized and requisitioning of agricultural crop surpluses was replaced by a tax on peasants, who were allowed to market their grain surpluses. A breathing spell was needed, and NEP was designed to provide it.

## The Bolsheviks ban opposition and take away their own freedom

The March 1921 congress was additionally noteworthy for Vladimir Lenin's ban on formal opposition groups within the party, a consequence of the Bolsheviks banning all opposition parties. In the debates preceding the congress, the Bolsheviks had split into three camps. Leon Trotsky and Nikolai Bukharin argued that the trade unions should be subsumed to the state and party. The majority of the party, including Lenin, Grigorii Zinoviev, Lev Kamenev and Josef Stalin, sought a middle course, arguing that the trade unions should act in the interest of the country and its nationalized economy, but that they should still remain autonomous organizations and protect the workers when necessary. Two formal opposition groups, the "Workers Opposition" and the "Group of Democratic Centralism," advocated a full return to workers' control, with trade unions and factory committees having control over the economy.

The more important of these two opposition groups was the Workers Opposition, which included many Bolsheviks with long pre-revolutionary years as organizers who were now union leaders. The group was headed by the first Bolshevik labor minister, Aleksandr Shliapnikov, and a former public welfare minister, Aleksandra Kollantai. Shliapnikov began factory work at age 13, becoming a skilled metalworker. He had joined the party in 1901, organizing unions and writing prolifically. Kollantai began underground work in 1899, organizing women workers, teaching at party schools in exile and tirelessly giving speeches in several languages.

The Workers Opposition published their platform in the leading party newspaper, *Pravda,* a few weeks before the congress, in which the group said the influence of unions had been reduced "almost to zero" and called for "involving the masses directly in the work of building the national economy" and for unions to "be built on the basis of workers' democracy, the elective principle and accountability of all organs from top to bottom."[51]

The document declared that "victory over ruin…is possible and achievable only through radical change of the existing system and of the methods of organization and management of the economy, now resting on an enormous bureaucratic machine, excluding the creative initiative and independent action of producers organized into unions."[52] Furthermore, "The existing bureaucratic approach to economic construction places obstacles in the way of achievement of the maximum of production results, which introduces discord, distrust and demoralization into the ranks of workers."[53]

The Workers Opposition demanded free apartments, heat, electricity, lunches, transportation and theater, and called for building and repairing of workers' dwellings to be the highest priority.[54] Unfortunately, the Workers Opposition did not say how this part of their program was supposed to be fulfilled, especially considering the dire straits in which the economy remained; the process of rebuilding industry had only just begun. The means of bringing to life even a small fraction of these demands for the free supplies simply didn't exist physically; however worthy these demands might sound, they were unrealistic at the time. Seven years of brutal war resulted in a decline in Russia's gross national income of more than 60 percent from 1913 to 1921[55] and a decline in its industrial output of 80 percent.[56]

Trotsky declared that the Workers Opposition "have made a fetish of democratic principles," declaring that it is "necessary to create among us the awareness of the revolutionary historical birthright of the party. The party is obliged to maintain its dictatorship, regardless of temporary wavering in the moods of the masses, regardless of temporary vacillations even in the working class."[57] Lenin dismissed the Workers Oppositionists as "anarcho-syndicalists," by which he meant they would disorganize society, and declared them a "direct political danger."[58] (Lenin had battled a syndicalist trend within Bolshevik ranks before World War I and had not become any more sympathetic toward anything that he deemed as overly decentralized.) Turning to his other flank, Lenin also admonished Trotsky and Bukharin for their proposals to reduce trade unions to subordinate instruments of state policy, saying that unions should be the schools, not the drill halls, of communism.[59] With a large majority behind him, Lenin's middle position had no trouble winning approval.

The Workers Opposition were able to muster only a small minority at the congress. Despite the failure of their ideas to gain traction, some of their leaders, including Shliapnikov, were re-elected to the Central Committee. Nonetheless, there were personnel changes in the party leadership that, in retrospect, provided another signal that the party was become something very different from what it had been.

At this point, it is appropriate to pause in order to sketch the basics of how the Russian Communist Party, as the Bolsheviks had renamed themselves, was organized.

- The party's most important body, on paper, was its congresses, held once a year until the mid-1920s. These were gathering of hundreds of party members (later numbering a couple of thousand) who, originally, were freely elected by the party rank-and-file. A congress set policy, and its resolutions were considered binding. A congress elected a Central Committee deputized to run party affairs and deal with day-to-day matters between party congresses. Before the revolution, the Central Committee had only a half-dozen or so members, but its size steadily increased until it contained dozens of members by the early 1920s. Because the Central Committee became so large, it in turn elected a Political

Bureau, usually referred to as the "Politburo" following the Russian custom of creating a new word out of the first syllables of multiple-word names. Just as the Central Committee was answerable to the next congress, the Politburo was answerable to the Central Committee. The Central Committee also elected Central Committee secretaries, who had administrative responsibilities. The secretaries represented a step between Politburo membership and a regular seat on the Central Committee.

- After the October Revolution, a party bureaucracy mushroomed. This bureaucracy included the Secretariat (headed by the Central Committee secretaries), which was responsible for personnel and also supervised administrative agencies; the Organization Bureau, or "Orgburo," which organized administrative work; and the Central Control Commission, which handled party discipline. As a consequence of the development of the one-party system, in which major decisions and policies were made by party leaders not subject to any control from outside the party, the most powerful people in this system were the members of the Politburo—the party was above the government. Eventually, the leading position on the Politburo became known as the "general secretary" because the first person to hold that title, Stalin, used his position heading the Secretariat to consolidate his grip on power.
- Separate from the party hierarchy was the national government, the leading positions of which were filled by the party with its members. The day-to-day functioning of the government was carried out by the council of ministers, the "Sovnarkom." The chair of the Sovnarkom was the country's prime minister; Lenin held this position but afterward it was a subordinate position to the party general secretary. In addition, the soviets continued to exist. The Supreme Soviet, as the national soviet came to

> be known, constituted a rough equivalent of a legislature, but as a rubber-stamp body without the authority a normal legislature has. Because the government was originally intended to be answerable to the soviets, the chair of the Supreme Soviet was considered the head of state, a ceremonial position similar to the president in parliamentary systems, except without the power to dissolve the government.

As the relevance of the soviets withered and the exercise of power was narrowed to smaller groups, decision-making power, even in theory, ceased to flow up from the congresses; instead, it flowed down from the Politburo.

Another consequence of the narrowing of the party's decision-making was that the personnel of the leading party bodies became highly important. Therefore, it was, in retrospect, a signal that the March 1921 party congress voted out the three Central Committee secretaries, Nikolai Krestinskii, Evgenii Preobrazhenskii and Leonid Serebryakov. Each was a highly able, independent thinker, but each had shown sympathy to the Workers Opposition, and they were replaced by the congress majority. (Each of the three would eventually join the "Left Opposition" of the later 1920s with Trotsky, losing a struggle with Stalin's faction.) In their place were elected less independent thinkers such as Lazar Kaganovich, Viacheslav Molotov and Emelian Yaroslavskii, already or soon to be unshakable followers of Stalin.

More significant at the time was the scrapping of war communism and the proclamation of the New Economic Policy (NEP), as well as the ban on party opposition groups and organized factions. Lenin was frank in proposing NEP, which was designed to give concessions to the peasantry:

> A [dose of] capitalism that we must and can accept, and to

> which we can and must assign certain limits, for it is necessary for the great mass of peasantry and to the trade that enables the peasants' needs to be satisfied. We must arrange things in such a way that the regular operation of the economy and patterns of exchange characteristic of capitalism become possible. It must be so for the sake of the people. Otherwise we should not be able to live...For the [peasants], nothing else is absolutely necessary; as for the rest, they must make the best of it.[60]

Restrictions on trade were removed, small enterprises were returned to private ownership and others were leased by the state, although large enterprises continued to be controlled by the government. Restrictions on farmers hiring labor were also eased, giving rise to big farmers, the "kulaks," who prospered under NEP. In the cities, merchants and traders also flourished; these "Nepmen" were resented by many as they took advantage of shortages to rapidly become wealthy, flaunting their new wealth while society as a whole still suffered from poverty. The peasants still comprised the overwhelming majority of the population and, with the urban merchants and traders, and the tsarist bureaucracy and intelligentsia, represented a formidable potential opposition to communist rule, which was glumly noted by party activists and supporters. But the party saw NEP as a necessary development, and intended that it would remain in place for at least several years.

At the same time that restrictions were greatly eased in economic spheres, and in cultural areas (the 1920s would become a golden age for Russian arts), political freedom was curtailed. That all political oppositions (Mensheviks, Socialist Revolutionaries, anarchists and others) unanimously hailed the Kronstadt rebellion, and encouraged the strikes in Petrograd and the peasant upheavals in the countryside, was read by the Bolsheviks as another danger to the revolution. The Bolsheviks believed that, if they were removed from power, the result would be a resurgence of the White armies, which would drown the country in blood and institute a savage Right-wing dictatorship.

The socialist oppositions were seen as unwilling or unable to sustain the revolution, and too weak to stabilize the country in the wake of threats from the Whites. An open election might well bring opposition parties to power, but they had already, in 1917, demonstrated that they were incapable of governing or coping with a collapsing economy, nor had they shown themselves capable of retaining power. The Bolsheviks were not about to hand power to the Whites, whom they had just defeated at such high cost.

But having taken away others' political freedom, the Bolsheviks had to take it away from themselves. They could ban opposition parties, but they could not make the ideas animating those oppositions disappear. With only one party permitted, and membership in that party a potential shortcut to career success, status-seekers and the personally ambitious flocked to join. Members of the now-banned parties who wished to remain politically active in Russia, or hoped to continue to promote their ideas, signed up as well. Moreover, the older members of any party will start to have deeper disagreements among themselves—four years in power is more than enough time for fissures to develop, and if the differences become deep and long-lasting, the potential arises for the party to split into two. How could a one-party system survive a split? The only way to prevent this from happening is by putting restrictions on the party's members. That is the pitiless logic of one-party rule.

The huge amounts of blood spilled to put down the Kronstadt rebellion fresh in their minds, the delegates to the March 1921 congress approved the ban on organized factions within the party. This was not yet a ban on all opposition. Lenin asked that party members of all shades of opinion be elected to the Central Committee and offered to publish opposing viewpoints in the party press, but said that any opposition should remain "diffuse" and not form into permanent groups. A secret clause authorized the expulsion of any party member, no matter how highly placed, for violating the ban on factions.

Lenin and Trotsky had intended the ban to be a temporary measure that would be lifted once the country achieved some stability, but it would not be revoked for 70 years. This ban was the instrument that would used throughout the 1920s to silence, then eliminate, various oppositions, until only Stalin's faction remained. Once a majority had formed on a given issue, the minority could be silenced by wielding this ban; party discipline steadily became more draconian under the momentum of the struggles at the top of the party. The Workers Opposition was only the first group to find itself unable to solve the contradiction of wishing to retain full freedom of debate while at the same time insisting that only one party could be permitted to exist.

The party had now traveled a long way from its earlier ideals; it had embarked on the revolution sure of its promises to create a much greater freedom than the capitalist states had or could provide. The form of the expanded democracy to be put in place after the revolution consolidated itself was to be a democracy where working people would participate in governing the country, ending their exploitation by a class that owned the "means of production": the factories and large enterprises.

In classical Marxist terminology, this democracy of mass participation is known as the "dictatorship of the proletariat." The theoretical conception of this phase is that it is a temporary measure during the transition from capitalism to socialism during which government power is exercised by working people (the "proletariat") while the deposed ruling class is excluded from power. Because working people constitute a huge majority of society in an industrial country, this simply means rule by that majority, which can be completely democratic. The "dictatorship of the proletariat" is temporary because, according to Marxist theory, a classless society would emerge in which everybody would be a full participant in society.

In a capitalist country, the class that owns and controls the means of production is the "bourgeoisie," and therefore, under the same theoretical conceptions, the class-based rule of capitalist countries is known as a "dictatorship of the bourgeoisie," even when they are governed with democratic forms as in Europe, North America and the Asia-Pacific region. Industrialists and financiers, regardless of whether they actually hold positions in a legislature or in a government, retain a preponderance of power in capitalist democracies through the enormous leverage their accumulated capital gives them. They have a stranglehold over the economy, enabling them to bend economic policy toward their favored positions, and are able to shape public opinion to their advantage through collective control of the mass media and their ability to diffuse their perspectives into a wide range of a capitalist country's institutions. A "dictatorship of the bourgeoisie" can take harsher forms—for example, the dictatorial governments of the Global South, often propped up by the United States, and of Europe's twentieth-century fascist dictatorships.

But instead of a democratic "dictatorship of the proletariat," the Bolshevik leadership was now proclaiming a dictatorship of the party, substituting itself for the working class it represented even though the working class, or at least the remnants of it, was now wavering in its support for the revolution. Among other assumptions, the Bolsheviks had assumed that once a working class took power, it would remain politically active and continue to support its party. That this was not so was an additional factor inducing them to exclude others from political power. The party decided it would act as a trustee until the working class would again exert itself, but having exhausted itself in the harsh years of civil war and having largely dispersed, Russia's working class would be unable to reassert itself. And as unemployment continued to be a problem throughout the NEP era, political loyalty became for many urban workers a necessary insurance against losing a job.

Yet economic recovery did occur, the country did get the breathing space it needed, and millions of people had a stake in the revolution, providing the régime with a solid social base. Portions of the working class would become active and take part in economic construction; and this grassroots support would continue to influence the party, even after the political dictatorship of the party further evolved into the far more thoroughgoing dictatorship of one person.

## Lenin rethinks his views in his final days, and Stalin sees his opportunity

The New Economic Policy did not fully restore capitalism; NEP-era Russia possessed a mixed economy. The agricultural sector remained, as it was even under war communism, overwhelmingly private. A minuscule number of collective farms did come into being during NEP, but Russian agriculture was completely dominated by 25 million individual farms. Most of these farms were, at best, self-sufficient; only a small number of them were large enough to provide a significant grain surplus, which was needed to feed the cities.

There was a decrease in the number of landless peasants and a large increase in the number of farms possessing a horse as a result of the massive land distribution carried out in the countryside, but the average size of farms sharply decreased.[61] It would now be more difficult to produce enough food to feed the cities and for export.

These millions of farmers represented a capitalist, or potentially capitalist, force in the eyes of those who looked toward a socialist future—and were therefore a source of anxiety. This anxiety became more acute as time progressed, because peasants gradually lost their fear that the old estate owners who had kept them in bondage would return. The peasants had largely sided with the Bolsheviks during the Civil War, knowing the Bolsheviks' triumph was the only way to prevent the return of the aristocracy, who would have taken back the land and wreaked revenge. With their holdings now secure, and the ruling party making a series of concessions to them, the peasants could afford to be more independent.

Differentiation in the countryside enabled a handful of farmers to grab a big enough plot of land that could not be worked without hiring employees. These big farmers were known as "kulaks." Concessions to the peasantry particularly benefited kulaks, who became relatively wealthy and, as an active element in the villages, often became local leaders. The great bulk of the peasantry remained poor, tilling a farm too small to break out of poverty, but content to work their plots—these peasants were still better off than they had been before the revolution. Despite the overwhelming numerical superiority of the peasantry, and the dispersal of the urban working class, which was only beginning to be reversed, the peasantry didn't constitute a dominant political force. Self-sufficient on their farms and so not dependent on social interaction, separated by distance, uneducated and mired in superstition, Russia's small farmers did not routinely band together for political purposes. All the more did this allow the kulaks to dominate the countryside.

The economic breakdown in the cities was much more complicated. Larger enterprises (the "commanding heights" of the economy) were state-owned. There were also mixed enterprises, partly owned by the government and partly owned by private investors; concessions and leased enterprises, which were owned by the government but operated by private interests who leased the operation from the government; and purely private enterprises, which were subject to regulation. The government maintained a monopoly in foreign trade, heavy industry, transportation and banking. Private enterprises were numerous but small, accounting for 88 percent of the number of enterprises in the early 1920s[62] despite the fact that, as noted earlier, 90 percent of the workforce worked for state enterprises. Private enterprises were concentrated in retail and trading, and artisans were prominent in producing consumer items. The socialist sector of the economy was expected to compete with the private sector, but also had to compete with the global capitalist system entrenched in its European neighbors.

"Russia's whole economic structure, viewed as a unit, faces in the world-market great capitalist systems," wrote Nikolai Bukharin in early 1922, about a year after the implementation of NEP.

> Conditions in the world-market may cause part of the excess value created in Russia, that created by strictly government enterprises, to flow into the pockets of the foreign bourgeoisie. Payments that we have to make to foreign Governments and the losses that we must incur, in consequence of the weakness of our whole social organization when we deal with other countries, will take this form. Apparently, therefore, even enterprises that are exclusively in the hands of the working people will have to yield part of their profits to others.[63]

Still another grouping that represented a potential leadership for a return to the old ways were the members of the holdover tsarist bureaucracy. Large numbers of them had opposed the Bolsheviks, or any of the socialist parties, but reconciled themselves to the new régime and continued to fill the ranks of the bureaucracy—educated men and women were at a premium and the working class was too lacking in education and practical experience to yet produce many people suitable to fill those posts. About 500,000 former tsarist bureaucrats worked in the government.

Meanwhile, the ranks of the party were swelling—about 700,000 were party members by the start of 1922. Grigorii Zinoviev estimated that those who were in the underground before February 1917 constituted only 2 percent of the party's membership.[64] Many who joined, particularly in 1917 and during the Civil War, did so out of honest convictions, but now careerists and bandwagon-jumpers were swelling the ranks. Calls for a purge of the party membership to root out careerists were heard, and it was none other than the Workers Opposition that initiated demands for a purge at the March 1921 party congress. Within a year, such a purge was carried out, and 200,000 were expelled from the party.[65]

Massive as such a purge was, it should not be confused with the later, lethal purges of the Stalin dictatorship. In this case, the only penalty was loss of party membership, nothing else, and there is no record of any expulsion resulting from oppositional viewpoints. This first purge was carried out completely in the open; any party member could speak for or against any other party member, and reasons were given for any expulsion.[66]

The Bolsheviks had once again instituted a practice that began reasonably innocently but would become an instrument of repression. And, again, many supported a program that seemed like a reasonable way of dealing with a problem, only to have it become a means of repression against themselves during future power struggles. But that such a massive reduction of its membership could happen also underlined that the Bolsheviks were already losing their composition as a free association of like-minded individuals and becoming something much more institutional.

Another change was the gradual withdrawal from party life of Vladimir Lenin. He became seriously ill in December 1921 and then suffered a stroke that temporarily left him partially paralyzed in May 1922; he was unable to work for long stretches during 1922. After returning to work later in the year, although never fully recovering his health, Lenin suffered another stroke in December 1922. He returned to only very limited work, but had decided, by March 1923, to remove Josef Stalin from power. Before he could act on his intentions, Lenin suffered a third stroke, leaving him without speech and permanently ending his active life. Stalin, once Lenin became sick, began accumulating power behind the scenes as part of a gradual, but steady, process. Lenin realized what was happening too late.

It was during Lenin's final months of active life that he more deeply analyzed the course of the revolution, producing five articles. Undoubtedly, Lenin would have developed his thinking further had he lived, but his mind was nonetheless in ferment.

Lenin started this final series of articles by noting the slow pace thus far of progress—a recent census had revealed that the literacy rate in Russia had improved only from 22 percent in 1897 to 32 percent in 1920. "[F]acts and figures reveal we are in a very bad way even [in comparison to] bourgeois culture," Lenin wrote. "It shows what a vast amount of urgent spade-work we still have to do to reach the standard of an ordinary West-European civilized country. It also shows what a vast amount of work we have to do today to achieve, on the basis of our proletarian gains, anything like a real cultural standard."[67] Literacy rates were lower in the countryside than in the cities, and Lenin saw a "duty" to establish links between urban workers and rural peasants: "[W]e must form a number of associations (Party, trade union and private) of factory workers, which would devote themselves regularly to assisting the villages in their cultural development."[68]

At the same time, Lenin sought to encourage the development of cooperative enterprises in sufficiently large numbers so that a majority of Russians would be involved in them.

All we actually need under NEP is to organize the population

> of Russia in cooperative societies on a sufficiently large scale for we have now found the degree of combination of private interest, of private commercial interest, with state supervision and control of this interest, that degree of its subordination to the common interests which was formerly the stumbling block for very many socialists.[69]

The cooperatives should be subsidized, he wrote:

> Cooperation must be politically so organized that it will not only generally and always enjoy certain privileges, but that these privileges should be of a purely material nature (a favorable bank rate, etc.). The cooperatives must be granted state loans that are greater, if only by a little, than the loans we grant to private enterprises, even to heavy industry.[70]

Cooperatives were distinct from private and nationalized enterprises—these were to be enterprises collectively run by their workforces. Although Lenin did not specify that coops should be concentrated in any particular industry, the implication was that much of them would be in agriculture, since farming was entirely in private hands. The pooling together of small farms, or the creation of cooperative small production or trading groups, would require subsidies—providing credit and other material incentives would make them more viable than small-scale individual production.

Lenin anticipated that the development of his proposed cooperative system would take a long time because of Russia's low cultural level.

> Therefore, our rule must be: as little philosophizing and as few acrobatics as possible. In this respect NEP is an advance, because it is adjustable to the level of the most ordinary peasant and does not demand anything higher of him. But it

> will take a whole historical epoch to get the entire population into the work of the cooperatives through NEP. At best we can achieve this in one or two decades. Nevertheless, it will be a distinct historical epoch, and without this historical epoch, without universal literacy, without a proper degree of efficiency, without training the population sufficiently to acquire the habit of book reading, and without the material basis for this, without a certain sufficiency to safeguard against, say, bad harvests, famine, etc.—without this we shall not achieve our object[ive].[71]

Lenin identified "two main tasks" to assist the massive task of raising Russia's cultural level: educating the peasantry and "reorganiz[ing] our machinery of state, which is utterly useless [and] which we took over in its entirety from the preceding epoch; during the past five years of struggle we did not, and could not, drastically reorganize it."[72]

He argued that there was now no choice but to create the conditions for future economic development because capitalism had not performed that task in Russia. "If a definite level of culture is required for the building of socialism…why cannot we begin by first achieving the prerequisites for that definite level of culture in a revolutionary way, and then, with the aid of the workers' and peasants' government and Soviet system, proceed to overtake the [capitalist] nations?"[73]

Lenin then came to what he saw as the centerpiece of a necessary struggle against bureaucracy. Unfortunately, it was a reshuffling of the bureaucracy, and a further merging of party and state—a measure also ironic because Lenin, less than a year earlier, had spoken at a party congress of the need to separate party and government. Because of the inefficiency and corruption of the bureaucracy, the Bolsheviks had created the "Workers' and Peasants' Inspectorate," a ministry to look over the shoulders of officials in other government ministries with a right to conduct inspections without notice of any other part of the government. Created in 1919, it had been headed by Stalin, another source of power for the future dictator since the Inspectorate oversaw the entire machinery of government.

The Inspectorate proved to be no more efficient or useful than the rest of the government; Lenin acknowledged this state of affairs as "an enormous difficulty." He now proposed that the Inspectorate be combined with the Central Control Commission (which oversaw party discipline), that the staff of the Inspectorate be reduced to 300 or 400 people, and that workers and peasants should fill the ranks of the body after undergoing special screening so that the "best of our workers" should fill those ranks, similar to the best workers forming the ranks of the Red Army during the Civil War.[74]

"Our state apparatus is so deplorable, not to say wretched, that we must first think very carefully how to combat its defects, bearing in mind that these defects are rooted in the past, which, although it has been overthrown, has not yet been overcome, has not yet reached a state of a culture that has receded into the distant past. I say culture deliberately, because in these matters we can only regard as achieved what has become part and parcel of our culture, of our social life, of our habits,"[75] Lenin wrote.

He argued that educating the members of the state apparatus and eliminating the useless "haste" of the previous five years were essential tasks.

> In all spheres of social, economic and political relationships we are "frightfully" revolutionary. But as regards precedence, the observance of the forms and rights of office management, our "revolutionariness" often gives way to the mustiest routine. On more than one occasion, we have witnessed the very interesting phenomenon of a great leap forward in social life being accompanied by amazing timidity when the slightest changes are proposed…[I]n our present life, reckless

> audacity goes hand in hand, to an astonishing degree, with timidity of thought even when it comes to very minor changes.[76]

Summing up, in the last words he wrote, Lenin said,

> [O]nly by thoroughly purging our government machine, by reducing to the utmost everything that is not absolutely essential in it, shall we be certain of being able to keep going. Moreover, we shall be able to keep going not on the level of a small-peasant country, not on the level of universal limitation, but on a level steadily advancing to large-scale machine industry.[77]

More firmly than ever, Lenin acknowledged the very low cultural level of his party, and the revenge that Russia's tsarist heritage was taking on it for that low level. But more bureaucracy doesn't seem the answer to the problem of bureaucratization. A further cementing of the merger of state and party, an unavoidable result of merging a government organ, the Inspectorate, with its party equivalent, the Central Control Commission, seems contradictory to the goal of reducing the weight of bureaucracy and to the goal of soon ending the bans on opposition parties and the formation of permanent groupings within the Communist Party, because such a merger, if carried out, would only reinforce the dominance of the party's majority viewpoint. Yet the Inspectorate had been another idea intended to boost workers' participation and prepare them to become administrators; elections to the body were held in September 1920 with the slogan of "Enter the [Inspectorate] and learn to govern the state!"[78]

By 1922, the Inspectorate had grown to 12,000 civil servants,[79] so Lenin's proposal did call for a drastic reduction in its size. But Lenin had also not clearly delineated to whom the new

Inspectorate would be responsible, and without a continuation of free elections to the body, the Secretariat would inevitably appoint its membership. Stalin was already general secretary and controlled the Secretariat; therefore he would be able to name his "watchers." Lenin had called for Stalin's removal as general secretary in his survey of the party's leading figures that became known as his "final testament" (written at about the same time as his final five articles), but had left potential control of not only the Inspectorate, but also the party and government apparatuses, in the hands of the general secretary, and therefore had done nothing to solve the problem of the concentration of power that Lenin saw as a defect.

The merger of the government and party oversight bodies did take place, but the resulting post-merger Central Control Commission became a tool in Stalin's hands, and would eventually play a prominent political role in the purges of the future.

Lenin's putting forth these final theses came at the same time his "final struggle" was taking place—his realization of Stalin's character and Stalin's plan for an extreme centralization and a trampling of the small nations on the "borderlands" of Russia.

Stalin had become the Bolsheviks' supposed expert on nationalities by something of a happenstance. Stalin spent almost the entirety of his pre-revolutionary career inside the Russian Empire, organizing among workers in the Caucasus region, or in jail or Siberian exile. On Stalin's third and last trip outside Russia, Lenin encouraged him to write an article on the "national question"; in it, Stalin faithfully parroted Lenin's viewpoint and he apparently received considerable help from Bukharin in preparing the article. Leon Trotsky remembered the article under the then-unknown signature of "J. Stalin," as "attract[ing] attention mainly because, through the banal monotonous text, there flashed occasionally original ideas and brilliant formulas."[80]

Stalin had remained aloof from the debates and schisms among the émigrés; he occasionally commented on them, but like most Caucasian underground activists, took a dim view of what he called "squabbling."[81] Stalin, after wavering, backed Lenin against other Bolshevik factions in 1911, and in the following year Lenin argued for Stalin's election to the Central Committee, but although other Caucasians were elected, the still-obscure Stalin was not.[82] The Central Committee, however, had the right to "co-opt" (unilaterally appoint) new members and Lenin soon succeeded in having Stalin promoted.

After Lenin's death, Stalin portrayed himself as Lenin's most reliable interpreter, although others, particularly Zinoviev and Lev Kamenev, were much closer and had worked with Lenin for a far longer period of time. But when Lenin's health declined, Stalin ceased to be a loyal follower.

The first serious breach between Lenin and Stalin came over the government's monopoly on foreign trade. Lenin favored the continuation of the foreign-trade monopoly on grounds that "foreigners will buy up and take home with them everything of any value."[83] Lenin was outvoted while he was on an extended sick leave during 1922, and when he returned to work he mounted an extensive lobbying campaign for the issue to be reconsidered. Lenin asked Trotsky to take up this cause, and eventually Lenin's viewpoint was approved over the considerable resentment of Stalin. When Lenin's poor health required him again to have an ally during his "final struggle"—the fight over treatment of national minorities, particularly in the Caucasus region—he again asked Trotsky to carry the fight.

Lenin believed that minority nations should be allowed independence or autonomy if it is the desire of those nationalities. Partly this was out of respect for the right of all people to organize themselves as they saw fit and partly it was because Lenin believed nationalism to be a force that obscured class interests; once a nation became independent, its working class and peasantry would see that its true oppressor is the ruling class of its own nation and not occupiers from another nation. Lenin also noted that "Great Russian chauvinism" had run roughshod over the nations of the tsarist empire's "borderlands" and therefore he consistently stressed the need to not replicate any behavior reminiscent of Russian bullying of other peoples.

Stalin, as commissar of nationalities, and enthusiastically assisted by Feliks Dzerzhinsky and Sergo Ordzhonikidze, were much more interested in centralization—under their leadership, the Red Army forcibly brought Georgia into the Soviet Union, and then the three hatched a plan to unilaterally merge the three Caucasian republics (Georgia, Azerbaijan and Armenia) into a single Transcaucasian Republic, and that the merged republic, along with Ukraine and Belorussia, would be completely subordinate to the Russian Republic, instead of each republic having its own government, with each, including Russia, under a federal multinational government.

At first, Lenin accepted the reports of Stalin and Dzerzhinsky, and wouldn't give consideration to the protests of local Georgian leaders. The irony here was that the renewed Russification of national minorities was being led by two Georgians, Stalin and Ordzhonikidze, and a Pole, Dzerzhinsky. Stalin issued a series of dictates intended to impose his centralization plan that local Georgian communists continued to resist in the face of party orders to conform to higher party decisions and Ordzhonikidze's speeches declaring that the independent tendencies of Georgian leaders should be removed "with a branding iron."[84]

Stalin decided to present his plan for approval to the party Central Committee in October 1923 without bothering to circulate the text beforehand. Lenin, upon seeing the text, announced his disapproval and proposed several changes to Stalin's plan, adding in a note to Kamenev that "Stalin tends to rush things too much."[85]

Lenin now sensed that things were not as Stalin was telling

him, and asked Kamenev to go to Georgia to talk to the local leaders. Kamenev told Stalin that Lenin "is going to war to defend independence"[86] and Stalin, evidently believing Lenin would not be returning to fully active political life, replied, "We should get tough with [Lenin]" and dismissed Lenin as being under the influence of "a few Georgian Mensheviks."[87] Stalin capped off his insults by accusing Lenin of "national liberalism."[88] In other words, Lenin was now not capable of formulating his own opinions, and even the opinions of Lenin were wrong on the sole basis of being different from Stalin's. But with Lenin showing some unexpected fight, Stalin backed down and, characteristically, incorporated Lenin's suggestions while claiming the revised text he was submitting to the Central Committee was his alone with only very minor adjustments.

The approval of the revised text did not end matters. Georgian officials continued to press their view that their republic should join a federation as equals, and Ordzhonikidze, backed by Stalin, built further pressure on them to knuckle under. In a meeting with Georgian leaders, Ordzhonikidze struck one of them, and when this got back to Lenin, he began to look at the situation in the Caucasus in a fresh light.

Lenin asked Trotsky to join him in a fight against bureaucracy, but suffered further declines in his health. It was none other than Stalin who was appointed to watch over Lenin's health and to report to the Central Committee. Stalin used this to his advantage—in early 1923 Lenin was not allowed to see material without the permission of Stalin, discovering this order second-hand, via one of his doctors.[89] Stalin also berated Lenin's wife, Nadezhda Krupskaya, for allowing Lenin to dictate notes, and tried to intimidate one of Lenin's secretaries into not providing news or information to the ailing party leader, blocking the release of documents to her as well.[90]

Lenin now became very interested in what was happening in Georgia. On 5 March 1923, Lenin asked Trotsky to take up the cause of the Georgians and sent a letter to Stalin demanding an apology for abusing his wife and asking if relations "should be broken off."[91] The following day, Lenin sent a letter to the Georgian leaders stating, "I am following your case with all my heart. I am indignant over Ordzhonikidze's rudeness and the connivance of Stalin and Dzerzhinsky. I am preparing for you notes and a speech."[92] Further, Lenin was now resolved "to crush Stalin politically,"[93] confiding this to Kamenev.

Lenin had already added a postscript to his "final testament," in which he had expressed unease at the "immeasurable power" Stalin had accumulated: "Stalin is too rude and this defect…becomes intolerable in a General Secretary. That is why I suggest the comrades think about a way to remove Stalin from that post and appoint another man who is…more patient, more loyal, more polite and more attentive to comrades, less capricious & etc."[94]

It was at this time that Lenin wrote, "I suppose I have been very remiss with respect to the workers of Russia for not having intervened energetically and decisively enough in the notorious question of autonomisation," referring to the problems in Georgia.

> If matters had come to such a pass that Ordzhonikidze could go to the extreme of applying physical violence, as Comrade Dzerzhinsky informed me, we can imagine what a mess we have got ourselves into. Obviously the whole business of "autonomisation" was radically wrong and badly timed. It is said that a united apparatus was needed. Where did that assurance come from? Did it not come from that same Russian apparatus which, as I pointed out in one of the preceding sections of my diary, we took over from tsarism and slightly anointed with Soviet oil?…I think that Stalin's haste and his infatuation with pure administration, together with his spite…played a fatal role here. In politics spite generally plays

the basest of roles.[95]

In asking Trotsky to take up his cause—the removal of Stalin from power, the demotion of Dzerzhinsky and the expulsion from the party of Ordzhonikidze—Lenin asked Trotsky to be firm and to trust no "rotten compromise" that Stalin might offer.[96] Instead of carrying out Lenin's intentions, Trotsky showed extraordinary magnanimity to Stalin, simply asking Stalin to promise to change his behavior, apologize to Lenin's wife and give assurances that national independence would now be respected. Stalin quickly agreed to these demands, and Trotsky declared himself opposed to Lenin's penalties.[97]

Just after this compromise, Lenin suffered his third stroke, permanently incapacitating him. Yet Lenin's intentions were still known. Stalin said to Trotsky that he had done all Trotsky had asked, and Trotsky agreed to not bring up Lenin's request at the Central Committee meeting and instead submit Lenin's notes to the Politburo, which promptly voted to suppress them.[98]

On the verge of losing everything, Stalin was now firmly in his seat of power. Although what the future had in store for the rest of them was unimaginable at this time, the party leaders had lost their best chance to unseat Stalin. And with Lenin now definitively gone from the scene, Stalin, in conjunction with Kamenev and Zinoviev, methodically tightened his grip on the party.

## The bureaucracy underpinning Stalin's power, and the party's desire to back the majority

Here again it is a necessity to delve into personalities. An irony of the Soviet system is that it was created by Marxists—men and women dedicated to the proposition that social forces (groups and classes of people acting under the impact of national and international socio-economic conditions, political relations and cultural traditions) are the primary vehicles of historical development—yet personalities were a dominant feature of that system. How is it that personalities—the "subjective" factor—became more predominant than in a typical capitalist democracy? A critical reason is the lack of controls.

The Bolshevik structure was organized to be run by selfless revolutionaries who were elected by, and responsible to, the rank-and-file party membership. But regardless of whatever aura may have attached to the leadership, it consisted of flesh-and-blood human beings, albeit human beings with extraordinarily large senses of responsibility to improve their world. During the long years before 1917, many people came and went, but slowly a leadership corps formed, some of whom had been with Vladimir Lenin since the 1903 split with the Mensheviks.

Both before and after the October Revolution, Lenin kept personal rivalries in check and exerted a strong influence on his party through "moral authority"; Lenin earned the respect of his colleagues through his ability to realistically analyze changing conditions and thoroughly prepare concrete strategies. His talents and intellect enabled him to persuade party opinion when he saw that a dramatic change of policy had become a necessity. In no sense was Lenin a "dictator"—he had to win votes, and accept it when he lost, which sometimes happened.

As Lenin's health declined and he was away from the day-to-day business of governing the country, his associates, most of whom had followed him for many years, began to assert their independence. By this time there was much less constraint on those at the top level of the party, the Politburo. The loss of relevance of the soviets, the centralization of the party, and the party's tight control over the government resulting from the intensity of the Civil War had placed extraordinary authority into a few hands. Even had all of those who possessed this extraordinary authority truly been selfless revolutionaries, concerned solely with the betterment of the country, this would have been an unhealthy development. But the members of the Politburo were flesh-and-blood human beings with the flaws of human beings, and these human characteristics led them to behave in a variety of ways, by no means without personal considerations.

Fatally aggravating this inherently unhealthy political condition was the fact that the genuine policy differences among them, and the highly differentiated attitudes toward the party's centralization and the array of questions of democracy posed by that centralization, were kept hidden. There had been a need to present a unified face to win the Civil War, and a desire to maintain unity in the face of continued hostility from the powerful capitalist countries contributed to keeping differences behind closed doors. This public unity was also partly a consequence of the ban on organized factions put in place in March 1921—the gradual constriction of the space for genuine debate made it increasingly difficult to challenge majority viewpoints.

The interplay of personalities began to take shape with Lenin's withdrawal from day-to-day politics imposed by his fading health. Part of the uneven struggle that now began—by no means the only important factor—were the different attitudes toward power among the seven other members of the Politburo, who were the contestants to succeed Lenin unless the Politburo could agree to work on a true consensus basis and replace Lenin "collectively." The differences in opinions on major policy questions, more so than personality conflicts, made such a collective system all but impossible. The differences in the attitudes toward power exacerbated those divisions.

- Leon Trotsky and Nikolai Bukharin were motivated to succeed in the onerous task of building socialism, or, more accurately, beginning the onerous task of making the transition from capitalism to socialism. But Trotsky and Bukharin came to have very different ideas on how to manage that transition, so although neither had any interest in power for its own sake, they found working together difficult. Temperaments played a role, too:

Trotsky saw himself as above squabbling with people he deemed not his equals, and Bukharin could be something of a loner. Trotsky and Bukharin were the outstanding theorists among the Politburo members, and the two most able to attract allies and followers among the most conscientious party activists, but they had also been aligned with Lenin for briefer periods of time than the other Politburo members. Trotsky had only joined with the Bolsheviks in 1917 (although he had a warm relationship with Lenin prior to the 1903 split when he joined the Mensheviks), and Bukharin was younger than the others. Nonetheless, both had distinguished backgrounds. Bukharin, the son of two teachers, had begun revolutionary activity at age 16 during the 1905 revolution, quickly rising to prominence. Forced into exile, he was a prolific writer who gained attention for his theoretical thinking. Trotsky became a revolutionary at a similar young age, quickly establishing himself as an outstanding writer; before escaping to exile, his popular commentaries had already earned him the nickname of "The Pen."

- Mikhail Tomskii and Aleksei Rykov were perhaps a little more interested in power, although more concerned with advancing their viewpoints and protecting the interests of those they represented. Tomskii headed the trade unions, defending the consumerist interests of workers and consistently working to retain some measure of independence for the unions (although what he advocated was nowhere to the degree sought by the Workers Opposition). Born into a working-class family, Tomskii began work as a printer when 13 years old and had a long career as a trade union organizer, work he carried out even before joining the party. Rykov, who succeeded Lenin as prime minister, was an advocate of the peasantry and held an important position as head of the Supreme Council of National

Economy. He was born into a peasant family and remained attuned to the moods of the countryside; cautious by nature, his reputation was that of a capable administrator. Tomskii and Rykov had stood with Lenin since 1903, and sided with Lenin during his pre-war factional battles with the syndicalists and "god-builders" that had divided Bolsheviks. They remembered Trotsky's pre-1917 polemics with Lenin; moreover, Tomskii had serious disagreements with Trotsky about the role of the trade unions while Rykov was in conflict with Trotsky over economic policy, eventually coming to believe that the Soviet Union could industrialize solely through internal capital.

- Lev Kamenev and Grigorii Zinoviev, as Lenin's closest associates for many pre-revolutionary years, tended to see themselves as Lenin's rightful heirs, and from here on always traveled together despite the significant differences in their personalities. Kamenev had no aspirations to succeed Lenin, but his cautious nature, belief in a collective post-Lenin leadership and desire to remain with the party majority, even when he initially disagreed with it, led him to oppose Trotsky. Kamenev had a power base by virtue of his leadership of the Moscow party organization, and Lenin repeatedly entrusted him with responsible posts despite the fact that he more than once resigned his office because of disagreements with party policy. Leaving law school to become a revolutionary, he had long served the party as a journalist between stints in prison and exile. Zinoviev joined the party at age 18, after he had begun work as a teacher, and was Lenin's aide-de-camp during long years in European exile. He was very interested in wielding power and was deeply jealous of Trotsky, bitterly resenting Trotsky as a "latecomer" to the party. Zinoviev was the head of the Communist International and of the Bolsheviks' Petrograd organization, and had a considerable reputation as an inspiring orator. But, as we saw in Chapter 1, Zinoviev was vain, egotistical and prone to panic. He had been entirely intellectually dependent on Lenin, and without Lenin to lean on he became unmoored politically and was motivated more by personal aggrandizement than any other consideration.

- Josef Stalin was motivated primarily by an all-consuming desire for personal power and a morbid need for ego gratification. Dull as a writer and speaker, he was a practical underground worker who organized strikes, wrote leaflets and set up presses. Much more controversially to many Bolsheviks and all Mensheviks, he also organized robberies of Caucasian banks (carried out by others) to fund underground work. Stalin grew up in poverty, and had no permanent address after getting kicked out of the seminary where he had been a student. The seminary's student body was a hotbed of radicalism; the grim rigidity of the school undoubtedly fed the militant moods of the students. In his early career, moving among homes of associates and safehouses, Stalin rarely left his native Caucasus region except for when exiled to Siberia, developing an animosity toward the intellectuals in European exile.

As Lenin withdrew from active participation, Kamenev and Zinoviev formed a bloc (a "triumvirate") with Stalin that was motivated more by a desire to block Trotsky from becoming Lenin's successor than for any other reason, although at this time Kamenev and Zinoviev had definite policy differences with Trotsky. Trotsky, by virtue of being almost co-leader of the October Revolution with Lenin, was a natural candidate to succeed Lenin.

Kamenev, Zinoviev and Stalin comprised half of the Politburo at the time of Lenin's decline and death (Bukharin was elected to the body soon after, becoming the seventh member) and because the three voted as a bloc, and the other Politburo members had differences among them, it was easy for the "triumvirs" to win all Politburo votes. The triumvirs would meet beforehand to decide the outcome of votes—technically they were in violation of the rule against organized factions. But while ignoring that rule for themselves, they wielded it as a club to prevent further discussion once a vote had been taken on the basis that the "majority" had decided the issue and further attempts to address the issue amounted to forbidden factionalism.

But significant as they were, it is a common mistake to overrate the role of personalities by focusing solely on the power struggles at the top of the party and on Stalin's personality. The common view that Stalin was extraordinarily paranoid with a morbidly sensitive ego and an extreme will to power merits no refutation; there is ample material in the historical record to support that view. But those personality traits don't explain anything; at best a study of them thrusts the question back one step. For Stalin could do nothing as an individual: He rose to absolute power at the head of a faction, a faction that gradually gained the following of the majority of the party during the 1920s.

It was the Stalin faction, a considerable body, that would carry out the purges, forced collectivization and shock-rate mass industrialization of the 1930s, driving the country to fantastic changes at horrific human cost. How a dull personality such as Stalin—inept and ignorant in theory in a party dominated by theorists, a crude inward-looking nationalist in a party led mostly by educated people with broad international horizons, a virtual unknown who played a small role in a revolution whose leaders became known around the world—rose to power is a question that must be answered in order to come to any kind of understanding of the Soviet Union's development and the rise of the Stalin dictatorship.

Stalin held multiple posts in the party and, after the Civil War, this enabled him to steadily amass power, without others realizing what was happening. During the revolution, Stalin received a small amount of attention from his post as editor of *Pravda*, the party's lead newspaper, but otherwise was little more than a footnote. His posts as minister of nationalities and minister of the Workers' and Peasants' Inspectorate were what enabled him to gather considerable power, and build a following, before becoming general secretary, the decisive post that enabled him to solidify an ever tightening grip on power.

The dozens of national minorities within Russia added up to about 45 percent of the country's population; other than the two non-Russian Slavic nations, Ukrainians and Belorussians, and a small emerging industrial working class in the Caucasus region, these minorities lived in undeveloped societies little changed from the worlds of their ancient ancestors. Stalin became the high party official that local ethnic leaders dealt with, and through whom they sought help in establishing the basis of modernizing their societies. As the revolution cooled into its New Economic Policy period, this large mass of underdevelopment made its influence felt, just as the large mass of the uneducated Russian peasantry did. Many of Stalin's closest followers came from these areas, in particular the Caucasian nations.

Stalin appears not to have paid much attention to the day-to-day functioning of the nationalities ministry during the Civil War, leaving that to deputies, although he did oversee its work and remained the ministry's public face. Stalin seems to have developed some of his methods of ruling here; in 1920, he created a five-person body, a "small collegium" in place of a much larger collegium, to run the ministry[99]—a much smaller top body is much easier to control. The ministry was intended to be the national minorities' representative in the national government and party, but Stalin, in a series of moves designed to tighten his grip on the ministry, instead intended to establish it, and therefore himself, as the overlord of the minorities. Among these moves was the downgrading of subcommittees for individual nationalities, centralizing control within the ministry.[100]

As head of the Workers' and Peasants' Inspectorate, Lenin's pet project to oversee, and root out inefficiency and corruption in, other government ministries, Stalin was able to have his hand in every aspect of government through what developed into a sort of police of the government, albeit a police as inept as the ministries it was overseeing. Simultaneous with these duties, Stalin, as part of his duties as a member of the party's Politburo, also acted as the Politburo's liaison to the Organization Bureau, the party body organizing administrative work that overlapped with the Secretariat's work of assigning personnel.

In 1922, Stalin left the Inspectorate and was elected by the Central Committee to the newly created post of general secretary. Here, personnel work would now be consolidated, making this office a huge fulcrum of influence, although that was something unappreciated at the time, at least by those who elected Stalin to it. Technically, Stalin did have a predecessor, Yakov Sverdlov. Here, again, the subjective factor inserts itself.

Sverdlov was the party's organizer of personnel, being elected as the Central Committee's sole secretary in 1917 after 15 years of underground organizing punctuated by stints in prison and Siberian exile. He escaped from exile to resume clandestine organizing, only to be captured and returned to a more remote Siberian exile inside the Arctic Circle. Shortly after the October Revolution, he became chairman of the Central Executive Committee of the soviets, then a crucial post because this was the body to which the government formally answered in the early months of the revolution. He chaired countless meetings of soviet bodies and others, including opening the ill-fated Constituent Assembly, with never-wavering calm. But it was his organizing skills for which the Bolsheviks most prized him; Sverdlov was seen as a matchless judge of talent and it was he who oversaw all personnel matters.

He had an "encyclopedic knowledge of the entire Party" in the words of Anatolii Lunacharskii, the first Bolshevik minister of education. "If the revolution threw up a large number of tireless workers who appeared to exceed the limits of human capacity, then Sverdlov must be placed in the front rank of such men. When he managed to eat and sleep I do not know."[101] Trotsky wrote that Sverdlov "was truly beyond compare…Time and time again it happened that [Lenin] would pick up the phone in order to propose to Sverdlov a particular emergency measure and in most cases the answer he got was: 'Already.' This meant the measure had already been adopted."[102] Trotsky remembered Sverdlov as the "central organization figure" whom party members repeatedly sought when a problem needing solving.[103] Despite all his achievements, Sverdlov had no power ambitions and seemed highly respected by all who worked with him, a most different character than Stalin.

Sverdlov died suddenly during the 1919 flu pandemic; he had carried out so much responsibility that three secretaries were elected to replace him. If Lenin had remained active just a little longer, he would have ended Stalin's career; if Sverdlov had lived, he would have held the key organizational posts instead of Stalin, and history would have turned out differently. But the social forces that Stalin rode to the heights of power would have still existed, so it is impossible to guess with any precision how different history would have been, other than that the mass bloodletting unleashed by Stalin would not have occurred. Russia's objective conditions, including the promotion into administrative or party posts of so many active working people, and the deaths of many more in the Civil War, the need for massive rebuilding, the ongoing internal and external threats the country faced, the lack of help from more industrialized countries, and the relative passivity of the working class reconstituted from an uneducated peasantry, would have existed just the same.

The size of the Secretariat, by the time of Stalin's appointment in 1922, had grown drastically from Sverdlov's day and personnel were badly needed in all areas of the country, needs that the Secretariat struggled, often unsuccessfully, to meet. One of Stalin's first moves was to reduce the number of positions to be directly filled by the Secretariat by about two-thirds.[104] The Secretariat would now fill 4000 senior positions in the party and government, ranging from the leading regional party bodies to the higher levels of the ministries.[105] Appointments to lesser positions would be entrusted to leading local officials—the Secretariat would have more assurance its appointees were "reliable" because it had to find a much smaller number than before; those "reliable" appointees would be more able to find "reliable" local personnel than would an overextended Secretariat in far-off Moscow.

A year later, regional and local party secretaries were given more power in selecting the personnel to fill local government and other official positions.[106] In part this was done to eliminate miniature power struggles among local officials, but the net effect was to further strengthen Stalin because the party secretaries who would select local cadres were Stalin appointees, diffusing his influence down to the lowest levels.

The rapid centralization of power and concomitant reduction in party democracy did not go completely unnoticed. Evgenii Preobrazhenskii, one of the three Central Committee secretaries who replaced Sverdlov but who were not re-elected in 1921 due to their sympathy with the Workers Opposition, said at a January 1924 party conference: "We must [encourage] a broad discussion of all crucial questions of intra-party life...such that issues of concern to Party members can be posed not only by Party committees, but also on the initiative of Party cells and even individual comrades."[107] Stalin's response was blunt: "Democracy is not something appropriate to all times and places...Democracy demands a certain minimum of culture from the members of [party] cells and organizations as a whole...Of course we need to retreat from it."[108]

Gone were all pretenses to control from below, and although Lenin had frequently lamented the low cultural level of the party, Lenin wished to raise that level as quickly as possible, whereas Stalin now made the low cultural level an excuse to cut off the party rank-and-file from all participation in decision-making, reducing them to the executors of orders from above.

This dismissal of popular participation was no aberration. A little later in 1924, at the party's Thirteenth Congress, Stalin made clear his view of the party:

> A cadre must know how to carry out instructions, must understand them, adopt them as his own, attach the greatest importance to them, and make them part of his very existence. Otherwise, politics loses its meaning and consists merely of gesticulating. Hence the decisive importance of the cadres department in the apparatus of the Central Committee. Every functionary must be closely studied, from every angle and in the most minute detail.[109]

In earlier days, Stalin had not infrequently listened to the complaints of ordinary party members during breaks in, or after, meetings, and he had spent most of his pre-revolutionary career organizing and living among industrial workers, creating an image of accessibility. Now he elevated himself far above the ordinary worker, far above party members, even higher-ranking party officials. Stalin had been entrusted with his positions because of his capacity for administrative work and was not visualized as a potential party leader. But with increased centralization and a lack of controls, the post of general secretary became immensely powerful because its extremely willful holder used it to pack the party and government apparatuses. The general secretary not only had a stranglehold on the assignment of personnel, but as chief of the Secretariat he was in charge of the body responsible for the carrying out of Politburo decisions, and so could twist those decisions to suit his purposes.

As Stalin increasingly controlled the personnel of the party, and could command the loyalty of that personnel, the lower bodies of the party could be packed with his loyalists, ensuring his candidates would gradually fill the higher party positions, eventually even the Politburo. In turn, Stalin's insistence on obedience to orders and his dismissal of democracy meant that the party's regional secretaries were now more secure in their positions, largely shielded from grassroots control, and this in turn promoted loyalty by them to Stalin. Loyalty of party secretaries was a key component of Stalin's ability to eventually control the slates that were elected to party congresses; it was the congresses that in turn elected the Central Committee, and the Central Committee the highest bodies, including the now all-powerful Politburo.

As the 1920s progressed, gone were the days when the party grassroots freely elected delegates to congresses, and the ability of the grassroots to shape party policy and leadership. As Stalin continued to command a majority on the Central Committee and on the Politburo, it was more difficult for the various oppositions to disseminate their ideas. That difficulty played a part in the majority support that Stalin (and whoever his allies were at a given time) was consistently able to muster—these were the ideas and platforms to which party members were exposed. Tactical considerations in political maneuvering were important in shaping these ideas and platforms; until 1929 the majority's ideas were almost always those of Stalin's allies as Stalin and his increasingly tightly controlled faction had few original ideas of their own. Sometimes Stalin would even appropriate opposition positions as he successfully maneuvered among the various factions.

## The origins of the cult of personality, and its effects on the struggle for control at the top

Another critical part of the puzzle of Josef Stalin's rise was his ability to gain the trust of millions of everyday working people—his presentation of himself as Vladimir Lenin's most loyal and most reliable disciple and interpreter. Stalin created a Lenin cult, then built his own personality cult on top.

Any sort of personality promotion was vehemently opposed by Lenin, who lived as a poverty-stricken "professional revolutionary" for virtually all his adult life before barely changing his living style after becoming Russia's leader. Karl Radek, who played a large role in German, Russian and Communist International affairs, once wrote of having to argue repeatedly with Lenin, during the return to Russia in 1917, to replace Lenin's boots, so old they were held together by nails, and buy a new pair of trousers; months later, Radek recalled, Lenin was still wearing the same trousers.[110]

Stalin launched the cult during the week of memorializing Lenin after Lenin's January 1924 death with the recitation of his "Oath to Lenin." Seemingly inspired by his boyhood education in the stifling seminary of Tiflis, Georgia, Stalin spoke with a religious fervor: "In leaving us, Comrade Lenin ordained us to guard the unity of our party like the apple of our eye. We vow to thee, Comrade Lenin, that we shall fulfill honorably this thy commandment, too...In leaving us, Comrade Lenin ordained us to guard and strengthen the dictatorship of the proletariat. We vow to thee, Comrade Lenin, that without sparing our strength we shall fulfill honorably this thy commandment, too."[111]

On the speech went, vows to fulfill a series of "commandments" without ever specifying any detail of Lenin's program.

Stalin's oath was part of a carefully stage-managed week of activity designed to put himself and his fellow triumvirs, Grigorii Zinoviev and Lev Kamenev, in the limelight, subtly promoting themselves as the heirs apparent. It was during this week that

Stalin concocted his scheme to embalm and place on display Lenin's body, disregarding the vehement protests of Lenin's family and the revulsion of much of the party. The commission formed to supervise Lenin's funeral and organize ongoing memorials to Lenin was headed by Viacheslav Molotov,[112] Stalin's loyal lieutenant who was already known as "Stalin's shadow." Much of the work in creating a mausoleum for Lenin's body was supervised by Leonid Krasin and Anatolii Lunacharskii;[113] both were now government ministers but the two had been leaders of the pre-World War I "god-building" faction of the party that Lenin had so vehemently opposed, a faction that had sought to appeal to Russians through religion and spiritualism.

As a further measure, when Leon Trotsky, who was in the Caucasus region having an illness treated, called Stalin on the news of Lenin's death to ask if he should immediately return to Moscow, he was told by Stalin not to bother because the funeral would happen before he would be able to return. Instead, there was a week of ceremony, and with other party leaders standing guard as Lenin lay in state, many wondered why Trotsky was absent. Trotsky returned when his son called to ask him why he wasn't in Moscow.[114]

Stalin had amassed power, but by no means had he secured his power, nor could he maintain it without allies. Stalin was in the process of gaining control over the party through the apparatus of the Secretariat and being part of a steady majority on the Politburo. He was relentlessly extending his control over the government and other bodies—in just his first year as general secretary, for instance, the number of party members among regional trade union leaders increased from 27 percent to 57 percent.[115] A Moscow party vote in late 1923 kept oppositionists from gaining control of the capital city through vote falsification.[116] Less than a year later, Stalin's control over the party machinery enabled him to pack the party congress, which then voted to increase the size of the Central Committee, placing Stalin followers in the new seats.[117]

Although considerable resistance to centralization remained in Moscow and elsewhere, Stalin was now gaining notice among ordinary workers and peasants through his simple language; the "Oath to Lenin" must have had an effect on many religious believers and undoubtedly on some of those not swayed by religious imagery but seeking something in which to believe. Stalin met with considerable success in his claim to be the most faithful follower of Lenin and the leader most qualified to continue the work of Lenin.

However absurd, even darkly comical, that last claim was to the educated veterans of the party—if they seemed to agree on one thing about Stalin, it was that he had no business mixing in theory—there were many rank-and-file members who believed it, and followed Stalin because they still believed in Lenin despite all the tribulations of life since the October Revolution. After Lenin became permanently incapacitated, the triumvirs decided to toss aside the normal high standards for admission to the party and admitted 250,000 "workers from the bench" in an effort to "proletarianize" the ranks; this mass influx became known as the "Lenin Levy."

For the most part, the new recruits were very raw, many recent migrants from the countryside, with little or no understanding of the party's principles and little knowledge of the party's history. The simple language of Stalin, as opposed to the more lofty rhetoric of other party leaders, and Stalin's success in stressing his working-class background, made him seem more accessible to the uneducated and undereducated people who still formed a large majority of the country's population. This formed one leg of Stalin's support. A second leg were the careerists who continued to enter the party despite periodic purges designed to root them out. They formed a natural support base, since failure to back the majority might cost you your job, no insignificant fate considering the persistent unemployment during the New Economic Policy years. And the middle levels of the party, including the regional secretaries, formed another prop of Stalin's rule because their positions were made secure by Stalin's continued tenure.

Stalin, however, still needed to command a majority in the Politburo, since that body decided all things and, should he lose his majority, could vote him out of all offices. Stalin had formed a bloc with Zinoviev and Kamenev, and although at the time there were policy disagreements among them, fear of Trotsky and a deep loathing of the idea of Trotsky becoming the party leader was much stronger. This loathing of Trotsky was the principal animating point of the bloc. The triumvirs' desire to maintain their grip on power was intensified by continuing resistance to centralization.

In the weeks before Lenin died, opposition was building within the party: 46 prominent party veterans, many of whom were heroes of the October Revolution, signed a manifesto calling for a return to democracy in the party and criticizing the party's leadership.[118] In the factories, strikes were breaking out; although some of these were due to frustration with the slow pace of economic recovery and the refusal of the trade unions to take up the interests of their members, others were explicitly political in nature, calling for freedom of discussion.[119] The opposition argued that a lack of economic coordination and increasingly bureaucratic rule had fueled the strikes, and leaders of factory party cells were sympathetic to their fellow workers' demands, often refusing to take any steps to prevent the strikes.[120]

The triumvirs put forth a call seeming to endorse the political demands, but at the same time began unleashing the political police against strikers, expelling some from the party and throwing others into prison. This new level of repression caused Trotsky to begin to voice his opposition to repressive party policies openly, and also inspired the manifesto of the 46. But Trotsky publicly, and in closed Politburo sessions, had vowed to abide by Lenin's rules against organized factions, now interpreted by the triumvirs to forbid any public discussion of any issue already voted on by the Politburo. Trotsky had voted for the rules at the 1921 congress, and this now boxed him in, enabling the triumvirs to openly attack him for alleged breaches of discipline and inconsistency.

The first stepping up of what became a steady stream of attacks on Trotsky was, on the surface, an amazingly irrelevant debate. This episode was noteworthy for the first serious falsification of history and therefore also noteworthy as the beginning of what would become a mainstay of Stalinist propaganda techniques in the coming years. Already, the "debates" were becoming venomous. At the party's Thirteenth Congress, in May 1924 (which was packed by Stalin), Zinoviev thundered denunciations of Trotsky, loudly demanding the party be "monolithic." Zinoviev had already demanded Trotsky's expulsion from the party, even his arrest, and now demanded Trotsky "recant" his viewpoints. Thus another pattern had emerged, in which Zinoviev and Kamenev fulminated, screaming for Trotsky's head, while Stalin appeared relatively reasonable, calmly disagreeing with his fellow triumvirs' demands and declaring at the congress that a party leadership without Trotsky was "unthinkable."[121]

Bound by ever tightening party discipline, Trotsky could not continue to put forth his now evolving views. Soon after, a book of Trotsky's speeches and writings of 1917 was to be published, and Trotsky wrote an introductory essay for it, "The Lessons of October." In the essay, Trotsky surveyed the social forces that create the conditions for a revolution, and the social forces that act against the revolution during the time of upheaval or that throw wrenches into the works after a revolution. As part of this, Trotsky criticized many members of the Bolshevik Old Guard, who did not share Lenin's attitude in the runup to the October

Revolution, and especially targeted Zinoviev and Kamenev for their outright opposition to the seizure of power.[122]

Trotsky's article caused a firestorm of criticism, not only for what he wrote but also for calling attention to Zinoviev's and Kamenev's attitude in October 1917 and therefore defying Lenin's "final testament" in which, in addition to his comments on Stalin, Lenin stated that Zinoviev's and Kamenev's opposition should not be held against them and Trotsky's past as a Menshevik should not be held against him. Although suppressed, the contents were known to the party leadership, and provided the triumvirs, and others in the leadership uneasy about Trotsky, a new opening to attack Trotsky.

A flood of articles challenged Trotsky, and Stalin invented a story that the Military Revolutionary Committee of Petrograd, which Trotsky had led, was not the organizing center of the revolution (which of course it had been), but that a separate party "center" on which Stalin sat actually led the uprising, a claim even Stalin's supporters "received at first with embarrassed irony."[123] But a precedent for falsifying the past was now set, and Trotsky's opponents now dredged out every criticism of Lenin that Trotsky had ever written, going back to 1905 and implying that any record of "deviation" demonstrated untrustworthiness. Although the immediate effect of this campaign was to throw mud on Trotsky's reputation and build up the authority of the triumvirs and those who supported them, it also had the effect of further constricting the scope of possible dissent and signaled what fate might befall anybody who did dare to persist in dissenting.

The power struggle was now on. The triumvirs eventually pushed Trotsky out of his post as army commander and isolated him on the Politburo, neutralizing him. Zinoviev and Kamenev were fully confident they were the senior members of their bloc when in fact Stalin had become the strongest member. With Trotsky out of the way, there was no more glue to hold the triumvirs together, a situation aggravated by the fact that serious programmatic differences had developed among them. Stalin was leaning to the more cautious, pro-peasant policies of the emerging "right wing" of the party leadership while Zinoviev and Kamenev were now switching their backing to the polices enunciated by the emerging "left wing" advocating faster industrialization. Stalin, heading what was now seen as the "center" of the party, next formed a bloc with right leaders Nikolai Bukharin and Aleksei Rykov to defeat Zinoviev and Kamenev. Zinoviev and Kamenev then formed a bloc with Trotsky (the short-lived "United Opposition"), which was defeated in an even harsher manner by a bloc of the Stalin-led center faction, now reinforced by new Politburo members sponsored by Stalin, and the right represented by Bukharin, Rykov and Mikhail Tomskii.

Stalin continued to let others make the harshest attacks in public meetings, although much of this campaign of vilification was now being directed from behind the scenes by him. During the showdown that led to the defeat of the United Opposition, it was, uncharacteristically, the normally affable, scholarly Bukharin who howled for repentance: "Come before the party with head bowed and say: Forgive us, for we have sinned against the spirit and against the letter and against the very essence of Leninism…Why do you not have the common courage to come and say it is a mistake?"[124] Despite the "well done" Stalin offered to Bukharin at this session, Stalin's henchmen soon began, at first softly, attacking Bukharin, and Stalin broke the bloc with the Bukharin-led right, defeating his final opponents in 1929.

Just as earlier the Bolsheviks banned opposing parties and as a consequence lost their own freedom, the same pitiless logic now forced a still more draconian stifling of opposition as the Stalinist faction, having banned opposing factions, now lost its freedom. Because the circle of those allowed to have a voice had become so much smaller, from a party to a faction of that party, harsher methods were needed to keep everyone else silent. Once the faction had won, severe discipline had to be imposed on it to prevent the ideas of the defeated oppositions from gaining traction inside the faction—the momentum of suppressing his own faction resulted in Stalin becoming a sole dictator.

This narrowing of power was further fueled by the fact that Stalin was the unchallenged leader of his faction; he was surrounded by sycophants who had no intention of unseating their master. The oppositions had each featured multiple leaders and had shades of opinion that were thrashed out among themselves; indeed, the oppositions, particularly the main left faction featuring Trotsky and the main right faction featuring Bukharin, possessed a range of ideas and sought to face the dire problems and increasing crises of the 1920s. The Stalinist "center" tended to vacillate but mostly followed the policies of the right faction, and this accounted for the left faction saving most of its harshest words for the party's right rather than for the Stalinist center.

The increasing harshness in the way that oppositions were treated, and the increasingly vehement demands for repentance, played a role as well in paving the road to the single-person dictatorship. By the late 1920s, gone were the days when agreeing to not re-address a controversy was sufficient. After the defeat of the "United Opposition," Zinoviev and Kamenev were allowed to remain in the party only by formally renouncing their own beliefs, and even then only after a "probation" period. Stalin and his followers could not resist kicking the prostrate.

Many others would soon also renounce their views, but having crossed the rubicon of self-abasement, the price of re-admission to the party would only become more humiliating, and the price for not living up to every demand more severe. All sides still believed in the single-party system, believing that the collapse of the country into chaos was the only alternative to continued Bolshevik monopoly of power, but alternative views could not be heard inside it. The oppositions were unable to square the closed circle within which their belief that there could be only one post-revolution party had trapped them.

Because of Stalin's adoption of Bukharin's policies and because the right held so many prominent positions, such as editorships of the leading newspapers, many on the left saw the imminent victory of the right. But Stalin's control of the party machinery made that belief an illusion. After the defeat of the "United Opposition," and as Bukharin was allowing himself to open his eyes to Stalin's intentions and started sending feelers to the defeated left, Trotsky declared: "With Stalin against Bukharin? Yes. With Bukharin against Stalin? Never!"[125] With the clarity of hindsight, that statement sounds astonishing. But Trotsky, in exile at the time of this statement, still believed that Bukharin would win because of the *appearance* that the right was in command, and his statement reflected the serious differences in programs between the right and left wings, which was as important as the oppositions' common desire for a return to party democracy.

The left still viewed the right's programs as appeasement of kulaks and NEP traders, and feared that further strengthening of those groups, and of a growing bureaucracy also receiving privileges, would lead to an overthrow of the revolution and the restoration of capitalism. Mere months after his confident public attacks on the left in which he demanded repentance, Bukharin fearfully told Kamenev of the "new Genghis Khan"—Stalin—and begged Kamenev to keep their discussion secret lest the Stalin-controlled secret police find out about it.

Why had so many followed this new Genghis Khan? It was never certain that Stalin would emerge as the final victor in the power struggle, or that there would even be a single victor. Even at this point, nobody could imagine the terrible vengeance Stalin would wreak on party, government and country, nor could they have imagined the "Great Change" of forced collectivization and speeded-up industrialization about to descend on the country that would have a more profound effect on the country than had the October Revolution.

The Stalin that so many began following in the 1920s either saw a different Stalin, thought the center faction's policies were the correct ones or simply thought their proper place was with the majority of the party. The one theoretical idea that Stalin promoted—it is unclear whether he or Bukharin actually came up with it, but it was Stalin who popularized the idea—was the concept of "socialism in one country." Stalin's primary reason for this slogan was to have something with which to oppose Trotsky's "theory of the permanent revolution." Simply put, Trotsky's theory was the belief that no one country could advance to socialism on its own, certainly not an undeveloped country such as Russia; it would take several industrialized countries having a revolution and forming a large enough bloc to survive the inevitable capitalist counterattacks. This belief, as we saw in Chapter 1, animated the Bolsheviks' staking Russia's revolution on European revolution.

Help from Europe not forthcoming, and surviving the capitalist world's attempts to undo the revolution by inflaming the Civil War, Russia needed a consolation. "Socialism in one country," the belief that Russia could advance to socialism all on its own with no outside help, was that consolation, and an understandably attractive one.

Nikita Khrushchev, Stalin's eventual successor, provides an example of a lower-level, but rising, party member who early on threw in his lot with Stalin. (Khrushchev's career was guided by Lazar Kaganovich, one of Stalin's chief lieutenants, also an example of Stalin's leading followers in turn promoting loyalty to them, and therefore to Stalin.) Khrushchev was elected as a delegate to the party's Fourteenth Congress, in 1925, where he met Stalin for the first time and was "very impressed."[126]

Stalin had agreed to sit for a photo with the Ukrainian delegation, of which Khrushchev was a member. (Kaganovich was the head of the Ukrainian branch of the party at the time.) The photographer was giving instructions on how to pose, Khrushchev wrote, when "Stalin remarked in a voice everyone could hear, 'Comrade Petrov [the photographer] loves to order people around. But now that's forbidden here. No one may order anyone else around ever again.' Even though he said this jokingly, we all took him seriously and were heartened by the democratic spirit he displayed."[127] Khrushchev then recounted a story about Stalin receiving a delegation from a city that had just renamed itself for Stalin and which asked the general secretary to send greetings back to the city's workers. Stalin refused on the grounds that the workers "weren't serfs on my farm," and said it would be "insulting" to them to write a letter of greeting. One of the delegates, Khrushchev wrote, "spread this story around to illustrate Stalin's democratic spirit, his accessibility, and his proper understanding of his place."[128]

At the next party congress, in 1927, Khrushchev supported Stalin wholeheartedly, and the Ukrainian delegation received their instructions from Stalin. At this time, "we had no doubt in our minds that Stalin and his supporters were right, and that the opposition was wrong," Khrushchev wrote in his memoirs, decades later.

> I still think that Stalin's ideological position was basically correct. We realized that a merciless struggle against the opposition was unavoidable. We justified what was happening in a lumberjack's terms: when you chop down a forest, the chips fly…Stalin was a powerful personality, and he had contributed greatly to the mobilization of the Party's forces for the reconstruction of our industry and agriculture and the strengthening of our army.[129]

Bukharin expressed the feelings of the party's rank-and-file in a different way, but with similar conclusions, in 1933, while on a trip to Paris. Bukharin, already doomed, was asked by a Menshevik émigré, Fedor Dan, how he and others could have entrusted their fate to such a "devil" as Stalin. Bukharin replied, "You do not understand, it was quite different; he was not trusted [by us], but he was the man whom the party [rank-and-file] trusted. This is how it happened: he is like the symbol of the party, the lower strata, the workers, the people, trust him. Perhaps it is our fault, but that's the way it happened, that is why we all walked into his jaws."[130]

Stalin had carefully presented himself as an ordinary worker raised up to help other ordinary workers. In a visit to Georgia in 1926, Stalin, in a speech, declared that "my first teachers were the Tblisi workers" and although he might have been a little better read than they, he said he had been "as a practical worker...without a doubt just an apprentice."[131]

## The surprising tepidness of change on the shop floor and in the countryside in NEP Russia

Despite the sweeping political changes, and continued labor militancy, everyday working conditions changed surprisingly little on the shop floors during the years of the New Economic Policy. A labor code enacted in November 1922, however, protected workers from dismissal except for flagrant violations.[132] A Rates Conflict Commission was created to arbitrate disputes; management and workers sat on this board in equal numbers.[133] Tens of thousands of cases were sent to the arbitration board until 1928, with workers winning a majority of cases, helping to dampen labor unrest.[134]

The way that work was organized showed less evolution. In the cotton mills, for instance, workers worked much the same as they had before the revolution. One reason for this was the age of the machinery. As late as 1927, more than 80 percent of cotton-industry machinery dated from 1909 or earlier, and about half from the nineteenth century.[135] Because of the cutoff of foreign trade there was little chance of importing newer machinery and, until Soviet industry could get back on its feet, little hope of significant machinery being produced internally. This was not unique to the cotton industry. Russia had always imported about 70 percent of its capital goods; it did not possess the ability to meet its machinery needs.[136]

The cutoff of imports also meant that lower-quality cotton from Soviet Central Asia had to be substituted for higher-quality cotton from elsewhere, and spinners had to repair the machines they worked on as there was a shortage of trained technicians, further lowering production.[137] The rhythms of the land also hurt efficiency; the staff of many cotton mills were comprised of peasants, large numbers of whom would return to the land at harvest time. Their ties to the land enabled them to resist periodic "speed-up" plans.[138]

Other patterns from before the revolution survived, some peculiar to specific industries. Younger workers were often treated badly in the printing industry, for example—they were frequently expected to run errands for the foremen, enduring this in the hopes of moving up when one of a limited number of openings emerged.[139] As a male-dominated bastion, the foremen and older printers had difficulty accepting women despite the revolutionary spirit that sought equality between men and women—women made up one-third of the printing industry personnel in Moscow in 1920; they had constituted 5 percent as recently as 1912.[140] The printers union journal regularly reported on sexual harassment; more egregious examples were sometimes punished by "comrades' courts."[141]

Despite the new gender egalitarianism promoted by the party, and some men's acceptance of an increased role in public life for women, women still bore the brunt of domestic duties. Women responded by organizing cafeterias so as to provide themselves with sufficient time to attend meetings.[142] Women working in metal factories also won the right to take two hours off per day to feed their babies.[143]

In contrast to blue-collar workers, white-collar workers saw more changes, and this strata's composition was subject to upheaval as factory workers were frequently "promoted" to white-collar jobs, with varying results. In a June 1929 speech, Mikhail Kalinin, the president of the Soviet Union (a post that was ceremonial), gave a speech at a trade union congress in which he lamented "mechanical affirmative action," noting that a "valued person makes good money in the factory, so don't promote a metalworker into a typist, don't make them into bureaucratic paper pushers."[144] Kalinin had noted that blue-collar workers who moved to an office were often miserable. With ideology playing a large role in the conduct of policy, the social position of office workers seemed to be a particularly difficult "problem" to solve.

This "problem" also manifested itself in higher education. Students wishing to be admitted to a university had their backgrounds examined to determine their "class status," and this led to young men and women proclaiming that they had broken all political ties with parents from relatively privileged backgrounds.[145] Despite the particular ambiguity of the class status of white-collar workers in the minds of Bolshevik officials, white-collar workers were equal in numbers to their blue-collar counterparts by 1926, and factory workers constituted only a minority of urban residents.[146]

At this point, the main union for white-collar workers, the Union of Soviet and Commercial Employees, was the Soviet Union's largest union, and it was a heterogeneous mix of many professions, from bankers to bookkeepers to members of the secret police.[147] The union had enjoyed the support of Lenin, but in the more uncertain political environment that evolved as the 1920s progressed, its leadership firmly backed Stalin,[148] although that support did not provide protection from purges.

Despite the surprising lack of change in work culture in many industries, the 1920s were nonetheless a decade of ferment in which opportunities for advancement and social mobility unfolded for millions who would have had no chance at this prior to the October Revolution. Enrollment in primary and secondary schools doubled by the late 1920s, wages had increased (albeit slowly), the average workday was reduced to seven and a half hours from ten hours, health care had significantly improved and with it social indications of health, and there was much more access to the arts, such as museums and theaters.[149]

But despite the improvements in so many areas, they fell short of revolutionary expectations, and urban workers harbored a multitude of resentments against "Nepmen" (those who flourished as traders under the New Economic Policy) and against kulaks. The party made a series of concessions to the peasantry, who had benefited the most from NEP. A desire for further improvements in living standards, continuing shortages of adequate housing in the cities and frustrations that their unions represented the state rather than the workers led to continuing urban unrest. Continuing high unemployment despite the growth of industry also played a role, and acted to suppress wages. Union officials calculated that 17 percent of their membership was out of work in January 1927.[150]

Not only did the arbitration board, the Rates Conflict Commission, provide the government with a safety valve, but the increasing regimentation imposed on workers and the subordinate role of unions contributed to a steady decline in work stoppages. The number of workers who struck fell by more than two-thirds from 1924 to 1927.[151] Those who did strike did so for a variety of reasons. In 1924, an attempt to require textile workers to be responsible for more machines was rescinded after a three-day strike,[152] and metalworkers repeatedly struck over pay and work conditions from 1922 to 1924, with mixed results.[153]

Nor was the political dimension missing—a shop representative in a metalworking plant demanded that "workers must know where funds are going, must control production. Layoffs were initiated in connection with the monetary reform. And what do we see? In the first instance, they lay off workers and employees. And in the trusts, everything remains as of old."[154] Corruption was also an issue—many NEP traders were state employees who used their official job to acquire scarce supplies with which to stock their private stores or to cut deals with their relatives.[155]

This unrest did sometimes lead to concessions; the higher ranks of the party were not kept in the dark. Reports supplied to them throughout the 1920s by the secret police tended to be critical of administrative and party bosses, and frequently vindicated the demands of workers, including those of strikers.[156]

Large numbers of soldiers demobilized from the Red Army at first were a significant contributing factor to the swelling of the ranks of unemployed, but as the 1920s progressed, steady streams of peasants seeking work continued to buoy unemployment rates. As many as three million peasants per year, primarily small farmers, sought work in cities,[157] mostly as permanent migrants but including some who worked seasonally before returning to the countryside. This stream of migrants appeared to many veteran factory workers to be a flood threatening to swamp their living standards; unions began responding to their members' fears of unemployment and wage cuts by advocating measures to stem this flow, and in 1928 the All-Union Central Council of Trade Unions tightened its regulations to make it more difficult for peasants to enter the unions.[158]

Despite this steady migration, the Soviet Union's population was nearly 80 percent rural by the end of the decade, and although the upheavals of 1917 had eliminated the landlord and the crushing debts imposed on the smallholder, rural culture seemed to be barely touched. Villagers remained deeply mired in a dense network of superstition; priests blessed houses and farms on feast days, blessed cattle in the spring with the use of whole eggs baked inside pierogies and "Holy Thursday salt," and were used on a myriad of other occasions, including to protect cattle from witchcraft.[159] An assortment of "midwives," "witches," "wizards" and "soothsayers" were also consulted on a huge variety of issues, including to heal sickness; this situation persisted despite the government establishing health clinics and hospitals.[160] Across the country, priests incited religious believers to believe that Soviet power would lead to the coming of the "Antichrist," the final judgment or "invasions of barbaric pagan hordes from China."[161]

One policy intended to modernize the countryside was a program to assist soldiers discharged from Red Army service in forming collective farms. This became more systematic in 1925, when the party Central Committee authorized funding for soldiers to be taught new trades.[162] Newly discharged soldiers usually met resistance from village elites when they made arguments for collectivization, and as a result set up collectives themselves and either organized their own local party bodies and soviets or contested local elections as a bloc.[163] Voluntarily created collective farms were created throughout the 1920s and provided grain surpluses for trade, although before 1929 they represented a minuscule fraction of the total number of farms.

Attempts at modernization met with some success in other fields during the 1920s. There was considerable experimentation with the penal system, and a linchpin of penal reform were court sentences of "obligatory labor," in which the convicted was to serve the sentence working at his or her regular job, with a paycheck deduction to cover fines.[164] There were also camps designed for convicted criminals in which the guilty worked during the day and then went home nights; but there was also a secret-police prison camp for political prisoners on the White Sea near the Arctic Circle.[165]

A new family code was put on the books in 1918, providing for no-fault divorce (a feat that would not be achieved in New York for more than 90 years), a guarantee of women's economic rights, the right to alimony and the right of all children, born inside or outside a marriage, to support. The code was designed to "establish absolute equality of men and women before the law," in the words of one of the drafters.[166] A 1925 revision recognized common-law marriages and granted alimony rights to unmarried partners.[167] Abortion was legalized and a birth control clinic was opened in Moscow.[168] But this modern code was in a sense suspended above the reality of the country.

More women were working, but, in 1926, earned only 65 percent of what men earned and, throughout the decade, suffered from higher rates of unemployment and longer periods of being out of work.[169] And the right to family support was curtailed by economic realities—paychecks were too small to support two families, as women whose husbands had left to form a new family often complained.[170]

Many gains by women, however, would be taken away by Stalin in the next decade.

The 1920s saw a tremendous flowering of the arts, with outstanding works in numerous disciplines, including painting, film, music, theater, poetry and fiction. Several movements in painting blossomed after the revolution, and several schools and institutes were organized by Anatolii Lunacharskii, the education minister from 1917 to 1929, while others were supported by the trade unions.[171] During the Civil War, Lunacharskii set up a purchasing commission to buy paintings for three dozen museums, providing an outlet for avant-garde painters that did not previously exist.[172] During the course of the 1920s, however, more conservative artists steadily eclipsed the avant-garde in the field of painting, although other arts continued to find creative expression. Nonetheless, artistic freedom was tightly constricted upon the victory of the Stalin faction. In March 1931, a decree was published criticizing "anti-

Soviet art" and demanding scrutiny over artistic production.[173]

Until then, for many, the freer air after the stifling censorship of the tsars was intoxicating enough; for others, a sense of opportunity opened. "For the first time," the novelist and playwright Valentin Katayev said, "we felt freed of all the weight and prejudice of the old world, from the obligations of family, religion and even morality; we were intoxicated by the air of freedom…The revolution opened up unlimited opportunities for us."[174] The poet Vladimir Mayakovsky was still more blunt when he wrote of the pre-revolutionary past: "Down with *your* love…down with *your* art…down with *your* régime…down with *your* religion."[175]

Mayakovsky became something of a "house artist" for the government, once writing a toadying ode to the secret police and its founder, Feliks Dzerzhinsky, but being simultaneously an official and an avant-garde artist is impossible. Mayakovsky, chafing under the inevitable boundaries within which he had placed himself, committed suicide in 1930.[176] Mayakovsky's fate was a grim foretelling of what lay ahead for artists.

## The debate over "socialist accumulation" and the gathering crises of standing still

Surrounding all the arguments, all the social ferment, all the struggles for power in the party, was a very basic question that could not be postponed indefinitely: Where would the Soviet Union find the means to create modern industry and modernize its agriculture? Massive investments were necessary for these goals, but where would the capital come from?

The revolution didn't, and couldn't, wave a magic wand and wish away the devastation, the grinding poverty, the massive illiteracy and lack of education. It couldn't build a better society without a massive effort and expenditure in raising the cultural and educational level of its citizens, and a massive effort and expenditure was needed even to begin to tackle the job of economic development.

The capital needed simply didn't exist. And with no elder brothers and sisters to lend a helping hand due to the lack of revolutions in Europe, and a virtual boycott of the country by the capitalist powers save a small, secret trade with Germany, still ostracized by the victors of World War I, there would be little foreign capital available.

The capital the Soviet Union needed could come only from within its borders.

This was the question that permeated political debates of the 1920s. Simply put, the capital could only come by extracting surplus value from workers and peasants and re-investing enterprise profit in economic projects. This meant suppressing wages of, and forcing greater productivity from, workers and extracting more surplus grain from the peasants. The party's economic debates centered on where this extraction of surplus value would come from and at what tempo. Because the peasantry formed an overwhelming majority of the country, most of the extraction of surplus value would come from farmers, no matter how far wages for urban workers were reduced or how much industrial productivity could be improved.

But with the countryside broken up into 25 million farms, most of which were small and could produce no more than enough food to sustain the family that worked it, and worked with wooden ploughs as mechanization was still a rarity on the farms, agriculture was at a miserably low level. Producing enough grain to feed the country would be something of a struggle; it would be difficult to generate the large surpluses necessary for export—grain exports were the commodity most likely to bring in badly needed finished goods or capital in return. The pooling together of these small farms into larger, more efficient units was an unavoidable necessity. But as the peasants were content with their new plots and freedom from their old landlords despite their ongoing poverty, incentives were needed to induce them to pool their land together to create the larger farms.

Creating these incentives was impossible without a larger industrial base than the country possessed. Larger farms could not be worked properly without tractors and other modern mechanized equipment, and the cities also had to produce finished goods with which to trade in exchange for agricultural products. The state had to make it economically advantageous for the peasant to join a collective farm and at the dawn of the New Economic Policy the means with which to do this did not exist. Because agriculture was in such a primitive state, it could bounce back quickly from the ravages of World War I and the Civil War, but the pre-war level was insufficient.

Industry was even further behind, and needed a much more prodigious effort just to rebound to pre-war levels, an effort hindered by the dispersal of the working class during the Civil War. But reaching the pre-war level of productivity would be grossly inadequate. A much higher level had to be reached if industry was to adequately meet the needs of urban workers, a population again steadily increasing, and also meet not only the consumer needs of farmers but create the equipment needed to make modernized agriculture work.

These huge needs required a sizable heavy-industry infrastructure that had to be built mostly from scratch. Not only would the capital required to build this infrastructure result in less capital being available, therefore reducing capacity to properly meet consumer demand (including basic needs like housing), but the capital would have to come, at least in part, from suppression of wages and speeding up work, still another source of lowered living standards for urban workers and their families.

This double-whammy was unavoidable and, given the desperate need for the peasantry to produce surplus grain, priority had to be given to meeting peasants' needs before urban workers' needs. Thus, the party that came to power as the representative of workers had to favor the peasantry instead. Compounding this situation was the difficulty in obtaining the raw materials needed to create industry because so many mines were destroyed either by the German and Austrian armies during World War I or by the White armies during the Civil War. Time and effort would be needed to re-create the means of supplying adequate raw materials.

The New Economic Policy was designed to provide a breathing spell, but NEP, with its re-institution of some capitalism in what became a mixed economy, was not a permanent solution. All sides were in agreement that progress had to be made in both the agricultural and industrial sectors; that the creation of collective farms and the development of industry were essential. But there were wide disagreements in tempo and emphasis.

The viewpoint of the party's left faction, that of the most rapid reasonably possible industrialization, was the first to crystallize, and was first articulated by Evgenii Preobrazhenskii in 1924. He first drew an analogy with Karl Marx's explanation of the early stages of capitalism, in which Marx outlined the brutal "primitive accumulation of capital," in which the newly ascendant capitalist class, or "bourgeoisie," conducted a "systematic plundering" of everything around it. In this manner, the early robber barons of the United States and their equivalents in other countries acquired massive, unheard-of wealth for themselves, but as a consequence also accumulated the capital on which a growing capitalist economy can be built. One need only think of Dickensian Britain or the nineteenth-century urban slums of the United States to be reminded of the horrors of this "primitive accumulation of capital." Preobrazhenskii did not propose anything anywhere near this harsh, but used this example to create the concept of "primitive socialist accumulation of capital."

The Soviet Union had to industrialize rapidly; it would fail otherwise, Preobrazhenskii argued. But with industry at such a small level, it could not produce more than a small fraction of the capital needed for rapid industrialization. Therefore, with little capital available from foreign sources, the primary source for that needed capital must be the private sector, a sector dominated by the peasantry. Unfortunately for his cause, he was less than tactful in proposing an extraction of wealth from the peasants, calling for increased prices for industrial goods and decreased prices for agricultural goods, "a price consciously aimed at the exploitation of the private economy in all its forms."[177]

Preobrazhenskii was also frank in stating that this policy would also mean differentiations in the cities because the shortage of consumer goods that would result from the emphasis on developing heavy industry would mean material advantages for skilled workers, technicians and administrators.[178] The Soviet Union would have to "take the productionist and not the consumptionist point of view…We do not yet live in a socialist society with its production for the consumer. We are only in the period of primitive socialist accumulation—we live under the iron heel of the law of that accumulation," he wrote.[179]

Only with increased societal wealth and education can these differentiations disappear. Until then, "This process of extending and consolidating the state economy can proceed both at the expense of its own forces and resources, that is, the surplus product of the workers in state industry, and at the expense of private, including peasant (itself including middle-peasant) economy. Can it be otherwise?"[180]

The use of the word "exploitation" provided critics favoring a slower rate of growth an opening to pounce on Preobrazhenskii, and he was forced to backtrack from that term. But his theory gained support among those on the left, including Leon Trotsky, although with certain reservations; Trotsky objected to the implication of Preobrazhenskii's theory that the Soviet Union could build socialism on its own nor was he convinced that the primitive accumulation would fall so heavily on the peasants.[181] The center and right factions would soon sneer that those on the left were "super-industrializers" and "anti-peasant," with Josef Stalin loudly making these accusations; only a few years later Stalin would adopt policies that would make the left's proposals look milquetoast in comparison.

It was Nikolai Bukharin, the best theorist of the right/center bloc, who developed a counter-theory. It might at first seem strange that Bukharin, who had consistently been to the left during all the major debates until the early 1920s, now found himself heading the party's right faction. This switch was a consequence of the failure of revolutions to take place in Europe. Bukharin's viewpoints had always been staked on his belief in imminent European revolution, and now Bukharin was forced to admit that Russia had to go it alone. Thus he now developed theories predicated on the unlikelihood of outside help. This meant, Bukharin was convinced, the need to go slow, and in principle going slow meant progressing at the pace of the least developed part of the economy: agriculture. Further cementing his new outlook was that there was no alternative to a strong alliance between the Soviet Union's workers and peasants. There would be nowhere else to turn.

The implementation of Bukharin's theory would mean continuing concessions to the peasantry and an encouragement of their consumerist interests; in practice, this meant the strengthening of the kulaks, the farmers with the most land. Bukharin's equivalent of Preobrazhenskii's "exploitation" remark was his call for the peasants to "enrich yourselves." In practice, that call meant for the kulaks to enrich themselves because only the numerically tiny upper strata of the countryside was in a position to accumulate wealth. The left objected to Bukharin's remark not only because it offended the notion of equality, which would have been bad enough, but because it was seen as dangerous to encourage kulaks, who, as the primary suppliers of surplus grain, possessed the power to starve the cities, a fear that was not without merit in light of kulak hoarding in 1925. Bukharin was forced by party opinion to disavow the remark.

The essence of Bukharin's theory was embodied in his slogan "Socialism at a snail's pace." The foundation for this program was an emphasis on trade. More trade would mean faster economic growth and thus a concomitant increased development of industry to meet this stimulated demand. Creating more commodities and accelerating their trade "would provide space for the fullest development of productive forces."[182]

To help stimulate this increased trade, Bukharin advocated lowering the prices of industrial products. Because the country remained predominantly peasant, the market for this increased trade would necessarily be dominated by peasant demand; therefore peasants had to be allowed to accumulate wealth and this would provide the stimulant to enlarge the overall economy. Thus, Bukharin argued, the peasants and even the "Nepmen" (private traders) would "objectively [be in] the service of socialist state industry and the economy of the whole" because the socialist sector's greater efficiency and resources would allow it to gradually displace the private sector.[183]

Bukharin summed up his ideas later, in a 1926 talk: "First, if commodity turnover in the country grows, this means that more is produced, more is bought and sold, more is accumulated: this means that our socialist accumulation is accelerated, i.e., the development of our industry…Second, from the capitalist elements which grow on this soil, we receive additional income in the form of growing tax revenues."[184]

Objections to Bukharin's policy, which had become the official party line with Stalin's backing, were not long in coming. In the summer of 1925, deliveries of grain dropped and shortages of food began to occur; from the point of view of the cities, making concessions to the kulaks did not appease them, and the people of Leningrad in particular raised an outcry.[185] This strengthened position of the kulaks alienated the far more numerous middle and poor peasants, who produced little surplus and so could not gain from policies favoring the kulaks, as one of Stalin's followers, Anastas Mikoyan, acknowledged when he declared later that year that "We are making great efforts to regain the middle peasant, who has become the kulak's political prisoner."[186] The Leningrad opposition was expressed by the party's city organization, controlled by Grigorii Zinoviev until Stalin pushed Zinoviev's followers out later in 1925, thereby silencing a significant source of opposition.

The slow pace of industrialization and negligible pace of agricultural rationalization caused the Left Opposition to continue to argue for a change in policy before further crises set in. In 1927, Trotsky authored the "Platform of the Joint Opposition," reflecting the temporary alliance of the Left Opposition with the followers of Zinoviev and Lev Kamenev. (The platform was forbidden to be published by Stalin.)

The platform argued that the lag in developing industry, transportation and electrification retarded the markets for agricultural products—for both internal consumption and for export—and therefore caused prices and production costs to rise. Further, official attempts at lowering prices were decreed only at the wholesale level; prices to consumers at the retail level remained high and therefore private traders were pocketing the difference with no extra capital made available for the development of the socialist sector.[187]

"The necessary acceleration of industrialization is impossible without a systematic and determined lowering of the costs of production and of wholesale and retail prices of industrial goods, and their approximation to world prices," Trotsky wrote in the platform.[188] He disapproved of the modest goals for the next few years set by the ruling group, and further complained that a modest projected drop in retail prices and modest projected increase in income would be offset by raising rents by 200 to 250 percent, in effect cutting the purchasing power of workers.[189]

At this point, the gathering crisis of standing still had to be acknowledged, and for the first time, the ruling bloc, led by Stalin and Bukharin, proposed stronger rates of industrialization, but proposed to finance this faster tempo at the expense of urban workers. In contrast, Trotsky proposed to increase the tax rate on private traders, who were accumulating fortunes and would be left nearly untouched by the official plans, and "to assure a collection from the well-off *kulak* levels…which should be collected in the form of a loan from those stores of grain."[190] In other words, kulaks would be required to give up some of the grain they were hoarding for speculation, but would be paid for it in the future, rather than immediately, in order to provide some economic relief—the "loaned" grain would be used to feed the cities and provide a surplus that could be exchanged for badly needed foreign products.

Trotsky also called for lowering retail and wholesale prices, and reducing the disparity between them,

> in such a way that the lowering of prices affects above all objects of mass consumption among workers and peasants…This lowering of prices should not deprive state industry of its necessary accumulations and should be carried out chiefly by way of an increase of the mass of goods, a lowering of the cost of production [through efficiency], a lessening of overhead charges and a cutting down of the bureaucratic apparatus.[191]

During the 1920s, the peasantry was divided into four groupings. Landless peasants hired themselves to other farmers or sought temporary work in industry. The poor peasants were those who did not have sufficient land to sustain themselves and thus had to hire themselves out to kulaks, and sometimes had to lease their land to kulaks, an arrangement that forced the poor farmer, as the owner of the land, to pay taxes on it while the kulak reaped the profits from the crops grown on it—another consequence of pro-peasant policies that were actually pro-kulak in practice. The middle peasants were those who were self-sufficient without hiring themselves out or hiring others, and could produce a small marketable surplus. The kulaks had the largest plots of lands and hired farmhands. Separate from all these individual farms were a minuscule number of collective farms, which yielded a higher percentage of marketable grain than did private farms of any size.

The commanding position of the kulaks was illustrated by a 1924 study by Kamenev that reported that 74 percent of individual farms were small, 18 percent middle and 8 percent kulak, yet 61 percent of the marketable grain was produced by the kulaks.[192] (Other studies tended to report smaller numbers of kulaks and small peasants and larger numbers of middle peasants.) But it was Stalin who ridiculed the notion that the kulaks represented any danger, saying, in 1925: "Those who are panic-stricken at the thought of this danger are prone to scream: 'Help, help, the kulak is coming! It is strange!"[193] Stalin declared suggestions that a struggle be directed against the kulaks "quite inappropriate"[194] and in 1928, on the eve of beginning his forced collectivization, declared that "people who think that individual farming is at the end of its tether and is not worth supporting…have nothing in common with the line of our party."[195]

The working class still had some influence on policy, and played a role even in as momentous a decision as the onset of forced collectivization and the struggle against kulaks. But even with the numerical recomposition of the working class, and its subsequent growth throughout the 1920s, the party apparatus tightened its control and centralized decision-making. There were many factors behind this development, as outlined in this chapter. Marxists had forecast an organized working class, a proletariat, that would govern society as a whole, and although the silence of the working class was somewhat exaggerated by the Left Opposition, a faction of the party leadership had substituted itself for the party as a whole, which had earlier substituted itself for the working class.

Bukharin, not long after the Civil War had ended, already was formulating a theory as to why this condition had come about. He believed that the traditional Marxist analogy of the transition from feudalism to capitalism with the transition from capitalism to socialism had to be reconsidered. The class that emerged from feudalism to take the helm of the nascent capitalist state, the bourgeoisie (industrialists and financiers), had built up its strength as feudalism broke down, and through its command of capital emerged as an elite and thus was culturally ready to administer the new state and mold it in its interests. But under capitalism, the bourgeoisie monopolized not only the means of production but also the means of practical education, shutting out all others from any meaningful societal role and thereby relegating the rest of society to backwardness, according to Bukharin.

"It is not possible for the working class, under the rule of capitalism, to so educate itself as to be capable of undertaking the leadership of society," Bukharin wrote in 1923.

> Under the rule of capitalism the working class is enslaved and oppressed. In order to rise, [the working class] must break down the capitalist shell which envelops society. It cannot train its forces, prove its powers of organization and undertake the leadership of society, until the period of the dictatorship [of the proletariat]. During this period the working class develops its real nature, the slave is trans-

> formed into creator and lord. This gigantic work is one demanding the utmost exertions on the part of the masses and their vanguard.[196]

A year earlier, Bukharin had written that the working class was unable "to prepare itself for organizing all of society. It is successful in preparing itself for 'the destruction of the old world'...[but] it ripens as the organizer of society only in the period of its dictatorship."[197] (To recapitulate, the theoretical concept of the "dictatorship of the proletariat" refers to an anticipated post-capitalist rule by working people, who constitute a huge majority in industrial countries, in contrast to the rule of capitalists in capitalist countries.)

Within this reasoning, however, is a kernel justifying the party's view of itself as a "vanguard," and thus entitled to substitute itself for the working class as a whole. With the vanguard arrogating decision-making to itself, inevitably a privileged strata will arise, which will exert itself to maintain its privileges. Trotsky saw Stalin as the leading exemplifier of this tendency; this was the basis for his formulation of Stalin as "the outstanding mediocrity in the party." And while the increasing dictatorial capabilities of a directing center and the non-participation of society is something of a "chicken or egg" problem, a confident, active society that is politically engaged won't allow itself to be dominated.

A leading theorist of the Left Opposition and a long-time collaborator of Trotsky, Christian Rakovsky (he had been the first Bolshevik leader of Ukraine and defended Ukraine's autonomy against Stalin's attempts at Russian centralization), puzzled over this problem from internal exile near the end of the decade. "No one today can ignore the terrible consequences of the political indifference of the working class," Rakovsky wrote.[198]

Examining the problem, Rakovsky continued:

> When a class takes power, one of its parts becomes the agent of that power. Thus arises bureaucracy. In a socialist state, where capitalist accumulation is forbidden by members of the directing party, this differentiation begins as a functional one; it later becomes a social one. I am thinking here of the social position of a communist who has at his disposal a car, a nice apartment, regular holidays, and receives the maximum salary authorized by the party; a position which differs from that of the communist working in the coal mines and receiving [a much lower salary].[199]

Because of the stratification that develops from this social differentiation, and as a result of the lack of education before the revolution, learning how to exert itself is something the working class as a whole has to learn:

> No class has been born in possession of the art of government. This art can only be acquired by experience, thanks to the errors committed, that is by each learning from his errors. No Soviet constitution, be it ideal, can ensure to the working class an exercise without obstacle of its dictatorship and its control over the government if the proletariat does not know how to utilize its rights under the constitution.[200]

As a result, Rakovsky wrote, "the psychology of those charged with the diverse tasks of direction in the administration and the economy of the state has changed to such a point that not only objectively but subjectively, not only materially but also morally, they have ceased to be a part of this very same working class." By equating the "factory director playing the satrap...in spite of his proletarian origins" and other "bureaucratic degenerations" with the "dictatorship of the proletariat," the party "only succeeds in discrediting the dictatorship without satisfying the legitimate discontent of the workers." Rakovsky lamented that most of the workers in the party joined it after 1923 and were without the education acquired in taking part in an organized struggle, and were "unable to acquire any part of this education" by the bureaucracy. "I naturally exclude, as an abnormal method of class education, the fact that our bureaucracy, by lowering real wages, by worsening conditions of work, by favoring the development of unemployment, forces the workers to struggle and awakens their class consciousness; but then this is hostile to the socialist state."[201]

Nothing short of a drastic reduction in the bureaucracy could reverse this state of affairs, Rakovsky wrote.

> In my opinion, the first condition necessary to make the leadership of our party capable of exercising an educative role, is to reduce the size and function of this leadership. Three-quarters of the apparatus should be done away with. The tasks of the remaining quarter should have strictly determined limits…The members of the party must recover their rights which have been trampled upon and be given worthwhile guarantees against the despotism to which the leading circles have accustomed us.

He lamented the "specious and erroneous line" of the party and the use of "anti-Semitism, xenophobia, hatred of intellectuals, etc." to stultify the minds of the lower ranks.[202]

Rakovsky sketched a formidable picture of where the revolution had traveled and outlined a solution, but tacitly acknowledged that he was providing an analysis without an immediate course of action. Given that the Left Opposition was now scattered across the vast country in internal exile, many in locations with climates detrimental to their health, or in prison, no immediate course of action seemed possible.

Progress in industrialization had been slow and without a supply of manufactured goods, and the tractors and other mechanized equipment necessary to work a larger farm, the economic incentives needed to attract peasants into collective farms still didn't exist. The country essentially had stood still in terms of tackling the larger problems connected with its future development. Even the Right Opposition had advocated a faster pace of industrialization than had occurred; in essence, Stalin had been to the right of the Right Opposition. He very soon would find himself far to the left of the Left Opposition.

## The social forces for collectivizing agriculture from below, and the harshness of commands from the top

Banned from publishing its platform in advance of the 1927 party congress, the Joint Opposition attempted to circulate it privately, but Josef Stalin had banned that as well. Stalin, becoming ever more unprincipled, arrested and immediately expelled from the party three prominent members, among them Evgenii Preobrazhenskii, for clandestinely making copies. Stalin accused the Joint Opposition of having an illegal printing shop set up by a former White officer who had served under Baron Petr Wrangel. This was the first time a Bolshevik faction was charged with being in league with veterans of the White armies who had tried to restore the monarchy during the Civil War. But it was soon revealed that the ex-Wrangel officer had been a spy for the government—an agent provocateur. Stalin then performed an about-face, claiming that there was nothing wrong with the government giving an opportunity to a former enemy to rehabilitate himself.[203]

In a further effort to discredit the Joint Opposition, Stalin suddenly announced a reduction in the workweek to 35 hours, with no cut in pay; Stalin's followers then told workers that the oppositionists were against the cut in working hours and therefore were lying in claiming they were on the workers' side. The Joint Opposition did oppose the cut in working hours on the basis of the seriousness of the country's economic situation, believing that the loss of productivity could not be afforded. Even Mikhail Tomskii, the head of the trade unions and one of the leaders of the Right Opposition, opposed the cut in hours. But the decree served to further undercut support for alternatives to Stalin.[204]

Mass expulsions from the party soon followed, to be followed by the exiling of Leon Trotsky over the strong protest of Nikolai Bukharin. Repression began to be used at the factory level in 1928, when arrests and deportations of rank-and-file Left Oppositionists dramatically increased, and followers of the party line routinely shouted down oppositionists at factory meetings and pushed through resolutions demanding "iron unity."[205] The Left Opposition now eliminated, the Right Opposition now found itself vulnerable. In December 1928, the trade union leadership was purged, and five months later Tomskii and his supporters were removed completely, putting the unions firmly under central control.[206]

Before the final showdown between the Stalinist center faction and the Right Opposition came a new crisis signaling that the New Economic Policy in its current state might not be able to continue much longer. When kulaks began withholding grain early in 1928, Stalin authorized searches for hidden stored grain, and this caused a further reduction in the amount of grain willingly marketed, leaving the cities short of a sufficient supply of food and making impossible any grain exports. Stalin's new policy also was intended to gain the support of poor peasants by granting them a 25 percent grain bounty as a reward for participating in the requisitions.[207] In July, the government reversed itself, adopting the demands of the Right Opposition by forbidding searches and increasing the price of bread by 20 percent.[208] But such a rise in bread prices antagonized urban workers. Nor did it placate the countryside; further withholding of grain occurred in 1929, compounded by the previous year's poor weather in Ukraine that culminated in a reduced crop.

Shortages grew sufficiently acute that consumer rationing was introduced for the first time since the Civil War.[209]

Stalin and his followers declared that the kulaks were withholding grain for political reasons, that they sought to overturn socialist construction by starving the cities. This accusation was readily believed in the cities, where opinion was inclined to be hostile toward the countryside. Trotsky, however, countered that "the kulak is little inclined to that kind of 'idealism.' If he hid his grain, it was because the bargain offered him was unprofitable. For the very same reason he managed to bring under his influence wide sections of the peasantry."[210]

Regardless of the motivation, the kulaks demanded prices too high for buyers to afford and the cities were faced with starvation unless a way out could be found. A summer 1928 drought in Ukraine, the Soviet Union's "breadbasket," led to a delayed October harvest, which was further hurt by early frosts that destroyed more crops; by April 1929 in parts of Ukraine and the neighboring northern Caucasus wheat and rye procurement fell to as low as one-eighth of the previous year.[211] In autumn 1928, this situation triggered inflation, speculation and fears of starvation. To overcome this latest crisis, the government looked to the Ural Mountains region and Siberia, where a record crop had come in. A higher quota for those regions was set as a consequence, but additional grain, above the quota, was needed to offset the losses elsewhere.[212]

Continued uncertainty over food supplies into early 1929 and concomitant bread-line queues and sharp price rises became the main issue at factory meetings ahead of the 1929 city soviet elections across the country.[213] The "emergency measures" of the first half of 1928 (the forced requisitions) had not worked, and could not have worked for longer than a short period of time.

Siberian regional party officials began experimenting with new methods to bring more of the surplus crop to market, including organizing "social boycotts" against hoarders of grain.

By March 1929, the "social influence" method was developed whereby peasants, in village meetings excluding kulaks, set delivery quotas binding on all villagers; social pressure and fines of five times the quota were to be applied against those who refused cooperation.[214] The quotas were higher on the kulaks but administered by the peasants, thereby gaining the support of poor and landless peasants. This methodology had its roots in Tsarist Russia's traditions of collective village responsibility for taxes and the parading of offending villagers—the tsarist government had engaged in forced requisitions in 1914 and the 1917 Provisional Government used the peasantry in grain procurement.[215]

The "social influence" method produced good initial results—the country's spring 1929 grain procurements overall were one-third higher than a year earlier, with particularly improved results in Siberia.[216] But this method, backed by the strong support of Moscow, would prove to be a short-term panacea only, and collectivization efforts had already begun in 1929, on a small scale.

During the course of 1929, brigades of Red Army soldiers and of factory workers fanned out into the countryside, not only to requisition grain, but to organize collective farms, provide repairs to equipment and rebuild the rural political infrastructure. The last of those tasks involved both qualitative and quantitative problems—party officials in Moscow did not believe that local officials in rural areas were capable of, or willing to, implement the new policies that called for pressure to be applied to kulaks. That belief was reasonable, but the campaign to overturn rural resistance was accompanied by the sort of overzealous zigzagging that Stalin would repeatedly display: The party had suddenly switched from a complete denial of even the existence of kulaks to thundering that kulaks had wormed their way into the party's ranks throughout the countryside.

Rural Soviet Union still contained 125 million people in 1929, with only 55,000 government officials, many of whom were uneducated, alcoholic or corrupt, and a party membership of less than 0.5 percent of the rural population.[217] Rural party officials were subjected to wholesale purges, with brigades of urban workers participating in these and often taking the places of the purged.[218] Trade unions actively encouraged their memberships to take part in these activities; likewise, the political administration of the Red Army sponsored programs to encourage discharged soldiers to form collective farms. Active-duty soldiers also formed special units to assist in collectivization and "dekulakization"; the Red Army, however, contained within its ranks considerable resistance to these policies, resulting in collectivization becoming dependent on workers' brigades and the secret police.

Demobilized Red Army soldiers were to be given land by the state to establish collective farms and soldiers from peasant families would be encouraged to join collectives; demobilized soldiers would also be given training to enable them to use tractors and work collective farms effectively.[219] A 1929 government order granted credit for machinery and seeds, and promised free farm implements from stocks earmarked for collective farms.[220] Collectivization was gathering momentum from regional party officials and trade unions, who sponsored campaigns and drew up plans for collectivization from summer 1929.[221] Workers' brigades from the cities also audited existing collective farms, frequently finding them disorganized or withholding grain that should have been marketed; their reports claimed these problems were due to kulak infiltration.[222]

Existing collective farms suffered from a myriad of problems. Many were poorly organized due to there not being any literate people on collectives formed by poor peasants; others suffered from a lack of equipment, an inability to repair their equipment or poor preparation. Some of the collectives dissolved, but there was enough momentum in favor that collective farms constituted about 4 percent of the country's farms by the end of 1929, double from the start of the year.

Perhaps 100,000 workers took part in these brigades, and they did earn considerable good will by fixing agricultural machinery for free. The brigades sent in a stream of reports proclaiming successes in collectivization and that the middle peasants were joining poor and landless peasants in forming collectives,[223] and this seems to have convinced Stalin of the possibility of all-out collectivization.

The inevitable debate of whether to allow kulaks to join collective farms also was debated early at the regional level. Party committees in four major agricultural regions during 1929 voted for resolutions banning kulaks from collective farms; in addition, metalworkers taking part in the workers' brigades called for purges of existing collective farms and reported opposition to collectivization as "kulak provoked."[224] A need for a supply of workers to staff new industries about to be developed also played a role; the party first secretary of the Ural Mountains region openly advocated collectivization in order to free up excess labor for work in forestry and mining.[225] Fewer farmers would be needed due to the efficiency of larger farms, creating a pool of workers who would require new employment.

In November 1929, the party Central Committee formally proclaimed the start of all-out collectivization. This was concurrent with Stalin's final victory over opposing factions. He had succeeding in removing Bukharin, Tomskii and other Right Opposition adherents from their posts in April, and in November, under a withering barrage of attacks in the press, the three chiefs of the Right—Bukharin, Tomskii and Aleksei Rykov—officially recanted, condemning their views as "mistaken." For good measure, Bukharin was expelled from the Politburo. Tomskii and Rykov would be, too, soon enough.

Stalin now controlled the Politburo and Central Committee completely, and he was now ruling by decree; the Central

Committee proclamation on collectivization merely rubber-stamped what Stalin had decided, which was quite different from the policy that the party had recently approved. For good measure, at the end of December, Stalin decreed that kulaks would be excluded from the collective farms. Kulak families would either be sent to work camps in Siberia, the Urals or Central Asia, become miners in Ukraine or migrate to the cities to become factory workers.

Concurrent with these developments, the five-year plan was thrown overboard and an all-out industrialization was declared. Stalin proclaimed that the period of capitalist equilibrium outside the Soviet Union had ended—all foreign communist parties were ordered to concentrate their fire on social democrats as the "twins" of fascists. The basis of Stalin's arbitrary decree was his claim that the capitalist countries had already become "fascistized," thereby increasing the threat of war, although at this time traditional parties still ruled in almost all capitalist states, including Germany.

In light of this new threat, only a greatly expanded base of heavy industry could provide the armament needed to defend the Soviet Union. Moreover, Stalin said, the party had to strike harder against its opponents because, as socialism draws nearer, the intensification of internal resistance from the defeated capitalist exploiters will increase. Bukharin noted that the last of these theses was "idiotic illiteracy"—that "enemies" become more powerful as they dwindle away makes no sense; moreover, the claim under Marxist theory that the Soviet Union was about to complete the building of socialism was nonsense.

"Socialism" in the theoretical sense is a stage based not simply on capitalist relations of production being transcended but when a full democracy is instituted with industry and agriculture built up during capitalist stages of development brought under popular control so that production is oriented toward meeting the needs of everyone instead of for personal profit by an individual owner. The Soviet Union was still in the process of eliminating capitalism within its borders, was largely undeveloped with the overwhelming majority of the population living with shortages of many kinds, where many people remained illiterate and where all decision-making was concentrated in a few hands.

Stalin's "theory" was fantasy, but with all rivals now eliminated and surrounded by sycophants, Stalin commanded ample force to impose his ideas. That the practical side of what he was now attempting was based on others' ideas (an increased tempo in industrialization from the Left Opposition, collectivization techniques from trade union brigades, dekulakization from regional party officials) and that the programs were based on the country's very real need to get out of its economic impasse, provided Stalin with enough support to enable their implementation. These programs, however, were implemented with a ferocity far beyond what any of the original developers had envisioned.

Worse, these dizzying changes were to be forced without any prior planning, causing vast discontinuities in the economy and upheaval in millions of lives, rural and urban. As late as August 1929, the central party newspaper, *Pravda*, had declared that "comprehensive collectivization is unthinkable without the large machine."[226] In January 1930, as all-out collectivization began, *Pravda* estimated that 1.5 million tractors would be needed for the full collectivization of Soviet farming.[227] Perhaps 25,000 tractors actually existed at the onset of collectivization.[228] Yet collectivization was to be completed by 1932. Moreover, the technicians to teach peasants how to use heavy equipment such as tractors were too few in number.

And no small part of the disaster that was about to descend on the Soviet Union was that millions of peasants wanted no part of the new collective farms. Friedrich Engels had written these words on collectivization: "We stand decisively on the side of the small peasant. We will do everything possible to make his lot more tolerable and to facilitate his transition to the co-operative, if he decides to take this step. If he cannot as yet bring himself to this decision, we will give him plenty of time to ponder over it on his holding." It was with these lines in mind that the Left Opposition had contemplated a collectivization based on subsidies and financial inducements. But Stalin arbitrarily declared Engels' statement suitable for Western Europe but inappropriate for the Soviet Union.[229]

There were collectives that formed on a voluntary basis, and some of the poor and landless peasants who were initially resistant came around when they saw that the kulaks would be expropriated and kulak property turned over to the new collectives. But if collectivization was a popular concept in the cities, with fresh memories of threats of starvation at the hands of kulaks, it was not in the country, where resistance was widespread. Village priests filled many peasants' heads with apocalyptic fears of judgment-day blacklists and the pending wrath of God unless everyone left the collective farms.[230]

Widespread opposition to collectivization on the part of soldiers was reported by Red Army political officers, and the identities of those who served on special brigades formed to assist in the collectivization had to be kept secret lest the volunteers be singled out for hazing by other soldiers.[231] Villagers frequently ambushed soldiers doing direct agitation work for collectivization, wounding or killing them as they traveled between villages.[232] The soldier volunteer brigades were put under the command of the secret police outside the normal military chain of command, and, as resistance within the ranks remained at considerable levels, by spring 1930 the Red Army was essentially withdrawn as a force to be used in collectivization.[233] Henceforth, the army's primary role would be to encourage its soldiers to volunteer in crop sowing and harvesting.

In its first months, collectivization was pressed in a frenzy of activity. Some kulaks, seeing the end, sold off their farms, animals and equipment before collectivization brigades could reach them; many others destroyed their crops and killed their animals, and encouraged middle and poor peasants to do the same. In 1930 alone, so many horses and oxen were killed that the loss in animal power exceeded the tractor power made available to the collectives.[234]

Party officials quickly took a two-faced approach, as exemplified in a January 1930 speech for a party audience by a Central Committee member, Andrei Andreyev, who claimed that the collective movement "will now destroy upon its road each and every obstacle," yet also said the sale by peasants of their implements and seed "is assuming positively menacing proportions."[235]

Faced with pandemonium in the countryside, Stalin decided to call for a breathing spell with his "Dizzy with Success" article in the 2 March 1930 edition of *Pravda*. This article was a classic piece of Stalin subterfuge. The dictator blamed his underlings for carrying out his policies, but there were just enough grains of truth to enable some to believe he was coming to the countryside's aid.

"But the successes have their seamy side, especially when they are attained with comparative 'ease'—'unexpectedly' so to speak," Stalin wrote. "Such successes sometimes induce a spirit of vanity and conceit: 'We can achieve anything!', 'There is nothing we can't do!' People not infrequently become intoxicated by such successes; they become dizzy with success, lose all sense of proportion and the capacity to understand realities."[236] And where might collectivist brigades have gotten such slogans? Nearly two years earlier, Stalin had declared, "There are no fortresses that the working class, the Bolsheviks, cannot capture."

Stalin, in his circular, repetitive writing style, continued in his

"Dizzy with Success" article:

> How could there have arisen in our midst such blockheaded exercises in "socialization," such ludicrous attempts to overleap oneself, attempts which aim at bypassing classes and the class struggle, and which in fact bring grist to the mill of our class enemies? They could have arisen only in the atmosphere of our "easy" and "unexpected" successes on the front of collective-farm development...To correct the line of our work in the sphere of collective-farm development, we must put an end to these sentiments.[237]

This article signaled an easing in rural policy, and many farmers left their collectives, although at least 25 percent of the country's farmers remained in collectives. The respite lasted only a few months, however, but when the drive for collectivization resumed later in 1930, it was at a much reduced tempo and with less harsh conditions for the peasants, including allowing them larger private plots. Despite the massive upheaval, good weather allowed for a strong harvest in 1930. But the massive loss of farm animals, which continued at a lesser rate for another couple of years, and destruction of seed left agriculture dangerously weakened.

There were nowhere enough tractors to go around and with fewer animals available, less land was sown. Extraordinarily bad weather in 1931 and 1932 tipped the balance in important growing areas, leading to food shortages in Ukraine, the Volga River basin, the Northern Caucasus, Kazakhstan and parts of Siberia, and in cities across the country. A survivor of the famine reported that no rain fell during the summer of 1932 where he lived in Ukraine, a time so dry that parched farmland had cracks in it and widespread fires destroyed most of the harvest.[238] (These memoirs were written in 1990, when the subject could be addressed, and the memoirist nonetheless blamed the famine on "the inhuman adventurist policy of the Stalinist leadership, drunk with plans for industrialization."[239])

Another first-hand account from Ukraine (this one by an urban planner with a long award-winning career in the United States and Canada who was forced to leave the Soviet Union in 1937) reported that

> the hot dry summer of 1932, which I had experienced... resulted in crop failure...Second, the struggle for collectivization had disrupted agriculture. Collectivization was not an orderly process following bureaucratic rules. It consisted of actions by the poor peasants, encouraged by the Party. The poor peasants were eager to expropriate the "kulaks," but less eager to organize a cooperative economy.[240]

The 1931 drought was widespread and severe, and these conditions were repeated in 1932 in most of the same places, including Ukraine, while some parts of Ukraine in 1932 were inundated with too much rain, causing widespread crop diseases that drastically reduced harvests and yields.[241] Compounding these problems was the fact that a considerable amount of grain was either not harvested or allowed to rot in 1932 as part of a systematic campaign of sabotage by kulaks and peasants, according to several eyewitness reports by foreign and Ukrainian nationalist observers.[242]

By 1933, the number of sheep and goats had fallen by two-thirds from 1929, horses by 55 percent and cattle by 40 percent. The inevitable result of this destruction of animals and seeds by kulaks and peasants, lack of preparation in creating the collective farms and two consecutive years of disastrous weather was food shortages. Food production had declined to the point that there was no margin for additional problems; severe drought in Ukraine now portended an insufficient supply of food. Grain quotas that took too little account of these problems, but rather were set to extract a surplus to be converted into capital earmarked to finance industrialization, exacerbated the looming crisis.

The Soviet leadership was not completely unaware of looming disaster. The 1932 grain-procurement quota (and that year's actual harvest) was much smaller than in any other year during the 1930s.[243] In May 1932, the grain quota was lowered by about 30 percent, and free-market trade in grain was legalized.[244] Nonetheless, calculations indicate that the total actual 1932 Soviet Union harvest was well below official statistics—possibly only 60 percent of the official 1930 total; the Ukrainian harvest was possibly less than 40 percent of the 1930 total.[245]

None of the above altered Stalin's pattern of applying force to a problem: He demanded grain be delivered, in August 1932 issuing a decree authorizing the death penalty for theft of grain from collective-farm fields.[246] In November, he declared that villages that didn't meet their quotas should be deprived of all consumer goods and demanded punishments for alleged sabotage and mismanagement.[247] Mixed with the punishments were a series of relief shipments of food, seed and flour from March 1932 to November 1933.[248] Grain exports were reduced in 1932, but could not be stopped altogether because bankers and government officials in Britain, Germany and elsewhere in the West threatened seizure of Soviet shipping and property in foreign ports and a cutoff of all credits if grain exports did not continue.[249]

Forced collectivization had been intended to make agriculture more efficient through economy of scale, enabling a reliable supply of food not subject to being cut off by a rural elite and sufficient to ensure a surplus for export, but hasty implementation had instead left the country vulnerable to disaster.

Nikita Khrushchev, in his memoirs written decades later, recalled it was "incredible" when reports of Ukrainian famine came to him in 1932 because "food had been cheap and plentiful" there three years earlier. He told the story of how he found out the true state of conditions in Ukraine:

> [Anastas] Mikoyan told me that Comrade Demchenko, who was then First Secretary of the Kiev Regional Committee, once came to see him in Moscow. Here's what Demchenko said: "Anastas Ivanovich, does Comrade Stalin—for that matter, does anyone in the Politburo—know what's happening in Ukraine? Well, if not, I'll give you some idea. A train recently pulled into Kiev loaded with corpses all the way from Poltava to Kiev. I think somebody had better inform Stalin about this situation." You can see from this story that an abnormal state of affairs had developed when someone like Demchenko, a member of the Ukrainian Politburo, was afraid to see Stalin himself...Demchenko decided to tell Mikoyan about what was happening in Ukraine because he knew Mikoyan was close to Stalin and might be able to get something done.

Khrushchev's conclusion? "The Stalin brand of collectivization brought us nothing but misery and brutality."[250]

## Material incentives and labor discipline in industrialization

Concurrent with mass collectivization was a dramatic upturn in industrial development. The flip-flop here was nearly as dramatic as in the agricultural sector. Josef Stalin had sneered at the Left and United oppositions as "super-industrializers" for their advocacy of yearly increases in industrial output of 15 to 20 percent. The first five-year plan adopted in 1928 called for fairly tepid growth, but then was repeatedly revised until in 1930 it called for a 47 percent growth for just that year; ultimately, the plan called for a more than doubling of industrial output from 1928 to 1932.

Dramatic increases in industrial capacity were achieved during this period, and throughout the 1930s. All the more did this stand out considering the Great Depression ravaged economies throughout the capitalist world. From 1929 to 1934, industrial output in the United States declined by a third, and in the larger European states by as much as 30 percent. Yet the Soviet Union's more than doubled.[251]

A February 1931 speech provides a good summation of Stalin's thinking. Declaring there could be no easing of the pace of industrialization, Stalin said: "To slacken the pace would mean to lag behind; and those who lag behind are beaten…[O]ld Russia…was ceaselessly beaten for her backwardness. She was beaten by the Mongol Khans, she was beaten by Turkish Beys…she was beaten by Anglo-French capitalists, she was beaten by Japanese barons…She was beaten because to beat her was profitable and went unpunished. You remember the words of the pre-revolutionary poet: 'Thou art poor and thou art plentiful, thou art mighty and thou art helpless, Mother Russia.'…We are fifty or a hundred years behind the advanced countries. We must make good this lag in ten years. Either we do it or they crush us."[252]

The drive to stamp "socialism in one country" on all aspects of policy had reached its logical conclusion. This speech is remarkable in a few ways. Stalin spoke as a Russian nationalist, thereby throwing overboard the entire internationalist thrust of Marxism. Further, the Soviet Union was a multinational state; ethnic Russians comprised perhaps 60 percent of the population and the non-Slavic minorities had been forcibly incorporated into the Tsarist Russian Empire by conquest. An appeal to Russian nationalism ignored the many national minorities and was additionally insulting because Stalin implicitly accepted the imperialistic origins of "old Russia."

By rehabilitating Tsarist Russia, he completely rewrote history in ignoring the horrors of the ancien régime. This was no momentary slip. Stalin would speak as a Russian nationalist for the rest of his life, and this would reach grotesque levels after World War II, even to the point of promoting anti-Semitism, still another trampling of Marxist ethics and another resurrection of an odious tsarist tradition.

Finally, Stalin called for an essentially inhuman pace of development. "Make good this lag in ten years": Stalin declared that the Soviet Union would travel, in ten years, the same path that capitalist industrialized countries had taken decades (more than a century in the case of the United Kingdom) to tread. Compressing that experience into such a short period of time seems an impossibility. Yet the Soviet Union did travel much of that distance in a prodigious effort, pushed all the way by a dictator who was indifferent to the individual human suffering such a fantastic leap would, and did, entail.

The human suffering caused by Western industrial development stretched over decades was enormous, and the industrialists who amassed gigantic fortunes under this capitalist-driven leap were themselves indifferent to the fates of those from whom the fortunes were extracted—their employees and the communities where they operated through the use of starvation wages, long hours, horrible working conditions and the formation of trusts and monopolies.

To make the same leap, in a single decade, unavoidably entailed huge costs. But the enormous sacrifices of tens of millions of Soviet workers theoretically were made to build a better future for all, not to enrich a minuscule capitalist class, a vision that sustained many of those workers. And, indeed, the Soviet Union would have been crushed; it could not have withstood the genocidal Nazi onslaught of World War II without the industrial infrastructure built during the 1930s. Without the extraordinary effort of the Soviet Union, it is difficult to envision Europe's triumph over fascism.

The mad pace of 1930s industrialization was marked by

declines in living standards for most, bloody purges and the introduction of forced labor, but nonetheless represented opportunity for many—there was unprecedented social mobility, dizzying leaps to management, and significant financial rewards for those willing to work at extraordinary paces. The onset of massive construction projects and the creation of factories across the country also meant a swift end to the persistent unemployment of the New Economic Policy era of the 1920s. Work was guaranteed to all, but severe labor shortages, especially a need for workers in areas newly opened for development, led to the creation of vast labor camps run by the secret police, a destructive, self-defeating measure that wasted human lives and ultimately proved to be economically disastrous, not to mention a horrific, inexcusable blot on what was supposed to be a "workers' state."

The immediate goal of the feverish industrialization was the development of heavy industry, and the capital to pour into heavy industry came at the expense of not only the agricultural sector, but urban workers as well. Consumer goods weren't a priority and received short shrift; living standards were further depressed by an astonishing shortage of housing. Neither of these problems was effectively solved even by the time of the dissolution of the Soviet Union in 1991 as the party never ceased to stress heavy industry, but this situation was particularly acute during the 1930s.

Official Soviet statistics state that 1932 living standards were only 80 percent that of 1928, and that the purchasing power of 1928 was not exceeded until the mid-1950s.[253] The real figure for 1932 was likely worse than the official figure; by some estimates, purchasing power declined by half from 1928 to 1932.[254] Suppression of wages only partly accounted for reduced living standards; inflation was also a factor as the amount of banknotes circulating in 1932 was more than four times that of 1928.[255]

Still another drag on living standards was a huge buildup of the military. The 1930s assumption of power by the Nazis in Germany, the aggressive militarism of Japan and the rise of fascist régimes across Europe made the creation of a strong army a priority, which could not be done without industrialization. The percentage of the national budget going to the military swelled from 3 percent in 1932 to 32.5 percent in 1940.[256]

To illustrate the dramatic growth in industry with one example, a new "steel city," Magnitogorsk, was created from scratch in the Ural Mountains (one of many new cities created at this time). After just one decade of existence, in 1940, a total of 51,000 were employed there.[257] Overall, the country's workforce in 1937 stood at 27 million, more than double the 12 million of 1928.[258] This expansion created opportunities: About 100,000 bench workers were promoted into administrative positions just from 1928 to 1932.[259] On the other hand, those workers in Magnitogorsk were mostly living in barracks,[260] far from a unique situation and not the worst living accommodation, either.

Various forms of individual incentives were created to stimulate production; this development was partly a consequence of the inability of sustained organized defense resulting from the subsuming of the unions. "Socialist competition" was introduced in 1929, in which individuals, shifts or enterprises challenged one another to perform greater feats on the shop floor—competition that was intended to raise the work levels of less productive workers. An offshoot of these challenges were "shock workers," who performed dramatic feats of labor; this technique frequently was used on large construction projects. Brigades of workers, often Komsomol (Communist Youth League) members, volunteered for those construction projects.

In 1931, Stalin decreed that equalization of wages, heretofore a sacrosanct Bolshevik principle, would be abolished. An increasingly stratified wage scale was introduced. From this point, Stalin regularly denounced equality in wages with his usual collections of vehement denunciations. Even piece rates, one of the most exploitative capitalist schemes, became a widely used wage structure, further stratifying workers.

One outcome of this development was the official celebrations of the "Stakhanovite worker," a worker who regularly produced well above the norms. Stakhanovites (the term was named for a "model worker," Stakhanov) were rewarded with wages and bonuses far in excess of other workers, including vacations, automobiles and partial subsidies of private houses. Thus, not only was a privileged strata of managers and, above managers, bureaucrats created, but also a "labor aristocracy" emerged, providing a social base for the Stalinist régime and also an example that could be used to induce greater productivity from the rest of the workforce.

These types of policies, serving as incentives and social pressure simultaneously, were augmented by increasingly rigid factory discipline as the ranks of industrial workers were flooded with peasants. Upon the formation of collective farms, many peasants were made redundant by the increased efficiency of larger agricultural units, and left with little choice but to migrate to the cities. Other peasants simply saw more opportunities in urban centers, and migrated on their own, a practice encouraged due to persistent labor shortages. But peasants, accustomed to working to the rhythm of the seasons, had to be "broken into" the discipline of the factory floor and so the whip was applied as well.

Stalin, characteristically, declared in 1930 that what working people want is repression: "The workers again and again complain there is no master, there is no system in the works. We can no longer tolerate our factories being transferred from productive organisms into parliaments. Our Party and Trade Union organizations must at length understand that, without ensuring one-man-management and strict responsibility for work done, we cannot solve the problem of reconstructing industry."[261]

Such sentiments were backed by a 1931 decree providing for

ten years' imprisonment for actions that caused delays in transport of materials needed for industry.[262] Stakhanovites were celebrated in newspapers, and their record-setting shifts used as examples to be emulated, but workers considered "breakdown prone" could be used as negative examples in the same newspapers.[263]

The harsh discipline could also act as a catalyst for "reverse migration"—workers frequently left their factory or construction job and returned to their native village, where they joined the collective farm, often with the connivance of the local administration.[264] Job mobility, however, didn't require flight to the country; job turnover in the years 1932 to 1935 was more than 100 percent.[265]

Administering industry was an increasingly complex bureaucracy. At first, there was the Supreme Council of the National Economy, headed in the early 1930s by Sergo Ordzhonikidze, one of Stalin's closest lieutenants and one of the leading centralizers attempting to harshly impose control over the Caucasian nations in the early 1920s. In 1932, the economy council was split into three ministries, one each for heavy industry, light industry and forestry products, with Ordzhonikidze placed in charge of heavy industry, the most important sector. Many of the leaders of these ministries didn't survive the purges of the later 1930s. Ordzhonikidze committed suicide, under pressure from Stalin, and both his top deputy and his successor, as well as the head of light industry, were all executed.

There were numerous branch administrations that directly supervised enterprises, as many as 37 alone for the heavy-industry ministry; and, further complicating the picture, the three industrial ministries were broken up into 22 ministries in 1939.[266] These ministries were run in rigid top-down fashion, mimicking the political structure that provided the marching orders and the now strongly enforced system of "one-man management" of the factories. Enterprises were responsible for fulfilling their share of the five-year plans, and in turn the branch administrations were responsible for seeing that the plan was fulfilled by all the enterprises under their supervision.

The manner in which this responsibility was to be carried out is exemplified in a 1934 order by Ordzhonikidze: "The plan, approved by the government, is the law. Any argument against an approved plan is a violation of party and Soviet discipline. Any director who speaks against an approved plan cannot remain a director."[267] Because the expected production was measured in quantity, quality was often sacrificed. Supplies of raw materials also became the subject of wrangling among various agencies, and the splitting of the economy into more and more units led to the proliferation of fiefdoms. Stalin condemned what he saw as "narrow departmental egoism,"[268] and while on the one hand the fragmentation of the bureaucracy introduced inefficiencies into the economy, the need for a supreme arbitrator reinforced Stalin's dictatorial rule.

Economic decisions by the government structure were ultimately the decision of Stalin, unless he allowed his lieutenants to decide a matter, paralleling the situation in the party leadership, which had been reduced to trying to influence Stalin into backing a particular proposal. Nonetheless, extreme centralization did not lead to high efficiency. "Shock" work, Stakhanovite working styles and "socialist competition" made output erratic and unpredictable, and the high intensity of work performed in these manners resulted in machine and tool breakdowns, all contributing to an inability to coordinate production of components or predict industrial output.[269] These were serious handicaps to a completely planned economy that could not be cured through punishing scapegoats.

## Fear at the top and terror below during the Great Purges

Josef Stalin had become an undisputed dictator, but he had not necessarily conquered power once and for all. The political structure of the Communist Party still existed and, theoretically, the Politburo or Central Committee could vote to remove Stalin from his positions, including as general secretary. Stalin, therefore, had to continue to fight to maintain himself in power. Although undisputedly in command of his faction, the oppositions embodied in the now-suppressed factions soon began to re-emerge inside his own faction, and a series of challenges were crushed with increasing vehemence.

Some of the leaders and followers of the various oppositions had decided to recant and took up responsible government posts (but were not returned to any party offices) and although they prostrated themselves in front of Stalin and condemned their past opinions, many were disillusioned and privately expressed vigorous disagreement with policy. Other oppositionists were in limbo, in internal exile or in labor camps. The various former and still-existing oppositionists, the potential new opposition from within the Stalin faction and the potential for widespread resistance by collective farmers and industrial workers who couldn't or wouldn't fit into the new structures added up to a formidable array of forces that theoretically could work to end Stalin's dictatorship, although it seems highly unlikely such extraordinarily heterogeneous groupings could have coalesced into anything resembling a unified front.

But with more officials believing that Stalin's policies, particularly that of forced collectivization, were leading the Soviet Union to an abyss, Stalin could not be certain of his grip on power. And that he had inflicted such humiliation on his opponents and used ever more ruthless methods, ratcheting up pressure and imposing increasingly draconian punishments, could only engender a hidden rage. Moreover, Stalin was trampling on the ideals that had carried the Old Bolsheviks through years in underground work and that wider party circles had worked toward in the early years of the revolution.

Outside its borders, the Soviet Union faced its strongest threats since the Civil War as the crises of global economic depression and increased militarization made the threat of war real; Hitler was threatening to rid the world of Bolshevism and it would have been folly to think those threats were mere bluff. The bungling that helped to allow Hitler to reach power also played a part in the loathing of Stalin within the parts of the party that were politically engaged, bungling encapsulated in Stalin's inane concept of "social fascism." This is the sort of radical posturing for which terms like "ultraleft phrasemongering" were invented, although even such an epithet seems inadequate considering the deadly consequences such a policy had; ideas far more lucid than this had been attacked as "infantile leftism" by Lenin.

In the years leading up to the Nazis being handed power, Stalin imposed on all communist parties the line that social democrats, such as those in Germany, were the "twins" of the fascists and "objectively" fascism had already triumphed in the capitalist countries; therefore communists in those countries should concentrate their attacks on the social democrats. By refusing all cooperation with other anti-fascist forces, the Communist Party of Germany shared responsibility for Hitler taking power without a whimper. (Although the Social Democratic Party of Germany bore a greater share of the responsibility by virtue of allowing the post-war Free Corps, terror squads that were the seeds of the Nazi stormtroops, to rampage unchecked; its demoralizing policies; refusal to join in a cooperative defense; and idly standing by as Hitler was handed the chancellery.)

Hitler was appointed as chancellor by President Paul von Hindenburg with no coherent response from German communists. The party's half-hearted call for a general strike had no credibility when its leadership continued to aim its attacks at the social democrats after Hitler's appointment, it had done nothing to organize armed resistance to the Nazis (whose climb to power was built on its widespread use of terror), and had in the recent past indulged in demoralizing antics such as endorsing and campaigning for a Nazi referendum to unseat the Prussian government, a vote that, had it been successful, would have benefited the Nazis.

Naturally, the Left in Germany could not forget the massacres of their leaders in 1919 and later, nor the blindness of the Social Democratic leadership that paved the road for the extreme Right to rise. A reluctance to link in common defense would have been understandable, but common defense was the only avenue remaining to stop the Nazis. Once appointed chancellor, Hitler needed only three months to completely consolidate his power, during which time he unleashed a savage wave of terror, shredding all vestiges of civil society, destroying the Communist and Social Democratic parties, the unions and any other source of political opposition, throwing leaders into concentration camps or killing them. Doing so unchecked enabled the Nazi terror to extend to Jews, homosexuals and other groups because the most militant sources of organized opposition had been eliminated.

As this catastrophe was happening, the Stalin-controlled Communist International declared its policy had been entirely correct, and launched the slogan of "After Hitler, our turn." The Communist Party of Germany was being physically exterminated by unchecked Nazi terror: Just how was it supposed to come to power? The Communist International, blinded by ideology, had mistaken ordinary capitalist states for fascist states—a mistake understood once actual fascist governments consolidated power.

So unrecognizable had Bolshevism become, so hydra-headed had the potential for opposition become, so unpredictable were the social forces that the "Great Change" had unleashed, so centralized had that power become, that Stalin had to strike ever harder to keep himself in the saddle. The bloodthirsty savagery that would be unleashed on party, government and bureaucracy in the Great Purges of 1937 to 1938 was a morbid manifestation of the extraordinary mutilation of Bolshevism, not least the all-pervasive cult of personality that piled comically pompous titles such as "Sun of the People," "Sublime Strategist of All Times and Nations" and "Choirmaster of Science" on Stalin.

There was nothing whatsoever "inevitable" about such a bloodletting, and its terrifying proportions reflected the personality of the dictator. But the dangerous internal instability Stalin's Great Change had unleashed and the growing external threats also played to Stalin's advantage as his high-level lieutenants believed only a "strong hand" could save party and government from overthrow or collapse, and rallied behind him as that strong hand. This enabled the easy defeat of new oppositions in the first half of the 1930s, although Stalin yielded when his lieutenants balked at his imposing the death penalty to punish what merely constituted political opposition.

Only by unleashing the Great Purges, aimed primarily at party members, government officials down to the city level, and high-level enterprise administrators (although such a widespread terror inevitably caught many ordinary people in its maw), could Stalin definitively reduce the party to a mere conduit for carrying out orders and establish an absolute dictatorship where even his top lieutenants could not dare to question a decision without putting their lives at risk.

The purges also served to continually overturn the bureaucracy, which had become a privileged strata but could not coalesce into a bloc with the potential of becoming a counterweight deriving from a common desire to maintain or expand its privileges or to press for political changes because its ranks were continually decimated. But as with other aspects of Stalin policy, the road to this outcome began in a complex mixture of local initiative, ad hoc crisis management, evolving party policy and a penchant for risky experimentation.

The Ural Mountains region, where officials left behind an extensive record in state archives, provide a good example of local initiative. Party officials at the end of the 1920s envisioned their region as a heavy-industry powerhouse and major supplier of forestry products. To that end, party leaders in the Urals region requested that central planners in Moscow triple the capital investment in their region for 1930, assuming that the sudden increased demand for workers this would entail would be filled by the high number of unemployed, a hangover from the New Economic Policy now ending.[270] Regional party officials envisioned farmers laid off due to collectivization and kulaks excluded from collective farms as two more sources of labor power to be tapped, and set collectivization goals well above levels set in Moscow while allowing abuses in recruitment despite admonishments from the capital.[271]

Poor working conditions and shortages of housing and food led to an inability to retain employees at newly built factories, and with forests being depleted in more populated central and southern districts, a desire to create a forestry industry in the unpopulated, remote northern reaches of the Urals presented another labor problem because few people lived there, nor would many people wish to endure the harsh climate there.[272]

Already in January 1930, the second-ranking person in the secret police, Genrikh Yagoda (who would be chief at the start of the Great Purges), ordered regions to draw up plans for dekulakization, and Urals officials quickly decided to expel kulaks from their home areas and send them to newly created forced labor camps. The Urals, like many regions, frequently had their requests for quotas reduced by half or more by Moscow officials, who frequently condemned as "appalling" the conditions of the camps, although little concrete seems to have been done to improve conditions.[273] This system expanded in 1931, with kulaks put to work in mining, steel plants and railroad construction, as well as further expansion of forestry, as local and provincial officials took advantage of vague orders and a lack of central control to use the official policy of dekulakization as a shortcut for overcoming labor shortages and fulfilling plan targets.[274]

Central control of the "Gulag" (General Camp Directorate), the forced-labor camp system set up in unpopulated areas of the Soviet far north and eastern Siberia, was much tighter, with entire cities and infrastructures built from scratch to exploit natural resources. But even the Soviet presence in Magadan, the city known as the "capital" of the Gulag, began on an innocent note, with a "cultural center" established to provide medical and educational services to the Indigenous peoples of the region. This program was headed by an Old Bolshevik animated by the ideals of the October Revolution before the Stalin government ordered it, and others in Siberia, closed upon the decision to exploit the area for its resources.[275]

Areas to the north of Magadan, a seaport, contained gold, and this was the impetus for the construction of camps, although the use of forced labor in the region went back to the tsarist mid-nineteenth century.[276] Labor shortages were particularly acute in such a remote area—it is a 9300-kilometer train trek from Moscow to Vladivostok, the main Pacific port and Trans-Siberian Railroad terminus, and then another 2600 kilometers by ship to Magadan.

The Gulag was created as a result of the desire of officials in the secret police and the interior ministry (which merged during the 1930s, with the secret police chiefs becoming heads of the interior ministry) to play a major role in industrialization. Control of the secret-police apparatus was an indispensable part of Stalin's control; therefore, interests coincided. Major infrastructure projects were built under this system, with the construction of the White Sea canal in 1931 and 1932 the first feat of forced laborers under interior ministry control.[277]

By the mid-1930s, about 500,000 forced laborers worked in all areas of the country,[278] with a steady supply of newcomers throughout the remainder of Stalin's dictatorship. The justice ministry had held on to its ideals of rehabilitation and of the judicially convicted serving labor terms on their regular jobs (the 1920s system), but lost its responsibility for penal institutions to the interior ministry and the Gulag in the early 1930s.[279]

Opposition within Stalinist ranks did not take long to manifest after the final defeat of the Right Opposition. A new Politburo candidate member and the newly installed premier of the Russian Republic (the largest administrative unit within the Soviet Union), Sergei Syrtsov, and a Central Committee member, Beso Lominadze, in mid-1930 circulated a memorandum sharply critical of the Great Change, demanding an end to the "baronial-feudal attitude toward the needs and interests of workers and policies."[280] Syrtsov and Lominadze had participated in the Stalinist center faction's defeat of the Left and Right oppositions, but, similar to many who had done so, became disillusioned at the harshness of the new policies.

Syrtsov had become disillusioned in more than one way. Upon his promotion, he remarked, "The Politburo is a fiction. Everything is really decided behind the Politburo's back by a small clique…It seems to me an abnormal situation when a whole series of Politburo questions is pre-decided by a particular group."[281] Needless to say, Stalin was a member of each group. Working through small groups and presenting orders to be co-signed by others on the Politburo would be the standard methodology from then until Stalin's death. Syrtsov and Lominadze called for a change of leadership, and were promptly expelled from the party.

In 1931, 14 ex-Mensheviks were put on trial for "wrecking," a trial notable for a tactic that would be used in the show trials later in the decade: a claim that an émigré Menshevik leader, Rafail Abromovich, had snuck into the Soviet Union to organize followers. A photo of Abromovich attending a meeting in Europe taken at the time he was alleged to have been in the Soviet Union, however, showed the charges were lies.[282] An opposition of government administrators in 1932 also surfaced.[283]

The most significant of these episodes was the "Riutin program" of 1932. This opposition centered on a 200-page document written by several prominent party officials, including the former party propaganda chief, Mikhail Riutin. This program came against a backdrop of party dissent; the famine was at its peak and labor productivity in the cities was suffering due to widespread food shortages.

According to the "Letter of an Old Bolshevik," a much-discussed article that was ghost-written by the Menshevik émigré historian Boris Nicolaevsky after a series of talks he had with Nikolai Bukharin, then traveling in Paris, and presenting Bukharin's viewpoints and inside information anonymously, "many influential Central Committee" members favored Stalin's removal and an anti-Stalin majority was forming in the Politburo.[284] Riutin advocated the abolition of collective farms and the removal of Stalin, who, "motivated by vindictiveness and lust for power, had brought the revolution to the verge of ruin."[285] Furthermore, Riutin wrote that "It is disgraceful and ignominious for proletarian revolutionaries to tolerate Stalin's yoke, arbitrary rule and the mockery of the Party and working masses any longer. Whoever does not see this yoke, does not feel this arbitrary rule and oppression, whoever is not exasperated by it, is a slave, not a Leninist."[286]

Stalin was furious, ordering all who had circulated the Riutin program arrested. Lev Kamenev and Grigorii Zinoviev were expelled from the party for a second time and sent to internal exile for the "crime" of reading the platform. Most ominously, Stalin claimed the Riutin program had called for his assassination (it did no such thing) and demanded Riutin be executed. This was yet another escalation of penalties, as the death penalty had not been seriously discussed for previous oppositions, not even for the Mensheviks the year before, although individual attempts at terror and breaches of trust within the secret police had resulted in executions.

Sergei Kirov, a staunch Stalinist, or so it seemed, who was Zinoviev's successor as Leningrad first secretary, led the arguments in the Politburo against executing Riutin, a debate that Stalin lost. Riutin was "merely" sent to a harsh internal exile. But opposition to Stalin slackened the next year, 1933, according to Bukharin via Nicolaevsky, when the first strong harvest in three years caused support to swing behind the dictator.[287] An additional factor was that dissent mostly remained at the grass-roots level; fear of what might happen if the government toppled and its leading officials had to face the wrath of peasants provided another rallying point. A belated realization of the threat posed by Hitler presented still another argument against a leadership change.

The behavior of leading party officials, now more than ever, revolved around trying to win over Stalin, and a brief political thaw set in, with prominent oppositionists re-admitted to the party, although they were required to sign humiliating statements extolling Stalin. In foreign policy, the ultra-sectarian tactics, such as the "social fascism" line, were thrown overboard. The Communist International now pursued "Popular Front" coalitions and the Soviet Union joined the League of Nations; in turn its international isolation was ending. But despite the relative calmness on the surface, differences of opinion never cease to occur, and, given the extreme rigidity of the political superstructure, dissent could develop a tangible form only within the Stalinist ranks. Kirov now became pivotal.

A complex figure, Kirov had been one of the firm hands of Stalinist rule, overseeing, for example, the White Sea canal built with forced labor, but he had also argued for a cessation of all uses of terror and supervised collectivization in the Leningrad region in a much slower and gentler fashion than had been done elsewhere. The product of a desperately poor childhood, Kirov joined the party as an engineering student in 1904, quickly demonstrating leadership qualities. He escaped police repression by moving to the Caucasus, where he organized military supplies during the Civil War and soon afterward rose to become the party chief of Azerbaijan, where he gained a reputation as a capable administrator for his work rebuilding the oil industry. Stalin appointed him Leningrad first secretary in 1926. Although a firm executor of Stalin's decrees—he could not have retained his posts otherwise—Kirov was known to advocate milder policies, and the latent hopes for a change in leadership seemed to find their focus in him.

These hopes subtly showed themselves at the February 1934 party congress, celebrated by its participants as the "Congress of the Victors" for consisting of only Stalin's followers. The ovation for Kirov was said to be as loud as that for Stalin; that alone might have been enough for Stalin to place Kirov on his list of people to be taken care of later. During the congress, several delegates met secretly at the apartment of one of Stalin's closest lieutenants, Sergo Ordzhonikidze, and suggested Kirov replace Stalin as general secretary, with Stalin assuming a lesser post, although most accounts of this meeting report that Kirov declined.[288]

As was customary at all congresses, the new party leadership would be elected. The system in place for this congress was a list of candidates for the Central Committee. The list contained the same number of candidates as seats, but voters could strike off names—each candidate had to receive more than half of the votes. Of the more than 1200 delegates eligible to vote, three struck the name of Kirov. But 292 struck the name of Stalin. That was not enough to deny Stalin a seat on the Central Committee, but it may have represented the most strikes against any candidate.[289] All but three of those 292 ballots were destroyed, so that Stalin's announced total would equal Kirov's. One version claims that Stalin's most ruthless henchman, Lazar Kaganovich, ordered them destroyed;[290] according to another, Stalin personally ordered the ballots destroyed.[291] Regardless of who gave the order, of the 63 members of the committee that oversaw the ballot, 60 were shot in the Great Purges.[292]

What is perhaps more interesting is that Stalin apparently was not re-elected general secretary; he was elected one of four secretaries. Kirov, too, was elected as a secretary and, most importantly, was designated to assume much of the oversight responsibility for the Secretariat in Moscow,[293] which was responsible for personnel throughout the country.

Not since 1922 had anyone but Stalin been assigned that responsibility, and it had been the key to Stalin's ascendancy and continued ability to remain in power. But Kirov was temporarily still Leningrad first secretary and was reluctant to move to Moscow, delaying his assumption of his new duties.

There is no "smoking gun" that pins the December 1934 murder of Kirov on Stalin, but there can be no doubt that Stalin was behind it. His most serious challenger—who potentially could have manipulated the levers of power to begin removing Stalin's followers from their positions, who had more popularity and who persisted in voicing differences in policy—was eliminated, and it gave Stalin an excuse to ratchet up the apparatus of repression and to use Kirov's assassination as a propaganda prop.

There is much that is suspicious about this case. Kirov's murderer, Leonid Nikolaev, was an unstable person who had held a number of low-level party posts but regularly announced his vehement opposition to the government and wish to carry out a terrorist act. He had recently been detained after being found to be carrying a gun, yet was sent on his way. Despite the heavy guard at the Smolny, the party headquarters in Leningrad, Nikolaev was able to walk into the hallway leading to Kirov's office. Kirov's bodyguard was out of sight when Nikolaev followed Kirov from behind and shot him dead. The bodyguard was killed in an automobile accident on his way to being questioned; nobody else was even injured in the accident.[294] The secret police didn't secure the murder site for 15 minutes and the Smolny wasn't surrounded for an hour and a half.[295] The bodyguard's wife was forcibly taken to a mental hospital, was interrogated as to what her husband might have said about the Kirov murder, and died shortly thereafter.[296]

On the night of Kirov's murder, Stalin, without bothering to obtain Politburo approval, ordered a "speed up" in investigations related to terror accusations and for the secret police to "execute the death sentences" of anyone convicted of a terror crime "immediately after the passage of sentences."[297] Stalin made a show of immediately leading a delegation to Leningrad to supervise the investigation, yet instructed Nikolai Yezhov, the secret policeman who would carry out the Great Purges, to "look for the murderers among the Zinovievites."[298]

Nikolaev and 14 others, accused members of a fictitious "center," were soon executed following a secret trial. Zinoviev and Kamenev were also put on trial as having "moral responsibility" because their past opposition "inspired" terrorism. Zinoviev was sentenced to ten years' imprisonment and Kamenev five in a separate secret trial, then Stalin agreed to exonerate them from any connection with Kirov's assassins in exchange for a statement from Zinoviev accepting indirect responsibility by "admitting" terrorists drew inspiration from his and Kamenev's earlier anti-Stalin statements.[299] By agreeing to such an admission, albeit an obviously untrue one, Zinoviev and Kamenev had fallen further down a slippery slope, and further discredited themselves.

Stalin now again showed two faces: Mass deportations followed the Kirov murder and a severe régime was introduced for political prisoners. Politicals held in prison previously had retained some rights, including the ability to communicate and circulate materials, even between prisons, but Stalin now ended all such rights, seeking to reduce oppositionists, through hard labor and privation, to an "animal-like existence."[300] Yet on the surface, another thaw set in, with amnesties and a large reduction in the overall number of arrests.

Stalin, however, was moving toward launching the Great Purges. He had set up a "personal secretariat" to spy on his lieutenants and carry out purges. In 1934, this body became the "secret political section" of the secret police, deploying a network of Stalin's spies in all party and government bodies, and it was through this body that the Great Purges were conducted. Yezhov and Stalin's long-time personal assistant, Aleksandr Poskrebyshev, were the chiefs of this secret body. Truly loathsome characters, Yezhov conducted the Great Purges without mercy, and Poskrebyshev is invariably described in terms such as "vile" by those who knew him.

Toward the end of 1936, Stalin decided to go ahead with massive purges, liquidating all opposition by the physical annihilation of anybody who had, or might, express a disagreement with him, or had done something that he had not forgotten. This final drowning in blood of the party spiraled out of control, reaching into all corners of the vast country: Stalin would have the enthusiastic backing of the secret-police apparatus, who fulfilled quotas for arrests, deportations and executions, then demanded higher quotas. A single secret-police directive, issued in July 1937, ordered that 225,000 people be sent to forced labor camps and another 75,000 shot.[301] Secret policemen now received significant privileges, such as vacation homes, and salaries five times higher than ordinary workers; higher-level secret policemen were paid 15 times more than a worker.[302]

Meanwhile, after 1934, Stalin ceased any pretense among his lieutenants about a collective leadership—by 1936, the party's top body, the Politburo, met less than once a month, one-tenth of its frequency in past years, and after 1939 seems not to have met at all.[303] Stalin simply summoned various subgroups whose composition differed from issue to issue and who simply signed whatever documents were presented to them.

That situation was in part a natural outcome of Stalin's denigration of objective conditions, absurd for someone who claimed to be a Marxist. Such an attitude had much more in common with the anarchist Mikhail Bakunin, who believed the "will" of activists is the decisive factor, regardless of material conditions, even if Stalin was using such a formulation for a program that would have horrified Bakunin and to consolidate a revolution rather than foment one. Stalin said in 1935 that "cadres decide everything,"[304] and from this, therefore, anything that went wrong was the fault of the person carrying out or supervising an assignment; never was it the fault of the plan decreed from above.

Oddly, this attitude of Stalin's, which resulted in plant managers being hit hard in the Great Purges, seems to have made work a little easier for ordinary workers. Shop-floor workers were encouraged to denounce bosses for "wrecking," and also provided a critical part of the audience for show trials. In early 1937, the party Central Committee issued instructions that regular meetings with Stakhanovite workers be held, to encourage criticism of managers.[305] This development came shortly after the show trial and execution of Yurii Piatakov, a former leading Left Oppositionist who recanted and became the second-ranking official of the heavy-industry ministry.

Complaints filed with unions against managers drastically increased in 1937, and denouncements became a regular feature of the workplace. In response, discipline of workers by managers slackened due to managers being afraid of being denounced as "wreckers" if they pushed too hard.[306] The space for workers to assert themselves was closed in 1940, however, when absenteeism and changing jobs without permission became criminal offenses, punishable by prison or sentences in labor camps; these laws remained in place until 1948.[307]

There were three main show trials. The first, of 16 defendants including Zinoviev and Kamenev, took place in August 1936 and served as a warmup for the Great Purges. The defendants were Zinovievists, Trotskyists and German communists who had fled Hitler—all oppositionists, some of whom were already in jail. The second, in January 1937, featured 17 defendants, including Piatakov, Karl Radek and other prominent officials who had recanted their earlier opposition and held high government posts when their turns came. The third, in March 1938, was a trial of 21 defendants drawn from the ranks of the Right Opposition and other figures who had recently held prominent posts outside of government or industry, most notably Bukharin, Aleksei Rykov, Christian Rakovsky and Yagoda. Between the second and third show trials was a one-day secret trial of Red Army generals including Marshal Mikhail Tukhachevskii, the Soviet Union's best military leader but who had been made a commander by Trotsky when Trotsky commanded the Red Army.

No evidence was ever presented. The show trials consisted of the defendants, guided by prosecutor Andrei Vyshinskii (a former Menshevik), "confessing" to astounding crimes, then stating they deserved to be put to death.

Kamenev, in his last plea, said, "Twice my life was spared. But there is a limit to everything, there is a limit to the magnanimity of the proletariat, and that limit we have reached."[308] K.B. Berman-Yurin declared, "I do not want to defend myself by any arguments. There are no such arguments…[T]he proletarian state will deal with me as I deserve. It is too late for contrition."[309] Ivan Bakayev said, "I am heavily oppressed by the thought that I became an obedient tool in the hands of Zinoviev and Kamenev, became an agent of the counter-revolution, that I raised my hand against Stalin."[310] Vyshinskii wrapped up his summation with his signature line: "I demand that dogs gone mad should be shot—every one of them!"[311]

The main theme of this first show trial was that the accused assassinated Kirov, and planned to assassinate Stalin and other top party officials, in a naked bid for power after having become fascists in league with Trotsky. But worse was still to come. A month after this trial, Stalin sent a telegram to Politburo members demanding that Yezhov be appointed secret police chief because Yagoda "was four years behind" in "unmasking the Trotskyist-Zinovievist bloc."[312] It had been four years since Stalin lost the vote to have Riutin executed. Yagoda had very little in the way of scruples—he could not have held his post otherwise—but had some limits. Yezhov had none.

In the second show trial, the defendants were accused not only of plotting assassinations, but of massive destruction of industry, seeking to restore capitalism and destroy agriculture, and plotting the partitioning of the Soviet Union in conjunction with Germany and Japan. Stalin's phantasmagoria reached even more delirious heights at the third show trial, when the defendants were accused of being part of a vast, global anti-Soviet conspiracy in league with all shades of Bolshevik opposition, other Russian parties, nationalists, foreign spy services of democratic and fascist countries, the anti-fascist Spanish partisans POUM and the violent United States ultra-racist group Ku Klux Klan. Moreover, the defendants, in league with those of the two previous show trials, were accused of having been in the service of foreign spy agencies, working for the overthrow of the Soviet Union, since World War I.

The fantastic accusations of the latter two show trials reflected the ever more dire foreign threats faced by the Soviet Union. Fascism was on the march across much of Europe, with no response from the other capitalist countries; Japan was aggressively expanding in East Asia and threatening the Soviet Union from the other side; and Soviet intervention in Spain was failing, although a large part of this was due to Stalinist sabotage of the

Republican side by, among other things, executing leaders independent of Stalin.

The lethal ultra-sectarianism Stalin's agents inserted into the Spanish Civil War was the latest manifestation of the wild zigzagging of Stalinist policy, and it occurred at the same time as a sharp swing rightward in overall foreign policy—a policy of participating and encouraging "united front" coalitions in which communists subordinated themselves to liberals and social democrats across North America and Europe. This tactic thereby acted as a brake on militancy at a time when militancy seemed appropriate because of the mounting crises of fascism and economic depression. This swing to the right followed the period of overly militant ultra-sectarian tactics during a period when tactics of cooperation were called for to block the ascension to power of Hitler. Moreover, such tactics of cooperation, had they been geared toward building a vigorous common defense, would have allowed for a contrast to the leaderships of social democratic parties, who were leading working people to disaster through their continual appeasement of national chauvinists, fascists and other extreme Right groups.

Trotskyists in particular attacked these Stalinist zigzags. They called for "united action" tactics whereby groups "march separately, strike together": All groups march under their own slogans, raise the demands they wish to raise and retain the right to critique the platforms of other groups within the "united action" at the same time that the focus is on the threats from the Right. Instead, communist parties alternated between refusing any cooperation with all other groups and passively tailing the organizations they previously denigrated as "social fascists," swinging from one extreme to the other without stopping at any middle ground.

There is no need to provide detailed refutations on behalf of the show trial defendants and the many others snared by the terror; the record is full of supposed meeting places that had ceased to exist and assorted other proofs that the accused couldn't have been where they claimed to have been. The "confessions" seemed completely unreal. In the second show trial, to provide an example, Leonid Serebryakov accepted blame for whatever Vyshinskii asked him to, rather too eagerly: "So you wanted to kill Stalin?" he was asked. "What a question, of course I did!" he responded. To this sensational confession, Vyshinskii merely replied, "Thank you. Be seated."[313] Serebryakov, incidentally, had voluntarily given his Kremlin apartment to Stalin during the Civil War when Stalin wanted an apartment better than the one he had.[314]

Moreover, how could the Soviet state have survived when almost all of its leadership was secretly plotting its overthrow, and why would those leaders have spent years, decades, in the underground, putting their lives at risk, suffering prison and exile, sacrificing themselves to institute socialism simply so that they could then subvert it? Then there is the political dimension of the question—acts of terrorism were inimical to the political ideals of Bolsheviks, as well as Mensheviks. Trotsky, once again a bitter opponent of Zinoviev and Kamenev after the collapse of their short-lived "Joint Opposition," encapsulated the impossibility of the two becoming terrorists in an analysis written just after the first show trial.

"Following the state prosecutor, the defendants now repeat they had no program, but simply were seized by an irresistible desire to capture the commanding heights of the state, regardless of the price," Trotsky wrote. "But we should like to ask: Just how could the assassination of the 'leaders' have delivered power into the hands of people who had managed through a series of recantations to undermine confidence in themselves, to degrade themselves, to trample themselves into the mud, and thereby forever to deprive themselves of the possibility of playing any leading political role?"[315]

Zinoviev and Kamenev, like all Bolsheviks, were embedded in

a political culture that believed history is made by social forces and classes, not by individuals or small groups acting in isolation. Working people, acting together, can emancipate themselves; emancipation cannot be delivered by small conspiratorial groups. This bedrock belief was the political chasm that separated Bolsheviks from Socialist Revolutionaries and the earlier People's Will. Assassinate an official, and there will be another official to take his or her place, and the authorities will take revenge by increasing their repression against society. Nothing would be gained by the assassination and conditions might well become worse. Any Bolshevik seeking to resort to terror would have to come up against this immense political wall.

"Let us suppose for a moment, however, that it actually occurred to Zinoviev and Kamenev to hope to gain power by a public disavowal of their past, supplemented by a campaign of anonymous terror," Trotsky continued.

> A hired killer who acts with the assurance of immunity given in advance—that is believable. But terrorists without an ideal or a profound faith in their cause, offering themselves up for sacrifice?—that is inconceivable...[In the show trial,] what is presented is *systematic* terror on an enormous scale. For the direct work of assassination, many dozens, if not hundreds, of fanatical, hardened, self-sacrificing fighters would have been necessary. Such people do not fall out of the sky. They have to be thoroughly imbued with the conviction that the only salvation lies in terror. Besides the active terrorists, reserves are needed. These can be counted on only if there are broad layers within the young generation inspired with sympathy for terrorism. Only by extensive propaganda in favor of terrorism can such moods be created, and such a propaganda effort would have an especially intense and passionate character, because the entire tradition of Russian Marxism

> goes against terror. This tradition would have to be broken down, and a new doctrine counterposed to it. If Zinoviev and Kamenev could not have repudiated their entire anti-terrorist past without saying a word, even less could they have steered their supporters toward this Golgotha without a critical discussion, without polemics, without conflicts, without splits and—without denunciations reaching the authorities. Such a drastic ideological rearming...could not have failed, in turn, to leave its traces in innumerable material ways...Where is the propaganda? Where is the terrorist literature? Where are the echoes of the internal struggles and debates? In the trial materials, there is not even a hint of all this.[316]

Trotsky then, hypothetically, wrote that if somehow the charges were true, the defendants would be the most "hard-bitten, cold-blooded, ferocious criminals." But, yet,

> these monsters suddenly renounced their past and themselves and pathetically confess one after the other. None of them defend their ideas, aims or methods...Yesterday's terrorists, saboteurs and fascists now prostrate themselves to Stalin and swear their ardent love for him. What in the world are these fantastic defendants—criminals? psychopaths? a little of both? No, they are the clientele of Vyshinskii and Yagoda. This is what people look like who have gone through the laboratories of the [secret police].[317]

Next we'll turn to the words of an actual self-declared terrorist, Maria Spiridonova. She is the Left Socialist Revolutionary who assassinated a tsarist governor, suffering torture, sexual assault and imprisonment in a remote Siberian exile, avoiding execution only because of a huge international campaign on her behalf, and then helped organize her party's waves of assassinations in 1918. In internal exile from the 1920s, a time during which she worked as an economist, Spiridonova and her fellow exile housemates were arrested in 1937 and charged with terrorism. While imprisoned, she left behind writings that were found when state archives began to be opened after the fall of communism. Spiridonova and the Left Socialist Revolutionary Party had ceased all political activity by the mid-1920s, nor did they have any scope for carrying out any.

"In all my years of exile, surveillance has been quite scrupulous," Spiridonova wrote, shortly after her 1937 arrest. "Where and how could I ever have conducted underground activity of any significance? I lived my life under an omnipresent bell-jar."[318]

Noting that her party had long ceased to have any mass connections, she wrote,

> And there was no hope of resurrection, since the workers and the peasant masses in our days will not be persuaded by slogans of the most seductive kind…Our working masses are [currently] absolutely incapable of initiating any voluntary military actions, struggles or uprisings. They are too tired of such struggle…Old bruises and wounds must first heal, a renewal must occur, children must be born, and lives that have been in turmoil must be stabilized through the passage of time. It is precisely this that wisely occupies the masses today. But there is another, more powerful basis for this than I have indicated; namely, that the workers of the Soviet Union…have abundant opportunities to build their lives and to improve them without recourse to aggression.[319]

Spiridonova wouldn't break, but her husband, like her also a Left Social Revolutionary Central Committee member, agreed to "confess" to false accusations under threats that his 80-year-old ailing father and 18-year-old son would be shipped to the Gulag if he didn't. Spiridonova was expected to confess to being a member of a "center" that hid bombs for future use. Scorning such a charge, she wrote, "Never has anyone been stupid enough to keep bombs in reserve for emergencies. They are not pickles to be salted away for future use. Anyone who keeps bombs around for a long time is an idiot, an ignoramus, an involuntary agent provocateur. Bombs are made just before they are used. This is an absolute law."[320]

Spiridonova was particularly insulted by a charge that she organized the installation of a faulty chandelier in the office of a local government official, presumably because the chandelier would fall onto him.

> As a professional I had a difficult time accepting the circumstances and the essence of this excessively vulgar version of my terrorist activities...It is difficult to imagine...that anyone but a total idiot or a provocateur, which I do not consider myself to be, would engage in such an ill-conceived adventure. In tsarist times I was in the position both of directing and carrying out terrorist activity. All to the last were masterfully organized, executed and guaranteed one-hundred percent...The Mirbach assassination [the German ambassador shot in 1918], which I directed at the behest of the [Left Socialist Revolutionary] Central Committee, was also carried off cleanly.[321]

Spiridonova had nothing to confess and didn't; only those who were coerced into making confessions appeared in a show trial.

Why did show trial defendants make their confessions? Psychological torture and vicious beatings, but, more importantly, a desire to save loved ones. Kamenev, in his trial, told his sons to devote their lives to "our great Stalin."[322] An interrogator who gave evidence in the hearings to rehabilitate victims of the terror, which were held after Stalin's death, testified that Nikolai Krylenko, who helped lead the taking of the Winter Palace in

1917 and was one of three Bolsheviks put in charge of military affairs in the first revolutionary government, finally gave in, "signed the record and added that his fate no longer interested him, that he was concerned only for the fate of his family."[323] Vyshinskii, the prosecutor at the show trials, regularly threatened to "annihilate the victim's family," among other tactics, during interrogations, according to eyewitnesses.[324]

It was not enough for Stalin to strike at his political opponents. He struck at their families as well and the press repeatedly thundered that all family members would be held responsible for any member's act. The show trial defendants expected that history would see the complete unreality of the charges, as indeed it does. Fear for family members was no idle threat: Even Stalin's most sycophantic lieutenants had family members taken away in a macabre attempt to prove loyalty: Kaganovich's brother was shot, and the wives of Mikhail Kalinin, Viacheslav Molotov and Poskrebyshev were all sent to prison or to labor camps.

The more important question is: Why did so many people believe the confessions were real? Outside the Soviet Union, communists wanted to believe so badly, had such an unquenchable desire to see a better world come into being, that they blinded themselves to the reality of the trials, mass arrests and what those portended. The trials were so unfathomable, and so bound up with byzantine internal Bolshevik struggle, they were difficult to comprehend, and the terror behind the show trials was hidden from public view, especially from foreign eyes.

As for anti-communists, who also readily believed the trials were legitimate, perhaps they simply enjoyed the spectacle. It certainly is curious to read reports of the trial from mainstream Western publications assuring their readers of the legitimacy of the show trials. What are we to make of this conclusion by a panel of prominent British and US lawyers: "We hereby declare that the accused were sentenced quite lawfully. It was fully proven that there were links between them and the Gestapo. They quite rightly deserved the death penalty."[325] With not a single piece of evidence presented?

Especially harsh conditions were imposed on political prisoners, including the old-fashioned tactic, familiar from many a capitalist and feudal country, of arming ordinary criminals and inciting them against the politicals. Political prisoners in forced-labor camps, in particular the Trotskyists, refused to work more than eight hours a day, engaged in hunger strikes and resisted the draconian camp regulations in an organized fashion until it became obvious to the Gulag administration that they would not break, leading to a series of executions in 1938.[326]

Executions of some of the few significant political oppositionists still alive occurred in 1941, well after the Great Purges had subsided. As the German army approached the prison where Left Socialist Revolutionaries and others were held, common criminals were evacuated but 157 political prisoners were shot. They had their death sentences pronounced with their mouths tightly gagged as German artillery shells exploded nearby.[327]

The death toll from Stalin's régime will never be determined with complete precision. The topic, alas, has been dominated by Western anti-Marxist demonologists, who often seem to be in a bidding war, and, since the fall of the Soviet Union in 1991, are joined in their bidding war by some in Russia. Thus far-fetched figures are thrown about: 20 million had once been the standard exaggeration, but a renewed bidding war has doubled or tripled that figure. To reach such fantastic figures, a historian would have to demand that Stalin should have surrendered unconditionally to Hitler, and then, because he did not do so, assign to Stalin all the deaths of World War II—approximately 27 million suffered by the Soviet Union alone, and 55 million overall. This is not scientific, or rational.

The number of people whose deaths are the responsibility of Stalin and his régime is horrifying; an incomprehensible waste of human life. Why is it necessary to inflate the numbers? Approximately 790,000 people were executed in the Soviet Union during Stalin's reign, including about 680,000 in 1937 and 1938.[328] If such a figure were quoted for almost anybody else, we would recoil in horror. Yet these figures, which come from careful studies of Russian archives by several groups of researchers, seem to induce paroxysms, with demonologists screaming that any figures lower than their fantasy figures is tantamount to a whitewashing or a defense of Stalin. Such yelling may serve propaganda purposes, but nothing more.

Formal executions, of course, are far from the end of the story when it comes to Stalin-era repression. The number of arrests during the Great Purges seems more subject to uncertainty than other figures, with estimates ranging from 1.5 million to 2.5 million. Perhaps 4 million were arrested during the full length of Stalin's reign. Most arrested were sent to prison, a labor colony or the "hard régime" forced-labor system (the Gulag). Many convicted of lesser, nonpolitical charges served their sentences at their regular jobs, but the labor camps steadily grew larger.

By March 1940, the Gulag camps held 1.3 million and labor colonies another 30,000.[329] The numbers dropped during World War II, but rose again afterward—from 1950 until Stalin's death in 1953, the total custodial population of the Soviet Union (Gulag, labor colony and prison) held steady at about 2.5 million.[330] That total is frightening, and it is sobering to think that the prison population of the United States in the early twenty-first century is roughly comparable at about 2.3 million[331]—about one-quarter of the world's custodial population.

Figures for deaths of inmates in the camps are usually quoted at about 1 million, but it is not clear what overlap, if any, with executions there are in that figure, as some camp inmates, in particular the politicals, were executed. But the large majority of the inmate-death total comes from the war years of 1941 to 1943, years of severe deprivation for the entire Soviet population, so it seems likely that several hundreds of thousands died from malnutrition, disease or other fatal conditions. That was a fate shared with many in the general population, especially those defending Leningrad against the Nazis during the 900-day siege, which cost more than 1 million lives. More than half of the population of the Gulag was released in 1953, following Stalin's death.[332]

From 1940, a significant number of those sentenced were for violations of the draconian labor laws.[333] Nonetheless, the Great Purges were aimed squarely at political dissent: actual, potential and imaginary. The purges spiraled out of control, but that the percentage of Gulag inmates with secondary or higher education was twice as high as the percentage of the general population[334] provides a clue as to the intended targets.

A more dramatic way to illustrate this phenomenon is to look at the fates of the political elite. Stalin is responsible for the early death of every member of Lenin's Politburo other than Lenin and himself. Of the 26 members of the Bolshevik Central Committee at the time of the October Revolution, 17 were still alive in 1929. Of those 16 men and women excluding Stalin, 13 were killed on Stalin's orders between 1936 and 1940.

There were 1966 delegates to the party's 1934 congress, the self-designated "Congress of the Victors" so-called because it consisted of only Stalin's followers; about 60 percent were shot.[335] Those delegates elected 139 members and alternates to the Central Committee, and 70 percent of them were shot.[336] Every provincial party secretary who held office in 1936 was removed the next year.[337] One-third of the armed forces officer corps was removed; some of whom were shot.[338] More than 60 percent of the top officials of Gosplan, the state planning agency, were shot.[339] Of the 33,000 "nomenklatura" positions—the leading posts in all spheres of the government and economy that were appointed by the Central Committee, half were replaced in 1937 and 1938.[340]

Finally, there is the toll from the famine of the early 1930s. This is a more difficult case to make a judgment on, because the destruction of animals, seed and farm implements by kulaks and kulak-influenced peasants was a significant contributor to the famine, but those desperate tactics were in response to the forced nature of the collectivization, and zealous grain collections were also a significant factor. The spell of priests on the rural population was another factor causing the peasants' resistance, but blunders in policy and hubris in implementation played no small role. The poor weather in 1931 and 1932 is yet another factor, the one that tipped the balance and which certainly is not the fault of the government.

There are no widely accepted figures totaling how many died in the famine, a topic that has long been hopelessly entangled with Ukrainian ultranationalist and Rightist politics. Almost all 1930s and 1940s "sources" for high estimates of Ukrainian deaths come from fascist sympathizers or people who falsely claimed to have been eyewitnesses.[341] (Indeed, the stories of intentional famine originated in Nazi Germany and the notorious newspapers of pro-Nazi William Randolph Hearst, a prominent US publisher with a long history of printing sensational fabrications for political reasons.) More recent attempts at quantifying the toll either uncritically repeat these earlier dubious originators or rely on statistical legerdemain. Whatever the true figure may be, it surely is horrific enough without the standard embellishments.

Ukrainian nationalists profess to wish to preserve the memory of the famine, yet they deny the famine victims outside Ukraine at the same time they inflate the numbers of victims inside Ukraine in a macabre effort to "outbid" the documented toll of the Holocaust. Thanks to these efforts, it has become something of a fad to assign the Ukrainian portion of the famine as a "crime of communism." If that is so, then intellectual honesty compels that the Irish Potato Famine and the British-induced famines in India be known as "crimes of capitalism." The British government was responsible for the Irish Potato Famine of the mid-1840s, resulting in 1.1 million deaths and an additional 1 million emigrants, in a pre-famine population of 8 million. If we were to accept the famine death figure of 3 to 3.5 million put forth by the most prominent Ukrainian nationalist historian,[342] that would represent a smaller proportion of Ukrainians than Irish who died in their respective famines. Are Ukrainian nationalists and their supporters willing to be consistent by raising a claim that the British intended to eliminate the Irish people?

Britain increased its exports of grain and livestock from Ireland during the Potato Famine years, sending off ships full of food under heavy guard, at the same time that it enforced multiple laws effectively blocking food from being sent to Ireland because of an unyielding "free trade" ideology.[343] The British government banned Irish from owning land or entering the professions, closed Ireland's food depots, and told the Irish they should raise money for their own relief despite the fact that much of the countryside lived on barter and had no money, nor were there any jobs.[344] Irish farmers had to pay exorbitant rents to their English landlords for land that had been taken from the farmers' ancestors by British conquerors.[345]

Famines in British-occupied India resulted in 10 million deaths from 1876 to 1879, another 19 million deaths from 1896 to 1902 and as many as 3 million in 1943. British policies of land and water confiscation, draconian taxes, one-sided tariffs, falling prices for local commodities and policies that destroyed fiscal autonomy—all imposed on India by Britain by force so that India's wealth would be transferred to Britain—directly led to the famines.[346]

Nor was forced labor the province of any one system. The British used widespread forced labor in Kenya as part of the campaign they waged against the Land and Freedom Army, the independence movement more often referred to by the derogatory British term "Mau Mau." Forced laborers held outside Nairobi, with no tools, built "the world's first handmade international airport."[347] The British systematically arrested every African in Nairobi, separated out members of "suspect" ethnic groups and sent them to concentration camps where they were forced to run through gauntlets of British settlers and gendarmes who beat them, and forced into cattle dips full of disinfectant in which many drowned.[348] Detainees, whether rounded up in cities or in rural villages, were whipped, beaten, sodomized, burned, forced to eat feces, had scorpions attached to their bodies, were subject to electric shocks and had sharp objects inserted into vaginas and rectums.[349] These tortures are comparable only to Nazi atrocities, and were committed merely a decade after World War II. As many as 300,000 Kenyans died in this campaign at the hands of the British.[350]

It would seem that moral opprobrium could be distributed more evenly.

## The results of a personal dictatorship and the morbid decay of a system stripped of all moorings

The Great Purges came to an end with Nikolai Yezhov's removal as interior ministry/secret police chief, and his replacement by long-time Stalin enabler and serial rapist Lavrenti Beria, who would hold the post until his arrest and execution in the months following Josef Stalin's death. Yezhov was declared responsible for the lawlessness of the purges and executed in 1940. Several thousand secret police officers were themselves shipped to camps or executed.

Meanwhile, Stalin signed a treaty with Hitler in 1939 whereby the two sides pledged not to attack each other while dividing Poland and the Baltic region between them. This pact was perhaps Stalin's most unprincipled act yet, although it did have an underlying logic in that Stalin was desperate to buy time. There was no longer anybody capable of acting as a check on Stalin. The Communist Party had completely ceased to be a "party" in any sense of the word; it now existed as a mechanism of force that issued orders. All political opposition had been physically annihilated, and only the most servile could survive in the party ranks. Nothing remotely comparable to the Great Purges would again occur, but that bloody example was not likely to be forgotten, and it was supplemented by relatively small new rounds of denunciations, purges and executions.

Opposition to the pact with Hitler could be expressed outside the Soviet Union, however, and many communists did express their disgust by leaving their parties. Many of them had joined because communist parties were energetically opposing fascism in the latter years of the 1930s after the earlier "social fascism" line was buried; that valuable recruiting point had been thrown away.

There is no reason to believe Stalin took Hitler at his word, and he did have every reason to want a breathing spell. In the summer of 1941, 75 percent of Red Army field officers had been in their posts for less than a year.[351] Worse, Stalin had massacred the Soviet Union's best military strategists, and it would pay dearly for the resulting disorganization when Hitler invaded in 1941. The remaining marshals were second-raters promoted by Stalin, many of whom had to be replaced early in World War II to avoid defeat, resulting in the release from forced-labor camps and return to command of officers such as Konstanty Rokossovsky.

But although much of Soviet industry was moved to the Ural Mountains, out of reach of the advancing Nazis, Stalin did not put to good use the time he had cynically bought. The result was that a superhuman effort on the part of the Soviet people was needed to defeat the Axis powers; Stalin turned the defense effort into a nationalistic "defense of the fatherland." Thanks to the harshness of the 1930s, there were many within the Soviet Union, particularly in Ukraine, who harbored illusions about the advancing Nazis. Those illusions were swiftly corrected.

"A member of the Soviet Communist Party told me how, on his [collective farm] in Ukraine, they had looked forward to the arrival of Hitler's army, the returning of land to the peasants, and the inauguration of paradise," wrote a Czechoslovak communist, Zdeněk Mlynář, in his memoir on the Prague Spring of 1968, here recounting his time at party school in Moscow, when he was already becoming disillusioned about the Soviet model. "When the Germans finally did arrive, they burned the village to the ground and shot everyone who didn't manage to get away. Those who escaped to the forests found a party secretary there organizing a unit of resistance fighters. And so they became partisans. Now they really did fight for all they were worth, knowing it was a matter of life and death."[352]

Millions fought for this most basic of reasons, some fought for patriotic reasons and others fought for the ideal of communism, hopelessly perverted now but, so it was believed, to be cleansed in the future when Stalin was gone.

All hoped that repression would become a thing of the past, that the loosening of the reins that occurred during World War II would be carried further afterward. But Stalin clamped down harshly at the conclusion of the war, tightly shutting all avenues of popular expression through the use of continuing mass deportations to Gulag camps, draconian labor discipline, shrill nationalism, escalating anti-Semitism, severe artistic censorship and crude ideological strictures on science. The pervasive control of a dictator who ruled as an omnipotent father watching over the helpless was not only unbearable but senseless. The revolution had happened only because of mass action, and the sons and daughters of those who made the revolution were becoming educators, engineers, technicians and managers numbering in the millions.

The Stalin dictatorship became ever more unendurable, yet resistance to it was weaker than ever. All political opposition having been annihilated, there were no organized sources of dissent nor any institutions in which new oppositions could be nourished. And the Soviet Union had been nearly destroyed in the carnage of World War II; much of the economic progress that had been made was wiped out and the country's people would be fully occupied with rebuilding for years to come. Reform could only come from above, and when it did, from 1953, it was halting and inconsistent—perhaps not surprisingly, considering there would be only Stalin's lieutenants to dismantle Stalin's system.

Stalin's foreign policy in the years following World War II was inconsistent and subject to zigzags; this was his normal pattern. All the more was this tendency compounded by his lack of knowledge of the world outside the Soviet Union and his contempt for foreign communists, intertwined with the lack of any internal current of opinion that need be considered. Stalin puffed on his pipe, thinking up a new line, and his lieutenants and all others patiently waited for him to make an announcement. Even the members of the Politburo were specialists who merely supervised sections of the economy and reported to Stalin, whom they did not dare question.

A good illustration of this relationship is provided by the Yugoslav communist turned dissident, Milovan Djilas, who in 1948 had a chance to observe up close. "[W]e came across places around Leningrad that still bore German names from the time of Catherine [the Great]. This caught Stalin's eye and he turned to [Andrei] Zhdanov, saying curtly, 'Change these names—it is senseless that these places still bear German names!' At this Zhdanov pulled out a small notebook and recorded Stalin's order with a little pencil."[353]

Djilas saw similar instances repeatedly, with the other Politburo members. At a banquet on the same trip, Djilas noted that Stalin had noticeably declined from 1945, but still was undisputedly in charge. "In one thing, though, he was still the Stalin of old: stubborn, sharp, suspicious whenever somebody disagreed with him. He even cut off Molotov, and one could feel the tension between them. Everyone paid court to him, avoiding any expression of opinion before he expressed his, and then hastening to agree with him."[354]

Djilas had been representing the Yugoslav government on an official trip shortly before the split between the two countries. Stalin had been trying to dictate to the Yugoslav leadership, an affront considering Yugoslavs had liberated their country from German, Italian and Croatian fascism in a punishing partisan war and were not in need of condescending instruction. More importantly, Stalin had been exploiting Yugoslavia economically and using a *capitalist* structure to do so, setting up a "joint stock company" that took capital out of Yugoslavia.

The head of the Yugoslav Economic Council, Boris Kidric, pulled no punches in recounting this treatment:

> Stalin treated us not as a socialist country but like any other nation which, as he and his associates felt, belonged to their sphere of influence—that is, under their hegemony, with all the economic exploitation that implied. The purpose was to keep Yugoslavia as an agricultural and raw-materials-producing appendage, which is why they opposed our setting up basic industries that would help us become independent.[355]

The Soviet negotiators demanded that a Soviet–Yugoslav joint venture be given a monopoly on all foreign air flights and the most profitable domestic routes, demanded that Yugoslavia put in the most capital, underestimated the Yugoslav contribution, overestimated the Soviet contribution, then allowed the Soviet side to extract enormous profits from this one-sided calculation without paying any taxes or customs duties.[356] A similar plan was demanded for shipping, with Yugoslavia contributing virtually all ships and the joint venture being given a monopoly over the Danube River, the main shipping channel.[357] Still worse terms were proposed for a bank that would have given the Soviet Union a complete stranglehold on the Yugoslav economy.[358]

The Yugoslav leadership balked at allowing the proposed bank to be formed, but did agree to the two joint ventures, with slightly modified, but still exploitative, terms. Vladimir Dedijer, a Yugoslav Politburo member, later wrote that there were several reasons for agreeing to such terms, including tense international relations, feeling threatened by the United States and ongoing boundary disputes. They believed the Soviet bloc was their only possible source of investment for their devastated country and for protection against a possible invasion; moreover, Yugoslav communists, believers in the ideals of Marxism, genuinely looked up to the Soviet Union and found it difficult to believe that it would exploit other peoples.[359]

Yugoslavia, in 1948, did break with the Soviet Union, canceling all the joint ventures. The split led to Yugoslavia helping to create the "Third World" as a group of states independent of the United States and of the Soviet Union. Stalin responded in typical fashion, threatening Yugoslav leader Josip Broz Tito and hurling an ever growing panoply of insults. Soviet and Bulgarian troops held maneuvers near the Yugoslav border; Stalin even sent a diplomatic note calling Yugoslavia's leadership "fascist bullies,"[360] the same sort of cartoonish lie familiar from the 1920s and 1930s. "Titoism" now replaced "Trotskyism" as Stalin's biggest bogey.

Stalin seems to have taken some time to formulate a post-war foreign policy. At first, he insisted on the removal of industry from Germany, and did shift Germany's borders to the west, converting German-populated areas into Polish territory, which seems to indicate that he had not initially decided on establishing a communist régime there—removing Germany's industrial base would not appear to be the best basis on which to build a socialist economy or earn good will.[361] Stalin had a tacit agreement with Franklin Delano Roosevelt and Winston Churchill that each side's system would predominate, but not dictate, in the areas that their armies had liberated; short of all-out war among the victorious Allies, such a result would have been inevitable. Believing that the Soviet Union needed breathing space because of its post-war devastation and therefore not wishing to provoke the Western powers in any way, Stalin stuck to this deal. Moreover, the phenomenon of the Stalin dictatorship was a product of isolation; it needed continued isolation to maintain itself. Stalin had never shown any enthusiasm for foreign revolutions, and would particularly loathe any revolution outside his tight control.

France and Italy were weak links in capitalism—traditional capitalist rulers in those two countries had been incapable of governing, which is why they had to hand the reins to fascists—and a desire to overcome those deficiencies led to a strong turn to the Left in both countries.[362] Communist leadership in the World War II Resistance reinforced the strength of the Left, and conditions arose in which a taking of power by a coalition of all social and political forces supporting a socialist alternative became possible.[363] It is impossible to know if such revolutions (which very likely would have been quite different from the Soviet model) would have occurred, but by ordering French and Italian communists to accept capitalist rule, and those parties' meek acceptance of that order, Stalin guaranteed there would be no revolutions.

Similarly, Greek communists capitulated to Stalin's demand to stand down even though, in 1944, they controlled almost the entire country and were backed by a popular army; Greek communists were in a much less favorable position when they rose after the war, succumbing to the Allies' military might as Stalin stood by.[364] The resulting instability culminated in the murderous military junta of the "four colonels" supported by the United States.

Stalin also consistently opposed any communist takeover in China; since the 1920s Stalin had persistently told the Chinese Communist Party to subordinate itself to Chiang Kai-Shek's nationalists, before and after Chiang had massacred communists in 1927. The communists were the strongest fighters against Japanese occupation, giving them moral authority to go with their military strength; the communist takeover there happened because Mao Zedong ignored Stalin's instructions.

The new setups in Europe did not last long—communists were pushed out in Western Europe, putting that region under US dominance; social democrats and others were pushed out in Central Europe, converting that region into the Soviet Union's defensive barrier. "Socialism in one country" became a slightly larger "socialism in one zone," but with Stalinist rigidity imposed on the countries of the defensive barrier, there were soon show trials rather than the previously encouraged "independent roads." Considerable communist movements existed throughout Central Europe, but nonetheless the Red Army hovering in the background was the catalyzing factor.

Strong desires to overturn the fascist and ancien régimes would have been enough for local communists to have received backing for locally inspired root-and-branch progressive changes, but the stifling Soviet model imposed on them, taking no account of local cultures and conditions, became seen as a foreign conquest in those countries. This poisoned legacy left the new régimes unstable and with insufficient legitimacy.

A harder rigidity was imposed within the Soviet Union. No discipline was spared absurd ideological fetters. Scientists in fields as diverse as physics and biology were forced to adhere to crude declarations that scientific discoveries made in the West were "bourgeois" and therefore automatically wrong, at times required to apologize for pursuing theories that implied variance with the political lines set down by the party leadership. Similarly, all artists, particularly writers, had to walk a tightrope. A slight move to one side from officially prescribed "socialist realism" led to verboten "bourgeois nationalism"; a slight move to the other side led to equally verboten "rootless cosmopolitanism."

Bourgeois nationalism in this context meant any expression that could be interpreted as a manifestation of any national group other than Russians, who were now the "big brothers" to whom all other nations in the Soviet sphere were expected to pay continuing homage. A leading party figure, in March 1946, declared,

> Every people in the Soviet Union understands perfectly well that the main decisive role in the achievement of victory in the Great Patriotic War [as World War II is called there]...was played by the great Russian people. For this reason, the prestige of the Russian people is so immeasurably high among the other peoples; for this reason the peoples of the USSR bear toward it boundless confidence and a feeling of tremendous love and gratitude.[365]

This attitude was expected from the Soviet bloc's Central European states, too, causing no small amount of friction in the ensuing decades. Zhdanov, the most zealous enforcer of censorship, later in 1946 declared, "Where can you find such a people or such a country as ours?"[366] This narrow nationalism, in a multinational state and trampling on all ideals and standards of the ideology in which it purported to rule, only escalated until Stalin's death. It was strong enough to have still found comic relief in the 1960s science-fiction television series *Star Trek*, in which twenty-third-century Ensign Chekov claimed that every invention had originated in Russia.

Such nationalistic attitudes, however, were not constructed

out of thin air. The Soviet Union was the decisive factor in winning World War II but was devastated, paying a price more severe than any other combatant. Much of the country was reduced to rubble—70,000 villages were razed, 32,000 enterprises were destroyed, the transportation infrastructure was wiped out and farm animals were killed in countless numbers.[367] The Soviet Union would require a monumental effort to rebuild itself, and Stalin was desperate to conceal this from the Western Allies. Nationalist themes had predominated during the war, and these would be employed to rally a decimated populace to rebuild. But Stalin's indifference to the concrete suffering of the people of the Soviet Union is illustrated by his signing an order for the erection of a monument to himself in Stalingrad (now Volgograd), authorizing the use of 33 tons of copper, at a time when people there were still living in huts.[368]

Another measure was the continued use of forced-labor camps, which, in addition to the moral issue, was economically disastrous. Throughout the 1940s, the interior ministry/secret police (known at this time as the "MVD" in one of many name changes) was a major supplier of metals and timber, but complained it could not feed inmates properly because other ministries were not paying it properly for the materials it was supplying, while other government agencies repeatedly requested that the secrecy shrouding the Gulag be lifted to eliminate irresponsibility and inefficiency.[369] Already in 1940, secret police chief Beria reported that well more than 100,000 prisoners were idle from lack of food or clothing.[370] An extraordinarily low expenditure rate was set for the prisoners, yet the value of what they produced was still lower and the MVD, supplied with a steady stream of new prisoners, had no interest in rationalizing this system.[371]

What is strikingly poignant among many political prisoners is their ability to continue to uphold the ideals of the greater good they still believed in despite the unspeakable misery unfairly heaped onto them. An Azerbaijani, Ayyub Baghirov—he was the tenth among the 11 members of the Baku city government's executive body to be arrested—remembered in a memoir written years later what a popular Old Bolshevik told him in a transit camp as they awaited a nightmarish sea voyage to Magadan and the Gulag camps. "Uncle Vanya, sensing our mood—especially among the young people—gave us some fatherly advice: 'Don't give up. Be strong in spirit. Brave the difficulties that are awaiting you. Maintain your devotion to our people to the end, and show your good work in developing this desolate land.'"[372]

"Uncle Vanya" had been a Bolshevik since 1903 and held responsible positions; he was a popular figure in Baku but he, too, had been arrested. Baghirov had been taken away for refusing to denounce a colleague he knew to be innocent. Working was also a means of survival:

> Let me add that along with hope, the main thing that helped us to survive the Far North was labor. Being actively involved with work was a necessity of life in the severe climate of the North. Work became a life-saving stimulus for us. Those who understood this truth from the beginning were the ones who survived in their struggle against the unforgiving landscape of the Far North.[373]

This system could not endure; a steady stream of letters from the prisoners, often secretly forwarded by camp administrators or local party cadres, reached Moscow. Eventually, heads of MVD production branches began requesting authorization to pay partial wages.[374] By 1948, wages and other reforms were introduced in the Magadan-area camps and, in 1950, wages were universally adopted, although strikes became widespread throughout the system.[375] The forced-labor system was breaking down, and during the first four weeks after Stalin's death the MVD's industrial directorates were transferred to civilian ministries, 1 million detainees were freed, others had their sentences halved and all those released had their civil rights restored, a reversal of past practice.[376]

Stalin's terror did not fail to reach into all cultural spheres. Stalin took a particular interest in artists, over whom he enjoyed holding life-and-death power. At times, that interest meant a disgraced artist could obtain a reprieve by appealing directly to Stalin, but did not always mean escape from a grisly fate. The theater director Vsevolod Meyerhold was beaten with rubber hoses during an interrogation, at age 66, then shot in 1940;[377] the Yiddish Theatre actor Solomon Mikhoels, who had tirelessly rallied Jewish support for the Soviet Union's war effort, was murdered in 1948.[378] Often, an artist's fate would change rapidly: The poet Anna Akhmatova was granted a single room in the best hospital in Tashkent while ill during World War II, an unheard-of luxury, but a few years later had her food-ration card taken away and her son arrested and interrogated in the notorious Lubianka Prison.[379]

That such repression fell hardest on cultural figures such as Mikhoels is not surprising because a furious anti-Semitic campaign was gathering steam; Jews were especially in danger of being denounced as rootless cosmopolitans. Yiddish Theatre figures and members of the Jewish Anti-Fascist Committee were arrested and their organizations closed. Jewish students were beaten in schools and adults began to lose their jobs; ominously, a 1952 editorial in a Kiev newspaper, after listing a series of generic Jewish-sounding names, declared they "arouse the profound loathing of the people."[380]

This campaign culminated in the infamous "doctor's plot," in which nine doctors with Jewish names were accused in January 1953 of murdering recently deceased party leaders and of plotting the deaths of Stalin and military leaders in language reminiscent of the Great Purges. Official harassment of Jews became systematic, including pogrom-like language in the press, and rumors circulated that Jewish writers and scientists were to be asked to sign a letter saying "they understood the guilt of their people" and that Jews should "atone for their crimes…by their labors" in Siberian camps.[381]

In conjunction with the anti-Semitism that Stalin had unleashed, he was preparing a new massacre of the party. In December 1952, Stalin suddenly called for a party congress, the first in 13 years despite party statutes calling for no more than three years to pass without one; congresses had been yearly events under Lenin. At this congress, the number of Politburo and Central Committee members was doubled; many of the names to fill the new seats were unfamiliar to Stalin's lieutenants.

Stalin had nominated understudies with the intent of having the understudies learn the jobs held by his lieutenants, who would then be killed. It can reasonably be concluded that Stalin not only was preparing a new round of purges intended to eliminate his witnesses within the party, but also to foment pogroms outside the party.

Stalin had already reinstated so many tsarist trappings—"courts of honor" to ensure eyes were closed to the West; a "table of ranks" and accompanying uniforms emulating that of Peter the Great recreated for the bureaucracy; and purges of the party and government echoing Ivan the Terrible's purges of the aristocracy—that the deadly anti-Semitic atmosphere was just one more manifestation. The cult of personality had reached such heights that *Pravda* daily printed birthday congratulations for months after Stalin's seventieth birthday in 1949 and failing to quote Stalin in any article, no matter the topic, was taking a serious risk. Fedor Burlatsky, future assistant to Nikita Khrushchev and Yuri Andropov, when a graduate student was "persistently advised…to include at least one least quotation from Stalin in my dissertation. I was stubborn, however, and argued that Stalin had written nothing about N.A. Dobrolyubov, the famous Russian critic of the 1860s who was the subject of my thesis."[382] Stalin had declared himself the leading expert on history, culture, linguistics and any other subject in which he took an interest at some point.

Marxism had become so perverted that individual study of it was banned—absorbing pre-digested bites with approved commentary in official study groups was the only permissible methodology—and the reports and transcripts of past party congresses were banned. A philosophy based on patient, rigorous analysis, a cry of freedom for millions shaped by successive theorists from all corners of the world, a living banner of rebellion for a world where so many hoped to put an end to millennia of exploitation, had been reduced to a catechism that meant whatever one person said it meant, even if what he needed it to mean today was the opposite of what he needed it to mean last week.

The momentum to another purge abruptly halted with Stalin's death in March 1953. There has been speculation that Stalin was actually poisoned by one or more of his lieutenants; no evidence, or even hint of a plot, has ever surfaced. They must have known they were likely doomed: Stalin violently denounced Viacheslav Molotov immediately after the December party congress and had sidelined Lazar Kaganovich. If the dictator's longest-serving acolytes were not safe, who was? His lieutenants had ample motivation for eliminating Stalin, saving themselves and the country, but they were also his servile shadows, awed by their master and ever ready to shout new panegyrics to him. They had energetically promoted the Stalin cult and meekly submitted to his every whim, no matter how monomaniacal; they had lived with the constant threat of disgrace and execution for so many years that there is no reason to believe they now behaved differently.

Despite unprecedented development and mass education, the dead weight of centuries of tsarist absolutism and the homage that Stalin continually paid it exerted a powerful influence;

byzantine rituals and ancient cultural remnants were inextricably woven into Stalinist rule. Siberian exiles, official brutality, forced-labor camps and similar barbaric nightmares were all products of tsarism. Only the show trials were a new invention, and these could not have occurred in tsarist times because electronic mass media did not then exist and because the tsars did not care about any opinion, domestic or international, whereas Stalin, a careful cultivator of his public image, did. Even the cult of personality had its roots in the past: Stalin elevated himself to demigod status, albeit a very different type of divinity from that of the Romanovs.

Now that leader was gone. Enormous crowds poured into the center of Moscow to see Stalin lying in state; fear of the unknown by a country that had been forced to yield so much initiative to one ruler underlay the resulting pandemonium. The scene was described vividly by the poet Yevgeny Yevtushenko:

> It was a terrifying and a fantastic sight. New streams poured into this human flood from behind, increasing the pressure. The crowd turned into a monstrous whirlpool. I realized that I was being carried toward a traffic light. The post was coming relentlessly closer. Suddenly, I saw that a young girl was being pushed against the post. Her face was distorted and she was screaming. But her screams were inaudible among all the other cries and groans. A movement of the crowd drove me against the girl; I did not hear but felt with my body the cracking of her brittle bones as they were broken on the traffic light...When I looked again the girl was no longer to be seen. The crowd must have sucked her under...At that moment I felt I was treading on something soft. It was a human body. I picked my feet up under me and was carried along by the crowd. For a long time I was afraid to put my feet down again. The crowd closed tighter and tighter. I was saved by my height. Short people were

> smothered alive, falling and perishing. We were caught between the walls of houses on one side and a row of army trucks on the other. "Get those trucks out of the way," people howled. "I can't do it! I have no instructions," a very young, tow-headed police officer shouted back from one of the trucks, almost crying with helplessness. And people were being hurtled against the trucks by the crowd, and their heads smashed. The sides of the trucks were splashed with blood. All at once I felt a savage hatred for everything that had given birth to that "I have no instructions."...It was the "no instructions" that had caused the chaos and bloodshed at his funeral."[383]

Later, when Yevtushenko returned home, after escaping the crush, he was asked by his mother if he had seen Stalin. "'Yes,' I said coldly.'...I hadn't really lied to my mother. I had seen Stalin. Because everything that had just happened—that was Stalin."[384]

No human being has ever done more damage to the idea of socialism than Josef Stalin.

## Notes to Chapter 2

1 Zvi Gitelman, *A Century of Ambivalence: The Jews of Russia and the Soviet Union, 1881 to the Present*, pages 4–6, 14 [Indiana University Press, 2001]

2 Kenneth F. Mailloux and Heloise P. Mailloux, *Lenin the Exile Returns*, page 23 [Auerbach, 1971]

3 Solomon Volkov, *St. Petersburg: A Cultural History*, page 11 [Free Press, 1995]

4 Lindsey Hughes, *Russia in the Age of Peter the Great*, pages 213–14 [Yale University Press, 1998]

5 ibid, pages 216–17

6 Volkov, *St. Petersburg*, pages 9, 14

7 Arno J. Mayer, *The Furies: Violence and Terror in the French and Russian Revolutions*, page 236 [Princeton University Press,

2000]

8 ibid, page 237

9 Vladimir Lenin, *The State and Revolution*, page 39 (emphasis in original) [Penguin Books, 1992]

10 ibid, page 40 (emphasis in original)

11 ibid, page 87 (emphasis in original)

12 ibid, page 90 (emphasis in original)

13 ibid, page 91 (emphasis in original)

14 ibid, page 86

15 T.H. Rigby, *Lenin's Government: Sovnarkom 1917–1922*, page 8 [Cambridge University Press, 1979]

16 Victor Serge, *Year One of the Russian Revolution*, chapter 4 ("The First Flames of the Civil War: The Constituent Assembly"), posted on the Marxist Archives website, www.marxists.org

17 Silvana Malle, *The Economic Organization of War Communism, 1918–1921*, page 47 [Cambridge University Press, 1985]

18 ibid, page 95

19 S.A. Smith, *Red Petrograd: Revolution in the Factories 1917–18*, page 212 [Cambridge University Press, 1985]

20 ibid, page 213

21 ibid, page 215

22 ibid, pages 215–16

23 Malle, *The Economic Organization of War Communism*, page 47

24 ibid, page 327

25 Kevin Murphy, *Revolution and Counterrevolution: Class Struggle in a Moscow Metal Factory*, page 65 [Haymarket, 2007]

26 Thomas Remington, "Institution Building in Bolshevik Russia: The Case of 'State Kontrol,'" *Slavic Review*, Spring 1982, page 98

27 ibid, pages 94–7, 103

28 Malle, *The Economic Organization of War Communism*, pages

50, 55

29 ibid, pages 50–1; Smith, *Red Petrograd*, pages 236–8; Ronald I. Kowalski, *The Bolshevik Party in Conflict: The Left Communist Opposition of 1918*, page 167 [Macmillan, 1991]

30 Malle, *The Economic Organization of War Communism*, pages 57–8

31 ibid, page 58

32 Kowalski, *The Bolshevik Party in Conflict*, page 165

33 Malle, *The Economic Organization of War Communism*, pages 56–60

34 ibid, pages 60–1

35 ibid, page 61

36 Rigby, *Lenin's Government*, page 160

37 ibid, pages 163–4

38 ibid, pages 170–1

39 Smith, *Red Petrograd*, pages 242–3

40 ibid, page 243

41 Murphy, *Revolution and Counterrevolution*, page 63

42 Malle, *The Economic Organization of War Communism*, pages 63–4

43 Murphy, *Revolution and Counterrevolution*, page 69

44 ibid, page 72

45 Smith, *Red Petrograd*, pages 228, 261

46 ibid, page 247–52

47 Moshe Lewin, *Lenin's Last Struggle*, page 9 [Random House, 1968]

48 Malle, *The Economic Organization of War Communism*, pages 63–7

49 Isaac Deutscher, *The Prophet Armed: Trotsky 1879–1921*, page 414 [Verso, 2003]

50 Richard B. Day, *Leon Trotsky and the Politics of Economic Isolation*, page 43 [Cambridge University Press, 1973]

51 "Theses of the Workers Opposition," *Pravda*, 25 January 1921; posted on the Marxist Archives website

52 ibid
53 ibid
54 ibid
55 William C. Rosenberg, "NEP Russia as a 'Transitional' Society," anthologized in Sheila Fitzpatrick, Alexander Rabinowitch and Richard Stites (eds), *Russia in the Era of NEP: Explorations in Soviet Society and Culture*, page 4 [Indiana University Press, 1991]
56 Stephen F. Cohen, *Bukharin and the Bolshevik Revolution: A Political Biography, 1888–1938*, page 123 [Alfred A. Knopf, 1973]
57 Deutscher, *The Prophet Armed*, page 424
58 Deutscher, *Stalin: A Political Biography* (second edition), page 224 [Oxford University Press, 1966]
59 Deutscher, *Prophet Armed*, page 425
60 Lewin, *Lenin's Last Struggle*, page 22
61 Malle, *The Economic Organization of War Communism*, pages 327–28
62 Cohen, *Bukharin and the Bolshevik Revolution*, page 125
63 Nikolai Bukharin, "Economic Organization in Soviet Russia," *Die Rote Fahne*, 8 March 1922; posted on the Marxist Archives website
64 Deutscher, *The Prophet Unarmed: Trotsky 1921–1929*, page 398 (note 12) [Verso, 2003]
65 ibid, page 15
66 ibid
67 Lenin, "Pages from a Diary," 15 December 1922; posted on the Marxist Archives website
68 ibid
69 Lenin, "On Cooperation," 4–6 January 1932; posted on the Marxist Archives website
70 ibid
71 ibid
72 ibid

73 Lenin, "Our Revolution," 16 January 1923; posted on the Marxist Archives website

74 Lenin, "How We Should Reorganize the Workers' and Peasants' Inspectorate," 23 January 1923; posted on the Marxist Archives website

75 Lenin, "Better Fewer, but Better," 2 March 1923; posted on the Marxist Archives website

76 ibid

77 ibid

78 Remington, "Institution Building in Bolshevik Russia," page 103

79 Lewin, *Lenin's Last Struggle*, page 120

80 Leon Trotsky, *Portraits Political & Personal*, page 209 [Pathfinder 1977]

81 Robert C. Williams, *The Other Bolsheviks: Lenin and His Critics, 1904–1914*, pages 119–21, 155, 166 [Indiana University Press, 1986]

82 ibid, pages 155, 166

83 Lewin, *Lenin's Last Struggle*, page 35

84 ibid, pages 46, 48

85 Lewin, *The Soviet Century*, page 22 [Verso, 2005]

86 Lewin, *Lenin's Last Struggle*, page 51

87 Lewin, *Soviet Century*, page 23; Alfred J. Rieber, "Stalin, Man of the Borderlands," *The American Historical Review*, Vol. 106, No. 5, online version at *71.

88 Lewin, *Lenin's Last Struggle*, page 52

89 ibid, pages 92–3

90 ibid, page 94

91 Lenin, "To Comrade Stalin," posted on Marxist Archives website

92 Lenin, "To P.G. Mdivani, F.Y. Makharadze and Others," posted on Marxist Archives website

93 Lewin, *Lenin's Last Struggle*, page 103

94 Lenin, "Letter to the Congress," posted on Marxist Archives

website

95 Lenin, "The Question of Nationalities or 'Autonomisation,'" posted on Marxist Archives website

96 Deutscher, *Prophet Unarmed*, page 74

97 ibid, pages 75–6; Lewin, *Soviet Century*, page 27

98 Deutscher, *Prophet Unarmed*, page 76

99 Jeremy Smith, "Stalin as Commissar for Nationality Affairs, 1918–1922," anthologized in Sarah Davies and James Harris (eds), *Stalin: A New History*, page 56 [Cambridge University Press, 2005]

100 ibid, page 57

101 Anatolii Lunacharskii, *Revolutionary Silhouettes*, posted on Marxist Archives website

102 Trotsky, *Portraits Political & Personal*, page 73

103 ibid, page 77

104 Harris, "Stalin as General Secretary: The Appointment Process and the Nature of Stalin's Power," anthologized in Davies & Harris, *Stalin: A New History*, page 69

105 ibid

106 ibid, page 74

107 ibid, page 75, citing the official party transcript

108 ibid, citing the official party transcript

109 Lewin, *Soviet Century*, page 32, citing Stalin, *Sochineniia*, Vol. 5, pages 210–11

110 Karl Radek, "Through Germany in the Sealed Coach," originally in Fritz Platten, *Die Reise Lenin durch Deutschland im plombierten Wagen*; posted on Marxist Archives website (English-language translation by Ian Birchall)

111 Deutscher, *Stalin*, page 270

112 Nina Tumarkin, "Religion, Bolshevism, and the Origin of the Lenin Cult," *Russian Review*, page 40, January 1981

113 ibid, pages 40–1

114 Deutscher, *Prophet Unarmed*, pages 110–11

115 Deutscher, *Stalin*, page 256

116 Murphy, *Revolution and Counterrevolution*, page 165
117 Day, *Leon Trotsky and the Politics of Economic Isolation*, pages 97–8
118 Deutscher, *Stalin*, page 260; Murphy, *Revolution and Counterrevolution*, page 169
119 Deutscher, *Stalin*, page 258
120 Murphy, *Revolution and Counterrevolution*, pages 87, 164–5
121 Deutscher, *Prophet Unarmed*, page 114
122 ibid, pages 126–8; Day, *Leon Trotsky and the Politics of Economic Isolation*, pages 98–100
123 Deutscher, *Prophet Unarmed*, page 128
124 Cohen, *Bukharin and the Bolshevik Revolution*, page 240
125 ibid, page 269; Deutscher, *Prophet Unarmed*, page 264
126 Nikita Khrushchev, *Khrushchev Remembers*, page 26 [Little Brown, 1970]
127 ibid, pages 26–7
128 ibid, page 27
129 ibid, page 30
130 Rieber, "Stalin, Man of the Borderlands," at *39
131 ibid, at *38
132 Donald Filtzer, *Soviet Workers and Stalinist Industrialization: The Formation of Modern Soviet Production Relations, 1928–1941*, page 21 [Pluto Press, 1986]
133 Murphy, *Revolution and Counterrevolution*, page 83
134 ibid, pages 92–3, 105
135 Chris Ward, "Languages of Trade or a Language of Class? Work Culture in the Russian Cotton Mills in the 1920s," anthologized in Lewis H. Siegelbaum and Ronald Grigory Suny, *Making Workers Soviet: Power, Class and Identity*, page 197 [Cornell University Press, 1994]
136 Day, *Leon Trotsky and the Politics of Economic Isolation*, pages 33, 166
137 Ward, "Languages of Trade," page 203
138 ibid, page 204

139 Diane P. Koenker, "Class and Consciousness in a Socialist Society: Workers in the Printing Trades during NEP," anthologized in Fitzpatrick, et al., *Russia in the Era of NEP*, page 47

140 ibid, page 46

141 ibid, pages 46–7

142 ibid, page 51

143 Murphy, *Revolution and Counterrevolution*, page 124

144 Daniel Orlovsky, "The Hidden Class: White-Collar Workers in the Soviet 1920s," anthologized in Siegelbaum & Suny, *Making Workers Soviet*, page 220

145 Fitzpatrick, "The Problem of Class Identity in NEP Society," anthologized in Fitzpatrick, et al., *Russia in the Era of NEP*, pages 14–15, 26–7

146 Orlovsky, "The Hidden Class," page 228

147 ibid, page 230–3

148 ibid, page 236

149 Cohen, *Bukharin and the Bolshevik Revolution*, pages 273–4

150 Douglas R. Weiner, "'Razmychka?': Urban Unemployment and Peasant In-Migration as Sources of Social Conflict," anthologized in Fitzpatrick, et al., *Russia in the Era of NEP*, page 146

151 Filtzer, *Soviet Workers and Stalinist Industrialization*, page 24

152 John B. Hatch, "Labor Conflict in Moscow, 1921–1925," anthologized in Fitzpatrick, et al., *Russia in the Era of NEP*, page 64

153 Murphy, *Revolution and Counterrevolution*, pages 96–9

154 Hatch, "Labor Conflict in Moscow," page 63

155 Alan Ball, "Private Trade and Traders during NEP," anthologized in Fitzpatrick, et al., *Russia in the Era of NEP*, page 91

156 Lewin, *Soviet Century*, page 41

157 Weiner, "Razmychka?," page 148

158 ibid, pages 149–51

159 Helmut Altrichter, "Insoluble Conflicts: Village Life

between Revolution and Collectivization," anthologized in Fitzpatrick, et al., *Russia in the Era of NEP*, pages 204–5

160 ibid, pages 206–7

161 Lynne Viola, "Notes on the Background of Soviet Collectivisation Metal Worker Brigades in the Countryside, Autumn 1929," *Soviet Studies*, April 1984, page 214

162 Mark von Hagen, "Soldiers in the Proletarian Dictatorship: From Defending the Revolution to Building Socialism," anthologized in Fitzpatrick, et al., *Russia in the Era of NEP*, page 166

163 ibid

164 Lewin, *Soviet Century*, page 113

165 ibid

166 Wendy Z. Goldman, "Working Class Women and the 'Withering Away' of the Family: Popular Responses to Family Policy," anthologized in Fitzpatrick, et al., *Russia in the Era of NEP*, page 126

167 ibid, page 128

168 Margaret Randall, *Gathering Rage: The Failure of 20th Century Revolutions to Develop a Feminist Agenda*, page 102 [Monthly Review Press, 1992]

169 R.E. Johnson, "Family Life in Moscow during NEP," anthologized in Fitzpatrick, et al., *Russia in the Era of NEP*, pages 113, 114

170 Goldman, "Working Class Women," page 133

171 S. Frederick Starr, introduction to *Russian Avant-Garde Art: The George Costakis Collection*, pages 20–1 [Harry N. Abrams, 1981]

172 ibid, page 25

173 John E. Bowlt, chronology to *Russian Avant-Garde Art*, pages 518–19

174 Volkov, *Shostakovich and Stalin: The Extraordinary Relationship between the Great Composer and the Brutal Dictator*, page 56 [Alfred A. Knopf, 2004]

175 ibid, page 54 (emphasis in original)

176 ibid, pages 70–1

177 Cohen, *Bukharin and the Bolshevik Revolution*, page 164

178 Deutscher, *Prophet Unarmed*, page 198

179 ibid

180 James R. Millar, "A Note on Primitive Accumulation in Marx and Preobrazhensky," *Soviet Studies*, July 1978

181 Deutscher, *Prophet Unarmed*, page 200

182 Cohen, *Bukharin and the Bolshevik Revolution*, page 177

183 ibid, page 181

184 ibid, page 179–80

185 Deutscher, *Prophet Unarmed*, pages 204–5

186 ibid, page 415 (note 66)

187 Trotsky, *Platform of the Joint Opposition*, chapter 4 ("State Industry and the Building of Socialism"), posted on the Marxist Archives website

188 ibid

189 ibid

190 ibid (emphasis in original)

191 ibid

192 C.L.R. James, *World Revolution 1917–1936: The Rise and Fall of the Communist International*, page 213 [Humanities Press, 1993]

193 ibid

194 Deutscher, *Stalin*, page 319

195 ibid

196 Nikolai Bukharin, "A Great Marxian Party," *The Communist Review* (United Kingdom), May 1923, Vol. 4, No. 1; posted on the Marxist Archives website

197 Cohen, *Bukharin and the Bolshevik Revolution*, pages 141–2

198 Christian Rakovsky, "The 'Professional Dangers' of Power," published in *Bulleten Oppozitsii*, 1929, No. 6; posted on the Marxist Archives website

199 ibid

200 ibid
201 ibid
202 ibid
203 Deutscher, *Prophet Unarmed*, pages 299–301
294 ibid, pages 305–6
205 Murphy, *Revolution and Counterrevolution*, pages 110–11, 172–6
206 Filtzer, *Soviet Workers and Stalinist Industrialization*, page 24
207 James Hughes, "Capturing the Russian Peasantry: Stalinist Grain Procurement Policy and the 'Ural-Siberian Method,'" *Slavic Review*, Spring 1994, page 80
208 Deutscher, *Prophet Unarmed*, page 359
209 Cohen, *Bukharin and the Bolshevik Revolution*, page 330
210 Trotsky, *The Revolution Betrayed*, page 26
211 Hughes, "Capturing the Russian Peasantry," page 81
212 ibid, page 82
213 ibid, page 84; Viola, "Notes on the Background of Soviet Collectivisation Metal Worker Brigades," page 208
214 Hughes, "Capturing the Russian Peasantry," page 75
215 ibid, pages 87, 91, 93, 95; Graeme Gill, *Peasants and Government in the Russian Revolution*, pages 107, 111 [Macmillan, 1979]
216 Hughes, "Capturing the Russian Peasantry," pages 101–2
217 Viola, "Notes on the Background of Soviet Collectivisation Metal Worker Brigades," pages 206–7
218 ibid, page 207
219 Roger R. Reese, "Red Army Opposition to Forced Collectivization, 1929–1930: The Army Wavers," *Slavic Review*, Spring 1996, page 29
220 ibid, page 30
221 Viola, "Notes on the Background of Soviet Collectivisation Metal Worker Brigades," pages 208–9
222 ibid, pages 209–10, 216
223 ibid, page 209

224 ibid, pages 210–12

225 Harris, "The Growth of the Gulag: Forced Labor in the Urals Region, 1929–31," page 267, *The Russian Review*, April 1997

226 R.W. Davies, "Stalin as Economic Policy-maker: Soviet Agriculture, 1931–36," S. Davies & Harris, *Stalin: A New History*, page 123

227 Deutscher, *The Prophet Outcast: Trotsky 1929–1940*, page 434 (note 110) [Verso 2003]

228 Mayer, *Furies*, page 634

229 Deutscher, *Stalin*, page 324

230 Viola, "Notes on the Background of Soviet Collectivisation Metal Worker Brigades," page 214, citing Trade Union of Metal Workers archives

231 Reese, "Red Army Opposition to Forced Collectivization," page 32, citing Russian State Military Archives

232 ibid, page 33

233 ibid, pages 32, 41

234 Mayer, *Furies*, page 638, quoting Davies, *The Socialist Offensive: The Collectivization of Soviet Agriculture, 1929–1930*, page 413

235 Trotsky, *The Revolution Betrayed*, page 30

236 Josef Stalin, "Dizzy with Success: Concerning Questions of the Collective-Farm Movement," *Pravda*, 2 March 1930; posted on Marxist Archives website

237 ibid

238 David R. Marples, *Heroes and Villains: Creating National History in Contemporary Ukraine*, page 39 [Central European University Press, 2007]

239 ibid

240 Douglas Tottle, *Fraud, Famine and Fascism: The Ukrainian Genocide Myth from Hitler to Harvard*, page 97 [Progress Books, 1987], quoting Hans Blumenfeld, *Life Begins at 65: The Not Entirely Candid Autobiography of a Drifter*, pages 153-

4[Harvest Books, 1987]

241 Mark B. Trauger, "Natural Disaster and Human Actions in the Soviet Famine of 1931–1933," pages 9–17, The Carl Beck Papers in *Russian and East European Studies*, June 2001

242 Tottle, *Fraud, Famine and Fascism*, pages 94–6

243 Trauger, "The 1932 Harvest and the Famine of 1933," *Slavic Review*, Spring 1991, page 71

244 ibid, pages 71–2

245 ibid, pages 72–85

246 Davies, "Stalin as Economic Policy-maker," page 131

247 ibid; *Famine in the USSR 1929–1934: New Documentary Evidence* (lead researcher Viktor Kondrashin), published by the Federal Archival Agency of the Russian Federation, derived from nine archives, documents 88–92, online at www.rusarchives.ru/publication/famine/famine-ussr.pdf

248 ibid, documents 76–82, 84–7, 93–5, 98

249 Trauger, "The 1932 Harvest," page 88

250 Khrushchev, *Khrushchev Remembers*, pages 73–4

251 James, *World Revolution 1917–1936*, page 362

252 Deutscher, *Stalin*, page 328

253 Lewin, "Concluding Remarks," Siegelbaum & Suny, *Making Workers Soviet*, page 385

254 Mayer, *Furies*, page 630

255 Trotsky, *The Revolution Betrayed*, page 28

256 Mayer, *Furies*, page 631

257 Stephen Kotkin, "Coercion and Identity: Workers' Lives in Stalin's Showcase City," Siegelbaum & Suny, *Making Workers Soviet*, page 280

258 ibid

259 Gábor T. Rittersporn, "From Working Class to Urban Laboring Mass: On Politics and Social Categories in the Formative Years of the Soviet System," Siegelbaum & Suny, *Making Workers Soviet*, page 256

260 Kotkin, "Coercion and Identity," page 274

261 James, *World Revolution 1917–1936*, page 296
262 ibid, pages 298–9
263 Kotkin, "Coercion and Identity," pages 291, 298
264 Lewin, *Soviet Century*, pages 69–70
265 Rittersporn, "From Working Class to Urban Laboring Mass," page 264
266 Paul R. Gregory and Andrei Markevich, "Creating Soviet Industry: The House That Stalin Built," *Slavic Review*, pages 790, 809
267 ibid, page 798
268 Oleg V. Khlevniuk, "Stalin as Dictator: The Personalisation of Power," S. Davies & Harris, *Stalin: A New History*, page 113
269 Filtzer, *Soviet Workers and Stalinist Industrialization*, pages 117, 121
270 Harris, "The Growth of the Gulag," page 266
271 ibid, pages 267–9, 273, 275
272 ibid, pages 269–71, 273
273 ibid, pages 273–6
274 ibid, page 279
275 James J. Nordlander, "Origins of a Gulag Capital: Magadan and Stalinist Control in the Early 1930s," *Slavic Review*, Winter 1998, pages 793, 795–6
276 ibid, page 794
277 Lewin, *Soviet Century*, page 115
278 Mayer, *Furies*, page 643
279 ibid, page 642; Lewin, *Soviet Century*, page 114
280 Cohen, *Bukharin and the Bolshevik Revolution*, page 343
281 J. Arch Getty, "Stalin as Prime Minister: Power and the Politburo," S. Davies & Harris, *Stalin: A New History*, page 86
282 Franz Borkenau, *World Communism*, page 350 [University of Michigan Press, 1962]
283 Cohen, *Bukharin and the Bolshevik Revolution*, page 348

284 Boris Nicolaevsky, "Letter of an Old Bolshevik," anthologized in *Power and the Soviet Elite*, page 28 [Praeger, 1965]
285 ibid, pages 11, 28–9
286 Arkady Vaksberg, *Stalin's Prosecutor: The Life of Andrei Vyshinsky*, page 58 [Grove Weidenfeld, 1991]
287 Nicolaevsky, "Letter of an Old Bolshevik," page 30
288 Amy Knight, *Who Killed Kirov? The Kremlin's Greatest Mystery*, page 172 [Hill and Wang, 1999]; Anton Antonov-Ovseenko, *The Time of Stalin: Portrait of a Tyranny*, pages 79–80 [Harper & Row, 1981]
289 Knight, *Who Killed Kirov?*, page 173
290 Antonov-Ovseenko, *The Time of Stalin*, pages 80–2
291 Knight, *Who Killed Kirov?*, pages 173–4
292 ibid, page 173
293 Nicolaevsky, "The Murder of Kirov," anthologized in *Power and the Soviet Elite*, page 96
294 Khrushchev, "secret speech" given to the Twentieth Congress of the Communist Party of the Soviet Union, 24 February 1956
295 Knight, *Who Killed Kirov?*, page 198
296 ibid, page 211
297 Khrushchev, "secret speech"
298 Knight, *Who Killed Kirov?*, page 201
299 Deutscher, *Stalin*, pages 356–7
300 ibid, page 358
301 Lewin, *Soviet Century*, page 100
302 ibid
303 Getty, "Stalin as Prime Minister," page 83
304 David Priestland, "Stalin as Bolshevik Romantic: Ideology and Mobilisation, 1917–1939," S. Davies & Harris, *Stalin: A New History*, page 195
305 Fitzpatrick, "Workers against Bosses: The Impact of the Great Purges on Labor-Management Relations," Siegelbaum & Suny, *Making Workers Soviet*, page 315

306 ibid, pages 321–4

307 Donald Filtzer, "From Mobilized to Free Labour: De-Stalinization and the Changing Legal Status of Workers," anthologized in Polly Jones (ed.), *The Dilemmas of De-Stalinization: Negotiating Cultural and Social Changes in the Khrushchev Era*, pages 157–9 [Routledge 2006]

308 "Report of Court Proceedings: The Case of the Trotskyite-Zinovievite Terrorist Centre," 23 August [1936] morning session, posted on the Marxist Archives website

309 ibid

310 ibid, 22 August evening session

311 ibid, 22 August morning session

312 Khrushchev, "secret speech"

313 Vaksberg, *Stalin's Prosecutor*, page 89

314 Trotsky, *Portraits*, pages 180–1

315 ibid, page 170

316 ibid, page 171–2

317 ibid, page 173

318 Alexander Rabinowitch, "Maria Spiridonova's 'Last Testament," *The Russian Review*, July 1995, page 441

319 ibid, page 442

320 ibid, page 439

321 ibid, page 440

322 Albert Fried (ed.), *Communism in America: A History in Documents*, page 310 [Columbia University Press, 1997], excerpting Charles Shipman, *It Had to Be Revolution*

323 Vaksberg, *Stalin's Prosecutor*, page 142

324 ibid, page 80

325 ibid, page 123

326 "M.B.," "The Trotskyists in Vorkuta Prison Camp," anthologized in Tariq Ali (ed.), *The Stalinist Legacy: Its Import on 20th-century Politics*, pages 187–96 [Penguin, 1984]

327 Rabinowitch, "Maria Spiridonova's 'Last Testament," page 445

328 Getty, Rittersporn and Viktor N. Zemskov, "Victims of the Soviet Penal System in the Pre-War Years: A First Approach on the Basis of Archival Evidence," *American Historical Review*, October 1993, page 1022; *Pravda*, 22 June 1989, and 14 February 1990, reporting a KGB press release (cited in Getty, et al., page 1023); Lewin, *Soviet Century*, pages 105, 106, 397–8, citing, respectively, the report of a special Communist Party investigation commission set up in 1955, E.M. Adreev, L.A. Karskii and T.L. Kharkova, *Vestnik Statistiki*, No. 7, 1990, page 44, and B.P. Kurashvili, *Istoricheskaia Logika Stalinizma*, pages 159–60 [Moscow, 1996]

329 Getty, et al., "Victims of the Soviet Penal System," pages 1019–20

330 ibid, page 1049

331 "One in 100: Behind Bars in America," Pew Center on the States report, February 2008

332 Getty, et al., "Victims of the Soviet Penal System," page 1041

333 Golfo Alexopoulos, "Amnesty 1945: The Revolving Door of Stalin's Gulag," *Slavic Review*, Summer 2005, pages 279, 299

334 Getty, et al., "Victims of the Soviet Penal System," page 1030

335 Khrushchev, "secret speech" (citing the report of a special party investigation commission set up in 1955)

336 ibid

337 Deutscher, *Stalin*, page 323

338 Mayer, *Furies*, page 657

339 ibid, page 658

340 Lewin, *Soviet Century*, page 109

341 Tottle, *Fraud, Famine and Fascism*, pages 5–12, 45–56

342 Stanislav Kulchytsky, various works (also cited in Marples, *Heroes and Villains*, page 49

343 Christine Kinealy, *A Death-Dealing Famine: The Great Hunger in Ireland*, pages 77–83 [Pluto Press, 1997]

344 Philip Gavin, "The Irish Potato Famine," posted on The History Place website, www.historyplace.com

345 Gavin, "The Irish Potato Famine"
346 Mike Davis, "How Famine Was Created," posted on the Infochange website, www.infochangeindia.org
347 Walter Rodney, *How Europe Underdeveloped Africa*, page 210 [Howard University Press, 1982]
348 Caroline Eakins, *Imperial Reckoning: The Untold Story of Britain's Gulag in Kenya*, pages 121–4, 134 [Henry Holt, 2005]
349 ibid, pages 66, 136
350 ibid, page 366
351 Lewin, *Soviet Century*, page 110
352 Zdeněk Mlynář, *Nightfrost in Prague: The End of Humane Socialism*, page 12 [Karz, 1980]
353 Milovan Djilas, *Conversations with Stalin*, page 148 [Harcourt, Brace & World, 1962]
354 ibid, page 153
355 Vladimir Dedijer, *The Battle Stalin Lost: Memoirs of Yugoslavia 1948–1953*, page 74 [Viking, 1971]
356 ibid, pages 77–8
357 ibid, pages 79–80
358 ibid, pages 91–2
359 ibid, pages 92–4
360 Djilas, *Fall of the New Class*, pages 109, 111 [Alfred A. Knopf, 1998]
361 Deutscher, *Stalin*, pages 501, 534–42
362 Fernando Claudin, "Stalin and the Second World War," anthologized in Ali, *The Stalinist Legacy*, pages 199–202
363 ibid, pages 202–3
364 ibid, page 209
365 Hans Kohn, *Pan-Slavism: Its History and Ideology*, page 299 [Vintage, 1960]
366 ibid
367 Mayer, *Furies*, page 674
368 Khrushchev, "secret speech"
369 Lewin, *Soviet Century*, pages 117–19, citing Marta Kraven

and Oleg Khlevniuk, *Cahiers du Monde Russe*, January–June 1995 and also citing the Russian State Economic Archive

370 ibid, page 118

371 ibid, pages 119–20

372 Ayyub Baghirov, *Bitter Days in Kolyma*, posted on the Azerbaijan International website, www.azer.com

373 ibid

374 Lewin, *Soviet Century*, page 120

375 ibid, pages 120, 122

376 ibid, page 122; Deutscher, *Russia After Stalin*, page 132 [Bobbs-Merrill, 1968]

377 Volkov, *Shostakovich and Stalin*, page 41

378 Gitelman, *A Century of Ambivalence*, pages 145–6

379 György Dalos, *The Guest from the Future: Anna Akhmatova and Isaiah Berlin*, pages 71, 77 [Farrar, Straus and Giroux, 1996]

380 Gitelman, *A Century of Ambivalence*, pages 152–3

381 ibid, pages 153–4

382 Fedor Burlatsky, *Khrushchev and the First Russian Spring: The Era of Khrushchev through the Eyes of His Adviser*, page 11 [Charles Scribner's Son, 1991]

383 Yevgeny Yevtushenko, *Precocious Autobiography*, collected in *Yevtushenko's Reader*, pages 85–6 [E.P. Dutton, 1972]

384 ibid, page 87

## Chapter 3

# The Destroyed Experiment of a Developed, Industrial State: Prague Spring

In the years following Josef Stalin's death, the leadership of the Soviet Union backed reforms with varying degrees of confidence that waxed and waned considerably. One development that provided fresh momentum for reform was the removal of Stalin's two most loyal lieutenants, Viacheslav Molotov and Lazar Kaganovich, in 1957. The nature of this ouster itself demonstrated that profound changes had been introduced into the workings of the top of the party structure. The Politburo had narrowly voted to remove Nikita Khrushchev as party leader, but Khrushchev appealed to the Central Committee, which voted to back him and instead remove Molotov, Kaganovich and others aligned with them.

The outcome of the appeal was remarkable because the Politburo, as the Communist Party's leading body, had long been all-powerful, imposing its decisions by fiat, although, on paper, the Politburo was accountable to the Central Committee, which elected it. (During the Stalin dictatorship the Politburo rubber-stamped Stalin's decrees but during other periods made group decisions.) Interesting, too, was the fate of Molotov and Kaganovich. Far from being shot, the fate they had unhesitatingly dealt to so many during Stalin's reign, they were demoted to minor posts, then retired and given pensions. These must have been comfortable retirements, for Molotov lived until 1989 and Kaganovich until 1991, only a few weeks before Mikhail Gorbachev banned the Communist Party following the failed attempt to remove him.

Sweeping changes, however, had come in the first weeks following Stalin's death. Mass releases from the labor camps and reduction of the power of the secret police, among other reforms, demonstrated that the era of a single-personality dictatorship had ended, although the top layer of the party continued to hold the reins of power very tightly. Stalin's last secret police chief, Lavrenti Beria, and Beria's top assistants were arrested and shot, due to the Politburo members' fear that Beria intended to reinstitute Stalin's terror. Further mass releases of political prisoners followed Khrushchev's "secret speech" at the conclusion of the 1956 party congress, when he documented and denounced many of Stalin's crimes in an hours-long presentation in a closed session. The shock and force of the exposure created fresh momentum for deeper reforms and signaled that a return to institutionalized terror would be impossible.

But unrest in Poland and Hungary later in 1956 resulted in a pulling back of reform efforts by the Khrushchev régime; the Soviet invasion of Hungary demonstrated the new hesitancy all too well. The 1957 removal of Stalin's closest lieutenants gave Khrushchev more room for reforms, but his penchant for risky experimentation and lack of consultation of other party leaders slowly created dissatisfaction with his leadership, culminating in Khrushchev and his erratic reforms being sent into "retirement" in 1964. Different currents of thought among Soviet leaders remained unreconciled; some party leaders remained in favor of reforms and others were opposed. Similar to a lack of consensus in 1953 leading to Khrushchev's ascension to the party's top post as a compromise figure because he was viewed as not being firmly in either camp, Leonid Brezhnev was selected as general secretary in 1964 as a compromise for what was widely assumed would be a short-term interregnum.

Instead, Brezhnev gradually consolidated his power, bringing the reform process to a halt and putting the Soviet Union into a deep freeze from which it would never recover. All of these developments would be reflected in the experiences of Central Europe, not excepting Czechoslovakia and its attempt to create a state that would be socialist in reality rather than the deformed system imposed upon it.

## A popular beginning is overtaken by a larger neighbor

The Communist Party of Czechoslovakia seemed to react to Soviet developments with considerable delay. The first delay, the taking of sole power in 1948, after the communist takeovers elsewhere in Central Europe, was a result of Czechoslovak cultural realities.

Czechs and Slovaks had suffered terribly under Nazi occupation, and Slovak Jews were particularly persecuted under Nazi puppet ruler Jozef Tiso, a fascist Roman Catholic priest who zealously implemented Nazi-style laws. Czechoslovak leaders and intellectuals were shipped to the Nazis' infamous Mauthausen concentration camp in Austria, where educated people were condemned to be worked to death as slave laborers. Communists, socialists, Jews and Slavic intellectuals made up much of the inmate population, not many of whom survived.

Czechoslovakia had been the region's sole stable democracy between the world wars. When it was reconstituted after its liberation, it was governed by a coalition system whereby four parties in the "Czech Lands" (Bohemia and Moravia, the Czech-speaking portion of the country that today is the Czech Republic) and four parties in Slovakia (corresponding to the present-day country of the same name) governed as part of a "National Front" coalition. This multi-party system reflected Czechoslovakia's pluralist traditions.

The leading vote getter in the National Front was the Communist Party, which won nearly 40 percent of the vote, more than double that of any other party. That vote total reflected a strong desire for socialism and nationalization, particularly firm among Czech workers. The Communist Party also enjoyed some backing from small farmers because it implemented land reform beneficial to them. In large numbers, Czechs and Slovaks believed capitalism to be moribund—capitalist instability had led directly to fascism and Europe's capitalist powers had handed Czechoslovakia to Nazi Germany. More than a dozen corporations had profited from slave labor at the Mauthausen concentration camp, profits made on the bodies of as many as 320,000 who were murdered there under the most inhuman conditions.

Nationalizations, land reform, universal health care and other progressive reforms could only be attained under a socialized economy. In an atmosphere polarized by the just-concluded war and in which turning a collective back on the past animated the minds of millions, a socialized economy was seen as the surest route to social justice.

Soon after liberation, in July 1945, one province's miners sent a delegation to the capital, Prague, to declare that they would oppose any government that left the mines in private hands, and miners from another province called a strike to back nationalization.[1] Employees of many other industries, including banks, also called for nationalization.[2] Workers across the country vigorously opposed university students, who at this time constituted a small, privileged social layer drawn from the pre-war elite; in 1947, the information minister, a communist member of the National Front government, said that "on more than one occasion we have had to restrain Prague's workers from taking action against reactionary students."[3]

Trade unions and newly formed "works councils" took the lead in voicing demands for nationalization, and by October 1945 large enterprises were nationalized and works councils were given official standing. These decisions were implemented by decrees issued by President Eduard Beneš, a moderate socialist who had been a popular leader before World War II. Trade unions played a role in the appointments of heads of the nationalized enterprises, and one-third of the members of the boards that managed enterprises were selected by employees.

Beneš's decrees approving nationalization and implementation of some workers' control of industry were widely popular, and there was a consensus for those steps within the National Front. Beneš, re-elected as president in 1946 after his nationalization decrees, supported these measures as part of his belief that large enterprises should be brought under community control. These developments were seen as part of an independent "Czechoslovak road to socialism" in which large enterprises were nationalized, while midsize and small firms would have cooperative or even private ownership. There was no thought of copying the system of the Soviet Union. There was, however, considerable support for deepening socialization while traveling a "Czechoslovak road to socialism"—works councils voiced this demand and hundreds of thousands marched through the streets of Prague, backed by mass strikes, demanding the country's Communist Party take sole power.

A dozen government ministers representing other National Front parties resigned their posts to pressure Beneš into calling early elections, believing that Beneš would not accept their resignations, but instead pressure from the streets induced Beneš to appoint a Communist government. The expected independent path as a "bridge between East and West" (to use Beneš's formulation) did not last much longer, however, under the pressure of the Cold War. The Communist Party, headed by Klement Gottwald, began implementing the Soviet system under intense pressure from the Stalin régime. As a result of this imposition, the trade unions became instruments of party control and the works councils were disbanded in 1949.

Enthusiasm to go forward remained for a time, even under the new top-down system in which central planning would be decreed from above. Czechoslovakia was already a heavily industrialized country, which Marxists believed to be a necessary precondition for socialism: It had no need, or desire, for a system designed to force an agricultural, undeveloped society onto a path of rapid industrialization. But the Soviet system was forced on it economically as well as politically. Czechoslovakia had possessed a diverse economy with a healthy consumer-products industry, but the Soviet formula of heavy stress on steel, iron and other producer goods was imposed, disrupting the country's economy. Democratic control from the shop floor was ended, but promotion of workers from the shop floor to management and technical positions became a priority; about 100,000 workers made this leap during the early 1950s.[4]

Czechoslovakia was the last country to join the European communist bloc, and the last of those under Soviet domination to stage show trials. Fourteen party leaders, including its second-ranking official, Rudolph Slánský, and Foreign Minister Vladimír Klementis were put on trial; 11 of the 14 were executed. Among Central European countries within the Soviet bloc, only the purges in Hungary were more lethal.

Gottwald and Slánský, in September 1949, finally agreed to conduct purge trials, yielding to intense pressure from Stalin and Stalin's faithful followers in Poland and Hungary. Gottwald and Slánský, Czechoslovakia's highest-ranking officials, telegrammed the Kremlin: "We ask the Central Committee of the Communist Party of the Soviet Union to send a few specialists to Prague who are, if possible, familiar with the Hungarian case,"[5] referring to trials then ongoing in Hungary. An affirmative reply came within a week. Soon after arriving, one of the Soviet "specialists," upon seeing hesitation among the Czechoslovak secret police, declared, "I didn't come here for discussions. I came to Czechoslovakia to see heads roll."[6] Control of the secret police and the army were to be key elements in Soviet domination of Central Europe, and would play a critical role in the 1968 invasion of Czechoslovakia.

Western intrigue seems to have played a role in Slánský's downfall. Czech émigrés working for United States intelligence services concocted a letter to be smuggled into Czechoslovakia offering Slánský asylum in the West, and informing him that confirming codes would be broadcast on Radio Free Europe. The letter fell into government hands before it could reach Slánský, who knew nothing of the plot, and when the codes were broadcast as promised, Gottwald finally agreed, under continuing pressure from Stalin's lieutenants, to arrest Slánský.[7]

Slánský and the other 13 defendants had the same familiar charges from Stalin's 1930s show trials heaped upon them, except "Titoism" was substituted for "Trotskyism," and were just as imaginary. Show trials are staged to forcefully put forth political lessons. These Stalinist show trials were aimed at party members who might be tempted to stray from official lines.

"Stalin and, under his influence, Klement Gottwald intended to use these political trials to nip every possibility of an independent road to socialism in the bud," was the assessment of Jiří Pelikán, an active member of the party at the time who would later become prominent among the 1968 reformers.

> That is how they succeeded in establishing the Soviet model, as well as the domination of the [Communist Party of the Soviet Union] within the international communist movement. [The 14 show-trial defendants]...did not oppose the Stalin and Gottwald line...They became victims not because of their views and deeds but because of a suspicion that one day they might oppose the Soviet Union's role as the sole centre, the pivot of world socialism.[8]

Gottwald's imitation of Stalin seemingly reached absurd proportions when he caught a flu at Stalin's funeral and, already ill, died a week later. The Czechoslovak party leadership's choice for a new leader was overruled by Soviet leaders, who imposed Antonín Novotný.[9] The hard-line Novotný had distinguished himself as a zealous defender of the show trials, and his dull, bureaucratic personality made him a logical candidate to enforce Soviet dominance; he had not a hint of independence in him.

The Czechoslovak economy did show strong growth into the early 1950s, averaging about 10 percent annual growth from 1948 to 1952, but growth had slowed to 3.5 percent by 1954.[10] Signs of unrest had also appeared, with revolts in the major industrial cities of Brno (in 1951) and Plzeň (in 1953). Much bigger rebellions happened in Poland and Hungary in 1956, which, although handled very differently from each other, brought reforms to those countries.

## An early attempt at establishing workers' councils in Poland and Hungary

Unrest in Poland exploded in the city of Poznań in June 1956 when workers in the Zipso locomotive factory, which employed 12,000 people, walked out. Zipso workers had sent a delegation to the capital, Warsaw, with five demands, including a 20 percent pay raise and reductions to the work quotas. The widespread use of piece-work pay schemes was especially detested. Five days later, there had been no answer and rumors that the delegation had been arrested began circulating.[11] In response, the Zipso workers went on strike. Demonstrations turned into riots, and as word of what was happening in Poznań spread, riots broke out in other Polish cities. Polish authorities ultimately sent troops into Poznań to put down the riots.

The demands and subsequent demonstrations in Poznań reflected building discontent among Poland's workers, which was acknowledged by the Polish communist party leadership. Edward Ochab, the party leader, admitted at a central committee meeting three weeks after the rising that "it is necessary to look first of all at the social roots of these instances which have become, for the whole of our party, a warning signal testifying to the existence of serious disturbances between the party and various sections of the working class."[12] A steady stream of letters complaining about economic conditions had been sent to the central committee.[13]

In October, another central committee meeting convened, to elect Władysław Gomułka as the new party leader. Gomułka had been purged in 1951 during Poland's Stalin-style purges, but was merely sent to jail because Polish leaders possessed enough independence not to execute their colleagues despite pressure from Moscow. Gomułka had popularity among Polish working people, not only for being a victim of the purges, but for the dangerous work he had performed as a party worker from 1926 and as a union official from 1930; the party was banned and violently persecuted before World War II, when Gomułka served three separate jail terms. Gomułka then became a leader in the anti-Nazi resistance during the war, again risking torture and death.

The Polish party leaders decided to make concessions following their use of force in Poznań, easing the conditions for workers and allowing farmers to disband collective farms. Gomułka was also seen as someone who stood up to the Soviet Union, further enhancing his standing. In the relaxed atmosphere, two workers' councils were formed by employees in Warsaw in September 1956, with a goal of obtaining increased efficiency through, among other demands, economic restructuring and more workers' participation in basic decisions.[14] The workers' councils were made legal in November, but were quickly undermined, rendering them irrelevant.

In contrast to Poland, the formation of workers' councils played a much larger role in grassroots activity in Hungary in 1956. Hungary, under post-World War II communist ruler Mátyás Rákosi, suffered more repression than any Soviet bloc country, excepting the Soviet Union itself during the dictatorship of Stalin. Hundreds of thousands were expelled from the party, and thousands arrested and imprisoned during the Hungarian purges. Gathering popular discontent began mounting; unrest gradually took concrete form in organized discussion groups that began meeting in April 1956. After the Poznań strikes of

Poland in June, Rákosi was openly criticized throughout Hungary, and mounting discontent led the Soviet leadership to force Rákosi to step down in July. But Rákosi's replacement was another hated hard-liner, Ernő Gerő, who was just as responsible as Rákosi for the violent repression of previous years. That shuffle at the top only fueled more discontent. Ample evidence of that discontent came on 6 October, when 200,000 lined the streets of Budapest, the capital city, for a ceremonial reburial of five executed victims of the purge trials who had been declared innocent of all charges, including former Foreign Minister László Rajk.

The Hungarian government began losing control on 23 October, when several thousand students demonstrated in Budapest with a 16-point program that included demands for the removal of the "criminal leaders of the Stalin–Rákosi era," a new government headed by reformer Imre Nagy, a new legislature with free elections, the right to strike and increases in salaries.[15] Nagy, born into a peasant family and starting work as a locksmith's apprentice at age 15, became a communist while a prisoner of war during World War I. After 14 years of exile in the Soviet Union, he returned to Hungary, overseeing the first land reforms under the initial post-World War II provisional government. Nagy held various ministerial offices after the communist takeover (although Rákosi had blocked his attempted reforms), and was widely seen as a more accessible figure. Indeed, Nagy was attending a popular wine festival as these events unfolded. Nagy had been removed as prime minister and expelled from the party only a year earlier and retained a strong level of popular support.

Later on 23 October, the demonstrators marched to the center of Budapest, joined by groups of working people who streamed in from across the city. Gerő spoke on the radio, denouncing the demonstrators as "counter-revolutionaries." The crowd grew still larger, and marched to a radio station, where the Hungarian secret police, the "Avos," opened fire.

After Gerő's speech, the Hungarian communist party leaders met and, during the meeting, Gerő called Nikita Khrushchev to ask that Soviet troops be sent in immediately to quell the demonstrations.[16] Tanks arrived in Budapest the next day. This display of weakness by the Hungarian leadership was seen as overkill by some Soviet leaders—Anastas Mikoyan and Mikhail Suslov sent a cable from Budapest to their Politburo colleagues in Moscow stating that the Hungarians were "exaggerating the strength of the enemy and underestimating their own strength."[17] Despite the Hungarian leaders' fears they did not expand their own apparatus of repression; only the Avos had the authority to fire on demonstrators. The army did not have that authority, and many soldiers joined the demonstrators.

The appearance of Soviet tanks only enraged the people of Hungary. On 24 October, Gerő was replaced as party first secretary by János Kádár, who had been imprisoned during the purges, and Nagy, freshly re-admitted to the party, was appointed prime minister. But the uprising spread—factory workers on Czepel Island, Hungary's largest concentration of industry, located just south of Budapest, occupied their factories and armed the rebels, and general strikes broke out across the country. The contempt shown by the Rákosi–Gerő government generated such anger that blind lashings-out occurred: One morning, the Budapest party headquarters was stormed and 45 Avos were lynched, as was the city party secretary. But the Avos who were lynched turned out to have been conscripts, drafted into the secret police instead of the army, and the party secretary had been an opponent of Rákosi and a veteran of the Spanish Civil War and the French Resistance.[18]

Simultaneous with the fighting, workers' councils formed across Hungary, many of which became the effective government in their cities. Their basic set of demands is embodied in a 23 October resolution passed by the Parliament of Workers'

Councils, a group with representatives from 24 major factories. The first of the nine main points went right to the point: "The factory belongs to the workers. The latter should pay the state a levy calculated on the basis of the output and a portion of the profits."[19] The councils did not propose to make each factory or larger enterprise an island unto itself, but stated they expected to pay taxes to benefit the greater good.

The workers' councils were declared to be the "supreme controlling body in the place of work," which would in turn elect an executive body to oversee all areas of policy and carry out decisions of the councils. The council was to elect the director and other top managers within enterprises, and to decide on all factory plans, pay raises, employment disputes, "social questions in the enterprise" and the use to which profits would be put.[20] The resolution also declared that 90 percent of Budapest's factory, office, institutional and university councils, along with "the Peasant Alliance" being set up, "have already accepted these proposals, and have taken the necessary steps to put them in operation."[21]

Councils were formed not only by industrial workers, but also by white-collar workers, farmers and army personnel. The councils received further backing when trade union leaders formed a new national organization, and issued a set of demands, including that a new government be formed that would include union representatives and be headed by Nagy.[22] The trade union leaders also demanded the establishment of workers' councils as the basis of workers' management of factories, pay raises for the lowest-paid workers, the establishment of a maximum wage, a speed-up of house building by the state, and negotiations with the Soviet Union and other countries to establish mutual economic relations on the basis of equality.[23] An estimated 2100 workers' councils were set up across Hungary[24]—by no means was the desire for socialist solutions limited to Budapest.

Fighting continued in all parts of Hungary, and a nationwide general strike, organized by the workers' councils, remained in force. The councils reiterated their demands on 29 October, as Nagy unsuccessfully attempted to calm the unrest with repeated pleas on Budapest radio; radio stations in most of the rest of the country had been taken over by the rebels. Nagy spent his first days in office trying to keep up with the rapid developments—on 30 October, Nagy announced the formation of a multi-party government after having earlier promised pay raises, an amnesty for rebels and the withdrawal of Soviet troops.

The same day, the Soviet army pulled out of Budapest. But the Soviet leadership had already decided that Nagy had lost control, and on 31 October decided to re-invade with a far larger force. On 3 November, Kádár and three other ministers went to the Soviet embassy and were to emerge as Hungary's new leadership when the second invasion began the next day. This time, the Hungarian experiment would be decisively ended.

Simultaneous with these events in Hungary, the British and French governments, in collusion with Israel, invaded Egypt in an attempt to seize the Suez Canal and overthrow Egyptian leader Gamal Abdel Nasser. A series of diplomatic maneuvers had led Nasser to nationalize the Egyptian company that operated the canal, with payments to shareholders at full market prices. About 3000 Egyptians died at the hands of the invading forces. The British and French, however, were forced to pull out in the face of displeasure by US President Dwight Eisenhower, who threatened economic punishment against the British. This episode represented the final moment when London and Paris could have retained delusions that they were not now definitively subordinate to the United States, and also rendered their protests over the Soviet invasion of Hungary hypocritical.

Meanwhile, the Soviet leaders knew they had a free hand in crushing the Hungarian workers' movement. On 22 October, the United States secretary of state, John Foster Dulles, had declared the legality of Soviet troops in Warsaw Pact states: "From the standpoint of international law and violation of treaties, I do not think you could claim that it would be a violation of a treaty."[25] That statement counted for much more than the encouragements to revolt that US-financed radio stations broadcast into Hungary. The US hands-off attitude was not a surprising development: The example of working people taking control of their places of employment and taking responsibility for economic decisions is a concept in opposition to the standards of the capitalist system. United States business leaders would have shuddered at the very thought with even more horror than the Soviet Union's hard-liners.

Nonetheless, a steady barrage of propaganda from the Soviet Union and organizations blindly loyal to it asserted that the unfolding events in Hungary were "counter-revolutionary." It is true that there were reactionary elements ready to take advantage of the situation, including those who would follow Roman Catholic Cardinal József Mindszenty, who was elevated to his post by the fascist sympathizer Pope Pius XII. Mindszenty vehemently opposed democratic republics, spending decades demanding a restoration of Hapsburg dictatorship and rigidly condemning Hungarians for mortal sins such as dancing.

Mindszenty was also a notorious anti-Semite, although he had that in common with other Hungarian Catholic leaders. He delivered an ambiguous speech on nationwide radio that was pointed to by Soviet and Hungarian hard-liners as "proof" that a conservative, or even a fascist, régime was about to be imposed. One problem with that thesis, however, is that Mindszenty made his speech on 3 November, three days after the Soviet Politburo decision to re-invade and as the tanks were closing in on Budapest. The uprising had managed to progress without input from the cardinal.

Interestingly, a Budapest organizer fleeing the country after the second invasion reported that farmers were uniformly disappointed in the cardinal's speech because they, too, inferred that he had called for a return of land to the pre-revolutionary estate owners, which they would have vehemently opposed; nonetheless it can never be known what paths Hungary might have taken, especially because the workers organizing themselves in the councils had not developed any clear ideas about how they might create a state that would animate their outline of democratic socialism.[26]

What was clear was a widespread desire to end the specific system imposed by the Soviet Union a decade earlier. The widespread desire to achieve this change is implied in a Left-wing British newspaper's report on 9 November:

> The Minister of the Interior, Ferenc Muennich, today issued instructions to all Hungarian troops to remain in their barracks—thus proving that none is fighting on the Russian side. They were ordered to dissolve their revolutionary committees, which were formed during the first Hungarian crisis. Civilian revolutionary committees were told they must reject counter-revolutionary elements. Political "advisers" will be appointed by the government and attached to them.[27]

Seventeen years later, the Kádár régime felt strong enough to at least partially tell the truth. A 1973 official history prepared by Hungary's Academy of Sciences contained some ritual references to "counter-revolutionary groups," but says of the 1956 Rákosi régime: "the leadership was held in such low esteem and the strength of opposing forces was so great…that the avalanche of events could no longer be stopped."[28] By then, a slow process of political and economic reforms had made Hungary the least orthodox member of the Soviet bloc, an evolutionary process that ultimately brought more changes than were achieved in Poland.

That was then, long after the final event of the period, the 1958 execution of Nagy. At the end of his trial, after the death sentence was pronounced, Nagy is reported to have said to the court,

> I have twice tried to save the honor and image of Communism in the Danubian valley, once in 1953 and again in 1956. Rákosi and the Russians prevented me from doing so. If my life is needed to prove that not all Communists are enemies of the people, I gladly make the sacrifice. I know that there will one day be another Nagy trial, which will rehabilitate me. I also know I will have a reburial. I only fear that the funeral oration will be delivered by those who betrayed me.[29]

## An increasing chafing at political and economic bottlenecks

The events in Poland and, in particular, Hungary did not pass unnoticed in Czechoslovakia, particularly by the many Communist Party members who were already concluding that significant reforms were needed there. Although dissatisfaction slowly grew, there was as yet no ferment in Czechoslovakia to match that inside Poland and Hungary, or that of East Germany in 1953, when countrywide strikes against work speedups turned into hundreds of thousands demonstrating in East Berlin for the resignation of the government. Just as the taking of power and subsequent implementation of a system dictated by Stalin was delayed in Czechoslovakia, the post-Stalin thaw was also delayed.

Young communists being groomed for future leadership roles who had left a relatively open Czechoslovakia and were surprised at the rigidity of Moscow when they arrived to further their studies, found themselves surprised anew when they left a Moscow that subsequently became more open to find a gloomy, grey apparatus fearful of speaking up. "The esprit de corps of a happy sect of young, ideologically pure Communists had vanished," wrote a future leader of Prague Spring, Zdeněk

Mlynář, of his 1955 return after five years of study in Moscow.

> The secretariats where we had once lived, debated and campaigned had been transformed into much larger bureaus, staffed by well-paid employees, ruled by a bureaucratic hierarchy…An atmosphere of fear reigned, even among young Communists. They no longer talked freely, except among their closest friends. The expression of civic, political loyalty had become a fossilized ritual, and the disagreements that in 1948 had been openly discussed among Communists were now deeply submerged and could only be surmised.[30]

Nikita Khrushchev's "secret speech" in 1956 loosened things up somewhat, helping less rigidly ideological communists start a process of thinking more critically about the political superstructure.

The outbreak of unrest in Hungary, however, gave pause for thought. Mlynář later admitted this as well, too:

> I would be lying if I said at the time that I was interested only in the general political and ideological problems raised by the "Hungarian events," as they were referred to. For apart from these problems was the quite concrete image of a lynch mob hanging Communists from the lamp posts. And from the conversations I had at the time with various Communists of various generations, I recall they were all preoccupied with the same thought as well. This was an important assistance to [party leader Antonín] Novotný in subduing the wave of criticism precipitated in the [Czechoslovak Communist Party] by Khrushchev's critique.[31]

Twelve years later, Mlynář notes, the party "was no longer afraid of lynch mobs, nor did it have any reason to be."[32] By then, the party was trying to bring about serious changes, and had the firm support of Czechs and Slovaks for doing so. But there were retreats and forward thrusts during those dozen years.

The entire Khrushchev period, for that matter, was one of thaws and retreats, not necessarily orderly. In 1956, for example, when Yugoslav leader Josip Broz Tito visited Moscow, Marshal Kliment Voroshilov wept at a dinner, saying, "What a dunce I am. What stupidities I had to mouth at Stalin's orders! How ashamed I am! Forgive me, please."[33] Yet soon enough, the same Soviet leaders exhibited little hesitation in invading Hungary.

Still, there were improvements in Czechoslovakia, thanks in part to a temporarily successful economic reform in 1958 and a very slow political thaw despite the hard-line approach of Novotný. More priority was put into building housing, and a reasonable, albeit not high, standard of living without the pressures of a capitalist-style rat race provided some material comforts, reducing incentives to revolt. But an absolute political monopoly, under which the average citizen had no chance to participate in public life, played a major role in so many Czechs and Slovaks retreating into their private lives.

On the political side, older members of the Politburo, holdovers from the Gottwald era, died, and Novotný was able to replace them with individuals of his own choosing, consolidating his rule. This turnover in the party's leadership created sufficient political space for an examination of the early 1950s, and what become known as the "Kolder Commission" (named for one of the new Politburo members, Drahomír Kolder) laid out the atrocities that had been committed during the purges. Novotný partially suppressed the findings, but enough information leaked out to result in more holdovers from the purge era forced out of their offices.

One of the young rising figures who had served on the Kolder Commission and who was elevated to the Politburo was Alexander Dubček. Kolder would eventually back Dubček when Novotný was forced from power at the start of 1968, although he also opposed most of the subsequent reforms. Another result of the Kolder Commission was that more space was opened for genuine political and economic discussion, although Novotný and his second in command, Jiří Hendrych, repeatedly tried to stifle it, and Khrushchev, in yet another zigzag, demanded a halt to talk of political reforms and examinations of the past during his last year in power.

Salaries were increased in the 1950s for everybody except those who worked in education and culture,[34] and Czechoslovakia became the country with the world's most egalitarian wage structure. But the reform of 1958 did not address deeper structural issues, and in the early 1960s the economy slowed again under the burden of over-centralization. Growth had been achieved through the expansion of productive capacity, but the limits to doing so had been reached. To achieve sustained growth, Czechoslovakia had to make its existing industry more productive through technical progress and more effectively putting to use the skills of its workers. The refusal to do either of these is reflected in the attitude of bureaucrats responsible for economic policy who were uninterested in practical advice from below.

Such bottlenecks can be illustrated by the words of a steelworker, whose plant had sent proposals to a party congress in 1962:

> When we steelworkers pointed out that we were turning out steel for the scrap heap, they nearly put us in jail because, they said, we were throwing mud at our socialist industry...When we protested again about the "steel concept" and showed it could only lead to bankruptcy, the people in Prague jumped down our throats—"Aren't you ashamed," they said..."You're reactionaries." Only I don't have to be dumb just because I'm a steelworker. What's the use of a thriving steel industry if the whole Republic is going to rack

and ruin?[35]

The Soviet-style emphasis on heavy-industry producer products, such as steel and iron, and productivity measured solely in terms of the volume of output, all formulated according to a plan imposed from above, was leading to waste. The centralized plans imposed on Czechoslovak industry called for specific quantities of products to be produced; the plan did not measure for quality, so inferior product could be produced without a penalty, but that inferior product could wind up on the "scrap heap."

Another bottleneck with tightly centralized planning was that directors would be penalized for not meeting their factory's quota under the plan, so directors had an incentive to ask for more raw materials than were necessary, to provide a cushion in the case of future shortages. Thus, sufficient raw materials weren't always available or sent to where they were more immediately needed, and the emphasis on quantity resulted in raw materials that were not always of sufficient quality, hurting the quality of finished products.

In short, reformers sought a way to loosen central control, to allow enterprises to have more scope for decision-making while retaining central planning as a controlling guide rather than as a rigid numerical target. An enterprise in the Czechoslovak socialist sense is the same as a corporation in a capitalist country; a large enterprise could be comprised of several factories in multiple locations, in the manner of a capitalist corporation. A director of an enterprise is the equivalent of a chief executive officer in a capitalist corporation, and directors had assumed considerable power in Soviet-style economies under the principle of "one-man management" as it was called.

A group of economists, headed by Ota Šik, worked out plans for more extensive economic reforms during 1963 and 1964, which were approved by the Communist Party Central Committee in January 1965. Only a very watered-down version of these plans was instituted in 1967, and the proposals were thus doomed to failure in the minds of many reformers. "Notwithstanding their limited character, these measures became a touchstone for a struggle between progressive elements, who insisted on their application, and the Party and State apparatus, which tried hard to obstruct them from the moment it suspected that its power monopoly might be in jeopardy,"[36] noted another reformer, Jiří Pelikán.

Another problem, not so easy to solve, was that Czechoslovak industry was geared toward producing machinery and weaponry for the entire Soviet bloc. "This production was the basis of our economy, and I had no power to change it—I could only maneuver within its bounds and try to limit its cost to our population,"[37] wrote Dubček in his autobiography. The basics of the program passed in 1965 were virtual elimination of obligatory targets, flexible competitive pricing and decentralization of investment decisions.[38] The plan foresaw a prolonged transition period, making it easy for its opponents to allow only small parts of it to be implemented.[39]

The economic commission under Šik was not the only major reform plan of the mid-1960s. A commission of political scientists and lawyers created a study on "the development of the political system in a socialist society," and another, comprised of members of the Academy of Sciences, studied the effects of scientific and technological developments on the socialist system.[40] The simultaneous studies and the contact among the members helped crystallize conditions for reform.[41] Pressures for reforms from below also increased, most notably in the resolutions passed by the Fourth Writers Union Congress in June 1967 that strongly criticized party policies and an October 1967 street demonstration in Prague that generated a huge police response.

Another factor that can't be overestimated was the ongoing ethnic tensions between Czechs and Slovaks, which had its roots in uneven historical development. During the centuries that both peoples lived under the Austria-Hungary Empire, there was a considerable divergence in their fates. The Czech Lands were in the Austrian half of the empire and although Czechs were politically suppressed, without any representation or say in the affairs of the empire, their area became Austria's industrial heartland by the end of the nineteenth century, and thus a middle class developed, along with requisite educational opportunities.

Slovakia, by contrast, was severely repressed by Hungary, which denied even the existence of the Slovak nation, referring to Slovakia as "Upper Hungary." During the second half of the nineteenth century, until the fall of the empire at the end of World War I, schools in Slovakia were closed, the Slovak language was banned and Slovaks were little better than serfs on the estates of Hungarian feudal lords. Slovak was not even a written language until the 1840s, and the almost total lack of education meant that, at the founding of Czechoslovakia, there were almost no Slovaks able to assume important positions, meaning the new state was dominated by Czechs. Between the world wars, little progress was made on tackling these inequalities, which included the fact that there was little industry in Slovakia, a further handicap in an industrializing country.

Progress was made toward easing this imbalance after the communist takeover, but as the party was dominated by Czechs, investment decisions often tilted toward the Czech Lands. Novotný's insensitivity toward Slovaks (he regularly made oafish insults toward them despite his public claims that he was a strong friend of the Slovak people) played a significant role in the ferment that led to the Prague Spring. This ethnic tension underlay the ability of Dubček to become in January 1968 the first Slovak to lead Czechoslovakia.

The population of Slovakia is only one-half of the Czech Lands, but a solid anti-Novotný front among Slovaks, including hard-liners, created the political conditions for Novotný's ouster by party leaders. Novotný more than once attempted to remove

Dubček from the Politburo, even going so far as launching a police investigation against Dubček that failed. That failure was another sign of Novotný's weakening grip on power. Novotný also disliked Dubček because Dubček, as the top party official for Slovakia, which had some autonomy from Prague, allowed a much greater freedom of the press than Novotný tolerated in the Czech Lands.

Still another political factor became embodied as the question of the "accumulation of offices." In the Soviet-style system, the leader of the Communist Party (the first secretary or the general secretary, depending on the local terminology) was the most powerful person. Posts such as prime minister and president would be held by other party leaders who sat on the Politburo, the highest decision-making body in a communist party. As general secretaries gained in power and were able to maneuver rivals off the Politburo, they could assume offices that had been held by their rivals, while retaining their key position of general secretary. Khrushchev and Leonid Brezhnev both did this. Novotný did this, too, and was president as well as party leader. When the political crisis came to a climax in January 1968, Novotný lost support on the basis of his "accumulation of offices," and was forced to yield the office of party first secretary, ending his grip on power even though he remained as president for another few months.

The catalyzing factor for those changes among the political elite was the mounting need for significant political, economic and cultural reforms, needs that had become too acute to further avoid. The top-down Soviet-style straitjacket was a poor fit for a country that already had a developed industry. (That system was designed for an uneducated, rural population that badly needed to develop an industrial base in a short period of time and was created under the impact of a series of dire crises and the specifics of Russian conditions, not excepting the burdens of Russia's backward cultural inheritance.) Further, the stifling, closed political system was completely inappropriate for educated people with a highly developed level of culture, and who, unlike the nations of the Soviet Union, had experience with democratic forms of government.

## A country in ferment begins to find its voice

Opposition to the Czechoslovak Communist Party burst into the open at the June 1967 Writers Union congress, which featured several speeches sharply critical of the party, speeches primarily made by long-time party members. Czechoslovakia has produced a remarkable number of outstanding artists, especially writers and movie directors, for a small country. In a country with such a high regard for culture, the open revolt of writers took on greater significance than it might have in many other countries.

This respected place in society was reflected in the content of the speeches. "Czech writers have borne responsibility for the very existence of their nation, and this is true even today because the standard of Czech writing, its greatness or smallness, courage or cowardice, provincialism or all-embracing humaneness, will to a large extent determine the answer to the nation's vital question: Is the existence of the nation even worthwhile?" said Milan Kundera, later famous for novels such as The Unbearable Lightness of Being. "Is the existence of its language worthwhile? These most basic questions, embedded in the foundation of the modern existence of this nation, are still awaiting a final answer. That is why everyone who—through bigotry, vandalism, uncivilized behavior or close-mindedness—undermines cultural progress is, at the same time, undermining the very existence of this nation."[42]

Such speeches brought a swift response. Jiří Hendrych, the second-ranking person in the communist hierarchy and the party official responsible for overseeing cultural affairs, condemned the writers with hard-line jargon and ritual accusations.

> It is difficult at this point to analyze the various speeches in the discussion and to define where they turned into outright attacks and slanders against the socialist system...against the Communist Party...Therefore, I will simply make a few brief remarks on views that every honest communist must repudiate...We can understand a certain lack of clarity, but we can neither understand nor tolerate a communist who publicly expresses criticism of the government's policy, [who] attacks his communist government at a time when fronts worldwide have precariously split apart and when shots are being fired.[43]

Two months later, Hendrych made good on his threats when the party Politburo started "disciplinary proceedings" against Kundera, expelled from the party three other writers, issued a reprimand to a fifth writer and removed another from the Central Committee.[44] The Writers Union newspaper was also banned by Antonín Novotný, the top party official. The days of Hendrych and Novotný, however, were dwindling.

The ferment reached the top layers of the Communist Party when its Central Committee met for a two-day session on 30 and 31 October 1967. This meeting primarily was intended to discuss a paper on the party's role in the political system approved by the Politburo earlier in the month despite unsuccessful attempts by Alexander Dubček to make changes to the paper, which failed to explore any real change and restricted criticisms of the party to local levels. But the Central Committee was less dominated by hard-liners than the smaller Politburo, and the Central Committee ultimately voted to reject the draft paper as formulaic and for it to be redrafted—an unprecedented rebuff by the Central Committee.[45]

Dubček was one of the first speakers at the Central Committee meeting, and was direct in his criticism. "Our main energy should not be concentrated on a defensive struggle against something, but on efforts to understand the causes of the problems, find a solution to them and to work for further progress—and I deliberately emphasize the word 'for,'" Dubček said. "We must deepen intra-party democracy...but we must also consolidate unified discipline of action by implementing this democracy. To lead the party consistently in a Leninist spirit toward the strengthening of its leading role means less ordering about and more practical work with communists whom the party has entrusted with jobs in any sector of its activity."[46] Dubček had not launched any sensational attacks, and had to remain within the bounds of the single-party system, but his words were a direct critique of Novotný and the immense power Novotný had accumulated.

Novotný detested any challenge to him, and responded with a speech in which his main themes were to point out the "errors" of those who had criticized him and to accuse Dubček of "nationalist deviation"—ideological jargon alleging that Dubček was concerned only with narrow Slovak interests. "I must stress that in my private conversations with Comrade Dubček I warned him that he was not pursuing a correct policy as first secretary [of the Slovak branch of the party]," Novotný said in his speech, which followed Dubček's. "I also warned him that he had fallen under the influence of incorrect parochial interests, that he did not confront erroneous views on a consistent basis, and that he was in the grip of certain narrow interests."[47]

Aside from some pro forma references about the need for modernization and the need for more development in Slovakia, Novotný did not address the issues raised by the reform-minded, and ended his speech with a formula familiar to many a country ruled by a leader uninterested in hearing differing opinions: "But I again confirm that the enemy is working exceptionally hard."[48]

Although an anti-Novotný majority had formed on the Central Committee, there remained a 6–4 pro-Novotný majority on the Politburo. There could be no serious reform until Novotný was removed as first secretary, and it was the Politburo that ordinarily selected the first secretary. The first secretary, as the holder of the highest office in a top-down, centralized system, held considerable power through the ability to make personnel changes; appointees throughout the party and government bureaucracies have a strong influence on the implementation, or obstruction, of reforms. They also are strongly influenced by a strong party boss. A first secretary who had many years in that post, as Novotný did, had appointed loyalists throughout the bureaucracies, and these appointees would not be eager to openly buck the system due to their ties with the leader.

A Politburo deadlock would throw the vote to the Central Committee. How to change a vote? Dubček carefully considered Novotný's allies and decided Hendrych was the most likely to change.[49] Dubček went to Hendrych's office one day, barged in and told him the separation of Novotný's offices was inevitable, adding, "So it occurred to me to ask you, wouldn't you be interested in one of these offices?"[50] Hendrych, despite being second in the party hierarchy, was staunchly loyal to Novotný and evidently hadn't considered moving up. "One way or another, a solution will have to be carried through," Dubček said to Hendrych. "But it would be difficult to replace the president in such a short order, so it is the office of first secretary that is at stake, of course. You can't stave it off, and if you go on opposing it, you too may fall."[51] Dubček recalled that Hendrych didn't say a word as his pencil slowly slipped out of his hand: "At least I had put a bee in his bonnet, I thought. And that I had."[52]

Novotný, seeing his position in trouble, asked Leonid Brezhnev, the general secretary of the Communist Party of the Soviet Union and therefore the most powerful person in the Soviet bloc, to come to Prague to bolster him. Brezhnev arrived in early December, talked to several Czechoslovak Politburo members one-on-one and left without making any overt effort to bolster Novotný. This is the series of meetings at which Brezhnev is widely quoted as saying, "It's your business" to the Czechoslovaks, but the quote is likely apocryphal. Of the many memoirs left behind, it is frequently quoted second-hand, but no one seems to have actually heard it. Brezhnev concluded that the dispute was a personality conflict, in part because reformers and orthodox figures advocated Novotný's removal.

Brezhnev's foreign policy adviser, who sat in on the discussions, recalled, "Most of the officials who took part insisted that Novotný was no longer capable of effectively leading the party and the country and had lost his authority. These accusations typically focused exclusively on personal matters, and none of the officials, as far as I remember, said even a word about changing course internally, much less in foreign policy."[53] And Dubček's bee had done its work: "[W]hen Brezhnev directly asked…Hendrych who, in his view, had sufficient skill and authority to replace Novotný in his posts (the secretarial and presidential), Hendrych immediately replied, without batting an eyelid: 'I do.' When Hendrych left the room, Brezhnev only shook his head in dismay and spat."[54]

Brezhnev's conclusion was that the main cause of the Czechoslovak difficulties was that Novotný appeared incapable of cooperation, taking too much upon himself and being incapable of participating in a collective leadership.[55] That is a more vigorous critique than it might initially appear to be, because that opinion mirrors Brezhnev's main critique against Nikita Khrushchev at the time of the 1964 deposing of Khrushchev; Brezhnev built his power as the Soviet party general secretary on the building of consensus.

Sure enough, Hendrych switched sides, and a 5–5 vote in the Politburo threw the question of the "accumulation of offices" to the Central Committee, where Novotný's support rapidly dwindled. Novotný yielded, offering his resignation as first secretary. A commission was formed to select candidates for first secretary; three candidates were put forth and a straw poll gave the most votes for Dubček, although Dubček had backed one of the other two candidates, Oldřich Černík (who would instead become prime minister in April). Dubček was the only candidate put forth at the 5 January 1968 Central Committee meeting that elected him as first secretary. The Central Committee also voted to add four new members to the Politburo, providing more support for reforms on the top party body.

Dubček was far from being the colorless bureaucrat who is the typical product of one-party systems. Through his intelligence, hard work and caution, he rose swiftly, earning a seat on the Politburo and simultaneously being named the top party official for Slovakia in 1963, only 14 years after entering the party's administrative ranks as a local official. Dubček had been in line to become the director of the factory in which he was working when he was asked to join the party administration; he took a cut in pay of more than one-half to do so, believing that his ideals and desire for a better world would be better served in the ranks of his party.

If there is one anecdote that summarizes the character of Dubček, it is the story of the funeral of Karol Smidke. A former party leader who lost his job as a result of the purges, Smidke died in 1952. Because Smidke was still in official disgrace, nobody was willing to give the eulogy until Dubček agreed to do so. Dubček had not known Smidke well, but Smidke was a friend of his father and had left a positive legacy, including helping to organize the Slovak National Uprising against Nazi occupation in 1944. Dubček wrote a glowing account of Smidke's life, but was advised to submit his eulogy text to a censor. The text came back full of deletions and changes that Dubček did not like, so he simply went ahead and gave the eulogy as he had originally written it. A friend who was aware of the differences between the two versions thought Dubček would find himself in trouble, but nothing happened; the censor did not monitor what was said at the funeral.

After Dubček's ascension as Slovak party leader, a careful observer might have noticed that when the press in Slovakia published criticisms that raised the ire of party leaders in Prague, Dubček might, when circumstances required, mildly lecture the writers in public, but would not take any action against them. Dubček also worked behind the scenes for a more rational policy of industrial development linked to the actual needs of the country's regions and to bring about rehabilitation for victims of the purges of the early 1950s.

It is easy, and simplistic, to grumble that these types of actions fall short of democratic ideals. Dubček, however high he had risen, was still part of a powerful apparatus, and he had to maneuver as best he could within that apparatus. As with all of the reform-minded party members, he had to be cautious. An overt display of opposition would have brought his career to an end; as it was, Novotný repeatedly tried to oust Dubček. Only a highly skilled politician could have successfully risen to the top of the party ranks with a reform agenda. Nor was Dubček hungry for power—by all reports, he was very reluctant to assume the post of party first secretary, a post with potentially awe-inspiring power but also one with huge responsibilities.

### A question of pace: Too fast, too slow, or irrelevant?

There was more anticipation than action during the first three months of the Prague Spring. There were multiple reasons for this, although perhaps none more important than that a clear-cut majority for reforms did not yet exist within the party hierarchy.

But that is not to say that January, February and March were spent simply marking time. In mid-January, Alexander Dubček won support for preparing an outline of the political, economic and cultural changes that had become necessary, which became known as the Action Program; pressure from Dubček and fast-moving public opinion induced Jiří Hendrych to allow the Writers Union newspaper to resume publication in February; the process of formally ending censorship began in early March; an accelerated facilitation of rehabilitations for victims of past purges began in mid-March; and a wave of resignations under popular pressure began in late March, including those of Antonín Novotný and Hendrych. These developments were a prelude to April's unveiling of the Action Program and significant government personnel changes that put the reform process on a stronger footing.

The early flurry of activity reversed the initial sluggishness that derived from poor communications. After Dubček's selection as party first secretary, only a terse announcement, with no details, was issued—the type of announcement consistent with past practice. Dubček could not obtain Politburo approval for a more informative explanation, but considerable disapproval of this silence in local and regional party bodies that were discussing the latest events resulted in a wave of resolutions demanding a full explanation.[56] As a result, further momentum to end censorship was created, a necessary condition for the planned significant structural reforms to be able to go forward. A prominent reform figure, Josef Smrkovský, wrote two articles explaining the background to Dubček's ascension and confirming support for a new course, which built confidence among the party rank-and-file, and among other citizens and intellectuals, that the party had become serious about reforms and was not simply paying lip service to the concept as it had done in the past. Smrkovský would become the head of the national parliament in April and was widely seen as Dubček's closest collaborator.

In the second of the two articles, published in the official party newspaper, Rudé Právo, Smrkovský stressed unity between Czechs and Slovaks, unity among the various societal groupings, the need for immediate rehabilitations and a need for the relationships among party, government, business enterprises and societal organizations to be "precisely demarcated."[57] The last item was a clear expression of the necessity of reducing the party's role in all spheres of life, and by itself served as a signal of an intention to make real changes.

Abolition of censorship helped speed the departures of hard-line holdovers such as Novotný and Hendrych. A scandal involving a general who had been close to Novotný, and who was suspected of possibly organizing a coup to save Novotný at the end of 1967, burst into the press in March 1968 when prosecutors found evidence of the general's sale of army supplies on the black market. The general fled the country, and the media began calling for Novotný to resign as president.

Ironically, there was some fear among some of the strongest proponents of reform that too much press freedom too soon might be counterproductive. This was the opinion of Zdeněk Mlynář, who was one of the main authors of the Action Program, still being worked on in March, and one of many reformers who believed the party should have moved much more quickly in its first months. Concern over a rapid unfettering of the press was a tactical consideration—it would be unwise to overly alarm Soviet leaders.

Upon hearing from Hendrych that the Writers Union newspaper would be allowed to resume publishing, Mlynář said he

> tried to persuade Hendrych that taking such a step before the Action Program was published would result in the press becoming far more radical than before and, in turn, less disposed to accept the limitations and framework of the Action Program. "That won't happen," claimed Hendrych. "I've already talked it all over with [the new editor]. They won't write against us." About a month later, Hendrych was forced to resign, one reason being that public criticism of him in the press was so harsh that he would have compromised the Dubček leadership by remaining in office.[58]

Mlynář already knew the Action Program would be bold in its general assertions, but would not have many specifics; in part this was so that reforms could continue to develop without preconceived, imposed ideas, but it was also in consideration of the knowledge that too radical a break with Soviet-style structures and formulations would generate considerable opposition in Moscow.

Already, concern was being expressed from Soviet leaders, and from Poland and East Germany. The hard-line leader of East Germany, Walter Ulbricht, had banned reporting on, and travel to, Czechoslovakia, and a late March Soviet bloc summit meeting had featured demands that Dubček put a stop to alleged "counter-revolutionary" developments. Shortly before that meeting, Polish leader Władysław Gomułka had listened to Dubček explain to him during a private talk that the rehabilitations of thousands would be necessary to renew confidence in the party. Gomułka replied, "I understand in a moral and human sense. But I am afraid that all this would bring about uncontrollable political consequences. It could undermine the position of the party."[59] Gomułka became a staunch opponent of any reform, upset at the spillover effect Czechoslovak events were causing in Poland. Gomułka had moved a long away from the reform figure he had been in 1956; in 1970 another series of uprisings in Poland would force his ouster.

One school of thought, held by many Czechoslovak reformers, was that much faster personnel changes in the party leadership were needed, in effect creating a "fait accompli" before Brezhnev & Co. would have sufficient time to react. It was understood by all shades of opinion in Czechoslovakia that the next party congress would lead to wholesale changes in the Central Committee and therefore in the Politburo, with hardliners and bureaucrats certain to lose their posts. The next party congress, the fourteenth, was scheduled for 1970. But, under party statutes, local and regional party bodies could ask for a congress to be convened early; enough did so that the Fourteenth Congress was re-scheduled for early September 1968. But the school of thought advocating faster changes argued that the congress should have been convened months earlier than September because forcing out the hard-liners sooner would have opened more space for reforms to take hold.

Not fully understanding the nature of the Brezhnev régime was part of the reformers' weakness, contends Jiří Hájek, who was the foreign minister in 1968. "We thought we could discuss things, not being aware of how little freedom of maneuver we were allowed," Hájek said in a conference 20 years later. "Furthermore, the group around Dubček was not homogeneous. We spent too much time in discussion, when it was really necessary to hold a party congress as early as February to give the reformers effective control of the movement. Thus, the enemies of reform had time to prepare for the military invasion, and we did not have time…Our real mistake was that we thought the people in Moscow would understand that our reforms were also essential to them."[60]

Many reformers advocated a faster pace, although not as radical as Hájek's, recognizing that preparations for a party congress and elections require some time. "[F]rom February 1968, I felt that the top priority for a successful reform program was to end this provisional state as rapidly as possible," Mlynář wrote, years later. He believed the Action Program should have been released in early March, simultaneously with local party meetings, thereby enabling the Fourteenth Congress to convene in May. In conjunction with scheduling local and parliamentary elections for June, those moves would have put in place a new ruling establishment at all levels.[61]

"The replacement of Stalinist and Moscow-controlled personnel would have taken place according to the party statutes and state laws before Moscow could organize any effective resistance," Mlynář wrote.

> Even with the totalitarian system erupting under continual pressure from below, expressed chiefly through the press (which roused the Kremlin into a fury), events in May had not yet reached a point where a military intervention could have been mounted. And after a party congress, Moscow could never have been able to set up a...government from among the [Czechoslovak party] leadership, nor would it be conceivable that a group of "party and government leaders" might "invite in the allied troops to save socialism."[62]

One problem with the above thesis is that there was not a clear-cut majority within the high levels of the party for major reforms before April. Not all of those who favored Novotný's ouster were in favor of reforms; they simply saw Novotný's removal as a necessity unto itself. And some reformers advocated a more cautious approach to reform, believing that a relatively rapid pace would alarm Moscow or that the reform effort might become uncontrollable. Communists' fears that the United States would attempt to exploit unrest were hardly unreasonable; US policy was aimed squarely at restoring capitalism. Its military might and dominant position within the NATO military alliance, and the huge resources the US poured into intelligence and covert operations, carried a potential for the United States to be able to bend events in its preferred direction.

A related argument to the "act faster" school is the belief that Dubček should have removed his opponents much faster. But a basic point of the reform movement was to break from the dictatorial methods of the past. This analysis was encapsulated by the head of Czechoslovak television in 1968, Jiří Pelikán:

> To foreign observers who regret that Dubček and his associates did not have the entire process well in hand and that they did not act like Ceaucescu, Kádár and Tito, one can only say that this might have helped Dubček remain in power

> and carry out some reforms, but that it would have meant the end of the Prague Spring—a symbol of a spontaneous popular movement, the expression of the aspirations and endeavors of a people to share responsibility for the decisions affecting their future.[63]

Dubček himself noted that he did not have a "crystal ball" to tell him when the Soviets would invade. Given the military might of the Soviet Union, which maintained firm control over the Warsaw Pact alliance, a much faster pace to the reforms might have accelerated the timetable for invasion. A more unified political leadership and a population backing that unified leadership undoubtedly would have created complications for Moscow, but if the imminent "threat" of wholesale changes in the composition of the party leadership, loosening of Moscow's ability to directly manipulate the Czechoslovak security apparatus and deep structural changes were enough to prompt an invasion, then it is difficult to accept that the actual implementation of these programs would not have similarly led to an invasion.

The idea that making all these changes before Moscow could organize an invasion would have led to an enhanced ability for passive, political resistance seems to have some merit, but, in the long term, a superior military engaged in a long-term occupation would have made a permanent implementation of reforms very difficult. It is not possible to replay history and a definitive answer is therefore not possible, but it is hard to believe that a program of accelerated reforms would have ultimately led to a substantially different result.

## A first foot forward: The Action Program

However delayed it may or may not have been, the Action Program, unveiled in early April 1968, provided the framework for a new type of society. After opening with a brief summary of the communist era and an acknowledgment of mistakes, the Action Program declared,

> We need a frank statement of what those mistakes and deformations were and what caused them so as to remedy them as soon as possible and concentrate on the fundamental structural change in our lives which we are facing at the present time...Dogmatic approaches impeded a full and timely re-evaluation of the character of socialist construction. The measures did not therefore bring the anticipated results. On the contrary, over the years, difficulties piled up until they closed in a vicious circle...This led to a precipitate expansion of heavy industry, to a disproportionate demand on labor power and raw materials, and to costly investments. Such an economic policy, enforced through directive administrative methods, no longer corresponded to the economic requirements and possibilities of the country and led to exhaustion of its material and human resources.[64]

The frank acknowledgment of economic difficulties early in the document reflected the fact that a stagnant economy was perhaps the single most important factor in creating the conditions for Prague Spring.

The program later tacitly abandoned the notion that the party always knows best:

> Using and unifying the manifold interests of social groups and individuals calls for the elaboration and implementation of a new political system in our lives, a new model of socialist democracy. The Party will strive to develop a state and social order that corresponds to the actual interests of the various strata and groups of this society and gives them a chance to express their interest in their organizations and voice their views in public.[65]

Such a formulation, to be consistent, must lead to a less central role for the party, although it would still play an active societal role:

> The Party's goal is not to become a universal "caretaker" of the society, to bind all organizations and every step taken in life by its directives. Its mission lies primarily in arousing socialist initiative, showing the ways and real possibilities of Communist perspectives, and in winning over all workers to them through systematic persuasion and the personal examples of Communists…Party bodies do not deal with all problems; they should encourage activity and suggest solutions to the most important ones. At the same time the Party cannot turn into an organization which influences society only by its ideas and program. Through its members and bodies it must develop the practical organizational methods of a political force in society.[66]

This was one of the most controversial portions of the Action Program, which reflected Dubček's conception that the party's "leading role" had to be continually earned. Some did not like this idea, because they believed the Communist Party should not have any sort of "leading role." Hard-liners did not like it because the Soviet-style conception of the party's "leading role" meant an uncontestable monopoly of power.

This was one of the more vague portions of the program, and that was probably unavoidably so because the political superstructure was a problem for which a solution required more time. Any proposal that intimated a restoration of a multi-party system would earn the wrath of hard-liners, especially those in Moscow. Nonetheless, the program at a later point declared: "Socialist state power cannot be monopolized by a single party, or by a combination of parties. It must be open to all political organizations of the people."[67]

That last passage acknowledged that, technically, Czechoslovakia was still governed by the National Front, the coalition of parties formed before 1948, and a loosening of Communist control would have led to a resumption of an independent existence for other National Front parties. But it also was based on the belief among many reformers that a revitalized parliament could have direct representatives of social organizations and workplaces, or other types of members, possibly in a separate chamber, and need not contain only representatives of parties.

From this conception naturally flows the ideal of socialism: a system under which people have more freedom than under capitalism, rather than the alternative set of bosses existing in a Soviet-style system.

> Socialism cannot mean only liberation of the working people from the domination of exploiting class relations, but must provide for a greater degree of self-fulfillment than any bourgeois democracy. The working people, who are no longer ordered about by a class of exploiters, can no longer be dictated to by any arbitrary interpretation from a position of power as to what information they may or may not be given, which of their opinions can or cannot be expressed publicly, where public opinion may play a role and where it may not.[68]

In addition to specifying freedom of information, including the right to view enterprise economic reports, the document also specifies that the parliament (the National Assembly) should be the "supreme organ of state power"[69] and that all forms of cultural censorship should be abolished. "It is necessary to overcome a narrow understanding of the social and human function of culture and art, over-estimation of their ideological and political role, and under-estimation of their basic cultural and aesthetic tasks in the transformation of man and his world."[70]

The portion of the Action Program dealing with the economy also began with a frank acknowledgment of the structural difficulties that helped lead to the stagnation of the 1960s.

> The system of protectionism—furthering economic backwardness, and maintained by our policy of prices, subsidies and grants and by the system of surcharges in foreign trade—continues to prevail in our economic policy. This confused system of protectionism creates conditions under which ineffective, poorly managed, backward enterprises many not only exist but are often given preferences. It is not possible to blunt the economic policy forever by taking from those who work well and giving to those who work badly...Differences in income between enterprises should reflect actual differences in the level of their economic activities. Nor is it politically correct for the consumer to pay indefinitely for inefficiency either directly in high prices and taxes or indirectly by different forms of siphoning off material from efficient enterprises.[71]

The single worst bottleneck in the economic structure was its top-down nature: A plan was handed down and enterprises simply fulfilled numerical quotas. Reformers believed that the producers of products, those responsible for carrying out the plan, are better positioned to determine needs.

> Decision-making about the plan and the economic policy of the state must be both a process of mutual confrontation and harmonization of different interests—i.e., the interests of enterprises, consumers, employees, different social groups of the populations, nations, etc.—and a process of a suitable combination of the long-term development of the economy and its immediate prosperity. Effective measures protecting

> the consumer against the abuse of the monopoly position and economic power of production and trading enterprises must be considered as a necessary part of the economic activity of the state. The drafting of the national economic plan and the national economic policy must be subject to the democratic control of the National Assembly and specialized control of scientific institutions.[72]

The program also called for enterprises to rationalize their internal operations as part of a broader economic evaluation and as part of the implementation of market mechanisms. The document warned, however, "we have in mind not the capitalist, but the socialist market, and not its uncontrolled but its regulated utilization."[73] The program concluded with a confirmation of Czechoslovakia's position in the communist bloc and affirmed its existing foreign policy, including membership in the military alliance of the Soviet-aligned states, the Warsaw Pact.[74]

Although this last portion could be interpreted as a sop to Moscow—and the writers of the Action Program were motivated to "assure" Soviet leaders—party reformers meant it. The pledge of remaining within the Soviet bloc reflected the fact that there was virtually no legitimate opinion among politically and socially active Czechs and Slovaks for a return to capitalism, and a belief among reformist party leaders that the protection of the bloc was the best guarantee for the wholesale renewal of socialism.

That does not mean Czechoslovak leaders were naïve about the negative attitudes already developing among the Soviet decision-makers, but they believed they could successfully either maneuver around those attitudes or convince the Soviet leaders that their reforms would mean a strengthening of socialism, not only because the economy would be put on a stronger footing but because the democracy being introduced to political, economic and cultural life would rally the population behind the party.

## A series of responses from inside and outside

The unveiling of the Action Program came amid a flurry of developments as the early period of sorting out personalities in top party and government positions concluded under rapidly increasing pressure from below.

Oldřich Černík was named prime minister, with a new lineup of government ministers, and Josef Smrkovský was named chair of the parliament (the National Assembly). With Černík and Smrkovský joining party leader Alexander Dubček, a strongly reformist lineup in the top positions was now in place. Ludvík Svoboda was selected by parliament to be the new president, replacing Antonín Novotný, on a groundswell of popular support, although Svoboda played a mostly ceremonial role because he did not have a party or government position and therefore had no base from which to exercise power, other than moral authority.

Svoboda was not involved in the discussions roiling Czechoslovakia nor was he looked to as a theorist, but his perceived independence and popularity (he had been commander of Czechoslovak armed forces fighting the Nazis during World War II and served as a bookkeeper on a farm after being purged in the early 1950s) made him a non-controversial choice for president. That Svoboda was also seen as someone with links to Moscow likely also served to make him a "safe" choice.

Černík, the son of a miner, worked as a metalworker until 1949. Avoiding getting caught in the purges, he held a series of local then provincial party posts during the 1950s. During the period of cautious attempts at reform during Novotný's latter years, when he had government responsibilities as energy minister and then chair of the state planning commission, Černík came to believe there was an unavoidable need to change the way the party operated to end the passivity of society.

A new Politburo was named by the Central Committee; six of the ten members, including Novotný, Jiří Hendrych and three other Novotný-era hard-liners, were replaced. A majority for reforms now sat on the most powerful decision-making body in Czechoslovakia, but by no means was there unanimity on it—the Politburo still contained hard-liners such as Vasil Bil'ak, who had an automatic seat by virtue of his becoming first secretary of Slovakia, the post previously held by Dubček. Bil'ak would eventually be one of the signatories of a letter asking Leonid Brezhnev to invade but, ironically, he was placed in his posts by Dubček because of the two men's friendship.

Other important developments at this time included the completion of formal rehabilitations for all victims of the 1950s repression; the election of another strong pro-reform personality, František Kriegel, as chair of the National Front (the "coalition" of pre-1948 parties that technically remained in power, on paper); and the formation of two independent social groups, K-231, a club of people who fell victim to the 1950s repression who were sentenced under a law numbered 231 in the national legal code, and KAN, the Club of Committed Non-Party People. A few weeks later, public discussions calling for the formation of new political parties were held as ordinary citizens continued to test the waters, encouraged by the continuing freedom of the press.

The response to the Action Program from neighbors, however, was sharply negative. Within a week of the program's unveiling, the Soviet ambassador to Czechoslovakia, Stepan Chervonenko, who throughout 1968 sent a steady stream of biased, wildly panic-mongering reports to Moscow, handed Dubček a protest note and Brezhnev telephoned Dubček to ask for a meeting.

Nor did the Soviets limit themselves to private attacks. Smrkovský and Kriegel were the two members of the new leadership who had extensive pre-World War II experience as communist activists, and it was probably not a coincidence that attacks from the Soviet Union and East Germany were aimed at those two, more so than other individuals. Both were independent thinkers possessing broad backgrounds of experience.

Smrkovský, born into a family of farmers, became involved in communist activities at age 19, holding various union and party posts. He was a leader of the Czech resistance during the Nazi occupation and was a major organizer of the Prague Uprising in 1945. He was arrested in 1951 at the height of the Stalinist purges and spent four years in jail. He then worked as a forestry worker until being rehabilitated in 1963 and was re-elected to the Central Committee in 1966.

Kriegel's youth was marked by poverty and anti-Semitism, and he saw the international movement of working people as the means to solve these social ills. He joined the Communist Party in the 1930s, serving as a doctor in the Spanish Civil War and with the Chinese partisans fighting the Japanese during World War II. Kriegel came home to serve as deputy minister of health from 1949 to 1952, then worked as a doctor after being purged before he, too, made a political comeback with his election to the Central Committee in 1966.

Smrkovský remained a staunch defender of the reforms and remained so after purges began anew in 1969; Kriegel distinguished himself by being the only member of the Czechoslovak "negotiation" team who refused to sign the dictated "Moscow Protocol" agreement following the August invasion.

Czechoslovakia's neighbors had also begun to demonstrate their displeasure—Czech newspapers were banned in Poland, East Germany and Ukraine.[75] In contrast to the entirely negative responses from Poland and East Germany, a sign that a mix of opinions still existed among the Soviet leaders was the varied responses of the Soviet press, much of which was hostile but some, including Izvestia, were cautious.[76] Izvestia was the official Soviet government newspaper and second in importance to party daily Pravda and therefore was responsive to the thinking of highly placed officials.

As a result of Brezhnev's request to Dubček for a meeting, Dubček, Smrkovský, Černík and Bil'ak traveled to Moscow for a 4-on-4 meeting with Brezhnev, two other leading Soviet Politburo members, Prime Minister Aleksei Kosygin and President Nikolai Podgorny, and the Central Committee secretary responsible for relations within the Warsaw Pact, Konstantin Katushev. Bil'ak, however, consistently echoed the arguments put forth by Brezhnev—"instead of being four to four, we were three to five," in the words of Smrkovský.[77] Most of this meeting was taken up by the Soviet side badgering the Czechoslovaks over minutiae; Brezhnev repeatedly read clippings of newspaper articles containing passages he did not like. Podgorny at one point interjected what seemed to be his primary interest: "It is very important that the press, radio and television remain under the control of the Central Committee, and that they carry out its wishes. Otherwise, any solution will be only so many words."[78]

Smrkovský later noted it would be impossible to know what was printed in every local newspaper, but that was not the point. "Our meeting took place a few days after May Day 1968, and we were disconcerted to find that they showed no interest whatsoever in May Day, where the [public] participation had been so impressive, so spontaneous, altogether there were millions of people [in cities across the country] who came out so enthusiastically for the party policy," Smrkovský wrote. "That didn't interest them. They were interested in meetings of KAN and K-231, attended by fifty or a hundred people, sometimes less. We were sickened by the whole business, because we realized they weren't interested in the facts, in our overall situation, but were looking for pretexts for opposing us."[79]

The obsession with press clippings was connected to the Soviet leaders' belief that any lessening of the party's grip would automatically result in a Right-wing dictatorship. "Under the guise of democratization, the press, radio and television, which have now eluded the party's control, are seeking to push malicious practice to the limit," Brezhnev said at the meeting. "I wish to emphasize, comrades, that this entire ideological machine is working in an organized way; all are aiming at a single target…All this bears the hallmark of being organized by a single center…[H]ostile parties and student organizations have been activated, and many other things are going on about which you, comrades, may not even be aware. I think all this is in preparation for the overthrow of the [Czechoslovak Communist Party] Central Committee and its policy and the overthrow of the current leadership."[80]

To press his argument further, Brezhnev later added: "In Hungary [in 1956], the same thing began with the activities of the writers' clubs, and it ended when they started hanging communists…And in your country the same kinds of threats are being heard in the villages. I don't want to be a prophet, but if you let things drift along, it might end up with communists being hanged in your country…If 1.7 million communists are done away with, then people will ask: And where was the [Communist Party of the Soviet Union], why did it not fulfill its internationalist duty?"[81]

The one concrete hope for the meeting held by the Czechoslovak leaders was for a loan by the Soviet Union to be used for modernizing industry. Without a loan from the Soviet Union, Czechoslovakia would have to accept a loan from Western countries. No Soviet loan was ever forthcoming, but Kosygin dismissed the need for it. "Kosygin didn't forget to remark—for whom did we want to manufacture consumer goods? For export? He said that the West didn't need our consumer goods and wouldn't want them in the future. So then we'd be wanting to get our goods on the markets of the socialist countries, especially of the Soviet Union, with the help of investment capital from the Western countries. But the socialist markets didn't want our consumer goods, either; it needed our investment goods," Smrkovský later wrote, paraphrasing Kosygin.[82]

"It was a very harsh and categorical attitude, favoring the old 'iron concept' of our industry which can only lead our economy by degrees not only into a complete unilateral dependence, but also into a state of permanent ineffectiveness, since we lack raw materials," Smrkovský wrote. "Their policy on trade with us was shown to be deliberately political, aimed at cutting off all our chances of sovereignty and firmly tying us to their policies."[83]

Not all the criticism of Czechoslovakia's post-Action Program policy came from those who thought matters were going too far; some inside the country thought reforms were happening too slowly. The solution, according to the signatories of the "Two Thousand Words" manifesto, was for more vigorous action on the local level—for ordinary citizens to take more control in their workplaces, for using all legal methods, strikes included, to force out officials who obstructed reform and to prepare to defend the country, arms in hand if need be, from any outside threat.

The manifesto was written by Ludvík Vaculík, one of the writers expelled from the Communist Party after the 1967 Writers Union congress before being reinstated early in 1968. Several dozen people signed it, and it appeared simultaneously on 27 June 1968, in the Writers Union newspaper and three daily newspapers. The manifesto was a completely independent initiative; Czechoslovak party leaders were caught by surprise by it, and Brezhnev & Co. reacted with fury.

The manifesto, officially the "Two Thousand Words that Belong to Workers, Farmers, Officials, Scientists, Artists and Everybody," opens with a lament that the welcoming of a socialist program in 1948 was so thoroughly trampled upon, but also noting that many communists were now trying to reverse the policies of the past.

> Let us not foster the illusion that it is the power of truth which now make such ideas victorious. Their victory has been due rather to the weakness of the old rulers, evidently already debilitated by twenty years of unchallenged rule. All the defects hidden in the foundation and ideology of the system have clearly reached their peak. So let us not overestimate the effects of the writers' and students' criticisms. The source of social change is the economy.[84]

The manifesto rejected the idea that a "democratic revival" could be achieved without the communists, but called for the party to "produce local Action Programs" so that "the issue will suddenly revolve around very ordinary and long-awaited acts of justice."[85]

Seeing the economy as the catalyzing factor for the new political season, the manifesto declares,

> The everyday quality of our future democracy depends on what happens in the factories, and what happens to the factories. Despite all our discussions, it is the economic managers who have us in their grasp...The workers, as entrepreneurs, can intervene in this battle by electing the right people to management and workers' councils. And as employees they can help themselves best by electing, as their trade union representatives, natural leaders and able, honorable individuals without regard to party affiliation.[86]

The "Two Thousands Words" does not read like a dramatic departure from the officially approved Action Program, except for the call to defend the country and the call to put direct pressure on hard-liners holding back progress. Those two passages did have a logic: The manifesto was issued as Soviet army units and other Warsaw Pact armies, including that of

Czechoslovakia, were conducting "training exercises" on Czechoslovak territory, which Dubček and the leadership around him had finally agreed to under continual pressure from Moscow.

The fact that for the first time in two decades there were Soviet army troops in the country, even if temporarily, put the question of a possible intervention into many minds. The signatories of the manifesto were not yet sure of the ultimate outcome of the reform process and wanted the hard-liners pushed out as soon as possible to increase the chances that the reforms would become permanent.

The Soviet leaders reacted very harshly to the publication of the manifesto, which the reform communists very well knew would happen. From a tactical standpoint, they believed the "Two Thousand Words" was an unhelpful development because it would be sure to harden viewpoints, an added difficulty at an increasingly sensitive time.

Because the manifesto was intended as a general call, and not as a personal opinion, "in practical terms…the conception of reform in 'Two Thousand Words' and not the Action Program was to become the focus for political discussions both in public and inside the [party],"[87] wrote Zdeněk Mlynář, at this time a Central Committee secretary and one of two people responsible for drafting official party statements, including the party's response to the manifesto. But because Czechoslovakia was not yet a formal democracy, the manifesto had a greater impact than it would have had in an established democracy. Mlynář believed that the signatories of the Two Thousand Words were concerned that not enough hard-liners would be removed, and that fear "blinded them to other circumstances far more serious and dangerous for the reform as a whole."[88]

Czechoslovak party and government leaders took the manifesto seriously enough to meet in an all-night session to decide how to respond; Soviet representatives had expressed displeasure the day it was published. Smrkovský understood that the signatories were well-intentioned, but that the publication was a bad move tactically, because of "the pretext it provided for the massive attacks on our cause."[89] Smrkovský also believed it was a mistake to arouse passions to that extent:

> I recalled what it led to in the 1950s, that in the end ten thousand resolutions came to the Party Central Committee demanding that the sentences in the trials should be even harsher, calling for more gallows, longer prison terms, and so on. I suggested that calls of any kind should be avoided; there's apt to be a big difference between a good intention and the way it may be understood. They certainly meant well, and in the end it turned against them, against us, against everyone it was horribly misused.[90]

The party ultimately gave the manifesto a mild rebuke, calling for unity around the Action Program. Kriegel, on his own initiative, later made public statements emphasizing the good will of the signatories.[91]

Two weeks later, five Warsaw Pact countries—the Soviet Union, East Germany, Poland, Hungary and Bulgaria—sent a letter demanding that the "counter-revolutionary" situation be immediately rectified, that the "danger" the party was supposedly facing be acknowledged and that censorship be reinstituted. The letter directly decried that "reactionary forces were given the opportunity, in public, to publish their political platform under the title 'Two Thousands Words'"[92] and hinted at possible intervention of some kind by declaring, "This is no longer your affair alone."[93]

The next five weeks saw two more summit meetings between the Czechoslovak leadership and its critics, but with no agreements other than ambiguous statements of general principles that each side could interpret as it wished.

## An acceleration of economic reform and the first formation of workers' councils

Concomitant with the developing political situation, work on economic reforms and radically increasing workers' participation in their workplaces gained momentum. The first workers' councils sprang into being in June 1968, and were spontaneous movements from below, helped along by new reform-minded trade union leadership. The movement for workers' councils developed sufficiently to prompt the government to respond with a general outline of how it envisioned the role of the councils. As a grassroots movement, the councils were more difficult to control than political and government bodies, and the creation of councils actually accelerated after the August invasion, and was not brought to a halt until well into 1969.

Forms of self-management had appeared during the first period of nationalization in 1945 to 1948, and the idea had not gone away once centralized, top-down management was instituted after the Communist takeover. The idea remained sufficiently alive that, in 1957, the state planning chief, a veteran party boss, found it necessary to declare that trade unions were the organization that would raise "the participation of the working people in management," while denouncing any changes to "basic principles" of what he called socialist construction.[94] Referring to the councils of a decade earlier, and to the then fresh creation of workers' councils in Hungary and Poland, the planning chief declared that "revisionist and opportunistic views which had recently appeared in some countries in discussions on the building of the socialist economic system found practically no support in [Czechoslovakia]."[95]

Support for changes, in spite of official condemnatory jargon, evidently did exist. The first mild economic reforms began only one year later, momentum for much more systematic reforms built from the early 1960s, and a desire for radically increased workers' participation from below became an early feature of

Prague Spring. This ferment at the shop-floor level helped push out recalcitrant leaders of the national trade union federation (known as the ROH); many ROH leaders had been Novotný followers and veterans of the top-down system in which unions acted to spur workers to increase production at the behest of the state rather than represent workers' interests. Local trade union branches and workplace party cells had begun issuing a stream of resolutions opposing that mindset, and the government finally had to force out the Novotný holdovers in the ROH in March.[96] Later that spring, new unions and other similar organizations sprang up and strikes broke out against incompetent management prior to the first formation of the councils.[97] By then, work was under way on proposed new laws to codify the councils, and the Communist Party Central Committee was sufficiently aware of the agitation to acknowledge in a 1 June resolution that the economic-democracy component of the Action Program had been taken up "only slowly, partially and with doubts and hesitation."[98]

The movement for workers' councils did have support in the high reaches of party and government; most particularly from Ota Šik, who had headed the commission on economic reform in the mid-1960s and continued to lead economic-restructuring efforts. Šik was appointed deputy prime minister for the economy in March 1968 and had a team of reform economists to work with who backed a serious restructuring, albeit with varying opinions on the desirability of workers' councils.

A component of this debate was: Who would the directors of factories and enterprises be responsible to? Under the top-down Soviet system, the enterprise director was directly responsible to government officials, the government hired and fired directors, and in turn the government was subordinate to the party. The new system contemplated by the reform economists under Šik, and sketched out in principle in the Action Program, foresaw the state ceasing to be the direct supervisor of enterprises. One possible alternative model would have managers assume control of enterprises. But that would be no democracy at all. The only way to bring democracy into the workplace, and therefore into the economy, is for the workforce to have a direct voice in the enterprise. On a larger, economy-wide scale, decision-making would have to be spread among various groups, horizontally as well as vertically in the production chain.

"The economy can only be harnessed to serve human ends by democratically decided, long-term and indirect measures to steer the course of income, investment and consumption, using one or another variant of scientifically based macroeconomic planning," Šik later wrote in exile.

> By making institutional provision for elected representatives of non-producer interests to share both in drafting alternate plans and in the final choice, the democratic element could be substantially reinforced. The common good would then stand a better chance of prevailing over the weight of the particular vested interests. With massive private appropriation of surplus value abolished, and distribution of national income a matter for public discussion and control, little would remain of the economic basis for narrow or self-seeking interests to dominate the political scene.[99]

Šik traveled a long path to become a reformer in a communist-ruled society. During the 1930s, he grew disgusted at the "nationalist and racist witch-hunting" and the "oppression and exploitation of working people" under capitalism. He joined the anti-Nazi resistance in 1939 at age 20 after becoming a communist, and after his arrest narrowly avoided death in the Nazis' Mauthausen concentration camp. But after the communist takeover, Šik became disenchanted by the lack of democracy and rigidity of the prevailing ideology and drew conclusions:

> The shock of Khrushchev's [1956 "secret"] speech was such that my former political activity lost all meaning for me. Naturally, I could not be satisfied with the ingenuous argument that the "cult of Stalin" was the root of all evil. I had to decide—either to leave the Communist Party, or to stay in order, by long-term, patient and systematic work, to help change the system. With a few like-minded friends I opted for the latter course.[100]

Although the enforcer of that system in Czechoslovakia, Antonín Novotný, was most certainly not among those "like-minded friends," it was under Novotný in the 1960s that Šik and other reformers began their work. It probably did not hurt Šik that he and Novotný had been interned in Mauthausen together and were personally close.

Workers' councils became a solution to two problems—the problem of creating a structure for employees to meaningfully exercise control over their workplaces and as a way to bind together different enterprises so that economic activity would benefit the country as a whole. The state was the owner of enterprises, carrying out all the prerogatives of ownership, including decision-making and appointments to managerial positions, without input from below although the state was in theory the "owner" in the concept of the "representative of," or "in trust for," the people of the country as a whole.

The enterprises were to remain formally in state hands but not be controlled by the state. A different structure would be necessary: If directors and other top managers of enterprises were to remain accountable to society as a whole, and if the workers of enterprises were to now shoulder responsibility for the economic viability of the enterprise, then accountability to the workforce would be the solution. Subsidies for poor performances would be withdrawn, putting the employees at risk of unemployment if the enterprise was not able to remain economically viable. It was only fair, the advocates of workers' councils argued, for the workers to have a large say in how their enterprise will be run if they were to shoulder the risks that would result from restructuring management.

The creation of the councils would bind together the enterprises, retaining the efficiency inherent in planning as opposed to the chaos of individual enterprises or factories each making decisions in isolation from all others, because the workers' councils would be connected horizontally through regional and national federations or congresses, which would help prepare national production plans based on the needs of producer and consumer goods at the local levels. A central plan would still exist, but it would cease to be a hard numerical total that had to be fulfilled no matter what, regardless of conditions or quality-control issues that might develop. Instead, the plan would become a guideline (this did happen in 1968 and 1969) that would suggest an overall output for economic sectors.

Enterprises were to use the guidelines as part of their processes of setting their own targets, but there would be no penalties if the total output of enterprises did not precisely equal the guideline. If the system had been allowed to develop, the cumulative output of enterprises undoubtedly would have become a significant factor in determining the following year's plan. In this way, the efficiencies of planning on a national scale could have been augmented with flexibility as enterprises adjusted according to changing conditions and demands.

Enterprise directors would become accountable to workers' councils, which would be made up of, and elected by, the employees. In the terminology of the Czechoslovak economic reformers, the councils would become the "entrepreneurs," since they would have responsibility for wages, distribution of income, overall planning for the enterprise and similar responsibilities, including making decisions on merging with other enterprises or shutting itself.

Individual employees would remain employees at the same time they would assume management duties by virtue of electing (or being elected to) the councils, although the latter role would be shared with all other employees on a collective basis. Thus, the trade unions, freed of their state shackles, would take up the traditional union role of representing the workforce as individual employees, and the workers' councils would represent the workforce in its collective role as managers.

Interestingly, the unions saw no difficulty with separate bodies, and unions took the lead in setting up workers' councils. Unions initiated the formation of about two-thirds of the councils that formed across the country in 1968 and 1969.[101] About half of the remaining third were formed by local Communist Party branches.[102] Embracing the duality, a national meeting of delegates representing local organizations of the ROH trade-union federation held in mid-June 1968 declared,

> The unions will continue without fail to demand a guarantee of real social security for the workers. We believe that the unions, in their fight to obtain and safeguard workers' rights, must use every available means, including the ultimate weapon of organized strikes…We call upon the trade unions to support…the experimental establishment and development of workers' councils.[103]

A more democratized economy still has to function as an economy. Among other issues that had to be worked out (and as with finding the proper balance between central planning and enterprise autonomy, there was far from enough time for proper experimentation) were the sources of investment money, pricing of commodities and methods of taxation.

Investments in industry financed directly out of the state budget were halved as the reforms were introduced;[104] reduced subsidies were introduced concurrently with a loosening of state control. Investment credits and loans issued by the state bank to enterprises, meanwhile, were doubled as a replacement for the diminished government subsidies.[105] Undoubtedly, there would have been further adjustments in the sources of investment money; possibly, loans could have been made in some sort of relationship with central plans, boosting somewhat the role of planning in the evolving relationship between national planning and enterprise autonomy.

Some freeing of commodity prices was seen as an integral part of the economic reforms, but this was a sensitive political issue. Prices had been set by fiat in the command system, and price increases in basic food items, for instance, had been the cause of unrest throughout the Soviet bloc. Moreover, because prices had been fixed, a sudden freeing of prices would unavoidably lead to inflation, touching off new economic problems. (This indeed was a very large problem two decades later when capitalism was introduced in countries previously ruled by communist parties or that had been attempting some sort of transition to a socialist system.) Fewer prices were set free than economists had wanted; political leaders are not as free as economists to ignore concrete political questions. By the end of 1968, most wholesale prices had become "controlled" (the government placed limits on how much prices could be raised), while most retail goods remained fixed; only a limited amount of goods were subject to free pricing.[106] The Soviet invasion disrupted the economy, leading to a refreezing of prices in 1969.[107]

The reform economists also believed that a rationalization of the tax system was unavoidable. Under the command system, wages and bonuses were based on an enterprise meeting its production quota under the central plan, and whatever money was left after paying wages and setting aside funds for planned investments in new equipment, upgrades and other improvements went into the state budget.[108] Because the money that went to the state was in effect the state's tax receipts, there was no consistency in what enterprises would ultimately provide the state; payments to the state budget were subject to wide changes. Economists' theory here was that a uniform tax rate combined with an equilibrium in prices would much better differentiate efficient from inefficient enterprises.[109]

There was not enough time to see how these reforms would have worked: The invasion cut off what would have been an extremely valuable experiment in socialist economic forms.

## A decision that reverberated for decades: The Soviet Union invades

Developments moved quickly in the final five weeks before the 20 August invasion. Soviet leaders, in particular Leonid Brezhnev, don't seem to have made the final decision to invade until a few days before, although the publication of the "Two Thousand Words" manifesto helped shape opinions. The catalyzing factor, however, was likely the early convening of the Fourteenth Congress. Although some reformers were critical of Alexander Dubček for not rushing to convene the congress in the spring, Dubček believed a more cautious sequence of events was unavoidable. The pressure of public opinion had caused hard-liners to retreat, but a "latent majority" against reforms still existed on the Central Committee, Dubček believed.[110] "The only way to change this situation was to convene an extraordinary Party congress to elect a new Central Committee,"[111] he wrote in his memoirs.

In Czechoslovakia, a congress, made up of elected delegates from all corners of the country, was convened every four years. A congress set party policy and elected the Central Committee, which in turn elected the higher bodies, most importantly the Politburo. The next congress was not due until 1970, but widespread support at the local level allowed an early convening under party statutes. Dubček also believed that there was no point in convening the congress until there was a program in place, which occurred in early April with the approval of the Action Program. A May 1968 poll of party members found that 85 percent supported the program[112] and this broad grassroots support was reflected in the composition of the congressional delegates, about 90 percent of whom were reformers.[113]

"When we decided in early June to convene the Congress," Dubček later wrote, "the Soviets happened to be urging—not by chance, I think—large-scale war games on our territory, and they went public with their criticism of our internal development. While it was now desirable to convene the congress as soon as possible, I was still reluctant to antagonize the existing Central Committee. That body's power would be intact until the congress, and we could not convene the congress overnight. District conferences had to meet and elect delegates to regional conferences, and regional conferences had to be held to elect delegates to the congress. It was also necessary to prepare congressional documents, resolutions and personnel proposals, all of which were demanding tasks."[114]

The hard-liners would certainly have been voted out when the Fourteenth Congress convened in early September; a separate meeting of Slovak communists was scheduled for late August, which would begin the wholesale renewal of the party leadership. Among those who would have been removed was Slovak party head Vasil Bil'ak, who had perhaps most consistently voiced opposition to any reform. Bil'ak had served under Dubček during the 1960s as the ideology and culture supervisor for Slovakia, carrying out Dubček's relatively lax policies. Trained as a tailor with little formal education, Bil'ak joined the party in the mid-1940s, holding various party and government posts. He came to oppose Antonín Novotný, but did not support any further reforms. He was not able to conceptualize any concept of socialism beyond the narrow, deformed Soviet example, and not long after his rise to a seat on the Politburo he was making speeches to party audiences complaining that the media had already gone too far. But Bil'ak did not limit his criticism to Czechoslovak party circles; he was also secretly meeting with a hard-line member of the Soviet Politburo, Petro Shelest. Shelest had been a close ally of Leonid Brezhnev since the 1964 ouster of Nikita Khrushchev, and at this time also served as party chief for Ukraine, which bordered Czechoslovakia. Shelest was already predisposed to stiff opposition to Czechoslovak reforms, and Bil'ak's lurid report to him in late May only reinforced those ideas.

Bil'ak told Shelest "it's urgently necessary that you conduct maneuvers of your troops on the territory of Czechoslovakia" in order "to cool off the hotheads."[115] Bil'ak spoke of supposed political murders and assorted mayhem, and Shelest reported this to the Soviet Politburo, hardening positions there.[116] In a second meeting in late July, Bil'ak repeated his allegations of "rightist forces" preparing for an overthrow of party and government, but also let slip what must have been his biggest concern: "Preparations for the Fourteenth Congress are going badly, and we're not sure that we'll be able to win out at this congress; although A. Dubček is placing all his hopes on victory, there is no basis for such hopes."[117] Bil'ak asked for armed intervention, and Shelest asked Bil'ak for a letter from like-minded colleagues requesting that.[118]

Augmenting Bil'ak's work, a steady stream of similar reports was sent to Moscow from the Soviet ambassador to Czechoslovakia, Stepan Chervonenko, and from the Soviet secret police, the KGB. Years later, the former KGB chief agent in Washington admitted,

> The KGB stirred up fears among the country's leadership that Czechoslovakia could fall victim to NATO aggression or a coup unless certain actions were undertaken. At about the same time, I reported from Washington that the CIA was not

> involved in the development of the Prague Spring. But my attempt at an even-handed report simply did not fit in with the KGB's concept of the way events were shaping up in Czechoslovakia, and therefore never got beyond the KGB. My information was wasted.[119]

The one-sided information stream had become a feedback loop, although the example of a spy agency tailoring its reports to what a political leadership wants to hear is hardly unique. The Soviet leadership was also irritated because many of its agents in the Czechoslovak army officer corps and secret police were being rooted out. The wholesale replacement of hard-liners from the Czechoslovak political leadership would have led to the completion of those purges, and this, too, was alarming to the Soviet leaders, accustomed to directing the affairs of the other Warsaw Pact countries. The Warsaw Pact army exercises, after which the Soviet troops were to leave the country, was to have ended in late June, but was extended well into July by the Warsaw Pact commanding officer, Soviet Marshal Ivan Yakobovskii. Two high-ranking Hungarian generals who took part in the exercises, irritated at being kept uninformed by Yakobovskii, flatly declared in a report to the Hungarian party Politburo, "The exercise was organized essentially for political reasons and with political objectives" and added, "In our opinion, there is no counter-revolutionary situation."[120]

After the exercises were finally ended and troops began leaving, two final series of talks were held, bilateral between Soviet and Czechoslovak leaders at the end of July and among the Warsaw Pact countries in early August. On the eve of the bilateral talks, a spontaneous display of nationwide support backed the Czechoslovak negotiators. The "Message from the Citizens" was written by a Writers Union veteran and party member, Pavel Kohout, and printed in several newspapers.

"The time has come when we are capable of demonstrating to

the world that socialism is not some emergency solution for underdeveloped countries but the only true alternative for civilization. We expected that this would be greeted with sympathy, above all by the entire socialist camp. Instead we are being accused of treason,"[121] the document stated. Addressing directly the party Politburo members, the Message points out the enormous responsibility they shouldered. "Over the next few days we will anxiously follow your deliberations in our thoughts, hour by hour. We are thinking of you. Think of us!"[122] The last two sentences rhyme in Czech. More than 1 million people signed their name to the Message,[123] in a country of 14 million.

The bilateral meeting featured a long string of insults and wild accusations of fomenting separatism in Ukraine by Shelest, and an anti-Semitic comment by Podgorny that prompted a walkout, temporarily halting the talks.[124] And when Dubček pointed to the support he and his policies were receiving, Brezhnev responded, "If I gave instructions, I too could have a ton of letters here in no time."[125]

The meeting ended with an ambiguous unwritten agreement, in which Dubček and Brezhnev agreed that all the Warsaw Pact countries would meet again in a week and rescind the harsh demands put forth by a Warsaw Pact summit meeting two weeks earlier, a set of demands backed by the usual assortment of false allegations and assumptions that became known as the "Warsaw Letter."[126] Brezhnev, however, had made several demands in the bilateral meeting, including the replacement of certain reformers he particularly disliked and the re-imposition of censorship.[127] Czechoslovak leaders later consistently said they made no formal agreements on these matters, promising only to take limited measures at future Central Committee meetings to rein in "excesses."

The early August follow-up meeting of the Warsaw Pact countries, the final summit before the invasion, took place in Bratislava, the Slovak capital, but produced only an ambiguous document with conflicting statements of principles that left the agreement open to interpretation. The most important occurrence of this meeting, however, occurred in a restroom. Following through on Shelest's earlier request, Bil'ak handed Shelest a letter, signed by him and four other hard-liners, asking Brezhnev to invade.

"In such trying circumstances we are appealing to you…with a request for you to lend support and assistance with all the means at your disposal," the letter said. "Only with your assistance can the Czechoslovak Socialist Republic be extricated from imminent danger of counter-revolution…In connection with the complex and dangerous course of the situation in our country, we request that you treat our statement with the utmost secrecy, and for that reason we are writing to you, personally, in Russian."[128] Joining Bil'ak in signing the letter was Alois Indra, who was designated by the plotters to take charge of the government after the invasion, with Bil'ak taking over the reins of the party.

Bil'ak was about to be ousted as Slovak party leader, and be replaced by Gustáv Husák,[129] in another irony. The extremely ambitious Husák had a reputation as a Slovak nationalist, serving a stint in prison in the 1950s because of it, and was publicly backing the reforms. Husák would eventually replace Dubček as Czechoslovak first secretary and become the gravedigger of the Prague Spring.

Brezhnev telephoned Dubček twice, on 9 August and 13 August, declaring that he felt deceived that Dubček did not carry out the "agreements" made at Bratislava. Evidently not getting the answers he wanted, Brezhnev joined the Soviet Politburo in the 17 August decision to invade. It is not known what the actual vote was at this meeting; the resolution uses a Russian word that translates as "unanimous in spirit" as opposed to a different word used to mean "unanimous vote."[130] The most probable explanation for that usage was that there was a broad consensus on going ahead with the invasion and therefore no need for a formal vote.

Although it's tempting to see "great power" geopolitical considerations as the motor force of the invasion—and that is part of the picture—a complex series of political issues, some internal, collided that summer. The Soviet leaders genuinely felt themselves under threat of a NATO invasion, and however legitimate (or not) that fear actually was, it was true that the Soviet bloc was encircled by military bases and the capitalist powers had tried to strangle the Soviet Union from its first days. The Central European countries that had come under Soviet domination after World War II acted as a defensive barrier against possible invasion in the eyes of Soviet military and political leaders, and that mentality could not be separated from those same leaders' genuinely held belief that their system was the best for ordinary citizens. In a closed political system, that belief had fossilized into a simplistic black-and-white idea that any change to this system was tantamount to the restoration of capitalism, or even outright fascism.

That defensive barrier and the perceived need to maintain as strong a defense as possible resulted in gigantic military outlays. Brezhnev once declared that the Soviet Union devoted 22 percent of its budget to the military, but "much more than that actually must be spent."[131] Brezhnev also was wary of Czechoslovakia becoming independent in the manner of Yugoslavia, and those two joining with Romania, the one Warsaw Pact member that showed an independent streak in foreign affairs, to form an alliance. In part, "great power" considerations did come into play here, an attitude not free of the idea that, because the Red Army liberated these areas from fascism at a staggeringly high cost, the Soviet Union was entitled to maintain its presence there indefinitely.

There was also the fraternal idea that communists stand together and coordinate with one another. Soviet leaders repeatedly accused the Czechoslovak leaders of not making good on their word—this accusation was angrily thrown at Dubček in the two August phone calls from Brezhnev. The Soviet general secretary once declared that "trust is very important in political and personal life. You know that in high and low politics personal relations have important significance."[132] More than once Brezhnev told Dubček that he needed no formal agreement, merely expecting him to carry out his word as a communist. But for Brezhnev & Co., this was a one-way duty. The Soviet leaders took as a given their right to dictate personnel changes in other countries, and the Czechoslovak leaders' refusal to allow that played a significant role in the decision to invade.

Another factor that shoudn't be underestimated is internal Soviet conditions. Brezhnev, as general secretary for four years, was indisputably the top leader, but was not so strong as to be able to dictate to the Politburo. There were other powerful figures in the leadership, including Prime Minister Aleksei Kosygin, President Nikolai Podgorny and ideology chief Mikhail Suslov. The last of these, who began his decades-long stint on the Politburo at the end of the Stalin era, was a hard-liner who exerted a very strong influence. Suslov had helped to organize the ouster of Nikita Khrushchev (as had Podgorny), and although he never posed any threat to Brezhnev's leadership he would have been a consistent voice for intervention. The leadership of the Red Army at this time had been forged in World War II under Stalin, and shared Stalin's foreign-policy conceptions of a strong defense against potential capitalist intervention, constituting an especially strong voice for invasion.

Brezhnev, for that matter, came to power as a result of party exasperation against Khrushchev and with a mandate to restore stability rather than experiment with reforms. The highly cautious Brezhnev was temperamentally suited for such a role, and the mandate for a return to orthodoxy dovetailed with his own views. But there were still those in the political leadership in favor of cautious internal reforms, such as Kosygin and (in contrast to his hard-line views on foreign policy) Yuri Andropov. Brezhnev had to navigate through a mildly heterogeneous leadership by reaching consensus.

Economic reform had been a topic of discussion among the Soviet leadership before 1968, and continued to be afterward. Indeed, just a year earlier, an official Soviet document declared that reform and change are inseparable from its official ideology because it is "a doctrine that is constantly being enriched and tested by historical practice. It is opposed to any kind of dogmatism and constantly develops on the basis of generalization of the experience recorded in world history and the achievements of the natural and social sciences."[133]

But attempts at meaningful reform within the Soviet Union went nowhere, most importantly due to the ideological viewpoint that only a continued party monopoly could guarantee continued development. For instance, the president of the Soviet Association of Political Sciences, a key ideological position, said that renouncing that monopoly

> would be tantamount to rejecting the need for political leadership per se and would almost certainly lead to anarchy and chaos and eventually degeneration of the system…The actual practice of socialism shows quite clearly that the one-party system is capable of serving as the instrument of social development and ensuring social progress at all stages of construction of the new society.[134]

The Soviet leadership's unshakable conviction of the rightness of their political monopoly guaranteed that any attempt at the loosening of party control in Czechoslovakia would be anathema. Nor would repeated assurances that there would be no break with the Soviet bloc or a withdrawal from the Warsaw Pact have any effect, despite Czechoslovak party leaders' convictions that they could only achieve their goals of renewing socialism with the protection of the bloc. The belief in political monopoly would have acted as a brake against any potential to widen divergences of opinion within the Soviet Politburo, although differences of outlook did not cease to exist and Brezhnev, to remain as general secretary, could not simply ignore those differences.

Although he exaggerated the degree of insecurity in his position, Brezhnev acknowledged his constraints in a conversation after the invasion with Bohumil Šimon, one of the most committed reformers among the Czechoslovak leadership. "You thought that when you were in power you could do what you wanted," Brezhnev said to Šimon. "But that's a basic mistake. Not even I can do what I'd like; I can achieve only about a third of what I would like to do. If I hadn't voted in the Politburo for military intervention, what would have happened? You almost certainly would not be sitting here. And I probably wouldn't be sitting here either."[135]

The invasion resolution approved on 17 August even included a draft proclamation for Bil'ak and Indra to announce the invasion as the new Czechoslovak leaders.[136] The draft announcement, in an effort to gain support of working people, decreed a rollback of consumer prices and acknowledged, "We are aware that current living standards still do not fully satisfy the growing demands of laborers."[137]

Bil'ak and Indra never had the chance to issue the decree, as their plans quickly unraveled and their promises to Shelest that they had a majority of the Czechoslovak Politburo and the country firmly behind them proved to be an illusion. The tanks rolled in on the evening of 20 August, with the Politburo meeting in Prague, and the Politburo then voted by a 7–4 majority to condemn the invasion. The four Politburo votes against the condemnation were cast by Bil'ak, Drahomír Kolder, Oldřich Švetska and Emil Rigo; the first three were among the five signers of the letter to Brezhnev. The other two signers, Indra and

Antonín Kapek, respectively a Central Committee secretary and a Politburo candidate member, the next-highest rungs in the party hierarchy, attended Politburo meetings without having a vote.

The tension evidently got to Bil'ak, because at one point he began pacing back and forth, yelling, "Alright, lynch me! Why don't you kill me?"[138] Švetska was also the editor of the official party daily newspaper, Rudé Právo, and attempted to halt publication of the communiqué condemning the invasion; Josef Smrkovský intervened to get the presses restarted.[139]

The conspirators, including Švetska, left after the communiqué vote, but the rest stayed, deciding they should not abandon their posts.[140] The invasion date was "recommended" by the Bil'ak group, and Brezhnev deemed that date and the plan worked out by them as "acceptable on the whole" at the 17 August Soviet Politburo meeting.[141] Bil'ak, Kolder and Indra planned to force a discussion on the "political situation" at the 20 August meeting of the Czechoslovak Politburo and Central Committee secretaries, which they expected to culminate in a vote that would depose the reformers.[142] The hard-liners would then reorient party policy and form a new government, which would then invite the Soviet Union to invade. Their move to change the meeting agenda failed, and they then lost the vote to condemn the invasion after it started.

Once the reformers decided to stay in the Central Committee building, there was nothing to do but wait. In a few hours, a unit of Soviet paratroopers, joined by a contingent of Czechoslovak secret policemen, arrived to arrest the leadership. The phone lines were cut and the reformers each had a gun pointed at the back of their heads before one of the secret policemen declared that they were about to be put in front of a tribunal of the "revolutionary workers' and peasants' government headed by Comrade Indra." Six of the reform leaders were forced into tanks and sent off; some lower-ranking ones were allowed to leave. But the plans went awry—there was no tribunal. Instead the arrestees were flown to Ukraine, then brought to Moscow for "negotiations."

By the time the Moscow talks began, three days after the invasion, the kidnapped reformers had no idea why their captors didn't seem to know what to do with them nor how the country was reacting to the invasion. After the initial shock of the news of the invasion on the night of 20 August, there was a quick unanimity among those at the Politburo meeting that there should be no armed resistance. The force invading was too strong to resist and the Czechoslovak army was not only under the partial control of the Soviet Union but was arrayed to protect against a NATO invasion from West Germany. Armed resistance would result in unnecessary bloodshed.

The Warsaw Pact generals knew there would be no military resistance. And consistent with the communiqué of the Czechoslovak Politburo, Defense Minister General Martin Dzúr, upon receiving news of the invasion, ordered all troops to remain in their barracks and "under no circumstances are weapons to be used."[143] At dawn on 21 August, Czechs and Slovaks began a nationwide passive resistance to the invasion, pulling down street signs, covering the cities in graffiti with slogans such as "Lenin awake! Brezhnev has gone mad!" and refusing to provide any assistance. The invaders' food, water and fuel supplies were very low for several days because they apparently believed these would be supplied in Czechoslovakia.[144] Groups of people argued with soldiers on their tanks, attempting to sway the minds of men whom they saw as exploited simpletons who did not know what they were doing.[145]

Meanwhile, the plans of Bil'ak and his fellow plotters had completely fallen apart; they tried to organize a Central Committee meeting two days after the invasion but only 50 people, about one-third of the membership, showed up.[146] The Soviet Politburo member designated to oversee the invasion by this point was already complaining that "our friends had gone somewhat haywire, but they really began to lose their nerve when the Soviet units were a bit late in arriving...Our friends have gone to pieces...We are doing everything possible to shore them up, but they have not yet recovered from the shock."[147]

In a final attempt to put together a "revolutionary workers' and peasants' government," the top party leaders not arrested by the Soviet forces or in hiding assembled in the Central Committee building. Although these mostly were the hard-liners, there were a couple of fence-sitters and two strongly reformist Central Committee secretaries, Zdeněk Mlynář and Štefan Sádovský. Several of the party leaders said no effort should be made to do anything without first ascertaining what had happened to Dubček and the other five who had been arrested and whose whereabouts remained unknown to them. A meeting was then set up at the Soviet embassy with Ambassador Stepan Chervonenko.

While the Czechoslovak delegation waited for the ambassador, Mlynář was greeted by a plainclothes KGB agent, who passed on greetings from a fellow student of Mylnář's from when both were at party school in Moscow in the early 1950s; the fellow student was now a KGB lieutenant colonel. Taking advantage of the situation, Mlynář asked to use the telephone and was provided with a secure line. Mlynář then telephoned his liaison at the clandestine Fourteenth Congress that had just convened and reported on the talks in the Soviet embassy. The Czechoslovak delegation, still waiting for the ambassador, was listening to a radio broadcast that reported on the congress and on their talks, causing the hard-liners to exclaim that they couldn't understand how the radio reporters knew they were negotiating in the embassy.[148]

Chervonenko asked the Czechoslovak delegation to form a "revolutionary government," but because the participants were aware of the public's knowledge of the talks and the near universal opposition to the invasion, a farcical discussion ensued in which people would propose others for various posts, but decline to accept one themselves (except for Bil'ak, who "reluctantly" agreed to be the new first secretary).[149] When no resolution was apparent, it was agreed that all should meet with Ludvík Svoboda, the Czechoslovak president. Svoboda rejected any "revolutionary workers' and peasants' government," and insisted he would go to Moscow and sort out all problems. Chervonenko was displeased by this development, but Svoboda was adamant, and took a delegation with him the next morning. Svoboda warned that a "great deal of blood would be shed" if the arrested leaders were not soon released, but also promised that Dubček and Prime Minister Oldřich Černík would resign, although he too had no communication with them.[150]

That bold move culminated in the negotiations that resulted in the forced agreement known as the "Moscow Protocol," in which the Czechoslovak negotiators (Svoboda's delegation and the arrestees) were forced to agree to several concessions, including nullifying the results of the Fourteenth Congress, re-imposing censorship and banning all non-communist social groups, plus an unwritten understanding that several strong reformers whom the Soviet leadership particularly disliked would be removed. Gustáv Husák, a member of the delegation that flew to Moscow with Svoboda, agreed with Soviet negotiators' demands that the congress be annulled; he did this on the basis that few Slovaks were able to attend it.[151] By doing so he broke the solidarity of the Czechoslovak side and signaled his defection to the hard-liners, cynically using Slovak nationalism to do so.

All but one, František Kriegel, signed, for the most basic of reasons: They believed they had no choice. "If you don't sign now, you'll sign in a week. If not in a week, then in a fortnight, and if not in a fortnight, then in a month," they were told.[152] In return for ceding so much ground, the Czechoslovak leadership had an agreement on the removal of the troops inserted and received a promise from Brezhnev that, although the Central Committee that existed before the Fourteenth Congress would remain in place, the CC would include some new members drawn from the list of people who had been elected to the now-annulled CC by the congress. But that the protocol was a diktat could not be disguised.

"We all hesitated," Smrkovský later recalled. "I hesitated for a long time, should I, shouldn't I...Nobody wanted to do it. I was aware of what a serious step this was."[153] Dubček stayed out of most of the talks and said had he been in Kriegel's position, he, too, would have refused to sign. But his responsibility was too great to refuse: "I had a clear and undeniable personal responsibility for the lives of thousands of people at home, who would have almost certainly taken my refusal to sign the 'agreement' as encouragement to active resistance. I did not believe I had the right to allow that, for it would lead to a bloodbath."[154] Dubček also believed there was enough ambiguity in the agreement to allow him to salvage some of the reforms.

Back home, those Fourteenth Congress delegates who could reach Prague—more than two-thirds—convened clandestinely. The meeting was held in a factory that had been one of the first to organize workers' councils, located on the outskirts of Prague. The meeting was guarded by members of the Workers' Militia, an armed group of ordinary citizens who were dedicated communists. That is significant, because the hard-liners and the Soviet leadership had expected the militia to back an invasion.

The congress had been scheduled to begin on 9 September 1968, but was convened on 22 August on the initiative of the Prague city party committee, a particularly strong hotbed of reformism led by Šimon. Because the invasion was likely timed to prevent the congress from convening, it is appropriate to look more closely at what so frightened hard-liners in the Soviet Union and Czechoslovakia.

The congress was assigned two main tasks—to elect a new

Central Committee and to discuss two working papers sketching the tasks of rebuilding socialist society, putting it on a proper democratic footing, redefining the role of the Communist Party and creating new social, political, cultural and economic structures. The starting point for these papers was an analysis of the wholly inappropriate Soviet model imposed in 1948. Since that time, the Czechoslovak party had no program of its own, instead imitating the Soviet model without taking into consideration the history, culture, morality and politics of the country, and a model that, additionally, was in conflict with the higher industrial, political and cultural development of Czechoslovakia compared to the Soviet Union.[155]

The two papers didn't lay out specific prescriptions, instead discussing the many areas where improvements were needed and the bases for making those improvements. The congress was to provide a starting point for the preparation of a more detailed program to be prepared by large working groups, submitted to extensive public discussion and eventually brought for approval to the future Fifteenth Congress.[156]

Simultaneous with these discussions, a presumed consensus for continuing the reform process was contemplated, in part by working out a new concept of the National Front with "truly independent" parties, open elections to a revitalized parliament that would include representation in multiple ways (geography, cultural institutions, professions and others), guarantees of civic freedoms and building a base for a new economic policy and managerial system.[157] One possible setup for parliament would have been for the creation of "ancillary" chambers—an industrial chamber elected from factories and trade enterprises, an agricultural chamber elected from collective and state farms, and a social services chamber elected from educational, health, cultural and similar institutions. These chambers would be in addition to traditional representation on the basis of geographic districts and would have special powers on legislation concerning their areas of expertise.[158]

New management systems were to include workers' councils and possibly other forms of self-management, and economic models would no longer be limited to state ownership; there also would be collectives and other forms.[159] These ideas were based on the need for a full realization of citizen participation in society. A congressional working paper stated:

> The whole purpose of socialism as a socio-political system is to mediate and guarantee those rights and freedoms, which in their totality form the actual content of a workers' state; this requires that use be made of representative democracy (in particular of parliament) and that direct and indirect democracy be linked, with a view to strengthening self-administration in every sphere of social life, in places of work as well as in areas of residence, where it can help overcome the shortcomings of representative democracy, where the conditions have been created for the free self-determination of man and widening of his real participation in decision-making.[160]

The congress was not able to substantially discuss these working papers; the one-day session instead mostly worked on electing a new Central Committee. It also voted to re-elect Dubček as first secretary.

The congress would soon be annulled under the pressure of the invasion, as the political sphere began shrinking. But with the invaders unable to control the country, August 1968 did not bring an end to all innovation—the workers' council movement had several months of life remaining, growing in strength, with most councils coming into being after the invasion.

## An experiment in economic democracy continues (temporarily) as more workers' councils are formed

At the time of the Soviet invasion, two months after the first workers' councils were formed, there were perhaps fewer than two dozen of them, although these were concentrated in the largest enterprises and therefore represented a large number of employees. But the movement took off, and by January 1969 there were councils in about 120 enterprises, representing more than 800,000 employees, or about one-sixth of the country's workers.[161] This occurred despite a new mood of discouragement from the government from October 1968.

From the beginning, this was a grassroots movement from below that forced party, government, and enterprise managements to react. The councils designed their own statutes and implemented them from the start. The draft statutes for the Wilhelm Pieck Factory in Prague (one of the first, created in June 1968) provide a good example. "The workers of the W. Pieck factory (CKD Prague) wish to fulfill one of the fundamental rights of socialist democracy, namely the right of the workers to manage their own factory," the introduction to the statutes stated. "They also desire a closer bond between the interests of the whole society and the interests of each individual. To this end, they have decided to establish workers' self-management."[162]

All employees working for at least three months, except the director, were eligible to participate, and the employees as a whole, called the "workers' assembly," was the highest body and would make all fundamental decisions.[163] In turn, the assembly would elect the workers' council to carry out the decisions of the whole, manage the plant and hire the director. Council members would serve in staggered terms, be elected in secret balloting and be recallable.[164] The director was to be chosen after an examination of each candidate conducted by a body composed of a majority of employees and a minority from outside organizations.[165]

A director is the top manager, equivalent to the chief executive officer of a capitalist corporation. The workers' council would be the equivalent of a board of directors in a capitalist corporation that has shares traded on a stock market. This supervisory role, however, would be radically different: The workers' council would be made up of workers acting in the interest of their fellow workers and, in theory, with the greater good of society in mind as well.

By contrast, in a capitalist corporation listed on a stock market, the board of directors is made up of top executives of the company, the chief executive officer's cronies, executives from other corporations in which there is an alignment of interests, and perhaps a celebrity or two, and the board of directors has a duty only to the holders of the corporation's stock. Although this duty to stockholders is strong enough in some countries to be written into legal statutes, the ownership of the stock is spread among so many that the board will often act in the interest of that top management, which translates to the least possible unencumbered transfer of wealth upward. But in cases where the board of directors does uphold its legal duty and governs in the interest of the holders of the stock, this duty simply means maximizing the price of the stock by any means necessary, not excepting mass layoffs, wage reductions and the taking away of employee benefits. Either way, the capitalist company is governed against the interests of its workforce (whose collective efforts are the source of the profits), and by law must be.

The Wilhelm Pieck Factory statutes were similar to statutes produced in other enterprises that were creating workers' councils. It was only logical for a national federation of councils to be formed to coordinate their work and for economic activity to have a relation to the larger societal interest. Ahead of a government deadline to produce national legislation codifying the councils, a general meeting of workers' councils took place on

9 and 10 January 1969 in Plzeň, one of the most important industrial cities in Czechoslovakia (perhaps best known internationally for its famous beers). A 104-page report left behind a good record of the meeting (it was also tape-recorded); representatives from across the Czech Lands and Slovakia convened to provide the views of the councils to assist in the preparation of the national law.

Trade union leaders were among the participants in the meeting, and backed the complementary roles of the unions and the councils. (Trade unions, as noted earlier, convened two-thirds of the councils.) One of the first speakers, an engineer who was the chair of his trade union local in Plzeň, said a division of tasks was a natural development: "For us, the establishment of workers' councils implies that we will be able to achieve a status of relative independence for the enterprise, that the decision-making power will be separated from executive powers, that the trade unions will have a free hand to carry out their own specific policies, that progress is made towards a solution of the problem of the producers' relationship to their production, i.e., we are beginning to solve the problem of alienation."[166]

Some 190 enterprises were represented at this meeting, including 101 workers' councils and 61 preparatory committees for the creation of councils; the remainder were trade union or other types of committees. The meeting concluded with the unanimous passage of a six-point resolution, including "the right to self-management as an inalienable right of the socialist producer."[167]

The resolution declared,

> We are convinced that workers' councils can help to humanize both the work and relationships within the enterprise, and give to each producer a proper feeling that he is not just an employee, a mere working element in the production process, but also the organizer and joint creator of this

> process. This is why we wish to re-emphasize here and now that the councils must always preserve their democratic character and their vital links with their electors, thus preventing a special caste of "professional self-management executives" from forming.[168]

That democratic character, and the popularity of the concept, is demonstrated in the mass participation—a survey of 95 councils found that 83 percent of employees had participated in council elections.[169] A considerable study was undertaken of these 95 councils, representing manufacturing and other sectors, and an interesting trend emerged from the data in the high level of experience embodied in elected council members. About three-quarters of those elected to councils had been in their workplaces for more than ten years, and mostly more than 15 years.[170] More than 70 percent of council members were technicians or engineers, about one-quarter were manual workers and only 5 percent were from administrative staffs.[171] These results represent a strong degree of voting for the perceived best candidates rather than employees simply voting for their friends or for candidates like themselves—because the council movement was particularly strong in manufacturing sectors, most of those voting for council members were manual workers.[172]

These results demonstrated a high level of political maturity on the part of Czechoslovak workers. Another clue to this seriousness is that 29 percent of those elected to councils had a university education, possibly a higher average level of education than was then possessed by directors.[173] Many directors in the past had been put into their positions through political connections, and a desire to revolt against sometimes amateurish management played a part in the council movement. Interesting, too, is that about half the council members were also Communist Party members.[174] Czechoslovak workers continued to believe in socialism while rejecting the imposed Soviet-style system.

The government did write a legislative bill, copies of which circulated in January 1969, but the bill was never introduced as Soviet pressure on the Czechoslovak party leadership intensified and hard-liners began to assert themselves. The bill would have changed the name of workers' councils to enterprise councils and watered down some of the statutes that had been codified by the councils themselves. These pullbacks included a proposed state veto on the selection of enterprise directors, that one-fifth of enterprise councils be made up of unelected outside specialists, and that the councils of what the bill refers to as "state enterprises" (banks, railroads and other entities that would remain directly controlled by the government) could have only a minority of members elected by employees and allow a government veto of council decisions.[175]

This proposed backtracking was met with opposition. The trade union daily newspaper, Práce, in a February commentary, and a federal trade union congress, in March, both called the government bill "the minimum acceptable." In a Práce commentary, an engineer and council activist, Rudolf Slánský Jr (son of the executed party leader), put the council movement in the context of the question of enterprise ownership.

"The management of our nation's economy is one of the crucial problems," Slánský wrote.

> The basic economic principlel on which the bureaucratic-centralist management mechanism rests is the direct exercise of the ownership functions of nationalized industry. The state, or more precisely various central organs of the state, assume this task. It is almost unnecessary to remind the reader of one of the principal lessons of Marxism, namely he who has property has power…The only possible method of transforming the bureaucratic-administrative model of our socialist society into a democratic model is to abolish the

> monopoly of the state administration over the exercise of ownership functions, and to decentralize it towards those whose interest lies in the functioning of the socialist enterprise, i.e. the collectives of enterprise workers.[176]

Addressing bureaucrats who objected to a lessening of central control, Slánský wrote,

> [T]hese people like to confuse certain concepts. They say, for example, that this law would mean transforming social property as a whole into group property, even though it is clearly not a question of property, but rather one of knowing who is exercising property rights in the name of the whole society, whether it is the state apparatus or the socialist producers directly, i.e. the enterprise collectives.[177]

Nonetheless, there is tension between the tasks of oversight and of day-to-day management. A different commentator, a law professor, declared,

> We must not…set up democracy and technical competence as opposites, but search for a harmonious balance between these two components…It would perhaps be better not to talk of a transfer of functions but rather a transfer of tasks. It will then be necessary for the appropriate transfer to be dictated by needs, rather than by reasons of dogma or prestige.[178]

These discussions had no opportunity to develop. In April 1969, Alexander Dubček was forced out as party first secretary, replaced by Gustáv Husák, who wasted little time before inaugurating repression. The legislative bill was shelved in May, and government and party officials began a campaign against councils. The government formally banned workers' councils in July 1970,[179] but by then they were already disappearing.

## A process of "normalization" turns into a rout

To bring the grassroots under control, it was first necessary to clamp down on political freedom. Because of the widespread national passive resistance, it took several months to begin the process of reinstituting the old system, and a year for mass repression to begin, aimed squarely at stamping out all traces of the Prague Spring.

It was within an already narrowed political space that the kidnapped Czechoslovak party leadership had to maneuver when they returned after six days. The first task was for the holders of the four most important posts—Communist Party First Secretary Alexander Dubček, Prime Minister Oldřich Černík, parliament chair Josef Smrkovský and President Ludvík Svoboda—to address the country after returning. Svoboda spoke first, but the speech by Dubček would be the most important one.

Speaking on radio on 27 August, this was the speech famous for minute-long pauses as the first secretary fought back tears. Dubček could only be circumspect, at one point noting, in regards to the resumption of a functioning government, "This activity, like the life of our people, will take place in a situation which does not depend on our will alone."[180] And alluding to the difficult path the party leadership was now embarking on, Dubček said, "It is necessary at any price to prevent...further losses, because that would not alter the real situation and the abnormal situation in our homeland would be prolonged. The fact that we are determined to prevent bloodshed does not mean that we want to passively submit to the situation which has been created."[181]

The reformers were under no illusions that their previous course would still be possible. The nationwide resistance was continuing, and the refusal of Czechs and Slovaks to be intimidated by the invasion force (a resistance that included clandestine radio stations and numerous newspapers appearing daily) seemed unshakable. But a population can't stay in the streets indefinitely; eventually, the necessity of eating, earning money and all the other basic activities of life intervene. At some point, and not in the hazy remote future, this reality would begin to sap the strength of the overt, albeit passive, resistance. And the physical limitations of indefinite life in the streets are further tempered by the emotional side. In the first week of the invasion, with anger still burning a vivid red, even if channeled into passive resistance, it was possible to believe that somehow the invading armies could be made to leave.

For now, the average citizen in the street could really believe they were winning. The kidnapped leaders had returned home, the reforms were still on, the grapevine and the mass media functioned at their side, the country was seemingly united against the invasion, and the Soviet Union faced international opprobrium, including from Western Europe's communist parties. What could an army even as powerful as the Soviet Union's do if everybody refused to cooperate?

But that emotional spur, too, eventually begins to flag. The invaders will still be there—the Red Army was not sent into another country only to be pulled out in a few weeks—and the very fact that such a drastic step was taken meant that the Soviet Union intended to re-impose a régime much like what existed before 1968. With all the physical force on its side, time as well was on the side of the Soviet Union Politburo. Physical and, much more importantly, emotional fatigue would inevitably set in among Czechs and Slovaks.

That doesn't mean all resistance would end, or that the invasion would in any way be accepted. But a realistic assessment of how effective this latent resistance would be had to be calculated at the time when emotions, and vigor, were at a peak.

So the party leaders, locked up in Moscow, half hostages and half government negotiators in the Kremlin, had to weigh all factors very carefully. Further violence was by no means excluded; this is an iron law of any show of force by a military, regardless of the motivation or the nature of the government that puts that military to use. That was a responsibility that the negotiators in Moscow could not duck. And they also had a political responsibility. However justified their actions of the previous eight months, however necessary the reforms were, however strong the popular opinion was behind their course, it was their political decisions that led to this impasse, and therefore their political responsibility to find a way out of it, salvaging what might be salvaged, gently dissuading the population from what they believed would be futile uprisings and avoiding further bloodshed.

By no means subordinated to these heavy, practical considerations was the matter of the political reforms themselves; without lasting political reform, all the other reforms would be impossible. The dynamic in the Moscow negotiations was that the reformers (those who were kidnapped and originally to have been put before a "revolutionary tribunal," and those who joined the negotiations later as part of Svoboda's delegation) had the most incentive to reach some sort of accommodation and were also the logical negotiating partners of the Soviet side. The Czechoslovak hard-liners, who wanted the invasion, would have signed anything, but their signatures alone would be worthless because Czechs and Slovaks had turned so decisively against them and it was known they were pro-invasion.

The reformers who signed did so not only out of what they saw as their moral and political duty, but also as the only way to salvage some of the reforms, wring a couple of concessions from the Soviet Politburo, and give themselves maneuvering room. Unity was the key to this conception: unity between the party and the people, but perhaps more crucially, unity within the party, specifically among the party leadership. If this unity held, if the Soviets couldn't find ways to split the Czechoslovak party, if, even after dictated personnel changes, there remained a broad consensus for limited reforms, then some of the Prague Spring could be salvaged. But if the unity frayed, if splits could be created and exploited, then the floodgates would be thrown wide open to a restoration of a harsh Soviet-style régime, complete with purges.

Unity, too, dictated that everybody sign. If some had signed and some had not, the likely result would have been personal opprobrium for those who did sign, despite their doing so for very real, practical reasons, and, in the worst case, a signal for an armed resistance against the Soviet troops, which could only have led to bloodshed. But with all having signed the Moscow Protocol (with the single exception, Kriegel), the reformers now had to explain the new, bitter reality. This was done not only with the national speeches on the radio, but with meetings that commenced immediately upon their return from Moscow.

Party unity, however, already was unraveling. As they returned home, the previously scheduled congress of the Slovak branch of the party was meeting in Bratislava, the Slovak capital. Here again, it is necessary to delve into the ethnic politics that continually asserted themselves in Czechoslovakia, tensions that would be skillfully used to remove reformers from their party and government positions and re-impose Soviet-style rule.

As is customary not only for a communist party, but for any political party that operates on a national level in any country, the communists had a national body with institutions in the national capital, and subordinate party organizations at the provincial, regional and city levels. But because Czechoslovakia, on a formal basis, was a federation of two republics, Czech and Slovak (similar to the United Kingdom being made up of England, Scotland, Wales and Northern Ireland), there was, above the provincial level but just below the national level, a Slovak party organization, with its own first secretary and parallel institutions.

A Slovak party existed because the Slovaks were a minority, with one-half the population of the Czechs, and were economically less developed due to the lingering effects of the long Hungarian colonization and the resulting wide disparity in economic development, a disparity that the pre-World War II republic had done almost nothing to address.

But there was another side to this, in the minds of many Slovaks: If there was no Czech equivalent of the Slovak party organization, then that is because the national party is the party of the Czechs. On the other hand, there were many Czechs who wondered why there was a separate Slovak organization but not one for the Czech Lands. Happily, there was a solution that solved both of these ethnic irritants: federalization. This aspect of the reforms translated into the creation of Czech party and government structures, identical to the Slovak ones, and a devolution of some powers to the two republican governments. The new federal model, too, was eliminated once the hard-liners had taken control, but Gustáv Husák portrayed himself as the strongest advocate of Slovak autonomy, using the momentum behind the creation and strengthening of these republican-level bodies as his route to power, before crushing them once he had become national party first secretary.

Returning to Czechoslovakia from Moscow with the rest of the negotiators, Husák traveled straight to Bratislava to speak at the Slovak party congress already in session. Because he had presented himself as a staunch supporter of Slovak autonomy and of the reforms, the ambitious Husák was elected as the new first secretary for the Slovak branch of the party, replacing the disgraced Bil'ak.

Husák promptly astounded the Slovak delegates by asking them to renounce the Fourteenth Congress that had just taken place. Most of the Slovak delegates to the congress were unable to travel to Prague because transportation was disrupted by the invasion. The clandestine congress acknowledged this problem and agreed that the Slovak party would have further opportunities to debate the resolutions that were passed, and the Slovak delegates who were in attendance urged their colleagues who could not attend to endorse the decisions. Indeed, the Slovak congress did endorse the results of the Fourteenth Congress prior to Husák's arrival.

Husák, however, argued that the congress wasn't representative because few Slovaks were able to attend, ultimately swaying the meeting by declaring that Dubček favored abrogating the results. Husák told the meeting, "I fully back Dubček's concept. I was present when it was formulated and I shall support him fully. I shall stand or fall with him."[182] (Of course, the formulation was the Soviet Politburo's, not Dubček's.) The Slovaks then reversed themselves, voting against accepting the Fourteenth Congress. Soon afterward, Dubček met in Prague with the members of the Central Committee elected by the congress and explained the obligation forced on them by the Soviets to annul the results of the congress, which they accepted.[183]

Dubček, though, had a trick up his sleeve. Although obligated to annul the congress, Dubček received two concessions: one, that the annulment was not explicitly stated in the text of the Moscow Protocol and, two, a verbal agreement with Brezhnev that some of the people elected by the congress to a new Central Committee would be added to the old Central Committee that would now be kept in place. Dubček named 87 of the Fourteenth Congress selectees (more than half of those elected) onto the CC. Doing so made Brezhnev furious—he called Dubček on the phone during the meeting where this arrangement was being made. But Dubček told Brezhnev that he had previously said he would add some of the members to the Central Committee and now he couldn't go back on making the additions, because everybody knew he was having this phone conversation.[184] "You did not say there would be so many," Brezhnev complained; Dubček responded, "Nor did you say how many there should be."[185]

Brezhnev & Co. were not without the ability to enforce their dictates, of course, and these abilities were not limited to the implied threat of force inherent in an armed occupation. A dirty-tricks campaign was hatched by the Soviet Union Communist Party Central Committee's propaganda department, aimed at discrediting and splitting the Czechoslovak leadership. "The KGB…will be preparing and publishing a series of articles in the foreign press about the ties of the anti-socialist underground in Czechoslovakia…above all with the intelligence organs of the USA and [West Germany]," a now declassified memorandum from September 1968 states. The memo went on to formulate strategies "to encourage the incipient trend toward a deep schism in the leadership of the [Czechoslovak Communist Party]."[186]

With overt and covert pressure from the Soviets, further concessions had to be made. At the same time as the Fourteenth Congress selectees were added to the Central Committee, several strong reformers in the party leadership, government ministries and other prominent posts had to be removed, but several hard-liners whom the Soviets had not specifically ordered kept in their positions were also removed. Some reformers, such as Jiří Pelikán, forced out as head of Czechoslovak television, were given other posts, among them ambassadorships.

More direct methods of pressure were brought to bear in October, when the Soviet leadership demanded Czechoslovakia immediately sign a treaty "legalizing" the stationing of Soviet troops. The troops had been pulled back into the countryside, but the Soviets threatened to reoccupy all the cities if the treaty was not signed immediately.[187] The gradual concessions were sapping the confidence of the citizenry; unrest was beginning to stir. The latest agreement with Moscow on the stationing of troops, along with the resumption of some press censorship, even if voluntary and not mandatory at this point, intensified this unhappiness.

In November, Soviet pressure to remove Smrkovský from his

post as parliament chair intensified, and that seemed to be the final straw as a four-day student strike, backed by several unions, took place in Prague and the major industrial city of Brno.

With the reforms in severe danger at this point, what would a proper strategy have been? Pelikán, among others, argued that the party leadership had become too isolated and should have rallied the citizenry behind them as the only way to prevent the end of Prague Spring. Arguing that abandoning active mobilization of the masses had led party leaders into a rearguard action that could not succeed, Pelikán wrote,

> The students' strike, the position of the workers and the population in general and the support of the progressive intellectuals gave Dubček a solid basis for going over to the offensive...But the way in which Dubček and the progressives—under pressure from Moscow and the Indra-Bil'ak group—surrendered Josef Smrkovský, the most popular champion of the "New Course," was in itself an indication of the disintegration of the collective leadership, which was by now incapable of resolute resistance.[188]

Unity between the party and the people had frayed, a critical link that once snapped would lead to popular withdrawal from politics—a sullen resignation that would provide the necessary political space for the hard-liners to go on the offensive. That frayed unity was the product of the lack of unity within the party. As hard-line pressure continued (pressure backed by the troops still in the country), the reformers, cornered into relinquishing some of their posts, increasingly were on the defensive. The reformers' defensive posture, vividly illustrated in the implicit direct challenge to them in the student strike and further implied in the continuing workers' council movement and union support for the student strike, had now developed far enough for the links between party and people to threaten to unravel altogether.

The students in Prague had originally planned to stage street demonstrations in support of reforms and in opposition to concessions. The composition of university students was now much different than it had been in the mid-1940s, when students formed an elitist reactionary bloc that was bitterly opposed by workers; in those days, students came almost exclusively from very privileged backgrounds. Now the student body mirrored the country much more closely, and student leaders sought out and established links with trade unions. "One thing was quite clear," a leader of the student strike wrote. "We did not intend to be complicit with the course of events that had started to prevail in Czechoslovakia. We were determined to show in one way or another our opposition to what we call 'the policy of the lesser evil'—'the policy of concessions.' We were determined to carry on resistance."[189]

All four top leaders—Dubček, Černík, Smrkovský and Svoboda—met with student leaders in an attempt to forestall the demonstrations, but the students were not dissuaded.[190] "I was very saddened about all this, because I did not see things that way," Dubček later wrote, referring to the student strike and union declarations that Prague Spring had been sold out. "Lines of communication and understandings between various components of the reform front were further weakened."[191]

The students did decide to switch tactics, instead occupying their campuses for four days rather than mounting street demonstrations. The students reached agreements with the metalworkers' union and the teachers' and academic workers' union. The unions endorsed the demands of the students, which centered on implementation of the Action Program, and the students endorsed the unions' demands for an end to government interference in the national trade union federation and for development of workers' councils.[192] The students were surprised at how strong they were during their sit-in: "During the strike, students acted as a mouthpiece for the masses…The voice of students is being listened to with much greater attention than ever before. Our problem now is to have meaningful things to say when we again have the chance."[193]

Despite widespread union support, the sit-in's effect was only temporary. The hard-liners' attack on Smrkovský resumed on New Year's Day 1969, and this time was successful. Putting his pose as a defender of the Slovaks to good use, Husák appeared on national television, surprising the rest of the leadership in Prague, to demand that the parliament chair be held by a Slovak, under the theory that the four most important political offices should be evenly divided between Czechs and Slovaks. This was a gambit to force out Smrkovský, a highly popular Czech who continued to be a strong defender of the reforms. Husák took advantage of the fact that the post was technically a new position, since the old parliament was being restructured to accommodate the new Czech–Slovak federal structure.

Four days later, Smrkovský stepped aside under the pressure, asking the unions not to strike on his behalf, which they had threatened to do. Another reformer had been pushed aside, although Smrkovský was kept on for a while as the deputy parliamentary chair.

The ability of the reformers to hold on, to salvage some remaining gains and stave off purges, was nearing its end. In late March 1969, the Czechoslovak ice hockey team defeated the Soviet Union to win the world championship, touching off mass street celebrations. Taking advantage, undercover Soviet agents planted a heap of paving stones in front of the Prague office of the Soviet airline, Aeroflot, and when the celebrants didn't take the hint, the agents themselves stoned the office. Soviet military leaders swiftly demanded an army attack on the celebrants, a re-imposition of total censorship and other demands, adding a flourish to their list by telling Dubček, "The counter-revolution must be beheaded."[194] At the next Central Committee meeting two weeks later, Dubček, now in the minority, was cornered into offering his resignation as first secretary. Husák had the backing of the Soviets (that he was not tainted by being one of the pre-invasion hard-liners worked to his advantage) and assumed the party's top post on 17 April.

As early as the Kremlin negotiations following the invasion, Brezhnev spoke of a period of "normalization." This so-called "normalization" now began to be accelerated. A month after Husák's ascension, a speech made in a Central Committee meeting by František Kriegel was censored—circulated, however, throughout the country as the first Czechoslovak "samizdat," or illegal literature.[195] In this speech, Kriegel said he refused to sign the Moscow Protocol "because I saw it as a document that would tie up our republic...The treaty wasn't signed with a pen but guns."[196] Kriegel, along with the economist Ota Šik and other prominent reformers, was soon expelled from the party. In September, Dubček was stripped of all his posts and the remaining reformers, including Smrkovský, were forced out, signaling the start of wholesale purges.

Under the gathering momentum that a wave of purges inevitably gathers, and with all political opposition silenced, 500,000 were expelled from the party—one-third of the membership. Supporters of the reform weren't simply stripped of their party membership; they were also forced out of their jobs as professors, doctors, lawyers and many other professions, and forced to take jobs as manual laborers. The Husák régime evidently saw this as an added punishment, but it only weakened the country's infrastructure. Not only did it have to replace so many skilled people, but the cost of the education of all those sacked men and women, borne by the state, was now wasted.

There were also massive purges in the unions. Near the end of 1969, a wave of purges hit several unions, including the militant metalworkers.[197] In May 1970, the entire executive body and most other leaders of the trade union council were removed from office; the chairman was sacked despite condemning himself for his previous reformist sympathies.[198]

Consolidation of the new/old régime could be considered to have been completed in May 1971, when the "official" Fourteenth Congress of the party was held, as if the earlier one had never happened. In his keynote speech, Husák reiterated his attacks on the 1968 economic reforms, but, consistent with his claims that he was not returning the country to pre-1968 days, he concentrated most of his fire on Antonín Novotný, for a wide variety of failings, although he failed to mention Novotný's repressions.[199]

Husák's own repressions, however, had already gone far beyond anything experienced under Novotný and were not stopping despite his feeling confident enough to hold the party congress after a long delay. Toward the end of 1971, and into early 1972, a wave of arrests began, and with them the first political trials. Just as in the Soviet Union, which the Czechoslovak hard-liners again were so slavishly mimicking, socialist opposition was feared more than any other source of opposition, and this was reflected in the fact that those arrested were public reform figures from 1968, members of the socialist opposition active at this time, or part of both groups.

The days of Stalinism were very much over, however, so there were no show trials. Trials there were, though, in the summer of 1972, and the defendants readily admitted their political activities such as handing out leaflets and printing newspapers.[200] Tacitly acknowledging that the public would see right through the charges of anti-socialist subversive activity, the identity of those on trial was not revealed in public for six months.[201]

Husák was a lifelong communist, joining the party at age 20 in 1933, but was completely consumed by a burning personal ambition, a quality by no means out of place considering that the party was now filled with opportunists and careerists. Husák's talents had enabled him to rise to prominence in the illegal party of the 1930s and he helped organize the Slovak Uprising against the World War II fascist puppet government. He then held a succession of offices before spending most of the 1950s in prison after his arrest during the purges. Following his official rehabilitation in the mid-1960s he refused to accept government ministry positions offered to him because he deemed the posts insufficiently high.

Dubček succeeded in bringing him back into the party leadership in 1968 and Husák initially supported the reforms. But when the winds changed, Husák quickly offered himself to the Soviet leadership and pitilessly carried out purges, sending opponents to jail to suffer systematic abuse and solitary confinement. Among those jailed were Husák's friends who had helped him after his own release from prison in 1960.

"He was an orthodox communist," said a Czech historian, Vilém Precan, who was a young reformist in 1968 and, at first, impressed by Husák's intellect. "That was his belief, but at the same time he was a great manipulator. He was a man of power. His fanaticism for power—to share in power and to occupy the top position was his ambition. And he was able to sacrifice everything in pursuit of this goal. He could sacrifice his name, his word and even his closest friends."[202]

Whether or not Husák wished to carry out repression on such a massive scale, to the point of political trials, does not matter—the logic of instituting a hard-line régime against the will of the overwhelming majority of a country must lead to persecution of at least some leaders of that opposition. Husák's position at the top of the party structure depended on Soviet force and he could only stay on top through applying his own force, implicitly backed by the force that underlay the Soviet Union's dominant role in Czechoslovakia. That was the price that Husák had to pay to fulfill his personal ambitions.

The top leaders of the Prague Spring, who were internationally known, people such as Alexander Dubček and Josef Smrkovský, were not arrested, although they suffered persistent harassment from the secret police. Vasil Bil'ak, back in power as a key member of the Politburo, made the hard-liners' strategy clear when he said in public, "We are not so foolish as to sentence Dubček and the others and thus give them a chance to attack us. It is quite sufficient to isolate them. But we shall punish, above all, the intermediate cadres, the journalists and intellectuals. No one will stand up for them: even the West is fed up with them."[203]

The socialist opposition issued manifestoes and did other work for several years, but eventually fell apart despite having a broad base—counting factory workers, former union officials, former party members and intellectuals in its ranks—as deaths and emigration dispersed the ranks. When the rock band Plastic People of the Universe and other musicians in a counter-cultural movement calling itself the "underground" were arrested in 1976, despite having no interest in politics, that proved to be the spark that led to the formation of the Charter 77 human-rights movement.

It is astonishing how backward and fearful the Husák régime had become—it claimed to rule in the name of a progressive cause, yet it energetically repressed rock 'n' roll music, something that one might expect in the most reactionary, preacher-dominated backwater in the rural South of the United States.

A lively cultural resistance continued, which produced hundreds of "samizdat" journals and books; eventually forbidden books were even surreptitiously printed in state printing houses.[204] Charter 77 from its beginning contained a wide variety of opinion. The initial signatories included a large number of socialist oppositionists who had been expelled from the Communist Party because of their ongoing pro-reform stances as well as religious activists, cultural leaders (including writers), and people from relatively privileged social positions who had until then constituted something of a grudgingly tolerated "official opposition," such as Václav Havel.[205] To represent the various currents of opinion, three spokespeople were appointed at the group's foundation, a custom that was continued as spokespersons stepped down or were arrested.

During the 1980s, a leadership developed within Charter 77, some of whom became famous as dissidents, most notably Havel, but this leadership isolated itself from the movement's rank-and-file and moved to the Right.[206] Left opposition within Charter 77, which opposed the leadership's policies and sought to democratize the movement's internal life, was marginalized because large meetings were not held, under the pretext of fear of police oppression, nor was there sufficient time for other organizations to coalesce when the communist régime collapsed at the end of 1989, so swift was the party's downfall.[207]

What would replace the discredited régime? A 1989 survey of Czechs and Slovaks showed that only 3 percent favored capitalism, with 90 percent of respondents split between the choices of a state-controlled economy or a mixed economy.[208] In the last months of their rule, communist authorities had, in a distant echo of 1968, introduced "workers' self-management" and a measure of autonomy for enterprises, but this reform was widely viewed as a trick.[209] During the final weeks of 1989, when the Communist Party made a rapid series of concessions in what quickly developed into an orderly process of relinquishing power, the Czech mass group Civic Forum grew out of Charter 77. The direction that Civic Forum, with its leadership in Prague, took would be decisive. But although capitalism was widely rejected, there were no plans for what might alternatively be installed.

"People know what they don't want; they do not yet know what they do want," said a former Charter 77 spokesman, Ladislav Hejdánek, at the time.[210] Moreover, many activists within Civic Forum believed that capitalism and socialism had become "obsolete" terms.[211] Civic Forum was loose and heterogeneous, but a Right bloc that coalesced around the newly appointed finance minister, neoliberal economist Václav Klaus, did not agree that political ideas had ceased to matter nor did it harbor doubts about what it wanted and therefore was able to decisively influence economic policy.

Thus, the stage was set for Civic Forum to move the country toward a harsh Thatcherite brand of capitalism. The Husák régime helped to bring about that capitalism by demoralizing and demobilizing working people and by repeatedly jailing Havel and other Charter 77 signatories; the more they were harassed and jailed, the higher the moral status of the leading dissidents became in the eyes of the world.

For most of the Husák era, however, the Charter 77 movement had little effect on the everyday lives of Czechs and Slovaks. Although a sullen disappointment with the outcome of Prague Spring played a significant role, a comfortable material standard of living did much to keep the country quiet for 20 years. Salaries were raised, food was in good supply and there was an adequate supply of material goods, including automobiles. Even a persecuted former leader such as Dubček, subjected to ham-fisted police spying until 1989, could build and use a summer cottage on a lake. And most of the traditional gap between Czechs and Slovaks was closed as considerable investments went to Slovakia; it did not hurt that the party first secretary, Husák, and the party's éminence grise, Bil'ak, were both from Slovakia. This was the classic Brezhnevite deal: Stay out of politics in exchange for a strong social safety net.

The secret police made sure to point out these factors to dissidents during their interminable interrogations. Milan Šimečka, a university professor who became a bulldozer driver after 1969, regularly was visited by the secret police because he continued to publish:

> They constantly threaten you and try to put the wind up you, because, as they repeat ad nauseam, their chief objective is not to punish crime, but to prevent it. Thus every hearing ends

> with the reproof: Why do you do it? Can't you see it's senseless, you are just hurting yourself and your family. You've got a flat and a car. You're not hungry. What else do you want? We'll manage to build socialism without writers, journalists and philosophers. Just get what you can out of it like everyone else and we'll leave you alone.[212]

Such vulgarity needs no comment. Miserably hypocritical as such an attitude was, at least people weren't expected to sacrifice their lives. Comparing the crushing of the Prague Spring with contemporaneous efforts to impose or re-impose capitalism provides an interesting contrast. The highest death toll from the Soviet invasion any organization has reported for Czechoslovak citizens is 100, most of whom died during the first six weeks.[213] The total number of Warsaw Pact soldiers to die was 20, all but one of whom died as a result of accidents.[214] By comparison, the United States invasion of Vietnam resulted in 3 million Vietnamese deaths, the destruction of that country's urban and rural infrastructures through carpet bombing, and 60,000 US deaths.

It might be argued that Vietnam resisted while Czechoslovakia did not. A comparison might then be made with the military coup in Chile in 1973, staged with the full support of the United States, which had carried out a well-financed campaign to destabilize the country. There was no mass resistance in Chile, not even the passive resistance of Czechoslovakia, but the new dictatorship was intended to impose a particularly harsh US-inspired capitalist régime and killed perhaps as many as 30,000 to do so. The river flowing through Santiago was full of corpses and the Chilean military traveled in "caravans of death"—mobile death squads. Czechs and Slovaks felt secure enough to argue with the Soviet troops in their streets; it would have been an act of suicide to confront one of Chilean dictator Augusto Pinochet's soldiers.

But it also can't be denied that the invasion and Husák's "real socialism," as his ideologists proclaimed the restoration, not only destroyed the chance to demonstrate what socialism could, and should, have been; it also trampled into the mud the very idea of socialism in many eyes. Repeated tries to break out of the Soviet straitjacket and create a true collegial society in Central Europe were repeatedly foiled. Capitalism was not the choice of Czechs and Slovaks, either, as noted earlier, nor would they be given a vote on its restoration. Removal of the detested one-party monopoly on public life was the goal at the time of the Velvet Revolution, but the resulting political vacuum would be filled by those with the most power behind them, not by popular preference.

The 1968 invasion also handed a propaganda coup to the Western capitalist powers, particularly the United States. Regardless of radio and other propaganda pumped into Czechoslovakia by US government agencies, the US had no intention of intervening militarily; the Warsaw Pact forces were too strong to contemplate any adventures. But US government understanding of the Prague Spring was muddied by ideological bias. Central Intelligence Agency reports at the time were generally superficial, focused on rivalries among political personalities and an underlying hope that the reform process would lead to a return to capitalism.[215] US big business elites, whose perspectives are seldom unheard in Washington, would not have wanted to see a successful example of working people taking charge of their lives and putting an economy on a democratic footing.

Nonetheless, the Husák régime's taking back of civil freedoms enabled the West to pull a cloak of moral superiority over itself while providing cover for the brutal results of US interference around the globe. Brezhnev, Husák, Bil'ak and their fellow hard-liners drove Czechoslovakia into the arms of Western capitalism, and it was they, and not 1968's reformers, who ultimately restored capitalism.

## Notes to Chapter 3

1 Robert Vitak, "Workers Control: The Czechoslovak Experience," *Socialist Register*, 1971, page 248, citing *The Czechoslovak Economy 1945–1948*, page 13 [State Pedagogical Publishing House, Prague, 1968]

2 ibid

3 John Connelly, "Students, Workers and Social Change: The Limits of Czech Stalinism," *Slavic Review*, Summer 1997

4 Vitak, "Workers Control," page 250

5 Igor Lukes, "The Rudolph Slánský Affair: New Evidence," *Slavic Review*, Spring 1999, page 172

6 ibid, page 173, citing a Czechoslovakia Communist Party Central Committee commission report on Slánský

7 ibid, pages 176–80

8 Jiří Pelikán, *Socialist Opposition in Eastern Europe: The Czechoslovak Example*, page 11 (emphasis omitted) [St Martin's Press, 1976]

9 ibid, page 12

10 Oldřich Kyn, "Czechoslovakia: Economic Reforms of 1960s," anthologized in Hans-Hermann Hohmann, Michael Kaser and Karl C. Thalheim (eds), *The New Economic Systems of Eastern Europe* [C. Hurst & Co., 1975]

11 Johanna Granville, "1956 Reconsidered: Why Hungary and Not Poland?" *Slavonic and East European Review*, October 2002, page 659

12 Andy Anderson, *Hungary '56*, page 42 [Black & Red, 1976]

13 Granville, "1956 Reconsidered," page 660

14 Roman Stefanowski, "Workers' Councils: 1956–1977," Radio Free Europe research, posted on the Open Society Archives website, http://www.osaarchivum.org

15 Paul Feldman, "Hungary's October Revolution" (a review of Victor Sebestyen, *Twelve Days: Revolution 1956*), posted on

the A World To Win website, www.aworldtowin.net
16 Granville, "1956 Reconsidered," page 668
17 ibid
18 Mervyn Jones, "Days of Tragedy and Farce," *Socialist Register*, 1976, page 68
19 Gerry Healy, *Revolution and Counter-Revolution in Hungary*, posted on the A World To Win website; Feldman, "Hungary's October Revolution"
20 Healy, *Revolution and Counter-Revolution*, Feldman, "Hungary's October Revolution"
21 Feldman, "Hungary's October Revolution"
22 Anderson, *Hungary '56*, pages 81–2
23 ibid, page 82
24 Csaba Békés, "New Findings on the 1956 Hungarian Revolution," *Cold War International History Project Bulletin*, Fall 1992, page 2
25 Anderson, *Hungary '56*, page 88, quoting *The New York Times*, 23 October 1956
26 Nicholas Krasso, "Hungary 1956: A Participant's Account," anthologized in Tariq Ali (ed.), *The Stalinist Legacy: Its Impact on 20th-Century World Politics*, pages 377–9 [Penguin, 1984]; Jones, "Days of Tragedy and Farce," page 78
27 Healy, *Revolution and Counter-Revolution*, quoting the *Manchester Guardian*, 9 November 1956
28 Jones, "Days of Tragedy," page 76
29 Noel Barber, *Seven Days of Freedom: The Hungarian Uprising, 1956*, page 231 [Stein and Day, 1975]
30 Zdeněk Mlynář, *Nightfrost in Prague: The End of Humane Socialism*, page 28 [Karz, 1980]
31 ibid, page 42
32 ibid, page 43
33 Vladimir Dedijer, *The Battle Stalin Lost: Memoirs of Yugoslavia 1948–1953*, page 225 [Viking, 1971]
34 Connelly, "Students, Workers and Social Change," page 333

35 Vitak, "Workers Control," page 251, quoting *Politika*, 31 October 1968, page 35
36 Pelikán, *Socialist Opposition*, page 16
37 Alexander Dubček, *Hope Dies Last: The Autobiography of the Leader of the Prague Spring*, page 105 [Kodanska America, 1993]
38 Kyn, "Czechoslovakia: Economic Reforms"
39 ibid
40 Pelikán, *Socialist Opposition*, page 16
41 ibid
42 "Proceedings of the 4th Czechoslovakia Writers Congress, June 27–29, 1967, and a Follow-up Resolution by the CPCz CC Plenum, September 1967," anthologized in Jaromír Navrátil (chief ed.), *The Prague Spring '68*, pages 8–9 [Central European University, 2006]
43 ibid, page 11
44 ibid, page 12
45 Dubček, *Hope Dies Last*, pages 115–16
46 "Speeches by Alexander Dubček and Antonín Novotný at the CPCz CC Plenum, October 30–31, 1967," anthologized in *The Prague Spring '68*, pages 13–15 (emphasis in original)
47 ibid, page 16
48 ibid, page 17
49 Dubček, *Hope Dies Last*, pages 119–20
50 ibid, page 120
51 ibid
52 ibid, page 121
53 "Andrei Aleksandrov-Agnetov's Memoir of the Pre-Crisis Period (Excerpt)," excerpted in *The Prague Spring '68*, page 24
54 ibid, pages 24–5
55 "János Kádár's Report to the HSWP Politburo of a Telephone Conversation with Leonid Brezhnev, December 13, 1967," anthologized in *The Prague Spring '68*, page 21

56 Dubček, *Hope Dies Last*, page 132
57 Josef Smrkovský, "What Lies Ahead," *Rudé Právo*, 9 February 1968, anthologized in *The Prague Spring '68*, pages 45–50
58 Mlynář, *Nightfrost in Prague*, pages 96–7
59 Dubček, *Hope Dies Last*, page 136
60 Kevin Devlin, "Exiles Look Back at Prague Spring 20 Years Later," Radio Free Europe research, 11 May 1988, posted on the Open Society Archives website
61 Mlynář, *Nightfrost in Prague*, pages 98–9
62 ibid, pages 99–100
63 Pelikán, *Socialist Opposition*, page 23
64 Dubček, *Hope Dies Last* (appendix), page 290 (emphasis in original)
65 ibid, pages 295–6 (emphasis in original)
66 ibid, page 297
67 ibid, page 302
68 ibid, page 303
69 ibid, page 308
70 ibid, page 329
71 ibid, pages 312–13 (emphasis in original)
72 ibid, page 317
73 ibid, page 318
74 ibid, pages 332–3
75 Jiří Valenta, *Soviet Intervention in Czechoslovakia, 1968: Anatomy of a Decision* [Johns Hopkins University Press, 1981], pages 23–4
76 ibid, page 34
77 Smrkovský, "How They Crushed the Prague Spring of 1968," anthologized in Ali, *The Stalinist Legacy*, page 395
78 "Stenographic Account of the Soviet-Czechoslovak Summit Meeting in Moscow, May 4–5, 1968 (Excerpts)," anthologized in *The Prague Spring '68*, page 115
79 Smrkovský, "How They Crushed," page 395

80 "Stenographic Account of the Soviet-Czechoslovak Summit Meeting," pages 120–1
81 ibid, page 121
82 Smrkovský, "How They Crushed," page 396
83 ibid
84 "The 'Two Thousands Words' Manifesto, June 27, 1968," anthologized in *The Prague Spring '68,* page 179
85 ibid, pages 179–80
86 ibid, page 180 (emphasis in original)
87 Mlynář, *Nightfrost in Prague,* page 138
88 ibid, page 139
89 Smrkovský, "How They Crushed," page 400
90 ibid, page 401
91 Mlynář, *Nightfrost in Prague,* page 143
92 "The Warsaw Letter, July 14–15, 1968," anthologized in *The Prague Spring '68,* page 236
93 ibid, page 235
94 Leason, "Dolansky on Czechoslovak Plan; Workers Rights," 6 March 1957, Radio Free Europe research, posted on the Open Society Archives website
95 ibid
96 Vladimir Fišera, *Workers' Councils in Czechoslovakia: Documents and Essays 1968–69,* pages 10–11 [St Martin's Press, 1978]
97 ibid, page 11
98 ibid, page 12
99 Ota Šik, *The Third Way: Marxist-Leninist Theory and the Modern Industrial Society,* conclusion [Wildwood House, 1976], excerpted on the Marxist Archives website
100 ibid, introduction
101 Vitak, "Workers Control," page 256
102 ibid
103 "Trade Unions and Workers' Councils," anthologized in Fišera, *Workers' Councils,* page 29

104 Kyn, "The Rise and Fall of the Economic Reform in Czechoslovakia," *American Economic Review*, May 1970
105 ibid
106 ibid
107 Kyn, "Czechoslovakia: Economic Reforms"
108 ibid
109 ibid
110 Dubček, *Hope Dies Last*, pages 154–6
111 ibid, page 155
112 Valenta, *Soviet Intervention*, page 172 [note 116]
113 ibid, page 42
114 Dubček, *Hope Dies Last*, pages 155–6
115 Mark Kramer, "Ukraine and the Soviet-Czechoslovak Crisis of 1968 (Part 1): New Evidence from the Diary of Petro Shelest," *Cold War International History Project Bulletin*, March 1998, pages 237–8
116 ibid, pages 236, 238
117 ibid, page 242
118 ibid
119 Kramer, "The Prague Spring and the Soviet Invasion of Czechoslovakia: New Interpretations," *Cold War International*, Fall 1993, page 6
120 "Report on the Sumava Exercises by Generals I. Oláh and F. Szücs of the Hungarian People's Army to the HSWP Politburo, July 5, 1968 (Excerpts)," anthologized in *The Prague Spring '68*, pages 199, 201
121 "'Message from the Citizens to the CPCz CC Presidium' July 26, 1968," anthologized in *The Prague Spring '68*, page 279
122 ibid, page 280
123 ibid, page 279
124 Dubček, *Hope Dies Last*, pages 167–9; Smrkovský, "How They Crushed," page 406–7
125 Dubček, *Hope Dies Last*, pages 168
126 ibid, pages 168–9

127 Smrkovský, "How They Crushed," page 408

128 "A Letter to Brezhnev: The Czech Hardliners' 'Request' for Soviet Intervention, August 1968," *Cold War International*, Fall 1992, page 16

129 Valenta, *Soviet Intervention*, page 119

130 "The Soviet Politburo's Resolution on the Final Decision to Intervene in Czechoslovakia, August 17, 1968, with Attachments," anthologized in *The Prague Spring '68*, page 377

131 "Remarks by Leonid Brezhnev at a Meeting of Top CPCz Officials, in Prague, December 9, 1967 (Excerpts)," anthologized in *The Prague Spring '68*, page 18

132 Kieran Williams, "New Sources on Soviet Decision Making during the 1968 Czechoslovak Crisis," *Europe-Asia Studies*, May 1996

133 Erik P. Hoffman and Robbin F. Laird, *Technocratic Socialism: The Soviet Union in the Advanced Industrial Era*, page 4 [Duke University Press, 1985]

134 ibid, page 174, quoting G. Kh. Shakhazarov, *Sotsialisticheskaia demokratiia*, pages 53, 102

135 Mlynář, *Nightfrost in Prague*, page 163

136 "The Soviet Politburo's Resolution on the Final Decision to Intervene," pages 380–3

137 ibid, page 381

138 Mlynář, *Nightfrost in Prague*, page 146

139 Smrkovský, "How They Crushed," page 412

140 ibid, pages 412–13; Dubček, *Hope Dies Last*, page 182; Mlynář, *Nightfrost in Prague*, pages 147, 151

141 Williams, "New Sources on Soviet Decision Making"

142 Dubček, *Hope Dies Last*, page 177

143 "Report by Defense Minister Dzúr, June 9, 1970, Regarding His Activities on the Night of August 20–21, 1968 (Excerpts)," anthologized in *The Prague Spring '68*, page 411

144 Valenta, *Soviet Intervention*, page 147

145 Mlynář, *Nightfrost in Prague*, pages 199–200
146 ibid, page 188; Valenta, *Soviet Intervention*, page 149
147 "Initial On-Site Report by Kirill Mazurov to the CPSU Politburo, August 21, 1968," anthologized in *The Prague Spring '68*, page 452
148 Mlynář, *Nightfrost in Prague*, page 190
149 ibid, pages 191–5
150 "Discussions Involving Certain Members of the CPCz CC Presidium and Secretariat, at the Soviet Embassy in Prague and CSSR President's Office, August 22, 1968 (Excerpts)," anthologized in *The Prague Spring '68*, page 463
151 Dubček, *Hope Dies Last*, page 207
152 Smrkovský, "How They Crushed," page 422
153 ibid, page 425
154 Dubček, *Hope Dies Last*, page 209
155 Charles Andras, "Pelikán's Book: Key Documents in Recent Czechoslovak History," Radio Free Europe research, 3 February 1970, posted on the Open Society Archives website
156 ibid
157 ibid
158 "Documents from the Fourteenth (Extraordinary) Congress of the Communist Party of Czechoslovakia," anthologized in Fišera, *Workers' Councils*, page 34
159 Andras, "Pelikán's Book: Key Documents"
160 "Documents from the Fourteenth (Extraordinary) Congress," page 32
161 Vitak, "Workers Control," page 258; Kyn, "The Rise and Fall"; Fišera, *Workers' Councils*, page 13
162 "Draft Statutes for Workers' Self-Management in the Wilhelm Pieck Factory (CKD Prague)," anthologized in Fišera, *Workers' Councils*, pages 39–40
163 ibid, pages 40–2
164 ibid, pages 42–3
165 ibid, page 47

166 "Workers' Councils: The Guarantee of Democratic Administration and Managerial Activity," comments of Kloknar, engineer, chairman of the Skoda Plzen Enterprise Trade-Union Committee, anthologized in Fišera, *Workers' Councils*, page 55
167 ibid, page 70
168 ibid, pages 70–1
169 Vitak, "Workers Control," page 259
170 ibid, page 260
171 ibid; Kyn, "The Rise and Fall"
172 Vitak, "Workers Control," page 260; Kyn, "The Rise and Fall"
173 Kyn, "The Rise and Fall"
174 Vitak, "Workers Control," page 261; Fišera, *Workers' Councils*, page 15
175 "The Bill on Socialist Enterprises," anthologized in Fišera, *Workers' Councils*, pages 82–6
176 Rudolf Slánský Jr, "Workers Councils – or Directors' Councils? Remarks of a By No Means Impartial Observer," *Práce*, 18 February 1969, anthologized in Fišera, *Workers' Councils*, page 109
177 ibid, page 110
178 "Specialist Technical Management and Democracy in the Industrial Enterprise," *Odbory a společnost* [Theoretical Journal of the Central Council of Trade Unions], 15 May 1969, commentary by Jiří Hromada, anthologized in Fišera, *Workers' Councils*, page 132
179 Fišera, *Workers' Councils*, page 14
180 "Dubček speech, 27 August 1968," transcription of Radio Czechoslovakia speech, Radio Free Europe research, posted on the Open Society Archives website
181 ibid
182 Andras, "Pelikán's Book: Key Documents," citing Radio Free Danube, 29 August 1968

183 Dubček, *Hope Dies Last*, page 217; Smrkovský, "How They Crushed," page 427
184 Dubček, *Hope Dies Last*, page 223
185 ibid
186 "Recommendations from the CPSU CC Propaganda Department on Efforts to Establish Political Control in Czechoslovakia, September 6, 1968," anthologized in *The Prague Spring '68*, page 497
187 Dubček, *Hope Dies Last*, page 228
188 Pelikán, *Socialist Opposition*, page 29
189 Pavel Tomalek, "Report from Prague: The Student Action," *New Left Review*, January–February 1969, page 14
190 ibid, page 15
191 Dubček, *Hope Dies Last*, page 231
192 "Co-operation Agreement between the Czech Metalworkers' Union and the Students' Union of Bohemia and Moravia," pages 102–3, and "Co-operation Agreement between the Czech Teachers' and Academic Workers' Union and the Students' Union of Bohemia and Moravia," pages 104–6, anthologized in Fišera, *Workers' Councils*
193 Tomalek, "Report from Prague." pages 19–20
194 Dubček, *Hope Dies Last*, page 237–8
195 Pelikán, *Socialist Opposition*, page 30
196 František Sládek, "Solitary Fighter František Kriegel," posted on the Portal of Prague website, www.praha.eu
197 "Massive Purges in Czech Trade Unions," Radio Free Europe research, posted on the Open Society Archives website
198 ibid
199 "Congress Opens: Gustáv Husák's Report," Radio Free Europe research, posted on the Open Society Archives website
200 Pelikán, Socialist Opposition, pages 66–8
201 ibid

202 Coilin O'Connor, "Gustáv Husák: Czech History's Forgotten Man," Radio Prague broadcast, 22 December 2004; transcribed on the Radio Prague website, www.radio.cz

203 Pelikán, *Socialist Opposition*, page 63

204 Ivan Klíma, *The Spirit of Prague*, pages 49–50, 114–15 [Granta, 1994]

205 Václav Havel's description of himself from Havel, *Disturbing the Peace: A Conversation with Karel Hvízd'ala*, page 126 [Vintage Books, 1990]

206 David L. Steinhardt, "The Last Czechoslovak Marxist: An Interview with Egon Bondy," *Monthly Review*, October 1991

207 ibid

208 Michael Parenti, *Blackshirts and Reds: Rational Fascism and the Overthrow of Communism*, page 73 [City Lights Books, 1997]

209 Petr Uhl, "The Fight for a Socialist Democracy in Czechoslovakia," *New Left Review*, January–February 1990, pages 116–17

210 Daniel Singer, "Czechoslovakia's Quiet Revolution," *The Nation*, 29 January 1990

211 ibid

212 Milan Šimečka, *The Restoration of Order: The Normalization of Czechoslovakia*, page 91 [Verso, 1984]

213 Kramer, "The Prague Spring and the Soviet Invasion," page 10, citing a declassified Czechoslovakia Interior Ministry report

214 ibid

215 US Central Intelligence Agency Freedom of Information Act website, www.foia.cia.gov; see especially, "Czechoslovakia: The Dubček Pause," 13 June 1968, and "Foreign Trade in the Economic Policy of Czechoslovakia," 1 July 1968

## Chapter 4

# The Destroyed Experiment of an Undeveloped, Agricultural State: The Sandinista Revolution

The Sandinista Revolution has traditionally been observed through ideological lenses. People from all points on the political spectrum have tended to see in it what they have wished to see, and so this much-scrutinized revolution has not been understood on its own terms.

Yet the Sandinista Revolution was neither closeted behind opaque barriers nor a palimpsest from which one could pick and choose at will. The doors were open to all who wished to see for themselves, the revolution's leaders consistently articulated their goals and strategies, and an extraordinary inclusiveness was not only enunciated but carried out. That inclusiveness cut in multiple ways. Urban workers, artisans, displaced agricultural field hands, small farmers, the numerically tiny middle class and others traditionally blocked from any meaningful participation in society began making decisions affecting their lives, and representative democracy was introduced along with experiments in direct democracy.

At the same time, a mixed economy was put in place and although an economy that incorporates an eclectic variety of economic forms (including state ownership; commonly owned collectives; marketing collectives composed of privately owned small farms; small-scale private businesses and independent farms; and private big-business manufacturing and agricultural operations left intact from before the revolution) might seem to be an interesting experiment, socialism and capitalism proved to be incompatible. Ultimately, the capitalist part of the economy triumphed, not because it was "better," but because Nicaragua's capitalists could call for help from the biggest capitalists of all, those in the United States.

Those bigger capitalists from the North and the local capitalists were willing to launch a devastating war aimed squarely at destroying the Nicaraguan economy. That war succeeded in devastating the country and yet the Sandinista government chose to peacefully hand over power to those capitalists' political representatives in the name of the democracy it had created. A remarkable contrast to the 50,000 deaths and widespread destruction inflicted on the country by the Somoza dictatorship as it cruelly fought to retain absolute power at any cost, backed by those same United States capitalists.

## Nicaraguan leaders provide "profitable investment," with one exception

The history of Nicaragua is a history of exploitation. Spanish conquest began in the early sixteenth century, with Spain coming to control the fertile Pacific coast and the adjoining highlands areas, and the United Kingdom holding sway over the Atlantic coast until the mid-nineteenth century, when United States interests began asserting themselves. The Central American Federation earned its formal independence from Spain in 1821, with Nicaragua and its neighbors becoming new countries when the federation broke up in 1843.

The Nicaraguan elite split into two factions, mirroring the Central American pattern: Conservatives and Liberals. The Conservative Party represented traditional plantation owners who had controlled society through their control of the land and sought to maintain Nicaragua's feudal social structure and organization. The Liberal Party represented newly emergent coffee exporters and a minuscule manufacturing sector that wanted "free trade" pushed ahead of any other value. Both groups ruled through naked force—each party suppressed the other (and Nicaraguan society) when in power and power changed hands only through violence.

The rivalry between Conservatives and Liberals provided ample opportunity for US business interests to keep Nicaragua from developing any stable political institutions and muscle out competing European and Japanese business interests. The first direct intervention came in 1855, when Liberals invited a US mercenary, Thomas Walker, to intervene in their civil war against the Conservatives; Walker promptly seized power for himself with his private army. Walker legalized slavery and declared himself ready to invade the other Central American countries to form a single state.[1] An armed coalition consisting of the threatened neighboring countries, the United Kingdom and a US transportation company ousted Walker.

The Conservatives then took control of the Nicaraguan government, ruling until 1893. Although foreign intrigue over a potential cross-isthmus canal continued to percolate, coffee now became the engine of Nicaraguan strife. The Conservatives made coffee exports the largest portion of the economy, facilitating the consolidation of large coffee plantations through force—ironically carrying out a Liberal program. Land communally owned by Indigenous peoples and some church land was taken through violence and given to plantation owners; subsidies and cheap credit were supplied to coffee growers; and those whose land was taken away or who had small plots coveted by plantation owners were converted into forced laborers through a prohibition on growing subsistence crops, crippling debt and the use of draconian "vagrancy" laws.[2]

When a Liberal dictator, José Santos Zelaya, was installed in 1893, the same policies were maintained. But Zelaya incurred the wrath of the United States by accepting a loan from British bankers instead of US bankers, then opened negotiations with Germany and Japan to build a new canal to rival the Panama Canal.[3] Zelaya resigned amidst a US invasion in 1909, culminating in the US installing a Conservative dictatorship. The president of the United States, William Howard Taft, then placed Nicaragua's customs collections under US control and the disapproved British loan was refinanced through two US banks, which were given control of Nicaragua's national bank and railroad as a reward.[4] These developments were not an accident, for Taft had already declared that his foreign policy was "to include active intervention to secure our merchandise and our capitalists opportunity for profitable investment" abroad.[5] Mission accomplished, the marines left in 1910, only to return in 1912 for an occupation that would last 13 years. Following the conclusion of that latter occupation, it would take only two months for the start of yet another US invasion that lasted 12 years.

US marines left Nicaragua in 1925 after the election of a Conservative–Liberal coalition government. A more hard-line Conservative promptly seized power in a coup, triggering a new intervention. The US "settled" the question by re-imposing the former Conservative dictator. The civil war continued, but was eventually brought to an end when a US envoy negotiated a deal in which the Liberals would return to power in the next "election" in 1928 in exchange for the Liberal insurgents ending the war and handing over their weapons to US marines. This unusual retreat happened in the wake of waning US public support following a July 1927 massacre by US soldiers of 300 unarmed people by bombing and machine-gunning them.[6] Because the Liberals were winning the civil war, the dwindling public support led the US government to negotiate a settlement.[7] The Liberals agreed to the deal, and the US government did have their candidate "elected" in 1928.

One Liberal general, however, refused to agree to this deal and turned his unit into a guerrilla army determined to force the United States out: Augusto Sandino.

Sandino worked as a mechanic and a plantation worker in Guatemala, Honduras and Mexico before returning to his native Nicaragua. These first-hand experiences as well as his childhood experience of being shunned by his land-owning father as "illegitimate" (his mother was an Indigenous servant on his father's plantation whom he joined in a debtors' prison at age 9) gave him a sharp understanding of injustice. Sandino founded his own army unit in 1926, joining the Liberal insurrection.

Sandino's army grew after he vowed that he would oppose any US interference in Nicaraguan affairs. Sandino had no choice but to create links with the rural population as Nicaraguan and US military forces conducted scorched-earth operations in the countryside where he operated. It was here that Sandino wrote the words that would be made famous by the Sandinista National Liberation Front four decades in the future: "The waverers and faint of heart will desert us because of the new character of the struggle…Only the workers and peasants will go all the way, only their organized strength will secure victory."[8]

Sandino's exploits earned him the support of progressive people around the world. A journalist working for the progressive US journal *The Nation* wrote this about Sandino: "He is a man utterly without vices, with an unequivocal sense of justice, a keen eye for the welfare of the humblest soldier."[9] Sandino simultaneously spoke as a nationalist, an internationalist and a representative of the oppressed. Upon starting his liberation campaign in 1927, he wrote that the "bonds of nationality" gave him the right to fight on behalf of Nicaraguans, but that fight was also for those of "Central America and all the continent that speaks our language."[10] Sandino declared "my greatest honor is having been issued from the womb of the oppressed."[11]

One organization that denounced Sandino, however, was the Communist International, completely dominated by Josef Stalin and which at this time was in its ultra-sectarian phase. Consistent with the confusion-inducing ultra-Left phrase-mongering it was promoting at the time, the Communist International absurdly claimed that Sandino wanted to give up his arms for a payoff and dismissed him as an anti-revolutionary would-be petit dictator.[12]

Sandino was no such thing, fighting on until 1932, when he agreed to lay down arms in exchange for a promise that the US marines would leave Nicaragua, for land that landless farmers could work as cooperatives and for 100 of his fighters to be allowed to remain armed.

The marines did leave in 1933, but they had left behind the Nicaraguan National Guard. The guard had been created by the US marines in the wake of the 1927 accords, and trained by them ever since. The marines also installed the commander of the National Guard, Anastasio Somoza. Somoza's father had sent the future dictator to business school in the United States, where Somoza learned to speak English, before his father ran his plantation into bankruptcy. After his return home, Somoza worked as a plumber, an electrician and a forger at various times, but his career received a big boost when he married the niece of Juan Sacasa, a prominent Liberal politician who would be handed the presidency in 1932.[13] Armed with his family connection and his ability to speak English, Somoza befriended the US ambassador, serving him as a translator, and when the marines left in 1933, Somoza was put in charge of the National Guard.[14]

There was still the matter of Sandino. The guerrilla leader had not only won his demand for the United States to end its occupation of Nicaragua, but the cooperatives he was organizing would set an undesirable precedent. Forced off their lands altogether or left with too little land to sustain their families, large numbers of Nicaraguan farmers had been forced to become seasonal workers working for starvation wages on plantations. This condition would be tougher to maintain if the example of cooperatives became a success. Somoza, firmly backed by the US ambassador, acted independently of Sacasa (the president and his wife's uncle), and began demanding that Sandino and his men turn in all their weapons. Sandino refused to do so, seeing that Somoza and his National Guard were a direct threat to the survival of their negotiated gains, and traveled to Managua, the capital, to negotiate with Sacasa.

Somoza resolved to assassinate Sandino and the armed guard Sandino brought with him. Somoza, in announcing his plans to his National Guard officers, said the US ambassador "assured me that the government in Washington supports and recommends the elimination of Augusto César Sandino, because they consider him a disturber of the peace of the country."[15] Somoza arranged to have his guardsmen arrest Sandino and his guards after they left a dinner with Sacasa, taken to an airfield and killed by machine-gun fire.[16] Somoza then sent his troops to the region where Sandino's followers were farming, and massacred them. A small number escaped, remained in the jungle, and decades later would train the first guerrillas of the Sandinista National Liberation Front.

Two years after the massacres of Sandino and his followers, in 1936, Somoza overthrew Sacasa, beginning a family dictatorship that would last 43 years and make him the richest person in Central America.

## Multinational corporations extract profits from Central America, with some assistance

Sadly, Nicaragua's experience is not unique. The United States has militarily invaded Latin American and Caribbean countries 96 times, including 48 times in the twentieth century.[17] That total constitutes only direct interventions and doesn't include coups fomented by the US, such as those in Guatemala in 1954 and Chile in 1973. Most of these invasions were for reasons along the lines articulated by former US president William Howard Taft: to ensure profits for one or more US corporations or to overthrow governments that did not prioritize the maximization of those profits.

An examination of the history of other Central American countries reveals a distinct pattern. Concurrent with Somoza beginning his ascendancy in Nicaragua, a US-backed general, Maximiliano Hernández Martínez, seized power in El Salvador in 1932. Shortly thereafter, Martínez drowned in blood a rebellion by the Pipil Indigenous nation, massacring 30,000 Pipils and executing Augustín Faribundo Martí, the communist leader of revolt in El Salvador.[18] Martínez then banned all unions, with US approval. After the general's ouster in 1944, members of "the 14 families" (that is how narrow the ruling oligarchy was in El Salvador) and army generals alternated control of the government,[19] but the generals ruled on behalf of the 14 families when directly in power.

Military and oligarchic rule was later supplemented by right-wing death squads as massacres continued throughout the 1960s and 1970s, until the 1980 assassination of Roman Catholic Archbishop Oscar Romero and the rape and murder of three nuns and a church lay worker signaled that government violence would become entirely unchecked. Taking office soon after those high-profile murders, the Reagan administration responded by increasing aid to El Salvador. Seventy percent of the US aid sent by President Ronald Reagan was for weapons and military assistance.[20]

The small geographic size of El Salvador left the rural population particularly desperate as elites gobbled up land to expand their export-oriented plantations; the percentage of rural Salvadorans without any land soared from 12 percent in 1961 to 60 percent in 1980.[21] Several opposition groups united to found the Faribundo Martí National Liberation Front, but the front faced a tougher time than did the Sandinistas in Nicaragua because in El Salvador the ruling class was firmly united, and in turn tightly linked with the military. This round of repression led to 70,000 Salvadorans being killed from 1979 to 1989.

For much of the twentieth century, the effective ruler of Guatemala and Honduras was the United Fruit Company. The company owned vast plantations in eight countries, and toppled governments in Guatemala and Honduras. The company also owned the railroads and ports that shipped its bananas, a formula also followed by United Fruit's main competitor, Cayumel, until 1930 when Cayumel was acquired by United Fruit.

It was Cayumel that overthrew the Honduran government in 1905 when the company's founder bought a surplus US Navy ship and hired a rebel army.[22] The new Honduran president installed in this manner quickly agreed to give Cayumel everything it wanted[23] and installed the leader of the company's mercenary militia as army commander.[24] So dominant were the two banana companies that Honduras' Liberal Party was financed by Cayumel and Honduras' Conservative Party by United Fruit; a 1925 civil war broke out between the two sides because of a railroad dispute.[25] The US government intervened in this war, its seventh military intervention in Honduras.[26] Eventually, United Fruit bought Cayumel, then put Cayumel's founder in charge of its Latin American banana operations.

These levels of intervention cannot be sustained without some local elites benefiting from the ongoing extraction of capital. Those elites in Honduras included the military that supplies the force that enables the plunder to continue. Cashing in on its many years in power, by 1980 the entire high command had become millionaires.[27]

For many years, United Fruit had an even sweeter deal in Guatemala. The company paid no taxes, imported equipment without paying duties and was guaranteed low wages.[28] During the 1930s, the Guatemalan dictator General Jorge Ubico asked United Fruit to not pay its employees more than 50 cents a day to prevent Guatemalans who worked elsewhere from asking for higher pay.[29] The company also possessed a monopoly on Guatemalan railroads, ocean ports and the telegraph.[30] Although United Fruit did build schools and medical facilities, this constituted an infinitesimally small portion of the taxes it would have paid under a fair régime.

Ubico was a fascist sympathizer who forced Mayans and other Indigenous people to perform forced labor on government projects and private plantations, and required them to carry internal passports restricting their movement.[31] After 13 years, the general was forced out of office in 1944 by a coalition of urban workers, dissident military officers, students and middle-class professionals[32] who helped bring about a general strike.

The mass action that brought down Ubico's dictatorship culminated in the free election of Juan José Arévalo, the country's first democratically elected president, who was an exponent of an ill-defined "spiritual socialism" that stressed "psychological" freedom but a firm anti-communist. He oversaw increased wages; enacted a labor code allowing for the right to strike, form unions and engage in collective bargaining; introduced a social security system; and obligated plantation owners to lease unused land to landless peasants.[33]

More than 70 percent of Guatemala's land was owned by 2 percent of the population, but Arévalo was not challenging the capitalist structure of the economy or the concentration of ownership, merely attempting to institute a more rational, modern form of capitalism. This, however, was unacceptable to United Fruit and the Guatemalan oligarchy; after all, Guatemala had offered an "ideal investment climate," in the words of a United Fruit executive in a book he wrote about the company.[34]

Arévalo was succeeded in 1951 by Jacobo Arbenz, a retired colonel who had helped bring down Ubico. Arbenz shepherded into law a program to expropriate unused land from the largest plantations and distribute it among the landless. The owners were to be compensated based on the land's 1952 value as declared by the owners for tax purposes and paid with 25-year government bonds, and low-interest loans would be provided to peasants to enable them to pay for the land.[35]

Arbenz further angered United Fruit by announcing he

would build a highway to the Atlantic Coast to end the company's monopolies—United Fruit's railroad was charging the world's highest rates.[36] When Arbenz did confiscate a portion of United Fruit's land—the company owned a total of 2400 square kilometers (600,000 acres), 85 percent of which was left unused—Arbenz offered to pay $1.2 million, the value the company itself had given to the confiscated land.

One hundred thousand families obtained small plots of land from this program, but Arbenz also was not challenging capitalist relations nor the agricultural basis of the Guatemalan economy. He was carrying further the reforms begun by Arévalo, converting nonproductive land to productive land and allowing the working people of Guatemala to share a little bit in the wealth the country's land created—wealth, after all, that was built on the sweat of those same working people. Nonetheless, tepid reforms had been considered an outrage by the corporations that operated there and by the US government that acted on their behalf, never mind a significant reform such as Arbenz's program.

A 1952 "national intelligence estimate" (a joint document put together by the Central Intelligence Agency (CIA) and other US intelligence agencies) described the situation from the United Fruit perspective in stark terms:

> If the company should submit to Guatemalan demands the political position of the Arbenz Administration would be greatly strengthened. The result, even if it were a compromise agreement, would be presented as a national triumph over "colonialism" and would arouse popular enthusiasm...The Government and the unions, under Communist influence and supported by national sentiment, would probably proceed to exert increasing pressure against other US interests in Guatemala, notably the Railway.[37]

A remarkable document. Note the use of quote marks around "colonialism," as if such a concept did not exist, and a privately owned railroad is a "US interest." Throw in the ritual reference to "Communist influence" (a phrase implying that Guatemalans, or anybody else subject to the formulation, are intellectually incapable of analyzing their own lives and experiences) and the recipe for an overthrow of a popular, freely elected government comes to completion.

United Fruit, even more than the typical large US company, had friends in very high places. CIA Director Allen Dulles and Secretary of State John Foster Dulles had both been partners in United Fruit's main law firm, Sullivan & Cromwell. When they were lawyers in the 1920s and 1930s, the Dulles brothers had distinguished themselves by facilitating US companies' business dealings with Nazi-connected firms in Germany, including those with industrialist Fritz Thyssen, the biggest bankroller and corporate recruiter for the Nazis from 1923.[38] Allen Dulles further distinguished himself at the conclusion of World War II by bringing into the United States Nazi "scientists" who had conducted inhuman experiments on concentration camp prisoners.[39] As CIA director, Allen Dulles met with a United Fruit official, promising that whoever the CIA would select as the next Guatemalan leader would not touch the company.[40]

United Fruit demanded $16 million from the Arbenz government for the unused land taken from it, instead of the $1.2 million representing the value of the land set by the company itself. But it was the US State Department, not United Fruit, that delivered this demand.[41] Rebuffed, the US government slapped an embargo on Guatemala, gave the CIA $20 million to overthrow Arbenz and regularly briefed United Fruit and other US companies on the status of the plans.[42] Training for the coup participants was conducted on United Fruit lands in Honduras.[43]

The CIA handpicked Carlos Castillo Armas to lead the coup, put together an air force (staffed with contract pilots from the

United States) that carpet-bombed cities to pave Armas's way, and broadcast radio reports falsely reporting that Armas's forces had scored one victory after another.[44] Arbenz lost his nerve, not putting up a fight nor arming peasant leaders who wished to fight the coup.[45] Armas was installed as president, and he promptly banned hundreds of trade unions; stopped all efforts at economic diversification; returned all the land to United Fruit and other plantation owners; reversed all the labor reforms; and unleashed a wave of murders and arrests of union officials and other Arbenz supporters.[46]

The US had instituted what would become a 40-year nightmare of state-organized mass murder. A series of military leaders, each more brutal than the last and fortified with US aid, unleashed a reign of terror that ultimately cost 200,000 lives, 93 percent of whom were murdered by the state through its army and its death squads.[47] The worst of these dictators was General Efraín Ríos Montt, whose régime murdered more than 1000 people a month during 1982. Ríos Montt was an evangelical Protestant preacher who declared that his presidency was the will of God. Reagan responded by paying a visit to Ríos Montt, declaring him "totally dedicated to democracy" and claiming that reports of human rights abuses were a "bum rap."[48] Reagan's military aid to Ríos Montt was supplemented by millions of dollars raised by a US evangelical television preacher, Jerry Falwell, and Falwell's followers.[49] Among the techniques used by Guatemalan dictators were dropping mutilated bodies from helicopters into crowded stadiums and cutting out the tongues of people who inquired about the "disappearances" of friends and family.[50]

Among other exploits in Latin America and the Caribbean, the United States backed a military coup overthrowing a democratically elected government in Brazil in 1965. The US ambassador to Brazil, who served in the Kennedy and Johnson administrations, said the coup would "create a greatly improved climate for private investment."[51] There were also, among others, a 1965 invasion of the Dominican Republic to install a Right-wing dictator and prevent the restoration to power of a democratically elected president; 1970s military coups in Chile and Argentina that instituted fascist-style systems, both guided by US advisers; and a series of invasions of Panama, where under US control there existed a racist apartheid system in the canal zone.

### Somoza offers bucks for friends, bullets for enemies

Nicaragua, too, would not be spared violence. Similar to other regional tyrants, Anastasio Somoza enjoyed the warm support of the US government, regardless of who was in the White House. Under Franklin Delano Roosevelt, US policy changed from military occupations to more quietly installing local dictators who would open their countries to exploitation by US multinational companies in exchange for steady support and the opportunity for their own wealth enhancement.

Somoza and his two sons, who succeeded him, were particularly skilled at playing this game. They lasted 43 years in the Nicaraguan palace, without being troubled by any calls from Washington for free and fair elections, nor did Washington trouble itself with noting the fact that the Somozas stood out even among their peers for their astonishing rapacity.

"Bucks for my friends, bullets for my enemies," was how Anastasio Somoza summed up his reign.[52] There were many enemies, and many executions, torture sessions and macabre punishments. Among the family's favorite punishments were electrical shocks of prisoners' genitals and placing prisoners in cages in a personal zoo, there to be displayed like the lions.

Nicaragua's plantation owners and industrialists didn't like Somoza muscling in on their action, but Somoza was careful to avoid taking their property and co-opted them by parceling out patronage and political positions to Conservatives and Liberals alike. The Liberal Party was reduced to a paper entity that existed to keep Somoza in power and the Conservative Party, with no actual politics to conduct, similarly became nothing but a patronage mill. Deep down, Nicaragua's plutocrats really couldn't complain too much—Somoza was following their own methods to enrichment. The dictator simply could amass wealth much faster by virtue of having the government at his personal disposal.

Coffee had been Nicaragua's chief exports for decades (based on coffee-growing plantations that had been created by forcibly taking land in the nineteenth century) but the fragile stability created by heavy reliance on one export crop was threatened when prices plunged after the Great Depression began in 1929. Plantation owners responded by planting more coffee, hoping that quantity would offset falling prices, and accomplished this strategy by displacing thousands of small farmers.[53] Those forced off their land during this round of unpaid confiscations became unemployed or migrated to the cities, where prospects weren't good, swelling the ranks of the discontented. Growing unrest, reflected in the birth of labor unions and the growth of Augusto Sandino's army, caused both Liberals and Conservatives to support Somoza's overthrow of Juan Sacasa.[54] There had already ceased to be any real difference between the two parties (personal rivalries had become the main source of conflict) so it was with little trouble that the two parties of the oligarchs could unite behind their common class interest.

Land confiscations by the plantation owners continued after Somoza took power, with small and medium farmers losing their land to the big landowners on manufactured excuses of "lack of title" or debt foreclosure.[55] Many of those who didn't escape to the cities effectively became indentured servants; agricultural workers couldn't legally leave their jobs if they owed debts to a company store as a result of buying food or tools.[56] Somoza, too, gobbled up some of this land. But that was only the start. He taxed illegal ventures such as gambling and prostitution, gave himself "commissions" when granting concessions to foreign companies, regularly raided the public treasury, and used public services for little or no payment.[57]

World War II brought new opportunities—Somoza confiscated all properties owned by Germans and Italians.[58] After the war, he pocketed export and import levies imposed on a variety of industries, acquired gold mining and lumber operations, and smuggled cattle.[59] When a political change in neighboring Costa Rica stopped his ability to smuggle cattle, Somoza would not allow anyone to transport cattle without his issuing a permit, would refuse to issue permits and then buy the cattle for a low price from the owners who were refused permits.[60]

Somoza did face increased labor unrest and organizing after World War II, when a recession aggravated economic difficulties caused by the loss of European export markets, at the same time that Conservatives were growing restless. Somoza first co-opted the nascent Nicaraguan Socialist Party and the unions by implementing a relatively progressive labor code.[61] This was simply a maneuver, however; once social unrest was quieted, Somoza cut a deal with the Conservatives, guaranteeing them one-third of congressional seats and ministerial positions.

Having taken care of the Conservatives, Somoza then took back his labor code, and arrested the leaders of the unions and the Socialist Party, forcing many to flee into exile.[62] (The Nicaraguan Socialist Party, despite its name, was an orthodox communist party that consistently followed the Communist Party of the Soviet Union. It would frequently play a deplorable role in the future, refusing until the last minute to join the Sandinista-led uprising that toppled the Somoza dictatorship, then later aligning with a conservative opposition bloc against the Sandinistas.)

In the 1950s, cotton prices had become very high, and plantation owners increasingly switched to cotton from coffee. Although coffee growing relies on a farmer's technique and labor (and therefore could be profitable for middle-sized farmers), cotton is much more capital-intensive, requiring machinery, considerable inputs and larger plots of land. Thus a new round of expulsions of small farmers from their lands ensued, plus massive expulsions of tenant farmers and sharecroppers, causing more displacement and leaving more without the means to adequately support themselves.[63] Those who did stay in the countryside were forced to become seasonal agricultural laborers, but work was only available about four months of the year—creating a large "agricultural proletariat" that would ultimately form a key part of the Sandinistas' base in the 1970s.

This process of land grabs by large plantation owners underwent yet another round in the late 1960s with the creation of large cattle ranches. Peasants pushed to marginal areas had cleared land to grow subsistence crops, but were then forced off these new lands by the cattle ranchers.[64] These successive waves of displacement in turn left less farming land available for subsistence crops, grown for the consumption of the small farmers themselves and for the country's urban population; coffee, cotton and beef were produced for export. The resulting lack of work for the landless rural population also kept wages severely depressed; most worked for less than the very low minimum wage.

With all political options cut off, a poet and printshop worker, Rigoberto López Perez, took matters into his own hands when he managed to sneak into a party and assassinate Somoza. Somoza's older son, Luis, became the new dictator and the younger son, Anastasio II, was named head of the National Guard. Although the assassin acted alone, the sons quickly unleashed a wave of terror, rounding up opponents real and imagined.

One of those arrested was Pedro Joaquín Chamorro, editor of the Conservative newspaper *La Prensa* and scion of a prominent Conservative family long involved in national politics. Chamorro would be assassinated by Anastasio II in 1978, an act that so revolted Nicaraguans that it jump-started the revolution that brought down the dynasty. On this occasion, in 1956, Chamorro was held incommunicado for months, suffering endless beatings, spotlights shone directly into his eyes, forced to eat cigarettes and forced to stay still in stress positions.[65] Still more savage tortures were meted out to others, including electric shocks, waterboarding and being lifted by the genitals.[66]

Following his imprisonment, Chamorro was sent to an internal exile near the border, and then slipped out of the country, but many of the thousands who had been arrested were executed. The United States government responded by steadily increasing aid, including military assistance, from 1953 to 1975.[67]

Luis Somoza reigned until dying of a heart attack in 1967; then it was his brother Anastasio II's turn until the 1979 revolution. The dynasty continued to weather various storms, although the latter outdid himself following the 1972 earthquake that leveled the capital, Managua. Ten thousand died and 250,000 were left homeless. Hundreds of millions of dollars in international aid flooded into Nicaragua, most of which went into Somoza's pocket. The pilfering was done via land speculation and a monopoly on construction materials, but also through founding his own bank.[68] This was too much even for the country's plantation and industrial elite. Somoza had muscled into too much business and now even the previously acquiescent bourgeoisie began turning against him.

Somoza still possessed a strong hand, however: the Nixon administration in Washington. Nixon's ambassador to Nicaragua, Turner Shelton, was an even more staunch friend of the dynasty than previous US ambassadors. Shelton was an executive with the sprawling corporate conglomerate of reclusive billionaire Howard Hughes, who rewarded Nixon with a $200,000 campaign contribution after Shelton's appointment.[69] Hughes was a business partner of Somoza, including owning a minority interest in Somoza's airline.[70] Shelton protected Somoza so rigorously that career embassy personnel had to smuggle to

Washington information about Nicaragua.[71]

The Nicaraguan economy rapidly deteriorated during the 1970s, and Somoza's only response was to increase repression. The National Guard consumed 11 percent of the national budget and thousands of guardsmen trained at the notorious School of the Americas,[72] the US military academy that trains military officers from repressive régimes across Latin America, many of whom return home to use torture and massacres to suppress popular resistance to dictatorial rule.

The mindset inculcated into the National Guard is embodied in a cadence chant used during drilling: "Who is the Guard?" "The Guard is a tiger." "What does tiger like?" "Tiger likes blood." "Whose blood?" "The blood of the people."[73]

## Sandinistas struggle to find the right strategy, cope with life underground

One of the ironies of the first Anastasio Somoza's ruthless repression and censorship was that his ego kept Augusto Sandino's words alive. Somoza wrote (more likely, it was ghost-written for him) a book denouncing Sandino in the usual ways, as a "bandit" and a "communist," but it also included some of Sandino's correspondence in an effort to discredit Sandino, thus making his words available for future opponents of the dynasty.[74] From Sandino's writings, Carlos Fonseca, a founder and the first theorist of the Sandinista National Liberation Front (FSLN), began to create the Front's ideology. It was Fonseca who began the eclectic process of combining Marxism, Sandino's writings, a skepticism toward both and a willingness to adapt to specific Nicaraguan conditions that would enable the FSLN to create a revolution.

Fidel Castro's guerrillas in the Cuban mountains provided inspiration to opponents of the Somoza dictatorship in the Nicaraguan mountains in 1958, from where a series of small uprisings arose, to little effect. But the memory of Sandino had been kept alive not only by remnants of Sandino's army and cooperatives still in the mountains, but by other oppositionists in the cities. One of those who discovered Sandino and his struggle was Fonseca, who arrived in the university city of León in 1952.

Fonseca joined the Nicaraguan Socialist Party (PSN), the communist party that continued to follow the Soviet Union's lead and which at this time was forced to operate underground because of Somoza's repression. The PSN maintained a rigid line that left no room for Nicaragua's actual conditions. Because the classical proletariat class (urban blue-collar workers in industry) represented a minuscule percentage of what was still primarily an agricultural state, the PSN saw no alternative to a strategy of peaceful participation in elections until the time was ripe for struggle, sometime in the distant future. Communist orthodoxy never swerved from this position; Moscow refused any help to the Sandinistas throughout the era of insurgencies.

Fonseca found in his studies of Sandino's writings a base to build upon, but the PSN continued to maintain the same negative attitude toward Sandino that the Communist International had exhibited in the 1930s. Alienated by this negative attitude and increasingly frustrated by the PSN's rigid ideological line, Fonseca and others seeking a revolutionary solution to Nicaragua's problems eventually broke with the party. Fonseca, in 1959, joined one of the small guerrilla bands that were carrying out uncoordinated attacks, was wounded and traveled to Cuba, where he met Che Guevara.[75] "Socialist and national demands are combined in the Sandinist People's Revolution," Fonseca wrote. "We identify with socialism, while retaining a critical attitude to the socialist experiences."[76]

Fonseca brought back to Nicaragua a belief in Guevara's "foco" strategy: the belief that a small band of dedicated guerrillas in rural areas, rooted among the local population, would provide an example that would inspire a general uprising, a strategy that succeeded in Cuba. In 1962, Fonseca, Tomás

Borge, Sylvio Mayorga and seven others founded the FSLN. (Only Borge would live to see the revolution triumph.) Guerrilla attacks in 1963 and 1967 both ended in disaster, and the FSLN decided to reassess its strategy. A long internal discussion of its failures began—among those failures were that, although by 1967 the FSLN had established clandestine cells in a few cities, it had failed to build an organization.

Fonseca's assessment was that the Sandinistas had lacked an effective revolutionary organization, failed to combine conspiratorial work with political work, failed to create an irregular guerrilla force to supplement the full-time guerrillas and gave too much priority to purely military considerations.[77] A new, evolved strategy would be necessary, and although they hadn't launched any offensives since 1967, in 1970 the Sandinistas formally suspended all military activity as they continued to work out a strategy of "accumulation of forces." That meant they would concentrate on building organizations, links among those organizations, and links between the organizations and the people.

Fonseca, meanwhile, embarked on developing further Sandino's ideas. Directly confronting the general level of political development at the time of Sandino's guerrilla campaigns, Fonseca wrote, in 1969, "The ideological obscurantism inherited from the colonial epoch has continued to decisively impede the people from going with a full consciousness into the fight for social change."[78] Because Nicaragua's peasants were "without any political awareness," the movement founded by Sandino "was incapable of continuity" after his death.[79] The FSLN's struggle could not be content with mere removal of the dictatorship, as Sandino would have been; the FSLN had to bring about wholesale changes to societal and political structures, Fonseca wrote.[80]

From these discussions, the FSLN in 1969 publicly announced its Historical Program. In this declaration, the Sandinistas said that, upon taking power, they would nationalize Somoza properties, the country's banks and foreign-owned mining and timber operations; give land to peasants who would work it; promote farming cooperatives; make credit available for small and midsized farmers for the first time; cancel debts owed to usurers; enable workers to participate in the administration of industry; provide free medical care through a nationwide system of clinics; and provide employment and housing for everyone.[81] Regardless of later tactical differences among the Sandinistas, there was no wavering from, or dilution of, this program. Although not all of these goals were reached, the FSLN ultimately fulfilled a remarkably high proportion of them given the underdevelopment of Nicaragua and the immense damage done to the economy by Anastasio Somoza II's backward economic policies and his scorched-earth warfare against the country's population and infrastructure in his last years.

Gradually, the tactical differences within the FSLN coalesced into three distinct currents of opinion, or "tendencies." This differentiation not only continued, but solidified, after the Sandinistas resumed military operations at the end of 1974. Fonseca was in Cuba, after escaping from a Costa Rican jail, and other leaders, such as Borge and Daniel Ortega, were in Nicaraguan jails. Perhaps there would have been more internal cohesion if the leadership had been able to remain intact. But the tactical differences were significant, resting in part on different analyses, and prominent leaders were represented in all three tendencies, so it is highly likely the same differentiation would have occurred, regardless of the ability to discuss strategies in person.

The strategy of "accumulation of forces" meant mobilizing and organizing broad masses of people directly rather than attempting to catalyze them indirectly; a task requiring extensive work in the cities and the countryside.[82] From this strategy grew the "Prolonged People's War" faction, although at first this represented the party as a whole and did not constitute a faction. One example of this strategy was the work of the head of the FSLN's Managua branch, Eduardo Contreras, who established links with branches in three nearby provinces and guerrillas in the mountains to the north, and developed unity among several student, workers' and peasants' organizations that had previously struggled individually in isolation from one another.[83] A key bulwark of the faction was the Revolutionary Student Front, one of the strongest Sandinista organizations.

Inherent in the Prolonged People's War strategy is a slow building up of forces in which there is no going on the offensive militarily until conditions are strongly in your favor; to go on the offensive prematurely leaves you open to decimation by the enemy. This strategy was inspired by the rural guerrilla strategies of Mao Zedong and Vietnamese General Vo Nguyen Giap and was based on holding liberated territories and building massive popular resistance in enemy-controlled areas—an alliance between peasants and urban workers.[84] Giap argued that the superior forces of an unpopular régime or occupier can be defeated because either it must concentrate its forces, thereby ceding wide areas to the resistance, or it must scatter its forces across broad areas, thereby ceding its numerical strength.[85] Forcing a régime into this choice can be accomplished only by successfully creating a guerrilla army large enough to operate across a country.

Critics of the Prolonged People's War strategy argued that it was too cautious militarily. The next distinct faction to develop was the Proletarian Tendency. It was the rise of the Proletarian Tendency that "created" the Prolonged People's War faction, since there had not previously been more than one organized current of opinion. This first serious split within the ranks of the FSLN ironically came about due to the Sandinistas' first military success.

Alienation in all segments of Nicaraguan society grew

following Somoza's pocketing of foreign aid after the 1972 Managua earthquake. Even the large capitalist industrialists began organizing themselves in organizations such as the Superior Council of Private Enterprise (COSEP), which was backed by the Roman Catholic Church and the Conservative daily newspaper *La Prensa*. Somoza's rule increasingly benefited not the entire class of large industrialists and large plantation owners but instead a small segment of that class with strong ties to Somoza himself. Somoza's rule became intolerable for most of them because the dictator's ever-expanding enterprises muscled in on more business sectors and pervasive corruption was becoming an economic bottleneck. And these industrialists and plantation owners saw themselves as the rightful rulers of Nicaragua; their equivalents ruled in any normal capitalist country.

A small but growing part of the population worked in industry and services in the cities, and were also ready to have a bigger societal role. The rural population was also ready to play a much larger role. Former smallholders who had lost their farms to plantation owners and were forced to work as seasonal subsistence field workers, as well as smallholders who continued to survive but nonetheless lived on the brink of ruin, shut out of any access to credit and at the mercy of a state that cared only for the plantation owners, sought a better life, too.

The "accumulation of forces" strategy of the Prolonged People's War (although it was not yet a faction) reached the next step in December 1974 with a spectacular return to military operations. Earlier in the year, Somoza was "re-elected" in another farce of an election, but, in an unmistakable sign of growing resistance across all classes, there had been boycotts. Both the Conservative and Liberal parties split, with the breakaway parties backing the election boycott. Following the "election," on 15 December 1974, a broad coalition was formed by supporters of the boycott: the Democratic Liberation Union.

This coalition included the breakaway conservative and liberal parties, but also the Social Christian Party, the Socialist Party of Nicaragua, civic organizations and two labor union federations.[86] Industrialists and plantation owners not aligned with Somoza, however, stayed far away from this anti-Somoza coalition.[87]

Twelve days later, on 27 December, FSLN guerrillas attacked a party honoring Turner Shelton, the US ambassador. The party was held at the house of a cotton exporter who had previously been a Somoza agricultural minister, and the 13 guerrillas carefully timed their assault to just after Shelton left the party. All in attendance were taken hostage, and the guerrillas were able to repel a National Guard unit sent to the scene by using a machine gun taken from the party's host.[88] Various ministers, Somoza relatives and industrial and banking leaders were taken hostage; in exchange for their release, the FSLN demanded the release from prison of several of their leaders (including Daniel Ortega), $5 million in ransom and the publication of two FSLN communiqués.[89] Somoza ultimately yielded, releasing 18 Sandinista prisoners, allowing the hostage-takers and freed prisoners to go to Cuba and providing radio time and newspaper space for the communiqués.[90]

Following this spectacular success, a flood of recruits swelled the ranks of the FSLN. Many of these recruits were urban intellectuals who brought with them a more traditional Marxist outlook. These points of views crystallized into the Proletarian Tendency faction. The Proletarian Tendency believed the focus had to be on organizing in the cities and that armed struggle in the mountains was no longer relevant, constituting a debilitating adventurism. The expansion of cotton exports and the creation of a Central American common market had sparked a rapidly growing base of industrial and service workers in the cities along with the rapid growth of a rural workforce that was the equivalent of the urban workforce, creating the need for a vanguard organization that could help develop this new, growing class struggle.[91] The faction argued that the FSLN should make its priority building trade unions and mass-participation groups such as neighborhood councils with a long-term goal of preparing nationwide political mass strikes supplemented by local uprisings.[92]

The Proletarian Tendency became an organized faction when the FSLN leadership resisted having the internal discussions necessary to work out these issues. Tomás Borge, a Prolonged People's War leader, later acknowledged that "We adopted authoritarian positions and tried to solve the problem by decree" because of being unprepared for the "strange and new phenomenon" of strategic and theoretical differences.[93]

The FSLN had bumped against a common problem: How can the need for internal democracy be balanced with the need for internal security in a necessarily clandestine organization? In a situation such as that in which the FSLN operated, the members have to accept a firm level of discipline. A ruthless state apparatus, equipped with a bloodthirsty military, was hunting down FSLN members in all corners of the country and would summarily execute not only any Sandinistas it found, but anybody who gave support to them. And short of outright execution, the state had plenty of tools at its disposal, including loss of employment (itself no small threat in a country where one-fifth of the working population was out of work) or destruction of farms and homes. These conditions necessitated not only that the FSLN and its range of organizing work remain clandestine, but that its organizers, guerrillas and other militants remain scattered. A casual get-together was simply impossible.

On the other hand, free discussion, particularly among the members with a stronger understanding of issues and the experience to analyze the complexities of society, is a necessity to keep the group alive intellectually and in other ways, and to allow the group to adapt its tactics, strategies and analyses to changing conditions. This free discussion is also necessary to enable the more experienced members to pass on their knowledge to the less experienced members, raising the overall political level of the group and helping those less experienced members to themselves work out the issues and come to higher understandings. Yet, at some point, a clandestine organization, facing harsh conditions in an acute struggle, has to be able to make decisions and carry them out. This is critical not only for the group's ability to be effective, but to keep its members alive. Self-discipline is indispensable to a clandestine group's survival.

One compromise between these competing needs is "democratic centralism." Originally conceived by Vladimir Lenin when Russia's Bolsheviks were a persecuted group that mostly conducted work clandestinely, democratic centralism means that there is a full and free discussion of an issue by all members, but once a vote is taken on the issue, that vote is binding on all members, regardless of their position during the discussions. In clandestine organizations, however, it is not possible for everyone to meet, so sometimes the leadership has to meet secretly, work out the issue, and make a decision for the organization. Theoretically, the leadership is put in place by a free vote of the membership and can be replaced, so there can be indirect democratic accounting in this situation.

But when those who crystallized into the Proletarian Tendency entered the FSLN after the 1974 hostage-taking episode, a leadership was already in place and wasn't willing to allow the discussion that the organization needed to have. Fonseca was aware of these interrelated problems in 1975 when he wrote,

> As is evident, clandestine methods predominate in the activities of the Sandinista Front. But it is necessary that our clandestine methods do not excessively limit the political life of the organization...[I]t is good to bring out the points that reflect the political concerns of the organs and members of the

> party...It should also be made clear that in attempting a constructive political life, neither should one fall into the other dangerous extreme which is ultra-democracy. Neither ultra-centralism, nor ultra-democracy. Our guide must be democratic centralism, and the conditions under which the Sandinista Front works demand that we do not neglect for a moment the necessary centralism.[94]

Those words of Fonseca were made more concrete a year later, when Fonseca was killed in a National Guard ambush.

The dominant Prolonged People's War faction "solved" the problem of competing tendencies by expelling the Proletarian Tendency faction, which, nonetheless, continued to carry out its work under its own leadership while still carrying the FSLN banner. The Proletarian Tendency, however, had to contend with another problem: urban workers' concrete conditions. The tendency did find much success in organizing city residents, but had to do so through neighborhood groups rather than workplace cells. "They thought that clandestine organizing in the factory would be detected and they did not have confidence in the ability of their fellow workers to resist the pressures of management and the National Guard," a tendency leader, Jaime Wheelock, said.[95] Those conditions also blocked the development of large Sandinista unions until Somoza's fall.

The expulsion of the Proletarian Tendency didn't bring an end to strategic and ideological differences. By 1976, there appeared a "third tendency," the Insurrectionists or "Terceristas." The Terceristas advocated more flexibility in tactics and broadening the social groups to be included within the FSLN. This faction advocated the organizing of urban workers carried out by the Proletarian Tendency and the building of rural guerrilla forces carried out by the Prolonged People's War, but wanted to also organize and recruit middle-class people in the cities and midsize farmers in the countryside, create coalitions with all anti-Somoza forces and favored immediate armed actions rather than waiting. Although the Terceristas agreed with the organizing being done by the other two tendencies, the stress on linking with other groups and a much increased tempo in armed actions represented a strong contrast to the other two tendencies.

Humberto Ortega, who became one of the leaders of the Tercerista faction, believed that if the FSLN did not begin to organize middle-class social groups such as white-collar workers, career-minded students, self-employed workers and small business operators, the alternative opposition coalescing around the anti-Somoza corporate elite and allied elite institutions would do so.[96] Nicaragua's corporate elite—industrialists and agricultural exporters—wanted to replace Somoza but retain his system. The United States government, under Jimmy Carter, was working toward the same goal, having decided that Somoza had become too much of a liability. Therefore, the Terceristas argued, the FSLN had to build its own multi-class coalition, going beyond peasants and blue-collar workers to include other social groups, including church groups and social christians. This was the entry point for Roman Catholic priests who advocated liberation theology in defiance of the church hierarchy and the urban and rural Catholics who followed them, becoming another pillar of the insurrection.

The leaders of the Terceristas were previously Prolonged People's War advocates, and the new, third tendency quickly displaced Prolonged People's War as the dominant faction, although each of the three FSLN factions grew in the next years. A key to the thinking of the Terceristas, and translated into practice in their readiness to immediately begin armed struggle, was that the masses were suffering now and had waited long enough for their conditions to improve.

"People in the underdeveloped countries got tired of paying the costs of waiting for economic advancement while barbarism proceeded,"[97] is the succinct conclusion of Orlando Núñez Sóto, who would become a leading Sandinista theorist. Núñez later wrote,

> History compels us to broaden revolutionary theory and practice. Diverse political experiences...have made it increasingly clear that the impetus for revolutionary change no longer comes only from Marx's working class or Lenin's worker-peasant alliance. Today, a *third* social force comprised of a variety of groups—the middle classes, the intellectuals, the urban poor, the petit bourgeoisie, and the ethnic and social movements—often plays a highly original role in social change.[98]

Although the Terceristas developed their insurrectionist strategy in an underdeveloped country of the Global South, their strategy has broad applications for the developed countries of the Global North, for similar social complexities and differentiations exist there. While no theory can be transplanted whole to another place or time, the Terceristas explicitly acknowledged, and acted upon, the fact that workers are not only blue-collar factory employees, but are also white-collar and other types of employees in a variety of settings, in offices and service positions, among others. Any revolution that seriously attempts to transcend capitalism, which means eliminating the immense power of the capitalist elite, has to include all these varieties of working people if it is to succeed in the twenty-first century.

In the Nicaraguan context, it was the Terceristas who became the dominant faction, in part because their strategy was "big enough" to include the other two tendencies and because its strategy was the one that brought about a successful revolution. Therefore, one of the Terceristas' leaders, Daniel Ortega, would become identified as the FSLN's leader. But that victory was another four and a half years in the future from the December 1974 hostage-taking that heightened the need to sort out these strategic and ideological questions. Those years would require immense sacrifices.

## Nicaraguan insurgency becomes a mass movement, defying organized terror

The return to the offensive in December 1974 proved a spectacular success, if just for the freed prisoners and mass-media communiqués. But such a success would not come without a heavy price: Anastasio Somoza II promptly declared martial law, imposed press censorship, suspended what few civil liberties there were to suspend and gave his National Guard free rein to terrorize the country. Repression against all areas of opposition activity, from wherever, was merciless. The newly formed multi-class anti-Somoza coalition formed by election boycotters, the Democratic Liberation Union, was paralyzed, but although the Sandinista National Liberation Front (FSLN) was forced underground, its factions continued to grow as the endless governmental violence caused more illusions of a peaceful solution to fall away. The Terceristas still managed the occasional scrimmage.

Having driven down living standards still further, believing that the FSLN had been finished off and wanting new military aid from the United States in exchange for lifting martial law, Somoza finally ended his state of emergency in September 1977. Nicaragua was in a dire state: falling wages, increasing unemployment and rapidly rising inflation. The country had begun industrializing in the 1960s, but because wages were so low, there was little internal market. Most of the manufactured products were exported and, in turn, the raw materials for these exports had to be imported; additionally, these new industries tended to be capital-intensive, so relatively few jobs were created, thereby further retarding the ability of an internal market to be created.[99] Profits for the industrialists increased, but wages and salaries steadily deteriorated in all major sectors through the

1970s.[100]

Rural conditions were even worse. Big plantation owners' taking of land from smallholders had gone on for so long that 1.5 percent of landowners owned 42 percent of the land (while most of the rural population did not own any land)[101] and although the total number of employers represented 3.5 percent of the rural population, they scooped up 63 percent of gross income.[102] Perhaps the most stark indication of Nicaragua's desperate poverty is that two-thirds of the country's children were undernourished.[103]

Within a month of Somoza lifting martial law, the FSLN launched a series of attacks on National Guard bases around the country, signaling that radical opposition had not gone away. The Conservative newspaper *La Prensa* then published a full-page appeal from 12 well-known economic, cultural and religious figures appealing for an end to dictatorship. *La Prensa*'s editor, Pedro Joaquín Chamorro, was assassinated on his way to work on 10 January 1978; Somoza now made it clear that no opposition, not even from the elite, would be tolerated. Somoza had sometimes used persuasion and bribery to keep the elites on his side, but, with this act, now would apply only a naked fist.

A series of coalitions, the Democratic Liberation Union the first among them, attempted to stitch together multi-class alliances in an attempt to remove Somoza from the country while leaving Somoza's system and National Guard in place. But Chamorro's assassination infuriated the population, which moved steadily Left, a process that culminated in the last multi-class coalition taking its leadership from the FSLN.

More than 100,000 people took part in Chamorro's funeral procession and a mass strike was called for 24 January. Even the Superior Council of Private Enterprise (COSEP), the federation of employers that wanted to retain Somoza's system without Somoza, joined the call for the strike. The mass strike did not achieve any concrete results despite being widely observed, but demonstrated unity across many social groups. Then the Indigenous population in the small city of Monimbó rose up, holding off the National Guard for a week until their rebellion was drowned in blood.

Nicaraguans were not cowed, however. A series of strikes, uprisings, armed attacks and defensive battles commenced. The most dramatic event came on 22 August 1978, when 25 FSLN commandos took over the National Palace, an even more daring act than the 1974 hostage-taking.

The FSLN commandos, dressed in National Guard uniforms surreptitiously put together using pieces acquired from several sources, pulled up in an official-looking truck. Somoza's standard practice when he made a public appearance was to have his personal Guard unit disarm the Guardsmen on duty, and the Sandinistas replicated this down to yelling, "Out of the way, here comes the chief," as they moved down the hallways. The Sandinistas burst into the National Palace's main chamber, ordering everybody to the floor; all complied, assuming this was the rumored National Guard coup come to life. "Operation Pigsty" was a breathtaking success, so far: In three minutes, hundreds of hostages had been taken, including several government ministers, two Somoza relatives and most of the congressional deputies.

The commander of this operation, "Zero," was Eden Pastora, and his subcommanders were "One," Hugo Torres Jiménez, who had taken part in the 1974 embassy-party attack, and "Two," Dora María Téllez. Shortly after the takeover, a National Guard helicopter began firing into the chamber through the Palace windows; in response, the more valuable prisoners were placed at the windows. "They were trembling with fear and believed that the guardsmen were going to kill them without further thought," Pastora later said. "It was at this moment that [Somoza's cousin] Luis Pallais and [Somoza's nephew] José Abrego telephoned Somoza and asked him not to leave them to die."[104] A mercenary from the United States brought a National Guard squad he commanded and was about to storm the National Palace, but was ordered to stop by Somoza, who was talked into giving the order by Pallais.[105]

In exchange for releasing all hostages, the Sandinistas demanded the release of 59 political prisoners, a plane to take the commandos and released prisoners out of the country, broadcasts over government radio of a communiqué, $10 million in cash and acceptance of the demands of striking hospital workers. The Sandinistas received all of it, except the cash, after two days of negotiations conducted by Téllez and Somoza through a team of intermediaries; the presence of his relatives induced Somoza to yield. FSLN supporters lined the streets for the 9-mile drive from the National Palace to the airport, where a huge throng gave the Sandinistas a hero's sendoff. The communiqué was broadcast, but, oddly, Somoza was not displeased by that, telling reporters that the world would now know what he was fighting.[106]

The presence of a woman, Téllez, among the commandos was not an aberration. Women had fought as FSLN guerrillas as far back as 1967, and fought in significant numbers shoulder to shoulder with the men. Several women were commanders and Téllez went on to be the top commander for one of the Sandinistas' most important "fronts," in the area of León, one of the country's major cities. Téllez became involved in the student movement in high school, then joined the FSLN as a medical student, first in a clandestine cell in a support role before becoming a guerrilla.

A similar path was followed by Nora Astorga, who first worked clandestinely for the FSLN while working as a lawyer and chief of personnel for a large construction company before going into the mountains and becoming a guerrilla; she would become the Sandinista government's ambassador to the United Nations.

"The social group into which I was born, in which I lived and moved, seemed so superficial," Astorga said in an interview granted shortly before she died at age 39 from cancer. "It was the Front that gave meaning to my life, gave me a sense of belonging to something...What changed me was seeing the people take the streets [during strikes], and feeling that the dictatorship would not be overthrown that way...I finally understood that armed struggle was the only solution, that a rifle cannot be met with a flower, that we were in the streets but if that force didn't get organized we wouldn't achieve much. For me, it was the moment of conviction: either I took up arms and made a total commitment or I wasn't going to change anything."[107]

Many other people also drew the conclusion that strikes alone would not be enough. In September 1978, FSLN forces attacked the National Guard in several cities, including León, sparking uprisings in each of them. When the Sandinistas were forced to retreat, thousands left with them in long columns—for good reason, as the National Guard let loose with savagery, massacring 6000.[108]

The masses were now starting to move ahead of the FSLN. "We could not say no to the insurrection," said Humberto Ortega, a Tercerista leader and future defense minister. "The mass movement had grown to such a size that the vanguard was incapable of leading it; all we could do was stand at its head, so as to lead it as much as possible and give it some direction...[W]e threw ourselves into the insurrection because of the prevailing political situation. Our aim was not to abandon the people to a massacre for...the people were already plunging into action."[109]

Retreating with thousands of people (FSLN guerrillas made up only a small number of the insurgents) proved that the people wouldn't be abandoned. Téllez, the FSLN commander for León, said,

> Without a doubt, it is difficult to retreat with hundreds,

> thousands of people like "Ruben" retreated [with] from Estelí [in a different action]: with old people, women and children. It seems crazy to retreat with so many people, but how are you going to leave the people behind?..."Ruben" decided to retreat with half of Estelí for the jungle. I do not know if that is the best solution...But there is one great advantage and that is that the people do not lose faith in their vanguard because it did not leave them to die alone.[110]

A final organizing step was the formal unification of the three FSLN tendencies. On 9 December 1979, the three tendencies issued a joint communiqué in which they said they "have decided to unite our political and military forces in order to guarantee that the heroic struggle of our people not be stolen by the machinations of yankee imperialism and the treasonous sectors of the local bourgeoisie. We unite our forces to carry on the armed revolutionary struggle until the definitive overthrow of the Somoza military dictatorship."[111]

The last of the series of multi-class coalitions designed to replace Somoza but leave his system in place had fallen apart after Somoza pulled out of talks with that coalition and the US government. The Left groups in that last multi-class coalition then joined a new coalition, the United People's Movement, that included all three FSLN tendencies and Sandinista-affiliated mass groups such as student, neighborhood and women's associations. The United People's Movement then linked up with other trade unions, a liberal splinter party and a christian social party to form the National Patriotic Front.

Meanwhile, the Carter administration made a show of displeasure at Somoza pulling out of the talks by suspending US aid to Nicaragua, but then the International Monetary Fund, which the Carter administration controlled, approved a large loan to Somoza.[112] In June, the Carter administration's ambassador to Nicaragua, Lawrence Pezzullo, promised Somoza that the National Guard would remain intact and receive "US assistance" if Somoza resigned.[113]

Finally, on 17 June 1979, a provisional government, the Junta of National Reconstruction, was formed in Costa Rica. The junta had five members: FSLN representative Daniel Ortega; the head of the United People's Movement coalition, Moisés Hassan; the head of an FSLN-affiliated group that previously participated in the earlier multi-class alliances, Sergio Ramírez; and two representatives of the corporate elite, Violeta Barrios de Chamorro (Pedro Joaquin Chamorro's widow) and industrialist Alfonso Robelo.

By now, Nicaraguans were revolting en masse. A 4 June FSLN call for an "insurrectional general strike" shut down the country. Coordinated attacks began in a series of cities, isolating units of the National Guard and forcing the Guard to stretch its forces too thin. By 16 July, almost every major city in Nicaragua was in insurgent hands and the régime was about to topple. The US government that day was still trying to negotiate a deal to block the Sandinistas from assuming power with the Roman Catholic archbishop of Managua (Miguel Obando y Bravo), various members of the anti-Somoza corporate elite and the Junta of National Reconstruction—this last maneuver was an effort to get the Junta to add a member of the National Guard and a member of Somoza's Liberal Party.[114] The Sandinistas, naturally, would have nothing of this. Sadly, the Moscow-aligned Nicaraguan Socialist Party joined with the anti-Sandinista bloc in these negotiations,[115] not the first or last time it would play a shameful role.

On 17 July, Somoza finally gave up and fled the country. The National Guard quickly melted away and two days later Sandinista columns marched into Managua in triumph. Four thousand National Guardsmen were taken prisoner, but several thousand more escaped to Honduras and the United States.[116] The Sandinistas released about half of the Guardsmen they captured, who then left for Honduras as well.[117] This act of magnanimity would be paid back by many of the Guardsmen organizing the Contras, who would soon launch a brutal war in an effort to destroy the Nicaraguan revolution.

Even now, at the moment of triumph, Nicaraguans could not avoid the massive toll their revolution had taken—Somoza's National Guard had killed 50,000, or 2 percent of the population, during the final insurrection. A similar proportion of the US population today would be 6 million! Industry was left in ruins; Somoza ordered the factories of opposition industrialists bombed. Cities suffered widespread destruction. Significant farming areas had not been planted, meaning a shortage of crops and exports loomed. More than one-third of the country was out of work. As a final insult, Somoza looted the national treasury, leaving it nearly bare.

On such ruins did the Sandinistas have to begin their work.

## New government begins process of rebuilding, with strains showing early

The nature of the enormous problems the Sandinistas faced had similarities to what the young Soviet Union faced in the early 1920s. A revolution had succeeded at enormous cost, with a civil war fought savagely by the revolution's opponents wreaking staggering economic damage; the revolution faced hostile, much stronger foreign powers; the country was dependent on agricultural exports and could adjust that dependency only with difficulty and at the risk of potentially wrenching changes internally; expanding a small industrial sector was desirable but a goal for which the fulfillment would be partly in contradiction to its agricultural base; and a population that had lived in miserable poverty expected its material needs and wants to be met faster than the country's shattered material base was capable of doing. Somehow these problems had to be solved by men and women with energy and determination but a lack of administrative experience.

Nicaragua's militants who had participated in the revolution and found themselves in responsible positions upon the revolution's victory had no experience in the affairs of state, because they had been shut out of public participation, and if their attempts at organizing became known to Somoza's authorities, the prisons and torture chambers of the National Guard awaited.

So mistakes, many of them, were made in the early days of the revolution. How could it be otherwise? It is not remarkable that the Sandinistas made mistakes; what is remarkable is their willingness to learn from them and often correct them, sometimes effecting sharp reversals of bad policies.

The early Bolshevik cadres, similarly, couldn't help but make mistakes when they were placed in responsible positions, having also been shut out of societal participation. But that is enough comparison; it would be too easy to overgeneralize and there were more differences than commonalities between the Soviet Union of the early 1920s and Nicaragua at the end of the 1970s. And the Sandinistas certainly carried out policies drastically different from those of the Bolsheviks, having the experience of many revolutions from which to learn, but also having carried out a revolution on their own terms, with a mix of ideologies and strategies rooted in their own and their country's historical experience. They could not have led a successful revolution otherwise.

And the Sandinista National Liberation Front (FSLN) did it with much help from inside the country, and very little from outside the country.

The Soviet Union's theorists had consistently held the position that conditions were nowhere near ripe for a revolution in Central America, and because challenging official dogma in the Soviet Union was anathema, that viewpoint could not in those years be challenged. Indeed, the Soviet Union, since Stalin's assumption of power, had opposed revolutions everywhere. True, it did use the Red Army to impose régimes in Central Europe, but that, too, went against the spirit of Marxism that believes revolutions can only be made by a people themselves, not imposed from outside. Stalin opposed home-grown communist revolutions in China, Yugoslavia and Greece—counseling revolutionary leaders to stop and instead back their nationalist capitalists in the first two and refusing to lift a finger for the third when its revolution was drowned in blood by the United Kingdom. All of Stalin's successors held fast to this refusal to back revolutions elsewhere; partly this was out of ideological rigidity tinged with a lack of confidence in other peoples, but perhaps more it reflected a desire to maintain peace with the capitalist West at any cost.

Tomás Borge, the only FSLN founder who lived to see the revolution, spoke frankly during an interview conducted eight years after the Sandinistas took power. "Since it was not easy to see the prospects for such a change—even revolutionary forces in the world had not grasped the imminence of victory and had adopted a rather indifferent attitude—we did not receive support during the war from any of the socialist countries, except Cuba," Borge said, without judgment.

> The Soviet Union and others did not support us because they believed that only the Latin American Communist parties were the representatives of revolutionary changes, and it was not possible for them to think otherwise at that time. They had been through a whole series of experiences, developing ideas in distant countries that divorced them from particular realities...I am not blaming those countries, simply pointing out an objective fact...It cannot be said—in that idiotic language that is sometimes used—that Nicaragua's revolution was the fruit of Moscow gold. Not even the Soviets, the Soviet revolutionaries, believed in revolutionary

> change in Nicaragua. So how were they going to help us![118]

Official commentary in the Soviet Union's leading theoretical journal stressed the prevailing viewpoint that armed struggle was hopeless and that Latin Americans should use peaceful tactics while participating in broad coalitions—a view echoed by the head of the El Salvador Communist Party, who went so far as to call those who advocated armed struggle "nihilists."[119]

The behavior of the Moscow-aligned Nicaraguan Socialist Party can best be explained in this context. The party was a participant in the Sandinista governing structure, but less than two months after the FSLN took power, it issued a formal resolution calling on the FSLN to

> be sensitive to the demands and interests of the capitalist class allies. Putting aside or neglecting those interests, in the name of excessive revolutionary radicalism, will not only lead to losing those allies but will strengthen the counter-revolution…[T]his revolution must be conducted in such a way as to prevent the influence of tendencies seeking to skip stages or leap arbitrarily over the necessary stages and their corresponding transformations.[120]

Overall, a statement quite consistent with the Nicaraguan Socialists' long-standing resistance to revolution. The party's resolution might reasonably be read as a warning against moving too fast, but regardless of how that resolution is interpreted, it is quite far removed from a "revolutionary" mindset. Continual shrieking about Soviet bogeymen under every rock ceases being comical at some point and becomes simply morbid.

Regardless, there was no need to worry about precipitous moves. The FSLN had consistently carried out its line of encouraging mass participation, creating the largest possible coalition in the final months of the insurrection and leaving plenty of room for political participation by sectors of society ranging from Marxist parties to its Left all the way to capitalist organizations on the moderate Right. Most of the 18 ministers in the first government lineup were capitalist figures and two of the five seats on the executive body of the provisional government, the Junta of National Reconstruction, were held by prominent capitalists.

The FSLN had adopted Augusto Sandino's motto, "Implacable in struggle, generous in victory," and applied that generosity even to the National Guard. Seeking to avoid a bloody revenge, Borge recalled, "When they tried to lynch the [Somozist] prisoners who were in the Red Cross building, I personally went to see the relatives of our martyrs...and convinced them not to do it by saying, 'So why did we make this revolution, if we are going to do the same things they used to do?'"[121] Borge had the moral authority to make that plea, for he had suffered through two prison terms in Somoza's prisons, undergoing torture and being held in solitary confinement, and his wife was tortured to death by the National Guard. Borge had been involved in struggles against Somoza since the late 1940s.

Borge was one of nine members of the FSLN National Directorate, which was the ultimate authority after Somoza fled. The directorate's structure was based on unity—when the three tendencies reunited, each tendency was represented by three leaders. Daniel Ortega, of the Tercerista tendency, as the one directorate member who also sat on the five-member Junta of National Reconstruction, became the Junta's chair.

Ortega assumed his roles because the Terceristas were the dominant faction due to their strategy proving successful and because their tactics could include the other two tendencies' strategies, giving them a moral authority within the FSLN. Ortega had a long history of political work, joining the student protest movement as a teenager despite the disapproval of his accountant father who had once been a fighter for Augusto

Sandino. Interestingly, Ortega also gave bible lessons when a student. He joined the FSLN at age 18 in 1963, becoming a resistance fighter before spending seven years in jail, where he was tortured.

The new Sandinista government may have shown generosity in victory, but it was going to consolidate that victory. An FSLN commander, Bayardo Arce, put it this way: "This is a Sandinista State; it is a state where the majority of our people subscribe to the political philosophy of Sandisimo, that is why the Council of State has to reflect this majority."[122] Arce was referring to a new legislative body that would soon be formed, but, more generally, he was noting the reality of Nicaragua. The revolution had been fought under the Sandinista banner, the Sandinistas had organized the insurrection and protected people from the wrath of Somoza's goons as best they could; there simply would not have been a revolution without them. So while Arce's words may have been difficult to hear for some, it was a plain statement of how most Nicaraguans felt.

Formally, the five-member Junta of National Reconstruction headed the government as a collective executive, and it ruled by decree for a year until the Council of State convened. Although the FSLN National Directorate was the true center of power, setting overall policy, the Junta worked by consensus in forming policies to implement the Directorate's broad policy decisions, and the capitalists also had opportunity to affect the carrying out of policy through their ministerial positions. The Directorate worked in a collegial fashion, creating a collective style of leadership. The Sandinistas did not wish to have a dominant personality, nor were there any candidates for such a role; only Carlos Fonseca, killed in a National Guard ambush in 1976, had any potential to do so and it is an open question as to whether he could have. Among other reasons, Fonseca advocated the Prolonged People's War line, not that of the Terceristas.

One of the Junta's first acts, in Decree Number 3, was to

confiscate and nationalize the property of Somoza, his family and a few very close associates. Somoza's business empire was so extensive that the Sandinistas' new state-controlled sector represented one-quarter of the economy. Included in the nationalization were Somoza's landholdings, which constituted 23 percent of the country's farmland.[123] More than 90 percent of the confiscated lands consisted of the largest plantations, those more than 3.5 square kilometers (875 acres).[124]

This decree was followed by the creation of the Nicaraguan Institute of Agricultural Reform, and, unlike other ministries, this important department was put in Sandinista hands from the start, under the direction of Jaime Wheelock, a National Directorate member and a Proletarian Tendency leader. Wheelock had originally wished to implement his tendency's more radical agricultural program, but a more modest program was implemented under Directorate consensus.[125] And, already, the Sandinistas were holding back landless agricultural workers from seizing more land.

The Rural Workers Association had emerged a few years earlier, organizing farm workers, particularly day laborers, and created a national organization by early 1978.[126] The association not only organized guerrilla units and coordinated armed actions with the FSLN, but in the final months before the takeover backed spontaneous land takeovers.[127] The land seizures assured there was sufficient food for the liberated areas; the seized lands were collectively farmed and managed, and not parceled into individual plots.[128]

Other early acts of the Junta were nationalization of banks, insurance and foreign trade. Nicaragua's banks, however, had collapsed; therefore taking them over meant taking over responsibility for the banks' debts. As that amounted to a bailout, the capitalists were happy to go along with this decree. But this aspect of the nationalizations had its firm logic, as well—the banks had played a large role in the massive corruption under

Somoza's reign and the insurance companies were unable to cope with the country's massive economic damage.[129] Nicaragua's foreign minister, Miguel D'Escoto, explained the banking and insurance takeovers in a letter to his embassies and consulates: "In this case, we were forced to act in response to economic necessity rather than ideological preference. The financial institutions were bankrupt. The nationalization of the banks was, in effect, the nationalization of their debt. In order to reopen the banks, the government has assumed an additional debt of $230 million."[130] That debt was on top of the $1.6 billion foreign debt that Somoza had saddled the country with, which the Junta agreed to honor.

The government takeover of foreign trade was also in effect a subsidy to capitalists, primarily agricultural exporters. The confiscation of Somoza's properties put some of this sector under state control, but private plantation owners still commanded about three-quarters of the country's agricultural exports, primarily cotton, coffee, beef and sugar. Maintaining agricultural exports was critical to economic recovery—they accounted for 80 percent of Nicaragua's exports.[131] Under the nationalization of foreign trade, the state sold imported inputs to exporters at the official exchange rate and purchased their production for export at guaranteed prices better than the exchange rates.[132]

The state was guaranteeing the exporters a higher price, with the state absorbing the difference between the guaranteed higher price and the price set by the international market. The beneficiaries of this subsidy were overwhelmingly large plantation owners. A government pamphlet later explained that "100 percent of the private sector's needs for working capital and investment" were now financed by the public, whereas never more than 70 percent of these needs had been subsidized under Somoza.[133] The pamphlet continued, "Despite the fact that the private sector has made significant profits [in 1980 and 1981], the producers in this sector have not been forced to use these profits to meet their own needs for working and investment capital."[134]

Despite subsidies and guaranteed profits, the big capitalists continued to chafe at not being in charge politically. A class that believes it is entitled to exercise political control found it increasingly difficult to remain part of the government, and the contradictions between what the big capitalists wanted and the many policies of the Sandinistas that sought to provide better wages, benefits and working conditions, and new democratic structures, for urban and rural working people—the overwhelming majority of the population and the classes who made the revolution—slowly intensified.

Those stresses caused a major shift in the cabinet. In December 1979 and February 1980, a series of resignations and reshuffles, along with shifts to the Left by other ministers, resulted in a radically different cabinet, with almost all ministries now headed by Sandinistas. Several members of the FSLN National Directorate assumed important ministerial positions. The work of the ministries was difficult at first; most of the bureaucrats who had worked in government before the takeover had fled. But the Junta asked lower- and middle-level employees to return, and about 90 percent did so.[135] A new culture of honesty in the ranks of the ministries was created, and dedication and sacrifice were rewarded; massive corruption had been the norm under Somoza.

A new type of temporary legislature, the Council of State, convened on 4 May 1980. The council had 51 seats, each reserved for organized groups—eight political parties, three mass-participation and community organizations, seven labor organizations, seven professional guilds, five employer organizations and the armed forces.[136] The Council originated most of the legislation and could pass or reject legislation introduced by the Junta of National Reconstruction, although the Junta could veto Council-passed legislation.[137]

There had been hope among the employers that they would

be able to control the Council of State, but when mass organizations aligned with the Sandinistas were granted seats, one of the capitalist members of the Junta, Alfonso Robelo, used that as an excuse to resign. Days earlier, the other capitalist Junta member, Violeta Barrios de Chamorro, had stepped down. Both were replaced by industrialists. The mass-participation organizations deserved representation, the Sandinistas argued, because of their massive growth during the past year. Robelo had wanted a guaranteed majority for capitalists on the Council, but walked out when a majority instead went to the organizations that had carried out the work of the revolution—the members of which had literally put their lives on the line for it and constituted a large majority of the country's population.

The Sandinistas were also faced with the massive task of building a court system. Unlike in the ministries, it would not be possible to use the bricks of the past to rebuild; the court system had been a completely servile instrument of Somoza's dictatorship. Plus there was the need to have trials for the thousands of imprisoned National Guardsmen. Special tribunals were created to try Somoza's war criminals in which the defendants were afforded vastly more rights than political defendants had been under Somoza, and the trials were open to the international press, another change.

"We didn't have anything," said Nora Astorga, a trained lawyer who was selected to be the prosecutor at the trials of the Guardsmen. "They gave you a job and you had to do everything from finding people to do it and a house to do it in, to inventing the mechanisms. From nothing. They'd say to you, 'You're in charge.' And you had to figure out how to do it."[138] Astorga found prosecuting Guardsmen difficult because many had wives and young children living in poverty. She had the authority to release them without trial, and did so in about one-fifth of the 6000 cases she handled, and most of those who were convicted received sentences of five or less years. No more than 15 percent received the maximum penalty of 30 years' imprisonment; the Sandinistas had immediately abolished the death penalty.[139]

Astorga said, "We had a group of compañeros who could go where the Guard member had lived to get information, to investigate why he joined the Guard, how he had behaved, what he had done...I'm not saying we were never unjust. It's difficult to be fair 100 percent of the time, but we made a tremendous effort."[140]

## Pressure from below shapes agricultural policy, with tensions

Sandinista agricultural policy began to take shape when systematic rural organizing began in 1976, and was shaped from below at the grassroots level. Committees of agricultural workers were formed by organizers with the Sandinista National Liberation Front (FSLN) and the Agrarian Promotion and Education Center, a group founded by liberation-theology Jesuit Catholics, but their organizing work frequently was stopped when the plantation owners would call in the National Guard.[141] As opposition to the Somoza dictatorship grew, the local committees united to create the Rural Workers Association, which had tens of thousands of members, including permanent agricultural wage workers, seasonal agricultural workers and peasant smallholders.[142]

The first land takeovers, shortly before the July 1979 overthrow of the Somoza dictatorship, were farmed and organized collectively. Because these takeovers of Somoza land were effected by politically motivated farmers, it is not surprising that they would have set them up as cooperatives rather than parceling out the land as individual plots. It also reflected the fact that they restarted production in a war zone, and had to work collectively to defend themselves from potential attack and to find the inputs necessary to make the land productive, so that sufficient food would be available.

Cooperatives were to be a part of the Sandinistas' agricultural policy, but not necessarily on large plantations such as those that were the objects of those first spontaneous takeovers.

The basis of Nicaragua's economy was agricultural exports, and for the moment that could not change. The lands confiscated from Somoza were among the country's most technically advanced and productive farms, and without the export crops produced on them (and on the big plantations remaining in private hands) the country would quickly slide into economic distress. At the same time, if these lands were parceled out to individual farmers, a new rural aristocracy might arise as those lucky enough to come into possession of these technically advanced farms would have huge advantages over other farmers, those not having the chance at this land and those who were smallholders. Conversely, if a large number of landless agricultural workers were given out small parcels of the land, breaking these plantation into tens of thousands of smallholdings, the efficiency inherent in the farms' scale of economy would be lost.

The Sandinistas also wanted to provide as many permanent jobs for the landless as they could. The Somoza farms had been run in the same profit-driven manner as the other plantation owners—by employing a small number of workers year-around (perhaps 10 percent were permanent employees) and the overwhelming majority as seasonal hands, for four months of the year at harvest times. By placing Somoza's lands in state hands and keeping them intact, more of these workers could be employed year round.

Another consideration was the surplus created by the plantations. Anastasio Somoza I had become Nicaragua's largest landowner by the 1950s, and Anastasio II became the richest person in Central America. This was in part through the family's massive manufacturing holdings, but their farms contributed significantly. With the farms going into state hands and remaining productive, their massive surplus would no longer go into a single family's pockets but rather would become a large source of income that could be put to use toward a variety of social necessities—to raise salaries, provide more jobs, create a nationwide network of free medical clinics, schools, infrastructure improvements and modernizing the country's industry.

For all these reasons, the Sandinistas discouraged "wildcat" takeovers of land not covered by Decree 3's confiscation of property owned by the Somoza family and their closest collaborators. Nor did the Sandinistas intend to break up the land acquired through the decree.

Added to these factors was the crisis atmosphere attending the new revolution—agricultural production had declined by one-third due to disruptions from the civil war that removed Somoza, and manufacturing had also declined significantly. Because so much urban infrastructure had been destroyed, and agriculture would be easier to restart, Nicaragua's export-crop earnings had become still more crucial. Many landless peasants expected land to be parceled out to them, sometimes taking matters into their own hands, and this desire created an early conflict with the larger needs of the country as the Sandinistas framed it. The top-down management style retained on the state farms became a second point of friction, and although the Sandinistas made this decision on the basis of what they interpreted as the interests of production, the decision on management style was much more debatable than the decision to keep Somoza's plantations intact.

One month after the Sandinista takeover, further seizures of land were banned, signaling a pause in the development of cooperative farms—the FSLN wished to concentrate resources on the state farmland confiscated from Somoza as the fastest way to boost production.[143] In addition to the factors just noted, the Sandinistas also wanted to give an assurance to the big plantation owners that their property was safe. The FSLN, in November, followed up by attempting to undo some of the "wildcat" confiscations when the court system attempted to hand unauthorized takings back to owners who were not closely linked to Somoza.[144] This represented a setback for peasants, who expected more land to be distributed to them, particularly land that was idle.

Pushing their demands, 30,000 agricultural workers and smallholders, led by the Rural Workers Association (ATC), the organization formed during the insurrection, demonstrated in Managua, demanding that their land occupations be made legal, that "not one inch" of land be returned to the original plantation owners and that interest rates be reduced.[145] The FSLN was prepared to yield to the ATC's demands, and Wheelock, the agricultural minister, spoke at the demonstration, telling the demonstrators, "We know that your demands are just, and this march gives us the confidence to advance and make further transformations."[146]

A few months later, the Junta of National Reconstruction issued a decree legalizing those "wildcat" occupations (excluding any land taken from smallholders), but with full compensation to the previous owners.[147] The two capitalist members of the Junta, Alfonso Robelo and Violeta Barrios de Chamorro, opposed this decree.[148] At the same time that the decision was a vindication for those struggling in rural poverty and a way to make idle lands productive, it was also a move that could not be accepted by the big plantation owners because capitalists' desire to maximize personal profits regardless of social cost was not given preference above the broader needs of society.

Nonetheless, the Sandinistas' commitment to a mixed economy and a strong agricultural-export sector (still dominated by the private big plantations, which was not going to change) remained strong, and the land subject to the latest decree was land that had been left idle and which the owners had refused to rent. Nor did the Sandinistas wish to see more spontaneous land takeovers. Further, the FSLN had begun harassing a Leftist union, Workers' Front, and the union's affiliated party, the Movement for Popular Action–Marxist-Leninist, which had been agitating for more raises for workers, and for all property belonging to the big capitalists to be expropriated. The crackdown was carried to the point of shutting the Movement's newspaper in January 1980.[149]

Although the lands originally taken from Somoza were to be kept intact and developed as state farms, those plantations spontaneously taken over, in particular those taken during the insurrection, were allowed to remain cooperatives. Those cooperatives become known as Sandinista Agrarian Communes, or "producer cooperatives." The Sandinistas also encouraged small and medium farmers to organize themselves into producer cooperatives, and provided access to state lands to landless agricultural workers who agreed to form producer cooperatives and raise subsistence crops. The farmers who agreed to do this were given unused state lands rent-free.[150]

This program also increased the farmland devoted to subsistence crops, mostly corn and beans consumed locally. Cooperatives that grew subsistence crops also received priority for obtaining help in transporting crops by the state.[151] Traditionally, these crops were grown almost exclusively by smallholders and medium farmers, and as smallholders had been pushed off more and more land during the twentieth century, Nicaragua began importing staple crops in the 1950s.

ATC efforts to boost the production of staple crops were so successful that the country had regained self-sufficiency in them by the end of 1980.[152] Food self-sufficiency was another important economic goal, because eliminating the need to import food would shift resources to other areas including helping to maintain a supply of consumer items, much of which had to be imported because of Nicaragua's low manufacturing capacity.

"Credit cooperatives" were another form of organization the Sandinistas encouraged. These types of cooperatives were organized among small and medium farmers who retained and worked their individual plots but collectively negotiated for and distributed loans and, in some cases, also collectively bought their inputs and equipment.

All cooperative forms were voluntary, but it was hoped that, in the long term, these would become a predominant form, although in the early years of the revolution, more attention was given to operating the state farms. As an incentive to form cooperatives, they were given loans with the lowest rates—producer cooperatives were given credit at 7 percent interest, credit cooperatives at 8 percent, non-organized smallholders at 11 percent and medium and large farmers at the Somoza-era rate of 14 percent.[153]

Despite these gains, many cooperatives struggled, with many of the early credit cooperatives dissolving. There were not enough resources or people to give the cooperatives the attention and technical assistance they needed, and many previously landless agricultural workers still wanted to be given their own plots of land. For many, a leap all the way to an advanced form such a cooperative was too much. "[The new member] had to learn collective practices," Wheelock said. "He has to learn a co-operative democracy, how to make collective decisions, whereas before he made decisions on his own. Now he has to be a piece of a complex organization and, at the same time, a collective leader. All this cannot be created overnight—it is an extremely difficult process."[154]

But thanks to the dedication of the earliest-created cooperatives and other politically motivated farmers who banded together, cooperatives became the most productive sector of Nicaraguan agriculture. Smallholders and cooperatives combined covered 14 percent of farmland a year after the revolution, but accounted for 20 percent of production. The capitalist sector (primarily the large plantation owners but also including far smaller middle-sized farmers) possessed 63 percent of the land and accounted for 61 percent of the production. The weak link was the new state sector, which covered 23 percent of the land but only 19 percent of the production.[155]

Reorganizing the state farms proved difficult, and a drop in their productivity had a direct impact, because there would be less surplus available to invest in improvements to the country's pressing social needs. The reduction in productivity was rooted in a reported 30 percent drop in the length of the working day on the state farms.[156] Also contributing was the fact that early attempts at workers' self-management were phased out in favor of top-down management, often by the same managers who were there before the revolution. Workers resented what they saw as a loss of their new rights and a concomitant loss of control over their working lives.[157] The ATC, which won the loyalty of the state-farm workers over unions to its left and right, developed a system of consultative councils to allow the workers to have some say in the management of the state farms, which were organized into a nationwide network of 45 Agrarian Reform Enterprises.[158] These councils had limited powers, however, and state-farm workers continued to seek ways of participating more in management. Nor did it help that there was a shortage of capable managers, and that many farms had been stripped of assets when the revolution was about to triumph.

The state farms did provide significantly increased full-time employment, however. Agricultural workers who continued to work on the private plantations also benefited—minimum-wage laws could no longer be ignored, and private employers had to offer sufficient pay and better conditions to be able to compete with the state sector. Big cotton growers acted more petulantly than some others and, in 1980, threatened to not plant the new crop if they did not received "guarantees" for their private property and access to credit, even though they had been given those all along, in addition to the subsidies they continued to receive and the fact that, although rural wages rose, the Sandinistas did not raise them as much as workers would have liked. Sharp declines in international cotton, coffee and sugar prices in 1981 and 1982 badly hurt Nicaragua, costing needed export earnings, yet the state absorbed some of those declines with its price subsidies—scarce money that went to big plantation owners instead of toward social and infrastructure projects.

Still, cotton plantation owners had been used to having immense power over the rural workforce, paying starvation wages, demanding a workday of 12 to 15 hours during harvest season and having the machine guns of the National Guard at their disposal should anybody open their mouth. The following hysterical answer upon being asked what he thought the government wanted from him following the revolution was undoubtedly not unique among plantation owners: "Obey. Produce as long as I want you to. I'll cut your throat when I want to. Be my servant. Do as I say until I'm ready to dispose of you."[159] That plantation owner seems to have described what his class had expected of its workforce before the revolution. Guaranteed profits and preferential treatment by the revolutionary government was not enough; absolute freedom to exploit others to the maximum possible amount was the real content of the "freedom" that the quoted plantation owner was lamenting had been lost.

Episodes like the threatened cotton slowdown and a need for efficient use of land led to a 1981 law that allowed confiscation of medium and large farms left idle. Much less land was confiscated under the new law than the government had expected, and less than half of it was distributed, leading to grassroots pressure to speed up transfers of land to the landless from the ATC and a new group created out of the ATC, the Union of Farmers and Ranchers.[160] The union, which represented small and medium farmers and ranchers, and the ATC, which would now concentrate on agricultural employees and the landless, were given control of the redistribution by the Agriculture Ministry in 1982, carrying it out in consultation with their membership.[161]

That devolution of control to the local level came at a time when the government began changing its agricultural policies. Although the policies were oriented toward the state farms, generating resentment, there was a vindication as the agricultural sector grew by 10 percent a year from 1980 through 1983,[162] when the Contra attacks on agricultural land became more sustained.

Starting in 1982, the Sandinistas began emphasizing production cooperatives, and the land being distributed was given out in that form. They also distributed some lands from the state sector. As a result, the cooperative (producer and credit) sector was as large as the state-farm sector by 1984, with both accounting for 19 percent of farmland.[163] But because there wasn't enough technical equipment nor enough trainers, 500 of the producer cooperatives were singled out for special state attention for modernizing production.[164] That left out most cooperatives, creating a new source of friction.

Sandinista agricultural policy, however, continued to evolve as it sought ways to meet the conflicting demands of plantation owners who resisted making any concessions and peasants who remained eager for land.

## Competing economic interests grow more irreconcilable, destabilizing the multi-class coalition

As significant as the problems of agriculture were, they probably weren't the toughest problems facing Nicaragua. The country's industry was in ruins, neighborhoods of many cities were in ruins and the country was broke. Although Nicaragua had a small manufacturing export sector, based on a handful of items such as pesticides and resins, there would be little capital available to restart the rest of the economy, must less to begin to build a larger manufacturing sector and diversify the economy.

The $1.6 billion foreign debt that the Sandinista National Liberation Front (FSLN) inherited was the highest per-capita debt of any Latin American country. Much of this debt was racked up by Anastasio Somoza II's arms buying. This debt accumulated so rapidly that the yearly repayments and interest charges owed by Nicaragua increased more than fourfold from 1970 to 1978.[165]

Because Somoza accumulated "odious debt," Nicaragua had a legal basis for refusing to pay. There are precedents for this: The United States government declared Cuba's debt to Spain canceled in 1898 because it was "imposed upon the people of Cuba without their consent and by force of arms."[166] Costa Rica was later declared able to cancel a debt it owed to the United Kingdom because an arbitrator said the money lent did not have a legitimate use.[167]

Yet the FSLN pledged to repay the debt in full except for a minuscule portion. The Junta of National Reconstruction issued a communiqué that said, "It is necessary to undertake an effort to preserve the prestige of our country among the international financial centers by assuming the payment of the international obligations contracted by the private sector."[168] Nicaragua then negotiated a new payment plan, and although the country did receive increased aid from the international community in 1980, it could ill afford to pay back that additional debt. The country received relief for 1979, but such understanding was short-lived—the debts it owed to international creditors rose sharply in 1980 and 1981 to well above the 1978 level.[169]

Simultaneous with dealing with the problems of the economy, the Sandinistas were also trying to cope with the massive poverty in the cities and the enormous job of tackling a grossly inadequate infrastructure. Money that was desperately needed at home was instead shipped off to international bankers to pay down Somoza's debts. In Managua, for instance, where one-fourth of the country's population lived, three-quarters of the city's residents lived in illegal subdivisions without utility lines or in slums where utility lines dumped raw sewage directly into nearby Lake Managua.[170] Yet there were large areas with complete utility lines that had been left empty; these were areas on which Somoza and his cronies were speculating.

Managua was still a patchwork with far too little adequate housing seven years after the 1972 earthquake. In response to the problems of Managua and other cities, a Ministry of Housing and Human Settlements was created, rent control was established, unused land in Managua's center was confiscated and new housing was built in the speculation areas with lakeside slum-dwellers moved there.[171]

One important reason for widespread urban poverty was the wretchedly low wages paid to working people. Wages were raised after the revolution, but a rapidly unionizing workforce wanted to see a faster improvement in their lives. With so much of the country's economy disorganized, and the material base at such a low level, it would take years for Nicaraguans to enjoy a significantly higher standard of living. Having brought a revolution to victory, at enormous cost, and having suffered miserable conditions, many people were not willing to wait years. Or months—a series of strikes, demonstrations and workplace occupations broke out from October 1979 to March 1980. The days of the bosses simply calling in the armed forces to machine-gun their workers were emphatically over.

One of the first of these actions was at a lumber company, a company partly owned by the government and administered by it. The lumber company was a rare producer of export products that had been left undamaged by the National Guard during the insurrection. Daniel Ortega and Victor Tirado, both members of the FSLN National Directorate, arrived the day the strike began, telling the strikers, "The old systems of struggle are not appropriate in this historical moment...If there exists a policy of restraining or limiting salaries, it is because the situation necessitates it."[172] These words were printed on the front page of *Barricada*, the official FSLN newspaper, highlighting the importance of patience that the Sandinistas already believed had become a necessity for the long-term health of the revolution.

Working people in the cities want higher wages, better working conditions and access to consumer goods. Concomitant with these components of a higher standard of living is a desire for not only plentiful food, but low prices for it. Farmers want all those material things, but of course wish to receive the highest possible price for the food they produce—something in direct conflict with the desire of the food purchaser to pay low prices.

Then there is the much more sharp contradiction embedded within the fundamental differences between the classes. The plantation owner and large business owner desire to accumulate money and are willing to leverage that tremendous wealth into domination of society. Reducing payroll and other cost-cutting measures, such as skimping on safety, inevitably become routes toward that accumulation, especially under the impact of competition among capitalists.

Although Nicaraguan big business was guaranteed profits after the revolution, there were now some constraints on the ability of capitalists to profiteer, because minimum-wage laws and other social legislation were now in effect and enforced. There could no longer be a "race to the bottom" because both regulatory and social constraints prevented private business owners from reducing wages and working conditions below certain levels. Faced with a rapidly organized and militant workforce demanding a better deal (backed by a state that, within constraints, was committed to giving priority to those demands) big businesses had to compete not only with each other but with the new state sector to retain employees.

At the same time, the state sector had significant constraints on it, because of the enormous damage done to the economy and the unavoidable period of disruption with so much of the economy changing from private to state hands. The state could, and was, creating a social safety net (a considerable improvement in material living standards by itself) but was in no shape to provide all the wage increases and other immediate concrete demands sought by a politically conscious general population.

Further, the capitalists were not in control of the country, as their counterparts are in any capitalist state, because the representatives of their workers had taken power in a revolution. Nicaragua's working people, with their revolutionary victory still fresh, naturally wished to assume political control, and the FSLN made it clear they would not be handing political power to the capitalists. Capitalists were free to participate politically as individuals, and, given their two representatives on the five-member Junta of National Reconstruction and their ministerial portfolios, they had government representation far above their actual numerical strength among the population. This status reflected the power they wielded through their economic might and the FSLN's desire for their continued participation in the revolution.

Nonetheless, decisive political power was to remain in the hands of the overwhelming majority of the Nicaraguan people, those who made the revolution through their sacrifices and blood. Or at least in theory—power was actually in the hands of the FSLN, which, although a top-down organization, was responsive to its supporters' demands.

This conflict between classes does not have a permanent solution short of the creation of a political system that grants full participation to all people, including the necessary economic restructuring required to create a true democracy. The alternative is that, ultimately, the political process will again be appropriated by those whose control of the economy ultimately guarantees their political dominance.

And that is the contradiction of a "mixed economy." For now, the two sides could agree to co-exist—most capitalists had grown to loathe Somoza and were glad to see him go because the dictator's greed cut into their own ability to accumulate wealth. The FSLN was in power based on its promise to all working people that the state would now be in their hands, enabling them to create a better life for themselves. But the FSLN had come to power with not only landless agricultural workers, struggling small farmers, middle farmers, street peddlers and other urban informal workers, industrial workers, artisans, service employees and the middle classes, all of whom, to differing degrees, suffered under Nicaragua's pre-revolution primitive capitalism. The upper middle class and even some capitalists had been a part of the revolutionary coalition, and they, too, sought to find a place in the new state. The factories had to be restarted, crops tended on the farms, commerce conducted, government offices staffed—in sum, the daily business of life had to return to normal.

The normal life of the country couldn't continue without its economic engines—and those engines were largely in private hands, most critically the agricultural-export sector, without which the country would not be able to pay for imports. In turn, the country was dependent on imports because it could produce little of what it needed, other than its food needs and basic consumer items. Nicaragua had difficulty even meeting its food needs, and had to import some agricultural products, because so much of its land went to export crops, a situation exacerbated by the large increase in cotton production from the 1950s.

Could Nicaragua survive trying to build socialism in a single country? Certainly not. The Soviet Union, underdeveloped and faced with international isolation in the early 1920s, felt it had no choice but to try to build socialism all on its own and could not do so. And that was the largest country, by far, on Earth—it covered one-sixth of the world's landmass and possessed enormous reserves of minerals, raw materials and productive farmland. And what of the richest country on Earth? The United States is not self-sufficient—its energy needs alone dwarf the amount of energy it can produce even with its prodigious industrial might and ample resources. No nation can be self-sufficient, not the Soviet Union of the 1920s and all the more so not a small underdeveloped country of 3 million people.

The economic rupture of expropriating all of Nicaragua's capitalists so early would have been immensely destabilizing to the economy, something that an economy already suffering could ill afford. Additionally, Nicaragua's capitalists had links with the capitalists of the United States, which possessed by far the world's largest military and, as history grimly demonstrates, the willingness to use it. Cuba was able to defy the United States, but at huge economic cost. Nicaragua's population is one-third of Cuba's, nor does it have the protection of being on an island without land borders that enable easy access to invading armies or proxy forces.

Nicaragua could survive an attempt to begin a transition to socialism only with strong links to a strong socialist bloc. But the Soviet Union had provided no help before the revolution, and while it and the Central European countries provided some aid and subsidized trade afterward, it was not nearly enough on which to survive because of the severe disruptions in trade caused by the US embargoes, US pressure on international financial institutions and other Western countries, and often fickle behavior by Western Europeans. Cuba provided what help it could, quietly, but Cuba and Nicaragua together were nowhere near big or strong enough to thrive on their own, isolated from and harassed by their neighbors and outside any supportive bloc.

The leaders of the FSLN could not ignore the likely response of the United States. The US was not happy with the outcome of the revolution (the Carter administration had tried to keep a Somozist system in place until literally the last minute) and an immediate move to expropriate Nicaragua's capitalists would have risked a swift response, possibly in the form of an invasion.

For the moment, however, the United States was not in a position to do anything. Capitalists were well represented on the Junta of National Reconstruction and, during the first months, in the ministries, thereby giving tacit approval to FSLN leadership. Somoza had been expropriated, but because even Nicaragua's capitalists approved that move, the US could not raise that issue effectively—especially as Somoza's family spirited out of the country uncounted millions of dollars that were indisputably the product of plunder. Most importantly, the revolution was a popular one, enjoying massive support. And Nicaragua was armed and ready. Having no illusions about US intentions, the FSLN guerrillas were swiftly converted into a conventional, standing army, and arms were pressed into so many other hands that the FSLN could boast a militia of 250,000 men and women. There was also a network of Sandinista Defense Committees: These were groups organized on the neighborhood level during the insurrection that, after the revolution, helped to provide social aid to their neighborhoods.

Days after the revolution triumphed, an FSLN leader, Luis Carrión, noted that maintaining the coalition that brought about that triumph would be Nicaragua's first defense. "It is preferable to confront imperialism in this way, rather than on the terrain of economic blockade and conspiracies," he said. "But it is clear that this situation will only last for a certain time; the revolutionary process will continue to press forward and deeper, and the two will eventually become incompatible," referring to the two opposite goals of, on the one hand, the FSLN and its backers' desire for a just, egalitarian society featuring economic, participatory and political democracy, and, on the other hand, the capitalists' goal of possessing the power to dominate all aspects of society. "Imperialism will then take up an openly aggressive stance. World experience is crystal clear. We don't have to look far or wide to be convinced this will happen. It is our duty to keep ourselves prepared."[173] Carrión and the Sandinistas did not have to wait long for imperialism's aggression.

The working people of Nicaragua may have seen the new state as their state, but that did not stop them from flocking to the several unions that now existed freely, nor from asserting their interests in the form of demands and strikes. Nonetheless, that did not mean they had ceased to be vigilant against sabotage of the national interest, and just as peasants in the countryside were quick to notice plantation fields left idle, workers in the cities were quick to notice factory owners trying to strip their properties of assets or letting them run down—an increasingly common process that soon became known as "decapitalization."

Big-business decapitalization of factories and other enterprises was financed by the generous credit policies of the government. Although credit was now available for the first time for small farmers and provided to them in large measure, most loan money still went to the capitalist sector. But rather than invest this money, loaned by the government and therefore ultimately capital created by the work of the entire country, many capitalists decided to pocket or launder it. A handy way of doing this was to take the loans, offered in the Nicaraguan currency, convert it into US dollars and send the money to banks in foreign countries. Speculation taking advantage of the differences between the official currency exchange rate and the black-market exchange rate was another method of enrichment.

Carlos Vilas, an economist who worked in Nicaragua, noted the impact of this speculation.

> Evidence exists that the financing handed over [to the private sector] was converted into dollars and taken out of the country through the free foreign-exchange market—a market lacking any effective regulation before September 1981...The result was a transfer of surplus from the public sector toward

> the private sector, and from the productive sectors toward the non-productive ones, contrary to what had been expected. While the nationalization of the financial system limits these movements somewhat, it has not been able to eliminate them totally. Nationalization [of banking and foreign trade] seems not to have been sufficient to eliminate the bourgeoisie's ability to maneuver, an ability that derives from its ownership of the means of production.[174]

Other methods of decapitalization included laying off needed employees; selling machinery or livestock to buyers outside the country; fake or inflated fees and commissions given to foreign firms as another way to send money out of the country; and owners paying themselves large salaries in advance.[175] To provide an example of decapitalization, a plastics factory steadily decreased its exports and made no investments despite receiving a large loan from the government. The factory union noticed this activity and notified the authorities. The factory owner had been trying to slowly bring production to an end by transferring operations to another factory he owned in Costa Rica. In response, the factory was nationalized.[176]

The original law against decapitalization was ineffective—it required such a high level of proof and took the courts such a long time that it was usually too late by the time action could be taken, and the law provided for an incentive to decapitalize because a nationalized property had to be paid for by the government at the full value of the original property even if nothing was left at the time of the takeover.[177]

The demands of the various parts of Nicaraguan society continued to diverge and became increasingly difficult to manage. Daniel Ortega noted this when he said,

> We hope to carry out a difficult task, i.e., maintain political pluralism and a mixed economy in a situation where the class

> struggle is reaching explosive dimensions. The main obstacle to our task, the reason for this polarization, is the lack of flexibility of the political representatives of the private sector. Everything is still possible, but it is important that this group, which does not represent the totality of all private industrialists, understand the revolution as a reality in which we can co-exist. At this time, their attitude only stimulates the class struggle.[178]

Nonetheless, the FSLN continued its policy of providing space for all classes. On the second anniversary of taking power (19 July 1981) a new law strengthening the government's ability to confiscate factories decapitalized or land left idle was implemented. That new law was denounced by big-business interests, but two months later, a state of emergency was declared, under which strikes and land seizures were banned. The war on Nicaragua by the Contras had already started, with destruction of economic targets and killings already becoming commonplace near the border with Honduras. In February 1982, the government provided further subsidies for private agricultural exporters.

Concomitant with these developments, conflicts in the political arena had been sharpening. Alfonso Robelo, one of the two original capitalist members of the Junta of National Reconstruction who had resigned earlier in the year, and his Nicaraguan Democratic Movement, a party based on cotton plantation owners, organized an anti-Sandinista demonstration in November 1980. Counter-demonstrators responded by attacking the Movement's headquarters. In retaliation, the Movement; the leading big-business group, the Superior Council of Private Enterprise (COSEP); and three allied parties and two conservative unions with links to the Movement and COSEP each pulled out of the Council of State, the government legislative body. In answer, 100,000 demonstrators rallied in support of the Junta and the FSLN. More ominously, that same month, the vice chairman of COSEP, Jorge Salazar, was killed in a shootout with police, who were attempting to arrest him. Salazar and three other people who held leadership positions in big-business organizations had been plotting to overthrow the government and assassinate Junta and FSLN leaders.

COSEP had organized the walkout from the Council of State to create a political crisis, but the group's leaders had not consulted other business representatives, and thus there was little immediate fallout from the walkout.[179] But regrouped ex-National Guard officers were already carrying out attacks from Honduras, and the conspiracy involving Salazar was the first proven link between big business and the Contras.

## Creating mass-participation democracy is one task, maintaining it is another

A critical question, one that has very different answers for different sectors of a society, is the one that is most basic and seems, at first, easy to answer, but turns out to be not at all simple. What is democracy? We might formulate an answer to that question in this way: the state of freedom, of being able to control one's own life and to be able to meaningfully participate in the decisions that affect one's life, at community and higher levels. But absolute freedom is not possible, for an action can have consequences for someone else, and one person's freedom can be another person's oppression. So if "freedom" cannot be absolute, then "democracy" cannot be absolute. If one person wishes to hoard much more than he or she needs, that person might well believe he or she possesses a "right" to acquire so much, but if, as a consequence, many others have to go without basic necessities, then at some point this "democracy" becomes distorted and ceases to be a system that functions for all its citizens.

Modern capitalism answers the question in this fashion:

Democracy is the ability to buy whatever you want. That is assuming you have the means to buy it, and it's your fault if you don't. There are ever more varieties of cola and more brands of food on the supermarket shelves—you can buy whichever one you want, or not buy them at all. Framing a definition of capitalist democracy in such utilitarian terms might seem cynical or flip, but is this not what the television and the rest of the mass media blare continually? Oh yes, you can vote for a candidate for political office, but these are advertised in the same way that soap or automobiles are. A catchy label or slogan and, if fate is smiling on a particular candidate, a memorable quip on a televised debate that is widely remembered often seems to be what distinguishes the candidates. Or a candidate or party is selected simply because a worse candidate or party might win unless blocked.

The modern capitalist state reduces the concept of democratic participation to consumerism and participating in an election once every few years. But these are passive "rights," easily reducible to spectacle and providing little control over one's life, nor any real say in how a country is run, how the country's resources are used, how the wealth is created and distributed, nor in determining to what purposes it is used.

A meaningful participation in society means popular control over the institutions of the state and its economic enterprises. In turn, popular control can't exist unless there is a measure of equality among citizens. A billionaire and a homeless person may both have the "right" to influence a senator or member of parliament, but it is the billionaire who gets to exercise that right. And when there are a handful of billionaires and millions of poor people, including legions of homeless people, then the billionaire is far more powerful. Those possessing enormous wealth are able to exert decisive influence over society and put the state at their disposal through an ability to mold public opinion by ownership of the organs of mass media, the ability to buy off potential opposition, privileged access to public officials whom they helped attain office, and power over working people's lives by virtue of the ability to grant or revoke employment, putting most people perilously close to financial disaster, depending on how much or little of a social safety net may exist.

The more social services are reduced, the more dependent on staying in the good graces of the boss one becomes. And what about having enough to eat and access to health care, education and housing? Are these not human rights? There are constitutions among those countries supposedly representing the apex of democracy that are entirely silent on these basic, everyday human needs.

For the Sandinistas, the construction of a democracy could not be separated from the construction of a just society. Speaking on behalf of the National Directorate at the conclusion of the 1980 campaign to end illiteracy, Humberto Ortega said,

> For the Sandinista Front, democracy is not defined in purely political terms, and cannot be reduced to the participation of the people in elections. Democracy begins in the economic order, when social inequalities diminish, and from there spreads to the spheres of government and culture. In a more advanced phase, democracy means the participation of the workers in the running of the factories, farms, cooperatives, and cultural centers. In short, democracy is the intervention of the masses in all aspects of social life, and it must be said once and for all: democracy neither begins nor ends with elections.[180]

Voting was included in the Sandinistas' 1969 Historic Program, along with the promises of land, free medical care and confiscation of Somoza property, and it was reiterated upon the 1979 victory. The 1980 literacy campaign that was the occasion of Ortega's speech was another example of a human right being put into concrete form. About 100,000 volunteers traveled to every corner of Nicaragua, including villages accessible only by mule, to teach men and women how to read and write. The literacy rate of the country was an astonishingly low 45 percent at the time of the revolution; the literacy program was such a success that the literacy rate rose to 86 percent in six months.[181]

Amazing as it might sound, there were capitalists who opposed the literacy program! Of course, there is self-interest here—those without education are easier to manipulate. For Tomás Borge, that opposition was an early "warning sign" of the opposition that was to come: "They very subtly opposed the national literacy campaign, saying that those who couldn't read or write had the right to remain that way and that nobody should force them."[182] How does one "force" someone to learn to read and write? But this is merely an unusually unguarded example of capitalists' crabbed approach to "freedom" and "democracy."

Before the revolution, did Nicaragua's capitalists recoil from the use of the National Guard to violently put down any challenge to them? Did they shed tears at the appalling, vast poverty that surrounded them? Did they worry about the ignorance that such widespread illiteracy carries with it? They did not. In a developed capitalist society arguments against reading and writing would never be made seriously because the system requires a nearly universal literacy, but only a literacy that serves the interest of the capitalists—an education that stresses technology and "business skills," but downplays or ridicules liberal arts and creativity. Thus battles over education assume ever larger roles.

But it is difficult to so simply tailor education, particularly higher education; the better educated are better prepared to participate in decision-making and less willing to accept being shut out of public participation. But an altogether different kind of education can prepare men and women for public participation—the dramatic, unprecedented surge of political consciousness during a revolution. Drawing direct conclusions from their own conditions and equipping themselves with a body of political thought that explained their conditions and showed a way to a better world, Nicaraguans acquired a wealth of knowledge and experience through *doing*. The Sandinista Defense Committees were born out of necessity in battle—nurses and doctors were needed to tend to the injured during the many urban combats, and neighborhoods gradually organized themselves to carry out these tasks and others. These neighborhood committees became the seeds for organizing others as the insurrection grew.

"They were political schools," a community organizer said of the committees. "We'd go to a neighborhood and look for kids to start up baseball or volleyball leagues, or whatever. We'd hold parties on the weekends...And we'd gradually win over youngsters to the FSLN to become guerrilla fighters. That was very effective. We discussed things with them, talked to them and increased their consciousness. I remember I started with five people and ended up with two FSLN squads that attacked the Ticuantepe barracks."[183]

The Sandinista Defense Committees were created across the country and provided a means for participation on a local level—they could provide mutual aid, help with social services, organize self-defense and serve as watchdogs. These were the most basic "mass-participation" groups, and were granted nine seats on the Council of State, the legislative body set up in 1980. There were also the Luisa Amanda Espinoza Nicaraguan Women's Association, the Sandinista Youth and several national unions, each of which was also represented on the Council of State.

More than half of the population of Nicaragua belonged to one or more of these organizations in the early years of the revolution. They were intended as instruments of direct democracy, through which people could work out their issues, press their demands in large groups and have direct influence on the workings of government, social policy and in the workplace. Having participated in a revolution that intended to allow everyone meaningful participation in society, Nicaraguans expected that government decisions would now reflect their wishes and needs. But because the FSLN maintained a top-down structure, failing to make the necessary adjustments from a necessarily clandestine militarized organization leading a dangerous struggle against a murderous dictatorship to a fully democratic post-victory party of government, it imposed the leaders of the mass-participation groups. Although an active membership forced those appointed leaders to continue to represent their interests, the leaders were also sensitive to the policies handed down from above by the party's top body, the National Directorate, leading to tensions and, over time, to reduced rank-and-file participation.

Another setback to the concept of mass participation was the institution of a conventional parliamentary system in 1984, in which representation was based on political parties only. The mass-participation groups no longer had direct legislative representation once the Council of State was replaced by the new parliament. The groups could, and did, continue to act as organized pressure groups and also continued to provide significant social services, but their original roles as agents of direct democracy withered.

In the absence of direct democracy, and the continued concessions and subsidies given to the plantation owners and industrialists, the capitalists slowly but steadily wrested more power for themselves. The capitalists did not hold political power in the revolution's early years, essentially holding a minority position in a coalition government through their government seats, but did hold economic power by virtue of owning most of the economy's means of production. That economic power would ultimately prove decisive.

## The United States funds a terror campaign, assisted by Sandinista high-handedness

Before the Contras became a severe problem, the Sandinista National Liberation Front (FSLN) was able to make progress on a variety of problems, despite the sharp downturn in prices for Nicaragua's main exports in 1981 and 1982 and a simultaneous rise in the cost of imported oil. By the end of 1981, the economy was growing strongly, unemployment had been halved, inflation reduced by two-thirds, the infant mortality rate reduced by close to half, and social security coverage and the availability of medical coverage greatly increased from where these indices stood in 1979.[184] Economic instabilities began surfacing in 1982 as the impact of the Contra war began to take a significant economic toll on the important farmlands and forestry industry of the northern highlands, compounded by the budgetary stress of having to divert resources to military defense and the internal inflationary pressures that had begun to build.

The November 1980 breakup of a coup plot following the shoot-out death of the vice chairman of the Superior Council of Private Enterprise, Jorge Salazar, signaled the beginning of what would become a well-funded, sustained war of attrition designed to bring down the Sandinista government. The 15 armed attacks launched by the Contras in 1981 were just the start—the number of armed engagements in Nicaragua escalated to more than 1600 during 1985.[185]

It had not taken even that long for US hostility to assert itself—the Carter administration's parting gift to Nicaragua was to cut off wheat shipments at the end of 1980. Two months earlier, just before Jimmy Carter lost the US presidential election to Ronald Reagan, one of the most influential business institutions of the Right, the Heritage Foundation, formulated the Reagan administration's policies. "Nicaraguan workers continue to have an emotional attachment to the revolutionary movement," the foundation's report said. "This attachment can be expected to weaken as the economy deteriorates...There are some indications of growing broadly based support to take up arms to overthrow the Sandinista government, and this support could increase as further economic problems develop."[186]

The goal of overthrowing the Sandinistas began to be put in motion on 1 December 1981, when Reagan signed an order that committed the US government to "Support and conduct paramilitary operations against...Nicaragua" (remainder of sentence blacked out).[187] This order was funded with $19 million. The start of hostilities against Nicaragua was whipped up by a "white paper" concocted by the US government that the primary author later admitted had parts that were deliberately "misleading" and "overembellished."[188]

The term "Contra" comes from the Spanish-language adjective for "counter" and is a shorthand for "counter-revolutionary." In every revolution there follows a counter-revolution by those who lost power in the revolution. The core of the Contras was the Nicaraguan Democratic Force, a militia formed by officers of Somoza's National Guard that operated out of bases in Honduras, attacking Nicaragua's north. Military officers on loan from Argentina's savage military dictatorship provided training, along with the National Guard officers. A second militia was the Revolutionary Democratic Alliance, which operated out of Costa Rica, to Nicaragua's south.

The political wing of the Contras was the Nicaraguan Democratic Movement, the big-business party based on cotton plantation owners headed by Alfonso Robelo that pulled out of the Council of State legislative body in November 1980 around the time when the first anti-Sandinista coup plot was foiled. Robelo was one of the two original capitalist members of the Junta of National Reconstruction, the executive body that would lead the government until the 1984 elections. Robelo helped found the Revolutionary Democratic Alliance. After going into opposition, Robelo tried to claim the mantle of Augusto Sandino for himself, a tactic sometimes used by the Contra groups. The FSLN, in 1981, countered the attempted usurpation by banning unauthorized use of Sandino's name or image.[189]

Reagan's order to begin "paramilitary operations" was carried out swiftly: That same month, the US Central Intelligence Agency (CIA) launched "Operation Red Christmas." The unofficial opening act was the bombing of a Nicaraguan airplane in Mexico City as it was being prepared to fly to Managua, an act widely believed by Nicaraguans to have been carried out by agents of the US government.[190] A small Contra group later claimed credit for the bomb,[191] which would have gone off in flight if the plane hadn't been late. The "official" start to the campaign was a series of attacks on 21 December 1981, in which thousands of Contra guerrillas launched attacks in an effort to establish multiple fronts and force the Sandinistas to commit enough defenders to leave Managua vulnerable.[192]

A focal point of the Contra attack was in the northeast of Nicaragua, an area primarily populated by the Indigenous Miskitu people. Many Miskitus were among the Contra guerrillas, although it was their own people whom the guerrillas were attacking. The Contras had been able to recruit Miskitus, and Nicaraguan peasants in the northern highlands, in part by misrepresenting themselves and their intentions and through propaganda by evangelical missionaries. Significant mistakes by the Sandinistas, however, were contributing factors, most notably an insensitive attitude toward the Miskitus and other Indigenous people, and land-reform policies that resisted giving landless agricultural workers their own plots of land coupled with sometimes heavy-handed execution of policy by officials sent from the cities.

The biggest mistake the FSLN made at this time—among the biggest mistakes the Sandinistas made in the 11 years of the revolution—was to evacuate the Miskitus from the war zone near the Honduran border. Although the evacuations were conceived as a measure to prevent non-combatants from being killed in crossfire, it was done without consultation with the Miskitus themselves and without any consideration of their traditions, and left the FSLN open to well-funded propaganda attacks damning (nonexistent) "concentration camps" and similar apocalyptic pronouncements. The CIA deputy director, for instance, claimed that Cubans had occupied part of Nicaragua and were building a military base, citing as his "proof" the appearance of a baseball diamond—an accusation "that caused amusement in Nicaragua, where baseball had been the national sport."[193] Indeed, Nicaraguans have played professional baseball in the United States at the highest level.

The eastern, or Atlantic, portion of Nicaragua comprises a little more than half of its land area, consisting of low-elevation rain forests. It is very thinly populated, with only about 8 percent of Nicaragua's population. Perhaps half of this region's population was Indigenous—primarily Miskitus but also two other, much smaller groups. The other half of the population primarily consisted of Spanish-speaking settlers from the western, or Pacific, side of the country, most of whom had been pushed east by being thrown off their lands by plantation owners. The balance of the population consisted of Black descendants of slaves and escaped slaves (a legacy of British colonial rule) and Jamaicans collectively known as "Creoles." The British had dominated the area until being pushed out by US interests in the latter part of the nineteenth century. The area was undeveloped and isolated from the rest of Nicaragua; not one road reached from the Pacific side of the country to the Atlantic coast before the revolution.

The Atlantic region was characterized by high rates of illiteracy, poverty, infant mortality and related problems; the area had been used for resource extraction for centuries without regard to the Indigenous peoples. Some Miskitus had taken part in Sandino's rebellion, and a Miskitu was one of Sandino's generals,[194] but the Indigenous peoples had little or no integration with the rest of Nicaragua and were almost untouched by the FSLN-led insurrection. When the FSLN took power, it saw backwardness and many problems of underdevelopment characteristic of the rest of the country, but failed to acknowledge the distinct cultural differences of the Miskitus and other Indigenous peoples. The Miskitus had long felt treated as second-class citizens by the Spanish-speaking migrants, and those migrants' attitudes toward the Indigenous peoples was not untinged by superior attitudes. Mutual wariness compounded the cultural gap.

"The initial focus of the revolution placed the emphasis on incorporating the Indigenous labour force into the wage sector, focusing on their extreme poverty, while at the same time interpreting certain practices of co-operative production and some characteristics of community life as survivals of primitive communism," wrote an economist who worked in Nicaragua, Carlos Vilas. "At the same time, this class-based culturalist reductionism reduced coastal ethnicity to its symbolic elements (different religions, languages, values) alone, while disregarding its socio-economic and political dimensions (productive practices, access to natural resources, relations to the power structure.)"[195] An example of the cultural gap was the nationalization of the forestry, mining and fishing industries, which was interpreted by Indigenous peoples and Creoles as the taking away of their traditional rights to access those resources.[196]

These tensions were ripe for exploitation by the CIA and by the missionaries of the Moravian Church. The Moravians arrived with the US Marines in the early twentieth century and never left, exerting a dominating colonizing influence. "The Moravians became influential in the structures of local leadership and created villages that become closed communities with an ideology of resignation to existing conditions and embracing the Moravian cult of obedience to God through the pastor,"[197] is the succinct summation of an organizer of Indigenous activists who made repeated trips to the Atlantic region of Nicaragua, Roxanne Dunbar-Ortiz. "[T]he Moravians worked closely with the US Marines and US fruit companies to turn the Miskitus into a cheap labor force, dependent on imported goods as they abandoned subsistence farming and fishing for purchasing Spam, Wonder Bread, Vienna sausages, and Ipana toothpaste from company stores to which they became indebted—an example of what development theorists called 'the development of underdevelopment.'"[198]

The outbreak of Contra attacks at the end of December 1981 resulted in the local Miskitu population fleeing in all directions. Many left for nearby Honduras, the southeastern part of which is part of the traditional Miskitu lands; similar to many Indigenous peoples, they paid little attention to the national border that ran through their lands. This theater of the Contra wars was in part a civil war, with Miskitus becoming bitterly divided. Those who didn't leave the war zone were evacuated by the FSLN to settlements about 50 miles to the south. Many who did choose to leave went north to Honduras, but found it unexpectedly difficult to return to Nicaragua—they found themselves trapped in camps controlled by the CIA and the Moravians, ruled through force by a Miskitu Contra group.[199]

Although there was some support for the Contras among the rural population of the northern highlands, the percentage of those who joined the anti-Sandinista paramilitary forces was considerably less than that of the Miskitus. Nonetheless, the Contras initially were able to find a foothold in parts of the northern highlands. The leader of the Union of Farmers and Ranchers, the organization of small and midsized farmers and ranchers, Daniel Núñez, noted that FSLN officials sent to the area acted arrogantly—an irony considering the fact that this area had been a prime area of support for the FSLN during the insurrection. "After the triumph, however, many comrades from the Pacific [coastal regions] were sent there who did not understand those peasants," Núñez later wrote. "They called them 'bourgeois' and 'counter-revolutionary,' and they began to harass them... This is why the counter-revolution found space to develop there."[200]

The Contras, however, quickly demonstrated that they had not strayed from their National Guard roots. Their goal was to inflict as much damage as they could, and they made a special target of the cooperative farms of the northern highlands—these were lands farmed by particularly strong supporters of the FSLN and an important backbone of the country's agricultural base. The Contras kidnapped and murdered cooperative members, and destroyed crops and machinery.[201] They also made a point of blowing up bridges and government buildings.

Forced recruitment under duress and kidnapping farmers became the principal forms of recruitment for the Contras. Contra squads would arrive in undefended villages, assemble the villagers and kill anyone they suspected of working for the Nicaraguan government or the FSLN, then demand the remaining able-bodied men join them.[202] Kidnapped boys and men were forcibly kept in Contra camps and those who refused to join the next attack were killed in front of others to set an example.[203] By 1983, one-third of the country's peasant population had been displaced by the war, adding additional economic setbacks, as new infrastructure had to be created in the areas where the displaced resettled, not to mention the disruptions forced migrations inflicted on agriculture.[204]

Funding for the Contras was being increased throughout this period by the United States, and the US government worked to unite the Contra paramilitaries working out of Honduras and Costa Rica, and to sabotage regional peace efforts. John Negroponte (who would go on to be one of the leading hardliners of the Bush II administration two decades later) was the US ambassador to Honduras and in this capacity was the chief enforcer for the US and the coordinator of the Contras. In April 1983, he wrote that the "southern front concept should be pressed hard" in order to pretend that Honduras wasn't the primary staging base for the Contras.[205] The US had constructed a fully developed military infrastructure, including airstrips and a dredged harbor, in eastern Honduras.[206]

Later in 1983, as the "Contadora Group" of regional countries attempted to negotiate a peace plan with the United States, Honduras and Nicaragua, Negroponte's goal was to divide the Contadora mediators, declaring his "greatest coup has been co-option of Costa Rica."[207] Negroponte later ordered the government of Honduras to provide full support for the Contras based there and "do nothing 'irreversible'" to them.[208] Simultaneous with Negroponte's strong-arm tactics, a high-ranking US diplomat, Richard Stone, met with the two main Contra groups in December 1983, then publicly announced, "I have all the information and now I will work on this, the fusion [of the Contras] is difficult but not impossible."[209]

The Sandinistas did learn from their mistakes, relatively sooner in the Miskitu lands and later in the northern highlands. Late in 1983, the FSLN declared a general amnesty for Indigenous people who been imprisoned or in exile, recognizing that its own mistakes had contributed to the problem and that the Miskitus who joined the Contras had been manipulated.[210] A ceasefire was agreed upon, the evacuated Miskitus were returned to their villages and a regional autonomous government was set up for the Atlantic region in which opposition groups participated.

Recognition of rights to natural resources, local leadership, official status for local languages and the right to reinvest proceeds from regional resources locally were among the agreements. The Sandinistas also increased the central government's investments in the region—the 1986 budget for the Atlantic region's investment, on a per capita basis, was ten times more than for the remainder of the country.[211] Nonetheless, tensions remained as Indigenous and Creole leaders subsequently complained both that the pace of implementing the new policies was slow and that the autonomy law did not provide a formula for the allocation of economic resources.[212]

Slowly, the tensions that the Contras had been able to manipulate in the northern highlands were reduced as the FSLN changed its rural policies. The FSLN National Directorate even went so far as to take direct political control of the region's provincial governments, pushing aside the cadres that had mismanaged their work and angered farmers.[213] More direct participation in planning and policy by the local population, a new sensitivity to rural concerns and a shift in land distribution policies to allow land to go to individual families all helped to ease tensions; the 1984 elections that gave the Sandinistas a sweeping victory while allowing full participation for all opposing political parties probably was another factor.

The Contras were never able to establish any base inside Nicaragua (it was due to that failure that they used terror as their primary tactic) and by the middle of the decade, it was obvious that the Contras had little support and no chance of achieving any victory on their own. But the US government would continue to fund and direct the terrorists, and use multiple means of economic aggression against Nicaragua, a policy nexus that severely aggravated inflationary pressures already building because of internal economic imbalances. The ongoing crisis of the Contra war also led to centralizing tendencies, a reversal of Sandinista political pledges that created new irritants in addition to economic difficulties.

### Colonialism is easy to understand when you are on the wrong end, harder from the power end

The Sandinistas, in their difficulties with the Indigenous peoples of the Atlantic, had not reflected on the irony of being on the opposite side of the nationalist equation than they were when, as the representatives of Nicaragua, they encountered the United States. It had not initially occurred to the Spanish-speaking majority of Nicaragua that they, too, walked in the shoes of a colonialist. Larger nations have long dominated smaller nations, but a nation can be both a larger and a smaller nation at the same time, in relation to various other nations.

Nicaragua, a small country of 3 million, was long the plaything of far larger neighbors. But Nicaragua is an artificial construct: the dominant people of Spanish descent are dominant because their ancestors decimated the people who had already lived there. The concept of a Nicaraguan nationality is itself a legacy of colonialism, but also the peculiarities of local geography. Why are there seven countries on the narrow strip of land between Mexico and Colombia? Five of those countries, all speaking the same language, were part of a single Central American Federation. Yet that federation broke apart, unlike Mexico, because communication and travel were so difficult due to the mountainous terrain.

Over time, patriotisms developed, separate in each country created by the breakup. Domination by more powerful countries, and repeated direct interventions in the twentieth century by the latest, and most powerful yet, of those more powerful countries helped forge strong national identities. But those identities did not include the people who were already there, and had seen their numbers decimated through war, disease and plunder—in plain language, through a hemispheric genocide. It is easy to understand a colonial relationship when you are on the wrong end; it is far more difficult to understand this when you are on the power side of the equation.

Nicaragua's nationalism was forged in its colonial relationship to the European powers and then to the United States. Augusto Sandino was able to articulate these feelings, and Sandino's writings and example were strong enough to form a key pillar of a movement decades later. But as the majority Nicaraguans found their voices, found the confidence to create a revolution and to attempt to develop their culture free of colonial domination, the minorities in their midst, the descendants of those Indigenous nations decimated centuries earlier, felt themselves oppressed by those very same people who were so motivated by their own oppression at the hands of the giant neighbor to the north.

The movement of the majority, the Sandinistas, were not oblivious to their country's history nor to the minorities of the Atlantic east, and were acutely aware of the poverty, underdevelopment and cultural trampling endured by the Indigenous minorities. But the Sandinistas had thought and acted in a mechanical manner, and so, initially, inflamed rather than soothed.

"The Left here did not incorporate anthropological concepts because it was married completely to the strict classical scheme: bourgeoisie versus proletariat without analyzing the cultural differences and the 'civilizing' conflicts that took place," is the assessment of journalist and feminist activist Sofía Montenegro, who was one of the leading figures of the official Sandinista newspaper, *Barricada*. "What has happened here is not a mixing of the races but a clash of two civilizations, the Occidental and the Indigenous, in which one imposed itself on the other but was never able to completely conquer it."[214]

Marxism's practitioners have often had a difficult time coming to terms with nationalism. The downgrading of the nation-state was articulated clearly in the movement's most important early document, *The Communist Manifesto* written by Karl Marx and Friedrich Engels in 1848. The two wrote: "The workingmen have no country. We cannot take from them what they have not got…National differences between peoples are daily vanishing, owing to the development of the bourgeoisie, to freedom of commerce, to the world market, to uniformity in the mode of production and in the conditions of life corresponding thereto."[215] Corporate globalization is not a new phenomenon, although of course the process has vastly accelerated since those words were written in the nineteenth century. Despite the increasing cross-cultural fertilizations in which better communications and increased commerce played no small role, the strength of nationalism only increased through the nineteenth century as disunited nations such as Germany and Italy struggled to unify their many pieces and other nations struggled to end their domination by stronger powers.

Those ongoing developments led to a current within Marxist theory that saw a difference between the nationalism of a colonial power and that of a captured nation seeking to throw off the hegemony bonding it. Self-determination for all nations had to be backed and therefore support should be given to independence movements. Independence was the right of all peoples in the name of self-determination. But it was also believed that national struggles were a "distraction" for the vast majority of a nation in that as long as they were oppressed by another nation they would not be able to fight for their emancipation as a class—they would not be able to free themselves of their domination by their native capitalists and aristocracy.

Humans can have multiple motivations, of course. World War I provided an excellent example: Nationalism was whipped up successfully in order to get millions to willingly fight a war that was fought to determine the capitalist division of the world's resources. There was no other way to get those millions to fight. The war had to be brought to an end when those millions started to think more in terms of class, and of their common interests with the soldiers in the opposite trench, rather than in solely national terms. Very different feelings were unleashed, thanks to bitter practical experience.

But the nonetheless still living body of nationalism continued to engender strong debates among the various strains of

Marxism. A forceful argument against advocacy of self-determination of nations was put forth by Rosa Luxemburg, one of the outstanding contributors to twentieth-century political theory. Regardless of how valid a reader finds Luxemburg's argument, she had the moral authority to make it. She was triply oppressed—as a woman in a male-dominated world, as a Jew in a Central Europe riddled with anti-Semitism and as a Pole (until the last days of her life, Poland was occupied and divided among three empires: Tsarist Russia, Prussian-dominated Germany and monarchal Austria-Hungary). Luxemburg adamantly refused to endorse independence for her native Poland, or any other nation.

"[T]he duty of the class party of the proletariat to protest and resist national oppression arises not from any special 'right of nations'...[but] arises solely from the general opposition to the class régime and to every form of social inequality and social domination, in a word, from the basic position of socialism...The duty to resist all forms of national oppression [under an apolitical 'right of nations'] does not include any explanation of what conditions and political forms" should be recommended, Luxemburg wrote in 1909.[216] Generic calls for self-determination don't provide any analysis of underlying social conditions and therefore cannot provide a guide to action.

A further basic weakness of generic calls for self-determination, Luxemburg argued, is that they do not take into consideration the highly differentiated status of nations. "The development of *world powers,* a characteristic feature of our times growing in importance along with the progress of capitalism, from the very outset condemns all small nations to political impotence," she wrote. "Apart from a few of the most powerful nations, the leaders in capitalist development, which possess the spiritual and material resources necessary to maintain their political and economic independence, 'self-determination,' the independent existence of smaller and petit nations, is an illusion, and will become even more so."[217]

Further, within each nation, there exist a multitude of interests that cannot be reconciled. "In a class society, 'the nation' as a homogeneous sociopolitical entity does not exist," Luxemburg wrote.

> Rather, there exist within each nation classes with antagonistic interests and "rights."...There can be no talk of a collective and uniform will, of the self-determination of the "nation" in a society formed in such a manner. If we find in the history of modern societies "national" movements, and struggles for "national interests," these are usually class movements of the ruling strata of the bourgeoisie, which can in any given case represent the interest of the other strata of the population only insofar as under the form of "national interests" it defends progressive forms of historical development.[218]

Luxemburg here argued that movements for national independence or self-determination are effectively controlled by the nation's capitalists who, by virtue of their economic dominance, will control the movement to establish their own narrow rule and thereby subjugate the working people of the nation. Therefore, only the widespread adoption of socialist economic relations can truly free the working people of any nation.

Seventy years after those words were written, the capitalists of Nicaragua indeed sought to control the liberation movement of their country. Nicaragua wasn't fighting for independence in the formal sense, but it was a country with very little self-determination. In the modern system of capitalism, the interests of local capitalists in subordinate countries align with the capitalists of the dominant nation. The interests of the Nicaraguan plantation owners and industrialists were simply to rid themselves of their local dictator, Anastasio Somoza, and establish their own rule. Rule by these local capitalists would be dependent on capitalists from the dominant power, through the medium of multinational corporations, and therefore compatible.

When direct rule of a colonized nation is no longer possible because of resistance, formal "independence" is granted, but a compliant dictator can be put in charge. When the rule of the dictator is no longer viable, a more "modern" form of domination is put in place, the rule of a local oligarchy. The local industrialists and plantation owners are ready to step in and assume domination of society; eager to fulfill what they see as their natural role, they seek to topple the dictator. Nicaragua's capitalists could not do that on their own (they are numerically minuscule) and so joined the rapidly building mass liberation movement in an attempt to wrest the movement's leadership from the Sandinistas. The capitalists were unable to do so because the working people of Nicaragua took an expanded, rather than narrow, view of self-determination, and this understanding led them to swell the ranks of Sandinista organizations.

But although Nicaraguans were aware of their class interests, and that their liberation necessitated changes in their societal institutions and social relations, nationalism played a significant role. Sandinista National Liberation Front co-founder Carlos Fonseca had helped create the FSLN's philosophy by skillfully blending the nationalism of Sandino with Marxism. The importance of nationalism was a consequence of the force of colonialism upon Nicaragua. Therefore, for the colonized, nationalism can potentially play a partly progressive role if it is combined with other political ideas. Another outstanding political theorist, Frantz Fanon, writing in the middle of the twentieth century at the peak of the Global South's national liberation movements, argued that nationalism is an important stage that can't be skipped.

National and racial differences are used to create and continue colonial situations, Fanon argued, and therefore, for the colonized, this divide adds to the complexities of a class analysis.

> In the colonies the economic infrastructure is also a superstructure. The cause is effect: You are rich because you are white, you are white because you are rich. This is why a Marxist analysis should always be slightly stretched when it comes to addressing the colonial issue. It is not just the concept of the pre-capitalist society, so effectively studied by Marx, which needs to be re-examined here. The serf is essentially different from the knight, but a reference to divine right is needed to justify this difference in status. In the colonies the foreigner imposed himself using his cannons and machines. Despite the success of his pacification, in spite of his appropriation, the colonist always remains a foreigner.[219]

The urban and rural working people of Nicaragua could not free themselves without "kicking out" the foreigner (the US commercial interests that dominated their country) and instead institute balanced trading relationships with interests outside their borders. No colonized country can attempt such a liberation without developing a sense of itself as a nation, and that sense of nationhood can't be separated from the differences between the newly awakened nation and the nation that dominates it. During Nicaragua's domination, just as throughout Latin America, the Caribbean, Africa and elsewhere, these differences were pointed to by the colonizing power as justification for the colonial nature of the relationship.

It is the recovery of nationalism, Fanon wrote, that provides the basis for an independence struggle. "A culture is first and foremost the expression of a nation, its preferences, its taboos, and its models...The nation is not only a precondition for culture...it is a necessity. Later on it is the nation that will provide culture with the conditions and framework for expression."[220] It is impossible to skip this stage of development. "Humanity, some say, has got past the stage of nationalist claims," Fanon wrote.

> The time has come to build larger political unions, and consequently the old-fashioned nationalists should correct their mistakes. We believe on the contrary that the mistake, heavy with consequences, would be to miss out on the national stage. If culture is the expression of the national consciousness, I shall have no hesitation in saying, in the case in point, that national consciousness is the highest form of culture.[221]

Fanon wrote as a Caribbean activist deeply involved in Algeria's 1950s struggle against brutal occupation by France, and so it may seem that his expressions of nationalism and equating those expressions with a definition of culture are too strong, but if a people are oppressed on a national basis, then it is only natural that a culture takes on that oppression in that form. It is not necessary to agree with Fanon's elevation of nationalism to such heights to find merit in his formulation. The course of the past century demonstrated the validity of Fanon's theories: Nationalism has been, and continues to be, an extremely powerful political force.

Fanon's integration of nationalism (grounded in profound sympathy for the distortions imposed by colonialism) with Marxism provides a more realistic analysis than Luxemburg's dismissal of national liberation movements. Not because Luxemburg's analysis of the lack of autonomy for the world's smaller nations is incorrect (in fact, it was fully accurate then as it still is today) but because it, to use Fanon's phrase, "skips" an important stage of development. A national consciousness bound together Nicaraguans in the struggle against Somoza, but rather than make that struggle a purely nationalist movement, the Sandinistas built upon nationalism, using it as a scaffolding upon which they erected a much larger understanding of what would be needed for Nicaraguans to liberate themselves. A struggle against an internal dictator, underdevelopment, lack of education and external domination is necessarily, in part, a cultural struggle.

Such a struggle by a national majority, however, inevitably contains differences from the concurrent struggle experienced by national minorities, and these differences, too, are cultural. The Sandinistas, to their credit, did come to understand, in a concrete manner rather than in their previous abstract theoretical manner, that they had to provide sufficient space for their own minority nations to develop their culture, and that those minority cultures had been stultified to a degree more severe than their own cultural underdevelopment.

## Elections instituted by a vanguard party demonstrate support for revolution, despite sabotage

One irony of the Sandinista National Liberation Front's 11 years in power is that it instituted free and fair elections despite coming to power as a vanguard and its capitalist opposition theoretically existing for the sake of contesting elections.

And despite the stream of lectures directed at the FSLN from Washington, the first elections took place five and a half years after the Nicaraguan revolution—the United States took 12 and a half years to have its first election.

Elections had been a part of the FSLN's pre-revolution program, and in 1980 the Sandinistas announced elections would take place in 1985. Ultimately, those first elections would be moved up to November 1984 to coincide with the US elections expected to return Ronald Reagan to office. By moving up the elections, Reagan would be constrained from launching an invasion of Nicaragua because of political considerations imposed upon him due to the need to avoid a military adventure during his own election campaign, nor would he have time to disrupt the Nicaraguan elections after winning the 1984 vote, when there would be fewer political constraints on him.

Work began in November 1981 on a law to create a framework

for the electoral process and to organize permanent government institutions. Debates, negotiations and study committees, which made frequent trips to other countries to study a variety of political systems, were centered in the Council of State, the legislative body that had been set up the previous year. The Council of State included seats for the Sandinistas, representatives of mass-participation groups and other organizations, including political parties, labor unions, professional guilds and employers' associations. Although the FSLN and organizations affiliated to it or in alignment with its political projects held a majority of the seats on the Council of State, it was a widely representative body despite periodic walkouts by capitalists upset that they did not control it. A corollary of Nicaragua's mixed economy was political pluralism—the Council of State had seats for all sectors of society, and permanent political institutions were intended to provide room for a multitude of parties to contest for power.

A Supreme Electoral Council would be created to supervise elections. The future head of the electoral council, Mariano Fiallos, a Sandinista, said in 1983:

> The political parties within our revolutionary process have the right to aspire to obtain political power by the legal means set out in the laws...I believe also that [parties] should not support the return to the political system of the Somozas or any similar political system. Within this framework, political parties should be able to act with all the liberty that the circumstances permit.[222]

Jaime Wheelock, that same year, acknowledged that there would be no return to the past: "We allow any type of opposition as long as it is within the rules of the new economic, social, and political system that we are trying to construct."[223] At this time, the Contra war was raging, and the Contras' US sponsors added their own direct interventions, such as mining Nicaragua's harbors and using explosives to destroy petroleum storage tanks. Somoza's National Guard officer corps formed the backbone of the Contras; it was no more unreasonable for the FSLN to ban the return of Somoza-style dictatorship than it is for Germany to ban a return of the Nazis or Italy to forbid a return of open fascism.

Work on the elections structure was temporarily halted in 1982, following the imposition of a State of Emergency under which political activity was restricted, but although the State of Emergency would remain in place until 1984 as the Contra attacks steadily worsened, free and open debate on the electoral law resumed later in 1982. The first milestone was the passage of the Political Parties Law in August 1983, which guaranteed access to the media and freedom to organize and express any current of opinion, excepting advocacy of the return of the Somoza political system. This law laid out the basis of elections, with a commission to formulate the specifics with input from, and negotiations with, all political parties. The law was followed in December 1983 by a blanket amnesty for all Contras except for the top leadership and ex-National Guard members.

Nicaragua now had 11 political parties, ranging from Marxist-Leninists who consistently criticized the Sandinistas for not expropriating the country's capitalists to hard Right groups affiliated with the Contras who sought a complete reversal of the revolution. Three of the four parties furthest to the Right formed a coalition, the Nicaraguan Democratic Coordinating Committee (CDN), that was dedicated to attempts to delegitimize the elections.

The new political pluralism in Nicaragua was reflected in the fact that there were now two social christian, two liberal and three conservative parties. The christian party further to the Right, the liberal party more to the Right and one of the conservative parties joined the CDN. Only one of these three parties—the Social Christian Party—had any real following. The CDN's real animating force was the Superior Council of Private Enterprise (COSEP), the big-business federation that had been the leading organization of the large agricultural exporters and industrialists since the 1970s. The CDN also included the main newspaper of the Right, *La Prensa,* which provided exhaustive coverage of the coalition, and two national trade union federations aligned with CDN political parties that had a combined total of less than 1 percent of Nicaragua's union membership.

CDN members had sometimes boycotted the electoral talks, and, two weeks after the amnesty for Contras was announced, the coalition issued a nine-point set of demands that included the abrogation of the statutes governing the country since 1979—essentially, a demand to reverse the revolution—and immediate, unconditional negotiations with the Contras.

The CDN positioned itself as the political wing of the Contras, supplanting the Nicaraguan Democratic Movement, which had been subsumed into the CDN. The Sandinistas refused to discuss the demands on the grounds that they either had nothing to do with electoral mechanics or were specious. (The CDN, for example, demanded "trade union freedom" despite the fact that there were six national trade union federations in the country, each of which operated independently.)

Despite CDN objections, talks on the details of the elections went forward. In early 1984, the date of the election was formally set for 4 November, and the CDN, which had long loudly demanded that the election date be moved up, now complained that the election date was too soon. CDN members sometimes boycotted the Council of State debates and began threatening an electoral boycott. Nonetheless, the Council of State passed the Electoral Law in March 1984.

Among the innovations in the new law was lowering the voting age to 16. Some argued that the Sandinistas insisted on the lower voting age because they enjoyed so much support from the young, but others thought it might hurt them because an unpopular military draft had recently been instituted to cope with the Contras. The law set up a hybrid system—a parliament with proportional representation but, instead of a prime minister from the party winning the most seats, there would be a directly elected president with strong executive powers. The new parliament, the National Assembly, would have 90 seats, elected on regional lists, and any presidential candidate who received more than 1.1 percent of the vote would be given a bonus Assembly seat in addition to the 90 contested seats.

Parties needed only 1.1 percent of the vote to earn representation in the National Assembly—an extraordinarily low figure designed to ensure the broadest possible representation. Each party participating in the election would receive a large sum of money for its campaign with no restrictions on raising additional funds, and each party would receive radio and television time. To further ensure clean elections, the Supreme Electoral Council was set up as an independent body and two separate oversight bodies were created, with each participating party guaranteed seats on them. Parties that boycotted an election, however, would lose their legal recognition.

In sum, a system was set up to maximize the participation of small political parties and holders of minority viewpoints—a system with much more representation than the winner-take-all system of the United States. The first task of the National Assembly would be to draw up a new constitution, a process that would include an extraordinarily high level of public participation. In the meantime, the Sandinistas sought to keep their oppositions engaged in the political process.

"We couldn't manufacture equality that did not exist—a two-party system," said Sergio Ramírez, a member of the Junta of National Reconstruction that continued to act as the government's executive until the new government was seated in 1984. "Our great fear was that our tiny opposition parties might not even win any seats in the Assembly, so we chose a system [of proportional representation] in order to permit them to survive and develop for the future."[224] Ramírez represented groups that had participated in the multi-class alliances that sought the toppling of Somoza during the final push to the 1979 revolution; he had not been a Sandinista. But he would become Daniel Ortega's vice presidential running mate in 1984.

Seven parties, including the Sandinistas, ran for office in 1984. The three CDN parties and the other far Right party, the most conservative of the three conservative parties and the fraction that most fanatically represented the largest plantation owners to the exclusion of even their own middle-class followers, ultimately declined to participate. That left the most moderate of each of the social christian, liberal and conservative parties, along with the Nicaraguan Socialist Party, the Communist Party of Nicaragua and the Movement for Popular Action–Marxist-Leninist.

The CDN's intention had been to boycott the election—and the coalition's patron, the United States government, saw to it that it did boycott, as the far Right's lack of participation would be the centerpiece of the Reagan administration's efforts to discredit the elections, in which it was widely assumed the Sandinistas would win a large majority. Arturo Cruz, a banker and COSEP leader who had been a member of the Junta of National Reconstruction before becoming one of the main organizers of the Contras, had this to say in a March 1984 *La Prensa* interview: "[I]n free and fair elections the Sandinistas would win since they enjoy considerable popular support."[225] That same month, Cruz began being mentioned as a possible presidential candidate for the CDN. Still playing coy, the CDN did not register election candidates that summer, even when the Sandinistas agreed to the CDN demand to extend the registration period for an extra month.

Behind the scenes, COSEP had been demanding a boycott of the elections, and sometimes its representatives did so publicly, but the three political parties within the COSEP-dominated CDN insisted they would participate—the Social Christian Party vice president went so far as to announce that boycott calls represented only "private enterprise" whereas "we political parties have a different view."[226] Cruz, however, would later admit that the CDN was "dominated by people who would never go through with an election" and who instead sought "to embarrass the Sandinistas by withdrawing."[227]

The leader of the Social Christian Party, the only one of the three CDN parties with more than a token following, Adán Fletes, had become the coalition's presidential candidate, but on 22 July 1984, three days before the extended registration period was to end, Cruz was named as the presidential candidate under heavy US pressure, with Fletes becoming the vice presidential candidate.[228] The next day, 23 July, Cruz arrived in Managua. (He had been in Washington for three years, where he worked for the Inter-American Bank, a regional institution similar to the World Bank and the International Monetary Fund that was enforcing an embargo on loans to Nicaragua under US pressure.) He was greeted by 300 people—this in a country where Sandinista rallies routinely drew 100,000. Cruz then jettisoned the first eight points of the nine-point set of demands issued in December by the CDN and now put forth only the ninth: immediate, unconditional talks with the Contras.

Simultaneously, the US Central Intelligence Agency brokered a fusion of the two main Contra groups. The fused leadership then declared its goal was to overthrow the Sandinistas within 12 months and that it backed Cruz.[229] The Sandinistas offered to negotiate with Cruz, but he declined, demanding they talk to the Contras first.[230] The remaining restrictions under the State of Emergency were lifted to provide for full campaign participation by all parties and, although the extended deadline to register for the election had passed, the Sandinistas again offered the CDN a chance to run, but the CDN again declined. This back-and-forth culminated in a mid-August declaration by the Contras that they would not enter into talks; the CDN promptly dropped its demand for negotiations with the Contras.[231]

Even before returning to Nicaragua, Cruz had confided to a US reporter: "I'm not really going to run. You know that."[232] Instead, Cruz, upon his return to Nicaragua, went on a nationwide tour in which he regularly denounced "communist dictators"—denunciations that received full coverage in the Nicaraguan media, including on live radio broadcasts. He also was being paid $6000 a month by the Central Intelligence Agency.[233]

Cruz was sometimes given more attention than he deserved, said Sandinista leader Tomás Borge. The CDN

> went out into the streets but failed to attract anyone. Then, with a stupidity unworthy of their cause, some people began to throw stones at them. Four nobodies in a kiosk or a fourth-rate cinema...and they began to throw stones at them! Of course each stone thrown at Arturo Cruz landed not on his head but on the big U.S. [daily newspapers], on all the press campaigns against the revolution. The stones fell in Europe too. I told them: "Cut that out!" and sent the police to restrain them, many times. But what were the police to do—especially as, for all I know, the police themselves had a tremendous urge to throw stones at Arturo Cruz.[234]

The election went ahead, and was declared clean and fair by the dozens of international groups that observed it. Seventy-five percent of Nicaraguans voted, and 67 percent of the vote went to the Sandinistas. The two moderate Right parties, the Democratic Conservative Party and the Independent Liberal Party, came in second and third with 13 and 9 percent of the vote, respectively. The Centrist party, the Popular Social Christian Party, won 5 percent and the three Left parties won 2 percent each. Daniel Ortega was elected president and the Sandinistas won 61

National Assembly seats, with the other six parties winning a combined 35 seats.

The Sandinistas had actually expected to do better, as did the runners-up, the Democratic Conservatives. Perhaps that in itself is an acknowledgment that the elections were as fair as possible. Democratic Conservative leader Clemente Guido was among those accepting the results, and he had only contempt for the boycotters.

"I was fairly happy with the election results, and I don't think that there was any cheating," Guido said.

> The results were within the limits of what could be expected. We received a little less than what we were hoping for: we had expected 30% and we got about half that. We attribute this lower showing to the fact that the [Democratic Conservatives] had to wage its battles on several fronts. We had to fight not only against the Sandinista Front, as was to be expected, but also against *La Prensa*, which portrayed us as a gang of self-interested politicians who were collaborating with the Sandinistas. We also had to deal with the [CDN], which spread the same story around outside the country...Finally, we had to confront the U.S. Embassy [which organized] an attempt to undermine our October convention and keep our party from taking part in the elections.[235]

The Sandinistas would have won decisively without a boycott. If every person who didn't vote had voted for the CDN (a highly dubious proposition), the Sandinistas still would have won just more than 50 percent. It is more likely that the opposition votes that were cast would have been spread among more parties had the CDN participated, and many who hadn't voted would not have voted anyway, simply diffusing the anti-Sandinista vote further.

The Contras increased their frequency of armed attacks in the month before the vote, and economic problems had already developed, yet the Nicaraguan people firmly voted for the revolution despite the war that was being waged against them for supporting that revolution. Although the mass-participation groups would now lose their direct political representation (the Council of State was dissolved with the election of the National Assembly) and labor unrest had sometimes been met with crack-downs, and concessions to the big plantation owners and the industrialists continued, Nicaraguans remained mobilized and saw the revolution as theirs, difficulties and all.

A joint statement issued during the campaign by the two largest unions in Nicaragua, the Sandinista Workers Federation and the Rural Workers Association, provides an idea of the militancy still felt after five revolutionary years:

> With the elections we are going to institutionalize the power of the workers, we are going to guarantee that not one single factory in the hands of the people is returned, not one single sugar mill, not one bank, not one inch of land. We are going to guarantee that the bourgeoisie never returns to power. With our votes, as with our bullets, we are going to guarantee the greatest aspiration of our class, the construction of socialism.[236]

Those votes did contribute to the electoral result they wished for, but that electoral result did not lead to the concrete result they wished for.

### Nicaragua provides another lesson in the high cost of the rich as the revolution is brought to an end

The day after the election, the response from the United States government was succinct: The election was a "setback for peace talks" and would "heighten tensions" with the US.[237] The Reagan administration was as good as its word in this case, pouring more money into the Contras and further stepping up its economic aggression. By 1985, the US embargo on Nicaragua was total and all assistance from multinational financial institutions had been cut off.

The mounting pressures of having to divert internal resources to military defense, scrambling to maintain at least minimal standards of living, shortages and export disruptions resulted in a small decrease in gross domestic product and an increase in unemployment in 1984. Economic indicators deteriorated further in 1985, and inflation reached 200 percent that year. In September 1985, when Nicaragua made its case in the World Court, the country sought compensation from the United States for damages totaling $1.7 billion—a figure near the total value of Nicaragua's exports for the previous four years. Nicaragua lost an additional estimated $1.1 billion during those four years as a result of the drastic decline in prices for its exports and increases in prices for products it needed to import.[238]

The Nicaraguan people, however, weren't buying Contra propaganda. An October 1985 analysis by an independent Nicaraguan news magazine noted,

> The internal anti-Sandinista front the Reagan administration wants to create through the economic crisis is prevented from developing by the many legal channels for dissent. Workers' organizations air their complaints about high prices and low salaries daily, although they tend not to place the blame for the material shortages on the revolution. Rather than translate into paralysis or violence, discontent is translated into an astute search for effective means of survival.[239]

To help people cope, the government guaranteed rations of rice and other basics at low prices (and many people planted vegetable gardens or relied on relatives in the countryside) and the government also abandoned agricultural development projects so it could divert more scarce resources to maintaining living standards.[240] Despite these enormous problems, Nicaragua's composite gross domestic product decline for the period of 1981 to 1986 was in the middle of the pack when compared to the other countries of Central America,[241] each of which followed a capitalist course and none of which faced any of the economic and military warfare directed at Nicaragua. The deep economic recession across Latin America, in turn, made it more difficult for Nicaragua to strengthen trade ties in the region. US banks, flush with deposits from oil-producing countries, aggressively loaned money to Latin American states, but when the Reagan administration pushed interest rates to extraordinarily high levels to attract foreign capital so that it could simultaneously finance a military buildup and massive tax cuts for the rich, debtors suddenly faced unaffordable increased interest costs. Coupled with high oil prices and having to pay for oil in dollars that had risen in value due to US monetary policy, Latin America fell into a debt crisis and a deep recession.

The continued wide support for the Sandinistas is borne out by the popular participation in the writing of a new constitution and the distribution of arms to militias, which supplemented the regular Sandinista army. By early 1986, the Sandinistas had distributed 300,000 rifles to the militias, and a Sandinista National Assembly leader, José Luis Villavicencio, said in defense of the arms-distribution policy: "If our government didn't have the support of the people, don't you think these guns would be turned against the government?"[242]

A clause in the new constitution, put into force in January 1987, declared, "The defense of the homeland and the revolution rests on the mobilization and organized participation of all the people in the struggle against their aggressors" and that the state "should promote mass participation" in national defense.[243] Given the Latin American tradition of militaries overthrowing governments and instituting murderous Right-wing dictatorships, the Sandinistas were not about to make the army an independent institution, separate and isolated from the rest of society.

Following the 1984 election, a 22-member constitutional committee was seated, composed of 12 Sandinistas and 10 from the opposition parties—a much larger opposition ratio than the ratio of their National Assembly seats. The commission met with a wide variety of religious, labor, professional, farmer and other groups, and discussed drafts at 84 open forums throughout the country. Among the opposition proposals that passed were those creating an independent judiciary, institutionalizing the loyalty of the army to the constitution rather than to the Sandinista National Liberation Front (FSLN) and leaving no role for mass-participation groups in the legislative process, ensuring that the National Assembly would remain open to political parties only.[244]

During the consultations at the open forums, a Leftist bloc had proposed a second legislative chamber, a Popular Assembly of Mass Organizations,[245] but opposition political parties were adamantly opposed, nor was it supported by the FSLN. That development was consistent with a constitution that enshrined the mixed economy. FSLN officials themselves readily admitted they had not put together a socialist document.

"The project we're discussing has some Liberal aspects to it, especially as it relates to the structure of the state," said the Sandinista National Assembly secretary, Rafael Solís, as the process was nearing its conclusion. "It follows the classical model of Montesquieu and other pioneers of French liberalism, who conceived of the state as divided into an executive branch and a judicial branch. This one follows the model of Liberal Latin American constitutions."[246] The constitution did improve upon the constitutions of capitalist democracies by enshrining the right to education, health care and housing. It also affirmed the nationalization of banking and natural resources.

Despite those features, the Left opposition agreed that this was a Liberal constitution, which met with their disapproval. The secretary of the Movement for Popular Action–Marxist-Leninist, Carlos Cuadra, complained,

> We consider it bourgeois because it guarantees private property [in the means of production, such as factories and plantations] and...attempt[s] an alliance or conciliation of classes, a social pact which, from the political point of view, is one of the principles proper to Liberal constitutions. The FSLN's quest for consensus reflects this desire for class conciliation...The mixed economy that the FSLN proposes and that appears in the Constitution guarantees capitalist relations of production.[247]

Capitalist representatives, naturally, sought a greater role for themselves in any mixed economy. "We believe that mixed economy means that there must be broad collaboration between private and state initiative; and that state initiative itself must be genuinely mixed," said the leader of the moderate Right Democratic Conservative Party, Clemente Guido. "That is to say, both state and private sectors would participate in state initiatives. For us, then, there must be two types of property: private and mixed (state-private)."[248]

Guido's conception meant a domination of the economy by capitalists, precisely what Cuadra feared. The parties backing the Contras were further to the Right than Guido's Democratic Conservatives, and would have preferred to do away with any public role in the economy and instead have capitalists dictate to the rest of the country.

The FSLN's Solís reiterated a commitment to both state and private property. He declared during the constitutional debates, "The mixed economy is the cornerstone of this revolution...Being realistic, in our time and located geographically as we are in the world, the principle of a mixed economy must be a fundamental one for our revolution. And it is. It's not a temporary or tactical matter."[249]

But that mixed-economy model, under the wrenching stresses of the Contra destruction, economic blockade, continued subsidies for plantation owners and industrialists, and the need to satisfy at least some consumer demands, was already becoming dangerously shaky. Another State of Emergency was put into effect in October 1985 following a massive Contra invasion from Honduras and the uncovering of Contra plots to destroy infrastructure in Managua, and although the decree mainly affected speech related to issues of national defense, it also banned strikes. Labor unrest, while not widespread and often unorganized and spontaneous, had continued since the FSLN implemented an austerity package earlier in 1985.

The austerity package included eliminating subsidies on basic foods and instead scheduling regular wage increases, an increase in prices paid to food producers, a drastic currency devaluation, cuts in government expenditures in all areas except defense, reducing imports of products that could be produced internally, freezing investment in urban infrastructure and cutting the number of government jobs. The FSLN hoped that these measures, while painful, would lead to increased production of basic foods, an end to speculation, the shrinking of the black market, and reductions in the fiscal deficit and in inflation.

Simultaneously, the Sandinistas altered their land-distribution policies, drastically speeding up the distribution of land in the form of individual plots to meet the desires of landless agricultural workers. In part, these programs were designed to improve the lives of the rural population, but those improvements would come at the expense of city residents, who would have to pay the higher food costs and bear the brunt of the layoffs. And all this sacrifice would not yield immediate results, requiring considerable understanding from a country already making major sacrifices, and against the backdrop of a US embargo that not only disrupted exports but cut off both consumer-product and food imports as well as parts and equipment necessary to maintain industry.

"The boycott must serve to push forward the process of rationalizing and reordering the economy," newly elected President Daniel Ortega said. "The whole population should mobilize to take an active role in the preservation, rationalization or replacement of the means of production."[250] The result, however, was an acceleration of inflation (700 percent in 1986), a breakdown in wage indexing and the weakening of the "social wage" that had previously offset inflation. The social wage included not only the greatly expanded social and health services, but workplace commissaries that sold lunch and consumer products at reduced, subsidized prices and the paying of some wages with finished products that could be bartered or sold for necessities.

The debilitating inflation was perhaps the worst economic plague Nicaragua faced. Inflationary pressures had started building soon after the revolution, although they started rising sharply only in 1984. A desire to provide increased living standards, especially in light of the cost paid in the last years before the revolution, fueled consumer demand. "We made an initial mistake of subsidizing normality in Nicaragua, whereas we should have used all resources for development after the victory of the revolution," is the assessment that Tomás Borge made in 1987. "The psychological conditions were there for belt-tightening, so that everyone would have to work even for their food, but instead we wanted everything to be normal…For everything to be normal we began to subsidize transport, food, the producers, everyone, and all the money we received [in foreign aid] went into subsidies rather than investment. Now we are paying the price of that mistake."[251]

That initial under-investment was later compounded by the

cutoff of foreign money and the limited help it received from socialist countries, meaning that the country now had to finance its investments internally. But that mistake was far from the only reason for the inflationary pressures now overwhelming Nicaragua. The FSLN had sought to raise living standards for working people in the cities and the countryside, provided large subsidies to the capitalists and was forced to fund an expensive military effort to defend itself. These factors were further aggravated by the US embargo, with the resulting shortages fueling inflation. The only way to support all these policies simultaneously was to print more money. The 1985 austerity program was designed to "rationalize" these competing interests by reducing consumer consumption through reductions in the earning power of wages while increasing subsidies for capitalists and small farmers to induce more production. But since the capitalists controlled a much bigger share of the economy than the small farmers did, the result was more subsidies for the already rich.

Thus "austerity" meant austerity only for working people—their reduced living standards would pay for the government money that would be channeled into capitalists' pockets. This was the true cost of the social pact among all the classes of Nicaragua.

Despite the concessions and subsidies they received, the capitalists continued to decapitalize and send money out of the country. From 1979 to 1987, the government provided 75 percent of total investment, while the capitalists provided only 14 percent—even though a majority of the investments went to the capitalists, instead of small businesses and small farmers.[252]

Rather than using government credits and subsidies to invest in their businesses, the capitalists put this money into speculation or simply sent it to banks in Miami. One study of the cost of these lost subsidies revealed that they equaled almost 10 percent of Nicaragua's gross national product.[253] Another study calculated the capital flight out of Nicaragua as $625 million during a two-year span from 1986 to 1988[254]—a siphoning that amounted to 15 percent of the country's gross domestic product for the period. This increased rate of capital flight and decapitalization came after the 1985 austerity package that granted the capitalists new subsidies.

The capitalists were quite happy to take public money and stuff their pockets with it; they had no interest in acting as the "patriotic bourgeoisie" that the FSLN still hoped they would become. Borge acknowledged this in the same interview in which he lamented the lack of investment immediately following the revolution. "The bourgeoisie is now a social sector of secondary importance. But it is not eliminated, nor do we plan to eliminate it; quite the contrary, we have made sustained efforts to keep it in existence as an economic force. What is happening is that the political element is also exerting an influence, because the bourgeoisie has not resigned itself to losing political power and is fighting with all its weapons—including economic weapons which threaten the very existence of the economy."[255]

Nicaragua's capitalists had the support of capitalists elsewhere, in particular the powerful capitalists of the United States, which was sponsoring a war of destruction designed to bring down the government of the mixed economy and instead put the capitalists in power. That a return to full capitalism would also mean the effective end of Nicaragua's sovereignty meant nothing to Nicaragua's capitalists. The country would again fall under US dominance but the local capitalists would get a cut of what the US capitalists would extract from the country, would no longer have social constraints on their accumulation of wealth and would have political control of the country in order to drive down employees' living standards, reverse the gains of the revolution and take back the property confiscated by the revolution, including the redistribution of the Somoza family's properties among themselves.

The capitalists believed it was their right to rule, and no

amount of guaranteed profits would divert them from this "right." Nicaragua's capitalists simply acted in their own interest and no amount of Sandinista pleading would induce them to cease acting in their own interest.

Borge continued: "It is no accident that the bourgeoisie has been given so many economic incentives, more even than the workers; we ourselves have been more attentive in giving the bourgeoisie economic opportunities than in responding to the demands of the working class. We have sacrificed the working class in favour of the economy as a strategic plan; but the bourgeoisie continues to resist, sometimes boycotting the economy for the sake of its political interests."[256]

Despite the sacrifices the country made on their behalf, the industrialists and plantation owners continued to seek the ouster of the FSLN by any means necessary. The ongoing Contra war not only caused economic pain; it also caused political pain as the State of Emergency remained in place and centralizing tendencies became difficult to resist because the population had to be mobilized for its defense. The government rations that were stopped in the 1985 austerity package had been distributed at the neighborhood level through the Sandinista Defense Committees, but now there was no need for this local initiative.

In general, the mass-participation groups became more vertical, with their leaders and agendas imposed from above. Centralization was a byproduct of the defense effort, although in part the vertical structures were a lingering remnant of the need for centralization during the pre-revolution insurrection. Even the women's organization, the Luisa Amanda Espinoza Nicaraguan Women's Association, which had been so effective in winning advances against gender discrimination and had vowed it would not postpone its demands, wound up subordinating itself to the defense effort, orienting its activity toward working with the mothers and wives of soldiers. The organization's top-down structure was a major reason for this retrogression, enabling the FSLN National Directorate (still composed of all men) to impose this duty upon the organization by appointing its top leaders.

The Women's Association was far from unique in this development, but the mass groups were able to remain active, assert themselves and become pressure groups that couldn't be ignored during the Sandinista years and when the post-Sandinista government attempted wholesale reversals of revolutionary gains from 1990. "There was a space. What happened was that it was constricted," said Luis Carrión, one of the nine members of the National Directorate that constituted the party's highest authority. "They were under pressure, but people tried to use those organizations and the proof is in the fact that they were authentic...One has to recognize that the revolution taught the people to defend their rights and they have rapidly learned to do that in the new situation [of the 1990 return of capitalist rule]."[257]

Pressure from farmers, agricultural workers and FSLN cadres influenced the party to make the policy reversals that helped eliminate the political spaces the Contras had exploited to gain footholds. From 1985 to 1987, farmland was distributed on an individual basis and, early in 1986, the law allowing confiscation of large farms left fallow was amended to allow midsized farms to be confiscated if left idle or abandoned. This change was implemented in consultation with the organization of small and medium landowners, the Union of Farmers and Ranchers, avoiding friction with the intended beneficiaries. The FSLN also began distributing lands from state farms.

These changes in policies enabled many more formerly landless agricultural workers to obtain land, and small farmers were provided with more services and access to equipment. In addition, the 1985 austerity program did meet the objective of increasing producer prices; the prices of the main subsistence crops, maize and beans, rose sharply in 1985. The Sandinistas also undertook an effort to make cooperatives work better and vowed to base their agricultural policies on what farmers wanted. New policies "should respect campensinos as our main sources of solutions to the problems of agrarian reform, abandoning any type of bureaucratic, highly administrative approaches," said Agricultural Minister Jaime Wheelock.[258]

These developments dried up support for the Contras, and combined with Sandinista military successes, eliminated the ability of the Contras to pose a serious threat to the government. But the Sandinistas faced considerable diplomatic pressure from the United States and several Latin American countries with governments subservient to the US to make concessions to the terrorists. Moreover, economic assistance from the socialist bloc began drying up, while the US embargo and the Latin American recession continued and Western European countries began withholding aid. Mexico and Venezuela had been suppliers of oil to Nicaragua, and when those two governments cut off oil exports, the Soviet Union stepped in. Except for Cuba, support from the socialist bloc had been spotty, failing to offset the economic aggression against Nicaragua from the capitalist countries.

A small state such as Nicaragua could prosper only by being integrated into a large bloc of countries organized on the basis of beneficial mutual relations, but Nicaragua did not have such a bloc to rely on, nor did it make any attempt to help the Leftist insurgencies in its region—in particular, the Faribundo Martí National Liberation Front of more industrial El Salvador. Latin American countries can assert their independence and create economies for the benefit of their own people only by uniting, a process that began to take shape at the end of the 1990s with Hugo Chavez's election in Venezuela and the following decade's series of Left electoral victories.

The Soviet Union, however, cut its oil shipments to Nicaragua by half in 1987; the Soviets had been Nicaragua's last supplier. The Soviet Union's ambassador to Mexico told a Mexican newspaper that the oil cutoff was intended to "demonstrate that [the conflict in Nicaragua] is a conflict within the American continent, and not an East-West dispute."[259] US aid for the Contras, however, continued.

Later in 1987, Nicaragua signed an agreement with Costa Rica, El Salvador, Guatemala and Honduras calling for national reconciliation and an end to all foreign aid to guerrilla groups. In response, the US Congress voted more aid to the Contras and Soviet Union leader Mikhail Gorbachev made it known that all trade with Nicaragua would be cut off unless the Sandinistas agreed to talks with the Contras. In January 1988, the Sandinistas agreed to the talks, lifted the State of Emergency and released thousands of Contras from prison. The Contras responded by demanding the Sandinistas immediately dissolve their government.

There was no longer a pretense on the part of the US government that the Contras were being used as anything other than a tool of harassment. A Pentagon official admitted that "2,000 hard-core guys could keep the pressure on the Nicaraguan government, force them to use their economic resources for the military, and prevent them from solving their economic problems."[260] And the terms of the Central American peace agreement were enforced against Nicaragua, but not against the other countries, a further constriction of diplomatic space.

Talks continued through 1988 with the Contras pulling out of negotiations and launching a series of guerrilla attacks. These attacks were repulsed, so the Contras resumed talks—at one point pulling out again after the Sandinistas substantially agreed to their demands, but this time not daring to resume sustained armed attacks. Although doing so was deeply unpopular among Nicaraguans, the Sandinistas did sign a peace agreement with the Contras, under which they agreed to free jailed National Guardsmen and open a dialogue with all Nicaraguan political parties, including the Democratic Coordinating Committee, the extreme Right coalition that boycotted the 1984 elections and acted as the Contras' political arm.

The US-sponsored terrorism of the Contras cost the lives of 31,000 Nicaraguans and ultimately cost the country $9.1 billion in damages[261]—the equivalent of a little more than four years of its gross domestic product.

As the Contra war lurched toward an end in 1988, the Sandinistas responded to renewed economic difficulties with what may have been the final insult to many of their followers: a full "structural adjustment." During this era, the major international lending institutions, in particular the US-controlled International Monetary Fund (IMF), were fond of forcing devastating austerity plans on countries in exchange for loans. These plans were always the same—governments accepting the loans had to eliminate social safety nets, provide subsidies for the rich, drastically reduce employment through massive layoffs and sell off public property at fire-sale prices to international speculators. Other than the fire sales, the Sandinistas imposed an IMF-style structural adjustment on themselves, only without the often dubious benefit of the loans and the accompanying debt burden. The Nicaraguan government had continued to print money to cover the subsidies it continued to give to its industrialists and plantation owners, and inflation reached an unimaginable 30,000 percent in 1988.

This self-imposed structural adjustment was intended to bring a halt to inflation by drastically reducing the supply of money and eliminating the difference between the official and the black-market currency-exchange rates. It also sought to stimulate exports and end speculation. Speculating on the difference between the exchange rates was the most profitable activity in Nicaragua—much more profitable than production.[262] Another set of traders took advantage of Nicaragua's overvalued currency (the cause of the difference in the official and black-market exchange rates) by buying products cheaply in

Nicaragua and selling them for far more in neighboring countries.[263] This behavior also contributed to shortages.

Smugglers and illegal traders also profited from speculation—speculators would buy beans, an important staple crop, at rates higher than the official price, then smuggle the beans into city markets and sell them for far above the official selling price, making huge profits and drastically increasing the cost to buyers, hurting consumers further as beans were largely diverted into the expensive black market.[264] This parasitic behavior enriched speculators at the expense of people doing productive work and effectively reduced city residents' living standards.

The steadily eroding value of the Nicaraguan currency was itself, in part, a result of speculation—in this case, international speculation. Under the modern capitalist system of leaving the exchange rates of national currencies to be set by the world's financial speculators through trading, small countries are vulnerable to rapid fluctuations in the value of their currencies. Speculators seeking new windfall profits can easily attack a currency, driving down its value. The small country whose currency is under attack can respond either by using its monetary reserves to buy its own currency on international markets (propping up the exchange value but also draining its own financial resources and leaving it less able to meet its own needs), or allow the value of its currency to plunge.

Although an orderly decline in a currency's value can have the short-term benefit of making a country's exports cheaper abroad, thereby stimulating an economy by theoretically boosting the volume of its export sector, a weakening currency also makes imports more expensive, reducing living standards for a country dependent on imports, and drives up the cost of its foreign debt, since its currency will now buy less of the creditor country's currency, in which it must pay its debt. The consequences of a steadily weakening currency were another source of difficulties for Nicaragua.

A further contribution to inflation was the inefficiency of Nicaraguan big business. As an example, small rice growers were 30 percent more efficient than large rice growers in terms of production yields compared to the costs of inputs.[265] Export subsidies to the plantation owners played a role, as well. The hyperinflation took a huge toll—wage raises couldn't keep up with inflation, until Nicaragua reached the point that a street peddler selling soda made more money than a government minister. Many office and government workers simply became street vendors. The significant loss of such white-collar workers further hurt productivity. But street vending or other informal work had its hazards—only 20 percent of informals were able to earn sufficient, stable incomes.[266]

The first round of the structural adjustment, in February 1988, was not immediately unpopular because it included, concurrent with a drastic devaluation, a new currency with limits on how much could be converted without a reasonable explanation of how the money was acquired, thereby liquidating illicit profits and also effectively confiscating money funneled to the Contras by the United States. In strong contrast to traditional structural adjustments administered by Western lending organizations, the Sandinista government's austerity plan also included wage increases and price controls.

But the hard side of the austerity soon was felt, and, in June, a second, harsher round of austerity was implemented. This time there would be no sugarcoating. The Nicaraguan currency was again drastically devalued, this time all the way down to the black-market rate. Prices were deregulated, and while private-sector wages were also deregulated, government salaries were only raised 30 percent. This meant that, coupled with the currency devaluation and price rises, government salaries were effectively cut by five-sixths.[267] Interest rates were also raised.

The purpose of these moves was to further wring out inflation and stimulate exports. But the effect of this structural adjustment would be to transfer income from employees, consumers, small farmers and small producers to the big agricultural exporters.[268] More subsidies for the rich. And salaries became so low that, for the lowest-paid government workers, the cost of commuting to work was greater than their wage. Private-sector salaries would also be driven down by this program.

A summation was perhaps best put forth by a plantation owner who was the head of a big-business organization who said, "I support and applaud the new measures of the Sandinista government."[269]

The goal of stopping inflation was met, but at the cost of 30 percent unemployment, reductions in living standards and decreased consumer consumption, sacrificed to boost exports.

Under such conditions did the Sandinistas seek re-election in February 1990. A proposal to raise the bar to gain entry into the National Assembly to 5 percent from the 1.1 percent bar of 1984 in order to encourage the many small parties to merge into larger, stronger groups met swift disapproval by those many small parties; therefore the 1.1 percent threshold was retained.

With 21 parties registered to run in the 1990 elections, they would have to unite to have a chance to defeat the FSLN. This they did—14 parties jointly ran a single presidential candidate and agreed to form a National Assembly bloc calling itself the National Opposition Union (UNO). The UNO was a heterogeneous coalition, consisting primarily of extreme Right and moderate Right parties, but also including the Centrist Popular Social Christian Party, the single-issue Central American Integrationist Party, the Nicaraguan Socialist Party and the Communist Party of Nicaragua.

The only thing that united this grab-bag of parties was a desire to defeat the FSLN. The UNO was dominated by industrialists and big plantation owners itching to reverse all the gains of the revolution that the Sandinistas hadn't already reversed themselves, in particular to take back state properties and farmlands distributed to the formerly landless. The Socialists and Communists gave cover to the capitalists by joining the UNO, yet another opportunist move by them.

The Socialists, still consistently following Moscow despite the dissolution of the Soviet bloc that was now under way, were, in their own way, at least consistent—the Soviet Union had abandoned the Sandinistas and had never believed in a Nicaraguan revolution, reducing the Nicaraguan Socialist Party to cooperating with capitalists while patiently waiting for "objective conditions" to someday align in its favor.

The Communists were a split from the Socialists and followed the unfortunate custom of orthodox communists of combining more-revolutionary-than-thou phrase-mongering with opportunism and capitalist collaboration in actual practice. The Communist Party of Nicaragua had proclaimed itself in favor of carrying the revolution further by demanding expropriation of capitalists, yet here they were in a bloc with those same capitalists, who were seeking the complete negation of the revolution.

The UNO decided to run Violeta Barrios de Chamorro as its presidential candidate, rather than one of the hard-line leaders of the larger Right parties. Chamorro was the widow of Pedro Joaquin Chamorro (the newspaper editor whose 1978 assassination helped to broaden the insurrection), and she had sat on the Junta of National Reconstruction in the first months of the revolution. The UNO platform was vague other than its denunciations of the FSLN that mirrored those of the US government and its call for a strengthened role for the private sector.

Chamorro herself had no defined political outlook—perhaps this helped her win the nomination. The UNO campaign really boiled down to one item: Vote for us so there will be no more Contra war and the United States will again give us aid. The Contras had not demobilized despite the peace agreement that had called on the other Central American states to insist on that demobilization; that detail was simply ignored. The Bush I administration that had succeeded Ronald Reagan in Washington wanted the Contras kept in reserve. The US government also supported the UNO with millions of dollars in funding.

The Sandinistas offered no radical change of direction, instead reaffirming its commitments. "We Have Won, and Now We Go Forward" was the FSLN's campaign slogan, echoing a platform that reaffirmed the mixed economy, with an intention of strengthening cooperatives in both small industry and farming. Their austerity program would continue, however, with renewed emphasis on increasing production. To that end, the FSLN sought to increase cooperation among private enterprise, the state and workers, although the owners of those private enterprises continued to be a bulwark of the opposition. The FSLN platform did say the unpopular military draft would continue, although in smaller numbers; the Sandinistas had already reduced the defense budget by one-third in 1989.

The 1990 election effectively was contested between the UNO and the FSLN, with little support for two independent Left parties, the Movement for Popular Action–Marxist-Leninist and the Revolutionary Unity Movement (composed mainly of ex-Sandinistas), nor for the bloc of a Miskitu regional party and the Center-Right Social Christian Party. And that choice between the FSLN and the UNO came down to a referendum on the 11 years of Sandinista government. The UNO promised Nicaragua would have peace if it won. But a UNO victory would also mean the end of the revolution, bringing to power a leadership bent on turning back the clock.

In a conventional capitalist democracy, a governing party that had overseen an economic implosion such as what the FSLN had presided over would surely be swept from office. But this was revolutionary Nicaragua—life had become very hard for the small and middle farmers and ranchers, the agricultural field hands, the street peddlers of the informal economy, factory workers, office workers and other city residents for whom the revolution was supposed to have been made, but these groups also retained significant gains that couldn't be attained in a capitalist country. More than 100,000 rural families now had land, credit and assistance that had never been available to such people in the past; ordinary people had means of organizing themselves and pushing for their needs through unions, youth groups, women's groups, professional associations and other organizations; a social safety net, in the form of health clinics, expanded educational opportunities and other benefits remained in place; and employees in state businesses, while not having the control from the floor they wished to have, were working for the greater benefit of society rather than for the benefit of a rich boss. The UNO was intentionally vague in its campaign, but, realistically, the revolution's advances would be in jeopardy with an opposition victory.

Nonetheless, exhaustion from war and fear of hostilities renewing were very real, significant factors. Polls indicated a win for the FSLN, albeit much narrower than in 1984, but the UNO scored a surprise victory. It is reasonable to presume the polling was accurate but that the FSLN's support was not firm, with many voters deciding to switch their vote at the last minute. Decisions to vote out a government often aren't reached until nearly the last minute; a decision to oust a party with such good will in its past would have been more difficult than most to oust.

Chamorro won 55 percent of the presidential vote to Ortega's 41 percent; the Revolutionary Unity Movement's candidate was the only other one to get a bonus seat in the National Assembly by reaching the 1.1 percent threshold in the presidential vote. UNO parties won 51 National Assembly seats to the FSLN's 39. A Miskitu regional party candidate won the only other seat.

Ortega quickly moved to affirm the results. "Of course, the FSLN as a political party fought with all its strength and organizational capacity," he said. "But the most global objective of the

FSLN has not been simply to win elections as a party, but to open up political space which has never before existed in Nicaragua, to enable the people of Nicaragua to choose between different options. So the great victory of the FSLN, of the revolution, of the people of Nicaragua, is that with these elections we are reaffirming democracy for Nicaragua."[270]

One way of looking at the results is this: The most powerful country on Earth, with 100 times the population and a monstrous military budget, had used its overwhelming might to overpower a small country, and left no doubt that it was willing and able to resume its offensive against them if Nicaraguans did not vote as they were told to, yet 41 percent decided to go ahead and vote against those explicit instructions, with all the attendant risks, in defense of their revolution and their country.

Nonetheless, a defeat is a defeat, and those threats from the North were not without effect. A political scientist who had worked with the Sandinistas captured the weariness engendered by constant pressure in this account: "The day after the election, a woman vendor passed by me sobbing. I asked her what was wrong, and she said, 'Daniel will no longer be my president.' After exchanging a few more words, I asked whom she had voted for. 'Violeta,' she said, 'because I want my son in the Sandinista army to come home alive.'"[271]

But it is also true that the revolution's agents had done much to reintroduce the hardships of capitalism—the rich were again getting richer, and at the quite obvious expense of everybody else. The revolution's theoretical beneficiaries were still suffering from structural adjustment, imposed by their own revolution. Thus the still sharp differences between the FSLN and the UNO were significantly blurred.

The Sandinistas had made their first significant mistake when they agreed to pay back the odious debt with which the Somoza dictatorship had saddled the country due to its arms buying; this helped to lock Nicaragua into the world capitalist system with its deck stacked against underdeveloped countries. The mixed economy, in which the country's capitalists maintained links with more powerful foreign capitalists, enabled the capitalist sector of the economy to steadily impose its will. The austerity program of 1988 was the result. The widespread struggle to maintain a minimal standard of living and a promise of peace was enough for a majority of Nicaraguans to vote against the agents of the revolution, there not being enough of the revolution remaining for them to decide otherwise.

## Nicaragua's women take some steps forward and some backward, mirroring historical experience

The severe difficulties of the 1980s forced social issues to the background. Or provided the excuse to sideline them, depending on your perspective. This experience was a vivid one for the women of Nicaragua. But not a unique one.

Women had participated in the Sandinista National Liberation Front as guerrillas starting in 1967 and fought in significant numbers—many FSLN commanders were women and women made up perhaps a third of the guerrillas. That fact alone created more social space for women, according to Dora María Téllez, a prominent commander during the insurrection and later vice president of the first legislative body, the Council of State, and then minister of health. "During a revolutionary process ideas change," she said. "Women participated in our revolution, not in the kitchens but as fighters. As political leaders. This gives us a very different experience."[272]

The FSLN, in its 1969 program, had declared its intention to establish "economic, political and cultural equality" for women. Upon taking power, the FSLN not only abolished outrageously antiquated laws such as those that had forbidden women to own land and allowed farm workers to collect their wives' salaries, but took concrete progressive steps that weren't so easy, such as banning the display of women's bodies in commercial advertising.

Although women made major advances during the Sandinista years, full equality proved elusive as advances were followed by setbacks—the same movement that implemented the advertising ban sponsored a beauty pageant nine years later, and abortion was still formally illegal.

Feminism and full equality for women have been difficult problems for Leftist movements. There are multiple reasons for the slow rate of development in women's equality, including the pervasive male privilege across societies and the reluctance of men to give up their privileges; the tenacious hold on social constructs this gender power imbalance has consistently had on virtually all aspects of human relations; the need of dominant classes in capitalist societies to maintain deep divisions among working people to enable the dominant to blunt challenges to those in dominant positions; and a tendency among Leftist movements to believe that eradicating capitalism and building socialism will automatically result in full equality for women. This last factor has tended to lead to an overly mechanical view of equality for women—pass a few laws, get women into the workplace and *voilá!* we shall have equality. Experience has proven this is very much not so.

A reluctance to discuss, and a trivialization of, the "personal realm," particularly when that "personal realm" is seen as the province of women (not unknown among many on the Left) has played its part as well. This is nothing new. In 1920, for instance, as revolutionary Russia was able to begin stabilizing itself, Bolshevik chief Vladimir Lenin expressed his indignation to a German Communist leader, Klara Zetkin, during a Kremlin discussion of how the parties should approach work among women. "I have been told that at the evenings arranged for reading and discussion with working women, sex and marriage problems come first," Lenin said with disapproval. "They are said to be the main objects of interest in your political instruction and educational work. I could not believe my ears when I heard that." Lenin proceeded to denounce what he called "this superabundance of sex theories," declaring, "There is no room for it in the Party, among the class-conscious, fighting proletariat."[273]

Lenin offered a simplistic solution to this issue: "Nowadays all the thoughts of Communist women, of working women, should be centered on the proletarian revolution, which will lay the foundation, among other things, for the necessary revision of material and sexual relations," he said to Zetkin. "For the German proletariat, the problem of the Soviets, of the Versailles Treaty and its impact on the lives of women, the problem of unemployment, of falling wages, of taxes and many other things remain the order of the day. To be brief, I am still of the opinion that this sort of political and social education of working women is wrong, absolutely wrong. How could you keep quiet about it? You should have set your authority against it."[274]

This conversation came in the context of Lenin asking Zetkin to take over organizing the work of a commission that was to report on women's issues at an upcoming Communist International world conference. Setting aside that Zetkin agreed with Lenin (according to her own memoirs), if a victorious revolution is supposed to grant women the right and space to organize and agitate on their own issues as they see fit, why should a trivialization of the "personal" be allowed to squelch discussion, and a mechanical reduction of women's issues to purely economic questions be tolerated? The personal realm, as it was directly experienced by women (including sexuality, desire and marital relations) cannot be disconnected from the larger issues of pervasive discrimination against women and the resulting imbalance of power between men and women. Unfortunately, overly mechanical attitudes became standard among many Leftist currents, but seem particularly strong among orthodox communists.

The Soviet Union achieved many revolutionary advances for

women in the 1920s, such as legalized abortion, rights to divorce and birth-control clinics, but by the end of the 1930s abortion had been made illegal and Josef Stalin was handing out motherhood medals to women who bore five children. An even more underdeveloped country, China, also took an economic approach after its revolution. During the Great Leap Forward in the early 1960s, the Chinese government facilitated women entering the workforce, particularly in small-scale industry it organized in the cities at this time. Because of a shortage of child care facilities, the lack of material means to provide adequate health care and birth control, and the persistence of traditional social attitudes, particularly in the countryside, economic advances for women were circumscribed.[275] The emancipation of women was also seen as an "evolutionary process" contingent on advances in household gadgets reducing household drudgery.[276] Although such advances were undoubtedly welcomed, feminists would point out that making housework less difficult does nothing to change imposed gender roles, instead reinforcing the notion that work in the house is a duty of women.

Chinese society placed a low value on this domestic labor, therefore it was not counted toward collective work and those who had to perform the domestic labor—women—had their ability to participate in political or social activities curtailed. The Chinese government believed the way out of this impasse would be increased production, with a resulting increase in family income enabling the buying of household labor-saving devices.[277] Neither this situation, nor its proposed solution, were far from unique to China, of course, and parties in highly developed countries were little better, and sometimes worse.

The French Communist Party, to take another example, still attempted to appeal to women as mothers and housewives into the 1960s, seriously moving to modernize its line only after the 1968 student uprisings. Despite increasing agitation among women, translating a more modern approach into its practice took until the late 1970s, when communists were in an electoral bloc with the Socialist Party.[278] At this point, the French Communist Party acknowledged that, although the subordination of women was codified in class-based capitalist society, socialism would not bring automatic equality and therefore further struggle for gender equality would be necessary under socialism. But as the Socialists became the much stronger part of the electoral bloc during the campaign, the Communists fell back on strictly economic themes, throwing overboard appeals to women based on anything other than as workers.[279] The party attempted to build a women's organization, but the party leadership still expected women activists to retire from party duties and devote themselves to raising children upon becoming mothers and stifled internal discussions, ultimately driving many women away.[280]

Sexual politics in revolutionary Nicaragua were similar to those faced in other countries. "A Nicaraguan woman—like a Nicaraguan man—is lively and intelligent and has the ability to give and take," noted Nora Astorga, the prosecutor of war-criminal National Guardsmen who later became ambassador to the United Nations. "But historically, society has been much harder on us; we've had less opportunity. It's a centuries-long history, a millennium of exploitation, during which we've carried an image of ourselves that isn't real. But since the men in our society, for so many reasons, have been irresponsible in paternity, women have had responsibility for their children's lives. This means that the real Nicaraguan woman isn't the one who wants to cry in the face of her tragedy, the apathetic woman. That was clear in the struggle against the dictator."[281]

Those ingrained attitudes against women, Astorga said, were also present in the FSLN and couldn't be eliminated overnight. "It's a problem of education, and we've eradicated it neither in the years of struggle nor in the years of our revolution," she said. "We women have had to struggle against it as well as the men.

Because at times we're more machista than they are and we educate our daughters different from the way we educate our sons. It's a very complicated problem."[282]

The FSLN created a cross-class women's organization in the early 1970s, and, when the revolution triumphed in 1979, the group became the Luisa Amanda Espinoza Nicaraguan Women's Association (AMNLAE). The mass-participation organization for women was named for the first Sandinista woman believed to have been killed in action, in 1970. The group was involved in organizing demonstrations, leading strikes, running safe houses and other work during the insurrection, and was determined to advance women's rights after the revolution. Unions, such as the Rural Workers Association, also fought and won improvements, such as 20-week maternity leave with partial pay, child care centers and communal kitchens.

During the early 1980s, when the Council of State was Nicaragua's legislative body, the AMNLAE introduced bills to advance equality, which it could do because it held a seat on the Council. The bills would be discussed in open forums around the country, and amended based on those discussions. But this advance was still subject to a counterweight—the bills would have to be signed into law. At one point, AMNLAE introduced two bills. One, a symbolic bill that required both mother and father to sign permission for a child to travel outside the country instead of only the father, passed easily. But the other, a more substantial bill that would require non-custodial parents to pay child support, was opposed by Sandinista men who claimed the proposed law would endanger national unity in the face of the Contra war by "dividing" men and women. The bill was not signed into law.[283]

Already, a few years into the revolution, liberation of women was being put on the shelf. Issues of gender equality were soon set aside: the FSLN leadership (its nine-person National Directorate all men) began pressing AMNLAE to become a support group for the mothers and wives of soldiers. The AMNLAE representative on the Council of State did argue for women to be included in the military draft, but the FSLN argued that women were needed at home due to the still insufficient level of social services provided by the state, and that a draft would only add to their burdens. Women countered that protective legislation was discriminatory.[284]

Sandinista army officials had sought AMNLAE help in combatting Contra bands in 1981, but only as cooks and similar support roles despite the fact that many women fought and commanded during the insurrection; the association responded by forming all-women's battalions to fight but were met by FSLN and broader social resistance.[285] It was not until 1986 that women were admitted into the army as volunteers, and only in noncombatant roles. Traditionalist male attitudes had reasserted themselves and the Sandinista leaders seemed reluctant to incur the disapproval of the Roman Catholic Church, which continued to bitterly oppose any advancement by women.

Despite setbacks, the AMNLAE held a nationwide series of 600 meetings in 1985 in which a range of issues, including sexuality, discrimination in the workplace and abuse by male partners, were discussed. Women observed that, although they made up 62 percent of the electorate, their issues were not a priority.[286] Nor did the FSLN open up its leadership ranks to women in large numbers—when the new government was sworn in following the November 1984 elections, only one of the 18 ministers was a woman and only 12 of the FSLN's 61 National Assembly members were women. Still, that was much better than the opposition parties—only one of the other 35 seats was held by a woman.

Women continued to organize and did earn gains in the 1987 constitution: a declaration of "absolute equality of rights and responsibilities" of men and women in the family, equal pay for equal work, a requirement that men contribute to child support, and a provision for sex education in schools. But equal work was frequently not available and courts found it difficult to enforce child-support rulings against men who fathered many children without the financial means to support them.

The Sandinistas also refused to legalize abortion. The FSLN leaders sometimes insisted that the Roman Catholic Church was too powerful to oppose, but President Daniel Ortega also sometimes said that the patriotic role of women was to increase the population to replace the soldiers killed by the Contras.[287] It would not have been unreasonable to expect the FSLN to pass legislation that the reactionary Roman Catholic cardinal of Managua didn't like—that was the point of the revolution! "Liberation theology" priests, and Catholics who subscribed to that dissident interpretation of church ideology, had long been one of the pillars of the Sandinista movement. Three priests served as government ministers through much of the 1980s despite the disapproval of church officials and being forced to choose between their clerical and political callings by Pope John Paul II.

Followers of liberation theology formulated a progressive interpretation in purely economic matters: acknowledging that horrific social inequalities and poverty are the consequence of unbridled greed freed of constraints under unfettered capitalism, thereby directly challenging traditional church dogma that portrays poverty as a "natural" condition that will always exist regardless of human development. They nonetheless clung to reactionary church dogma in many social matters, including those concerning women.

This had the effect of seriously retarding progress for women. How could a woman be considered a fully independent human being if she did not have control over her own body? The situation was serious enough that, in the late 1980s, more Nicaraguan women died as a result of illegal abortions than for any other reason. Nonetheless, legal abortions for medical reasons continued to be made extremely difficult to obtain.

The Sandinista leadership had shown itself incapable of putting its theory into practice when it came to women. The AMNLAE accepted the FSLN National Directorate's mandates, setting aside the battle to end discrimination despite having vowed they would not let that happen. Because the leadership of the AMNLAE was imposed from above by the National Directorate, ignoring the demands of the rank-and-file was easier; the organization's leaders did not have to put themselves to a vote. Perhaps another factor was a decision on the part of many AMNLAE activists to shift their work to other organizations. A 1987 analysis on the status of women reported that many AMNLAE members believed that "they could be more effective as a movement with a presence throughout other existing organizations than as a separate or autonomous organization. They argue that because women are a part of every sector of Nicaraguan society, it does not make sense to continue to function as a women's organization per se."[288]

Although other, smaller independent groups took up the cause of abortion rights and other rights, and injected activism into other places, the lack of an effective mass base advancing feminism made further advances difficult, and may have contributed to an atmosphere of backsliding in which women could be paraded at beauty contests. Women made giant strides under the Sandinistas, and went backward after the Sandinistas lost power, but the revolution nonetheless failed to take fully seriously the emancipation of women.

A Sandinista leader, Mónica Baltodano, a military commander during the insurrection and later one of the first five women to be named to the National Directorate in 1994, said in 1991, a year after the FSLN was voted out of power, that she regretted not pushing more. "I believe that we were too timid in many things and this was as much because of the perpetual threat under which the revolution lived as because of a series of internal mechanisms in our political life," Baltodano said. "Many struggles were not even begun because of fear of the war and of U.S. imperialist attacks...At this moment, I feel that we are very much behind and disjointed and that our women's organization is very weak. This lost ground in the struggle for women's rights is lamentable."[289]

But the activist Margaret Randall, who spent two decades in Nicaragua and Cuba, laments that concerns for issues such as sexuality were dismissed as "elitist" and that, all too often, the womanizing of male political leaders and other sexist behavior was not challenged. "We always *said* that the personal is political (and even broke with the old left over this conviction), but to put the idea into practice proved much more difficult. The superhuman effort required to survive when people are forced to confront an enemy so much more powerful than they, produced a situation in which there was rarely time for reflection," Randall wrote shortly after the FSLN lost power. "One result of this inability to clearly see how male mechanisms clouded our perceptions was our acceptance of male privilege—even in some of its grossest manifestations—*as if it had nothing to do with an ongoing analysis of social change.*"[290]

Heterosexual women at least could be visible. Lesbians and gay men had many more restraints on them, and the FSLN was unprepared to understand their liberation. Lesbians and gays who worked in the FSLN or with the government were transferred to break up their relationships or fired from their jobs and expelled from the party.[291] In at least one case, however, a group of gay men in an AIDS education group expelled from the party talked to Téllez, at this point the health minister, who quietly gave them logistical and material support to continue their educational work combatting AIDS and homophobia.[292] Despite official disapproval, Sandinista gays and lesbians marched with black T-shirts and pink triangles in the 1989 parade marking the tenth anniversary of the revolution, making sure the leadership would see them.[293]

Homophobia had been worse in Cuba—although there is a large gay and lesbian community there, until the 1990s it had to remain underground because the ruling Communist Party was unable to advance from traditional societal homophobic attitudes. A successful revolution does not mean that oppression of homosexuals will magically go away; it, too, has to be fought for.

Changes in social structures sometimes run ahead of changes in social attitudes. In an ideal world, everybody will march together to bring freedom to everybody. In practice, uneven development has stunted the development of revolutions that have declared themselves socialist and those that have some socialist elements while remaining an experiment in a mixed economy. But although these revolutions have failed to bring full freedom to women, they made more rapid progress than possible in capitalist democracies. Gays and lesbians have fared less well, a shameful blot on those revolutions and a painful reminder that a socialist revolution carries with it the potential for providing the space for full freedom, but not a guarantee.

A different reminder, that progress can be rapidly reversed, was quickly administered after the Sandinistas were voted out of office.

## The Sandinistas learn to become an opposition force, but develop into a conventional party

Upon being voted out of office, Daniel Ortega quickly accepted the results, but said the Sandinista National Liberation Front would not go quietly into the night, vowing that the FSLN would "rule from below." That vow was kept, as Sandinista unions organized strikes and the FSLN scrambled to pass legislation designed to institutionalize what it could of the revolutionary gains, mainly allowing farmers to retain the plots of land that had been distributed to them.

The Sandinistas had made a critical mistake by not codifying the revolution in the constitution and in the law, and now had no choice but to organize as the Right was poised to take back everything it could. Despite their electoral promises, the National Opposition Union (UNO) government in its first months brought renewed hyperinflation and intensified structural adjustment—another new currency, 25 devaluations of the currency, an increased budget deficit, layoffs, threats of mass firings of strikers, armed gangs throwing small farmers off their land and a scheme to sell off state property at fire-sale prices. Nor did the promised aid from the United States materialize: The US pledged less than one-third of what the UNO claimed Nicaragua would receive if it were elected; the US then failed to pay most of the reduced pledge.

As bad as these developments were, it would have been much worse without the organized Sandinista resistance. The FSLN was the only coherent mass political party in Nicaragua, and the contradictions within the heterogeneous UNO began splitting apart the coalition's 14 parties as soon as it took office. And it took office with some constraints on it, following two months of negotiations with the FSLN during the transition period following the February 1990 elections.

Although new President Violeta Barrios de Chamorro was able to get the Contras to disband in her first year in office, she generally left the details of government to her ministers, a group of technocrats headed by her son-in-law, Antonio Lacayo. The fractious nature of the UNO and Chamorro's lack of identity with any specific political grouping provided space to enable Lacayo and the ministers to determine government policy, much to the anger of the more conservative, Contra-aligned elements within the UNO that had wanted a swift retribution. Lacayo's willingness to negotiate with the FSLN headed off more serious disorder but further infuriated the UNO hard-liners. Lacayo also sealed a deal with Humberto Ortega, allowing the Sandinista defense minister to remain as the head of the army in exchange for Ortega resigning from the FSLN. A series of strikes that shut down Managua, led by Sandinista unions, helped bring Lacayo to the negotiating table. Now freed of a duty to support government policies, the mass-participation groups and unions formed by the Sandinistas quickly asserted independent, more militant stances.

Three more mass strikes took place in 1991 and another in 1992, but these were defensive in nature, merely slowing down the UNO. The new capitalist régime set up a privatization corporation to sell off Nicaragua's 351 state enterprises. For now, the telephone, electric and water utilities were left alone, thanks to union pressure, but all other state businesses were split into more than 1500 pieces; all but 39 of which were sold.[294] Pressure from Sandinista unions, although unable to stop privatization, did result in an agreement that workers would receive a 25 percent share of sold-off enterprises, although the new owners often tried to muscle the workers out of their share.[295]

The privatization of farmland was more difficult for the UNO to carry through because much of the land distributed by the Sandinistas was now in the hands of more than 100,000 families; additional land was in the hands of collectives. The FSLN, assuming it would never be voted out, had not created new, formal titles for the distributed farmland. Failing to do so provided an opening for attempts at reclaiming their old (stolen) lands by former National Guardsmen, the Somoza family's cronies and large landowners who left the country after cashing out the value of their land through mortgages—these attempts at land grabs were often made through violence. Unused land in the cities that had been held for speculation by the Somoza family and their cronies had also been distributed, for badly needed housing for poor families. The FSLN dealt with these problems by passing three laws in the interregnum between their election loss and the new government's swearing-in: Law 85 granted property rights to occupants of houses belonging to the state, but not more than one property; Law 86 gave rights to occupants of urban land, also not more than one property; and Law 88 granted full property rights to farmers on confiscated land.

Chamorro, after taking office, issued two decrees providing for the selloff of land held by the state or by cooperatives, and setting up a commission to examine all other lands; these decrees were backed by attempted evictions by former Somoza-era landowners and UNO-backed invasions of cooperatives, some carried out by Contras.[296] The Nicaragua Supreme Court ruled the decree setting up the commission illegal; Chamorro's acceptance of the ruling headed off a constitutional crisis and gave a victory to small farmers.

A series of constitutional crises developed during Chamorro's six years in office, usually caused by her own UNO National Assembly group. The FSLN alternated between confrontation and cooperation with Chamorro, but by 1993 a bloc of a disciplined FSLN and the moderates within the UNO gave Chamorro a narrow legislative majority, further frustrating hard-liners. The new alignment also made it more difficult for the hard-liners to change the constitution, although the UNO did have considerable latitude in interpreting it because so much of the 1987 work was written in ambiguous language.

Nor did constitutional or legal niceties stop big capitalists from attempting to run roughshod over everybody else. And in this, they had a big helper in an extreme Right Republican Party senator in the United States, Jesse Helms. He demanded that all aid to Nicaragua be cut off unless all properties previously held by US citizens immediately be given back or paid for at full value—and Helms included people who were naturalized US citizens but were Nicaraguan citizens at the time they abandoned their property. Two of Luis Somoza's sons, both naturalized US citizens, were among those pressing for former family possessions.[297]

Many of these rich landowners, who constituted about 70 percent of the total claimants, had taken out mortgages on their property, then took the money out of the country. The Sandinistas paid off those mortgages, but Helms now demanded that the rich be paid a second time for their old properties. Helms' loud demands suited the Bush I administration, which was in power in Washington during the first two Chamorro years and withheld aid to underscore its demand for faster privatization. During the subsequent Democratic administration of Bill Clinton, little changed—Helms was effectively the US secretary of state as the Clinton administration allowed him to dictate foreign policy to it and the Senate meekly allowed Helms to run amuck.

The Chamorro government succeeded in passing a November 1995 law that allowed those in small houses or farming small plots of land to remain, with the government compensating the former owners. Larger properties had to be vacated unless the former owner agreed to be compensated by the government. The new law exempted only properties that had been directly owned by the Somoza family. National Guard war criminals and Somoza family cronies who received their properties through corruption, violence or theft, and those who had already received money for their property through mortgages or previous Sandinista government compensation, were fully covered by the new law.

To pay for all of this, the Nicaraguan telephone company, Telcor, would be privatized, with the proceeds used to pay off those making compensation demands. Proceeds were also to be used to redeem bonds the Chamorro government had previously given to others seeking compensation, although most of these bonds had been sold by the former property owners to financial speculators.

The sudden rush to sell off Telcor was also the result of

pressure from the International Monetary Fund, the US-controlled bank that was now dictating Nicaraguan policy on behalf of multinational corporations. Telcor had just invested a large sum of money to upgrade its infrastructure and expand its service, and it was healthy enough to do so by using its own revenue while also generating a substantial profit for the state.[298] This profit was large enough to subsidize the Nicaraguan social security system, a benefit that would be lost with privatization.[299] The Chamorro government handled this sale in an opaque manner, as it had the fire sales of state companies earlier. No public accounting of the state selloffs was made, but it was rumored that the cost of the process was greater than the sales earned for state coffers.[300]

The deals the Chamorro government made with the International Monetary Fund and World Bank were also secret, with no consultation with the National Assembly. But what details did leak out revealed provisions violating Nicaraguan law and international treaties, including revoking labor rights directly in violation of International Labor Organization treaties to which Nicaragua was a signatory.[301] The International Monetary Fund and World Bank also demanded that cooperatives be converted into single-owner properties[302]—in effect ordering a supposedly sovereign country to adopt US-style economic relations.

And economics was not the only sphere in which the country went backward. Sixty of the 70 rural infant service centers established by the Sandinistas were closed, with the remainder offering reduced services. Women were particularly hard hit by layoffs despite a woman sitting in the presidential seat. And a Christian fundamentalist-inspired "anti-sodomy" law made homosexuality between consenting adults a crime punishable by three years in prison.[303]

The FSLN, meanwhile, also had to grapple with a serious internal issue: Just what was it to become? Remain a movement with a restricted membership? Become a conventional political party that works only within the system with an open membership? The party did not decide this fundamental issue when it held its first-ever congress in 1991, but did begin to democratize its internal structure by instituting secret-ballot elections for party posts; making congresses regular events, which would elect party leaders; and investing an expanded and no longer appointed Assembly with final decision-making powers on some issues previously the province of the National Directorate. But it also acted to create a single leader by creating the new post of general secretary and electing Daniel Ortega to it—enabling Ortega to remain firmly at the party helm for the next quarter-century.

The 1994 congress featured an open struggle between a majority headed by Ortega that advocated that the FSLN be an extra-parliamentary organization that intimated a possible return to armed struggle and a minority led by former Vice President Sergio Ramírez that wished the FSLN to be a strictly in-the-system political party. The majority group won ten of the 15 seats on the newly expanded National Directorate, with the minority group winning four seats.[304] Five of the 15 members of the National Directorate were women—the first time women had sat on the body and a response to the anger resulting from no women getting elected to the body at the 1991 congress. The 1994 congress passed a rule requiring that at least 30 percent of party positions be held by women, and this was also reflected in the composition of the Assembly.

But just as the militant union members who thought a Sandinista victory in the 1984 national elections would lead to socialism wound up with a very different result, those who thought they had voted at the 1994 congress for a militant party carrying on a struggle also wound up with a very different result. By the time of the 1996 national elections, the FSLN had become a conventional party. Ortega was once against the FSLN presidential candidate, but his vice presidential running mate was a cattle rancher and member of the Superior Council of Private Enterprise (COSEP), the big-business federation that had so vigorously opposed everything the Sandinistas had done to improve the lives of the poor and the middle classes.

The FSLN's 1996 election campaign not only attempted to appeal to business with a "neoliberal-lite" campaign, but also promised to name a Contra commander with a brutal reputation as interior minister, which would put him in charge of the police, and to negotiate with reactionary Roman Catholic Cardinal Miguel Obando y Bravo over the defense and interior ministries. Obando y Bravo had also bitterly opposed the Sandinistas every step of the way.

The 1996 election was essentially a two-ticket race between the FSLN and the Liberal Alliance, a coalition of the Constitutional Liberal Party and three other Right parties. The Liberal Alliance was headed by José Arnoldo Alemán, who ran on his record of paving the streets of Managua as mayor, but who in reality was the main hope of the extreme Right, which hoped that he would succeed in imposing the full neoliberalism that Chamorro had not accomplished in her six years as president. Most of Alemán's financial support came from Nicaraguan and Cuban exiles in Miami.

The UNO had completely collapsed, with most of its parties running individually this time, among a bewildering total of 24 parties. The election was marred by irregularities, with the reported results giving Alemán's Liberal Alliance a comfortable victory over the FSLN. A handful of parties trailed far behind.

Upon taking office, Alemán immediately demanded that the 1995 property law that allowed those living in small homes or farming small plots of land to stay put be scrapped. Violent forced evictions were attempted, with Right-wing judges signing eviction orders in defiance of the law. The Sandinista grassroots countered with strikes and street barricades. The Liberal Alliance and the FSLN ultimately negotiated a new settlement that weakened the 1995 property agreement but gave Alemán's backers less than they wanted. Poverty continued to worsen under Alemán, who added a Somoza touch when he and his cronies pocketed much of the international aid given to Nicaragua after its Atlantic coast was devastated by a hurricane.

Alemán's vice president, ex-Contra and former COSEP head Enrique Bolaños, was the Constitutional Liberal Party candidate for president in the 2001 election; presidents could no longer be re-elected. Ortega again ran for the FSLN. This time, the race was sure to be between these two because Alemán and Ortega had signed "The Pact" in 1998, a deal that changed electoral rules to favor their two dominant parties. The deal also guaranteed Ortega immunity from facing charges that he had sexually abused his stepdaughter for a decade—a scandal that neither the FSLN nor the Nicaraguan courts would address.

Alemán, meanwhile, had continued to run Nicaragua on behalf of multinational corporations and under the pressure of US dictates, with the result that the country's foreign debt grew to six times its gross domestic product; 70 percent of Nicaraguans lived in poverty; unemployment skyrocketed; large numbers of urban workers fell into the informal sector; and a sharp reconcentration of land and wealth into a few hands occurred due to a lack of credit and no protection from cheap imports, which devastated small farmers, cooperatives and small industrial shops.[305] The International Monetary Fund had dictated a long list of privatizations, mass layoffs, wage freezes, institution of fees for education and abolition of directed credit; in addition, the IMF demanded that payments to foreign lenders be made a priority to the point that half of Nicaragua's government revenue went to paying foreign debt during the 1990s.[306]

Although the FSLN National Assembly bench was becoming more accommodating to these policies, the United States government was determined that Ortega be defeated in the 2001 elections. To that end, it pushed for strong Conservative candidates to drop out in favor of Bolaños and allowed Bolaños to be photographed handing out US aid. Nicaraguans feared that the US would once again wage economic war—the new Bush II administration was stocked with veterans of the Reagan administration, including John Negroponte, who had directed US policy in the region as ambassador to Honduras. Those fears were reinforced by Bolaños ads linking Ortega to religious fundamentalist terror financier Osama bin Laden, then the number one enemy of the United States following the 2001 terrorist attacks in New York and Washington. Bolaños came from behind to win.

Ortega and the FSLN did return to power in the 2006 election, helped by the Liberal vote splitting between two parties. Neoliberalism had continued to devastate the country—1 million Nicaraguans were now working in Costa Rica,[307] and privatizing the electricity company had led to a collapse of the power system, featuring daily blackouts of five to ten hours a day.[308] On returning to office, Ortega began a Zero Hunger Campaign and canceled a planned privatization of the water system. But he kept other Constitutional Liberal economic policies in place and pledged to pay the large debt owed to speculators who bought bonds issued to bail out banks that collapsed under murky circumstances in 2000 and 2001. Ortega also cut a deal with Obando y Bravo to make abortions illegal under all circumstances. As a result, pregnant women with life-threatening illnesses, including AIDS, malaria, cancer and obstetric complications, are routinely refused treatment because doctors can be sentenced to years in jail if the fetus dies, regardless of medical professionals' intentions or what standard medical protocols deem appropriate treatment.[309] It is not known how many women have died from denial of care or due to botched illegal abortions because the Ministry of Health does not gather such information.[310]

A critical factor in the trajectory of the FSLN's first time in power was that there was little in the way of a socialist bloc to provide assistance; the decision to create a mixed economy with a reliance on the capitalist sector flowed from that situation. The Sandinistas, however, had done nothing to break out of their isolation by not helping Leftist movements in neighboring countries.

Ortega's second administration—a personal government in contrast to the collective FSLN government from 1979 to 1990—made no attempts at social or economic transformation, merely to somewhat ameliorate the conditions of the worst-off. The FSLN became a deeply dichotomous party—Ortega's thundering revolutionary rhetoric and a mobilized grassroots following regularly taking to the streets existed simultaneously with continued austerity to meet the expectations of international financiers and an ever growing number of Sandinista leaders with long years of service going back to the insurrection against Somoza denouncing the betrayal of the revolution.

The contradictions of Ortega's rightward move inherent in that dichotomy is illustrated by Ortega obtaining approval of the International Monetary Fund for an economic plan that cut health, education and social projects at the same time that he received generous aid from the Left government of Venezuela—aid used to give pregnant cows to small farmers, but which has not been used to create permanent jobs and much of which appears to have been diverted to Ortega and his closest associates with no public accounting.[311] Ortega also moved to suppress his critics, acting with particular vehemence against Sandinista oppositionists and women's groups.

Despite Ortega's moves to the right, the FSLN return to power occurred at a time when a growing Latin American bloc was attempting to find a course different from neoliberalism. A country-by-country account of the 1980s and 1990s would make for dreary reading as increasingly unfettered capitalism devastated the region. A 1990 report by the Pan American Health Organization estimated that almost one in eight children born in Central America would die before age 5.[312] A World Bank report said debt-service payments by developing countries to industrialized countries exceeded inflows of money by $43 billion in 1989 alone.[313] That figure increased to $120 billion in 1999.[314] And while there are almost no studies of how much wealth has been taken out of Latin America by the corporations of the North, estimates range up to a staggering $950 billion for the period 1975 to 2005.[315]

And all this was done through a mixture of invasions, military coups, dictatorships and terror. Several hundred thousand were killed to achieve these neoliberal results, with devastating psychological results in addition to the material distress. A clinical director in Chicago who treats Guatemalan survivors of that country's four-decade dirty war, in which 200,000 were murdered, summarizes the grim toll: "The terror in my country created a psychological disaster. So many were tortured to death that if the army took you into custody and you survived, those in your circle would suspect you as a traitor. Women who were raped were too ashamed to return to their homes. Families and communities just disintegrated. Even though we [now] live in [the United States], most Guatemalans still dare not organize themselves in public."[316]

The US government played a major role in enabling successive Guatemalan dictatorships of the Right to sustain their reign of terror by training police and military units in techniques to hunt down dissidents, better organize surveillance operations and improve the national system of recording fingerprints—evidence for all of which was uncovered when the archives of the disbanded Guatemalan national police were opened.[317]

The wave of Left governments that began taking power across South America starting with Hugo Chávez's sweeping 1998 electoral victory in Venezuela over the country's two traditional capitalist parties opened new possibilities. A US-assisted coup in 2002 by Venezuelan big business failed—Chávez's supporters put him back into power after two days. Argentina is another country that began shaking off neoliberalism, after unfettered capitalism and International Monetary Fund-style structural adjustments reached their logical conclusion with the implosion of the country's economy.

The fascistic military dictatorship of 1976 to 1983 laid waste to the Argentine economy while the junta killed, tortured or forced into exile hundreds of thousands. A civilian president, Carlos Menem, imposed an austerity program in the early 1990s in conjunction with selling off state enterprises at below-market prices. This fire sale yielded $23 billion, but the proceeds went to pay foreign debt mostly accumulated by the military dictatorship—after completing these sales, Argentina's foreign debt had actually grown.[318] The newly privatized companies then imposed massive layoffs and raised consumer prices. By 1997, about 85 percent of Argentines were unable to meet their basic needs with their income.[319] During this period, Argentina's debt steadily mounted, leading to a scheme under which the debt would be refinanced. A brief pause in the payment schedule was granted in exchange for higher interest payments—Argentina's debt increased under the deal, but the investment bank that arranged this restructuring racked up a fee of $100 million, the latest in a series of financial maneuvers that shipped a billion dollars to investment banks in ten years.[320]

It all finally imploded at the end of 2001, when the government froze bank accounts and the country experienced so much unrest that it had five presidents in two weeks. The people had no choice but to find solutions themselves, and did: They set up barter clubs and created a system of popular assemblies, creating dual government structures at the local level. Workers in factories that had been shut down simply took them over, restarting production and converting them into cooperatives. A new president, Néstor Kirchner, suspended debt payments. These developments soon reduced unemployment from 50 percent to 17 percent and created a budget surplus.[321] The outstanding debt, however, remained—had Argentina resumed scheduled payments in 2005, interest payment alone on the debt would have consumed 35 percent of total government spending.[322] Kirchner announced that Argentina intended to pay only 25 percent of what was owed and any group that refused negotiations would get nothing; in the end, Argentina paid 30 percent.

A country had finally stood up to the International Monetary Fund and the capitalist powers that animate it. But only a large enough bloc of countries collectively strong enough to stand against the offensives of the capitalist world will be in a position to ultimately transcend capitalism.

## Notes to Chapter 4

1 Henri Weber, *Nicaragua: The Sandinist Revolution*, page 4 [Verso, 1981]; Neill Macaulay, *The Sandino Affair*, pages 21–2 [Quadrangle Press, 1971]

2 John A. Booth, *The End and the Beginning: The Nicaraguan Revolution*, pages 20–1 [Westview Press, 1985]

3 Weber, *Sandinist Revolution*, page 7; Macaulay, *Sandino Affair*, pages 22–3

4 Juan Gonzalez, *Harvest of Empire: A History of Latinos in America*, page 75 [Penguin Books, 2000]

5 Macaulay, *Sandino Affair*, page 22, quoting Henry F. Pringle, *The Life and Times of William Howard Taft*, Vol. II, pages 678–9 [Farrar & Rinehart, 1939]

6 Gonzalez, *Harvest of Empire*, page 75

7 Macaulay, *Sandino Affair*, pages 29–30

8 Weber, *Sandinist Revolution*, page 13

9 Macaulay, *Sandino Affair*, page 106, quoting Carleton Beals, "With Sandino in Nicaragua," *The Nation*, 22 February – 11

April 1928

10 ibid, page 74

11 ibid

12 Weber, *Sandinist Revolution*, page 14

13 ibid, pages 15–16

14 ibid, page 16

15 Macaulay, *Sandino Affair*, page 253, citing the testimony of Abelardo Cuadra, an officer at the meeting who later defected to Costa Rica, and accounts of Anastasio Somoza and Alberto Medina

16 ibid, pages 253–6

17 "Just the Facts: US Military Interventions," *Envío*, February 1990 (English-language version, online at www.envio.org.ni), citing US congressional record, 23 June and 10 September 1969, and updated by *Envío* staff

18 Gonzalez, *Harvest of Empire*, page 133; George Black, "Central America: Crisis in the Backyard," *New Left Review*, September–October 1982, page 7

19 Gonzalez, *Harvest of Empire*, page 133

20 ibid, page 135

21 Black, "Central America: Crisis in the Backyard," page 14

22 Clifford Krauss, *Inside Central America: Its People, Politics and History*, page 185 [Summit Books, 1991]; Stephen Schlesinger and Stephen Kinzer, *Bitter Fruit: The Story of the American Coup in Guatemala*, page 68 [Doubleday, 1982/Harvard University Press, 2005]

23 Schlesinger & Kinzer, *Bitter Fruit*, page 68

24 Krauss, *Inside Central America*, page 185

25 ibid

26 "Just the Facts," *Envío*

27 Black, "Central America: Crisis in the Backyard," page 12

28 Schlesinger & Kinzer, *Bitter Fruit*, page 70

29 ibid

30 ibid, pages 70–1

31 Gonzalez, *Harvest of Empire*, page 135, citing Carol Smith (ed.), *Guatemalan Indians and the State: 1540 to 1988*, pages 141–2 [University of Texas Press, 1992]

32 James F. Petras and Morris H. Morley, "Anti-Communism in Guatemala: Washington's Alliance with Generals and Death Squads," *Socialist Register*, 1984, page 263; Gonzalez, *Harvest of Empire*, page 136

33 Petras & Morley, "Anti-Communism in Guatemala," page 263

34 Schlesinger & Kinzer, *Bitter Fruit*, page 73

35 Gonzalez, *Harvest of Empire*, pages 136–7; Petras & Morley, "Anti-Communism in Guatemala," page 264

36 Schlesinger & Kinzer, *Bitter Fruit*, pages 74–5

37 Krauss, *Inside Central America*, page 30

38 John Loftus and Mark Aarons, *The Secret War against the Jews*, pages 357–61

39 Alexander Cockburn and Jeffrey St Clair, *Whiteout: The CIA, Drugs and the Press*, pages 146–50 [Verso, 1999]

40 Schlesinger & Kinzer, *Bitter Fruit*, page 120

41 ibid, page 76

42 Petras & Morley, "Anti-Communism in Guatemala," pages 265–6

43 ibid, page 266

44 Krauss, *Inside Central America*, page 31

45 ibid

46 Petras & Morley, "Anti-Communism in Guatemala," page 267; Gonzalez, *Harvest of Empire*, page 137

47 Guatemala Commission for Historical Clarification official report, February 1999

48 Petras & Morley, "Anti-Communism in Guatemala," page 273

49 Black, "Central America: Crisis in the Backyard," page 29

50 Gonzalez, *Harvest of Empire*, page 137, citing Barry, *The Central American Fact Book*, page 225

51 Noam Chomsky, "The Victors (Part II)," *Z Magazine*, January 1991
52 Booth, *End and Beginning*, page 61
53 ibid, page 62
54 ibid
55 ibid, page 64
56 ibid
57 Weber, *Sandinist Revolution*, page 16
58 Bernard Diederich, *Somoza and the Legacy of US Involvement in Central America*, page 22 [Waterfront Press, 1989]
59 ibid, pages 23–4
60 ibid, page 24
61 Booth, *End and Beginning*, page 65
62 ibid
63 Carmen Diana Deere and Peter Marchetti, "The Worker-Peasant Alliance in the First Year of the Nicaraguan Agrarian Reform," *Latin American Perspectives*, Spring 1981, page 44; Booth, *End and Beginning*, page 66
64 Deere & Marchetti, "The Worker-Peasant Alliance," page 45
65 Booth, *End and Beginning*, pages 72–3
66 ibid, page 73
67 ibid, page 75
68 Weber, *Sandinist Revolution*, page 17
69 Booth, *End and Beginning*, page 76
70 ibid, page 77
71 ibid, page 76
72 ibid, page 86
73 Roxanne Dunbar-Ortiz, *Blood on the Border: A Memoir of the Contra War*, page 9
74 Macaulay, *Sandino Affair*, page 307
75 Weber, *Sandinist Revolution*, pages 20–1
76 ibid, page 21
77 Donald C. Hodges, *Intellectual Foundations of the Nicaraguan Revolution*, page 225 [University of Texas Press, 1988]

78 Steven Palmer, "Carlos Fonseca and the Construction of Sandinismo in Nicaragua," *Latin American Research Review*, Vol. XXIII, No. 1 (1988), pages 99–100
79 ibid, page 100
80 ibid, pages 100–1
81 Katherine Hoyt, *The Many Faces of Sandinista Democracy*, page 104 [Ohio University Press, 1997]
82 Hodges, *Intellectual Foundations*, page 227
83 ibid, page 228
84 ibid, page 230
85 ibid
86 Weber, *Sandinist Revolution*, page 39
87 ibid
88 Booth, *End and Beginning*, page 142
89 ibid
90 ibid
91 Hodges, *Intellectual Foundations*, page 234
92 ibid, page 235
93 ibid, page 233
94 Hoyt, *The Many Faces*, pages 45–6
95 ibid, page 41
96 Hodges, *Intellectual Foundations*, page 240
97 Hoyt, *The Many Faces*, page 90, quoting Orlando Núñez, *La insurreción de la conciencia*, page 29
98 ibid, page 93 (emphasis in original), quoting Núñez and Roger Burbach, *Fire in the Americas: Forging a Revolutionary Agenda*, page 7
99 Booth, *End and Beginning*, page 78
100 ibid, page 79
101 Weber, *Sandinist Revolution*, page 27
102 Forrest D. Colburn, *Post-Revolutionary Nicaragua: State, Class, and the Dilemmas of Agrarian Policy*, page 32 [University of California Press, 1986]
103 Hoyt, *The Many Faces*, page 11

104 Diederich, *Somoza and the Legacy of US Involvement*, page 179
105 ibid, pages 180–1
106 ibid, page 183
107 "Nora Astorga in Her Own Words," *Envío*, April 1988
108 Weber, *Sandinist Revolution*, pages 45–6
109 ibid, page 46
110 Hoyt, *The Many Faces*, page 43
111 "Communique to the Nicaraguan People," reprinted in *Latin American Perspectives*, Winter 1979, page 127
112 Weber, *Sandinist Revolution*, page 48
113 US State Department cable, posted on the National Security Archives website, www.gwu.edu/~nsarchiv
114 Alan Benjamin, *Nicaragua: Dynamic of an Unfinished Revolution*, pages 10–11 [Walnut Publishing, 1989]
115 ibid, page 11
116 Hoyt, *The Many Faces*, page 50
117 ibid
118 Frederick Jameson, "Tomás Borge on the Nicaraguan Revolution," *New Left Review*, July–August 1987, page 55
119 Ilya Prizel, *Latin America through Soviet Eyes: The Evolution of Soviet Perceptions during the Brezhnev Era 1964–1982*, pages 32, 142–3 [Cambridge University Press, 1990]
120 Benjamin, *Nicaragua: Dynamic of an Unfinished Revolution*, page 20
121 Booth, *End and Beginning*, page 185
122 Colburn, *Post-Revolutionary Nicaragua*, page 32
123 Deere & Marchetti, "The Worker-Peasant Alliance," page 51
124 ibid
125 Booth, *End and Beginning*, page 198
126 Gary Ruchwarger, "The Campesino Road to Socialism? The Sandinistas and Rural Co-operatives," *The Socialist Register*, 1988, pages 222–3
127 ibid, pages 223, 230
128 ibid, page 230; Deere & Marchetti, "The Worker-Peasant

Alliance," page 51

129 Colburn, *Post-Revolutionary Nicaragua*, page 123

130 Benjamin, *Nicaragua: Dynamic of an Unfinished Revolution*, page 20

131 Colburn, *Post-Revolutionary Nicaragua*, page 24

132 Richard Stahler-Sholk, "Stabilization, Destabilization, and the Popular Classes in Nicaragua, 1979–1988," *Latin American Research Review*, Vol. XXV, No. 3 (1990), pages 61, 83

133 Benjamin, *Nicaragua: Dynamic of an Unfinished Revolution*, page 21

134 ibid

135 Booth, *End and Beginning*, page 190

136 ibid, page 193

137 ibid, pages 192–4

138 "Nora Astorga in Her Own Words," *Envío*, April 1988

139 ibid

140 ibid

141 Deere & Marchetti, "The Worker-Peasant Alliance," pages 49–50

142 ibid, pages 50–1

143 Ruchwarger, "The Campesino Road to Socialism?," page 228

144 ibid, page 230

145 ibid; Benjamin, *Nicaragua: Dynamic of an Unfinished Revolution*, page 26

146 Ruchwarger, "The Campesino Road to Socialism?," page 230

147 ibid, page 231; Benjamin, *Nicaragua: Dynamic of an Unfinished Revolution*, page 27

148 Benjamin, *Nicaragua: Dynamic of an Unfinished Revolution*, page 27

149 ibid, page 24

150 Deere & Marchetti, "The Worker-Peasant Alliance," page 55

151 Michael Zalkin, "The Peasantry, Grain Policy, and the State," *Latin American Perspectives*, Fall 1981, page 71

152 Deere & Marchetti, "The Worker-Peasant Alliance," page 64
153 ibid, page 57; Ruchwarger, "The Campesino Road to Socialism?," page 229
154 Ruchwarger, "The Campesino Road to Socialism?," page 233
155 Deere & Marchetti, "The Worker-Peasant Alliance," page 58
156 ibid, page 60
157 Marvin Ortega, "Workers' Participation in the Management of the Agro-Enterprises of the APP," *Latin American Perspectives*, page 72
158 ibid, pages 73–5
159 Colburn, *Post-Revolutionary Nicaragua*, page 56
160 Ruchwarger, "The Campesino Road to Socialism?," page 224
161 ibid, page 225
162 ibid, page 229
163 Carlos Vilas, "War and Revolution in Nicaragua: The Impact of the US Counter-revolutionary War on the Sandinista Strategies of Revolutionary Transition," *The Socialist Register*, 1988, page 190
164 Ruchwarger, "The Campesino Road to Socialism?," pages 231, 233
165 United Nations Statistics Division common database, unstats.un.org
166 Noam Chomsky, *Rogue States: The Rule of Force in World Affairs*, page 101 [South End Press, 2000]
167 ibid
168 Benjamin, *Nicaragua: Dynamic of an Unfinished Revolution*, page 21
169 United Nations Statistics Division common database
170 Roberto Chavez, "Urban Planning in Nicaragua: The First Five Years," *Latin American Perspectives*, Spring 1987, page 227
171 ibid, pages 228, 230

172 Colburn, *Post-Revolutionary Nicaragua*, page 109
173 Weber, *Sandinist Revolution*, page 69
174 Benjamin, *Nicaragua: Dynamic of an Unfinished Revolution*, page 35, quoting Carlos Vilas, *The Sandinista Revolution: National Liberation and Social Transformation in Central America*, page 162 [Monthly Review Press, 1986]
175 ibid, pages 35–6
176 Weber, *Sandinist Revolution*, page 77
177 Benjamin, *Nicaragua: Dynamic of an Unfinished Revolution*, pages 35–6, quoting Joseph Collins, "The Failed Partnership: Big Growers and the State," in Peter Rosser and John Vandermeer (eds), *The Nicaragua Reader: Documents of a Revolution under Fire*, pages 319–20 [Grove Press, 1983]
178 ibid, page 37, quoting *Le Monde*, 27 March 1981
179 Deere & Marchetti, "The Worker-Peasant Alliance," pages 67–8; "The National Forum," *Envío*, July 1981
180 William I. Robinson and Kent Norsworthy, "Elections and US Intervention in Nicaragua," *Latin American Perspectives*, Spring 1985, page 88
181 Weber, *Sandinist Revolution*, page 185
182 Jameson, "Tomás Borge on the Nicaraguan Revolution," page 55
183 William Grigsby, "You Can't Organize People and Raise Consciousness by Decree," *Envío*, September 2007
184 Stahler-Sholk, "Stabilization, Destabilization, and the Popular Classes," pages 60, 70
185 Vilas, "War and Revolution," page 187
186 Benjamin, *Nicaragua: Dynamic of an Unfinished Revolution*, page 45
187 Presidential signing statement, posted on the National Security Archives website
188 Philip Brenner, "Waging Ideological War: Anti-Communism and US Foreign Policy in Central America," *The Socialist Register*, 1984, page 243

189 Palmer, "Carlos Fonseca and the Construction of Sandinismo," page 109
190 Dunbar-Ortiz, *Blood on the Border*, pages 119, 122–3 (Dunbar-Ortiz was waiting to board the plane)
191 Holly Sklar, *Washington's War on Nicaragua*, page 116 [South End Press, 1988]
192 Dunbar-Ortiz, *Blood on the Border*, page 118
193 ibid, pages 131–2
194 Dunbar-Ortiz, "Indigenous Rights and Regional Autonomy in Revolutionary Nicaragua," *Latin American Perspectives*, Winter 1987, page 47
195 Vilas, "War and Revolution," page 201
196 ibid, page 203
197 Dunbar-Ortiz, "Indigenous Rights and Regional Autonomy," page 46
198 Dunbar-Ortiz, *Blood on the Border*, page 220
199 ibid, pages 225–7, 230; Dunbar-Ortiz, "Indigenous Rights and Regional Autonomy," page 50
200 Vilas, "War and Revolution," page 217
201 ibid, page 195
202 Sklar, *Washington's War on Nicaragua*, page 117
203 Vilas, "War and Revolution," page 217
204 ibid, page 200
205 US State Department telegram, 5 April 1983, posted on the National Security Archives website
206 Brenner, "Waging Ideological War," page 252
207 US State Department telegram, 15 November 1983, posted on the National Security Archives website
208 US State Department telegram, 8 August 1984, posted on the National Security Archives website
209 Robinson & Norsworthy, "Elections and US Intervention in Nicaragua," page 109
210 Vilas, "War and Revolution," page 204; Dunbar-Ortiz, "Indigenous Rights and Regional Autonomy" pages 50–1

211 Patricia A. Wilson, "Regionalization and Decentralization in Nicaragua," *Latin American Perspectives*, Spring 1987, page 247
212 Stephen Durham and Susan Williams, "The Nature of the Nicaraguan State (Part two)," supplement to *Freedom Socialist*, May–July 1991, page 12
213 Vilas, "War and Revolution," page 196
214 Hoyt, *The Many Faces*, page 85
215 Karl Marx and Friedrich Engels, *The Communist Manifesto*, page 90 [Washington Square Press, 1964]
216 "The National Question and Autonomy (Excerpts)," Rosa Luxemburg, anthologized in Paul Le Blanc (ed.), *Rosa Luxemburg: Reflections and Writings*, page 128 [Humanity Press, 1999]
217 ibid, pages 133–4 (emphasis in original)
218 ibid, pages 136–7
219 Frantz Fanon, *The Wretched of the Earth*, page 5 [Grove Press, 2004]
220 ibid, page 177
221 ibid, page 179
222 Hoyt, *The Many Faces*, page 26
223 Robinson & Norsworthy, "Elections and US Intervention in Nicaragua," page 87
224 Booth, *End and Beginning*, page 281
225 Robinson & Norsworthy, "Elections and US Intervention in Nicaragua," page 96
226 ibid, page 99
227 Susanne Jonas and Nancy Stein, "The Construction of Democracy in Nicaragua," *Latin American Perspectives*, Summer 1990, page 17
228 Robinson & Norsworthy, "Elections and US Intervention in Nicaragua," page 101
229 ibid, page 103
230 Tony Jenkins, "Nicaragua's Elections: Another Battlefront,"

*NACLA Report on the Americas*, page 8

231 ibid, page 7

232 Jonas & Stein, "The Construction of Democracy," page 16, citing Roy Gutman, *The Nation*, 7 May 1988

233 ibid, page 17

234 Jameson, "Tomás Borge on the Nicaraguan Revolution," page 61

235 "An Interview with Nicaragua's Second Political Party," *Envío*, January 1985

236 Robinson & Norsworthy, "Elections and US Intervention in Nicaragua," pages 90–1

237 Jonas & Stein, "The Construction of Democracy," page 19

238 Benjamin, *Nicaragua: Dynamic of an Unfinished Revolution*, page 57, citing Francisco Mayorga, "The Economic Trajectory of Nicaragua 1980–84: An Overview," Occasional Paper No. 4, Florida International University, 1985, page 46

239 "A Survival Economy," *Envío*, October 1985

240 ibid

241 Vilas, "War and Revolution," page 213

242 Benjamin, *Nicaragua: Dynamic of an Unfinished Revolution*, page 52

243 ibid, page 51

244 Jonas & Stein, "The Construction of Democracy," page 20

245 Benjamin, *Nicaragua: Dynamic of an Unfinished Revolution*, pages 50, 56

246 "Political Parties View Constitutional Debate," *Envío*, November 1986

247 ibid

248 ibid

249 ibid

250 "A Survival Economy," *Envío*, October 1985

251 Jameson, "Tomás Borge on the Nicaraguan Revolution," page 62

252 "Nicaraguan Revolution in Retreat: The End of Sandinista

'Third Road,'" *1917: Journal of the International Bolshevik Tendency*, Winter 1988–9

253 Benjamin, *Nicaragua: Dynamic of an Unfinished Revolution*, page 65, citing John Miller and Joe Riccardi, "Nicaragua's Other War," *Dollars and Sense*, January–February 1989

254 ibid, page 63, citing Mario Arana, et al., *Deuda, Establización y Ajuste: La Transformación en Nicaragua, 1979–1986*, page 15 [Coordinadora Regional de Investigaciones Económicas y Sociales, 1987]

255 Jameson, "Tomás Borge on the Nicaraguan Revolution," page 58

256 ibid

257 Hoyt, *The Many Faces*, page 55

258 Ruchwarger, "The Campesino Road to Socialism?," page 237

259 Benjamin, *Nicaragua: Dynamic of an Unfinished Revolution*, page 109

260 Jonas & Stein, "The Construction of Democracy," page 23, citing *The Los Angeles Times* and *The Nation*

261 David Closs, *Nicaragua: The Chamorro Years*, page 28 [Lynne Reiner Publishers, 1999], citing Paul Oquist, "The Sociopolitical Dynamics of the 1990 Nicaraguan Elections," in Vanessa Castro and Gary Prevost (eds), *The 1990 Elections in Nicaragua and Their Aftermath*, page 8 [Rowman & Littlefield, 1992]

262 Stahler-Sholk, "Stabilization, Destabilization, and the Popular Classes," page 74

263 "Economic Reform: Taking It to the Streets," *Envío*, April 1988

264 Durham & Williams, "On the Nature of the Nicaraguan State (Part one)," *Freedom Socialist*, February–April 1991, page 16

265 "Economic Reform: Taking It to the Streets," *Envío*, April 1988

266 Stahler-Sholk, "Stabilization, Destabilization, and the

Popular Classes," page 75

267 "The New Economic Package—Will a Popular Model Emerge?," *Envío*, August 1988

268 ibid

269 ibid

270 Jonas & Stein, "The Construction of Democracy," page 10

271 Roger Burbach, "Et Tu, Daniel? The Sandinista Revolution Betrayed," *NACLA Report on the Americas*, March–April 2009, page 36

272 Margaret Randall, *Gathering Rage: The Failure of 20th Century Revolutions to Develop a Feminist Agenda*, page 42 [Monthly Review Press, 1992]

273 Klara Zetkin, "Lenin on the Women's Question," posted on the Marxist Archives website, www.marxists.org

274 ibid

275 Phyllis Andors, "Politics of Chinese Development: The Case of Women, 1960–1966," a Far East Reporter pamphlet, September 1977, page 11–12

276 ibid, page 17

277 ibid, pages 27–8

278 Jane Jenson, "The French Communist Party and Feminism," *The Socialist Register*, 1980, pages 123–7

279 ibid, pages 128–30

280 ibid, pages 133, 141

281 "Nora Astorga in Her Own Words," *Envío*, April 1988

282 ibid

283 Hoyt, *The Many Faces*, pages 49–50

284 Randall, *Gathering Rage*, page 42

285 "Becoming Visible: Women in Nicaragua," *Envío*, December 1987

286 Randall, *Gathering Rage*, pages 47–8

287 Ann Ferguson, "Lesbianism, Feminism, and Empowerment in Nicaragua," *Socialist Review*, July–December 1991, pages 81–5

288 "Becoming Visible: Women in Nicaragua," *Envío*, December 1987
289 Hoyt, *The Many Faces*, page 63
290 Randall, *Gathering Rage*, pages 58–9 (emphasis in original)
291 Ferguson, "Lesbianism, Feminism, and Empowerment in Nicaragua," pages 88, 91
292 ibid, pages 91–2
293 Randall, *Gathering Rage*, page 71
294 Closs, *The Chamorro Years*, pages 132–4
295 ibid, pages 77, 133–4
296 ibid, page 163
297 "The $100 Million Poker Game," *Envío*, August 1992
298 "Privatizing Telcor: Not the Only or Best Solution," *Envío*, December 1995
299 ibid
300 ibid
301 Hoyt, *The Many Faces*, page 141
302 ibid, page 137
303 Randall, *Gathering Rage*, pages 79–80, 184
304 "FSLN Holds Extraordinary Congress 'For Sandinista Unity,'" Weekly News Update on the Americas supplement, Nicaragua Solidarity Network, online at home.earthlink .net/~nicadlw
305 Alejandro Bendaña, "Washington and the Caudillos: Calculation and Miscalculation in Managua," *NACLA Report on the Americas*, January–February 2002, pages 13, 16
306 Adolfo Acevdeo, "Sixteen Years Lost in Five Agreements with IMF," *Envío*, April 2008
307 William I. Robinson, "Latin America, State Power, and the Challenge to Global Capital," Global & International Studies Program, posted on the eScholarship Repository website, repositories.cdlib.org
308 Phil Stuart Cournoyer, *Socialist Voice*, posted on the ZNet website, www.zmag.com

309 Amnesty International July 2009 report, "The Total Abortion Ban in Nicaragua: Women's Health and Lives Endangered, Medical Professionals Criminalized," pages 7–9, 12–13, 17–20, 27–8

310 Human Rights Watch October 2007 report, "Over Their Dead Bodies: Denial of Access to Emergency Obstetric Care and Therapeutic Abortion in Nicaragua," pages 8, 12

311 "Stones in Their Shoes," *Envío*, January 2010; "What to Add, What to Subtract, How to Multiply, Who To Divide?," *Envío*, December 2009; Victor Hugo Tinoco, "Corruption Is the Most Serious Aspect of the Ortega-Chávez Relationship," *Envío*, September 2009; Burbach, "Et Tu, Daniel?," pages 33–7

312 Chomsky, "The Victors (Part I)," *Z Magazine*, November 1990

313 Chomsky, "The Victors (Part II)," *Z Magazine*, January 1991

314 Chomsky, *Rogue States*, page 97

315 Petras, "Latin America, the EU and the US: The New Polarities," *Dissident Voice*, 22 May 2006

316 Gonzalez, *Harvest of Empire*, page 143

317 Kate Doyle, "The Atrocity Files: Deciphering the Archives of Guatemala's Dirty War," *Harper's*, December 2007, pages 60–2

318 Pablo Pozzi, "Popular Upheaval and Capitalist Transformation in Argentina," *Latin American Perspectives*, Spring 2000, page 70

319 ibid, page 75

320 Colin M. MacLachlan, *Argentina: What Went Wrong*, pages 169, 171 [Praeger, 2006]

321 ibid, page 177

322 Alan Ciblis, "Argentina and the IFIs," posted on the ZNet website

## Chapter 5

# The Dissolution of the Soviet Union

A peculiarity of political science is that there was never a consensus on the proper description of the Soviet Union. In contrast, the United States, the other Cold War-era superpower, was universally acknowledged as a capitalist country without debate. The Right routinely called the Soviet Union "communist," a designation almost invariably preceded by the scariest possible adjective they could conjure. The Communist Party called it a "developed socialist society." Many on the Left called it simply "socialist." Others invented the category of "state capitalism" for the Soviet Union—a term intended to signal that *capital* continued to distort economic and social relations in the sense that party and government controlled production and investment, and thus concentrated decision-making power in their hands. Nonetheless, the concept is at best highly misleading, although some find the term useful because it is amorphous with no accepted definition and therefore served as a convenient way of signaling a dislike of the Soviet system while simultaneously opposing the capitalism of the West.

Perhaps the best shorthand description of the Soviet Union would be simply "post-capitalist." Because the country's rulers insisted they were governing according to tenets of Marxism, it is fair to make a judgment on those terms. From the standpoint of a strict Marxist definition, the Soviet Union never came close to being a socialist state. It remained frozen in a deformed transitional stage from capitalism. But it was not a capitalist state—the capitalists of the West certainly knew that, which is why so much time, energy and money was poured into attempting to defeat the Soviet bloc. Thus "post-capitalist" provides a neutral term that acknowledges that capitalist economic relations had been abolished without suggesting a transition to a higher state had been completed, without sorting out the details. That does not mean a lack of interest in the details; on the contrary, sketching the details will be the focus of this chapter.

Not the least of those details is: Who ruled? To a surprisingly large degree, it was a deeply hierarchal bureaucracy that enforced its will and not the party that monopolized political power. Working people in the Soviet Union, guaranteed employment, were able to wrest some control in the workplace, including the ability to slow the pace of work. Nonetheless, they were also subject to hazardous environmental and safety conditions and those areas where they could assert themselves were penumbral—control ultimately resided in the hands of a bureaucracy whose rule rested on social atomization.

There was no capitalist class that maintained its rule by virtue of owning the means of production, able to maintain power through decisive influence over a range of social institutions and thus diffusing and mystifying the roots of power. The Soviet bureaucracy, by contrast, could maintain its privileges only through undisguised direct political force.

Democracy in all aspects of life for everybody is a basic goal of socialism, and that was glaringly lacking no matter how loudly Soviet ideology insisted its system was "socialist." Josef Stalin declared that socialism had been achieved in the 1930s and that declaration remained sacrosanct dogma for decades, the fitful decade of de-Stalinization that followed the dictator's death not excepted.

Soviet rulers' insistence that the country had achieved socialism and only their model constituted socialism had tragic consequences for the reformers of the Prague Spring, among others, and acted as a prophylactic against necessary changes in the Soviet Union itself. Thus the 18-year rule of Leonid Brezhnev became known in Russian history as the "era of stagnation." The end under Mikhail Gorbachev, however, began when elements of capitalism were introduced into the system, unraveling the dense network of ties that had bound it together.

## Sometimes yes, sometimes no: The contradictions of Khrushchev's reforms

When Stalin died in 1953, only those who had unquestionably executed his will were in a position to succeed him. All oppositions had been physically annihilated, leaving Stalin's most servile and unimaginative lieutenants to dismantle what they had helped to create. The post-Stalin Communist Party leadership (simultaneously a new and a holdover leadership) brought an end to political terror and radically reduced repression in everyday life, yet the political superstructure that had been created during the Stalin dictatorship remained. This meant that there was still little meaningful political freedom: The party (and therefore Soviet society as a whole) continued to be ruled in an autocratic, top-down manner and immense power could be concentrated into the hands of the party leader, the general secretary.

The dramatic arrest of Stalin's last secret police chief, Lavrenti Beria, three months after Stalin's death, and the subsequent execution of Beria, brought an emphatic end to the use of Stalin-style purges, and the intellectual ferment unleashed by Nikita Khrushchev's "secret speech" at the 1956 party congress denouncing Stalin definitively brought an end to the possibility of mass repression. A lack of consensus among the Politburo members also was a factor softening party policy. Upon Stalin's death, the Politburo, the party's top decision-making body, was roughly divided between hard-liners and reformers, viewpoints that could now be expressed.

Khrushchev, one of the newer members of the Politburo, was a compromise selection as general secretary because he was not seen as being on either side. There was also a desire to split the posts of party leader and government leader so as to not concentrate too much power in the hands of Georgii Malenkov, who become prime minister immediately following Stalin's death.

But Khrushchev, like his peers, had come of political age while rising through the ranks of the Stalin party faction and was unable to overcome his limitations. Khrushchev pinned all the blame on Stalin in his "secret speech," portraying the Politburo members as forced to act under coercion and therefore blameless, even helpless. They had been in continual physical jeopardy—the machinery of repression would have finished off any of them had they challenged the dictator—but were also responsible for elevating Stalin to power and keeping him there. By ignoring the blood that was also on the hands of Stalin's lieutenants, Khrushchev, in his own way, continued into the post-Stalin era the Stalin faction's tradition of seeking scapegoats and pinning all responsibility on them.

Party leaders continued to believe it was unthinkable to question the punishing defeat of the various Bolshevik oppositions of the 1920s and the super-centralized command structure. They did not think that a small number of officials making a vast array of decisions in politics, economics and culture was unnatural. It should be acknowledged that Khrushchev sincerely wished to bring about meaningful reforms, bury the Stalin cult and create a better life for the Soviet Union's citizens, but his limitations blocked him from making sufficient progress in any of these areas.

The entrenched opposition of the country's elites also acted as a brake on reform. Khrushchev was able to concentrate political power into his hands by virtue of the inherent powers of the post of general secretary, although he had nothing resembling the absolute powers wielded by Stalin. Khrushchev was strong enough to demote challengers, but the bureaucracy, no longer subject to purges, was able to coalesce into a formidable strata capable of exerting its interests. Opposition to Khrushchev at the highest levels of the party (the Politburo and the Central

Committee) also had the ability to crystallize, culminating in his smooth ouster in 1964.

Khrushchev's reforms did begin with positive results. From 1953 to 1958, agricultural output grew rapidly following a significant rise in the prices paid for collective farm produce and the development of new farmlands.[1] The first attempt at serious decentralization, however, soured after some initial success. In 1957, Khrushchev abolished the central industry ministries and replaced them with regional economic councils scattered across the country. The Soviet Union had 200,000 enterprises and 100,000 construction sites centrally managed from Moscow[2] through government ministries that supervised individual industries. The proponents of Khrushchev's decentralization plan believed enterprises should be allowed to deal directly with other local enterprises rather than go through ministry officials in Moscow. The decentralization resulted in improvement in industrial output along with a decline in paperwork.

The reform marked Khrushchev's political apex. Discussions about the reform were conducted in April 1957, with the conspicuous absence of long-time Politburo members Lazar Kaganovich, Vyacheslav Molotov and Malenkov (the last of whom had already been demoted from the post of prime minister). Soon all three would be forced out by Khrushchev and not long afterward a fourth member of Stalin's inner circle, Nikolai Bulganin, would be dismissed, with Khrushchev taking the post of prime minister in addition to his position atop the party.

Khrushchev's Politburo rivals had opposed him on a variety of issues—not only the large investment made to open new farmlands in Central Asia and the decentralization of economic planning, but also his "secret speech," his attempts to place less stress on heavy industry in favor of consumer products, and his reconciliation with Yugoslavia's independent communist policy and Yugoslav leader Josef Broz Tito. The bureaucracy opposed decentralization as a threat to its power, but nonetheless ministry officials were sent off to the provinces to staff the regional economic councils.

The new decentralized system developed its own problems as officials began to favor their local area over other regions, cutting back shipments to other places and hoarding local production,[3] introducing new bottlenecks. The breakdown of management into geographic segments also tended to waste the specialized, industry-specific knowledge that had accumulated within the ministries, and the regional economic councils, unlike the former central ministries, were separated from research offices and did not have the authority to implement new technology.[4] Opposition mounted, and the old system of centralized ministries was swiftly recreated after Khrushchev's ouster.

There were positive developments during Khrushchev's decade in power, such as the introduction of pensions, the establishment of a minimum wage, the reduction of the workweek to five days, and increased pay for those on the low end of the wage scale or who worked in hazardous jobs. He also abolished some of the privileges of the party's higher ranks and tried to introduce term limits for party posts. Those last two moves, needless to say, were resented by those who would be affected, further weakening his support within the party, and Khrushchev began to lose the support of the broader public when retail prices for food were sharply increased in 1962. Farmers resented Khrushchev's arbitrary decree banning personal ownership of cattle on collective farms; instead the general secretary offered them lectures on the importance of planting maize.

Unrest resulting from increasing economic pressures exploded in the city of Novocherkassk, where the price rises came on the heels of wage cuts. On 2 June 1962, the city's factory workers marched on the city center, carrying red banners and portraits of Lenin, halting when they reached a cordon of armed soldiers. The crowd began to chant, "Make way for the working class!" and the soldiers allowed the demonstrators to pass. When no party official would talk to them, they stormed and seized the party headquarters and when they learned of the arrests of some of their fellow demonstrators, they then attempted to seize the police station.[5] More troops were sent in to quell the uprising; the reinforcements obeyed orders by opening fire, killing 23.[6]

Khrushchev's régime was becoming more erratic, a weakness compounded by continuing attempts at micromanaging public life. Although attacks on culture were not bloody in the style of the massacre in Novocherkassk, they nevertheless demonstrated the party's insecurities. Fiction and poetry long held a particularly exalted place in Russian culture, and a flowering was seen in these arts after Stalin's death. Public appearances by poets such as Yevgeny Yevtushenko, Bella Ahkmadulina and Andrei Voznesensky were major events—the size of the crowds who came to hear them was too large for bookstores and sometimes filled stadiums. Poetry was regularly published in Soviet newspapers, avidly discussed by readers. Although the official literary establishment, riddled by careerists and bureaucrats, could be hostile to popular writers, those writers nonetheless continued to reach a large audience. Yevtushenko, for example, often was given denunciatory reviews at the same time his books sold out, newspapers printing his verses would quickly vanish from newsstands and he received congratulatory letters by the thousands.[7]

During a period of a few years, anti-Stalin works were give permission to be published—even Aleksandr Solzhenitsyn's *One Day in the Life of Ivan Denisovich*—but the new spaces for culture gradually gave way to crude attacks. One example, by no means the only, of Khrushchev's meddling comes from an account by Voznesensky. Summoned to a ceremonial hall, Voznesensky, while speaking, was interrupted by someone shouting over a microphone, "Get out of our country!" Startled, the poet turned around to see it was Khrushchev doing the shouting: "The head of state jumped up, shaking his fists in the air. 'Mr. Voznesensky! Out! Comrade Shelepin will issue you with a passport.' A quite monstrous flood of words followed…For a long time, I could not comprehend how one person could combine the best hopes of the sixties and all those powerful changes with such an obstructive old way of thinking, such philistine tyranny."[8]

Voznesensky did not in fact leave the Soviet Union, and continued to give well-attended readings at home and abroad. But Khrushchev's increasingly erratic behavior eroded all sources of support. Thus when the party's Central Committee and Politburo decided to replace him in 1964, he would find himself with almost no defenders. A Central Committee employee, Georgi Arbatov (who would go on to head a major institute under Brezhnev and become a key adviser to Mikhail Gorbachev) recalled sitting among a film audience a month before the ouster and being startled by audience laughter when Khrushchev appeared in a newsreel. "Such a show of mass disrespect for the leader was still most unusual," he wrote.[9] Two weeks later, at another film, "there was loud and unabashed laughter in the audience. We left the theater with a sense of foreboding."[10]

Although it was Leonid Brezhnev who became the new party general secretary, the coup against Khrushchev was actually organized by Aleksandr Shelepin with Mikhail Suslov, Nikolai Podgorny and the chief of the secret police (the KGB), Vladimir Semichastny. Each of these four had been promoted to their positions by Khrushchev; Brezhnev had become the unofficial "second secretary" of the Politburo under Khrushchev.

Shelepin saw Brezhnev as a temporary figure—Shelepin was far from alone in that forecast—and wasted no time in beginning maneuvers designed to propel himself into the top job. As a Politburo member and a Central Committee secretary, Shelepin had control over personnel appointments and had placed several of his associates in responsible posts. Those associates made no secret of their belief that Shelepin would soon be general secretary and Shelepin apparently did nothing to dampen those boasts.

Brezhnev may not have known much about theory, economics or most any other intellectual body of knowledge, but he was skilled at maneuvering within the party apparatus and knowing who was, and wasn't, with him. When Shelepin's ambitions had become too obvious, he stopped in the Siberian city of Irkutsk on the way home from a trip to Mongolia to loudly praise Brezhnev at a regional party committee meeting.[11] It was already too late. In autumn 1965, Shelepin lost his post in charge of appointing personnel and was demoted to overseeing the food and consumer goods industries.[12] Shelepin was later removed from the Politburo when he made a demand that a protest note be sent to the United Kingdom over a perceived insult or he would resign; his overreaching backfired when no note was sent and his resignation was accepted.[13]

Unlike Brezhnev, who carefully avoided standing out in any way on his way to the top, Shelepin was a hard-liner who routinely made his views known and was feared by many who were afraid of a rollback of the post-Stalin reforms. Brezhnev, meanwhile, began his reign by concentrating on securing his position.

## Ideology over intellect: The parallels of Leonid Brezhnev and George W. Bush

It may seem strange to pair together Leonid Brezhnev and George W. Bush. It might be tempting to see both as representative of the decay of their respective systems, and there would be some truth in that, although the analogy shouldn't be pushed too far. The United States under Bush was stronger than was the Soviet Union under Brezhnev: The latter's 18-year "era of stagnation" put his country into a sufficiently weakened state that it was able to implode within a decade, but it is safe to say that the United States won't be splintering into smaller republics any time soon.

Yet both men symbolize a political crisis in that they were woefully under-equipped intellectually to be at the head of a superpower and found themselves in their positions by virtue of considerable help from others. Both represented and upheld the interests of elite sections of their societies at the expense of the overall health of their countries. It would be unfair to conclude that Brezhnev had no interest in the lives of ordinary Soviet people, but his was a deeply paternalistic concern; he assumed he knew what was "best" for working people and had no need for fundamental reforms. Brezhnev did not have the élan to do anything significant—his base was the party apparatus and he kept his base happy with his policy of "stability in cadres."

Those surrounding Bush were by no means free of similar paternalism, although Bush himself could not be bothered to convincingly pretend to care about ordinary people; his base was the superrich and the corporate elite, and he expended his energy in making them even more rich and even more powerful. And, unlike Brezhnev, Bush was something of a figurehead since his vice president, Richard Cheney, gave every impression of actually being the one in charge.

The elites who engineered Bush's accession to the US presidency had a use for an amiable dunce (although the amiable part was the artificial creation of his handlers) and Bush, handed everything in life, provided no reason to counter the impression that he believed the natural order of the universe was himself (or his family) at the top of the pyramid with his foot on everybody else's neck. That Bush did not have the intellectual capacity to actually be president was confirmed by his administration's first treasury secretary, Paul O'Neill, who reported that Bush remained silent during cabinet meetings, while Cheney ran them. One-on-one meetings weren't much different, O'Neill's biographer revealed: "[Bush] threw out a few general phrases, a few nods, but there was virtually no engagement...O'Neill had been made to understand by various colleagues in the White House that the President should not be expected to read reports. In [O'Neill's] personal experience, the President didn't even appear to have read the short memos he sent over."[14]

Somewhat similarly, a Soviet speech writer and theorist working in the Central Committee apparatus, Fedor Burlatsky, recalled his encounter with Brezhnev when attempting to counter arguments by a group of hard-liners seeking to effect a reversal of the Khrushchev reforms. "I began to expound our position to Brezhnev point by point," Burlatsky wrote.

> The more I explained, the more his face changed. It began to look tense and drawn until we realized, to our horror, that Leonid Illyich had hardly understood a word. I brought my fountain of eloquence to a halt and he said with winning sincerity, "It's hard for me to grasp all this. On the whole, to be honest, this isn't my area. My strong point is organization and psychology," and he made vague circular motions with his fingers spread wide open. What was most dramatic—and this became clear very soon—was that Brezhnev was entirely unprepared for the role which had suddenly fallen to him.[15]

Burlatsky wrote that Brezhnev insisted his reports and briefings be read to him, as he disliked reading and writing, but tried to cultivate the impression he was a theoretical thinker by having his assistants ghost-write nine volumes worth of his "works."[16] Similarly, Bush had to have his two- or three-page "presidential daily briefings" read to him, but was not above having his handlers once claim that he had been reading the French-Algerian existentialist writer Albert Camus. The Camus episode was quickly dropped as few in the United States were familiar with Camus, and those who did know who he was could only laugh at the idea of the famously anti-intellectual Bush reading him seriously.

Another commonality between Bush and Brezhnev is the culture of corruption that surrounded both. Bush and Cheney invaded Iraq in part to hand that country's resources over to their backers, who had the potential to profit greatly from a forced privatization of the Iraqi economy. Indeed, the US government was used as a piggy bank for the Bush administration "base"—the well-connected benefited from no-bid contracts, weakened regulations and the dismantling of government oversight agencies, among the policies that culminated in the economic collapse that began in Bush's last year in office. Brezhnev presided over marked increases in privileges for his base, the elites of Soviet society, although what was grabbed by Brezhnev's supporters paled in comparison to the trillions of dollars scooped up by Bush's backers.

What Brezhnev did understand was how to use the power inherent in the position of general secretary. Khrushchev was ousted, among other shortcomings, for "subjectivism"—meaning he had made too many decisions by himself. The new general secretary, then, wisely demonstrated his willingness to work in a collegial style and avoided making any significant public pronouncements. One of Brezhnev's advisers noted that "He had a well-earned reputation as a poorly educated man of limited vision. But those who portray Brezhnev as a fool are wrong. Brezhnev was capable of showing political savvy, common sense and know-how. Immediately…he chose to follow a line of action that proved to be very correct and advantageous. It assured him success."[17] One of those actions, in his first months in office, was to spend two hours each morning calling Central Committee members, and republican and provincial party secretaries, to ask their opinion on various subjects.[18]

Indeed, while Brezhnev was cunning enough to gradually push out all his rivals for power and gently replace lesser party officials who were insufficiently behind his policies, he usually strove to reach a consensus on the Politburo before acting, consolidating his hold on power during the 1970s. The last two people who could potentially unseat him, ideology chief Mikhail Suslov and Prime Minister Aleksei Kosygin, continued to have influence but accepted Brezhnev's political leadership. Other rivals who did not accept that leadership, such as Shelepin and Podgorny, eventually were pushed out of the Politburo. And because party and government bureaucrats were secure in their positions, there would be no rumblings in the party's middle ranks.

How does such a mediocrity ascend to the highest post in such an immense country? By having a patron who rose through the ranks and never deviating from the ideological line of the day. After a career as an engineer, Brezhnev became a minor party official in the mid-1930s, and began rising to higher posts in the late 1930s with the support of Khrushchev, serving as the party chief in out-of-the-way cities and regions before being named party boss of the small republic of Moldova. Because so many posts became open due to the wide net cast by the purges, there was the opportunity to ascend the ranks much more quickly than would ordinarily be possible. Brezhnev was promoted to the Politburo in 1957 when much of the Stalinist old guard was removed; once again he was in the right place at the right time. Because he was such a grey figure who was not associated with any trend of opinion, he became the compromise figure selected as general secretary in 1964.

He was expected to be a temporary transition figure, but instead he stayed as party leader longer than anybody other than Stalin. "I've served my time and here I am," Brezhnev said soon after making it to the top.[19] That statement is not only a summation of his career, but reflects the fact that he had no program of any kind; he simply wanted power for its own sake. That was fine by his followers, who wanted nothing else but to secure their positions and privileges, and especially valued Brezhnev for his ability to blunt any and all attempts at meaningful reform.

## Look down below: Reform plans and intellectual ferment under the surface of stagnation

Leonid Brezhnev's 18 years as general secretary are known as the "era of stagnation," but that stagnation was not a necessity. Evidence of bottlenecks that had the potential to strangle the economy steadily mounted, and there was no shortage of conscientious people in scientific academies, in government planning agencies and in the Central Committee departments who realized the necessity of serious political, economic and cultural changes. Nor was there any shortage of ordinary working people in the supposed "workers' state" who lived and worked with the dispiriting results of the stagnation and sullenly refused to continue to cooperate. Nor was knowledge of the need for changes unknown at the highest level. The first attempt at reform was authored by the prime minister, Aleksei Kosygin, in 1965.

Kosygin dwelled on the fact that the regeneration of the centralized ministries, with their vast array of decisions made in Moscow, recreated the problem of over-centralization. As prime minister, Kosygin oversaw the economy and was distressed at the volume of decisions that were made by the council of ministers. He asked: "Why should the government have to concern itself with the quality of the sand being supplied to the glass industry and other industrial branches? There are ministries and a state standards agency: why don't they meet and resolve the issue?"[20]

Kosygin sought to cautiously remove some of the over-centralization by introducing incentives at the factory and enterprise levels through monetary rewards for technological innovation or strong results while allowing them some measure of autonomy. Kosygin also wished to introduce cooperatives and other forms of property, but made no headway with his Politburo colleagues with this idea. The incentive plan was implemented on a limited basis and showed positive results, but ran into bureaucratic opposition, which led to cutbacks in enterprise independence; the plan was also limited by the fact that the basic indicator by which the country's production was measured remained numerical volume totals, without regard for quality or other factors.[21]

One interesting feature of the Brezhnev years was that a multitude of academic institutions were set up to study all aspects of Soviet performance, which issued a steady stream of reports, recommendations and suggestions. Mostly they were ignored. Detailed criticisms of the economic structure (and, by implication, the stifling role of the party) appeared in the Soviet press. To provide one example, a group of economists contributed to an article published in 1964 in the party's leading theoretical journal, *Kommunist*, that set forth a detailed critique of the system of material supply and distribution and pointed out that the accompanying provision of capital to enterprises at no cost encouraged inefficiency and requests for more capital, deepening inefficiencies.[22] Books, too, appeared on these themes, one of which declared, in 1965, that "a system which is so harnessed from top to bottom will fetter technological and social development; and it will break down sooner or later under the pressure of the real processes of economic life."[23]

Concurrent with these economic debates, hard-line party members in responsible posts were conducting a debate on whether the "attacks" on Josef Stalin (as they termed the post-1956 discussions and artistic works directly challenging Stalin's crimes) should continue—or even if Stalin should be "rehabilitated." These debates represented one form of struggle among the various opinion currents in the party's ranks and served as a surrogate for directly debating the myriad of developmental problems the Soviet Union faced.

The debate was fully engaged by writers, and a continual back-and-forth raged in Soviet newspapers and periodicals. But ominous signs began appearing. A political trial, held without outside observers, to silence novelists Andrei Sinyavsky and Yuri Daniel for "anti-Soviet propaganda" was held in 1967, complete with denunciations, signaling an end to the relative openness that had carried over from the Khrushchev years.[24] This constituted the first resemblance to a show trial since the Stalin dictatorship, and both novelists spent five years in custody.

The events in Czechoslovakia in 1968 created more nervousness, embodied in a more open campaign for Stalin's rehabilitation and the awarding of a state prize for a toadying poem praising Stalin.[25] The debate reached its climax in December 1969, the ninetieth anniversary of Stalin's birth, when *Pravda*, the leading party newspaper (and therefore the most important barometer of official thinking), seemed about to print a two-page article that would have signaled the start of an official rehabilitation and sent chills down spines across the country. But the article was killed and replaced with another emphasizing the "mistakes and distortions arising out of the cult of personality."[26] The worst fears—a reversal leading backwards to a restoration of some aspects of the Stalin dictatorship—could now be put to rest. But the space to debate the mounting problems the Soviet Union faced nonetheless was steadily closing.

Organized dissent began appearing in the late 1960s, but increasing repression and the heterogeneous nature of opponents prevented them from coalescing into any organized force. A prominent socialist oppositionist, Zhores Medvedev, argued that it was very difficult to put forth a positive program. That difficulty is a problem that recurs in all societies—it is much easier to be against conditions than to articulate how to change those conditions for the better.

The dissidents broke into three broad camps: a messianic nationalism seeking a return to the tsarist empire tied to a rigid hostility to democracy rooted in an authoritarian Right, exemplified by Aleksandr Solzhenitsyn; a Western orientation seeking to replicate much of the features, real or imagined, of the capitalist democracies, exemplified by Andrei Sakharov; and Leftists seeking radical change to bring about the full promise of political, economic and cultural democracy embodied in socialism. Medvedev noted that "It was much more difficult to develop genuinely new social ideas than to fall back on religion or nationalism or to become a so-called 'westerner.' The great majority of dissidents, unfortunately, had virtually no education in political science—their knowledge of world history, contemporary states or comparative social systems was very superficial."[27]

Despite the congealment of ideology, not even Brezhnev & Co. could remain oblivious to the need for some reform, particularly because of the ongoing rapid development of technology around the world. But the need to adopt new technology had to be squared with the demand by the leadership that technological development be contained within its rigid ideological constraints. Although there would be no return to a Stalin-style rule, Stalin's arbitrary 1930s declaration that the Soviet Union had established "socialism" had to remain in force because the political superstructure that overlay Soviet society had been built upon such ideological pronouncements and was therefore sacrosanct. Khrushchev's boast that the Soviet Union had begun to build "communism" was an arbitrary fiction based on that.

To recapitulate, the Marxist definition of "socialism" is a stage not only based on capitalist relations of production having been transcended but when a full democracy has been instituted with industry and agriculture built up during capitalist stages of development brought under popular control so that production is oriented toward meeting the needs of everyone instead of for personal profit by an individual owner. The development of socialism would be followed by "communism," a theoretical stage in which the coercive powers of the state would wither away, all forms of exploitation would have ended and production would be fully rationalized to align with community need.

Karl Marx's conception of communism was that of a "free association of producers" (producers here being individual people) in which members reach decisions through some form of collective decision-making. Freed of alienation, exploitation and the coercive effects of subordination to wage work and the power of capital, all people would be able to fully develop their human potential.

But the foregoing is a very loose theoretical construct; moreover, although "socialism" in this sense is a transitional stage to "communism," the Soviet Union remained mired in attempting a transition from capitalism to socialism, revealing the complexity of post-capitalist development. There are no formal benchmarks that can be pointed to that such-and-such a stage has been "reached," and Marx and Friedrich Engels purposefully avoided sketching out the future in any detail because such a blueprint is impossible. The wide differences in human societies would be enough to make any blueprint a hopeless task; the details of a new and better world can only be created in the process of creating it.

Even by the very loose, generalized standard sketched in the preceding two paragraphs, the Soviet Union of the 1930s had a vast distance to travel and still had yet to fulfill the basic requirements in the 1970s. The abolition of capitalist economic relations by means of forced industrialization and farm collectivization imposed at the beginning of the 1930s was the basis for Stalin's boast that his régime had established "socialism." But ending traditional capitalist relations, by whatever mechanism and in whatever form, is simply a precondition, not the actual content, of socialism. And by no means did popular control exist over the means of production: Capital was no longer in private hands, but it was concentrated in party and state bureaucracies. Decades later, the domestic and foreign policies of the Soviet Union continued to rest on the belief that it had found the one path to socialism.

Fortunately, although the dogma of "achieving socialism" could not be questioned, it was not difficult to simply ignore Khrushchev's boast that his régime had begun the process of "building communism"—Khrushchev was ignored by the official media immediately following his removal from power, and thereafter. So in 1967 Brezhnev put a different ideological "update" on the decades-old boast of "achieving socialism" by declaring that the Soviet Union had become a "developed socialist society." The Soviet Union would use the ongoing "scientific-technological revolution" to achieve further advancements.

Hard-liners and reformers could agree on the need to embrace this revolution; the former believed technological refinement would solidify the existing system while the latter believed it would provide a path for needed structural changes. The official viewpoint was well expressed by a social theorist in a 1976 book: "Developed socialism is not an independent or self-sufficient phase but only a new stage in the maturing of a socialist society. The construction of developed socialism occurs after the complete transition from capitalism to socialism. Developed socialism speeds our transition to communism by immeasurably accelerating the tempo of social progress."[28]

The "scientific-technological revolution" was perceived as a tool to assist the process of gradually creating harmony among the various groups of society and thereby breaking down barriers among them; to better coordinate central planning; and to assist party leaders in making better decisions through having more scientific information provided by specialists.[29]

But the so-called revolution was reduced to tinkering. Perhaps a more representative quote, considering the stagnation to come, comes from a Central Committee meeting in 1965, when Brezhnev summarized his views of Kosygin's proposed economic reforms: "What's he dreamed up? Reforms, reforms…who needs them? Nobody will understand them. People have to work better. That's where the whole problem lies."[30]

Regardless of how hard people did, or did not, work, economic growth continued to slow. Annual growth was about 5 percent around 1970, less than in the 1950s although still respectable, but was more like 2 percent in the early 1980s. Worse, growth in industrial output steadily fell more short of what was planned, so that in the late 1970s only 56 percent of planned growth was actually attained.[31] Part of the problem was that adding more productive capacity was becoming more expensive. As early as 1970, the director of the research institute at the Soviet economic planning agency, known as Gosplan, wrote a report warning of coming problems "primarily because growth in basic capital assets is outstripping growth in output."[32] Less return was received from investment, a problem that steadily grew more acute.

Quite aware of the state of the economy, sociologists and economists in the Academy of Sciences institute in the western Siberian city of Novosibirsk spent two years intensively studying Soviet agriculture and in 1983 a conference was held to further discuss the issue. The lead paper for the conference was written by Tatyana Zaslavskaya, who assessed frankly the grave problems in agriculture, factors that could more broadly be applied to the economy as a whole. The conference noted, inter alia, the parasitic nature of the bureaucracy, the revival of authoritarian methods of management, a breakdown of public ethics and the strong fetter these developments placed on production.[33] For their troubles, Zaslavskaya and institute director Abel Aganbegyan (who would soon become an adviser to Mikhail Gorbachev) were put through an investigation by the KGB secret police after a copy of Zaslavskaya's paper was leaked to the Western press.[34]

That sort of reaction had become more common. A year

earlier, two scholars at another institute, the Institute of World Economics and International Relations in Moscow, were arrested and an investigation into the institute was organized by Viktor Grishin, a notorious hard-liner who sat on the Politburo. The director of the institute was hounded so furiously that he suffered a fatal heart attack, but before more damage could be done, two of Brezhnev's advisers interceded with the general secretary, who had been unaware of the investigation. Brezhnev placed a telephone call to Grishin, putting an end to the witchhunt.[35]

The deaths of Brezhnev and Mikhail Suslov in 1982 raised hopes that a path out of the mounting problems might begin to be blazed, but Brezhnev was followed by Yuri Andropov and Konstantin Chernenko, both in ill health and neither lasting much more than a year. And rapid change of such a rigid system is not so easy—the investigation of Zaslavskaya and Aganbegyan happened during Andropov's reign.

The country was now approaching the end of the rule of people who had begun their career during Stalin's dictatorship. The son of poor peasants, Suslov became a party activist during the Russian Civil War, eventually becoming a professor at Moscow State University before switching careers. He ascended the party ranks in the 1930s, catching the eye of Stalin's most ruthless lieutenant, Lazar Kaganovich, while carrying out purges as a member of the party and state oversight bodies. Suslov was voted onto the party's Central Committee in 1941, eventually to be put in charge of ideological matters by Khrushchev.

As ideology chief under Brezhnev he had vast responsibilities, overseeing print and broadcast media, science, propaganda, and secondary and higher education. These duties were carried out in the most monotone manner possible—socialist dissident Roy Medvedev noted that "Although Suslov's obituary writers describe him as a 'major party theoretician' his actual contribution to party theory was nil; he never said an original word on the subject."[36] Suslov saw his job as that of chief censor, relentlessly excising from texts anything that deviated from official dogma.

One of those whom Suslov helped raise to power was Andropov. Despite his connections to Suslov, high hopes were pinned on Andropov, who upon becoming general secretary following Brezhnev's death immediately launched a serious crackdown on corruption and removed many notorious officeholders. In return, he sought better discipline in the workplace.

Andropov was widely credited by those who worked under him earlier in his career for his unusual openness to ideas challenging party orthodoxy and for his immunity to the temptations of corruption, a strong contrast with much of the party leadership of this time. But he was also very cautious—too cautious in the minds of many who had worked under him—and so the organs of party control changed little from Brezhnev's last years. Andropov was also suffering from a kidney disease. He died after only 14 months in office, leaving him too little time to effect much serious change, although there is a consensus among those who worked with him that he sought a thorough restructuring of the economy.

Andropov's replacement was, disappointingly, Chernenko. Gorbachev by now was widely seen as the heir apparent, a reformer with a reputation for having overseen improvements in agriculture. But instead Chernenko, Brezhnev's sidekick, was selected as party general secretary. This was despite the fact that he was in poor health due to emphysema and heart diseases. He lasted little more than a year as general secretary. Chernenko had spent his career in the party apparatus, essentially acting as Brezhnev's chief of staff during Brezhnev's later years.

Chernenko continued to stress Brezhnev's concept of "developed socialism." Shortly after becoming general secretary in 1984, he declared that the "fusion of two revolutions—the scientific-technological and the social—should be given fitting reflection" in party policy, proclaiming that the "formation of the classless socialist society will be an important stage on the path to complete social homogeneity and will, no doubt, entail substantial changes in all superstructures."[37]

Chernenko was promising nothing less than sweeping social and technological changes that would radically overhaul Soviet society. Nothing so dramatic was going to come from Chernenko, as those who pushed his candidacy knew, but nor were those merely empty words. A special Central Committee session on the technological-scientific revolution was scheduled to convene during Chernenko's term, with Gorbachev tasked with giving the main report, but a Politburo majority scuttled it.[38]

Nonetheless, Chernenko did insist on Gorbachev being named to the important post of second secretary, over the objections of other Politburo members,[39] nor did he reverse Andropov's crackdown on corruption. The interregnum, however, could not continue beyond Chernenko's death, as even Politburo hard-liners realized.

The doctrinaire Grishin could have been Chernenko's successor as general secretary and was openly maneuvering to grab the top post. But realizing that the Soviet Union's ever mounting problems finally had to be tackled, one of the last holdovers from the Stalin era, Andrei Gromyko (who had been foreign minister since 1957) put forth Gorbachev's candidacy, smoothing the way to a quick ascension. *Perestroika* and *glasnost* would soon become household words around the world.

## Fruits of stagnation: The complexity of structural dysfunction

A basic structural issue to be tackled was that the Soviet economic (and political) system had become out of date.[40] The command system no longer functioned well, nor could it. Soviet industry was constructed in the 1930s on a system centered on an all-powerful dictator at the top, with an entourage that strictly oversaw all aspects of production, handing down a plan that had the force of uncontestable law. The entourage, Politburo members who directed ministries that oversaw various industrial branches, had to master an enormous amount of knowledge to cope with their duties.

Such a system can be efficient only with managerial possession of "perfect knowledge," or at least very close to perfect. The ministers and their deputies have to know intimately the production capacity of all factories and facilities in their charge, have to ensure that their orders are fulfilled, have to accurately calculate what raw materials are needed, ensure that the raw materials arrive as ordered and ensure that the finished products are distributed to where they are needed. As an economy develops and becomes more complex, it is impossible for a single person, or for a small group of officials, to possess such a breadth of information.

Socially, such a command system becomes alienating for those who work in it. In the 1930s, the Soviet Union had just begun the process of educating its citizens—the mass industrialization came at horrendous human cost, but it did provide opportunity for millions of people to rise into managerial positions who would never have had such opportunities in the pre-revolutionary past. Nor was there a shortage of enthusiasm for "building socialism." Fear alone—although there was certainly no shortage of terror and draconian labor laws—could not have produced the unprecedented development of the 1930s. But regardless of the motivations of the tens of millions whose herculean efforts built Soviet industry, such a system still entails the taking of orders and unquestioningly carrying them out. An educated society, which the Soviet Union became after World War II, naturally chafes at not having any control in the workplace or having any political voice.

After Stalin's death, life became much easier for working people, culminating in the unwritten Brezhnev "agreement"—

stay out of politics in exchange for an array of social guarantees such as full employment, easy access to health care and secure pensions. The ongoing need to increase economic output also helped to loosen conditions on the shop floor. Persistent labor shortages and factory managers' needs to not drive out workers so that there would be sufficient personnel to fulfill their assigned plans provided space for workers to wrest some control on the shop floor, and regular wages were so consistently supplemented by bonuses for reaching or exceeding plan targets that jobs would be advertised by including the bonuses as part of the expected pay.

Nonetheless, alienation became more widespread. Labor unions were not independent from the state and consistently sided with management, leaving working people without an organized voice for better conditions and pay. There was no real opportunity to give input into the organization of work. Workers could "vote with their feet" by leaving for another workplace, but the same basic conditions would be there as well.

A strong sense of egalitarianism pervaded Soviet society, with official ideology backing those sentiments, so the privileges afforded higher officials bred considerable resentment. Those privileges were minuscule compared with the immense wealth amassed by the elite in capitalist countries, but were real enough in a country that believed in equality and suffered from ongoing shortages of consumer products. A distinct "us versus them" attitude developed, and these factors jelled into a deep alienation.

Those shortages also bred alienation. During the latter years of the "era of stagnation," consumer consumption had continued to increase—for example, meat consumption was three-quarters higher in 1985 than in 1965 and the ownership of television sets had increased fourfold in the same time span. More consumer products were available, easing people's lives, yet this is when the desire for more became more acute. In part this was due to the fact that the quality and availability of consumer goods in the

Soviet Union lagged behind that of the advanced capitalist countries by a considerable margin and that shortages persisted in all manner of goods. A hidden inflation had also taken root in the early 1980s—official prices of consumer commodities tended to remain unchanged for years, but cheaper, more basic items would disappear from the shelves, leaving only more expensive variations available. The prices for the respective variations remained the same, but because only the more expensive item could be bought, the substitution amounted to price inflation.

Acute housing shortages were another factor in lagging material living standards. The massive movement of the Soviet population from the countryside and smaller towns to the major cities could not be kept up with by new housing, creating years-long waiting lists in cities such as Moscow. The combination of chronic labor shortages, better opportunities in Moscow and a shortage of work in outlying areas, particularly in the Central Asian republics, created a second-class group of people termed the *limitchiki*. These internal migrants received a five-year permit to live in Moscow, where they worked in substandard conditions for low pay and lived in temporary housing such as dormitories. (A permit was needed to live in the capital because authorities wished to slow the steady flow of people seeking to move there; the infrastructure was already inadequate for the existing population.) After five years, during which time they were at the mercy of their factory managers, they could receive a permanent permit to stay in Moscow but only then join the queue for permanent housing. (The lives of the limitchiki were often featured in Soviet newspapers.)

The bureaucracy coped by continuing to pour investment capital into creating new production capacity that could not be fully utilized, rather than upgrading an aging industrial infrastructure. Here it is necessary to differentiate between the two sets of officials (and this duplication was yet another problem). There was the bloated party bureaucracy, a group collectively known as the *apparat*; its members were "apparatchiks." The apparatchiks essentially duplicated the work of the government ministries by overseeing their work in minute detail and imposing themselves in the smallest details. The party Central Committee contained large departments to supervise all sections of the economy.

But over time, the decisive bureaucracy was that of the government. This bureaucracy was known as the "nomenklatura." The term, which comes from the Latin, literally means "list of names." It was just that. All top posts in the ministries, throughout the government and in the economic enterprises, were filled by the party from a list of approved names. The nomenklatura, who enjoyed considerable privileges, were all party members in good standing and so enjoyed a dual status as important officials in government or industry.

The nomenklatura essentially controlled the economy through their direct management of it. The party's Politburo and Central Committee continued to issue a steady stream of directives, to which the nomenklatura were doubly subjected as the managers or ministry officials responsible for the fulfillment of the plan and also being under strict party discipline, but as the command structure created in the 1930s decayed, the nomenklatura were able to act with increasing independence. The party leadership was unable to force compliance with its orders, in large part due to its inability to possess enough reliable data to know what should or could be produced. There were too many enterprises, too many factories and places of production, for any small group to know well.

As is typical in any tightly controlled, top-down organization, the party's leadership at national, republic, regional and local levels tended to reproduce itself. Grey, unimaginative figures incapable of independent thought but willing to carry out all orders from above constituted a large number of those who moved up the ranks and they in turn pulled up those like themselves, perpetuating mediocrity. From the same pool came the nomenklatura. With no popular control and answerable only to those above, and where the top level of the party had lost its ability to impose its decisions, the bureaucracy was able to develop into a privileged strata.

The state planning agency, Gosplan, continued to issue state orders to enterprises to fulfill the five-year plans, and enterprises continued to be judged solely on their fulfillment of plan targets. Enterprise management handed down their orders to their individual factories and production units, and directors and managers continued to be responsible for implementing the plan directives on the shop floor. But labor shortages, alienation and other social factors left the workforce with little incentive to produce more than the plan, and continual shortages of raw materials, aging equipment and poor working conditions often impeded quality.

Management would be judged by whether it met its target—everything was based on reaching a hard numerical total. Quality was not factored in nor was increased efficiency through technological or other innovations. Worse, a technological innovation that resulted in an improved product that used less raw material could actually result in being judged to have failed to meet a quota because the resulting improved product weighed less than the previous product. Therefore, neither those working on the shop floor nor management had incentive to concern themselves with quality, and because the components sent to them by their suppliers were created under the same conditions, poor-quality inputs were added to a poor-quality product that often did not perform well or, if the product was in turn a component of a more finished final product, that final product's quality was hurt by the poor quality of its components.

Another factor promoting inefficiency was that, because a certain volume had to be reached, extra personnel were kept on the payroll in case production had to be increased to reach the target. Extra raw materials and inputs had to be stockpiled for the same reason and as a hedge against possible future shortages. The hoarding of inventories above plan allotments could prevent needed supplies from reaching another enterprise that needed them, creating still more imbalance.

In effect, management's interest was to hide capacity so it would have sufficient reserves to reach its target during periods of raw materials shortages and to prevent their factories or enterprises from receiving higher production quotas. The workforce counted on bonuses given for reaching targets to supplement chronically low wages, and higher targets might prompt some workers, in continuing conditions of labor shortage, to quit and work elsewhere. Therefore, the workforce and management both had incentive to keep information away from the nomenklatura and party bosses who made all of the decisions.

Because of their lack of knowledge, the planners could not adequately create plans. And because there were insufficient mechanisms to study consumer demand, it was difficult for the system to produce adequate consumer products. The lack of quality in consumer items also played a role in depressing consumer spending because there was a lack of demand for low-quality products, leaving large amounts of unsold inventory. The lack of quality also impacted industry and research as institutions sometimes sought to buy equipment from outside the country to avoid having to use internally made equipment that did not work well.

Yet another factor was a chronic, built-in imbalance in producing for heavy industry as opposed to light industry, including food and consumer products. Soviet industry was created in the 1930s with an extreme emphasis on heavy industry. Stalin had wanted to create a massive industrial infrastructure in ten years where little had existed, and with little access to capital from outside the country other than through agricultural exports, the capital needed to effect this manic development could only come internally from industrial workers and farmers. The extraction of that capital came through reduced living standards that were suppressed through lowered wages, a lack of consumer products and a starvation of residential construction.

After Stalin's death these conditions were drastically eased, but the mania for heavy industry remained. Therefore, by 1985, Soviet industry still concentrated on producing machinery and parts to be used in industry, failing to shift a sufficient portion of its capacity to fulfilling consumer demand. Compounding this problem was that profits from light industry were confiscated to provide subsidies to heavy industry, making it difficult to find the capital necessary to finance increased production of consumer items.

Production of consumer items was often concentrated in a single entity, and the resulting lack of competition was seen as contributing to quality problems. The widespread low quality was often contrasted with the Soviet Union's prowess in military hardware, which was seen as being in "competition" with hardware made in other countries. Sophisticated technology, including that of computers, went into the military, but because of excessive secrecy, very little spinoff was seen in civilian industry, in contrast to the technological spinoff generated in capitalist countries. And the extraordinarily high amount spent on the military was another drain on the economy. Leonid Brezhnev had decided that military prowess would be the route to international respect, and the fact that the KGB chief, and the defense and foreign ministers, each sat on the Politburo reflected that belief.

Yet it cannot be denied that, overall, living standards rose during the course of the Brezhnev years and that production continued to grow—at ever-slowing rates but without any recessionary drops as seen in capitalist countries. Nonetheless, a range of problems, including shortages, seemed to become more intractable. The accumulated result of all these problems was a continual decrease in productivity and a steady decline in the ability to obtain an adequate return on investments.

The impressive growth of earlier years was based on a steady increase in productive capacity—more factories equaled more production. The command system set up under Stalin could produce growth as long as the investment capital it extracted from industrial workers and farmers was used to build new, productive capacity. Eventually, new equipment wears out and must be replaced. Old equipment can be replaced by new machinery of later vintage, theoretically more productive and therefore increasing the capacity of an existing plant.

But instead of replacing worn, outdated equipment, Soviet planners went on building new plants and putting them online alongside the existing facilities. But the older equipment that remains in service breaks down more often and doesn't work as well when it is operating; capacity at an older plant declines until new equipment is installed. So although the economy receives the benefit of the new capacity with better capabilities, this new capacity is partially offset by the deterioration of the older facility. But sometimes there was not enough capital to finish the new plant, so the capital that went into an unfinished capacity would be wasted and the declining capacity of existing facilities would become magnified. At other times, a new facility was built without taking into account that a labor shortage already existed in its location, so the new capacity would be underused.

The poor quality of much new machinery further retarded the potential of new facilities. The net result of all these factors was that the value of output as compared to the value of the investment made was 40 percent lower in 1985 than it was in 1960—a phenomenal drag on the economy. Put another way, Soviet industry required continually rising amounts of resources to produce the same quantity of material.

This massive array of problems was what confronted Soviet leaders when the widely anticipated new era arrived in 1985.

## Steel teeth and a fast start: Gorbachev makes his first moves as general secretary

Leonid Brezhnev's "stability in cadres" had not made an exception for the Communist Party's highest body, the Politburo. From January 1982 to March 1985, a three-year period culminating in Konstantin Chernenko's death, five full members of the Politburo and two candidate members died—and the average age of its membership was still 68. New blood in the leadership was desperately needed and, unlike a year earlier, when the terminally ill Yuri Andropov had unsuccessfully sought to have Mikhail Gorbachev replace him, this time the Politburo's youngest member was given the nod.

Andrei Gromyko's endorsement and his comment to the Central Committee that Gorbachev "may have a nice smile, but he has teeth of steel" provided an enormous boost for the new general secretary. Regardless, there was a consensus on the Politburo and Central Committee that serious reform was needed, a viewpoint shared by many of the party's several dozen provincial first secretaries, who by themselves constituted a significant bloc on the Central Committee.

Gorbachev wasted no time in reshaping the top of the party. Within his first three months, he pushed out one of his hard-line rivals, Grigori Romanov, from the Politburo, removed Gromyko from the foreign ministry after 28 years by promoting him to the ceremonial office of president, and replaced Romanov on the Politburo and Gromyko as foreign minister with his long-time friend, Eduard Shevardnadze. By the beginning of 1986, Gorbachev had removed two other Politburo hard-liners, Prime Minister Nikolai Tikhonov and Moscow party boss Viktor Grishin, as well as the top three economic officials and one-quarter of the country's regional and local first secretaries.

Gorbachev's twin themes were *perestroika* (restructuring) and *glasnost* (openness). These basic concepts were to be applied across society. Upon taking office and throughout the rest of

1985, Gorbachev stressed the "strengthening of discipline" and meant it—one of his first acts was to announce a crackdown on alcohol, banning the sale of alcohol before 2 p.m. and threatening government officials who drank excessively with penalties.[41]

From the start, Gorbachev was a Soviet leader very different from his recent predecessors. In May 1985, he told an audience at the Smolny, Bolshevik headquarters during the October Revolution, "Try to get your flat repaired: you will have to find a moonlighter to do it for you—and he will have to steal the materials from a building site."[42] Indeed, a large percentage of home and appliance repairs were done by people earning some extra money on the side because getting such work done through official routes could be futile. Later in the year, Gorbachev told another audience, "You can understand the consumer who wonders why we know how to make spaceships and atomic-powered ships, but often produce defective modern household gadgets, shoes and clothes."[43] No Soviet leader had spoken in public like this since the 1920s.

Not all of the early initiatives went as planned. The alcohol crackdown caused some economic problems because vodka production accounted for a staggeringly large percentage of the Soviet economy. It was also hidden. A samizdat researcher, Mikhail Baitalski (writing under the pseudonym "A. Krasikov"), a Red Army soldier in the Civil War who later worked as a journalist and as a metalworker but who also spent 11 years in Stalin's camps for the "crime" of being a "Trotskyist," was able to calculate that 25 percent of the Soviet Union's collected sales taxes came from vodka and that it accounted for 28 percent of all food and drink sold in state and cooperative shops—the largest single commodity of any kind.[44] It took research to discover this because, in the late 1970s, vodka came under the heading of "other foodstuffs," a column that accounted for one-third of all expenditures, while foodstuffs accounting for less than 1 percent were listed individually in official statistical reports.[45]

Nonetheless, Gorbachev's most important move in 1985 was to announce an adjustment to the current five-year plan. For 1986, consumer consumption would not see much improvement; instead there would be a large increase in the production of new machine tools. At first glance, this seems like a continuation of the past overemphasis on heavy industry, but there was a difference this time. About 45 percent of the equipment used in heavy industry during perestroika was considered "totally worn out."[46] Gorbachev's initiative was to emphasize new machine tools to replace old equipment instead of bringing still more capacity online.[47]

Machine tools were also a focus of the first government reform—Gorbachev created a "super-ministry" of machine tools in October 1985, followed a month later by the merger of five ministries into a single agricultural super-ministry.[48] Meanwhile, a steady stream of exhortations appeared in party newspapers across the country during 1985 calling on party officials to conduct their work more honestly and openly.

This momentum carried into the party's congress at the end of February 1986, when Gorbachev would be able to make more changes in the party's top ranks. Signaling his intentions, the general secretary declared, "A ruling stratum lies between the leadership of the country and the people, who wish for change, who dream of change—the apparat of the minister, the apparat of the party, which does not want transformation, which does not intend to lose certain rights tied to privileges."[49] Forty-one percent of the new Central Committee's membership were elected for the first time, an extraordinary turnover, and the Congress also replaced 14 of the 23 Central Committee department heads.[50]

New party rules adopted at the congress demanded "collectivity of work" in all organizations and declared that collective work is a "reliable guarantee against the adoption of volitional, subjective decisions, manifestations of the cult of personality, and infringements of Leninist norms of party life."[51] Certainly explicit words, but even with all the personnel changes, there was yet no guarantee that these words would be put into action.

Two months after the congress, the Chernobyl nuclear disaster happened. There was official silence for ten days, until radiation measurements downwind in Europe created international pressure to put an end to the lack of information. The Soviet Union then began providing information, and this development seemed to propel forward perestroika's twin, glasnost. The new openness led to the release of Andrei Sakharov from internal exile and the pardon of his wife and fellow human-rights activist, Yelena Bonner, at the end of 1986, followed by the release of the country's last 200 or so political prisoners. This period also saw the end of jamming Western radio broadcasts, and the long-awaited publication of Anna Akhmatova's poem *Requiem* and Anatoli Rybakov's novel *Children of the Arbat*—two highly regarded literary efforts about Stalin's purges that had been long censored and the publication of which was still opposed by hard-liners.

Concomitantly, the Soviet justice minister announced that the notorious Article 70, banning "anti-Soviet propaganda and activity," would be dropped in the new legal code being formulated.[52] And seriousness in the fight against corruption was unmistakably signaled when the first secretary of the republic of Kazakhstan, Dinmukhamed Kunayev, who also had a seat on the Politburo in Moscow, was forced into retirement. Kunayev was the notorious chief of a tight group of associates that maintained an iron grip on the Central Asian republic while skimming off considerable wealth for itself.

The Kunayev group's grip on Kazakhstan was so tight that Gorbachev appointed a Russian as the new republic leader in an effort to break the culture of corruption there. An orchestrated riot in the Kazakh capital followed the news of a non-Kazakh's appointment, demonstrating both the resistance to restructuring in the party apparatus and the latent nationalism that six decades of Russian chauvinism had engendered. These two awakening tendencies would become prominent during the next few years.

Still, all this represented no more than a start, albeit a necessary start, particularly with the end of censorship. How could the country solve its problems without frankly discussing them? The economy still awaited a solution, and the first serious attempt at reform came in 1987.

## More stick than carrot: Uneven implementation of the enterprise law of 1987

The first major shakeup in the Soviet Union's economic organization—the Law on State Enterprises—was approved in June 1987 by the Central Committee. The basic concept of the enterprise law was to liberate enterprises from some of the more rigid controls of the ministries, put them on profit-and-loss accounting, reduce the amount of product required to be produced for the state plan, reduce subsidies in order to make enterprises more efficient, and bring a measure of democracy into the workplace with the creation of "labor-collective councils" and workforce elections of enterprise directors.

State planning remained in force, but would become less of a hard numerical total and more of a guide, although the requirement of fulfilling the (reduced) plan requirements would continue. Production sold to the state under the plan would still constitute most sales and would continue to be paid at rates specified by the state, but production beyond plan fulfillment could be sold at any price, subject to volume limitations to prevent unnecessary production beyond any reasonable social need.

In conjunction with these reforms, measures were implemented aimed at putting pressure on wages. Basic wage rates were increased, but individual output quotas (or "norms") were also raised, to make it much more difficult to earn bonuses. Bonuses would no longer be essentially automatic; they could only be earned through more effort—and the new wage levels made up only part of the differences between the new basic wage and the old basic wage plus bonus.

Put plainly, workers would have to work harder to earn the same amount of money. Bonuses, in turn, would no longer be given simply for meeting quotas, but would now also depend on quality and efficiency and be dependent on the results of an entire unit. And further pressure was applied by forcing workers into lower skill grades (grade inflation had sometimes been used to enhance wages) and a larger wage differential between the grades was implemented.[53] The new wage system was implemented immediately, but otherwise the enterprise law was to be phased in, taking effect in half of the country's enterprises on 1 January 1988, and the other half one year later.

The basic idea behind these sets of reforms was to introduce a mechanism that would provide a better understanding of demand while retaining central planning. In turn, more efficiency would be wrung out of the system through the use of shop-floor and enterprise-wide incentives and the introduction of some workplace democracy, thereby alleviating both some of the alienation on the part of the workforce and the incentive of management to avoid introducing technological or other improvements. Further, the decrease in mandatory production to fulfill state orders and a new ability to arrange direct sales would encourage mutually beneficial relations between producers and suppliers, reducing the fetter from the over-centralized system that required enterprises to make all deals through the ministries.

Gorbachev also sought to use the new law as a springboard for further changes in the party. "The party cannot accept that perestroika sets the pace for the economic, social and moral progress under way; that the changes in the lives and moods of the people surpass the party's understanding of them," he said, adding that the country was facing an "economic stagnation"[54]—an unmistakable comparison with the era of Leonid Brezhnev.

The contradictions within these plans included that the sprawling bureaucracies of Gosplan (the state planning agency) and Gossnab (the state supply and distribution agency) would remain intact and therefore, because most production and supply would still go through them, enterprises would have no control over prices. A critic of the new law, Leonid Abalkin, a reformer who headed a Soviet economic institute, said, "By continuing to opt for purely quantitative, volume economic growth we are unable to solve the problems of fundamentally improving output quality, retooling the national economy, and improving its efficiency, and we cannot turn the economy around towards the consumer."[55]

But there were macroeconomic problems as well, not all in the Soviet Union's control. An important factor was a large decline in revenue from oil exports—oil and gas exports accounted for more than half of the country's export earnings but prices of both commodities were sharply lower in 1985 through 1988 as compared to 1984.[56] Another blow to the economy came with the crackdown on vodka. Primarily due to the large decline in vodka available through official channels, the national collection of sales taxes declined 13 percent in 1986 from 1984.[57] Drinkers responded by brewing more of their own vodka, which in turn created a shortage of sugar.[58] The combination of reduced sales-tax revenue, reduced income from oil and gas, and the emphasis on machine tools to provide a necessary overhaul to productive capacity—more consumer goods couldn't be produced until there was more equipment to make them—resulted in a decline in the availability of consumer goods by 1988. This was one disappointment for working people. A bigger disappointment, however, was the lack of results, for them, from the enterprise law and the wage-restructuring package.

The wage reforms were originally supposed to have been

implemented slowly, concurrent with implementation of the other reforms and the preparation of enterprises for the change to profit-and-loss accounting. Demotions to lower skill grades were not supposed to be implemented without a chance for targeted employees to appeal and take a skills test, but instead managements frequently imposed unilateral demotions.[59] Although many male workers suffered from these actions, women were frequently the specific targets of skill-level demotions and were also more prone to illegal dismissal from jobs because of the looser job protections resulting from the package of reforms.[60]

Management was not subject to this taste of market mechanisms, and the egalitarian streak of workers was inflamed because workers believed they were again bearing the brunt for what was not their fault and sacrificing once again to subsidize the bloated bureaucracies, both the apparatchiks of the party and the nomenklatura of the government ministries.

Unilateral management dictates were possible because the workplace democracy was stillborn. Only a minuscule number of the "labor-collective councils" actually functioned as intended, by giving the workforce a genuine voice. In most factories, either there was no council, it did nothing or the enterprise director headed it, neutralizing its potential. The trade unions, as before, did nothing to intervene, remaining silent or backing management.

Top-down orders in the old fashion continued in even the rare factory where management actually was elected, as an automobile factory labor-collective council chair complained in a labor newspaper:

> Although all managerial personnel in the factory are elected, so far this democratization is more external than deep. In its relation with the labor-collective council, management, as before, adheres to the military code: an order from a higher rank is not open to discussion. For example, the adminis-

> tration orders the workers to appear on their days off, and neither the labor-collective council nor the trade union even tries to protest, even though we have passed the limit of [legally] allowed overtime.[61]

After the first year of the enterprise law, polling showed that a mere 15 percent of industrial workers, technical specialists and managers felt the reforms yielded positive results.[62] The intention of democratizing the workplace was conceived as a way to reduce alienation and as a necessary balance to the increased power that would be possessed by management. Mikhail Gorbachev himself had said, "The well-being of the worker will depend upon the abilities of the managers. The workers should, therefore, have real means of influencing the choice of director and controlling his activity."[63] But the enterprise law text was ambiguous—it made references to "one-man management," the foundation of the existing top-down command structure; did not specify the powers of labor-collective councils and the workforce; and stated that, although directors are elected, those elections must be confirmed by a ministry, a veto power supposedly needed to avoid cases of unspecified excesses.[64]

But not only did managements remain unanswerable to workforces, government ministries refused to relinquish their grips. The nomenklatura owed their privileges and power to the ability to command, and naturally most of them did not relish losing such positions. Ministry officials continued to issue detailed orders to enterprise managements that left no room for enterprises to make their own decisions and continued to require enterprises to buy from a specific supplier, acting as a crucial brake on democratization; they also continued to impose management personnel.[65] The traditional top-down economic structure remained largely untouched. It appears that no more than 20 percent of enterprise directors were ever elected[66] and, after 1988, the councils became more irrelevant until the entire experiment was ended in 1990.

The party remained deeply divided, and so could not act to enforce the reforms in any consistent manner, thereby ceding its potentially powerful supervisory role. But, additionally, because the dense network of industry, agriculture and commerce spread over a vast country was simply far too large, and far too complex, for a small body at the top of the party structure to possess anywhere near enough knowledge to oversee it, power continued to devolve to the nomenklatura. Each industrial-branch ministry could continue to run its fiefdom as it wished. Those factors, combined with the inability of the workforces to have any real voice (partly because there was no mechanism to enforce it and because workers remained unorganized and demoralized after almost six decades of political pressure against their organizing) left the nomenklatura free to continue to exert control, and therefore maintain their privileged status.

Some progress was made in the political realm, although there were those in local party bodies, and in Moscow, who continued to resist this as well. But with the economy continuing to be run in a top-down manner, and the problems inherited in 1985 largely left unsolved, the question of democracy in reality, as opposed to theory, was raised more urgently. If there is no democracy in the workplace, no popular control over decision-making in the economy, could there be any real democracy at all?

Thus far, all the decisions on perestroika and glasnost had been made at the top with only indirect input from the grassroots level. Little improvement in people's living standards had been seen. These conditions had to be changed, soon, or Gorbachev's entire project would founder.

### Differences come out in the open: The party is not so monolithic after all

Self-interest played the lion's share in the list of reasons that could be formulated in answer to the question of why so much of the party was resistant to the reforms. In a one-party state, there is no need to contest for political power through ideas; and in the Soviet Union the one party's rule was codified in the constitution, guaranteeing the supremacy of its ideology.

In such a situation, the party is less a political organization than a supervisory body and the best route to a career. And because that party's ideology becomes fixed (there is no countervailing force to oppose it, unless it arises from within the party or from an organized movement entirely outside the system) the surest route to a career is through adopting that ideology and never visibly deviating from it, and gaining the mentorship of someone who had done exactly the same thing. And with that career comes access to privileges. So why rock the boat? Careerists did what would be expected—they resisted change to protect their privileges and power.

Mikhail Gorbachev was doing something highly unusual for the leader of a single-party system—he was trying to make significant changes to the prevailing ideology and to the methodologies used to govern. In effect, he attempted a "top-down" restructuring, a process that potentially could develop into a top-down social revolution. Not a more thoroughgoing political revolution; Gorbachev did not want to scrap the Soviet system. Rather he sought to implement the long overdue changes it needed so that actual reality came much closer to the promises of socialism. But what Gorbachev and his party allies needed to do was to provide sufficient political space to enable the grassroots to create their own movements.

The "bottom-up" side of perestroika and glasnost was missing. Nearly six decades of atomization that was the bequest of the Stalin dictatorship and the political superstructure that had lived on, repeated disappointments in the previous much less ambitious reforms of Nikita Khrushchev and later leaders, and the lack of democracy in the workplace and in politics left the Soviet people deeply wary. Perestroika and glasnost, intended to create the conditions to move the country toward the creation of a true socialist democracy (or at least bring improvements in living standards and provide more space for a civil society), would not take hold without fundamental changes in the political superstructure. Thus far, the new freedom of the press meant that complaints of every sort filled the pages of newspapers and periodicals, and although an important development, writing letters to editors still constituted the main avenue of redress. Official channels had to be opened.

Gorbachev would now need to democratize the party, making it more of a party and less of a managerial body. That would be no easy task.

The prime minister at this time, Nikolai Ryzhkov, who had chaired the party Central Committee's economics department when Yuri Andropov was general secretary, was aware that the independence that had devolved to the government's industrial-branch ministries would be difficult to counteract. "Both the Central Committee and the [government] Council of Ministers had been lacerated by departmentalism" by the early 1980s, Ryzhkov later wrote. "Every department tried to take the blanket for itself because there was not a composite department in the Central Committee that could formulate overall economic policy."[67]

Another outcome of the June 1987 Central Committee meeting that passed the enterprise law was a decision to convene a special party conference in June 1988. A conference was akin to a miniature congress. Party congresses were held every four years, although the date could be moved up, and it was at these gatherings that broad policy decisions were approved and a new Central Committee elected, after which the Central Committee could, and usually did, make changes in the lineup of the ruling Politburo. In the past, the party had sometimes convened conferences to make policy and personnel shifts that would ordinarily be made at a congress without the trouble of preparing a full congress. This party conference would be the first such gathering since 1941.

The Central Committee resolved that the delegates to the conference would be elected by secret ballot and that the special gathering would take "measures for the further democratization of the life of the party and society."[68] Gorbachev's calculation was that the party grassroots would elect delegates that would be firmly behind perestroika and glasnost, and the binding measures approved by these delegates would speed up needed reforms by bypassing the recalcitrant party bureaucracy. Gorbachev also concentrated his fire on the lower ranks of the party bureaucracy, at the city, regional and republican levels. In part this was due to the difficulties the general secretary was having with the central party apparatus in Moscow, but also reflected the fact that, in many localities, entrenched local elites were openly hostile to any lessening of their considerable powers over local matters.

A *Pravda* commentary pulled no punches on the severity of that problem:

> Mutual relations among workers based on servility and sycophancy have to this day not been eliminated in the apparatus of some party, soviet and economic bodies. Here you still find a collection of rules which can essentially be described as "Know your place." There are leaders who are unashamedly proud of the obedience of their subordinates, who unthinkingly carry out any assignments but are totally incapable of initiative. This kind of style does not accord with the times. Party-minded, civic activeness is today demanded of everyone.[69]

Differences among those at the top of the party leadership were also becoming more defined, and began to come out into the open. In turn, Gorbachev increasingly sought to find a middle course between those who wanted faster and more thorough reforms and those who agreed with the consensus that changes were necessary but believed that Gorbachev was moving too fast. Those among the former included many of his advisers and an increasingly active intelligentsia; those among the latter included many Politburo and Central Committee members. The outright opponents of any change and the flamboyantly corrupt had been removed from the Politburo by autumn 1987, at which point Gorbachev had named a majority of the Politburo and a majority of the next most important party layer, the Central Committee secretaries. But that did not mean that all the new appointees were faithful followers. Nor did it mean that new opposition to Gorbachev's policies would not develop, at all levels of the party.

Gorbachev acknowledged the intricate, many-sided struggle that was developing when he told a group of newspaper editors that "the old and new are living side by side, comrades, side by side, and they are in conflict," producing "an intricate mosaic of moods, confused thoughts, illusion, impatience, irritation."[70] Some of the societal confusion undoubtedly was a result of Gorbachev not having a thought-out plan—there was a certain improvisational flourish to his moves, but as time went on he had more difficulty navigating among the multiple currents of opinion. But the general secretary was helped by the fact that there was no consensus on the way forward, and therefore no bloc that could coalesce into a defined alternative movement.

The second-ranking member of the Politburo, Yegor Ligachev, a Gorbachev appointee, emerged as the leading voice of caution—he opposed changes being made too rapidly without sufficient preparation as well as those changes that he believed would lead to the imposition of capitalism, arguing that a reliance on only market relations would result in unacceptable unemployment, homelessness and social injustice. Ligachev did back glasnost and perestroika (he would not have held his seat on the Politburo for almost all of the Gorbachev era otherwise), doing so, for example, in this *Pravda* commentary: "We must actively utilize market, commodity-money relations within the framework of socialism, with the aim of revealing all of its advantages and possibilities."[71]

Uncertainty about the depth of the commitments to reform, however, came to the surface in March 1988, with the full-page publication of an article titled "I cannot renounce principles" in the official newspaper of the Russian republic government, perhaps the most authoritative paper other than the central party daily *Pravda* and the central government daily *Izvestia*. The article was an apologia for Josef Stalin and an all-out attack on all the reforms of the past three years, complete with an attack on "cosmopolitanism," Stalin's notorious code word used to condemn international ideas that carried unmistakably anti-Semitic undertones. The article, written by an unknown chemistry professor, Nina Andreyeva, was published as Gorbachev was about to leave on a trip to Yugoslavia.

Ligachev was widely accused of being the hidden hand behind the publication of the letter, and in a meeting of newspaper editors was said to have praised the article as an example to emulate. Ligachev, however, consistently said he did not know of the letter before it was published—in his memoirs he said rumors of his involvement were "absurd and thoroughly malicious" and a "primitive invention."[72] He also wrote that the meeting where he discussed the article had previously been scheduled, that the meeting was at first taken up by the scheduled discussion of agricultural topics and that his praise was limited to the portion of the article opposing a blanket condemnation of the entire past.[73]

Regardless of who made the decision to publish, the Andreyeva letter caused a sensation, in a negative way. When there was no immediate official response to the article, widespread fear that reform had come to an end took hold—

despite the new press freedom, "official" newspapers remained important and continued to be read for signals of shifts in party policy. For three weeks, Gorbachev was silent in public, choosing not to overreact. Finally, an official response was published in *Pravda*, the most authoritative newspaper in the Soviet Union, vehemently attacking the Andreyeva article and thereby putting the matter to rest.

The episode had been a tempest in a teapot. But that it had occurred at all underscored the top-down nature of the reforms and the lack of pressure from grassroots social forces. Glasnost had provided the ability for people to complain and discuss freely, but organized social movements that could put the reforms on more solid ground had not been created. Three years had elapsed since Gorbachev became general secretary with a mandate for serious reform, but the panicked reaction to the Andreyeva article demonstrated clearly that the reforms, thus far, were not on a sufficiently solid footing and that they remained dependent on political alignments at the top of the party.

Because the party continued to be a top-down organization, the dependency on alignments at the top would continue to be decisive until sufficiently strong social movements emerged—these could be some combination of renewed or new independent trade unions, a labor-collective council movement radically changed through seizure by rank-and-file memberships, or new forms of social organization outside the workplaces. But these types of grassroots movements faced strong impediments to coalescing because the centralized nature of the Soviet system concentrated power in the hands of party and government bureaucrats and the enterprise directors, making workplace organizing in particular difficult. Yet without strong grassroots pressures through national organizations, the people of the Soviet Union would continue to be unable to affect the changes buffeting their country.

Steadily diverging ideas about Soviet history added an extra complication. Debate about this history was inevitable, healthy and long overdue, but many reformers who wanted a faster pace and a greater reliance on markets also had such a pent-up desire to examine the past critically that they began presenting the past in entirely negative ways. A desire for a more nuanced examination of history was behind Ligachev's disapproval of those he believed were working to "discredit" the entirety of Soviet history.

"To move forward successfully, society had to go through a process of self-cleansing and re-thinking much of what happened in the past," Ligachev wrote in his memoirs. He agreed that striving for justice in examining the past was "salutary," but believed that many writers "narrow-mindedly relish[ed] the misfortunes that had befallen earlier generations…The past rose up from the pages of the right-wing radical press not as a diverse and contradictory combination of achievements and errors but in exclusively gloomy if not pitch-black tones."[74]

Ligachev already had a lengthy career behind him when Gorbachev promoted him to the Politburo shortly after becoming general secretary. And Ligachev was no stranger to Stalin-era repression—his father-in-law had been one of the generals executed in Stalin's mass purge of the Red Army in 1937 and he himself had been investigated for the "crime" of being a "Trotskyist" in 1949 before being cleared.

Not a careerist, Ligachev was content to spend two decades as party first secretary for a western Siberian province, where he earned a reputation for personal honesty and refusing to tolerate corruption. As a provincial first secretary, he supervised the construction of academic, cultural and industrial institutions in an area that previously had been a backwater. But Ligachev also experienced the limitations of a regional post when on a trip to Moscow he sought permission to raise a memorial in a provincial village that had been a forced-labor camp for waves of political opponents of the tsars and then again in the 1930s, only to be curtly refused any discussion by the powerful party ideology chief, Mikhail Suslov, because Stalin's victims would have been memorialized along with tsarist victims.

Ligachev was brought to Moscow by Andropov to serve as the Central Committee official in charge of personnel with a firm mandate to root out corrupt provincial party officials. Ligachev also was responsible for advancing the career of a very different personality who would eventually eclipse Gorbachev.

Boris Yeltsin was trained as an engineer in Sverdlovsk (a city that today is once again known by its original name, Yekaterinburg), beginning his career in the construction industry, where he rose from foreman to director of a construction enterprise. By then, Yeltsin had joined the party to further his career. He was given a regional party post overseeing the construction industry before working his way up the party ladder to become the first secretary of Sverdlovsk, the industrial center of the Ural Mountains. Yeltsin's rise through the ranks of industry and then the party demonstrates that he was an energetic and capable administrator, but he also had a reputation for being difficult to work for, shifting responsibility to his subordinates when something went wrong and unhesitatingly carrying out party orders.

Yeltsin was brought to Moscow on the recommendation of Ligachev to become head of the party Central Committee's construction department. Months later, when Viktor Grishin, a hard-liner who was the potential alternative to Gorbachev in 1985, was dismissed from the Politburo and as Moscow party boss, Gorbachev replaced Grishin as Moscow first secretary with Yeltsin, who also became a candidate member of the Politburo.

Yeltsin was tasked with rooting out corruption in the Moscow branch of the party and immediately adopted a populist style. On his first day, he chose to eat in the regular city committee cafeteria instead of the one reserved for top officials, ordered the special cafeteria closed on his second day and then closed several special stores reserved for high officials to buy goods not available to the general public.[75] He subsequently fired the mayor of Moscow, most of the city government department heads and most of the secretaries of the city's district party organizations.[76]

Yeltsin, however, also had an abrasive personality, and he overreached when, in a party meeting, he bitterly attacked Ligachev (this was before the Andreyeva affair) and more generally denounced what he believed was the too-slow pace of perestroika. His criticisms rejected, Yeltsin demanded that he be allowed to resign; instead, he was removed from the Politburo and as Moscow first secretary. Yeltsin, however, gained popularity when details of the meeting were published.[77]

Navigating through these affairs, buffeted from all sides, Gorbachev hoped that the June 1988 special party conference would provide him with a boost. Despite these expectations, candidates of the party apparatus won a majority of the seats to the conference due to many local party bosses arranging elections in the old-style ways—only allowing their approved candidates to be put forth—although some of the irregularities were reversed under public pressure.[78] One key reform that Gorbachev won was a drastic reorganization of the Central Committee apparatus, scrapping the myriad of departments and replacing them all with six commissions. Further consolidation in the party bureaucracy at lower levels was also proposed, with the expectation that the size of the party apparatus would be cut by 30 to 50 percent.[79]

Further ideological changes were not neglected, either, as Gorbachev called for the party to use all progressive theory and practice from abroad and won approval for the creation of a new parliament that would act as an independent legislative branch of government.[80] The new parliament, the Congress of People's Deputies, would in turn elect a new Supreme Soviet invested with real powers, and the Supreme Soviet would elect the president, creating an executive for the country not named directly by the party. This arrangement would help separate state from party and reduce party control over day-to-day government functions.

The Central Committee restructuring entailed a shuffling of personnel, and resulted in a demotion for Ligachev, who remained among the leadership but was removed as ideology chief and unofficial second secretary and put in charge of the new CC agriculture commission. The six commissions were to study problems and formulate regulations,[81] a change from the previous Central Committee departments that were direct supervisors. Andrei Gromyko was pushed into retirement, with Gorbachev replacing him as president, and a close Gorbachev associate, Vadim Medvedev, was promoted to the Politburo and put in charge of the new Central Committee ideology commission.

The current position of president was a symbolic post in itself. The president was technically the chair of the existing Supreme Soviet, a rubber-stamp body with no independent decision-making authority; its holder could possess power by virtue of being an influential Politburo member. From 1953 to 1985, it was held by a succession of prominent party leaders, sometimes the general secretary, as a symbol of authority. The exception to this tradition was Gromyko, who had no real influence in the post but was made president by Gorbachev to give him a dignified exit from his long term as foreign minister. The office as it had existed would be eliminated during the next year, 1989, when the new legislature elected a new, more powerful president from within its membership. That president would be Gorbachev, providing him with a power base outside of the party—another weakening of the organization that had ruled the country since 1917.

Some seats in the Congress of People's Deputies were reserved for the Communist Party and for professional organizations, but most were contested on a geographic basis. The elections became a resounding defeat for the apparatus—the party first secretaries of 38 cities, including Leningrad and Sverdlovsk, were defeated, and Yeltsin staged a comeback by winning a seat easily in what was widely seen as a race against the Moscow party apparatus.[82] Yeltsin was helped by a "throw them out" mood—34 of the 38 Moscow party officials who ran lost.[83] Although some apparatchiks did get in, the overall results represented "a rude awakening to the inadequacy of our knowledge of the society we live in," a *Moscow News* commentary said.[84]

The Communist Party's political monopoly was beginning to end as, in the course of the campaign and the seating of the deputies, nascent political parties emerged, although this process was more advanced in the three Baltic republics (Estonia, Latvia and Lithuania), where national fronts calling for autonomy already operated and won most of the seats.

## Pushing back: Unrest develops as the slow pace of reforms fails to improve living standards

There may have been a quickening pace of events in the political sphere during 1988 and 1989, but everyday matters such as the economy and living standards stagnated. Failing to see sufficient improvement from the promises of perestroika, working people began to take a more direct approach—by striking. The first mass strike was conducted by the country's miners in 1989.

Mikhail Gorbachev continued to meet directly with the public (a 1988 visit to the Siberian city of Krasnoyarsk in which he heard complaints about food, housing and services was nationally televised[85]), but after three or four years, patience was running out. Working people were also able to make some improvements to their working conditions through organized action, but the changes that could be made through existing institutions were limited.

Workers in a truck engine plant in Yaroslavl and in the vast Tolyatti automobile works in 1987 defeated attempts by their managements to make them work several Saturdays in the next year in exchange for a ten-minute reduction in the workday. In Yaroslavl, the workers organized a strike after the union and the labor-collective council (the latter headed by the director!) endorsed the schedule; but the rank-and-file workers used a clause in the 1987 enterprise law to collectively vote the plan down.[86] In Tolyatti (in a rare example of a fully democratic union, in which posts from shop steward to the chair had been freely elected) the union took the lead in successfully opposing the Saturday plan.[87] Far more common, however, were workplaces in which the union refused to take the side of those it was supposed to represent. From such a situation arose the July 1989 miners' strike.

More than 400,000 miners ultimately walked out, mostly in the Soviet Union's two main coal-producing areas—the Donetsk basin in eastern Ukraine and the Kuznetsk basin in western Siberia—but also in Vorkuta, a Ural Mountains city near the Arctic Circle, and in Karaganda in the Central Asian republic of Kazakhstan. Production in Donetsk had become particularly difficult, even by the standards of coal mining, because coal had been extracted there since the nineteenth century, forcing miners to descend more than a kilometer deep to find new veins, and because investment had so lagged behind what was needed. "My fellow cutters and I are using the same jackhammers as fifty years ago. This state of affairs has to be corrected immediately," a Donetsk miner told the 1986 party congress.[88]

An electrician at a Kuznetsk mine put conditions still more bluntly in a trade newspaper:

> Not long ago our Berezovskii [the electrician's city] greeted guests with the brave slogan, "The city born at the dawn of communism will be a communist city." Neither the guests, nor even more so the inhabitants, believed this slogan. Because the city, born at the dawn of communism, instead of flourishing

> has instead withered at the roots. Indeed, they built it not for the good of its inhabitants, but with one aim only: to pump out coal as quickly as possible...And this predatory administrative economic system destroys not only the town, but human souls.[89]

Several small local strikes had already occurred; one strike in Vorkuta did not end until the government minister for the coal industry arrived to meet with strikers' representatives.[90] The mass strike began when management and the union ignored the demands of miners in a Kuznetsk pit for higher wages and improved conditions. Within a week, miners struck across the Kuznetsk basin in response to a call for solidarity, followed by miners in other regions. The critical problem of Soviet coal mining was that the entire industry had been planned to run at a loss and was consistently underfunded, so the resources did not exist to ameliorate the poor working conditions, substandard housing and low wages.[91]

Although they had not started the mass strike, it was the Donetsk miners who moved the quickest politically. Strikers there occupied the square in front of the regional party headquarters, and all 21 area mines sent representatives to occupation meetings. Abandoned by their union and all other institutions, the miners set up their own strike committee, and began making contact with the striking miners in other regions, who then also set up committees. The strike committees became the effective local governments, setting up patrols, acting as arbitrators for problems citizens brought to them and closing all sources of alcohol.[92] Strikers this time refused to negotiate with the coal industry minister,[93] and would only end the strike when Prime Minister Nikolai Ryzhkov signed a detailed agreement and Mikhail Gorbachev announced his personal approval.[94]

The strikes, at best, ended with mixed results. Most of the demands won in the agreement weren't honored; despite that development, miners did not go back on strike that year, except for a brief strike in Vorkuta that did not spread.[95] But the miners did learn how to organize—a most important lesson. About one-quarter of the members of the strike committees were rank-and-file party members,[96] but local party leaderships in the mining areas had refused to support the action.

The Donetsk party boss afterward gave this self-criticism to the local party: "Our greatest tactical error was in trying to prevent the strike when we should have been leading it. We all supported the miners' demands. I suppose we were afraid of what the higher echelons would say. That's the old style of thinking dominating us."[97] The strike committees remained intact and union leaderships were replaced, but the movement of the miners did not catch on elsewhere—this could have been a movement containing the potential for self-management and workplace democracy, but the failure to replicate these grassroots structures in other industries allowed this potential to dissipate.

The example of striking did take root, as an average of 130,000 people per day struck during the first months of 1990.[98] These were often strictly local affairs, however, and there was little attempt at national coordination, rendering them politically ineffective. The Soviet trade union central umbrella was widely seen as irrelevant, but new unions that began to form by 1990 were very small and unorganized, and even the very few unions that did work well had no links with other unions.[99]

The early promise of perestroika, which had initially provided some benefits, was forgotten as the 1980s drew to a close, and Gorbachev became widely unpopular, an unpopularity that, thanks to glasnost, was voiced unceasingly within the Soviet Union. This internal view was in marked contrast to much of the rest of the world. Gorbachev's initiative and persistence had resulted in arms-reduction treaties, withdrawals of troops, and an easing of tensions that had accumulated as United States President Ronald Reagan had begun a massive arms buildup and pressured European governments to agree to host new US weapons systems against the will of European peoples.

Gorbachev had also pulled the Soviet army out of Afghanistan, eliminating another source of international tension. (Although the Soviets had gone in to shore up a régime that sought to modernize the country and provide education to girls. It was the latter policy in particular that inflamed the religious fundamentalists that the US heavily armed and forged into an army that later begat al-Qaeda, the Taliban and the Islamic State.)

Gorbachev, Foreign Minister Eduard Shevardnadze and their advisers seemed to believe that if they made enough concessions to the United States, they would buy peace. Instead, the Reagan and Bush I administrations simply saw concessions as signs of weakness. Nor did it buy the Soviet Union a voice in international affairs in the eyes of the United States government. When Gorbachev volunteered to attempt to broker an agreement with Iraq dictator Saddam Hussein to secure the withdrawal of Iraqi troops from Kuwait when US President George H.W. Bush was maneuvering to start the first Persian Gulf war, Bush simply told Gorbachev to mind his own business.

The Soviet Union did need to reduce its military spending significantly (money that would have been better spent on modernizing its aging industrial infrastructure and improving living standards through more investment in consumer production and housing), but Gorbachev and Shevardnadze seemed to talk themselves into believing that the capitalist world, in particular the United States, had not spent the entire history of their country attempting to destroy it.

A widely noticed article in the official publication of the Soviet foreign ministry declared:

> By pursuing the logic of anti-imperialist struggle, we allowed ourselves—contrary to the interests of our fatherland—to be drawn into an arms race, and helped to introduce the "enemy

> image" and to set up technological and cultural barriers between the Soviet Union and the United States…If, however, one takes a look at the United States monopolist bourgeoisie as a whole, very few of its groups, and none of the main ones, are connected with militarism. There no longer is any need to talk, for instance, about a military struggle for markets or raw materials, or for the division and redivision of the world.[100]

Following the October Revolution, the capitalist countries, as soon as they could stop fighting each other by bringing an end to World War I, united in a 14-nation bloc to strangle the revolution at its inception. The United States was one of those 14, and never relented in its hostility, except during World War II when the Soviet Union was needed in the struggle to defeat Hitler. Could this history truly be forgotten? And what should be made of the "discovery" that the corporate elite that dominates the United States has little or no connection with militarism? The US economy has long been run as a war economy—for two decades after the fall of the Soviet Union, the US military budget was roughly equal to the military spending of the rest of the world combined.

Leonid Brezhnev, as earlier noted, once said that military spending accounted for 22 percent of the Soviet budget.[101] By way of comparison, military spending officially accounted for 21 percent of the United States government budget for fiscal year 2008, according to the US government, but independent analysts calculate that the true amount of military spending that year, when accounting for all factors, including off-budget "supplemental" war funding, totaled 51 percent of the budget![102] (The figures are not directly comparable because the US economy was larger than that of the Soviet Union, and the Soviet Union's budget accounts for a far larger portion of gross domestic product than does that of the US—but it's still a huge number.) The fiercest lobbyists within the United States for expanding the

NATO military alliance were its military contractors, some of the largest and most powerful corporations on Earth, which would profit by supplying arms to the new NATO members that would be required to replace their military equipment with NATO-compatible materiel. And production of components for US weapons systems and military craft is intentionally spread among as many states and congressional districts as possible to generate support for military spending.

One factor behind the scaling down of the Soviet military was the most basic of reasons—freeing up scarce resources to better tackle internal problems. Shevardnadze put this plainly to legislators in a session of the new Supreme Soviet: "The People's Deputies know how many needs and how little money and resources there are. But today we can redirect the budget and the plan toward the social sphere and we can invest resources where we can expect to receive a return that will improve the Soviet people's well-being. Would this have been possible at all if our political environment had remained as it was, say, before the period of restructuring?"[103]

A second factor was a desire on the part of reformers to expand economic contact with the capitalist world as a response to the lagging quality of Soviet-made products. A senior scholar at a leading Soviet economic institute in the summer of 1989 put this policy plainly: "No longer regarding ourselves as an alternative model of development for the whole world community, and having realized the fundamental weak points of our own economic and political systems, we are deliberately trying not to hinder Western-style international economic contacts. On the contrary, we would like to integrate with that system and adapt ourselves to its already existing structures."[104]

Gorbachev and, it is likely, many of his advisers still sought to strengthen the Soviet socialist system, hoping to introduce market mechanisms to make the economy work better, without having a thought-out idea of how this goal might be accomplished. But statements such as the one in the preceding paragraph demonstrated that faith in perestroika was waning.

Nonetheless, the isolation of the Soviet Union from most of the world economy, and the resulting cutoff from technology developed outside its bloc, was a factor in the poor quality of Soviet products. Innovation is a global phenomenon, and throughout history, but especially since the industrial revolution began gathering steam, technological and other developments have spread rapidly. Because of that rapid spread, less developed nations are able to leap technological stages by taking advantage of the latest technologies. The first countries to industrialize, such as the United Kingdom, traveled a long and painful path. The "second wave" of countries to industrialize, such as Germany and the United States, could do so more quickly, albeit still painfully for those who had to work in the factories, by taking advantage of existing technology and learning from the mistakes and successes of the earlier-developed economies.

In turn, even a completely backward country like Tsarist Russia (representing a relatively late wave of industrialization) could nonetheless build up minuscule islands of industry in St Petersburg and Moscow, featuring very large factories and highly concentrated industry with modern technology in its two main cities in an otherwise agrarian, backward empire. Russian industry was barely a couple of decades old when the revolutions of 1917 came. Who would have expected technological innovation in Russia at that time? Russian industry then was based on technology imported from more advanced countries and much of it was owned by foreign firms.

Today, many countries readily copy and use technology developed elsewhere. For instance, countries that developed earlier laid out a network of telephone lines; much of the landscape in the United States features wires strung high above the ground, tied to an endless series of wooden poles. This sight is so ubiquitous that the poles and wires aren't ordinarily noticed.

But in the last years of the twentieth century, many countries in regions such as Latin America primarily used wireless mobile telephones. They skipped over the stage of land lines to the latest technology.

These countries did not develop this technology; they acquired technology developed elsewhere. Because they are connected to the global capitalist system, it does not occur to commentators to reproach them for not having developed their own communications technology. There is no need for them to invent what is already invented. When such a country does make an innovation, it will go into the general global pool of ideas.

The largest countries naturally develop most of the new technology, in the first place the United States due to its immense population augmented by (prior to 2001) its willingness to encourage talented foreign students to study at its universities. But although Third World countries are never rebuked for using technologies developed elsewhere, it was considered a scandal for a Soviet bloc country, in particular the Soviet Union itself, to adapt a technology developed elsewhere. Technological development lagged in the Soviet Union in the 1960s and later. That is supposed to be "proof" that the Soviet Union, or any non-capitalist country, was incapable of technological development. But that lag in technology, which did grow larger, was in part a byproduct of the Soviet Union being cut off from the rest of the world's developments by economic boycotts.

Any single country or group of countries cut off from the rest of the world's technology would suffer the same fate; no country or bloc develops all of its products or innovations, not even the United States or the European Union or Japan. What if successful socialist revolutions had taken hold in Western Europe? Those industrialized, developed countries would have shared their technology with Russia, helping it build its own industry in a far more rational manner, and a big enough bloc certainly could have more than held its own in any technological "race," particularly because such a bloc would have had more rational governance due to different culture heritages and more developed starting points. As it was, the Soviet Union was able to develop its military prowess and became the leading spacefaring country during the 1950s and early 1960s, although it is reasonable to ask whether it would have been better off developing technology more useful for everyday life rather than projects designed primarily for international bragging rights.

The Soviet Union was no Third World country, having built up an industrial complex, so it had more capacity to develop technology than most countries. Here the glasnost side of reform comes into play—the widespread alienation in workplaces, the lack of initiative that develops in an inflexible command system and a production system centered on quantity instead of quality all played their part in Soviet industrial mediocrity.

If Gorbachev's foreign policy didn't win him much outside the country's borders, his reforms didn't count for much inside, either. All social groups seemed to lose faith in perestroika. By 1990, polling found that 85 percent believed that economic reform had achieved nothing or made the situation worse.[105] As the miners' strike, the failure of the labor-collective councils and mounting disillusionment demonstrated, efforts by the reformers to gain the support of working people had failed.

Two important reasons for this failure were the ongoing shortages of consumer goods, which, if anything, were becoming worse, and the realization that the economic reforms were, in large part, going to come on their backs. The timid effort at workplace democratization through the labor-collective councils was intended to compensate people on the shop floors for the harsher work conditions and lower basic pay, and when the councils proved a farce the reformers were empty-handed.

The 1987 enterprise law meant that enterprises had to sink or swim on a profit-and-loss accounting basis, and employees were expected to take on some of that risk through the new wage structure—but they had no ability to affect their enterprises' results. The nomenklatura (ministry officials who handed down and administered state plans and the directors and factory managers of the enterprises) still had control, and continued to resist giving up their privileges. The top officials of the enterprises, however, had limited control over profit and loss—most of their production still had to be sold to the state to fulfill the five-year plan; they had little or no control over their suppliers, which were becoming ever more erratic; wage boosts increasingly were necessary to keep the workforce from leaving, gradually counteracting the wage cuts initially imposed; and they remained subject to the dictates of the ministries.

In the crisis situation they faced, enterprise managers frequently took the easiest shortcut to increased profits—they cut production and raised prices. Frequently they had no choice but to cut production because sufficient supplies were not arriving. The suppliers were under similar pressures.

The attitudes of those in the Soviet Union who were often referred to as the "technological intelligentsia"—the equivalent of white-collar personnel such as engineers, middle management and skilled office workers—had soured along with other employees. This group felt itself underpaid, and many did earn less money than industrial workers, but they also had more privileges and, obviously, less strenuous working conditions. The Soviet educational system produced more engineers than did any other country—more than it needed. Many engineers and technicians felt frustrated by uninspiring work and many others worked as laborers because they could make more money doing so. These workers had been promised higher pay, commensurate with what they felt they deserved, but their pay went up only a little more than that of manual workers, engendering further resentment. Even with the little bit of privilege the technological intelligentsia possessed, they, too, were hit hard by the deterioration of the economy.

Collective farmers perhaps had the most ambiguous relationship to perestroika. Farmers had done better under Leonid Brezhnev than many others; one of Brezhnev's first moves was to reinstate the private plots each farm family was allowed to use for itself, and then the allowable allotment was doubled in size because the private plots were far more productive than the common land of the collectives. But farmers were subjected to bureaucracy, too—the agricultural ministries gave orders to collective-farm directors, who in turn gave orders to the farmers. Farms had to meet their quota, as with factories, but could sell their extra produce in farmers' markets at whatever price they could receive. There was less upheaval in agriculture than elsewhere in the economy, but here, too, bureaucratic obstruction played its part.

The 1987 enterprise law, in addition to the profit-and-loss accounting and its other reforms, also legalized "cooperative" retail and service enterprises. Small-scale production was also legalized, with a prohibition against producers hiring employees. These cooperatives, although not altogether new, helped exacerbate shortages and trigger inflation. Farmers' markets, which sold produce at higher prices than charged in state markets while offering greater variety, were long a part of Soviet retail, as was street trading and peddling. But the new cooperatives quickly took advantage of the differential between what the new market would bear and the level of prices set in state shops.

For instance, when a shipment of meat would arrive at a state store, where it was intended to be sold at the low, state-controlled price, more than half of the shipment would be illicitly resold to a cooperative, which would then sell it at a far higher price, leaving a shortage in the state store.[106] Another report found that, although the Soviet Union enjoyed an excellent harvest in 1990, only 58 percent of produce that was supposed to be delivered to state stores actually made it there; the remainder was siphoned off by black marketeers or rotted due to a distribution system that was breaking down.[107] Consumers feared future shortages, which became self-fulfilling prophesies when widespread hoarding helped empty store shelves.

Shortages also fueled inflationary pressures, previously a virtually unknown phenomenon in the Soviet Union. Shortages of goods naturally put upward pressure on prices, but because the output of goods significantly lagged behind the wages that were paid, the amount of savings parked in banks by Soviet consumers rose sharply—there was more money than could be spent, effectively increasing the supply of money. An oversupply of money makes money less valuable, which is a form of inflation. The continuing depression in prices for oil and gas exports, and the need to import food from the West to make up for the inefficiencies in agriculture, added fiscal pressure, to the point that by 1989 the Soviet Union suffered from a rapidly widening fiscal deficit, further constricting the government's ability to provide investment capital.

Yet another factor that accelerated the disorganization of the economy was internal protectionism—at the republic and city level. Late in 1989, the three Baltic republics, where separatist sentiment was already forming, banned the sale of meat and appliances to anyone not a republic resident. Leningrad, near the Estonian border, was dependent on supplies from the Baltics, creating shortages there and prompting city authorities to restrict sales there to city residents. This triggered a similar ban on Leningrad residents in a nearby city.[108] Moscow was perhaps the best-provisioned city in the country, and people who lived outside the city regularly traveled there to buy goods not available in outlying areas. But panic buying emptied the food shelves of Moscow in May 1990 after Prime Minister Nikolai Ryzhkov gave a speech outlining a proposed introduction of elements of a market economy; the Moscow government responded by restricting sales of consumer goods to city residents.[109] The surrounding areas in turn responded by blockading shipments to the capital until the Moscow mayor agreed to back down.[110]

Nationally, the textile industry was particularly hard hit in 1989 as raw materials trade virtually halted; when a government oversight body attempted to negotiate supply contracts, suppliers refused to send material to mills on that contractual basis.[111] Suppliers either wanted much higher prices paid for their materials or they sought barter deals to cope with the mounting shortages.

## Man without a plan: Unable to make a decision, Gorbachev opts for capitalism

In addition to the question of their own privileges, many among the nomenklatura pondered the associated problem of passing their privileges to their sons and daughters. In contrast to the corporate elite in a capitalist country, the nomenklatura did not own the means of production. Their privileges were based on their management of the Soviet Union's industry and commerce, and this control rested completely on the state ownership of that property.

This social strata had tended to resist all reforms—after all, reform targeted their privileges and positions—but some of the nomenklatura began to think of life outside the constraints of the Soviet system. These privileges had become greater thanks to the opportunities for corruption during the Brezhnev years. But these privileges (access to automobiles without the years-long wait others had to endure, dachas in the country, access to special stores stocked with otherwise unavailable consumer goods, and relatively high wages) were minuscule compared to what the economic elite possesses in capitalist countries, especially the staggering wealth accumulated by financial speculators and industrialists.

Imports of luxury items for Russia's privileged had diverted money that could have gone to meet basic needs for the rest of the population, and the black market grew, in part, to meet these desires for luxuries. A criminal underworld that operated black-market networks had formed during the Brezhnev era, and these sometimes had the protection of elements among the nomenklatura, and sometimes alliances were formed.

Some among the nomenklatura began to dream of capitalism—then they would be able to dramatically upgrade their lifestyle. Economic malaise was becoming more pervasive as the dense web of threads that held the Soviet system together were starting to be snipped through corruption, local protectionism and supply disruptions, the last of which was exacerbated because many component parts were produced in only one factory. The move to profit-and-loss accounting helped to bring about an "all against all" mentality: Instead of simply continuing to manage state property, why not grab it for yourself?

Distribution bottlenecks helped fuel black-market activity and fed into nascent nomenklatura desires to grab state property. The single massive agency for supply and distribution, Gossnab, was responsible for distributing all raw materials, tools, supplies and equipment across the Soviet Union. Gossnab employed 130,000 people and was responsible for facilities in all parts of the country; it was also responsible for the supply bottlenecks that plagued production.[112] Because of chronic difficulties in obtaining raw materials and supplies, enterprises employed an army of official procurement agents tasked with obtaining needed materials (there were more than 700,000 of these by 1970) and an additional shadowy network of unofficial "pushers" who traveled to Gossnab warehouses to "speed up" delivery or to use connections to obtain material that could not be procured otherwise.[113]

Black-market profiteers did the same work as pushers for their illegal operations and sometimes the two groups overlapped. Official corruption raged unabated during the Brezhnev years, allowing the black market to grow, along with criminal syndicates. (Those are not to be confused with the legal "second" or "unofficial" economy consisting of repair work and other consumer services that were acceptable, and necessary due to the state's inability to provide them, as long as taxes were paid on the income earned.[114])

It was against these backdrops that Gorbachev began to abandon his efforts to renew the system he inherited and to introduce capitalism. Yet the general secretary who presided over this unprecedented change had a conventional party background and could not have risen through the ranks if that had not been so.

One of Gorbachev's grandfathers was imprisoned and the other spent two years in a forced-labor camp during the 1930s, childhood experiences that left a deep impression on him. Both grandfathers were collective farmers. (The one who was sent to a camp was the chair of his collective.) Gorbachev himself, after World War II, worked on a collective farm and, at age 16, was awarded an Order of the Red Banner of Labor for his part in helping to bring in a record crop. The honor, extraordinary for someone so young, helped him gain admission to the Soviet Union's top university, Moscow State University.

After graduation, he steadily moved up in the party ranks, attending the 1961 congress as a delegate and becoming first secretary for his home region, Stavropol, in 1970. A year later, Gorbachev became a Central Committee member after his work in improving agriculture in Stavropol attracted notice and he eventually was voted onto the Politburo in 1979, having secured the patronage of Yuri Andropov. Gorbachev continued to have responsibility for agriculture, giving him something of a technocratic reputation, and, by the time of Leonid Brezhnev's death, he also had earned the reputation of a reformer.

After Andropov became general secretary, Gorbachev began meeting with intellectuals working in Soviet institutions, later recalling that his safe was "clogged" with proposals.

> People were clamoring that everything needed to be changed, but from different angles; some were for scientific and technical progress, others for reforming the structure of politics, and others still for new organizational forms in industry and agriculture. In short, from all angles there were cries from the heart that affairs could no longer be allowed to go on in the old way.[115]

And now, five years after this reformer was selected as general secretary, Gorbachev moved to eliminate the Communist Party's monopoly on power, sacrosanct since 1921. Gorbachev had already sought to weaken the grip of the party apparatus by creating an enhanced post of president attached to the new parliament, the Congress of People's Deputies and the new Supreme Soviet elected by the deputies. He would now act more decisively to create a firmer power base completely separate from the party by relinquishing the party's monopoly, which he would achieve with the help of the party rank-and-file.

Centrifugal forces continued to tear at the party—as 1989 ended, the Lithuania Communist Party declared itself "independent" of the Communist Party of the Soviet Union[116] and the first two months of 1990 saw rank-and-file revolts overthrow local party first secretaries across Russia and Ukraine.[117] The separatist sentiments of the Baltic parties were condemned in Moscow, but those parties were scrambling to keep up with mounting nationalist sentiments. Denounced or not, nationalism had an effect—a Russian "bureau" was created inside the party and long-standing official opposition to relinquishing the party's monopoly on power was suddenly reversed.

The Soviet Union was comprised of 15 republics, and all but Russia had their own separate party structures that were, nonetheless, completely subordinate to the center. A similar structure for Russia was almost a redundancy—the Russian republic comprised about 80 percent of the country's land mass and ethnic Russians dominated Soviet institutions. But under the impact of ethnic tensions that were arising across the country, including among ethnic Russians who believed they should have their own republic institutions, it was decided to create the Russian bureau as a new Central Committee department. This bureau would be headed by the general secretary, and while creating the bureau was something of a paper move, it planted a seed that, before long, would grow into a full-fledged republic party body—assisting the process of Russian nationalism that would be used by Boris Yeltsin to, in the following year, bring down the Soviet Union. But such a development was as yet unimaginable.

The more immediate, and dramatic, development was ending the party's monopoly. Channeling rank-and-file pressure, Gorbachev met with representatives of miners on the eve of the crucial February 1990 Central Committee meeting. *Pravda* gave the talks with the miners front-page coverage, noting the miners' hostility to the party apparatus, which was followed by the miners being unilaterally named (or "co-opted") as delegates to the Central Committee meeting.[118] Just before the meeting, 250,000 demonstrated in Moscow, with the front of the march featuring a giant banner proclaiming, "Seventy-two years—to nowhere."[119]

Gorbachev, at the meeting, declared that the party had to earn its right to govern. "In a society that is renewing itself the party can exist and fulfill its vanguard role only as a democratically acknowledged force," he said in his speech. "This means that its position should not be enforced through being constitutionally legitimized. The [party] naturally intends to do this strictly within the framework of the democratic process, renouncing any and all legal and political advantages, putting forward its own public and political forces, constantly working among the masses, living their interests and needs…This process can also lead at some stage to the creation of parties."[120] That stage would come quickly, as elections to city and regional councils went forward, with a variety of still-coalescing movements winning seats.

A month after the Central Committee voted to renounce the party's monopoly (helped by the rank-and-filers co-opted as delegates), the Supreme Soviet changed the Soviet constitution to eliminate the "leading role" of the party and voted to elect Gorbachev to a yet again enhanced office of president. The office would now formally be an executive post in the manner of a strong-presidential system, except that election was by the parliament rather than by a popular vote. (The president was to be directly elected by popular vote in the future.) Gorbachev now had a secure base of power outside the party, although he remained party general secretary.

The new-found power was soon used to begin to introduce elements of capitalism. To bring about these "market reforms," the limited ability of working people to defend themselves had to be eliminated. A series of laws designed to do this began with a new enterprise law stealthily passed by the Supreme Soviet in June 1990. Gorbachev continued to insist that market reforms were to remain within the boundaries of a socialist system (and there was a widespread belief in the country that the conditions for an outright restoration of capitalism didn't exist), but in reality from this time the debate within Gorbachev's government and among his closest advisers was about how far and how fast the transition to a capitalist-type system should go.

Those in the party already opposed to perestroika now dug in their heels at any change; the hard-liners, too, were trapped in the same poverty of imagination that could visualize only orthodox Soviet-style centralism or capitalism. Gorbachev's support among those who backed reforms but opposed a return to capitalism eroded as well and his support among working people evaporated as the reality of the latest changes hit them.

Employees had gained a small amount of control in the 1987 enterprise law, although the labor-collective councils that were to have given them a measure of democracy within their places of work were largely ineffective or co-opted by managements. Ongoing labor shortages, enabling workers to switch jobs easily, were a perhaps more consistent source of employee ability to wrest some control from management. The new 1990 enterprise law was designed to eliminate both these sources of limited workforce empowerment.

The 1987 enterprise law had been expected to generate a wave of layoffs and, although it was also anticipated that most workers would be able to find work in other areas, the labor shortage would be eliminated. Yet labor shortages persisted into 1990. The "cooperative" private enterprises in retail and service industries that had been legalized in 1987 thrived on the differences between official state prices and market prices—as noted earlier, these enterprises often illegally obtained food and consumer products at the subsidized state price and resold them at far higher prices. These enterprises were able to pay higher wages as a result, resulting in an exodus of workers from state industry, creating continuing labor shortages and also taking skilled workers from jobs for which it was difficult to train replacements.

A second factor was the exodus of women from industrial jobs. The partial reversals during the 1930s of earlier improvement of women's lives and subsequent refusal of Soviet authorities to tackle sexism in any serious way resulted in women being segregated into jobs with low pay and/or poor working conditions. Women also bore the brunt of having to stand for hours in queues for food and their low pay had increasingly little purchasing power, giving them reasons to withdraw from work;[121] in an economy where virtually everybody who could be mobilized to work had been, there was no available pool of replacements in a situation of labor shortages.

The 1990 enterprise law reduced by administrative means the

ability of employees to defend themselves—it eliminated the labor-collective councils and declared that enterprises would now have private owners with the right to impose management. The labor-collective councils, ineffective as they had been, were to be replaced by "enterprise councils"—bodies in which half of the membership would be designated by the workforce and half by the owner, although these new bodies would have no say in the hiring of managers or in enterprise administration. These new councils were given responsibility for issuing ownership shares in their enterprises.[122]

Thus, even very limited workers' control would be eliminated and a mechanism for privatization was created, through new bodies designed to be controlled by top management—management would be able to impose its viewpoint on its appointees, while the employee representatives would reflect an inevitably disunited, or even atomized, workforce. The Supreme Soviet passed the new law without public input and with no advance publicity.

The new law had come as a surprise to those affected by it, and the Soviet central trade union, true to form, refused to oppose it in any way.[123] The trade union apparatus continued to form a bloc with management; the head of the union for autoworkers declared not only that the labor-collective councils "[were] no longer needed," but that the central trade union leadership accepted the imposition of a market economy "in principle."[124]

At the same time, the Supreme Soviet was discussing a new employment law that would set up a system of benefits for those who became unemployed, but the benefit would be pegged to basic earnings only, excluding earned bonuses, extra pay for hazardous duty or overtime.[125] This time, the unions actually argued against this formula, and sought to have unemployment benefits be based on full pay, but these demands were simply ignored.[126] Until now, employment was guaranteed to all able-bodied people; that a need for a system of unemployment insurance had become necessary was another sign of coming capitalist-style changes.

A further complication that had only just begun to emerge was the emergence of a second pole of government power—in essence what would become a situation of "dual government." A dual government can arise during revolutionary or potentially revolutionary situations; it is an inherently unstable situation and cannot last long. One or the other must prevail. This duality was the situation that developed in Russia in 1917 (and also in Germany at the end of 1918).

That was not yet the situation in the Soviet Union; the union center still held sway. But the centrifugal forces already weakening the country would enable the rise of the government of the Russian republic, and Yeltsin as an alternative figure to Gorbachev, to counterpoise itself to the Soviet government. Yeltsin would come out in the open during the course of 1990 for an all-out restoration of capitalism.

In May 1990, members of the Russian parliament elected Yeltsin the body's chair, effectively making him the top official of the Russian republic and handing him the bully pulpit he craved. Parliamentarians elevated him on the force of his strong stands for Russian sovereignty over Soviet institutions, which was what mattered to them. (The parliament was a new body elected by popular vote; Yeltsin won a seat based on his populist public image as someone who curbed the privileges of local party bosses.)

The following month saw the foundation congress of a Russian Communist Party, equivalent to the party organizations of the other 14, far smaller Soviet republics. Already, the Russian "bureau" created in the central party apparatus earlier in the year was seen as inadequate. The Russian party, however, at its start was dominated by local party bosses from outlying areas seeking to return to the days of Leonid Brezhnev, and a hard-liner was elected as first secretary of the new Russian party over a candidate supported by Gorbachev.

Thus those opposed to perestroika now possessed a base at the same time that those who sought far greater changes than those that had occurred, or were contemplated by the central Soviet government, possessed a base in the Russian republican government. This foundation congress for the Russian party was also notable for two factions that came out into the open, the Democratic Platform and the Marxist Platform. This marked the first time since 1921 that formal groups put forth programs; organized factions had been banned from the party at its 1921 congress and that ban had never been rescinded.

The Democratic Platform primarily concerned itself with the party itself—it advocated transforming the party into a parliamentary organization that would compete in multi-party elections and not have a single ideology, and proposed that party leaders be elected.[127] The Marxist Platform advocated power being put in the hands of mass social groups, rather than in a parliament, and accepted a transition to market mechanisms but insisted that any market be kept under popular control.[128] These factions again made their presence felt at the Soviet party congress convened two weeks later. This congress, the twenty-eighth, would be the last. Little in the way of concrete results would come out of the congress, however—the party apparatus was able to manipulate the results so that apparatchiks and nomenklatura formed a majority of the congressional delegates.

Dramatic changes were occurring all around, yet the party could do little but reshuffle its hierarchy. The all-powerful Politburo was changed into a body based on territory—it would now consist of the general secretary, the holder of the new post of deputy general secretary, the first secretaries of the 15 republics, and seven people chosen by the Central Committee.[129] The Central Committee was also substantially overhauled. The new format of the Politburo (creating a body that would be difficult to convene because of its members' geographic dispersion), plus the passing of a new rule granting autonomy to the republican parties, served to further weaken the party center.[130] Nor did the party, riven by deep divisions, approve any program.

The congress was notable for a definitive speech on the transition to a market economy by Gorbachev, although he attempted to situate the transition within a socialist system.

> Our history has shown the fruitlessness of attempts to escape the poverty in which both the state and citizens find themselves by darning and patching the command-distribution system. The advantages of a market economy have been shown on a worldwide scale and the question is now only whether we can, under market conditions, assure a high degree of social security and the other characteristics of the socialist system. Here is my answer: it is not only possible, but it is specifically a regulated market economy that will allow us to build a social wealth that will improve the standard of living for everyone…The ideology of socialism is not a textbook, where everything is spelled out, chapter and verse. It will develop along with socialism itself, as we help the country to become well fed, comfortable, civilized, spiritually rich, free and happy…We inherited from Marx, Engels and Lenin a strong methodology, the dialectic method of thinking, on which we shall rely in both our theory and our practice. But we must not allow everything created by the classics to become another "short course" [a reference to Stalin's notorious ghost-written book of gross lies about the history of the party that had the force of absolute law until Stalin's death]…This will be fatal for perestroika and for society. This must not happen.[131]

Gorbachev was re-elected as party general secretary by the

congress, and he included Yeltsin on his slate of candidates for the Central Committee. But Yeltsin said he could not be subject to party discipline while carrying out his duties as chair of the Russian parliament; he therefore resigned from the party, removing himself from Gorbachev's slate.[132] The mayors of Leningrad and Moscow, both aligned with Yeltsin, also resigned from the party.

Perhaps the only tangible result from this congress was that the party had become weaker. The main question facing the country—what reform package would be adopted?—would have to be decided by the government. During the spring and summer of 1990, two competing plans emerged.

One plan, developed by a commission headed by Prime Minister Nikolai Ryzhkov and Gorbachev's economic adviser Leonid Abalkin, sought to phase in changes over five years, with reductions in state subsidies, and concomitant rises in prices, for basic food items, although the prices would remain regulated by government.[133] The plan proposed a "regulated market economy" with central control to remain in force during the five-year transition period.[134]

Ryzhkov, one the reformers who wished to implement change in a more orderly manner, began his career as a welder, eventually rising to be a chief engineer and then a factory manager in one of the Soviet Union's largest industrial complexes. He, too, was brought into the party Central Committee by Andropov. Gorbachev named him prime minister in 1985, a post he held until he stepped down after suffering a heart attack at the end of 1990. The advocates of a slower reform pace lamented the decline in living standards after 1988 that resulted from hasty withdrawal of economic planning without a new structure in place.

"I am a staunch opponent of 'great leaps,' including those in the areas of economic reforms," one of Ryzhkov's allies, Yegor Ligachev, wrote.

> To be well grounded and gradual is a major assurance of success. Such an approach in no way implies that the introduction of innovations has to be dragged out. A gradual approach means not a lengthy process, but an orderly, carefully conceived sequence of changes, in sharp contradistinction to both the new "ideological assault" in which everything is to be destroyed for the sake of market principles, and economic romanticism, which fails to take the realities of life into account.[135]

A precipitous decline in housing construction, for example, occurred due to the decline of state orders resulting from the reforms of the enterprise law of 1987 that began to be implemented in 1988, an aggravation of living standards that could have been avoided by phasing in changes to social services, rather than a precipitous removal of all controls, according to Ligachev.[136]

The competing plan, developed by a group headed by Stanislav Shatalin, another adviser to Gorbachev, and Grigorii Yavlinskii, deputy prime minister in the Russian republic government, called for a rapid selloff of state enterprises, allowing prices (except for basic foods) to be set by market forces and for all taxes to be collected by the republics (which in turn would send some of the proceeds to the central government).[137] Although the plan's authors declared it "a program of transition to a different development model,"[138] it lacked details specifying how its sweeping program would be accomplished.[139] Yet it was to be completed in 500 days.

By this time, Gorbachev's two closest allies were Aleksandr Yakovlev and Vadim Medvedev, and they used their control of the press to consistently attack the Ryzhkov plan while promoting the "500-Day Plan."[140] (Yakovlev had appointed the top editors of newspapers and journals since 1986 and Medvedev had been the party official in charge of ideology since 1988.) Yakovlev, who had once advocated very different positions when he held a key ideology post under Leonid Brezhnev, was now perhaps the most energetic among Gorbachev's top officials in arguing for a swift transition to capitalism.

Yakovlev had earlier rejected the 1987 reforms that were to have enabled workers to elect factory managers: "Free elections should be confined to the political sphere, not the economic. In production you need discipline and one-person management."[141] The concept of "one-person management" had been in force under Communist Party rule since 1918 and had been sacrosanct since the frantic industrialization of the 1930s, but Yakovlev now backed the concept because capitalism could not be imposed otherwise.

Gorbachev, however, refused to formally choose between the two economic plans because he faced pressure from republic-level officials to include their input. In September, he asked for the two groups to meet and synthesize their plans. The effort failed—the Supreme Soviet refused to adopt either plan and Yeltsin effectively ended the discussion by getting the Russian parliament to approve the 500-Day Plan, with his eye fixed on the portions of the plan that devolved authority to the republics. Yeltsin had begun the process of arrogating more power to himself, at the expense of Gorbachev, the central government and the Communist Party.

While leaders at the elite political levels continued their debates, moves and counter-moves, failing to find any sort of consensus on an overall economic plan, the economy went from stagnation to contraction, and the nomenklatura began their own privatization program. That stealth privatization, in turn, occurred as more focused laws passed by the Supreme Soviet further turned the screws on working people while opening the road for the grabbing of state property. There was no need for an official, formal economic plan for the stealth privatization to begin.

In a series of moves following the passage of the new enterprise law in June 1990, wages were completely freed of any central control in October, reducing wage labor to a commodity as it is in capitalist countries; guarantees to investors, including compensation in the event that future legislation affects an investment, passed in December; the debated law on employment, creating unemployment insurance but failing to authorize any money to pay for it, was passed in January 1991; and draft legislation was passed for the privatization of state enterprises in February.[142] All these measures were passed by the Supreme Soviet. The state planning agency, Gosplan, forecast in 1990 that 16 million people would lose their jobs by 2000, although it expected most would be re-employed elsewhere.[143]

Unemployment, planned or spontaneous, would soon be inevitable. Among many people of the Soviet Union, there did not seem to be a realistic idea of what a return to capitalism would actually mean—some thought that there would be a cost-free cornucopia and others believed that unregulated market mechanisms could be introduced without capitalism. Would it possible to have the consumer goodies of the West coupled with the extensive social guarantees of the Soviet system?

Unfortunately, all too many Russians seemed to get their ideas of what life is like in places like the United States from Hollywood movies: "Nowadays, the Russians I meet know much more than I do about…a whole host of Western stars," a French analyst reported in 1988. "And they have an almost magical ability for picking up unexpected details in Western films. Russians who had seen *Kramer Versus Kramer*, for instance, could tell me the size of the rooms in the American divorcees' apartment to the nearest metre. They explained to me that in Russia, newly divorced couples were often forced to go on living under the same roof—which really is a form of mental cruelty—because they had nowhere else to go. In their view, it is socialism that is to blame, and they imagine that under a different régime everyone in the USSR would have a big apartment like the Kramers."[144]

In New York City, however, couples who have split also sometimes find themselves forced to continue living together because a separate apartment is too expensive.[145] And typical New York City apartments do not look anything like those portrayed in television series such as *Friends*; real apartments there are a small fraction of the size of what is seen on that show.

Those who were more realistic about life under capitalism, including union officials and reformers within the party apparatus, believed that introducing market mechanisms would not lead to the imposition of capitalism and all the social ills associated with it. Either "workers would not accept a radical market reform short of its being forced upon them by an authoritarian government"[146] or "there is great resistance toward it here. There is a strong spiritual basis in this society which does not accept the excesses of capitalism."[147] These sorts of opinions were expressed in the city of Tolyatti on the Volga River (named for the popular post-World War II Italian communist leader Palmiro Togliatti). The world's largest auto plant was there, and it was a well-run enterprise (built with the help of the Italian automaker Fiat) that exported about 40 percent of its vehicles; the hard currency thereby earned kept the shops in the city full.[148]

The Tolyatti autoworks represented a rare example of not only management being elected by the workforce, but all union posts as well; as a result, there was a measure of workplace democracy and very strong social services.[149] This status also represented a rare example of a strong labor-collective council. After the stealth passage of the June 1990 enterprise law, the autoworks management decided it would privatize the enterprise, with ownership shares to be sold abroad. The labor-collective council opposed this move, and demanded that the enterprise instead be given to it, making the workforce the collective owners.[150]

A movement of labor-collective councils was then organized to press these demands elsewhere, but the individual councils elsewhere were concerned only with control of their own factory and made no effort to work out a new relationship among the enterprises that would be taken over by their workforces, instead accepting that market relations would govern the economy.[151] Failing to coalesce into a national movement (just as the miners' strikes failed to jell into a large movement), the council movement quickly faded, and the autoworks shares were sold as the management had wished.

As 1990 ended and 1991 progressed, nomenklatura and Communist Party privatizations, although not yet widespread, occurred more frequently. Selling shares, but with most shares reserved for top management, paid for with state funds, was a popular methodology. There was also maneuvering to be able to take the maximum advantage of the massive privatizations expected in the near future.

In Moscow, for example, the newly elected city council and the city party organization attempted to wrest control of property from each other, so that the respective bureaucracies would be able to distribute the properties among themselves and those connected to them.[152] With the adoption of the 500-Day Plan by the Russian government, property was close to being ripe for the taking. Meanwhile, shortages became so acute in the capital that a tobacco riot broke out.

A Moscow city council deputy, Boris Kagarlitsky, who was in opposition to the council's controlling Communist–Yeltsinite coalition that mostly concerned itself with divvying up property, recorded the scene:

> When the Yava tobacco factory closed down for repairs, the city was left without cigarettes and crowds of angry smokers

surged onto the streets and began to loot the few cigarette kiosks where some packs could still be found. When astonished passersby asked what was going on, the looters answered: "Privatizing cigarettes." The Moscow hooligans must be given their due: they understood the essence of privatization a lot faster than did many Ph.D.s.[153]

## Grabbing power: Yeltsin creates a dual government

As 1990 drew to a close, many reformers became convinced that Mikhail Gorbachev had gotten cold feet, and would call a halt to reform or even turn back. His appointment of hard-liners as prime minister (Valentin Pavlov), interior minister (Boris Pugo) and vice president (Gennadii Yanayev) fueled this fear; enough so that Gorbachev's long-time ally and foreign minister, Eduard Shevardnadze, resigned in December with a warning that "dictatorship is coming."

Those fears threatened to come true when in January 1991 Red Army and Interior Ministry troops seized the communications center in the Lithuanian capital of Vilnius, killing 14 in the process of knocking Lithuanian television and radio off the air. The attack was part of a sustained effort to thwart independence bids by the Baltic republics. Pugo and Defense Minister Dmitry Yazov ordered that attack on their own without Gorbachev's approval, but this raises the question of who was in charge.

Force was becoming the only way for party hard-liners to assert themselves as the party rapidly disintegrated throughout 1991. Almost one-quarter of the party membership left in a period of 18 months; city, regional and provincial governments confiscated party buildings; the size of party bureaucracies was slashed by half or more; local party organizations ceased to exist or paralyzed themselves waiting in vain for orders from higher up; and party organizations were increasingly expelled from enterprises and institutions.[154]

Boris Yeltsin pressed the political attack, calling for

Gorbachev's resignation and threatening to withhold taxes from the central Soviet government (he backed off on the latter). Although the final months of the Soviet Union are often seen as a personalized battle between two outsized personalities, Gorbachev and Yeltsin—and there is some truth in that view as both sought to outflank the other—the question of power, and to what use that power would be used, was more pertinent. Yeltsin, with his endless stream of decrees, ostentatious disregard for the central government and bold assertions of autonomy for himself and for the Russian republic, had set himself up as the head of a second governing center, creating a dual government.

Gorbachev, until the end, maintained that he was committed to a long-term strengthening of socialism through the introduction of market mechanisms, although the concrete results of the decisions that he and the Supreme Soviet took from June 1990 formed a reality of a phased transition to capitalism. The appointment of hard-liners to sensitive positions in his government and his silence during the January Baltic bloodshed suggested, on the surface, a partial backtrack to the old ways, but in reality the appointments of authoritarian officials were necessary to continue to implement more elements of capitalism, which were sparking off unrest—at some point, working people across the Soviet Union might yet decide that enough reform had been done at their expense.

The steady drumbeat of legislation pushed through by the Supreme Soviet following the stealth passage of the 1990 enterprise law demonstrated that Gorbachev was irrevocably committed to his path, no matter how much the hard-liners he appointed might have liked to turn back the clock. The continued weakening of the party, through Gorbachev's moves and due to its evaporating credibility, signaled that a forcible turning back would not be possible.

Yeltsin, in contrast to his populist image and public proclamations in favor of democracy, stood firmly for a much more rapid transition to capitalism—when the time came, the change would be so sudden and so cruel it would become known as "shock therapy." Yeltsin was already assembling a team of young technocrats itching to upend the entire economy, and there would be absolutely no popular consultation nor any consideration of the social cost. He was also a very skilled political tactician; he turned back an attempt by the Russian parliament to remove him as parliament chair by calling for demonstrations in his support and gathering enough support so that a referendum to create a new post of Russian president could be put to voters.

Voters approved, and in June 1991 Yeltsin was elected president of the Russian republic. The dual government was more firmly in place.

In the highly unstable situation of a dual government, the two sides can be in relative equilibrium for a brief period only: Power must flow to one or the other. Power flowed to the Bolsheviks in 1917, but this time the momentum was against their descendants—the August putsch pushed all the weights on the scale to Yeltsin's side.

In July, a month after his election as Russian president, Yeltsin issued a decree banning all party organizations within all departments of the Russian government, effectively a ban against communists. Gorbachev did not publicly protest this decree, the Central Committee confined itself to "studying" the constitutionality of the ban, and the ban did go into effect.[155] Yeltsin, however, was not afraid to use the communists when it suited him. Another of his decrees set up draconian ballot-access rules so that the badly weakened communists, who had no chance of winning a popular vote, would be the only opposition to the caucus aligned with him in the Moscow city government elections.[156]

As the struggle for power, and the struggle to set the pace of change, continued, life became more difficult. Gross domestic product had declined by 3 percent in 1990 and the decline was accelerating in 1991. Although some food and medicines were exempt, many prices were liberated in April 1991; despite government caps, prices for many consumer items doubled or tripled. The price rises were the work of the new prime minister, Pavlov, and Gorbachev seemed curiously detached, later writing in his memoirs: "Perhaps the chief shortcoming of the price reform of 1991 was that it had been developed and implemented outside the overall context of economic transformation. Pavlov's attitude did not help. There were no grounds to complain about his lack of activity. He started many things, but he acted impulsively, haphazardly, unsystematically."[157] Who was in charge?

Miners across the Soviet Union had again been on strike when prices were freed; but this strike, unlike the 1989 action, was only partially observed. A general strike broke out in Minsk, the capital of the republic of Belarus, in response to the April price rises, but was not sustained. In part due to the failure of their strike to spread, the miners, too, went back to work. Both groups of strikers failed to win the wage increases they had sought to offset the price rises; Russian miners went back to work when Yeltsin promised the mines would be transferred from Soviet to Russian jurisdiction and given financial independence.[158] But this agreement was another maneuver by Yeltsin—although the mines were transferred to Russian jurisdiction, they had long operated at a planned loss under central planning and there was no money to upgrade their operations to make them competitive on the world market.

Workers in Minsk demanded compensation for the price increases, the repeal of a new sales tax and the removal of the Communist Party from all Belarus institutions.[159] But their general strike was called off without winning any demands. The strikes in Minsk and in the mines did not spread and the movement died out—the working people of the Soviet Union had not rallied to their own defense. Brief sporadic strikes had broken out in several enterprises across the country, but local authorities would quickly agree to negotiations, inducing employees to immediately return to work without winning significant concessions. Neither a new federation of unions nor new political parties emerged during this period, nor had they in the earlier years of glasnost and perestroika. The lack of coordination helped seal the fate of the mass strikes of the miners and the general strike in Minsk.

The Soviet Union was a very different country in 1985 than it had been at the end of the Stalin dictatorship in 1953, as demonstrated by the spread of democratic activity and unrest in contrast to the 1950s. But no true popular mass movement developed. There are various parts to the puzzle of why no mass movements arose; among them would be that six decades of working under a rigid command structure with no means for self-organization had thoroughly atomized working people. The accompanying 60 years of propaganda blaring that the centralized command system was the only true form of socialism now boomeranged, causing significant numbers of people throughout the Soviet bloc to reject socialism in any form or be unable to visualize different forms of a society based on cooperation, and therefore to develop an idealized and naïve view of capitalism.

If the creation of a better society, with popular control over all aspects of life, including the workplace, was in a position to happen, it was now, before widespread privatization. The workers of Czechoslovakia had begun working out a national system of workers' control and self-management during the Prague Spring; they could attempt to create an economic democracy because the economy was in the hands of the state, and therefore could be placed in collective hands under popular control. But once the means of production become private property, the task of wresting control becomes vastly more difficult. The owners of that privatized production dominate a capitalist economy, enabling the accumulation of wealth and the ability to decisively influence government policy; the state becomes an agent of the dominant class, and the force available to the state is used to reinforce that dominance.

The Soviet bureaucracy had only political force available to it to maintain its privileged position, in contrast to a capitalist elite's variety of mechanisms, particularly economic coercion, to maintain itself in control. Moreover, all capitalist economies are connected to a global capitalist system that reinforces the power of capitalists in any given country.

Although it probably is impossible to overstate the exhaustion of Soviet society as a factor in the failure to develop national grassroots organizations, perhaps the people of the Soviet Union didn't believe that they had nothing left to lose as their ancestors had believed in 1917. Back then, Russians lived in miserable material conditions and under the constant threat of government violence. By no means were material conditions satisfactory during the period of perestroika, but they were not comparable to the wretchedness endured under tsarist absolutism nor did the urgency of having to remove a violent dictatorship exist. A social safety net, tattered and weakened, still existed, and most Russians believed that, despite whatever dramatic economic and political changes still lay ahead, they would be able to retain the social safety net they were used to under Communist Party rule.

Pushing back against economic and political changes, hard-liners thought they would be able to turn the clock back and reinstitute some variation of the orthodox Soviet system. They, too, did not understand the social forces that were gathering. The Soviet Union could not stand still—if it could not find a path forward to a pluralistic, democratic socialist society that would be defended across the country, then capitalism was poised to burst in as if a dam holding back a sea burst.

The Soviet Union could not find such a path—working people were unable to create a society-wide movement, perestroika was unable to solve the massive economic problems that had only become worse, and introducing capitalistic reforms had severed the supply and distribution links among enterprises without putting anything in their place.

The Soviet command system did not function well and had been long overdue for radical changes to convert it into a more modern system—but it did function. What had begun to replace it, elements of capitalism, disorganized the country's economy into disaster. But the old command system could not be put back together; doing so was economically, politically and socially unfeasible. Having reached a dead end, the question was not would there be a change, it was what change would there be.

Blinded by their ideology, the hard-liners misunderstood the situation more than anybody else.

## Steel into air: The August putsch brings down the curtain

Rumors of an attempt to overthrow Mikhail Gorbachev circulated in the days before the putsch of August 1991. Those rumors were noted in Soviet newspapers, those who were close to the president gave private warnings, and some observers believed that Prime Minister Valentin Pavlov's June request to be given emergency powers (swiftly denied) was something of a dress rehearsal.[160] The date of the putsch, 19 August, was timed to block the imminent signing of a treaty by Gorbachev and republic leaders that would have changed the Soviet Union into a federal system granting considerable autonomy to the republics; talks to achieve this goal had gone on all summer.

It is likely that an additional factor was the deal Gorbachev had sealed with the leaders of the seven most powerful capitalist countries, the "G7" group. In July, Gorbachev had sent a letter to the G7 leaders stating that

> We feel that the time has come to take resolute steps to undertake coordinated efforts for a new type of economic

> interaction that would integrate the Soviet economy—with its vast productive, scientific-technical, and human potential, its rich natural resources, and its colossal domestic market—into the world economy. This would reinforce the positive political process in international relations as well.[161]

A week later, the G7 leaders agreed to implement a "special association for the Soviet Union with the [International Monetary Fund] and with the World Bank."[162] But these leaders were not going to underwrite a new competitor, and the IMF and World Bank, as we saw in Chapter 4, are blunt instruments whose policies relegate most of the world's countries into roles as economic vassals of the most powerful states. No matter how noble the intentions of Gorbachev, the reality of "integration" would soon enough prove to be no miracle cure.

The putsch leaders were all government officials who were close to Gorbachev, including his new prime minister (Pavlov), interior minister (Boris Pugo) and vice president (Gennadii Yanayev); the appointment of each had sparked considerable controversy. Defense Minister Dmitry Yazov and the head of the KGB secret police, Vladimir Kryuchkov, were also among the putsch conspirators. Gorbachev was on vacation in Crimea when a delegation arrived unannounced to demand he hand over his powers to his vice president, Yanayev. Gorbachev argued with them, and the delegation left without his cooperation, but all communication was cut and Gorbachev was placed under house arrest.

A "state committee for the emergency" declared itself in charge, claiming that Gorbachev's health had failed. Although only a handful of conspirators were behind the putsch, Communist Party bodies took a wait-and-see attitude—the failure to mount any opposition swept away the party's last scraps of authority. At the top of the party, for example, the Central Committee demanded to be allowed to meet with

Gorbachev, saying it could not give an assessment of the emergency without such a meeting.[163]

The putsch leaders' worst mistake, perhaps, was for some of them to appear on national television. They could not articulate any reason for their actions, and numerous personal accounts of the attempted coup recalled the shaking hands of the plotters and the relief felt at seeing that. The television press conference seemed to counteract the sight of tanks rolling through the streets of Moscow. Some of those tanks parked in front of the Russian government building, the imposing "White House." It was here that Yeltsin joined the crowd surrounding the tanks to make a speech, thereby symbolizing resistance to the putsch. Yeltsin, in his account of this episode, later wrote: "I greeted the commander of the tank upon which I was standing and talked with the soldiers. From their faces, from the expressions in their eyes, I could see they would not shoot us. I jumped down from the tanks and was back in my office in a few minutes."[164]

The crowds remained in front of the White House and some among them gave food to the soldiers, who had not been provisioned. The emergency committee's decrees were ignored. The committee's plans falling apart, Kryuchkov, the KGB chief, decided against arresting prominent Soviet and Russian government officials. Yeltsin and the Russian government loudly condemned the putsch as illegal, in strong contrast to the silence of Communist Party bodies.

On the third day of the putsch, however, it appeared that an attack on the White House was about to start, and Yeltsin's aides began to take him to the United States embassy, across the street from one of the rear wings of the White House. The embassy had offered to take in Yeltsin, but at the last moment the Russian president decided it would give the appearance of too much interference in Russian affairs by the US, and he refused to leave the White House.[165] Later that day, the troops were removed from Moscow; the military had refused to attack the rows of civilians who still stood in front of the government building, and key army commanders refused to back the putsch.

The putsch failing, several of the emergency committee members flew to Crimea to see Gorbachev, who had remained under house arrest. "When the plotters turned up," Gorbachev later wrote, "I gave orders that they should be arrested, and I issued my demand that I would not speak to any of them until the government telephone line was reconnected."[166] Gorbachev was soon back in Moscow, the plotters were in custody and all political momentum decisively flowed to Yeltsin.

Three days after the putsch collapsed, Gorbachev resigned as Communist Party general secretary, told the party Central Committee to disband, banned the activity of the party in all government and security institutions, and ordered local governments to take into their possession all party properties. He believed he had no choice but to draw firm conclusions: "The Secretariat, the Politburo and the Communist Party's Central Committee did not take a stand against the coup d'etat...Among the conspirators were members of the party leadership. A number of party committees and the mass media supported the action of the state criminals. This places millions of Communists in a false position."[167]

During those three days following the collapse of the putsch, Yeltsin suspended six party newspapers, including *Pravda,* and formally recognized the independence of the three Baltic republics. The Supreme Soviet of the Soviet Union "suspended" the party on 29 August and in November Yeltsin banned the Soviet and Russian communist parties from the territory of the Russian republic. The ban was illegal because a party could be banned only by a court order, not by a presidential decree, but there was little public protest.[168] The party had become so discredited that its lead newspaper, *Pravda,* was reopened as an independent collective by its reporters and editors, outside of any party.

Gorbachev, however, continued to seek a way to keep the Soviet Union intact; he summoned the Supreme Soviet and the broader Congress of People's Deputies to resume work on the new union treaty that was about to be signed before the putsch, and he refused demands by deputies that he step down as president.[169]

Not only was the party disintegrating, but the Soviet government structures were as well. Yeltsin named the leader of his corps of young technocrats, Yegor Gaidar (who would soon administer shock therapy), as the Russian republic's deputy prime minister. On Gaidar's first day on the job, 5 November, he walked into the Moscow headquarters of the Soviet Union's planning agency, Gosplan, armed with Yeltsin's decree and a police officer—he and his team had arrived to dismantle all remaining central planning.[170] That Gosplan was a Soviet agency, not a Russian one, and therefore not at all under Yeltsin's jurisdiction, had ceased to matter. Power had flowed irrevocably to Yeltsin. Gorbachev could no more assert himself than could Aleksandr Kerensky on the eve of the October Revolution. The period of the dual government had already passed.

The October Revolution took place in the capital city with the city's residents filling the streets, occupying strategic buildings and electrifying the world with their cascade of motion and unity of purpose, backed across the country with civilians, soldiers and sailors asserting their collective will. The end of that revolution 74 years later happened in a secret meeting, in a forest outside a provincial city, and involved all of three people.

Yeltsin met with the leaders of the two other Slavic Soviet republics—Leonid Kravchuk of Ukraine and Stanislav Shushkevich of Belarus—in the Belovezhsky Nature Reserve, a forest outside Minsk, the capital of Belarus. The three signed an accord declaring that the Soviet Union had ceased to exist. A follow-up agreement confirmed that Russia would be the legal successor to the Soviet Union, including the retention of the

USSR's permanent seat on the United Nations Security Council. "I was convinced that Russia needed to rid itself of its imperial mission," Yeltsin later wrote, "nevertheless, Russia needed a stronger, harder policy, even forceful at some stage, in order not to lose its significance and authority altogether and in order to institute reforms."[171] Perhaps not only for those stated reasons—his Russian government had just declared itself the owner of all Soviet gold and diamond deposits and of petroleum.[172] Yeltsin could unilaterally sign the pact to dissolve the Soviet Union because he had gotten the Russian parliament to grant him extraordinary powers to rule by decree.

His country having ceased to exist, Gorbachev was left with nothing to do but announce his resignation as Soviet president on 25 December. The party that had created that country traveled a remarkable path—from a persecuted group of revolutionaries to new leaders struggling in a hostile world to a monolithic "single piece of steel" to a bureaucratic dictatorship that couldn't control its own bureaucracy to rapid decomposition. From steel to air.

Liquidation complete, Yeltsin could not resist a final insult. Gorbachev and Yeltsin had agreed that Gorbachev would vacate his Kremlin office by 30 December. But Yeltsin was in a hurry: "[O]n the morning of the 27th, I received a telephone call from the Kremlin reception-room," Gorbachev later wrote. "I was informed that Yeltsin [and two Yeltsin aides] had occupied my office at 8:30 a.m. and held a party there, emptying a bottle of whisky…This was a triumph of plunderers—I can find no other word for it."[173] Gorbachev's presidential apartment had even been sealed the day he gave his resignation speech.[174]

Yeltsin rather gleefully gave his side of this affair, recounting his conversation with Gorbachev following the signing of the Belovezhsky agreement: "At that point, I said to him: there's no more Union, don't you see? And there's no turning back."[175]

Why recount such a personal detail? Because that lack of human feeling, beginning a few days later, would be projected onto a vast country.

## Shock therapy: Unprecedented collapse as the "Chicago School" conducts an experiment

More than half a century earlier, a remarkable prediction had been made. The theorist who foresaw the potential path of the Soviet bureaucracy mostly used his formidable pen to analyze the events of his day, and so the prediction was not widely noticed. Or perhaps it seemed too fantastic to take seriously. After decades of thinking, writing and struggling, Leon Trotsky wrote these words in 1936:

> Let us assume…that neither a revolutionary nor a counterrevolutionary party seizes power. The bureaucracy continues at the head of the state. Even under these conditions social relations will not jell. We cannot count upon the bureaucracy's peacefully and voluntarily renouncing itself in behalf of socialist equality…[I]t must inevitably in future stages seek support for itself in property relations. One may argue that the big bureaucrat cares little what are the prevailing forms of property relations. This argument ignores not only the instability of the bureaucrat's own rights, but also the question of his descendants. The new cult of the family has not fallen out of the clouds. Privileges have only half their worth, if they cannot be transmitted to one's children. But the right of testament is inseparable from the right of property. It is not enough to be the director of a trust; it is necessary to be a stockholder. The victory of the bureaucracy in this decisive sphere would mean its conversion into a new possessing class. On the other hand, the victory of the proletariat over the bureaucracy would ensure a revival of the socialist revolution.[176]

Two years later, Trotsky would take those thoughts to their

logical conclusion: "[E]ither the bureaucracy, becoming ever more the organ of the world bourgeoisie in the workers' state, will overthrow the new forms of property and plunge the country back to capitalism; or the working class will crush the bureaucracy and open the way to socialism."[177]

If the bureaucracy were to be left in power, it would eventually appropriate the Soviet Union's economic assets for itself, Trotsky had said. And that is what happened. Although, after a few more years, a handful of "oligarchs" who mostly had not been party officials or among the nomenklatura would ultimately own most of the economy, in raw numbers most of the new owners of factories and businesses would come from the ranks of the nomenklatura. There would be few winners, however, as the greatest economic collapse in modern world history would leave scores of millions destitute.

The Yeltsin government's dramatic implementation of new economic policies imposed from above known as "shock therapy" would provide the greatest opportunity imaginable for a very specific ideological experiment—a "pure" capitalism. "Pure" because this would be capitalism without constraints, without government. A perpetual barrage of propaganda has maintained that freeing markets of any and all regulations would lead to paradise. Perhaps the most vigorous proponents of this ideology are the "Chicago School" economists trained at the University of Chicago in the United States under the utopian theories of Milton Friedman. (A primary wellspring of the policies popularly known around the world as "neoliberalism.") Boris Yeltsin's economic advisers, headed by Yegor Gaidar and Anatoli Chubais, had fallen under the sway of the Chicago School ideology, and were determined to implement it at all costs.

The term "shock therapy" was coined by Friedman on a 1975 trip to Chile to tighten the economic policies Augusto Pinochet's military dictatorship was imposing,[178] policies designed and implemented by Friedman's acolytes. Moreover, Friedman repeatedly used the word "shock" in his follow-up letter to Pinochet laying out his prescriptions.[179] In short, economic shock therapy is the sudden simultaneous lifting of all price and currency controls and withdrawal of state subsidies in conjunction with rapid mass privatization of public assets and properties. The immediate purpose of such a program is to place everything into private hands so that as much profit as possible can be extracted, in conjunction with the concomitant broader goals of blocking the creation of more socially harmonious economic models. The foreign capitalists who promote shock therapy also seek to buy property in the "shocked" country as cheaply as possible.

The formal ideological justification offered in public for these policies is that private businesses would take advantage of the resulting higher prices by increasing production, which in turn would dampen inflationary pressures. Chicago School economists believe that inflation is a result of imbalances in a country's supply of money—thus the formal name for them is "monetarist." Austerity programs of all sorts (including shock therapies) are alleged to be necessary to eliminate inflation or the threat of inflation, a particular obsession of monetarists. (The reason is that inflation hurts the value of speculators' assets.)

The Chicago School is an ideologically driven belief system based on mathematical formulae, divorced from the conditions of the actual, physical world, and which seeks to put human beings at the service of markets rather than using markets to provide for human needs.

What would happen if markets were left entirely to themselves with effectively an absence of government? An all-out scramble in which the strongest, or, more accurately, the most ruthless, would grab whatever they could in whatever way they could. Russia, and the international financiers who cheered on the Russian "reformers," would soon see the results of this experiment on the bodies of 150 million Russians. But this would not be an entirely unprecedented experiment—Chicago School economics imposed by dictatorship had already led to grisly results in Chile, as well as Argentina and Uruguay, in the 1970s and 1980s.

The democratically elected government of Salvador Allende was overthrown in a violent coup in 1973 following a well-funded destabilization program carried out by Chilean and US big business and the US Central Intelligence Agency. The CIA, among other exploits, routinely meddled in elections, funded Right-wing mass media, organized mass social groups, conducted an "economic offensive against Chile,"[180] and paid Chile's truck drivers more to go on strike than they would have made by working.[181] Four days after the military coup, six of Chile's most prominent businessmen were honored by Pinochet and the three other coup leaders for their role in toppling the Allende government, and one of the businessmen was given a post as an economic adviser.[182]

Shock therapy was enforced on Chile with devastating results—lavish subsidies were given to large corporations, public spending was slashed and the social security system was privatized. The privatized social security system was so bad for Chilean working people that a working person retiring in 2005 received less than half of what he or she would have received had they been in the old government system.[183] The military, naturally, exempted itself from the privatization, and the six companies that administer almost all of the private plans rake in huge profits.[184]

Chile's poverty rate skyrocketed to 40 percent, real wages had declined by a third and one-third of Chileans were unemployed during the last years of the dictatorship.[185] Unemployment figures do not include the many urban Chileans who worked as "car minders" by "waving orange rags at motorists pulling into parking spaces and taking their coins to insert them into parking meters—in exchange for a small tip."[186] Chile's planning minister, one of the Chicago School partisans who oversaw the Pinochet dictatorship's economic policies, declared that the car minders made a good living from collecting tips and "with all the new cars we are importing, they will have more work than ever."[187]

Argentina's military dictatorship was even more lethal than Pinochet's. Argentina was an industrialized country with agricultural abundance that had active union and Left-wing movements, and a sizeable middle class. But the country's economic elite and the multinational corporations that operated there wanted Argentina turned into a low-wage haven, and only extreme violence could accomplish this goal in the face of widespread organized opposition. The Argentine military, assisted by two Right-wing death squad organizations, seized power in a coup and handed control of the economy to the former head of the country's largest steel company, who also was a major landowner with ties to Argentina's rural, industrial and banking elites. Bans on unions and strikes, elimination of social programs and sharp rises in prices followed.

The result was a 50 percent reduction in real wages in the first year, mass unemployment, further drops in production and wages, and an increase of more than fivefold in Argentina's foreign debt.[188] This occurred as the military dictatorship's "dirty war" of "disappearances," mass torture and execution raged against the population. (This régime also trained Nicaragua's Contras.) The US financier David Rockefeller, whose loans helped finance the régime, famously declared, "I have the impression that Argentina has a régime which understands the private enterprise system."[189]

Tens of thousands were killed, hundreds of thousands were arrested and tortured, and hundreds of thousands were forced into exile to implement shock therapy in Chile, Argentina and Uruguay. Friedman claimed that he gave only "technical economic advice" and that Chile's economic and political policies were totally separate, but also wrote that people who demonstrated in favor of human rights at his speeches were "fanatics."[190] Even by the standards of conservative economists Friedman was unusually disingenuous, so let us turn to an unusually honest Chicago School economist, a Chilean who was a protégé of the planning minister who said the "car minders" made a good living. The economist acknowledged in a 1984 interview that "[i]t would have been difficult to apply this kind of economic policy without a military régime."[191]

This interview was conducted by a Chilean journalist, Patricia Politzer, who noted the difficulty in getting anyone to admit to being a "Chicago Boy" in light of the freefall the Chilean economy was then suffering. This self-declared Chicago Boy, however, believed that 80,000 to 100,000 people had been killed by the Pinochet régime yet said that a coup capable of producing such a death toll was an acceptable "lesser evil," declaring that "freedom ought to be restricted, because it is good up to a certain point and then it begins to endanger society."[192]

Far less armed force would be needed in Russia because Russians were so disoriented from the dizzying collapse of the Soviet Union's institutions and also had an almost total lack of sustained organizing (in contrast to the populations of Chile and Argentina). Nonetheless, Russia's shock therapy of 1990s was applied without any democratic discussion. Capitalism could not have been implemented otherwise.

The very breakup of the Soviet Union was undemocratic—a referendum in early 1991 had resulted in about 78 percent of those voting expressing a desire to keep the country intact, and the agreement to dissolve the country was signed in secret. The plans for shock therapy were not placed before the public or the Russian parliament; they were presented only to the International Monetary Fund.[193] A large majority of Russians opposed full privatization, instead backing the transformation of enterprises into cooperatives and state guarantees of full employment.

Yeltsin was ruling by decree at the end of 1991, and his team of reformers used the president's authority to force through their plans. At the same time that Yegor Gaidar had strolled into Gosplan headquarters with his decree in hand as the newly appointed deputy prime minister and finance minister, Anatoli Chubais was appointed privatization minister and chair of the newly created State Property Committee, tasked with preparing state enterprises for privatization. Yeltsin, on Chubais' recommendations, issued a series of decrees at the end of 1991 to help speed the process.[194]

One week after Mikhail Gorbachev's resignation the shock therapy would begin, on 2 January 1992, with complete liberation of prices (except for energy), the concomitant ending of all subsidies of consumer products and for industry, and allowing the ruble to float against international currencies instead of having a fixed exchange rate. Gaidar's strategy was to radically reduce demand, a devastating hardship considering that most products were in short supply already. The freeing of prices meant that the cost of consumer items, including food, would skyrocket, and the ruble's value would collapse because the fixed value given it by the Soviet government was judged as artificially high by international currency traders. This combination would mean instant hyperinflation.

Here we might note the irony of a plan bound to cause punishing inflation implemented by economists who preach that harsh medicine must be applied to eliminate even the possibility of inflation. Partisans of Chicago School economics will claim that hyperinflation unleashed by eliminating all price controls at once is not actually inflation, because prices are merely conforming to prices set by world markets.[195] To put it another way, the (theoretical) increase in production spurred by higher prices and (concrete) reduction in demand would enable prices to reach an equilibrium point; that the resulting high prices would be beyond the reach of consumers was another "technical" issue. Regardless, no such equilibrium was reached.

Due to the desire to implement these policies as quickly as possible, the plans to implement this program were not well thought out. Upon accepting his new post, Chubais contacted one of his associates from his earlier stint working in the St Petersburg city government and asked him to draw up a privatization plan in 24 hours.[196] The associate later recalled that he and the rest of Chubais' team had to write "twenty normative laws" in the last month and a half of 1991, a time he called "a really romantic period."[197]

Another Yeltsin adviser was rather less flowery in his description of the eve of shock therapy: "[T]he most favorable condition for reform" is a "weary public, exhausted by the previous political struggle," he said. "That is why the government was confident, on the eve of price liberalization, that a drastic social clash was impossible, that the government would not be overthrown by a popular revolt."[198]

Romantic or not, Russia's privatizers also had expert advice. The chief economist of the World Bank in the late 1990s, Joseph Stiglitz (a Keynesian economist who was forced out of the institution by the US Treasury Department because of his dissents from monetarist policy), later disapprovingly summarized the thinking of Western economic advisers: "Only a blitzkrieg approach during the 'window of opportunity' provided by the 'fog of transition' would get the changes made before the population had a chance to organize to protect its previous vested interests."[199] Yeltsin himself, in an infamous statement, promised Russians they would have to endure six months of pain, and then everything would get better.

They did not. Inflation for 1992 was 2600 percent and for 1993 was nearly 1000 percent—that alone wiped out all savings held in banks. The excess cash that had accumulated in banks, instead of being put back into circulation by stimulating demand or used toward productive investment, was simply made worthless. A very large surplus of personal savings parked in banks had built up during the previous three years because there had not been enough production for consumers to buy. Gaidar considered liquidation of the money in savings accounts part of the effort to reduce Russia's "monetary hangover."[200] In other words, Russians possessed too much money—another "technical" issue because too large a supply of money causes inflation, Chicago School economists believe, a problem cured here through hyper-inflation.

For the first seven months of 1992, Russian Vice President Aleksandr Rutskoi reported that industrial output fell by 18 percent and agricultural output by 27 percent.[201] Because credit was cut off to enterprises at the start of the year, it became impossible for most enterprises to pay their workers because their customers paid them late; enterprise debt as a result of the economic upheaval rose from 39 billion rubles at the start of 1992 to 3.2 trillion rubles by July.[202] The first half of 1992 saw the equivalent of 15 billion US dollars of capital taken out of Russia.[203]

In the first days of January, what little food was available in state stores completely disappeared, as state-store managers diverted their supplies to private operators for a cut of their profits. State enterprises were also crippled by new high taxes levied only against them. Reduced to penury, Russians took to the streets to begin peddling their personal possessions to survive.

For a handful, however, the mass misery merely meant more opportunity to take advantage. Millionaires had already appeared in 1991—dollar millionaires, not ruble millionaires. One of those millionaires, Mikhail Friedman—soon to be one of the seven oligarchs who would effectively run Russia—had made a fortune through smuggling consumer items and exporting oil, the latter particularly lucrative because the oil was bought at extremely low subsidized Soviet prices and sold abroad at international market prices.[204]

Another millionaire, a former physics professor, also became rich in 1991 by buying subsidized oil and selling it abroad at a price 40 times higher.[205] These profits were taken out of the country to be parked in foreign banks; without the speculation of these "middle men," the oil they sold at world market rates could have been sold by the state to instead be used to invest in desperately needed industrial retooling or social spending.

Having set up the privatization agency (the State Property Committee), Chubais and Gaidar wished to get as much property into private hands as fast as possible. For the purpose of making privatization appear to be fair, a voucher system was created in the summer of 1992—all Russians would be issued one voucher that could be redeemed for shares in newly privatized enterprises. The vouchers were worth 10,000 rubles, but this amount was already worth little because of the hyperinflation, and the remaining value dwindled further as inflation raged throughout 1992 and 1993. One Russian writer, noting that his family's vouchers wound up in a scrapbook, put the value of these vouchers succinctly: "Shortly after it was issued, a voucher could at most buy a loaf of bread."[206] The writer was among many who refused to exchange his voucher at such a low price, but the vouchers were canceled, without possibility of redemption, in 1994.

Russians found the low value of the vouchers insulting, wondering how their share of such a vast economy could be worth so little. Gaidar and Chubais set the value by making very low estimates of the value of enterprises, then taking 35 percent of that figure and dividing the sum by the population of Russia.[207] Most of the vouchers were bought cheap by speculators looking to buy enterprises for a minuscule fraction of their worth or were given to swindlers who promised large payoffs but in fact ran ponzi schemes that collapsed.

To help expedite this process, a prominent Western

investment bank was brought in. (The same investment bank that "earned" 100 million US dollars for restructuring Argentina's foreign debt, the single deal that in the long run increased interest payments mentioned at the end of Chapter 4. The bank acted no differently than its competitors would have.) A 26-year-old itching for revenge because his ancestors, tsarist military officers, went abroad after the October Revolution and a 32-year-old ideologue who couldn't speak Russian were sent to put enterprises on the sales block. Once again, the ideological imperative to place everything into private hands trumped all caution. One of the two described their methodology this way: "In typical investment banking fashion you kind of bluffed your way through and made believe that we had some highly developed incredible plans."[208]

In many cases, however, speculators would not be able to win control of their targets because 51 percent of the stock of privatized enterprises was to be made available first to the enterprises' management and workforce. But thanks to hyperinflation, few had any money with which to buy these shares. Enterprise directors were able to induce or coerce their employees into selling their shares and vouchers to them because the employees desperately needed some cash due to being wiped out by inflation or because they were not being paid because of the general economic dislocation. These managers wound up owning about two-thirds of privatized enterprises[209] (although large numbers of them would later lose control to Russia's emerging oligarchs).

High officials in government ministries overseeing natural resource industries managed to privatize themselves, converting these ministries into Russia's largest commercial operations. For instance, the Soviet Ministry of Coal converted itself into Coal of Russia, a company containing 88 of the ministry's 112 Russian enterprises, including mines and engineering plants.[210]

The first operations to declare themselves private were the

supply and warehouse operations within the centralized distribution system, a naked taking of state property.[211] The parallel black-market networks were the nucleus from which grew the pervasive organized-crime networks that controlled much early business in cities such as Moscow and St Petersburg and from which rose the oligarchs.

Unemployment had become so pervasive with the closing of everything from factories to scientific institutes—as well as widespread lack of pay for those still employed and the hyperinflation that reduced paychecks to nothing—that Muscovites were reduced to growing vegetables at their country dachas in order to be able to eat.[212] Those who were able to survive were those who spent their days and nights in open-air markets, selling whatever they could get their hands on. But becoming a merchant was highly dangerous—open-air peddlers and those renting commercial real estate space could expect to pay 25 to 30 percent of their profits to organized-crime groups or be treated with red-hot irons or shot if they underpaid.[213]

Against this backdrop, the Russian parliament asserted itself to demand that Gaidar, who had been promoted, be sacked as prime minister. (Russia had a French-style "strong president" system in which the president appointed the prime minister and the government.) Fearful that Russians might yet rise up against the misery imposed on them, Yeltsin removed Gaidar and named Viktor Chernomyrdin as the new prime minister. Chernomyrdin had been minister of gas during the last years of Gorbachev, and oversaw the conversion of the Soviet gas ministry into Gazprom, a company that dominates Russia's vast natural gas industry but in which the government retains a controlling interest.

That control at this time represented almost the last thread of the former social safety net—Gazprom sold its gas at extremely low rates to Russian customers, preventing Russians from freezing to death during the winters. Reflecting the general state of the country, Chernomyrdin took office with a promise to "put an end to the impoverishment of the population."[214]

Gaidar, however, did not disappear—he and Chubais remained Yeltsin's two indispensable lieutenants with varying duties (and sometimes without holding government posts) depending on what direction the political winds were blowing at a given moment. Chernomyrdin, too, would be in and out of government as Yeltsin would repeatedly shuffle his government ministers. But Yeltsin's removal of Gaidar as prime minister near the end of 1992 did not mean he had ceased to think of the parliament as an annoyance to be dispensed with.

In March 1993, the parliament voted to revoke Yeltsin's powers to rule by decree; the authorized one-year decree period had already expired. Yeltsin responded by declaring a "state of emergency," granting himself the right to continue to rule by decree. The constitutional court ruled the declaration was illegal, but Yeltsin ignored the court ruling. Disapproving of the Russian parliament's effort to ameliorate shock therapy, the then-deputy US treasury secretary, Lawrence Summers (a neoliberal economist who had previously worked for the World Bank), demanded that "the momentum for Russian reform must be reinvigorated and intensified to ensure sustained multilateral support."[215] In other words: Do as you are told, Russia.

That was no problem for Yeltsin. Here is what Yeltsin himself said in his memoirs:

> My priorities had been constant: political stability, clarity, definition. Enough of this pulling the blanket back and forth like an old couple. Enough of this fiddling with the legislation… Russia would no longer tolerate our squabbling at the Congress. If this kept up, a new Russian Stalin would emerge who would crush this intellectual fussing with democracy with his little finger. I therefore chose my option for stabilization.[216]

Never mind that the parliament was freely elected, represented the Russian people who were sick of shock therapy and that these same parliamentarians had stood with Yeltsin against the August putsch two years earlier. Moreover, they had voted for his economic policies and granted him the power to rule by decree. The president decided to eliminate the threat of dictatorship that a parliament represented in his mind by declaring a dictatorship: He announced that the constitution was abolished and parliament dissolved despite having no legal authority to do either.

The constitutional court again ruled against Yeltsin, and the parliament voted to impeach Yeltsin and replace him with Vice President Aleksandr Rutskoi, who had become a consistent critic of shock therapy. Yeltsin responded by cutting off electricity and heat to the parliament building and surrounding it with troops, tanks and water cannons.

Yeltsin also issued decrees banning trade unions and strikes, and he banned independent newspapers; his security forces had already routinely attacked demonstrations in Moscow earlier in the year.[217] Once again, government officials and staff opposed to a coup occupied the White House; once again thousands of people stood in front of the building to defend it.

One difference this time was that there was a more clear-cut choice. At the time of the August 1991 putsch, the lack of organizing and independent political movements with the potential to steer perestroika into a truly democratic direction left two elite projects to contend—one a forcible return to Brezhnevite stasis that had no chance to succeed and the other a definitive passing of power into the hands of Yeltsin, who intended to use his power to force shock therapy on a Russian public that did not realize what was being prepared for them.

Now, in 1993, there was a choice between, on the one hand, an ineffective parliament that nonetheless represented some measure of democracy and a potential rolling back of some of the hardships of shock therapy and, on the other hand, a naked power grab that could only promise more pain. A victory by the White House defenders held the possibility (with much follow-up work) to begin to create a democratic movement that could enable a long-term project to institute popular control over society. Such a development, of course, would not have been the only possible outcome of a victory by the White House defenders nor would it necessarily have been a likely outcome given the exhaustion and atomization of Russian society, although a victory against a coup can serve as a spark for an upsurge in grassroots organizing.

When troops started talking with the demonstrators, they were replaced by other troops from outside Moscow who were forbidden to fraternize; the troop commander supplemented those orders by ordering attacks on anybody in the vicinity, including people standing in kiosk queues and those inside a nearby subway station.[218] A week into the standoff, an unarmed contingent of demonstrators marched to a television station, where troops opened fire with machine guns, killing about 100 people. The next day, Yeltsin ordered an all-out assault on the White House—thousands of troops and dozens of tanks pounded the building with artillery shells and machine-gun rounds, setting the building on fire. The troops then stormed the White House, killing about 500 people and wounding another 1000. Yeltsin ordered the parliament disbanded and, for good measure, also disbanded the Moscow city council.

One of the defenders of the White House who had stood against the 1991 putsch had this to say about the 1993 version: "What we got was entirely the opposite of what we dreamed of. We went to the barricades for them, laid our lives on the line, but they didn't keep their promises."[219] Boris Kagarlitsky, a member of the Moscow city council in opposition to Yeltsin, was in an automobile in another part of the city at the time of the attack on the White House when his vehicle was stopped by police. He and the council members with him were then arrested and beaten by police officers who screamed, "You wanted democracy, you sons of bitches? We'll show you democracy!"[220]

This crackdown was loudly praised as "democracy" in the United States—Russia had been made safe for capitalism. Indeed, the World Bank's chief economist for Russia declared, "I've never had so much fun in my life."[221]

## "Chopping the Gordian knot": Capital slices through democracy

Taking advantage of his free hand, Boris Yeltsin issued further decrees deepening shock therapy, and the Russian economy continued to contract. Yeltsin's approval rating would eventually drop to 3 percent, and he would be faced with creating a scheme to keep himself in office when his term was up in 1996. There was also the matter of the largest state enterprises, those involved in natural resources, which had not yet been privatized. The "solution" to these two issues would be found together.

Although most businesses paid protection money to organized-crime groups, few of them paid taxes, leaving the government starved of revenue. And although 122,000 state enterprises had been privatized,[222] the government had received almost nothing for them—an estimated 160 million US dollars,[223] a minuscule fraction of the value of the properties and far less than the money that had been taken out of the country by the new owners. Organized-crime groups were among the few to do well in this environment—Russian crime-fighting authorities estimated they faced 100,000 mobsters organized into more than 4000 groups.[224]

The country's seven biggest businessmen—who, naturally, did not wish to pay taxes—came up with a scheme that became known as "loans for shares." In contrast to the nomenklatura that had been content to take over a factory or piece of state or party property they had previously managed, these seven had built huge companies by parleying the profits from their early private businesses into the capital necessary to grab other enterprises and then form banks that won exclusive government accounts or engaged in other activities that enabled them to begin to dominate the Russian economy. Six of these seven bankers essentially were products of the black market, setting up sham "cooperatives" to cover their previously illegal black-market activities and raw materials speculation. The seventh was a foreign ministry official who used his connections to set up a bank that had the massive assets of a state bank transferred to it followed by being given contracts to handle the accounts of two large government departments.

These seven bankers offered Yeltsin a bargain: In lieu of paying taxes, they would make loans to the government so it could meet its expenses, such as actually paying its employees. In return, the government would give the bankers collateral in the form of shares of the big natural-resources enterprises that were soon to be privatized. If the loans were repaid, the bankers would give the shares back. If not, the bankers would hold auctions to sell the collateral. The government had no ability to pay back these loans, but Yeltsin issued a decree sealing the deal in August 1995.

The bankers used their own banks to conduct the subsequent auctions, and, through a mix of rigged terms and conveniently closed airports, won them all at prices that were small fractions of the enterprises' reasonable market value. These enterprises represented Russia's enormous reserves of oil, nickel, aluminum and gold, and a minority share in the dominant gas company, Gazprom.

These seven bankers all became billionaires through the "loans for shares" scam. They became the biggest of the perhaps two dozen wheelers-and-dealers known as the "oligarchs" who would now cement their control of the Russian economy. By the end of 1996, after they had engineered Yeltsin's "re-election," these seven bankers alone controlled about 50 percent of the country's gross domestic product and almost all of its mass media. Yeltsin would need all of that power to remain in office. So hated had he become that even his 1994 war against the tiny province of Chechnya (started at the behest of his bodyguard and his defense minister, who predicted it would be over in "a few hours" and thereby provide a popularity boost) failed to rally Russians because the war quickly became a quagmire.

By late March 1996, less than three months before the presidential election, Yeltsin appeared headed to a sure defeat against the leader of the Communist Party of the Russian Federation, Gennadii Zyuganov. Although he promised voters a "return to socialism," Zyuganov mostly campaigned on nationalist themes. The Russian communists were by no means monolithic, although the faction around Zyuganov sought to renationalize banking; stop capital flight but leave smaller businesses in private hands to end the impoverishment of Russians; and lead a multi-class coalition including workers, intellectuals and "patriotic capitalists" in a struggle against "rampant capitalism" that had resulted in "the colonization of Russia."[225] Zyuganov had been an instructor in the Soviet party Central Committee's propaganda department during the 1980s and was named ideology chief of the Russian republic party at its 1990 formation. He became head of the Communist Party of the Russian Federation at its foundation in 1993.

Yeltsin reacted to his deep unpopularity by deciding to cancel the election, as he later admitted in his memoirs:

> I kept thinking, "It's too late"…There is no point in hiding it: I had always been inclined toward simple, effective decisions. It had always seemed to me that chopping through the Gordian knot was easier than spending years untying it. At some stage, when I compared the two strategies proposed to me by two teams [of advisers], I came to the conclusion that we couldn't

> wait for the results of the June elections. We had to act now…I had to take a radical step. I told my staff to prepare the documents. Decrees were written to ban the Communist Party, dissolve the Duma [as the newly reconstituted parliament was now known], and postpone the presidential elections.[226]

A majority of Yeltsin's staff approved, and he gave himself 24 hours to make a final decision.[227] Preparations went ahead—the security forces fabricated a bomb threat to empty the parliament building, sealed the building with troops and searched the offices of Communist deputies.[228] But before that 24-hour period expired, Yeltsin's daughter Tatyana asked him to reconsider, and brought in Anatoli Chubais,[229] still Yeltsin's fixer whether in or out of government. The two convinced Yeltsin that the election would be taken care of: "And finally I reversed a decision that I had *almost* already made."[230] What had Chubais cooked up?

At the just concluded World Economic Forum in Davos, Switzerland—the annual gathering of the world's capitalist elites—Chubais gathered together the seven big bankers, who had been feuding with each other and with Chubais. Putting aside their differences, they sealed a deal under which the bankers would use their money, and their ownership of the mass media, to keep Yeltsin in office, and Chubais would run the campaign in exchange for 3 million dollars.[231] The oligarchs spent an estimated 100 million dollars (33 times the legal limit) and provided 800 times more television coverage of Yeltsin than was provided to his opponents.[232] One of the seven bankers, Boris Berezovsky, summed up the buying of the election succinctly: "It is very simple. Big capital is not altruistic—we needed to protect our business."[233]

Why were the capitalist leaders of the West so eager to place the Russian economy in private hands, regardless of the disorganization the process would impose on the economy and of the asset-stripping the new owners would use to amass their billions? Why was the dictatorial rule that enabled this disorganization and inflicted misery so lavishly praised as "democracy" and "freedom"? The most basic reason was to eliminate any alternative example. The modern growth of capitalism and its assortment of permutations—whether we call these harsh policies "Chicago School" or "neoliberalism" or "Reaganism"—is built on an ideological foundation that insists, using the concentrated corporate ownership of the mass media as a bullhorn, that "there is no alternative."

Concentration of wealth and power, and the concomitant impoverishment and harsher struggles of working people, are systematically presented as the culmination of human development into the most "modern" system. Such an assertion can only have a chance to be widely accepted if there are no examples of different systems that are more humane. The repressive nature of the Soviet system unfortunately did much to buttress the capitalist elite's insistence on its modernity.

It is true that Western capitalist elites, especially those in the United States, wished to grab much of the newly available Russian property for themselves, but couldn't because ties within the bureaucracy remained strong even when the country's institutions were crumbling and because of Russian oligarchs' nimbleness and willingness to use force; the immense size of the country also made it difficult for foreigners to quickly gain control. Many of the leading cheerleaders for privatization did profit nicely—investment bankers as well as some of the advisers who arrived in Moscow from the US—but privatization overwhelmingly materially favored Russian oligarchs and the nomenklatura.

From an ideological standpoint, however, that was not a big problem, because the principle that everything should be converted into a source of profit for a minuscule class of owners was firmly put in place. As early as 1990, groundwork for the

Russian shock therapy variant of privatization was being laid. Jeffrey Sachs, a Harvard University professor who had already overseen shock therapy in countries such as Bolivia and Poland, did not mince words in describing the process he wished to implement in Russia: "[T]he overriding aim should be to transform state enterprises into private corporations, with transferable ownership shares, rather than, say, into cooperatives or firms self-managed by their workers."[234]

But where are the capitalists to come from? A country cannot have capitalism without capitalists. During the centuries of time it took for capitalism to supplant feudalism, factory owners, plantation proprietors and traders built up commercial empires until a handful of robber barons were able to amass gigantic fortunes vastly beyond anything humanity had previously seen. This process necessitated forcing farmers off their land, seizing farmland through one-sided laws, and driving people into cities to work long hours for little pay in factories because they had been stripped of any other way of surviving, along with the accumulations of capital built on exploitation of slave labor, colonialism and the forced extraction of precious metals.

But here was something unprecedented in human history—large-scale industry had already been constructed and had to be given to people who had not created it. That property had been built by the sweat of the working people of the Soviet Union, first by the enormous sacrifices they made in the 1930s and 1940s, and financed in later decades by reductions to their living standards. Yet they would be shut out, by design, under shock therapy. The only way to create a capitalist elite would be through sanctioning looting and stealing.

That was the lesson that the institutions of capitalist governments (such as the World Bank and the International Monetary Fund) and neoliberal "advisers" (such as Sachs and Lawrence Summers) had sought to impose on countries as small as Nicaragua and as large as Russia. Multilateral institutions such as the World Bank and the IMF (and the US government that is the ultimate power animating the two banks) are simultaneously exploitative and paternalistic, believing that they know what is best for all countries. That one-size-fits-all approach is perhaps inevitable when they are run by economists under the sway of the Chicago School, which became a dominant ideology by the end of the 1970s. Such an ideology is not the product of a conspiratorial cabal; it is simply a direct descendant of earlier economic schools employed to justify the harsh one-sided policies of their day. (A further discussion of capitalist economics will be found in Chapter 6.)

Chubais, in a private moment with one of his associates, demonstrated this belief that the privatized ends justify any means: "They steal and steal and steal," he said of Russia's oligarchs. "They are stealing absolutely everything and it is impossible to stop them. But let them steal and take their property. They will then become owners and decent administrators of this property."[235]

"Take" property they did. But can the looting of Russia's oligarchs be considered the work of "decent administrators"? The ideologues of shock therapy have frequently had to resort to contortions and ever shifting excuses to explain away the results of their advice. Let us briefly examine the writings of Anders Åslund, perhaps the most prominent of the Western non-governmental advisers other than Sachs. (To call Åslund "self-assured" might be an understatement—one reviewer of his books wrote, "His scalding prose is not of the sort belied by a mild presence: in person, Åslund has an impressive glower, looking as if he ought to carry a fan to dispel the steam rising from his ears."[236])

Åslund has one simple explanation for Russia's instability: "Post-communist transformation is the history of the war for and against rent seeking."[237] One dictionary definition of "rent" in this macroeconomic sense is "a return derived from [an] advantage, as in a monopoly in natural resources."[238] Åslund, however, provides a broader definition: "A useful definition of rents is 'profits in excess of the competitive level.'"[239] Writing about the final three years of Gorbachev's administration, Åslund declared:

> At the collapse of communism, the opportunities for rent seeking were probably greater than at any other time in world history. Huge resources lay unguarded. Large rents arose from arbitrage between free market prices and state-controlled prices, aggravated by multiple exchange rates...Rents faded away with time, but successful rent seekers bought politics to impose new rents. A vicious circle of self-reinforcing rent seeking evolved. Finally, the rent seekers privatized the state enterprises, which ironically turned them into profit seekers and caused high economic growth.[240]

The first part of this passage is factually correct and the entire passage, except for the last sentence, seems reasonable on the surface. But on closer examination, it quickly falls apart. The object of a capitalist enterprise is to amass profit and to do so by defeating the competition. Inherent in this competition is a quest for monopoly—successful big businesses ultimately seek to eliminate competition in their core line(s) of business. It is not necessary to place a moral judgment on such behavior, for it is inherent in capitalist competition. Most industries are not reduced to a single monopolistic producer, but a typical industry is dominated by a small number of large corporations, a situation that inherently contains the potential for those dominant enterprises to form a cartel, in essence a collective monopoly. (Such companies can maintain a joint dominance even when they compete for market share among themselves, one reason why Western antitrust law continually evolves.)

In newly capitalist Russia, this process was dramatically

accelerated and, because of the lack of any regulation or organized countervailing social pressure, the field was clear for the most ruthless to dominate not one business, but many businesses. So many businesses that the oligarchs could dominate an entire economy. Those who grabbed property and feverishly extracted wealth from it—looting, to use a more precise word—were simply amassing profit, albeit crudely. It was very true that this activity would be harmful in the long term for the property and was immediately harmful to the employees of these properties and Russian society as a whole. But when a system is set up to enable naked greed to run amuck, then the most greedy will do so. That is the logic of capitalism—and similar behavior is what touched off the global economic collapse that began in 2008.

Åslund's intimation is that the Soviet nomenklatura was behind all the excesses—that is why he is careful to confine his commentary about "rent seeking" to the Gorbachev years. It is true that the nomenklatura, freed to sell some of their production at their own discretion in the latter Gorbachev years, sought to profit unfairly by producing less and charging higher prices, helping to disrupt the economy. But, again, this was the result of a rapid introduction of market relations, precisely what Åslund and the other Western advisers pressed Soviet leaders to do.

Furthermore, the large-scale "rent seeking" Åslund deplores was conducted by the oligarchs whom he lovingly extols as the embodiments of virtue. Russian and Ukrainian oligarchs "are responding rationally to the prevailing conditions to maximize profit and security," Åslund wrote, a few pages later declaring that "[t]he emergence of the oligarchs must be understood as a natural consequence of the prevailing economic, legal and political conditions in the aftermath of communism and needs to be accepted by the public. This requires that the public understands and embraces the fundamental principles of capitalism."[241]

Oligarch behavior was "rational" only in the cold-blooded sense that it is naked self-interest to seek the maximum possible personal profit if the opportunity arises. The oligarchs were by far the most aggressive "rent seekers," emerging from the shadows of the black market to rack up astounding profits from the differences between market and state prices—that is how they accumulated the capital enabling them to become oligarchs. Their most audacious "rent seeking" came during the Yeltsin years, when Åslund would have us believe there was "high economic growth" in an era of ordinary "profit seeking."

One example of the oligarchs at work will suffice, and the fact that, under the foregoing distinction, this example constitutes approved "profit seeking" rather than disapproved "rent seeking" would likely provide little consolation. The object of this specific oligarchal work is the vast automobile plants of Tolyatti, the factory complex discussed earlier where the workers had organized themselves and enjoyed strong social services but ultimately lost their struggle to convert the plants into self-managed enterprises.

Instead of the factory complex providing a high standard of living for all the people of Tolyatti through cooperative ownership and management, it wound up in the hands of a single oligarch. Berezovsky, whom we just met in his later role fixing the 1996 election to keep Yeltsin in power, had been a mathematics professor during the Soviet era, and began his second career as a trader and as a consultant to the Tolyatti autoworks, now known as Avtovaz. Berezovsky teamed up with the Avtovaz director to form an auto dealership to sell the cars and a pyramid scheme to draw in investors.

Berezovsky's new sales company kept the money from the sales of the automobiles, which were transferred to it from the Avtovaz complex in opaque transactions, while the factory was saddled with the debts and taxes, sometimes without the ability to pay its employees.[242] In essence, all the value created by the complex and its workforce was appropriated by Berezovsky through his sales company. The Russian government, not wanting Avtovaz to become bankrupt, provided cheap loans or forgave its tax debts[243]—in effect another subsidy for Berezovsky, who was now on his way to becoming a billionaire.

A slice of that fortune went toward keeping Yeltsin in power. But the bottom had not yet been reached—1998 would bring a currency crisis and another economic collapse. Among the consequences of shock therapy was Russia's rapid integration into the global capital markets on disadvantageous terms. Despite having had the world's second-largest economy during Soviet times, Russia was treated as an undeveloped country whose main role would be to provide raw materials for other industrialized countries. The collapse of the Russian economy under shock therapy made it more vulnerable to the whims of international speculators.

Speculators had fueled construction booms and stock-market bubbles across Southeast Asia in the mid-1990s, causing an inflation in the local currencies until it was no longer profitable to speculate on the exchange rates. At that point, speculators pulled their money out, causing the value of those currencies to plunge and triggering the region's 1997 economic collapse. Speculators then sought new "emerging markets" in which to place their enormous fortunes. One of these places was Russia, helping to create a stock-market bubble there. The economic crisis in Southeast Asia had also caused a strong drop in demand for oil and metals, triggering declines in prices for the commodities, exports of which Russia was heavily dependent on due to its collapse of industry and agriculture.

A loan from the International Monetary Fund helped bring about Russia's 1998 ruble collapse—instead of stabilizing the underlying weakness of the Russian economy, the loan merely provided a pause in the downward spiral, time that speculators used to pull their money out.[244] Because it failed to collect taxes from Russia's wealthy or from big businesses, a shortfall compounded by the loss of revenue from falling oil and metal prices, the Russian government was dependent on foreign investors buying its bonds to continue to function, and had to offer extraordinarily high interest rates of 150 percent to keep foreign capital flowing. Because it was not tenable to continue to pay such interest rates, Russia obtained a loan from the IMF to be used, in part, to exchange its bonds for longer-term loans with lower interest rates.

The terms of the IMF loan were typically harsh, in the manner of the fund's standard one-size-fits-all austerity. Russia had to agree to cut government programs and policies that benefited primarily average Russians and small enterprises; increase revenue with new regressive value-added and sales taxes on consumers; freeze pay for workers; cut pensions for retirees; and simultaneously reduce the income tax for the wealthiest Russians, allegedly to induce them to invest in the Russian economy.[245] Nonetheless, Russia's economy continued to deteriorate: In August 1998, the month following the IMF loan, the Russian government would need to spend 11 billion rubles (about US$1.8 billion) more to service interest on its debt than it collected in monthly tax revenues.[246]

Aware that Russia's situation was not sustainable, foreign speculators stopped buying the high-interest government bonds and fled Russian securities, triggering a stock-market crash. The speculators were able to do so at a profit because the IMF loan temporarily maintained the ruble's exchange rate. No longer able to continue making payments on its ballooning debt nor to continue spending massive amounts of money on the foreign-exchange market to prop up the value of the ruble, Russia defaulted on its debt and ended its support of the ruble's exchange rate. More than half of the defaulted debt, however, was owed to Russia's big banks, which in turn needed the high-interest payments received from the bonds to pay off their debts to foreign creditors.[247] Most of those banks closed, becoming insolvent because the value of the defaulted government bonds fell by 85 percent.[248]

The government had spent more than twice the amount of money owed to Russians in unpaid back wages in an effort to prop up the value of the ruble in the international currency-exchange market, in vain—the ruble swiftly lost three-fourths of its value as speculators punished the currency. Because of the bank failures, the small number of people who had managed to put money in the bank now lost their savings again. And the resulting new burst of inflation, coupled with the ruble devaluation, resulted in a de facto halving of salaries.

By the end of 1998, Russia's economy had contracted 45 percent from 1990, when capitalism began to be introduced. Investment in industry declined by almost 80 percent in the same period and the murder rate skyrocketed to become one of the world's highest.[249] Two million children were orphaned with more than half of them homeless.[250] The World Bank estimated that 74 million Russians lived in poverty; 2 million had been in poverty in 1989.[251] In the Ural Mountains, competing organized-crime groups fought armed battles for control of factory complexes, backed by different police forces, with the winners then proceeding to strip the assets.[252]

Women suffered particularly harshly. Women were pushed out of their jobs in large numbers—they made up 60 to 80 percent of Russia's high number of unemployed and most of Russia's single mothers were out of work.[253] The Yeltsin government's concern with this problem was summed up in 1993 by its labor minister: "Why should we try to find jobs for women when men are idle and on unemployment benefits? Let men work and women take care of the homes and their children."[254]

Unemployment, skyrocketing levels of violence at the hands of male partners, the elimination of the Soviet-era social safety net, the pervasiveness of organized crime, and ubiquitous television and other mass media images glamorizing prostitution and the consumption of the rich of the West resulted in hundreds of thousands of Russian women trafficked into prostitution.[255] The extent of sexist culture that capitalism had unleashed was illustrated in a 1997 survey of 15-year-old young women that found 70 percent aspired to be prostitutes; ten years earlier, 70 percent said they wanted to be cosmonauts, doctors or teachers.[256]

Yeltsin's response to ongoing crises was to repeatedly shuffle his government, with personnel changes often being made at the direct request of the oligarchs. He went through five prime ministers in his last two years as president. One reads Yeltsin's memoirs in vain for the slightest acknowledgment of the immense difficulties his policies caused Russians. The passage closest to doing so is a typically self-indulgent, egotistical paragraph in which Yeltsin appears to believe he personally suffered more than any other Russian: "By choosing the path of shock therapy, I did not choose it for some immature Russia or some abstract people. I chose this path for myself as well. The first person who would have to suffer this shock—and suffer it repeatedly with savagely painful reactions, having to strain all resources—would be me, the president."[257] Perhaps some of the retirees who were reduced to hunting for discarded bottles in parks so they could scrape together enough money to eat because their pensions had become worthless might differ on who suffered more.

The last act of Yeltsin's presidency was to resign on the final day of 1999, and name his latest prime minister, Vladimir Putin, as his replacement in exchange for Putin issuing a blanket pardon to Yeltsin and his family. Three months later, the oligarchs saw to it that Putin was elected to a full term in the previously scheduled election. The Russian economy ended a streak of nine consecutive years of contraction in 1999, but the growth was primarily due to a strong rise in oil prices, augmented by imports becoming so expensive as a result of the collapse of the ruble the year before that Russians had little choice but to buy domestic products, thereby providing a spur to local production.

Russia's economy steadily grew during Putin's first set of terms as president, but this was due to extraordinarily high prices for oil and gas; the country had been reduced to being an exporter of natural resources. Total manufacturing in the Russian Federation in 2006 was only two-thirds of what it was in 1990 and agricultural output that same year was 80 percent that of 1992.[258]

Health trends were also sharply negative. Separate studies published in peer-reviewed medical journals found that post-communist countries participating in International Monetary Fund restructuring programs experienced significant increases in tuberculosis rates[259] and countries undergoing mass privatization experienced large increases in adult male mortality rates.[260] Capitalism has de-developed Russia.

Meanwhile, Putin cut taxes for the rich while reducing benefits for pensioners. Corruption became so rampant that, in Putin's first years as president, the amount of money spent on bribes exceeded the amount of revenue paid to the Russian government.[261] Putin has stressed nationalism during his reign, wielding it as a shield to deflect attention from the use of the state for narrow economic interests while adding tsarist touches such as making Russian Orthodoxy again the official state religion—in an echo of tsardom, the ruler and the church are reinforcing one another.

It is true that Putin jailed and confiscated the assets of a couple of oligarchs who attempted to challenge him politically, but the drastic weakening of government institutions during the Yeltsin years not only enabled the oligarchs to grab hold of the Russian economy but also badly weakened civil society, creating a power vacuum that potentially could be (and was) filled by an authoritarian leader. The weakness of Russian institutions, both cause and effect of the oligarchs, had the perverse effect of enabling a vigorous proponent of nationalism to grow strong enough to change one important ground rule. The oligarchs could continue to enrich themselves (and use government institutions to do so), but had to accept the political leadership of Putin and that the state would become a competitor in natural resources. There would be no domestic cost to Putin for muscling out the targeted oligarchs because Russians widely believed, not without reason, that all of the oligarchs amassed their fortunes by stealing.

The gangster capitalism of Russia was the child of Soviet orthodoxy and the Chicago School—a seemingly impossible mating possible only because each saw the other as the only other possible structure for societies anywhere on the globe.

## Notes to Chapter 5

1 Tatyana Zaslavskaya, *The Second Socialist Revolution: An Alternative Soviet Strategy*, page 30 [I.B. Tauris & Co., 1990]

2 Moshe Lewin, *The Soviet Century*, page 221 [Verso, 2005]

3 Marshal I. Goldman, *What Went Wrong with Perestroika*, pages 54–5 [W.W. Norton & Co., 1992]

4 Lewin, *Soviet Century*, page 222

5 David Mandel, "'Revolutionary Reform' in Soviet Factories: Restructuring Relationships between Workers and Management," *Socialist Register*, 1989, pages 102–4

6 Lewin, *Soviet Century*, page 185

7 Yevgeny Yevtushenko, *Precocious Autobiography*, collected in *Yevtushenko's Reader*, pages 95–103, 110–22 [E.P. Dutton, 1972]

8 Fedor Burlatsky, *Khrushchev and the First Russian Spring: The Era of Khrushchev through the Eyes of His Adviser*, pages 142–3 [Charles Scribner's Son, 1991]

9 Georgi Arbatov, *The System: An Insider's Life in Soviet Politics*, page 108 [Random House, 1992]

10 ibid

11 Burlatsky, *Khrushchev and the First Russian Spring*, page 217
12 Arbatov, *The System*, page 121
13 Zhores Medvedev, "Russia under Brezhnev," *New Left Review*, September–October 1979, page 7
14 Ron Suskind, *The Price of Loyalty: George W. Bush, the White House, and the Education of Paul O'Neill*, pages 148–9 [Simon & Shuster, 2004]
15 Burlatsky, *Khrushchev and the First Russian Spring*, pages 213–14
16 ibid, pages 72, 216, 222
17 Arbatov, *The System*, pages 124–5
18 Burlatsky, *Khrushchev and the First Russian Spring*, page 217
19 ibid, page 211
20 Lewin, *Soviet Century*, page 224, quoting T.I. Fetisov, *Prem'er—Izvetnyi i Neizvestnyi: Vospominanii o A.N. Kosygine* [1997]
21 ibid, pages 225, 249; Zaslavskaya, *The Second Socialist Revolution*, pages 35–6
22 Lewin, *Soviet Century*, page 250
23 ibid, page 252, quoting V. Nemchinov, *O Dal'neishem Sovershenstvovanii Planirovaniia i Upravleniia Khoziaistvom*, page 53 [1965]
24 Zaslavskaya, *The Second Socialist Revolution*, page 36
25 Roy Medvedev, "Stalinism after the Twentieth Congress of the CPSU as the Reflection of Internal and International Problems of the USSR," anthologized in R. Medvedev (ed.), *Samizdat Register 2: Voices of the Socialist Opposition in the Soviet Union*, page 15 [W.W. Norton & Co., 1981]
26 ibid, pages 20–1
27 Z. Medvedev, "Russia under Brezhnev," page 24
28 Erik P. Hoffman and Robbin F. Laird, *Technocratic Socialism: The Soviet Union in the Advanced Industrial Era*, page 34 [Duke University Press, 1985]
29 ibid, pages 38, 100–1

30 Burlatsky, *Khrushchev and the First Russian Spring*, page 220

31 Zaslavskaya, *The Second Socialist Revolution*, page 39

32 Lewin, *Soviet Century*, pages 215–16

33 Zaslavskaya, *The Second Socialist Revolution*, pages xii–xiii, 2, 45–6

34 ibid, page xiii

35 Arbatov, *The System*, pages 236–40

36 R. Medvedev, "The Death of the 'Chief Ideologue,'" *New Left Review*, November–December 1982, page 63

37 Hoffman and Laird, *Technocratic Socialism*, pages 23, 29

38 Yegor Ligachev, *Inside Gorbachev's Kremlin: The Memoirs of Yegor Ligachev*, pages 45–8 [Westview Press, 1996]

39 ibid, pages 30–1

40 This section, in part, draws on Donald Filtzer, *Soviet Workers and the Collapse of Perestroika: The Soviet Labour Process and Gorbachev's Reforms, 1985–1991*, pages 2–3, 30, 47, 72–4, 149–52 [Cambridge University Press, 1994]; Zaslavskaya, *The Second Socialist Revolution*, pages 63–75; Lewin, *Soviet Century*, pages 203–11, 320, 330–3, 357–66; Arbatov, *The System*, pages 222–5; Hoffman & Laird, *Technocratic Socialism*, pages 63, 70–3; Harry Magdoff and Paul M. Sweezy, "Perestroika and the Future of Socialism," anthologized in William K. Tabb (ed.), *The Future of Socialism: Perspectives from the Left*, page 132 [Monthly Review Press, 1990]; Z. Medvedev, "Russia under Brezhnev," pages 8, 13–18; Marcus Mulholland, "The Soviet Model and the Economic Cold War," posted on 21st Century Socialism website at 21stcenturysocialism.com; and Mandel, "'Revolutionary Reform' in Soviet Factories," pages 104–6

41 Goldman, *What Went Wrong with Perestroika*, page 81

42 Patrick Cockburn, *Getting Russia Wrong: The End of Kremlinology*, page 53 [Verso, 1989]

43 ibid

44 A. Krasikov, "Commodity Number One," anthologized in

R. Medvedev (ed.), *Samizdat Register 2*, pages 168–71
45 ibid, page 165
46 Filtzer, *Soviet Workers and the Collapse of Perestroika*, page 150
47 Goldman, *What Went Wrong with Perestroika*, page 86
48 ibid, page 89
49 R. Medvedev and Giulietto Chiesa, *Time of Change: An Insider's View of Russia's Transformation*, page 10 [Pantheon, 1999]
50 Graeme Gill, *The Collapse of a Single-party System: The Disintegration of the Communist Party of the Soviet Union*, page 24 [Cambridge University Press, 1994]
51 ibid, page 28
52 K.S. Karol, "Gorbachev and the Dynamics of Change," *The Socialist Register*, 1988, page 35
53 Filtzer, *Soviet Workers and the Collapse of Perestroika*, pages 59–60
54 R. Medvedev & Chiesa, *Time of Change*, page 111, quoting *Pravda*, 26 June 1987
55 Cockburn, *Getting Russia Wrong*, page 38
56 ibid
57 Goldman, *What Went Wrong with Perestroika*, page 135
58 ibid, pages 157–8
59 Mandel, "'Revolutionary Reform' in Soviet Factories," pages 112–13; Filtzer, *Soviet Workers and the Collapse of Perestroika*, pages 65–6
60 Mandel, "'Revolutionary Reform' in Soviet Factories," page 113; Filtzer, *Soviet Workers and the Collapse of Perestroika*, page 24
61 Mandel, "'Revolutionary Reform' in Soviet Factories," page 120, quoting *Trud*, 15 June 1988
62 Filtzer, *Soviet Workers and the Collapse of Perestroika*, page 64
63 Mandel, "'Revolutionary Reform' in Soviet Factories," page 108, quoting *Pravda*, 28 January 1987
64 ibid, page 109

65 Zaslavskaya, *The Second Socialist Revolution*, pages 154–5, 175–7

66 Filtzer, *Soviet Workers and the Collapse of Perestroika*, page 82

67 Lynn D. Nelson and Irina Y. Kuzes, "Russian Economic Reform and the Restructuring of Interests," *Demokratizatsiya*, summer 1998, pages 484–5

68 Gill, *The Collapse of a Single-party System*, page 45

69 ibid, page 49, quoting *Pravda*, 14 November 1987

70 Cockburn, *Getting Russia Wrong*, page 30

71 Jeffrey Surovell, "Ligachev and Soviet Politics," *Soviet Studies*, Vol. 41, No. 2 (1991), page 355, citing *Pravda*, 2 September 1988, page 2

72 Ligachev, *Inside Gorbachev's Kremlin*, pages 299–300

73 ibid, page 301

74 ibid, page 285

75 R. Medvedev & Chiesa, *Time of Change*, page 135

76 Gill, *The Collapse of a Single-party System*, page 61

77 R. Medvedev & Chiesa, *Time of Change*, pages 129–30

78 Gill, *The Collapse of a Single-party System*, pages 57–9

79 Zaslavskaya, *The Second Socialist Revolution*, page 209

80 Jonathan Harris, "Vadim Andreevich Medvedev and the Transformation of Party Ideology, 1988–1990," *The Russian Review*, July 1992, pages 364–5

81 Gill, *The Collapse of a Single-party System*, page 72

82 Vladimir N. Brovkin, "The Making of Elections to the Congress of People's Deputies in March 1989," *The Russian Review*, page 441

83 Gill, *The Collapse of a Single-party System*, page 201 [note 4]

84 Brovkin, "The Making of Elections," page 440

85 Cockburn, *Getting Russia Wrong*, pages 27–8

86 Leon Panitch and Sam Gindin, "Perestroika and the Proletariat," *The Socialist Register*, 1991, pages 33–4

87 ibid, pages 38–9

88 Lewis Siegelbaum, "Perestroika from Below: The Soviet

Miners' Strike and Its Aftermath," *New Left Review*, May–June 1990, page 6

89 Filtzer, *Soviet Workers and the Collapse of Perestroika*, page 96

90 ibid

91 ibid, page 98

92 Siegelbaum, "Perestroika from Below," pages 10–12

93 Filtzer, *Soviet Workers and the Collapse of Perestroika*, page 97

94 Siegelbaum, "Perestroika from Below," pages 18–19

95 Filtzer, *Soviet Workers and the Collapse of Perestroika*, page 99

96 Siegelbaum, "Perestroika from Below," page 11

97 ibid, page 25

98 Goldman, *What Went Wrong with Perestroika*, page 151

99 Panitch & Gindin, "Perestroika and the Proletariat," pages 35, 36, 51

100 "Perestroika: A Pandora's Box," *1917: Journal of the International Bolshevik Tendency*, Summer 1989, online version at www.bolshevik.com

101 "Remarks by Leonid Brezhnev at a Meeting of Top CPCz Officials, in Prague, December 9, 1967 (Excerpts)," anthologized in Jaromír Navrátil (chief ed.), *The Prague Spring '68*, page 18 [Central European University, 2006]

102 War Resisters League, New York

103 Glenn R. Chafetz, *Gorbachev, Reform, and the Brezhnev Doctrine: Soviet Policy toward Eastern Europe*, 1985–1990, page 68 [Praeger, 1993]

104 ibid, page 111

105 Filtzer, *Soviet Workers and the Collapse of Perestroika*, page 87

106 Panitch & Gindin, "Perestroika and the Proletariat," page 31

107 "Soviet Stalinism in Extremis," *1917: Journal of the International Bolshevik Tendency*, third quarter 1991, online version at www.bolshevik.com

108 Goldman, *What Went Wrong with Perestroika*, page 147

109 Boris Kagarlitsky, *Square Wheels: How Russian Democracy Got Derailed*, page 44 [Monthly Review Press, 1994]

110 ibid, pages 49–50
111 Filtzer, *Soviet Workers and the Collapse of Perestroika*, page 139
112 Lewin, *Soviet Century*, pages 357–9
113 ibid, pages 359–60
114 ibid, pages 360, 364
115 John Gooding, "Perestroika as Revolution from Within: An Interpretation," *The Russian Review*, January 1992, page 46, quoting *Pravda*, 12 February 1990
116 Gill, *The Collapse of a Single-party System*, page 93
117 ibid, page 98
118 Gooding, "Perestroika as Revolution from Within," page 53
119 Kagarlitsky, *Square Wheels*, page 11
120 Gill, *The Collapse of a Single-party System*, page 99
121 Filtzer, *Soviet Workers and the Collapse of Perestroika*, pages 51–2
122 ibid, page 88
123 Panitch & Gindin, "Perestroika and the Proletariat," pages 34–6, 48–9
124 ibid, page 35
125 Filtzer, *Soviet Workers and the Collapse of Perestroika*, page 33
126 ibid
127 Gill, *The Collapse of a Single-party System*, page 123
128 ibid, page 125
129 ibid, page 139
130 ibid, pages 140–1
131 Mikhail Gorbachev, *Memoirs*, page 365 [Doubleday, 1995]
132 ibid, page 370
133 Goldman, *What Went Wrong with Perestroika*, pages 218–19
134 David Michael Kotz and Fred Weir, *Russia's Path from Gorbachev to Putin: The Demise of the Soviet System and the New Russia*, page 84 [Routledge, 2007]
135 Ligachev, *Inside Gorbachev's Kremlin*, page 270
136 ibid, pages 268–9
137 Goldman, *What Went Wrong with Perestroika*, pages 217–19;

Gorbachev, *Memoirs*, page 378–82
138 Kotz & Weir, *Russia's Path*, page 84
139 Jerry F. Hough, *Democratization and Revolution in the USSR, 1985–1991*, page 363 [Brookings Institute Press, 1997]
140 ibid, pages 358–61
141 Jonathan Steele, "Alexander Yakovlev: Key Intellectual Who Backed Gorbachev's Perestroika," *The Guardian* of London, 20 October 2005
142 Filtzer, *Soviet Workers and the Collapse of Perestroika*, pages 35, 71, 129
143 ibid, page 16
144 Karol, "Gorbachev and the Dynamics of Change," page 35
145 The author of this book personally knows people who have been in such situations
146 Panitch & Gindin, "Perestroika and the Proletariat," page 44
147 ibid, page 54
148 ibid, page 37
149 ibid, pages 38–9
150 Filtzer, *Soviet Workers and the Collapse of Perestroika*, pages 90–1
151 ibid, pages 91–3
152 Kagarlitsky, *Square Wheels*, pages 28–9, 72–3
153 ibid, page 62
154 Gill, *The Collapse of a Single-party System*, pages 154, 157–61
155 ibid, pages 161–2
156 Kagarlitsky, *Square Wheels*, page 120
157 Gorbachev, *Memoirs*, page 394
158 Filtzer, *Soviet Workers and the Collapse of Perestroika*, pages 103–6
159 ibid, pages 108–12
160 Arbatov, *The System*, pages 342–3
161 Gorbachev, *Memoirs*, page 612
162 ibid, page 615
163 Gill, *The Collapse of a Single-party System*, page 174

164 Boris Yeltsin, *The Struggle for Russia*, page 69 [Times Books, 1994]
165 ibid, pages 92–3
166 Gorbachev, *The August Coup: The Truth and the Lessons*, page 36 [HarperCollins, 1991]
167 Serge Schmemann, "Gorbachev Quits as Party Head; Ends Communism's 74-Year Reign," *The New York Times*, 25 August 1991, pages 1, 14
168 Gill, *The Collapse of a Single-party System*, pages 175, 176, 244
169 Gorbachev, *The August Coup*, pages 49–66
170 Chrystia Freeland, *Sale of the Century: Russia's Wild Ride from Communism to Capitalism*, page 24 [Crown Publishers, 2000]
171 Yeltsin, *The Struggle for Russia*, page 115
172 Goldman, *What Went Wrong with Perestroika*, page 243
173 Gorbachev, *Memoirs*, page 672
174 ibid
175 Yeltsin, *The Struggle for Russia*, page 121
176 Leon Trotsky, *The Revolution Betrayed*, chapter 9 ("Social Relations in the Soviet Union"), posted on the Marxist Archives website, www.marxists.org
177 Trotsky, *The Transitional Program of the Fourth International*, posted on the Marxist Archives website
178 Orlando Letelier, "The Chicago Boys in Chile," *The Nation*, 26 August 1976, citing El Mercurio, 23 March 1975
179 Milton and Rose D. Friedman, *Two Lucky People: Memoirs*, pages 591–4 [University of Chicago Press, 1998]
180 "Covert Action in Chile, 1963–1973" (US Senate report also known as the "Church Report"), posted on the US Department of State Freedom of Information Act website, foia.state.gov (representing what the CIA would admit)
181 Patricio Guzmán, *Battle of Chile*, Part Two [film]
182 Mary Helen Spooner, *Soldiers in a Narrow Land*, page 93 [University of California Press, 1994]
183 Pete Dolack, "Retiring at 100 under Social Security

Privatization," *Z Magazine*, November 2005, page 14

184 ibid

185 Steve Kangas, "The Chicago Boys and the Chilean 'Economic Miracle,'" The Truth About Pinochet website, www.lakota.clara.net; Spooner, *Soldiers in a Narrow Land*, page 184

186 Spooner, *Soldiers in a Narrow Land*, page 145

187 ibid

188 David Rock, *Argentina 1516–1987*, page 375 [University of California Press 1992]; "Cry for Argentina," *CCPA Monitor* (Canadian Centre for Policy Alternatives), September 2000; Jayati Ghosh, "Argentina: A Cautionary Tale from South America," International Development Economics Associates paper

189 "Cry for Argentina," *CCPA Monitor*

190 Friedman, *Memoirs*, pages 398–408, 597

191 Patricia Politzer, *Fear in Chile: Lives under Pinochet*, page 212 [New Press, 2001]

192 ibid, pages 204, 212

193 Karol, "After Perestroika," *The Socialist Register*, 1993, page 177

194 Goldman, *The Piratization of Russia: Russian Reform Goes Awry*, page 79 [Routledge, 2003]

195 The author of this book has had this argument made to him personally

196 Freeland, *Sale of the Century*, page 55

197 ibid, page 56

198 Naomi Klein, *The Shock Doctrine: The Rise of Disaster Capitalism*, page 224 [Metropolitan Books, 2007]

199 Joseph Stiglitz, preface to Lawrence R. Klein and Marshall Pomer (eds), *The New Russia: Transition Gone Awry*, page xxii [Stanford University Press, 2001]

200 Hough, *Democratization and Revolution in the USSR*, page 363

201 Karol, "After Perestroika," page 174, citing *Moscow News*, 23

August 1992

202 ibid, citing official government statistics

203 ibid, page 175, citing Russia's central bank

204 Freeland, *Sale of the Century*, page 117

205 Karol, "After Perestroika," page 179

206 Vladimir Kartsev, *Zhirinovsky!*, page 110 [Columbia University Press, 1995]

207 Goldman, *The Piratization of Russia*, page 86

208 Freeland, *Sale of the Century*, page 64

209 ibid, page 91

210 Filtzer, *Soviet Workers and the Collapse of Perestroika*, page 220

211 Lewin, *Soviet Century*, page 370

212 Anna Politkovskaya, *Putin's Russia: Life in a Failing Democracy*, page 87 [Metropolitan Books, 2004]

213 Kartsev, *Zhirinovsky!*, page 132

214 Karol, "After Perestroika," page 188

215 N. Klein, *The Shock Doctrine*, page 226

216 Yeltsin, *The Struggle for Russia*, page 224

217 Kagarlitsky, *Square Wheels*, pages 193, 197–8

218 ibid, pages 202–4

219 N. Klein, *The Shock Doctrine*, page 229

220 Kagarlitsky, *Square Wheels*, page 212

221 N. Klein, *The Shock Doctrine*, page 230

222 Paul Quinn-Judge, "Russia's Regent," *Time* magazine, 9 December 1996

223 Goldman, *The Piratization of Russia*, page 93

224 ibid, page 182

225 Peter Gowan, "The Passages of the Russian and East European Left," *The Socialist Register*, 1998, pages 138–9, 143

226 Yeltsin, *Midnight Diaries*, pages 23–4 [Public Affairs, 2000]

227 ibid, page 24

228 Freeland, *Sale of the Century*, page 207

229 Yeltsin, *Midnight Diaries*, page 24

230 ibid (emphasis in original)

231 Freeland, *Sale of the Century*, pages 192–7
232 N. Klein, *The Shock Doctrine*, page 232
233 Freeland, *Sale of the Century*, page 237
234 Nancy Holmstrom and Richard Smith, "The Necessity of Gangster Capitalism: Primitive Accumulation in Russia and China," *Monthly Review*, February 2000, quoting *The Economist*, 13 January 1990, page 23
235 Freeland, *Sale of the Century*, page 70
236 David Woodruff, "The Economist's Burden," *New Left Review*, January–February 2009, pages 143–4
237 Anders Åslund, *How Capitalism Was Built: The Transformation of Central and Eastern Europe, Russia, and Central Asia*, page 48 [Cambridge University Press, 2007]
238 *Funk & Wagnalls New Comprehensive International Dictionary of the English Language*, page 1067 [Publishers Guild, 1972]
239 Åslund, *How Capitalism Was Built*, page 48
240 ibid
241 ibid, pages 267, 273
242 Freeland, *Sale of the Century*, page 136
243 ibid
244 ibid, pages 311–12
245 Joel C. Moses (ed.), *Dilemmas of Transition in Post-Soviet Countries*, page 6 [Burnham, 2003]
246 ibid
247 ibid
248 Kotz & Weir, *Russia's Path*, page 236
249 Vladimir Popov, "Russia Redux?," *New Left Review*, March–April 2007, pages 43, 46–9
250 Holmstrom & Smith, "The Necessity of Gangster Capitalism"
251 N. Klein, *The Shock Doctrine*, page 238
252 Politkovskaya, *Putin's Russia*, pages 126–38
253 Donna M. Hughes, "Supplying Women for the Sex Industry: Trafficking from the Russian Federation," page 6, paper

posted on the University of Rhode Island website, www.uri.edu

254 Ana Muñoz and Alan Woods, "Marxism and the Emancipation of Women," posted on the In Defence of Marxism website, www.marxist.com

255 Hughes, "Supplying Women for the Sex Industry," pages 2–6, 11

256 ibid, page 15

257 Yeltsin, *The Struggle for Russia*, page 149

258 United Nations Statistics Division common database, unstats.un.org

259 PLoS Medicine, article available 22 July 2008, at medicine.plosjournals.org

260 *The Lancet*, 31 January 2009, online summary at www.lancet.com

261 Tony Wood, "Contours of the Putin Era," *New Left Review*, March–April 2007, page 65

## Chapter 6

# Imagining a Better World Is the First Step

The Soviet Union remains a giant bogey. As long as the Soviet system is believed to be, or is presented as, the only possible system of socialism, many minds inevitably will remain closed to possibilities beyond capitalism. Authorities in the capitalist countries consistently told their working people that they enjoyed a higher standard of living and more political and cultural freedom that did those living in the Soviet bloc and asked them why they would want to lose what they have already.

The actual situation was more complicated than this standard presentation—social gains such as full employment, greater potential for upward mobility, and free education and medical care were as much a part of that world as were the shortages, long queues and poor quality of services—but it is a real enough argument that this "lesson" remains vivid. Those on the Left who unconditionally defend the Soviet Union, agreeing with the Soviet line that only the Soviet system constitutes "real" socialism, serve to buttress the capitalist world's ever-present self-congratulations that it represents the culmination of historical development. Until the emergence of different models, democratic in all senses of that word and capable of meeting expectations of stability and economic wellbeing, mounting a final challenge to capitalist orthodoxy will be immensely difficult.

That challenge will be particularly acute if the alternative to capitalism is given the word "socialism." (Although *any* system proposed to supplant capitalism would be similarly demonized.) But there is no single idea, plan or model that can claim any sort of exclusivity to the word "socialism." The more realistic of the philosophers searching for a better world than their Dickensian nineteenth-century capitalist societies—those philosophers whose works can still be read seriously today—made no attempts at designing blueprints. And if they had, could a construct made a century or more in the past remain relevant after all the changes of the twentieth century? Nor could any of us today invent a system that would continue to function perfectly for our descendants in the twenty-second century.

For this reason socialist pioneers such as Karl Marx and Friedrich Engels scorned as "utopians" those who would attempt to create a perfect society through a preconceived plan or believed they had exclusive insights into a better world, or who would impose their idea of a perfect society through undemocratic means. Marx and Engels were appropriated and converted into utopians by Soviet bloc rulers who claimed to possess sole knowledge of the proper organization of society, a knowledge those rulers believed entitled them to impose a particular model until people accepted that this was what was good for them. This model was the product of historical accidents and rooted in one country's cultural heritage and economic underdevelopment—it was a fallacy to see such a model as universal.

In this final chapter, there will be no attempt at creating a blueprint. Rather, the intention is to stimulate discussion on the meaning of "political democracy" and "economic democracy," and offer rough sketches of the basics of how these separate but interconnected concepts might be fused together and grounded in political, social and economic institutions. These institutions would be different from the institutions of the modern capitalist state. In short, thinking about the basic contours of a better world is a prerequisite to becoming effective in bringing about a better world.

Thinking about a better world is inseparable from analyzing the world we currently have. Because the formal form of the large capitalist countries of the North is democratic, it is natural to believe that existing democratic forms can be used to expand freedom and slowly evolve toward a better, more rational society. But the bitter lessons of Europe's pre-World War I social democratic movements provided a harsh rebuke to such hopes, and those lessons have been reinforced repeatedly. Analyzing these limitations is part of the process of imagining a better world—we have to ask ourselves what it is we don't want today that can be changed tomorrow.

But there is no escaping the past. Countless millions in the world of that past were motivated by the idea that socialism will inevitably follow capitalism—and that the fall of capitalism would not be far in the future. That prediction appears to us, today, as spectacularly wrong. So perhaps it is best to begin this chapter by examining why the predictions of capitalism's demise have not come true.

## Explorations in theories of transition to and from capitalism

It would be impossible to isolate any single factor, or group of factors, as to why predictions of capitalism's demise have proven so wide of the mark thus far. No serious discussion of this question, however, should exclude these factors:

- The early pioneers of the socialist movement seriously underestimated the ability of capitalism as a system to adapt and therefore did not foresee the ability of working people to extract concessions for themselves.
- The early pioneers failed to understand the buoying effect that would be provided by imperialism (for the leading capitalist countries).
- Many of the early pioneers clung to an overly mechanical (mis)understanding of social development that led to a passive belief in an automatic unfolding of revolution that implied, incorrectly, that powerful capitalists would

simply sit back and allow themselves to be overthrown.

- Many leaders during the Soviet era continued to hold to a similar overly mechanical belief in future revolution while at the same time failing to grasp the nuances of capitalist development.
- An overly centralized world movement that retarded the theoretical developments needed for local conditions, blocking the creation of innovative leadership while at the same time discouraging existing local leaderships from attempting revolutions.
- A too narrow conception of "working class" or "working people"—a tendency to visualize only blue-collar manual workers as working people, a declining percentage of the population in increasingly technological capitalist societies. Such narrow horizons served to exclude a large proportion of wage workers, with the result that movements purporting to be organizations of working people instead divided them at the start.

Before exploring these factors in more detail, a more fundamental question to ask is this: Is the very prediction wide of the mark? Predicting the eventual demise of a system by critics who themselves acknowledge it as the most powerful and dynamic yet to emerge—and foreseeing the transcending of this new system when it was still young and had conquered only a small part of the globe—certainly seems audacious. The belief that capitalism is destined to collapse is rooted not only in Karl Marx's groundbreaking study of the capitalist system but in the philosophy that he developed. That philosophy ("historical materialism" as Marx called it) developed directly out of the philosophy of dialectics conceived by Georg Wilhelm Friedrich Hegel.

At first glance, the previous sentence might seem odd. Hegel, after all, became a favorite philosopher of conservatives thanks to his exaltation of the Prussian police state of his early nineteenth century and his belief that religion represents humanity's highest expression of consciousness. But it was the methodology of Hegelian analysis, not Hegel's limitations, that was useful for Marx.

Hegel's method of dialectical thinking is sometimes simplified into the triad "thesis–antithesis–synthesis": An idea contains within it incompleteness, giving rise to a counter-idea; this conflict gives rise to a higher idea, which in turn generates a new counter-idea, continuing the process. Ideas develop because only the final totality is true—the stages or phases that lead to the whole are partial and therefore partially untrue.[1] The "absolute concept" develops from the preliminary stages that culminate in it.[2] Hegel's insight that things and conditions change and develop as opposed to being static was a dramatic development in philosophy, but Hegel also believed that the "absolute concept"—the final stage of his dialectical process—would complete development. The limitations of his philosophical system enabled Hegel to declare constitutional monarchy as the endpoint of political development and that freedom could not be achieved at the individual level, only through social institutions.[3]

In the years following Hegel's death, a group of his followers who became known as the Young Hegelians began to push beyond the limits of Hegelian dialectics, publishing their work during a brief political thaw in Prussia before censorship clamped down on them. The Young Hegelians came to believe that Christianity was a historical development and subject to change because it was a product of history—this conclusion was in direct conflict with the "absolute concept," and if Christianity is subject to historical changes, then neither could the state achieve a final endpoint.[4]

Two of the Young Hegelians, still in their twenties, were Marx and Friedrich Engels. Forced into exile and soon going beyond the Young Hegelians, Marx realized that ideas and social development do not reach absolute attainment; rather, dialectical progress continues into the future. In essence, Hegelian dialectics was now used to contradict Hegel's ideas, and therefore transcend the originator.

"But precisely here lay the true significance and the revolutionary character of the Hegelian philosophy…that it once and for all dealt the deathblow to the finality of all products of human thought and action," Engels wrote. "Truth lay now in the process of cognition itself, in the long historical development of science, which mounts from lower to ever higher levels of knowledge without ever reaching, by discovering so-called absolute truth, a point at which it can proceed no further and where it would have nothing more to do than to fold its hands and admire the absolute truth to which it had attained."[5]

Marx would always consider himself a student of Hegel, despite his statement that dialectics in Hegel's hands "is standing on its head. It must be turned right side up again, if you would discover the rational kernel within the mystical shell."[6]

Marx called the philosophical system he developed "historical materialism" because it was a dialectic based not on philosophically derived abstractions but on observations made in an empirical way and on accurate descriptions of concrete (or material) conditions.[7] Historical materialism is a theory of human social development rooted in the view that the motor force of history is economic struggle.

Engels, Marx's lifelong close collaborator, and Grigorii Plekhanov, one of the most important Marxist theorists in the two decades following Marx's death and whom history remembers as the "Father of Russian Marxism," built on Marx's foundation, developing the broader philosophy "dialectical materialism." Although Engels did much of the work, Plekhanov is usually credited with coining the latter term, which refers to an expansion of Marx's concept from a social science to encompass the natural sciences.

To give a simplification similar to the triad shorthand that frequently is used to describe Hegelian dialectics, Marxist materialism posits that anything of human creation contains its opposite, that a contradiction inevitably arises from the tensions between the opposites, and in the process of resolving the contradiction a new, higher form develops. But the new form, although it contains elements of its precursors, is not permanently stable, either, and contradictions will arise here, too, continuing the process.

Plekhanov, in the 1890s, sketched this concept in vivid fashion:

> It follows that a man has two qualities: first of being alive, and secondly also being mortal. But upon closer investigation it turns out that life itself bears in itself the germ of death, and that in general any phenomenon is contradictory, in the sense that it develops out of itself the elements which, sooner or later, will put an end to its existence and will transform it into its own opposite. Everything flows, everything changes; and there is no force capable of holding back the constant flux, or arresting the eternal movement.[8]

That flow and movement takes varying directions, and far from always in an expected direction. As the concept of "flow" implies, history, and social development, do not consist of discrete steps or stages. Philosophical, political and religious ideas (which are built on the materials of their predecessors); the prevailing culture (which includes traditions shaped in the conditions of the past that have survived into the present); and local geographic factors not only influence each other, but also influence economic conditions. What was a cause can become an effect, and an effect can become a cause. These forces are given concrete form within a state, the form of which (including its legal structure) is based on the material conditions of life—the economic structure is the foundation on which society is built and which therefore shapes social consciousness.

Marx applied his theory of constant dynamic motion and development to an intensive study of capitalism, discovering the exploitative relations inherent in it. Capitalism evolved from older systems—specifically, feudalism. A historical materialist analysis proposes that feudalism not only had to have contained contradictions within it that eventually resulted in it being transcended, but there had to be specific feudal elements that carried the seeds of the future capitalist system. (That does not necessarily mean that capitalism was inevitably the system to have followed.) Because the dialectical process continues indefinitely, no system or state can be the final culmination of human development; therefore, capitalism, too, must reach its limits and the contradictions that will eventually spell the end of capitalism are contained within itself.

To carry out this line of study, the transition from feudalism to capitalism could not be neglected. If feudalism, despite the centuries it endured in the European countries that would become the first to develop capitalist economic systems, ultimately contained instabilities or contradictions that led to its breakdown and also contained within it seeds that germinated into capitalism, such a discovery would not be simply a vindication of a materialist approach to history, it would also provide support for the idea of a transition from capitalism to socialism.

But such a theory of transition could not be overly broad or a sweeping generalization; different countries had different versions of feudalism just as present-day countries have different versions of capitalism. Nor were they on the same schedule—capitalism began appearing in nations such as England centuries earlier than latecomers. Nor was the tempo the same; capitalism developed much more rapidly in the latecomers than in the earliest nations to undergo the transition. The reason for that lies in the fact of capitalism's expansionist dynamic. Once it gains a foothold, it must expand; unchecked, it grows into a tsunami that washes over less developed spaces and, under the force of its dynamism, dramatically accelerates the pace of development in areas subject to it and the pace of those less developed spaces' integration into the world capitalist system.

The gradual breakdown of feudal economic relations and their eventual replacement by capitalist economic relations began as a very slow process; capitalism initially was anything but a tsunami, taking centuries to establish itself firmly. Exploitation, naturally, existed long before capitalism did—slavery, serfdom, other forms of feudalism, theocratic dictatorship, absolute monarchy and other historical forms provided a grim existence for most of humanity. Capitalism, however, represented an entirely new, more economically efficient form of exploitation.

As slowly as life moved in feudal society, there were slow evolutionary changes that eventually began to tip the balance. Two basic factors provided seeds for modern capitalism: one, feudal lords pushing their peasants off the land to clear space for commodity agricultural products and, two, the capital accumulated from trade by merchants growing large enough to create the surpluses capable of being converted into the capital necessary to start production on a scale larger than artisan production.

Many students of history are partisans of one of these two factors. Those who stress the peasant-removal theory point to the "enclosure movement" that forced peasants off the land and accompanying draconian laws, and assert that merchant capital floats on whatever economic system is in place, simply circulating whatever commodities are available. Because capitalism requires the accumulation of surpluses created through the employment of labor, merchant capital on its own is not capable of catalyzing a transition from one economic system to another, according to partisans of the theory of peasant dispossession from the land.

Those who stress the merchant-capital theory argue that the increase of trade between towns stimulated the development of production and commerce, creating a money economy that undermined the feudal lords. This by itself was sufficient to overturn feudalism because it provided an initial dynamic toward capitalism from within autonomous towns, partisans of the merchant-capital theory believe, who also argue that the forced removal of peasants from the land was not necessarily prevalent outside of England.

Interesting as this debate is, it seems a bit schematic in that both factors were present, and these two theories are not at all incompatible. One or the other could play a larger role in different localities and the two developments often reinforced each other. Moreover, the early development of capitalism cannot be understood without a frank examination of the slavery of African and Indigenous American peoples and the ruthless exploitation of the natural resources of the Americas. All these factors contributed to the rise of the capitalist economic system in Europe. The dominance of European capitalist nations could not have happened without slavery and colonialism.

Nor was feudalism the stereotyped era of acquiescence in which serfs contentedly tilled the soil of their lords; in itself repeated unrest is partly responsible for variations in the administrative and legal forms of peasant exploitation during the centuries of European feudalism. Peasants did push back when they could—for example, winning much better conditions because of labor shortages resulting from the destruction of one-third of Europe's population from the Black Death of the fourteenth century.

Peasant uprisings, often with explicit demands for equality, repeatedly broke out across Western and Central Europe in the fourteenth through sixteenth centuries.[9] Strong religious movements challenging the feudal order, and therefore a direct challenge to the Roman Catholic Church that maintained that order, were mercilessly drowned in blood in the early sixteenth century, effectively ending two centuries of direct challenges to feudalism from below.[10] Moreover, the church stepped up its Inquisition and its burning of non-conforming women as "witches" as part of the effort to subjugate peasants and town-dwelling working people and to foster divisions within those large groups.[11] But as yet there was no class that could challenge the rule of the lords—peasants were isolated and illiterate, and artisans in the towns were highly heterogeneous.[12]

Peasants produced for themselves and, under compulsion, for their lord through payment-in-kind of a percentage of their crops, delivering firewood and finished agricultural products, and performing chores. Although they were kept tethered to their lord legally through courts presided over by the lords, and ideologically by church officials (who were themselves landowners),[13] peasants were not economically dependent on lords and therefore capable of resisting—a strengthening of peasant resistance reduced what lords could extract from them and therefore also reduced tax transferred to the state, one cause of later feudal instability.[14] English peasants, for example, successfully reduced what they paid to their lords, and the lords could not regain their former level of exploitation without re-imposing serfdom, a political impossibility as serfdom had long been abolished across Western Europe.[15]

Serfdom continued for some time further east, however; for example, in Poland, estates were self-sufficient and lords were able to reduce peasant holdings to barely enough for peasants' physical survival.[16] These harsh Polish estates were so self-sufficient that lords could continue to enforce serfdom even when they sold their estates' surplus on markets, in contrast to Western Europe, where estates gradually became entangled with international markets.[17] Procurement of luxury items for lords and their families gradually stimulated commerce.

English feudal lords began throwing peasants off their land in the sixteenth century, a process put in motion, in part, by continuing peasant resistance. The rise of Flemish wool manufacturing (wool had become a desirable luxury item) and a corresponding rise in the price of wool in England induced the wholesale removal of peasants from the land.[18] Lords wanted to transform arable land into sheep meadows, and began razing peasant cottages to clear the land.[19] These actions became known as the "enclosure movement." This process received further fuel from the Reformation—the Roman Catholic Church had owned huge estates throughout England, and when these church lands were confiscated, the masses of peasants who were hereditary tenants on these lands were thrown off when the confiscated church lands were sold on the cheap to royal favorites or to speculators.[20]

Forced off the land they had farmed and barred from the "commons" (cleared land on which they grazed cattle and forests in which they foraged), peasants could either become beggars, risking draconian punishment for doing so, or become laborers in the new factories at pitifully low wages and enduring inhuman conditions and working hours.

Force was the indispensable factor in creating the first modern working class. Late feudalism was hardly a paradise for small farmers, but Western European peasants, some of whom were independent smallholders, had wrested better conditions for themselves. They had no reason to enter willingly the new workplaces and the Dickensian conditions they would endure there.

The historian Michael Perelman, in his appropriately titled book *The Invention of Capitalism*, notes that "Simple dispossession from the commons was a necessary, but not always sufficient, condition to harness rural people to the labor market."[21] A series of cruel laws accompanied the dispossession of the peasants' rights, including the period before capitalism had become a significant economic force.

"For example, beginning with the Tudors, England created a series of stern measures to prevent peasants from drifting into vagrancy or falling back onto welfare systems," Perelman wrote.

> According to a 1572 statute, beggars over the age of fourteen were to be severely flogged and branded with a red-hot iron on the left ear unless someone was willing to take them into service for two years. Repeat offenders over the age of eighteen were to be executed unless someone would take them into service. Third offenses automatically resulted in execution...Similar statutes appeared almost simultaneously in England, the Low Countries, and Zurich...Eventually, the majority of workers, lacking any alternative, had little choice but to work for wages at something close to subsistence level.[22]

Supplementing these laws were displays of military power. A widely quoted document claims that 72,000 were hanged during the early sixteenth-century reign of King Henry VIII,[23] throughout which England experienced a series of peasant uprisings.[24] Regardless of what the true number may have been, Henry, who reigned as the enclosures reached their peak, did have large numbers of people executed for being "vagabonds" or "thieves"—in reality for not working.

Systematic state force enabled factory owners to steadily gain the upper hand against artisans, although those nascent capitalists possessed no production innovations at the time. "Early factories employed the same techniques of production as putting-out [assemblers of finished products working from home] and craft organization, and there were no technological barriers to applying them to these more traditional forms," according to economist Herbert Gintis. "The superior position of the capitalist factory system in this period seems to derive not from its efficiency sense, but its ability to control the workforce: costs were reduced by drawing on child and female labor, minimizing theft, increasing the pace of work, and lengthening the workweek."[25]

A process of intensifying exploitation enabled early factory owners to accumulate capital, thereby allowing them to expand and amass fortunes at the expense of their workforces; they were also able to force artisans out of business, forcing artisans to sell off or abandon the ownership of their means of production and become wage laborers. Greater efficiencies can be wrung out through economies of scale, which in turn leads to the ability to introduce new production techniques because the accumulation of capital also provides funds for investment. Such efficiency, in turn, is necessary for the capitalist to take advantage of opportunities for trade. (Many early manufacturers were merchants, which also tends to dilute the enclosure movement/merchant capital dichotomy.)

The gathering pressures of competition eventually ignited the Industrial Revolution and fueled the rise of the factory system. A flurry of inventions useful for production shaped the Industrial Revolution that took root in Britain in the second half of the eighteenth century. The Industrial Revolution emerged not only due to technological and economic factors, but also as a result of capitalist class relations that had already become established.[26] The introduction of machinery was a tool for factory owners to bring workers under control—technological innovation required fewer employees to be kept on and de-skilled many of the remaining workers by automating processes.[27]

As industrial resistance gathered steam in the early nineteenth century, the British government employed 12,000 troops to repress craft workers, artisans, factory workers and small farmers who were resisting the introduction of machinery by capitalists, seeing these machines as threats to their freedom and dignity—more troops than Britain was using in its simultaneous fight against Napoleon's armies in Spain.[28]

This period coincided with a "moral" crusade promoted by owners of factories and agricultural estates in which the tiny fraction of commons that had survived were taken away by Parliament; the measure of independence that rights to the use of commons provided wage laborers was denounced for fostering "laziness" and "indolence"—defects that could be cured only by forcing full dependence on wage work.[29] Organizing, in the forms of unions and other coordinated activity, soon supplanted machine-breaking, reinforcing capitalists' desire to use technical innovation to render their workforces docile.

Reinforced with the power of the state that would enforce capitalists' economic coercion, the capitalist system gained ground against rival systems, and as it gained traction in more areas it steadily became more able to expand to new areas through the command of money resulting from increased accumulation of capital. This accumulation of capital that fuels the entire system is created by extracting surplus value from the workforce—the owner pays the employee much less than the value of what the employee produces.

Sometimes far less value. The process of accumulation by European capitalists was greatly accelerated by slavery and colonialism, simultaneously impoverishing Latin America, Africa, South Asia and other regions. Christopher Columbus, on his first encounter with the natives of the Caribbean, initiated their enslavement; within 15 years at least three-quarters of the population of Hispaniola had been killed.[30] From the beginning, the Spanish demanded that the Indigenous peoples provide them with a steady supply of gold—Columbus wrote in his journal, "of gold is treasure made, and with it he who has it does as he wills in the world and it even sends souls to paradise."[31] Columbus was qualified to make those pronouncements because one pope had approved the slavery of non-Christians and another pope divided the world outside of Europe into Spanish and Portuguese possessions.[32]

Gold and silver were the mediums of exchange in Europe, Asia and Africa, and currencies were based on these metals. Indigenous peoples in Mexico and the Andes were skilled at mining, creating a supply of both metals that they themselves used for ornamental purposes. Silver shipped to Spain from Latin America by 1660 totaled three times more than the entire pre-existing supply in all of Europe.[33] During this period, silver production in the Americas was an estimated ten times that of the rest of the world combined,[34] all of which was shipped to Spain. This vast wealth enriched the empires and monarchies of Europe, except for Spain—the metals it imported mostly were delivered to foreign creditors, and the rest spent on the Crusades, the Inquisition and importing manufactured items.[35] Spain imported everything it needed while other countries threw up trade barriers and developed their industries.

The brutality with which this extraction of wealth was carried out led to the reduction of Indigenous populations by an estimated 95 percent. The imperial solution to this genocide was to import slaves from Africa. A steadily increasing number of slaves were shipped from the early sixteenth century as plantations grew in size. During the seventeenth century, Caribbean sugar supplanted mainland precious metals as the mainstay of wealth extraction; for three centuries the European powers would engage in continual struggle for possession of these islands. This sugar economy was based on the slave labor of kidnapped Africans; conditions were so horrific that one-third of the slaves who made it to the Caribbean died within three years.[36] It was more profitable to work slaves to death and buy replacements than to keep them alive.

The slave trade, until the end of the seventeenth century, was conducted by government monopolies.[37] European economies grew on the "triangular trade" in which European manufactured goods were shipped to the coast of western Africa in exchange for slaves, who were shipped to the Americas, which in turn sent sugar and other commodities back to Europe. Britain and other European powers earned far more from the plantations of their Caribbean colonies than from North American possessions; much Caribbean produce could not be grown in Europe, while North American colonies tended to produce what Europe could already provide for itself.

Britain profited enormously from the triangular trade, both in the slave trade itself and the surpluses generated from plantation crops produced with slave labor. Proceeds from the slave trade were large enough to lift the prosperity of the British economy as a whole, provide the investment funds to build the infrastructure necessary to support industry and the scale of trade resulting from a growing industrial economy, and ease credit problems—early industrialists had extremely large needs for investment capital and commercial credit because of long delays in returns on investment due to the slow pace of trade transport.[38]

Profits from the slave trade and from colonial plantations were critical to bootstrapping the takeoff of British industry and modern capitalism in the second half of the eighteenth century into the early nineteenth century.

This early buoying of capitalism can be obscured because slavery is a system best suited for accumulating agricultural surpluses; slavery's association with plantations, however, can't be disassociated from the use of plantation profits. Those surpluses provided investment capital for capitalist development despite slavery having been abolished within the internal British and other Western European capitalist systems.

Slavery, as well as serfdom, is incompatible with industrial capitalism's need for "flexible" workforces that can be hired or fired at will and for large numbers of consumers who can buy the capitalists' products. A concomitant factor is that capitalism requires a workforce with formal education—an educated person is more difficult to enslave.

"Britain undertook a major series of investment programmes: in the merchant marine, in harbours and docks, in canals, in agricultural improvements and in developing new industrial machinery," wrote the sociologist Robin Blackburn in his comprehensive study *The Making of New World Slavery*. "The profits of empire and slavery helped to make this possible, enlarging the resources at the command of public authorities, [land-]improving landlords, enterprising merchants and innovating manufacturers. Because of the prior transformation in agriculture, and in British society as a whole, colonial and mercantile wealth could be transmuted into capital employing wage labour."[39]

This extraction process had opposite effects in those colonies undergoing the most intensive exploitation. The Caribbean countries were reduced to monoculture production, forbidden to manufacture anything, because their agricultural products were so profitable. The mainland colonies that would one day become the United States, by contrast, were allowed to develop the industry and varied agriculture that would in the future enable rapid growth of their economy.[40]

African development also was stunted because rulers of coastal kingdoms could buy goods and weapons from Europe while profiting by enslaving Africans from other kingdoms;[41] wealth there was used to buy from imperial powers and thus did not stay in Africa.

The widespread use of slave labor also necessitated that further social divisions be instituted, while institutionalizing global trade. "With its immense concentration of workers and its captive labor force uprooted from its homeland, unable to rely on local support, the [Caribbean and Latin American] plantation prefigured not only the factory but also the later use of immigration and globalization to cut the cost of labor," wrote Marxist feminist theorist Silvia Federici in *Caliban and the Witch*. "In particular, the plantation was a key step in the formation of an international division of labor that (through the production of "consumer goods") integrated the work of slaves into the reproduction of the European workforce, while keeping enslaved and waged workers geographically and socially divided."[42]

Slavery had long existed before this time, nor were national chauvinism, religious intolerance, sexism, invasions, wars of conquest and theological extremism something new in human history. Europe and most of the rest of the world had long featured a full assortment of such backward ideologies and exploitative relations. In classical Greek thought, non-Greek "barbarians" were believed to be "natural slaves" needing direction from those endowed with "civilization"; Roman Empire slaves were captured from an assortment of conquered peoples and codified under Roman law as chattel without regard to the slaves' origins; and early Christianity's most influential theologian, Saint Augustine, declared that slaves were "fortunate" because their sinfulness, a state they shared with all humans, was receiving earthly punishment, relieving part of their burden, a doctrine consistent with Christianity's acceptance of slavery.[43]

Slavery in the Roman Empire, however, began to break down under the pressure of slave revolts and an increasing inability to find markets for the agricultural surplus generated by slave labor as the empire disintegrated. A new form of bondage, serfdom, supplanted slavery in Europe during the continent's Dark Ages. Control of horses, mills, trade routes and superior means of violence enabled the class of lords to subjugate local populations as serfs,[44] and although conquered peoples frequently were serfs under lords of a different, conquering nation and subject to national and religious hatred, national oppression was by no means essential to this class-based system of feudal exploitation.

Slavery had not disappeared, however, remaining common in the Ottoman Empire and northern African kingdoms, where most of the slaves were Black Africans.[45] The first European slave traders were able to tap into existing networks that captured slaves for transport across the Sahara Desert. Growing demand for plantation labor in the New World, and a complete lack of scruples as to how profits were generated, resulted in a huge expansion of the slave trade—trans-Atlantic transport of slaves became many times larger than ongoing trans-Sahara transport.

Slavery in the Ottoman Empire differed because slaves there were used mostly as domestic servants; military, administrative and agricultural-labor slaves were far less numerous.[46] The Ottoman economy thus reaped little accumulation from its slave labor although slaves were steadily imported into the region for more than ten centuries and occupied a variety of roles.

The economic exploitation was vastly more intense on Europeans' Caribbean and Latin American plantations, and slaves constituted a far bigger percentage of the population. Plantation dependency on slavery grew so large that existing Christian, Greek and Roman "justifications" for slavery were no longer sufficient; legal and other methods would be developed to maintain control over an increasingly large population of slaves.

At first, White indentured servants and Black slaves were treated similarly by plantation owners on the North American mainland, excepting the significant fact that the servants had seven-year terms in contrast to the slaves' lifetime sentence.[47] Many indentured servants were English felons given the choice between execution or agreeing to be shipped to North America, a process given considerable assistance from English law listing more than 300 felonies meriting punishment by death, including pickpocketing and shoplifting.[48]

"Sheriffs handed over reprieved felons directly to merchants who carried them to the colonies and sold them as indentured servants...By the mid-seventeenth century, transportation of felons was a private enterprise, and a lucrative one,"[49] noted feminist historian Ann Jones.

Black slaves and White indentured servants socialized

together, helped each other escape and joined in rebellions, seeing each other as being in the same predicament.[50] In response, plantation owners implemented draconian laws in the late seventeenth century, codifying slave owners' "right" to kill slaves for minor infractions, banning interracial marriage and enacting laws requiring recaptured indentured servants to spend extra time serving the owners of slaves whom they assisted or escaped with.[51]

The justification of slavery through ancient Greek and Roman texts approving the enslavement of those captured in "just" wars was difficult in the face of the obvious fact that there was no "war" with African nations. To counter these developments, racism began to be developed as an ideology to counter solidarity between Blacks and Whites and to counter poor White settlers who left the colonies to live among Indigenous peoples, whose non-hierarchical lifestyle was more appealing to thousands of them.[52]

To facilitate this process, freed servants were given small privileges not available to slaves to give them the illusion of having a stake in the aristocracy-dominated social order; Whites who rebelled were not punished as severely as Blacks; and poor Whites were forced to move inland due to the monopolization of coastal land by elites, thereby exacerbating tensions with Native Americans—these were among the strategies used to divide the people who had the potential to unite against the oppressive aristocracy.[53]

Another exploitable division was that between men and women—the exploitation of male wage workers depended on the exploitation of women within the family. Drastic declines in wages throughout the sixteenth century and well into the seventeenth century across Europe, accompanied by repeated famines and widespread starvation, led to continuing unrest and a declining population.[54]

Although the Inquisition had been under way for centuries,

the witch hunts peaked during this period. Women were systematically excluded from wage work, in part to force them to bear children that would replenish the supply of workers in an era of falling population[55] and in part to enable the sustainability of the male wage worker through enforced housework.[56] Destroying the autonomy that women had exercised over their sexuality and reproductive capacities was a necessary element of this process;[57] thus the witch hunts centered on imaginary female sexual perversions and "insatiable" lust that brought men to ruin.[58]

"When labour became waged labour, the work of reproduction became unwaged housework," wrote the economist Antonella Picchio. "The biological aspects of human reproduction were used to hide the historical and social aspects of gender division of labour…The separation between the process of production and that of social reproduction of labour implied that the division of labour between men and women took new forms and shaped new power relationships within the traditional context of women's subordination."[59]

The witch hunts, although often carried out by local authorities, were well-organized campaigns orchestrated by state and church working in concert.[60] The economic element of the witch hunts could take different forms in different areas.

In Germanic states and principalities, lawyers and "commissions" organizing witch hunts, trials and executions earned very lucrative fees and payments, while governments confiscated most of the property of accused witches.[61] "The blood-money of the witch-hunt was used for the private enrichment of bankrupt princes, of lawyers, doctors, judges and professors, but also for such public affairs as financing wars, building up a bureaucracy, infrastructural measures, and finally the new absolute state," wrote the sociologist Maria Mies. "This blood-money fed the original process of capital accumulation."[62]

In the British Islands, by contrast, witch hunts mostly

targeted poor peasant women, accused by wealthy individuals who were part of the local power structure, in areas where most of the land had been enclosed—such women, who were often older, were a personification of the fear of "lower classes" by the upper classes and a socially broader superstitious fear of "magic."[63]

Although research into this still understudied subject continues, a scholarly estimate is that approximately 200,000 women, perhaps more, were accused of witchcraft over two centuries, charges that usually led to torture and/or execution.[64]

The scale on which trade began to be conducted, the ability to invest because of large accumulations of wealth, and the pressure of competition marked a significant break from feudalism. The concomitant need to grow created a need to do business in larger areas—small principalities and frequent borders blocked trade and became barriers to expansion. Capitalists, therefore, worked to create "free trade" through the elimination of borders. Nationalism became a useful ideology because its logical demand at this time was for nations to unify. There were dozens of German states in the early nineteenth century, for example, and all but Austria had been united in a single Germany by the late nineteenth century.

The high cost of trade imposed by borders in the form of institutional regulation and tariffs imposed obstacles to agricultural growth in the feudal economy, and the lowering of barriers reduced the revenue that lords could extract, weakening their positions.[65] Incessant warfare among lords built up larger territories, reducing the number of feudal monopolies, enabling the systematizing of legal codes and creating larger markets—such centralization created an institutional basis for capitalism.[66]

Knowledge could also be transferred, shared and copied much more easily once feudal blockages were eroded. The high cost of travel, lack of codification and the fact that technical knowledge was contained within the expertise gradually attained by scattered individuals blocked innovation in feudal societies, but greater urbanization in late feudalism enabled technology to spread much more readily,[67] another factor helping capitalism to take root.

Thus, the seeds of capitalism were contained within feudalism, although it took centuries for those seeds to sprout fully because of the slow pace of life and glacial pace of innovation. Feudalism itself contained elements of still earlier systems, including slavery. The foregoing discussion of the transition from feudalism to capitalism in itself does not "prove" that a further transition from capitalism is inevitable, but it does provide validation for a materialist theory of history.

## Explorations in theories of the continuing dominance of capitalism

Frequently in this book, reference has been made to the fact that, to use a Marxist standard, the Soviet Union never reached the status of a socialist state. As noted in Chapter 5, this standard is offered simply because it is how the country judged itself. A realistic judgment—again, there are no benchmarks or definitive accomplishments where one can hold a ceremony and pronounce "this is it"—is that the country remained in a deformed transitional state between capitalism and socialism. The transition from feudalism to capitalism unfolded over centuries, but although a transition from capitalism could hardly be expected to happen overnight, events do move much more quickly today. It is therefore justified to ask about the first attempt to move beyond capitalism: What sort of transition is it that lasts 74 years? Moreover, it is reasonable to ask that if "building socialism" or "transitioning to socialism" is so difficult that three-quarters of a century go by without getting past this stage, why should anyone attempt to do it?

To answer these questions, it should be noted that the Soviet Union was born, and had to be constructed, in extremely unfavorable circumstances, including facing hostile capitalist encirclement alone and the underdevelopment it inherited. Spectacular development was achieved (at very high cost)—from 20 percent literacy to producing more engineers than any other country in the span of two generations—but the centralization that enabled rapid development by marshaling scarce resources eventually developed dialectically into its opposite, becoming a fetter to further development. The congealment of the peculiar form of Soviet ideology into uncontestable orthodoxy blocked necessary changes, as we saw in chapters 3 and 5.

The very basis of historical and dialectical materialism is that evolution and development are continual processes: There is no permanent ideal state that can be reached nor can any element of human thought become a final, unappealable truth. Soviet orthodoxy routinely paid lip service to this concept, while trampling on it in actual practice. The writings of Karl Marx, Friedrich Engels and Vladimir Lenin were treated as absolute truths that could only be interpreted by official party specialists and leaders, an orthodoxy put in place during the Stalin dictatorship and continued (in less severe forms) for decades afterward by party leaders who had begun their ascent up the party hierarchy during Stalin's dictatorship. It did not help that most top Soviet leaders understood those writings only on a superficial level and carried them into practice in arrogant and crude ways.

The result of those institutionalized failings was the conversion of Marx and Engels into infallible utopians despite the fact that they forcefully condemned the utopians of their own days. The unreality of that conversion can easily be condemned even on the basis of "orthodox Marxism," as the philosopher and literary critic Georg Lukács did as early as 1923: "Orthodox Marxism, therefore, does not imply the uncritical acceptance of the results of Marx's investigations. It is not the 'belief' in this or that thesis, nor the exegesis of a 'sacred' book. On the contrary, orthodoxy refers exclusively to *method*."[68]

If what is at the core of Marxist materialism is a methodology, then it is by definition a living philosophy that cannot reach a final state nor posit that a particular form of organization is inevitable or mandated. The methodology provides the student with tools that can be used to understand capitalism's democratic and fascist forms, as well as understand post-capitalist Soviet bloc societies. Tools, however, must be mastered—they can provide assistance but can't substitute for the user's own brain power. What Marxism emphatically is not is a set of magic formulae, a shortcut to enlightenment or a blueprint for the future.

The root of Soviet orthodoxy's insistence on its mastery of truth was anchored in the expansion of historical materialism (a social theory pertaining to history and human development) into dialectical materialism (a broader philosophy encompassing the natural sciences and purporting to constitute general scientific laws). The Marxist movement of the late nineteenth century believed it needed a philosophy with which to counter its opponents, and Engels took up the task, providing the outlook that became known as dialectical materialism in his most influential book, the *Anti-Dühring*.

Engels wrote that what had begun as a polemic turned into an "exposition of the dialectical method and the communist world outlook."[69] Engels argued that the world is a complex of processes, not fixed and static things, writing that the then new rapid series of discoveries uncovering dynamic change in astronomy, biology, chemistry and physics demonstrated dialectics in the natural world—the laws of motion in nature are the same as those of history.[70]

Critics argued that extending dialectics to nature erased the subjectivity and consciousness that are unique to history; that physical and chemical matter are not dialectical; and that the proper terrain of Marxism is the structure of society.[71] This argument raged for decades. Engels, and others following him, certainly were correct in seeing development in the natural world as a process begun far in the past and destined to continue in the future (in strong contrast to erroneous "steady state" and "hand of God" beliefs that had predominated), but processes such as species evolution or chemical transformation are at most merely analogies to human social development.

Regardless of whether or not it was a mistake to expand to natural sciences, that it was done was the kernel that Soviet orthodoxy seized to claim it had a monopoly on truth. Pre-World War I Marxists readily grabbed onto Engels' dialectics, in whose hands it was rather benign, but the concept reached absurd proportions during the Stalin era.

Of the latter, the sociologist Michael Löwy has written,

> With Stalinism, a new and unprecedented phenomenon appears in Marxism: an attempt to "ideologize" the natural sciences themselves. It is true that Engels and Lenin ventured into the field of the natural sciences, but (rightly or wrongly, it is irrelevant here) they did so in order to develop philosophical considerations relating to natural facts (their dialectical or materialist character) and not in order to impose ideological norms on research on the natural sciences as such. The idea that the existing natural sciences are "bourgeois" is quite alien to classic Marxist thought…Stalinism…fail[ed] to recognize the specificity of the human sciences and the methodological differences between them and the natural sciences.[72]

Within the human sciences (returning to the original concept of historical materialism as a social theory), it is also necessary to guard against ideological distortions. It is important to emphasize that postulations of post-capitalist society are not prophecies. Capitalism contains the seeds of a newer, better society because productive capacities are raised sufficiently high to enable everyone to have an adequate standard of living if only production were distributed rationally and fairly. Nonetheless, it does not follow that any better society, whether it be some variant of socialism or some other form of more expansive democracy, must automatically follow. Concrete conditions and human actions will determine the contours of the future.

Those factors have determined the contours of the past. Studying the development of capitalism enables the puncturing of the mythologies that accrete to it. From the system's earliest days, myth-makers claimed that capital accumulation originated in Protestant frugality. The sociologist Max Weber exemplified that belief in his 1905 work *The Protestant Ethic and the Spirit of Capitalism*, in which he argued that the asceticism of Calvinism, Puritanism and other Protestant sects, and the individual links these religions posit between believers and God, as opposed to the centralizing medium of the Roman Catholic Church, produced a work ethic that induced people to develop enterprises and accumulate wealth. Weber argued that these religions discouraged luxuries and wasteful spending, giving rise to savings that created the investment pools needed to develop capitalism.

Weber, however, did not seem to account for the fact that Catholic Spanish monarchs sponsoring trans-Atlantic voyages, Catholic Italian traders and financiers, Jewish merchants, luxury consumer items imported from Asia, metals extracted from the New World and (not least) slavery seemed to have something to do with early accumulations of European capital—the initial "primitive accumulation" providing the base for later capitalist accumulation. To accept Weber's thesis, it would be necessary not only to ignore the violence accompanying the foundation of capitalism; it would also require ignoring the fact that belief in Protestant exceptionalism is inextricably bound up with both anti-Catholic claims that Catholics act only at dictates of popes and bishops and more virulent anti-Semitism, both of which flourished for centuries in Europe and North America.

Marx, in typically direct style, had this to say about often-promoted mythologies concerning the origins of capitalism in the first volume of *Capital*:

> [P]rimitive accumulation plays in Political Economy about the same part as original sin in theology. Adam bit the apple, and thereupon sin fell on the human race. Its origin is supposed to be explained when it is told as an anecdote of the past. In times long gone by there were two sorts of people: one, the diligent, intelligent, and, above all, frugal élite; the other, lazy rascals, spending their substance, and more, in riotous living. The legend of theological original sin tells us certainly how man came to be condemned to eat his bread in the sweat of his brow; but the history of economic original sin reveals to us that there are people to whom this is by no means essential. Never mind! Thus it came to pass that the former sort accumulated wealth, and the latter sort had at last nothing to sell except their own skins. And from this original sin dates the poverty of the great majority that, despite all its labour, has up to now nothing to sell but itself, and the wealth of the few that increases constantly although they have long ceased to work. Such insipid childishness is every day preached to us in the defence of property.[73]

("Property" here refers to the means of production, not personal possessions.)

Pre-capitalist forms of economy were transcended by capitalist forms when the contradictions within those forms became fetters on production. Artisan production gave way to large-scale production—production became "socialized" in the sense that it was now accomplished by groups of people working together. Production becomes ever larger in scale, and enterprises must become ever larger to survive competition. Fewer enterprises can survive—this is the tendency toward monopoly or, at the least, oligopoly. In order for profits to increase, the owners of the means of production (or in the typical large corporation of today, the executives at the top of the corporate pyramid) have to extract more from the workforce, in the form of lowered wages and benefits and speeded-up work. But the "socialization" that modern production creates—that is, the bringing together of masses of working people—creates a necessary condition for those working people to band together to throw off the fetters imposed on them by the capitalists and the state that serves the interest of the capitalists.

To put all this another way: The long trend of human history has, with a great many zigzags, sidesteps and reversals along the way, been toward greater freedom. The vision of transcending capitalism represents further steps along this long journey.

Future advancement is not guaranteed—only that humanity can go forward to more democracy or it can go backward to something worse than modern capitalism. There is no stasis.

A particular vision of the future envisioned by millions of people has not happened. At the beginning of this chapter, six factors were offered as among the reasons as to why this future has not arrived. The first of these factors is that the early pioneers of the socialist movement seriously underestimated the ability of capitalism as a system to adapt and therefore the ability of working people to extract concessions.

Many early Marxists believed that what we would today refer to as the middle class would be wiped out; that capitalist society would become deeply divided into capitalists and destitute workers. The "middle class" that existed at the dawn of the Industrial Revolution, people such as artisans, by and large did go under, becoming subsumed into the working class. But a sizable modern middle class eventually formed in the leading capitalist states (albeit only a minuscule middle class formed slowly in the Global South).

The modern middle class is very heterogeneous, including office workers in a vast range of industries and manual workers who earn a living wage thanks to their organizations, in addition to shopkeepers and self-employed professionals. But this heterogeneous group mainly consists of blue- and white-collar employees who exist, however precariously, as a direct result of the ability of working people to extract concessions through self-organization. We saw in Chapter 1 how working people were able to win many advances by virtue of the threat to capitalism posed by a well-organized socialist movement, particularly during the uprisings immediately following World War I.

It is no accident that the first country with universal health care, Germany, had the strongest movement. The later onset of the Great Depression brought renewed strong movements, again threatening the capitalist order—many more social advancements were won. The ability to form unions was a crucial gain, and organization within the workplaces coupled with new social guarantees allowed millions of people to rise above poverty into a comfortable life with some security.

Note, however, that all those gains were created against the will of capitalists and ordinarily with much resistance by the governments of the capitalist states—a middle class was created, social gains were won, but all of it because of struggle by working people. These same struggles also made more people politically active, and all these factors would eventually lead to dramatic gains in civil rights in the advanced capitalist countries in the 1960s and 1970s. Once again, it was struggle by working people that accomplished this, in the teeth of resistance of governments that are under the sway of the capitalists who wield so much power. But there was another factor in this rise of material living standards in the advanced capitalist states, which brings us to the second of our six factors: that the early pioneers failed to understand the buoying effect that would be provided (for the leading capitalist countries) by imperialism.

Capitalists, under compulsion of competition, expanded into what today is called the Global South. Taking advantage of undeveloped institutions, a badly undereducated population and a local ruling class (plantation owners at the start of the process) willing to allow nearly unlimited exploitation in exchange for a share of the proceeds, capitalists from the North could move in and ship massive profits back home while leaving the local populations destitute and forced to work for starvation wages. This process of primitive accumulation, not much different from the sort of primitive accumulation that occurred in England and elsewhere at the dawn of capitalism, kept local elites happy but, more so, fattened the wallets of the corporate elites who set up operations. (We saw examples of this in Central America in Chapter 4, but this process went on elsewhere as well.)

This transnational profiteering, a process known as imperialism, primarily filled bulging corporate coffers, but inevitably some tiny amount of it filtered down for some working people in the North. Jobs for administrators, sales representatives, warehouse workers and others related to supporting exports as new markets are forced open would be a direct manifestation, and manufacturing jobs tied to the expansion of production destined for export are created. But competitive pressures inevitably force production to be moved to countries with much lower wages—thus the age of buoying living standards through export of locally made products comes to an end, supplanted by corporate globalization that moves jobs overseas and drives down wages.

Nonetheless, imperialism has not been without benefit to the North. Some of the wealth amassed by corporate elites is converted into those elites' personal consumption, although that has a distorting effect as the consumption mostly consists of luxury items. This wealth, however concentrated at the top, is money funneled into Northern economies, boosting wealth there—but it is money subtracted from the economies of the South, plunging people there deeper into debt and poverty. This capital flow is the other side of so-called "free trade" between unequal countries on which the relative "prosperity" of the stronger country is partly based. This process does (temporarily) buoy living standards in the North, a factor dampening militancy by the working peoples of the advanced capitalist countries. The net effect has been to provide more stability than would otherwise have existed.

The third and fourth of our six factors—an overly mechanical belief that revolution would somehow unfold automatically, a belief held before and after the establishments of post-capitalist governments—was compounded by the tendency of timely capitalist concessions. Working people who stop struggling for gains, accepting the concessions on offer (although without further struggle those concessions are gradually taken back), lose their militancy and movements dissipate. Long periods of relative quiet simply don't jibe with unrealistic, mechanical concepts of a continual unfolding of an automatic process.

Men and women must press their demands in organized fashion, whether for reforms or, during revolutionary moments, for something new. When demands aren't pressed, there is not only no momentum toward revolutionary change (or at least some meaningful reforms), but the status of working people begins to go backward. Concessions are taken back, harsher working conditions and cuts to average wage levels are imposed simultaneous with backlashes against social groups who achieved recent gains, and clampdowns are pursued against non-traditional social groups and other non-conformists.

The original conception of future terminal crisis was that capitalist development would eventually become a fetter on production: The monopolization of production by fewer capitalists and their increasing confiscation of wealth created in production would conflict with the socialization of the labor necessary for that production; the immiseration and exploitation of working people under these conditions and their gathering in large groups to carry out production would give them incentive and ability to organize in revolt; and the monopolization of education and intellectual leadership by a narrow class hinders development by constricting the range of allowable ideas and blocking all but a small elite from contributing their talents to social betterment.[74] Working people, who constitute the vast majority, can transcend those contradictions by taking control of production themselves, a process that, if undertaken, would culminate in the abolition of classes in a society in which work would be carried out by free associations of individual producers.

Such a revolution requires material conditions to reach a point where enough is produced for everyone to have a reasonable standard of living and, crucially, for working people to collectively possess the consciousness necessary to achieve their own emancipation. The theory that a struggle was necessary for the transcending of capitalism was sidetracked by a reformist belief that socialism would develop automatically; that history unfolds in a series of specific stages. A further detour came in the form of an overemphasis on waiting for conditions to ripen, which in practice meant accepting capitalist conditions and hoping for small reforms because those ripe conditions were far in the future.

The fifth of our six factors—an overly centralized world movement that retarded the theoretical developments needed for local conditions and blocked the creation of innovative leaderships—underlay the continued isolation of the Soviet Union and its long path to the Stalin dictatorship analyzed in Chapter 2 and is central to the fate of the Prague Spring discussed in Chapter 3. Movements need not arise from any single party, nor from this or that group or this or that particular interpretation. Movements need local leadership and must be grounded in theory and practice based on experience and actual material conditions, at the same time they are connected to other places and nations. Capitalism is a global system and the response to it must be global as well.

To return to the idea of understanding Marxism as a methodology, a canonization of texts is inseparable from over-centralization. Such over-centralization was first effect and later cause of a lack of confidence by local leaderships and an inability to adapt tactics and movements to concrete local conditions. An irony of canonization is that those texts so treated aren't necessarily studied closely; the ideas within them become distorted into oversimplifications. Theory withers into a reduced body of work shorn of its original subtleties. Under the pressure of day-to-day struggles in challenging social and economic environments, the temptation of simply falling back on formulaic, simplified versions of ideas can be difficult to avoid. But to do so is to cease adapting to new conditions and challenges.

A prominent US communist leader, Dorothy Healey, put it this way in looking back at her long movement career:

> Marxism had been taught as a set of formulas, and most Party members had neither the time nor interest to look beyond those formulas. I know from my own case that it took nearly two decades of practical experience before it occurred to me that the "theory" I was reading in books by Marx and Lenin had much of anything important to do with my practical activity. That was in part my own fault, but it was also the fault of the intellectual atmosphere within the Party. We weren't encouraged to think of Marxism as a *methodology,* as an open system of thought that could change in a changing world...[T]reating Marxism as a methodology means having the ability to look dialectically at contemporary reality and not to be content with one-sided arguments or formulas from

the past.[75]

Theory divorced from practice loses its relevance, and practice without replenished theory loses its coherence. A centralization substituted for such a disassociation ultimately accelerates breakdowns of movements.

Movements can't be commanded from any single location or by any single group. Participants in the anti-corporate globalization movement that burst onto the world's stage in Seattle in 1999 understood this concept, and although it faded after a few years, the example of autonomy and consensus in decision-making provides models that merit further development. At the same time, too much decentralization leads to the disintegration of movements without their leaving any permanent institutions.

The sixth factor—a too narrow conception of "working class" or "working people"—requires a firmer divergence from traditional readings of texts. The tendency has been to visualize only blue-collar manual workers as working people, who represent a declining percentage of the population in increasingly technological capitalist societies. By no means is this narrow concept of who constitutes a "worker" confined to the Left; it seems a rather widespread idea. The author of this book need only think of his father (firmly on the Right) who soon after entering the world of labor decided (in his words) "this working is for the birds," put himself through college and had a long career as an engineer. He went to his job every morning for more than 35 years—how could this be anything but working?

The blue-collar worker has much different conditions than does the white-collar worker, meaning there are divergences in some interests, and the term "white collar" is itself quite heterogeneous. Nonetheless, white- and blue-collar workers are similarly exploited economically, contribute to the economy and endure subservient relationships to capitalists just the same. Their interests ultimately converge in a capitalist system;

moreover, white-collar workers outnumber blue-collar workers in technologically advanced countries. These are examples of where ideological calcification must be chipped away; the cities of modern capitalist states are not primarily populated by families of manual laborers as was the case in the nineteenth century.

This basic census does not alter the fact that, in an economic crisis deep enough to threaten capitalism, many middle-class people will be plunged into poverty. Some of those cast out of the middle class will continue to psychologically consider themselves as middle class and continue to resist the idea of thinking of themselves as working people and joining with those who had been below them on the economic scale, but in doing so would be acting against their own interest. All working people, regardless of collar color, have a common interest because sustainable improvements can only be won (and defended) through collective struggle.

Working people are all men and women who are employees earning wages; all those who are in the "informal" sectors; and those who work on freelance or temporary bases, who are in essence wage workers without any job security subject to periodic stretches of unemployment. These groups collectively constitute an overwhelming majority of any advanced capitalist country. Any movement of working people has to reflect this reality; traditional interpretations that narrow definitions will remain exclusive of too many people to be useful.

Many advances in the conditions of working people have been achieved, thanks to their own struggles—life is certainly better than it was in the early years of capitalism. Can the democracy that has been carved out within capitalist countries be pushed further to create some new vision of a society without domination? Regretfully, no. There are limits to the conception of democracy within capitalism, and when we start to examine society in a broader sense, conceptualizing democracy for all spheres of life, the practice of democracy under capitalism is revealed as more formal than actual.

## Conceptualizations of the economic barriers to democracy under capitalism

The ideology that pervades capitalist societies is built on two concepts: That citizens enjoy more freedom than elsewhere and enjoy more economic prosperity than elsewhere, and that these two are linked. Any analysis of contemporary capitalist society will have to confront not only that this official ideology is widely disseminated, but that it is widely accepted. As long as this ideology continues to be widely accepted, there will be little in the way of serious movement toward radical reform, much less the still more radical step of revolutionary change.

Corporate power has become dominant in the advanced capitalist societies, a fact that is also widely accepted. This acceptance isn't necessarily inconsistent with acceptance of the theses of freedom and prosperity. Some people simply accept corporate dominance as the "price" to be paid for freedom and prosperity and may well decouple, in their minds, this corporate power from the exercise of political power, seeing their right to vote for the political party of their choice in elections as a symbol of continuing freedom.

Other people are more sensitive to corporate power and may go so far as to see political elections as very limited, but fall into resignation, believing that the system is far too powerful to fight—an attitude that we might as well leave things as they are. Still other people observe the limitations in their corporate-dominated society, perhaps are skeptical about voting even while participating in elections and aren't so defeated as to give up a desire to effect serious changes. But there are copious consumer goods and freedom of expression, so maybe we shouldn't tamper with the basics but rather seek to reduce the concentration of power and money. Those who enjoy their concentration of power and money are not eager to part with either, so a commitment to this sort of path can be difficult to sustain, and if we wish to bring about this sort of reduction (and a concomitant income redistribution) within the current capitalist framework, the work becomes still more difficult.

There certainly is wealth in the advanced capitalist countries. But who enjoys this wealth and how is it created? There certainly is formal freedom of expression in the advanced capitalist countries. But who actually gets to put to use this freedom of expression? Is this freedom, created by centuries of struggle, the limit of attainable freedom, or can we go beyond it?

These concepts must be analyzed together, and because the concentrated economic power that is personified by the corporation is increasingly ubiquitous, critiquing the economic side of the equation is indispensable.

Wealth is said to be derived from profits. Very well. But where do profits come from? On this critical point, there is a surprisingly wide divergence of both opinion and theory. Moreover, some theories are designed to obscure and others to illuminate. There are many schools of economic theory, but those that have come to dominate debate are those collectively known as "neoclassical." These are theories of unbridled capitalism, and its believers see themselves as the descendants of Adam Smith, the eighteenth-century Scottish economist who is to capitalism as Karl Marx is to anti-capitalism.

Neoclassical theories are most closely associated with the "Chicago School" centered on the University of Chicago economics department and the department's best-known professor, Milton Friedman. (The actual application of these theories is popularly known as "neoliberalism.") It is the Chicago School that developed Chilean dictator Augusto Pinochet's brutal economic policies, spawned the twin ideologies of Reaganism and Thatcherism, and fomented the pitiless top-down imposition of capitalism through "shock therapy" in Russia (and elsewhere) in the 1980s and 1990s. It is the Chicago School that helps to supply the intellectual justification for International Monetary Fund and World Bank programs imposing harsh austerity on the people of the South while insisting the countries of the South open themselves unconditionally to the economic might of the North.

Such an ideology flows naturally from the Chicago School's antecedent, the Austrian School, whose leader, Friedrich Hayek, went so far as to claim that human civilization consists of a long struggle against "primitive instincts" such as solidarity, benevolence and a desire to work for the needs of the community.[76] Such an elevation of selfishness to an organizing principle of the world found its echo later in Margaret Thatcher's statement to a British magazine that "There is no such thing as society."[77] There are only individuals and families autonomous from all others, the prime minister said, yet actual humans seem strangely absent from conservative economics.

Standard neoclassical economics is highly abstract, built on mathematics and based on concepts such as "perfect competition" rather than on the real world.[78] The model of perfect competition assumes that all prices automatically calibrate to optimum levels, and that there are so many buyers and sellers that none has sufficient power to affect the market.[79] Summing up these assumptions, economist Robert Kuttner wrote,

> Perfect competition requires "perfect information." Consumers must know enough to compare products astutely; workers must be aware of alternative jobs; and capitalists of competing investment opportunities...Moreover, perfect competition requires "perfect mobility of factors." Workers must be free to get the highest available wage, and capitalists to shift their capital to get the highest available return; otherwise identical factors of production would command different prices, and the result would be deviation from the

model.[80]

In the real world, workers do not have the ability to freely find jobs at the highest wages, nor do capitalists have sufficient information to always earn the maximum possible profit. Corporate secrecy, a requirement imposed by the rigors of competition, makes it impossible for capitalists or working people to ever possess sufficient information to achieve anything close to these ideals. Friedman tap-danced around this problem by arguing that it does not matter whether an assumption is empirically true as long as it is internally consistent and the model is not refuted by data.[81] Chicago School economists, however, don't believe there are any data that refute their assumptions—any economic difficulties, such as inflation or high unemployment, are always the result of government interference. This attitude is exemplified by a Chicago School economist, Frank Knight, who wrote in a leading academic economic journal that professors should "inculcate" in their students that these theories are not debatable hypotheses, but rather are "sacred feature[s] of the system."[82]

This is not abstraction for its own sake, but for a cause. Thus, Chicago School economists could gleefully institute their ideology in 1970s Chile simultaneous with (in fact, because of) Pinochet torturing and killing tens of thousands. It is just such a mindset that led a major New Orleans developer to declare, days after Hurricane Katrina devastated the city in 2005, that "I think we have a clean sheet to start again. And with that clean sheet we have some very big opportunities."[83] Friedman himself, in his last public statement, said the fact that "most New Orleans schools are in ruins" offered "an opportunity to radically reform the educational system" by handing them over to "private enterprise"[84]—by which he meant privatizing the schools for corporate profit. So what that one of the world's culturally unique cities had to be destroyed to create this "opportunity."

Neoclassical theory can be seen as a theory of equilibrium in exchange, with production and distribution as afterthoughts, in which firms and individuals are not part of a social structure; initial factors such as wealth and property are taken as given.[85] Production is alleged to be independent of all social factors, the employees who do the work of production are in their jobs due to personal choice, and wages are based only on individual achievement independent of race, gender and other differences.[86]

Given the unreality of the preceding, it is not surprising that so much capitalist ideology resorts to the "magic of the market" and the "invisible hand." Yes, magic must account for dramatic imbalances in income and power! Don't laugh just yet—here's how a prominent Chicago School economics professor invoked supernatural forces to defend "junk bonds" (high-risk debt created to finance takeovers of companies by speculators who did not have the money to buy them):

> My own view is that the fact that the invisible hand could work its magic through mere humans is an essential part of Adam Smith's insight. Not many thousands of years ago, men like this would have clubbed each other over hunting rights. A few hundred years ago, they would have hacked each other with axes and swords. Now they yelled at trainees while they brought together the supply and demand of home mortgages on a world-wide scale.[87]

Those feudal lords hacking at each other with axes and swords undoubtedly believed they were doing God's work, too. For his part, Smith himself wrote that "Providence" guarantees that everyone, including the poor, has enough to eat: "When Providence divided the earth among a few lordly masters, it neither forgot nor abandoned those who seemed to have been left out in the partition."[88] And it is a small step from there to the proposition that without regulation business activity will invariably be honest and benefit all.

Panegyrics to magic and invisible hands aside, the closest neoclassical economic theory seems to get to an explanation of profits is the cliché of "buying low, selling high." Profits appear out of thin air, or thanks to the business acumen of the capitalist. But if somebody is buying low, then someone else is selling low. Selling something for more than was paid for it explains how one individual earns a one-time profit, but does not explain how the system as a whole generates profit. Otherwise, the economy would function as one giant flea-market, which it does not.

There must be something inherent within the capitalist system that ultimately is the source for the profits it generates. We need a more material explanation than "magic."

Indeed, there is a source of profit—labor power. Specifically, labor power produces surplus value. Labor power is not the same as labor: Labor is the actual activity of production whereas labor power is the workers' mental and physical capabilities that are sold to capitalists. Nature is the source of much wealth; by no means is labor power the sole source. But it is labor power that is used to extract natural resources and produce the commodities that are to be sold.

Surplus value is the difference between what an employee produces and what the employee is paid—the surplus value is converted into the owner's profit. This is a complicated concept and initially seems counter-intuitive. Machinery is a part of modern production and does not machinery increase efficiency? The machine presumably costs less over its life than the worker; isn't that why capitalists buy machines, so they can employ fewer workers and increase productivity? True on both counts. But the value of machines is consumed in production. It is the physical labor of production that produces the commodity that is sold for more than was paid for the materials used to make it. This concept is easier to understand when it is applied across the life of a commodity rather than narrowly within only the enterprise that physically produced the final product.

Any product made for sale has an "exchange value." This value is not necessarily the same as its "use value"—the intrinsic value a product has to the user of it. If it takes eight hours for an individual to make a shirt for herself, then the shirt might be said to have a use value of eight hours of labor. Perhaps instead of wearing it herself the shirt-maker wishes to barter the shirt for a pair of shoes. But if the shoes require 16 hours to make, the shoemaker is not likely to see that as a fair exchange. But if the shoemaker needs two shirts, then the labor that went into each side of the exchange is equal (assuming the skill and intensity of work are close to equal)—the pair of shoes can be said to have the value of two shirts.

In a capitalist mode of exchange, the shirt or shoe is sold for money—its exchange value is the amount of money paid for it. But the shirt-maker working for a wage paid by a manufacturer will receive only a portion of that value. The difference, the surplus value, is the source of profit. If the capitalist willingly paid to his employees the full value of what they produce, he wouldn't be a capitalist—there would be no profit.

The owner of the factory is not altruistic; he intends to extract surplus value. But that owner does not keep all the surplus value—he must share it with those who help circulate the commodity. (Distributors and merchants assume the cost of circulation, part of the expense of a commodity, while sharing the surplus value.[89]) In the following hypothetical case, the surplus value is shared with the distributor and the merchant. Let's say the factory owner pays a wage that is equal to $8 to each worker for each widget. The owner sells the widget to the distributor for $10, the distributor sells it to the merchant for $12 and the merchant sells the widget for $14. When the worker goes to the store to buy a widget, she pays $14 although she was paid only $8 to make one. Thus, the widget is worth $6 more than what the factory owner paid to the worker, not the $2 difference between the wage and what the factory owner received for it.

The distribution of that surplus value can change among the capitalists. These capitalists compete against each other to earn a bigger profit, at the same time they cooperate in getting the product to market. The widget manufacturer might miscalculate the demand and overproduce, causing a glut that requires a reduction in prices. Or a giant merchant chain becomes so big that it has the power to force lower prices—the chain wishes to sell the widget for less to undercut its smaller competitors, and possesses sufficient clout by virtue of its size to negotiate a discount, forcing the manufacturer to cut its wholesale prices.

If the manufacturer does not wish to see its profits reduced, it has to reduce its costs. The primary way it can do so is to lower its labor-power costs. This can mean cuts to wages or benefits, increased workloads or layoffs ("increased efficiency" in official economic jargon): In each of these cases, the capitalist is buoying profit levels by extracting more surplus value. More will be extracted from the workforce through suppressing pay or an intensification of work. That is the power of capital.

The above example is of course an oversimplification. The business owner has costs other than labor power, and employees do not create the widgets solely with bare hands. (And, in reality, the employee will be paid far less than the 80 percent of the factory owner's proceeds in our hypothetical example.) There is machinery in the manufacturing process, and raw materials (here including manufactured components) are needed to make the widgets. If the company's stock is traded on a stock exchange, the shareholders will be expecting a hefty cut of the profits. (Among larger such companies, management is mostly separate from ownership; the top executives of the company assume the role of ownership and take correspondingly large parts of the surplus value; the legal owners, the holders of the common stock, likely number in the thousands and are too diffuse to exert any significant influence on management as individuals. But the stockholders nonetheless expect steadily increasing profits and rising share prices, and collectively will punish a company that fails to provide them by selling off shares, which forces share prices lower and thereby puts pressure on management to meet shareholders' expectations. Large institutional shareholders—particularly investment banks, hedge funds and rich speculators seeking short-term profits—are often the most aggressive in fueling this tendency to elevate maximizing immediate profits above all other values.)

Labor power is the source of surplus value because raw materials and the value of the machinery are consumed in production while labor power produces more value than is paid for it.[90] That does not mean that machines aren't productive nor that they don't raise the productivity of those who work with them. They do both. The surplus value contained in the machines placed in production was realized by the manufacturer of the machine upon selling it; the machines transfer their value to the commodities produced using them.[91] (Payments might continue to be made on the machine after it is put into service, but the payments go to the lender who financed the machine's purchase; interest is another sharing of surplus value. Rents and mortgages are as well.)

A commodity is produced with direct labor, machines and raw materials, but the machines and raw materials assist labor in producing the surplus value—machines make labor more productive, enabling more surplus value to be extracted from each worker.[92] Raw materials and other commodities are bought by the capitalist so they can be sold in a new form for a higher price; raw materials and natural commodities can't do that by themselves—labor power is the only commodity that can add the value that becomes surplus value.[93]

Marx demonstrated this concept at the beginning of Volume III of *Capital*. He wrote,

> Let us say that the production of a certain article requires a capital in expenditure of £500: £20 for wear and tear of the instruments of labour, £380 for raw materials and £100 for labour-power. If we take the rate of surplus-value as 100 per cent, the value of the product is 400c + 100v + 100s = £600. After deducting the surplus-value of £100 [the "100s" in the equation], there remains a commodity value of £500, and this simply replaces the capital expenditure of £500. This part of the value of the commodity, which replaces the price of the means of production consumed and the labour-power employed, simply replaces what the commodity cost the capitalist himself and is therefore the cost price of the commodity, as far as he is concerned.[94]

In this example, the capitalist, assuming the finished product has been sold at the market value of £600, has realized a profit of 20 percent. Because £200 was realized by the capitalist above the total £400 cost of raw materials (£380) and machine-use (£20) while only £100 was paid in wages (the "100v" in the equation), £100 in surplus value was extracted by not paying the employees for half of what they produced. It is by calculating labor power separate from other inputs that the source of profit is discovered.

This crucial point is obscured when the cost of labor power is subsumed in the overall expenditures; the capitalist's profit appears to him or herself simply as the difference between the sum total of his or her costs and the sale price. Thus the profit *appears* to derive from the circulation (sale) of the commodity while in reality circulation is the *realization* of profit.[95]

The explication of labor power is an achievement of Marx; nonetheless, the labor theory of value is not an invention of Marx. In fact, the theory predates capitalism—it was first developed in 1377 by a diplomat and government official who served many Arab governments before becoming a scholar. The diplomat, Ibn Khaldûn, wrote that labor is the source of value, arguing that even when profits result "from something other than a craft, the value of the resulting profit and acquired [capital] must include the value of the labor by which it was obtained."[96]

The idea of labor adding value was picked up in the seventeenth century, most influentially by John Locke. In *The Second Treatise of Government*, Locke wrote that what is taken from the earth through labor rightfully becomes the property of the laborer; it follows that labor provides value. Cultivated land is more valuable than fallow land as a result of labor, Locke wrote, and he extended his concept to acknowledge that all manufactured products are given value by labor.[97] Among those who accepted this concept in the following century was Adam Smith.

Although it seems surprising coming from him because of the way that his writings have been used, Smith wrote that the value of any commodity "to the person who possesses it and who means not to use it or consume it for himself, but to exchange it for other commodities, is equal to the quantity of labor which it enables him to purchase or command. Labor, therefore, is the real measure of the exchangeable value of all commodities."[98] Smith later wrote, "Labor alone is the ultimate and real standard, or real price; money is the nominal price."[99]

Smith also realized that there would be an imbalance deriving from the command of labor.

> It is not...difficult to foresee which of the two parties [employers and employees] must...have the advantage in the dispute (over wages), and force the other into compliance with their terms. The masters, being fewer in number can combine much more easily; and the law, besides, authorizes or at least does not prohibit their combinations, while it prohibits those of the workmen.[100]

These quotations are inconvenient for neoliberal apologists. But happily for Smith's present-day acolytes, he believed that capitalists and landowners have to be rewarded for risk-taking; therefore, upward redistribution of income was required to ensure they would employ the resources they owned.[101] Smith's ability to reconcile his acknowledgment of the value added by labor with his belief that upward flow of money was a proper result rests on his theory of the division of labor.

He argued in *Wealth of Nations* that the factory facilitates the division of labor, which vastly increases the productive capacities of individual laborers by breaking down the production of an item into discrete parts accomplished by separate people.[102] Smith wrote that fixed capital (such as machinery and factory buildings) increases the productive power of labor but can produce nothing without circulating capital (such as money and inventory)—from these starting points he concluded that the circulation of capital not only furnishes raw materials and the wages of labor, but is the source of profit.[103] Here we have the origination of the "buying low, selling high" cliché that purports to explain profits.

Smith's conclusion that capital is the source of profit, nonetheless, contradicts other passages in *Wealth of Nations* in which he wrote that command of labor is the source of value—if the latter is so, profits must originate from the differential between what labor is paid and the value of what labor has produced.[104] The value of the commodity would be the same if the workers kept the full value of what they produced rather than having some of it taken by the capitalist; the surplus value taken by the capitalist, not the circulation of the commodity, is therefore the source of the capitalist's profit.[105]

Smith, despite his exaltation of capitalists, did believe that labor also was entitled to be rewarded. He concomitantly believed that capital accumulation inevitably leads to increases in employment and wages, that commercial exchange leads automatically to moral behavior and that a free market without restrictions would restrain big merchants and manufacturers while benefiting employees and consumers.[106] What appears to us today as extraordinary naïveté is ameliorated by the fact that Smith wrote at the dawn of the Industrial Revolution; that such platitudes are repeated with a straight face today is of an altogether different motivation.

Smith's regard for working people, however well intentioned, reflected that of an elite member of society. His opinion of working people can be glimpsed in this extract: "In mercantile and manufacturing towns where the inferior ranks of people are chiefly maintained by the employment of capital, they are in general industrious, sober and thriving."[107] Modern concepts of noblesse oblige were already taking shape in the eighteenth century.

Modern capitalist monoculture seems to have been prefigured at this time as well. Smith's contemporary and rival, the economist James Steuart, believed that the military-barracks culture of ancient Sparta represented the ideal society, writing that the emerging world of industry and trade promised the same "utopia." Steuart wrote:

> The whole republic was continually gathered together in bodies, and their studies, their occupations and their amusements, were the same. One taste was universal; and the young and the old being constantly together, the first under the immediate inspection and authority of the latter, the same sentiments were transmitted from generation to generation. The Spartans were so pleased, and so satisfied with their situation, that they despised the manners of every other nation. If this does not transmit an idea of happiness, I am at a loss to form one. Security, ease, and happiness, therefore, are not inseparable concomitants of trade and industry.[108]

These ideas have been further refined by modern corporate culture's public relations techniques so that individual consumers are bombarded with messages celebrating their uniqueness at the same time they are inundated with messages to consume the same mass-produced products as their peers; the drive to make one consumerist taste universal must be obscured with continual affirmations of individual choice.

Steuart is largely forgotten today, completely eclipsed by Smith, although his work is not without influence. The work of their era's "classical" economics, in particular Smith's "invisible hand," has developed into modern neoclassical economics. Smith, for example, believed that commodities have "natural" prices; although changes in supply and demand will cause price fluctuations, these are temporary deviations from the natural price.[109] He believed that workers will be paid commensurate with what they contribute toward what society wants, manufacturers will produce only what is desired and prices will always quickly revert to natural levels because competition is a built-in regulator that keeps the economy in balance.[110]

What Smith did not trouble himself with is how workers would always be paid their full value if employers "have the advantage" and can "force the [workers] into compliance with their terms." Neoclassical economists have not strained themselves pondering how it is that unemployment, boom/bust business cycles, crises of overproduction, inflation and persistent price imbalances (none of which should exist according to their theories) are such persistent features of capitalism. Pinning blame on scapegoats such as regulation or immigrants is the usual method of dealing with these "anomalies."

Neoclassical economics, and capitalist ideology, which flows from that body of work, treats all economic activity as a simple exchange of freely acting, mutually benefiting, equal firms and households in a market that automatically, through an "invisible hand," self-adjusts and self-regulates to equilibrium.[111] Households and firms are considered only as market agents, never as part of a social system, and because the system is assumed to consistently revert to equilibrium, there is no conflict.[112]

This obfuscation masks both the exploitation and hierarchy inherent in capitalism and serves as a convenient ideology that hides the exploitation, erases any recognition of conflict and makes the hierarchy appear as a "natural" order so obvious there is no need to pay attention to it.

The nature of the structure that has been built up by the capitalist system doesn't at all preclude that most capitalists genuinely believe their propaganda. And, ultimately, if exploitation and hierarchy are inherent in capitalism, then it does us little good to fixate on any individual capitalist or to make moral judgments about this or that capitalist. We may well have good reason to see the greedy exploiter as an immoral character, but the immoral character is able to act in such a way only within a particular system. Replacing a specific immoral character will solve very little, if anything at all, because another person will step into the role and receive the same benefits deriving from the privilege of extracting surplus value. It is the impersonality and normal functioning of the system, not specific personalities, that drive exploitation.

That does not mean that personalities have no effect on the capitalist system. Modern-day large corporations did not grow like plants, but were built under the leadership of specific personalities. Many made lasting contributions, good and bad (although the good, such as libraries, hospitals and charitable giving, typically represents a minuscule portion of what they extracted in the first place as surplus value), but the wealth that enabled them to do so was accumulated because particular personality traits such as greed and competitive drive were so heavily rewarded.

Capitalism, by virtue of its dynamism, is therefore also very elastic. The dynamic growth of the system (through the introduction of machinery and new production techniques, but also through expansion and imperialism) has enabled higher money wages and more consumer goods than humanity has ever seen (for some). The spaces within the modern capitalist republic have provided openings for social movements that have improved the lives of those not at the top rungs of the capitalist hierarchy.

The contradictions here, however, should be noted. The higher wages are replaced by lower wages and structural unemployment when competitive pressures convert traditional imperialism into corporate globalization, eroding the manufacturing base and thereby making the cornucopia of consumer goods unaffordable. Moreover, the democratic spaces for social movements were never designed into the capitalist system, but are openings that could be taken advantage of because of the nature of the state machinery that is necessary to adjudicate the persistent differences and conflicts among the capitalist class.

Democracy was seen as incompatible with capitalism for most of the system's existence—we've already seen the force that was necessary to bring the system into being and the force necessary to expand it. Smith and another influential classical economist, David Ricardo, among many others, opposed universal suffrage. Ricardo was prepared to extend suffrage only "to that part of them [the citizenry] which cannot be supposed to have an interest in overturning the right to property."[113]

Smith's reluctance seemed to be rooted in his honest assessment of how few are able to enjoy that right to property: "For one very rich man, there must be at least five hundred poor, who are often driven by want, and prompted by envy, to invade his possessions."[114] Not long afterward, the influential British politician and writer Thomas Babington Macaulay said universal suffrage would be "the end of property and thus of all civilization."[115] (Again, "property" refers to the means of production, not personal possessions.)

Higher pay, for a time, is not necessarily inconsistent with the flow of wealth to the top because increased productivity makes possible both increased rates of exploitation and increased income for wage earners at the same time—in fact, a study showed that precisely this pattern did happen in Germany, Sweden, the United Kingdom and the United States for the overall period of 1895 to 1960.[116] This means that, despite higher wages, employees nonetheless were receiving smaller portions of the value of what they produced. Since the 1970s, moreover, wages have stagnated or fallen in many countries at the same time that productivity continues to increase—essentially, all productivity gains have been taken by capitalists, and an increasing share of surplus value diverted to financiers.

Increased productivity is one method to keep the system functioning; another is expansion. There are physical limits to how much productivity can be increased, however—in the long run, the capitalist has no alternative to growing bigger. This can be achieved through defeating the competition, thereby taking more market share, but there can be only so much market to supply. The capitalist enterprise, then, must turn to expanding the market—the remainder of a national territory that has not already been covered, and then on to other countries.

Rosa Luxemburg, the German theorist who dissected German social democracy's drift toward capitulation to war in the years leading up to World War I, also demonstrated the inevitably of imperialism as the capitalist system continued to expand. Capitalists use their profits both for personal consumption and to invest in further production, and as production is expanded some of the production is in excess of what the total market of capitalists, workers and all other strata can consume, Luxemburg wrote.[117] With nobody remaining who is able to buy this excess production, it must be disposed of through penetration into new areas, and this need for expansion results in capitalist enterprises creating new markets by moving into non-capitalist areas.[118] Competition mandates growth—a capitalist that doesn't expand risks being run out of business by competitors who do. The competitor who successfully expands accumulates more through an expanded market and the greater productivity that derives from economy of scale and an enhanced ability to finance new production techniques.

Luxemburg's study of imperialism, interestingly, was shouted down in the pages of German social democratic newspapers by party leaders. That was because she used her development of the idea of imperialism to point out also the ossification of the party as it made one concession after another to German militarism, a process that provided cover to bloody military conquests in Africa and China and culminated in the party's support of World War I—all of which served to strengthen greatly the power and security of Germany's capitalists.

Not mincing words, Luxemburg wrote, nearly a century ago:

> [T]he apparent theoretical "expert knowledge" and infallibility of official [German] Marxism, which blessed every practice of the movement, turned out to be a grandiose façade hiding its inner insecurity and inability to act behind intolerant and insolent dogmatism. The sad routine moving along the old tracks of the "tried and tested tactics," i.e., nothing but parliamentarism, corresponded to the theoretical epigons who clung to the master's formula whilst renouncing the living spirit of his teachings.[119]

The process of imperialism is more advanced today, and more subtle. The mid-twentieth-century uprisings of colonized people across the world ended formal colonialization (with a few exceptions) but ushered in the era of the multilateral financial institution. Today, markets rarely are expanded through military conquests but instead through "structural adjustment programs" imposed by the World Bank, the International Monetary Fund and similar lending organizations controlled by the advanced capitalist countries. But capital's expansion will ultimately reach its limits—when capitalism has penetrated into every corner of the world, there will be nowhere else to expand: The only way to generate more profits will be to reduce wages and benefits.

Physical limits to the level that productivity can be raised further emphasize the necessity for capitalists to cut costs in order to increase profits. Ultimately, there will be a point where no more reductions can be tolerated, because working people will be driven to fight back because their living standards will have been reduced to intolerably low levels, and if wages are driven so low that increasingly smaller portions of production can be bought with wages, there will be overproduction that can't be sold, and production will collapse from a lack of buyers. The limits of the system will have been reached, just as limits were reached in earlier systems.

Intermediate crises, long before that final limit is reached, are a regular feature of capitalist economies. Because there is no mechanism to determine social need, products of all sorts are produced until there is a glut, causing prices to fall and capitalists to reduce production through mass layoffs and shutting down facilities—in essence, destroying productive capacity until shrinking inventories create shortages that again stimulate demand. Layered over this dynamic is the deprivation created by the accumulation of capital into fewer hands.

"The process of exploitation leaves purchasing power in the hands of a proletariat that enables it to purchase only an inadequate portion of the total products just turned out," the economist John G. Gurley wrote.

> The large remainder of the output must be fashioned and purchased by capitalists as part of the accumulation process. There is a continual threat, therefore, of too heavy a burden being placed on capitalist accumulation, a "burden" that stems from the exploitation of labor…"Underconsumption" does not indicate that during phases of rapid accumulation

> and prosperity [the "boom" portion of the business cycle] wages are depressed...[T]he opposite occurs. But, while workers in these exhilaration phases are thus entitled to raise their consumption levels somewhat [because of their increased wages], it is never enough to lighten significantly the "burden" on the capitalist class, which is soon made intolerable by a falling rate of profit. Thus, accumulation slows down until the previously favorable conditions for capitalists have been restored; and this involves principally the destruction of capital values and the replenishment of the reserve army of labor.[120]

In other words, offices and factories are shut down and employees are sent to the unemployment office.

The deprivations engendered by the accumulation process are by no means limited to the economic. Those deprived see their choices in life constrained "to the point where intellect, creativity, compassion, and commitment are stunted or destroyed," writes an institutionalist economist, Marc Tool. (Institutional economics is a school that believes economic and social behaviors are cultural phenomena, conditioned by cultural parameters, and incorporates a focus on the deployment and concentration of power, in particular the role of institutions in shaping economic behavior.) "We then live in a layered or tiered community suffering from elitism and privation alike. This would appear to be inefficiency of really monumental proportions."[121] Tool argues that competitive market economies are inefficient because they provide no way for wants and preferences to be appraised, leaving it instead to media advertising to create demand artificially, and that markets fail to address the problems of gross income inequality, creating the problems noted above.[122]

## Conceptualizations of the sociological barriers to democracy under capitalism

This system couldn't continue to endure unless it continued to retain a significant level of popular support. The corporation has become the dominant player in all advanced capitalist countries, and the firmer the grip capitalism has on a given country the greater the power of corporations.

A modern advanced capitalist country has a great many institutions other than the corporate—presumably, these institutions have different interests and ideas. Yet the idea that everything should be "run like a business" seems to become ever more pervasive. Political parties win elections based on the premise that they will run government like a business. Most people do not like the job they are forced to go to every day, so presumably are not necessarily enamored of the corporate form. Yet this ideology is incessantly promoted, across society. Where does this state of affairs come from?

No single answer could suffice, and an ideology that becomes dominant in a formally democratic society has to rest on multiple pillars, nor can it be seen as being imposed by force. Such an ideology has to be seen as a natural development so that its often subtle reinforcements recede almost to the background. This environment provides fertile soil for the rise of aggressive mass media outlets that blare harsh versions of nationalism ("patriotism") and unyielding versions of capitalist economic relations as part of a regular scapegoating of minority groups or opposing political philosophies, but such ham-fisted propaganda can be effective only to (or, more likely, serve to provide reinforcement for) a small number of maleducated holders of extremist views.

It is frequently argued that, although only a tiny minority are swayed by these sorts of ravings, it makes less extreme and less loud versions of orthodox corporate capitalism or relatively moderate Right-wing viewpoints seem "rational" in comparison, and therefore serves to elevate capitalist orthodoxy. That view seems too deterministic—ranting is still ranting—and the dissemination and acceptance of that orthodoxy must be accomplished in more subtle and diffuse ways.

One of the pillars on which mass acceptance of an ideology rests is sociology. Ideas found useful by elites within a society can be given a scientific veneer by "experts" and given popular form through media personalities. These ideas don't have to be, and sometimes aren't, overtly propagated. Nor must they directly promote the interests of economic elites; ideas can simply substitute idiosyncratic, individualistic or other reasons for social outcomes in place of rigorous structural analysis. Such ideas simply have to lead to useful applications for powerful social groups.

Two broad schools of sociology and psychology have been used to help shape consciousness in developed capitalist countries. One, with roots in nineteenth-century upper-class revulsion against popular uprisings, became in the twentieth century grounded in Freudian psychology and theories of irrationality. The other school, with roots sunk by the German sociologist Max Weber, asserts that consciousness exists only at the individual level.

The first of these two schools was based originally on an idea that mental function is bifurcated into emotional and intellectual, and that the ideas of a dominant class are rational and intellectual while ideas from elsewhere are irrational and emotional.[123] (This same set of labels was just as easily applied to majority/minority racial or national groups and to men/women, making it a most effective divide-and-conquer tool.) The work of Sigmund Freud later provided a supposed "scientific" basis for this specious duality: Freudian psychology asserts that destructive, selfish human nature is held in check by social constraints; that the social, as opposed to the individual, is rational; and that a separately established intellect battles with the unconscious.[124]

This basic concept has produced numerous offshoots. One is a body of work that claims that political ideas are associated with varying degrees of irrationality, perhaps most famously in the view that pathological movements such as fascism arise from the unconscious.[125] Authoritarian nationalism, including extreme manifestations such as fascism, surely is irrational, but such movements nonetheless have a "rational" underpinning in the sense that they serve the interests of powerful segments of a society, whether they are created by the powerful interests directly or powerful interests find ways of first co-opting and then strengthening movements that develop at the grassroots level.

Grounding these types of movements in personal psychoses obscures completely that fascism, for example, is a dictatorship that is established through, and maintained with, terror on behalf of big business when capitalists can no longer maintain profits and control within a democratic system, and which uses nationalism, among other ideologies and symbols, to create a social base that is mobilized in its support but is badly misled since the fascist dictatorship acts directly against the interest of this social base.

In part this underpinning can be obscured because fascism is a dictatorship *for* big business, not *by* big business—fascist propaganda often sounds populist in its condemnations of bankers or "unpatriotic" big business, but such condemnations are scapegoating in the service of creating a misled mass movement. The leadership of a fascist movement shows its true colors as soon as it gains power, but because huge amounts of money have been poured into a movement led by megalomaniacs it remains independent of the capitalists who earlier became its financiers at the same time that its dictatorial policies directly serve the interests of those capitalists.

It should not be surprising that economics plays such a large role. Even Erich Fromm, who developed a rigorous and challenging body of work that stressed the psychological underpinnings driving authoritarian movements, had no hesitation in resting his theory on an economic foundation. Fromm, in his classic work *Escape from Freedom*, wrote that "the mode of life, as it is determined for the individual by peculiarity of an economic system, becomes the primary factor in determining his whole character structure, because the imperative need for self-preservation forces him to accept the conditions under which he lives."[126] That does not mean that psychological factors are not significant—they are—but they are not wholly independent nor properly dismissed as simply "irrational" and therefore outside normal society.

Another application of Freudian psychology was its use in the creation of the modern consumer. Freud sought to locate the conflict between industrial society and individuals in the "fixed nature" of individuals, thereby precluding any social or political transformation that could alter the existing social order—and because Freudian psychology's aim was to benefit "civilization," it was oriented toward adapting the individual to the prevailing social order.[127]

By the 1920s, the industrialists and financiers who dominated US society sought to create a consumer society. Such a development would provide stimulus to corporate profits through the increase of commerce from heightened consumer spending, substitute the "freedom" of buying mass-produced products for freedom of choice in political or social life, and atomize society. A nephew of Freud, Edward Bernays, is prominent among those who helped to lay the foundation for modern consumer society.

Bernays, in an influential book he wrote in 1928, when the process was already under way, made little attempt to disguise this project. The first paragraph of his book, unambiguously titled *Propaganda*, reads: "The conscious and intelligent manipulation of the organized habits and opinions of the masses is an important element in democratic society. Those who manipulate this unseen mechanism of society constitute an invisible government which is the true ruling power of our country."[128] The elitist view of society that underpins Bernays' project was put to use by the most powerful capitalists of this time. Bernays himself believed that the "intelligent few" are tasked with influencing and directing the attitudes of a public that possesses little ability to understand or act upon the world in which they live.[129]

Bernays put his manipulative theories into action by persuading a group of debutantes to hide cigarettes while walking in a New York Easter Day parade, then lighting up and smoking them simultaneously at a signal.[130] This was in the 1920s, when social mores strictly frowned upon women smoking; the sight of these women smoking, captured in newspaper photographs, caused a national sensation and definitively smashed social mores that had opposed women smoking—and increased cigarette sales, the goal of the demonstration. Soon, in 1928, Herbert Hoover would be elected president of the United States. Hoover cemented his place in history as the cold-hearted head of state who would not lift a finger to help working people during the Great Depression. After his election, Hoover told a group of advertisers and public relations agents: "You have taken over the job of creating desire and have transformed people into constantly moving happiness machines. Machines which have become the key to economic progress."[131]

Hoover, who had served as secretary of commerce for the previous two presidents, carrying out austerity policies, had articulated a pithy phrase summarizing the creation of a controlled society as envisioned by industrial and financial elites.

Such a "concept of managing the masses takes the idea of democracy and turns it into a palliative, turns it into giving people some kind of feel-good medication that will respond to an immediate pain or immediate yearning but will not alter the objective circumstances one iota," said Stuart Ewen, a social scientist who has written several books on public relations and the manufacturing of consumerist society, in an interview for the BBC documentary *Century of the Self*. "The idea of democracy at its heart was about changing the relations of power that had governed the world for so long; and Bernays' concept of democracy was one of maintaining the relations of power, even if it meant one needed to stimulate the psychological lives of the public. And in fact in his mind this was what was necessary. That if you can keep stimulating the irrational self, then leadership can go on doing what it wants to do."[132]

Democracy is thereby reduced to an empty slogan that does not touch in any way the prevailing alignments of power.

"It's not that the people are in charge, but that the people's desires are in charge," Ewen said. "The people are not in charge; the people exercise no decision-making power within this environment. So democracy is reduced from something that assumes an active citizenry to the idea of the public as passive consumers driven primarily by instinctual or unconscious desires and if you can in fact trigger those needs and desires you can get what you want from them."[133]

Still another application of Freudian psychology is to provide a basis on which to divide and conquer. Bernays' use of Freudian psychology to convince women they would be "empowered" by smoking cigarettes contains an extra edge because of the deep sexism of Freud. Just as Freudianism saw industrial society—and, implicitly, its sharp class divisions—as natural and immutable, it also believed that women were "naturally" inferior to men. The individual problems of women were a byproduct of "natural" and unchangeable forces, and psychology therefore sought to help the patient "adjust" to these "natural" social conditions, thereby accepting their domination.[134]

A school that claims that broad numbers of people are irrational is useful since it is a short step to pronouncing ideas coming from supposedly irrational people as irrational.

Not all of modern psychology derives from artificially created ideas of irrationality and inferiority. The second broad school of sociology and psychology that has helped to shape consciousness, with the roots going back to Weber, rejects the idea that rationality is restricted to privileged people or classes, but asserts that rationality is confined to individuals—a class can have no clearly defined interest or collective consciousness.[135] Class consciousness is seen as ambiguous; any class interest that may exist is nothing more than an amalgam of individual interests at a given moment and cannot have an objective referent, nor can a class have intrinsic interests that can be defined.[136] Society is said to be composed of individuals with no permanent common interests—this is an ideology useful in terms of providing a basis for the atomization of society.

Very much in the tradition of nineteenth-century Enlightenment thinking, Weber believed that modern industrial development under capitalism brought efficiency through organization, bureaucracy and rationalization, to the point of writing glowing tributes to the efficient structures created by bureaucratic organization. On the other hand, Weber also believed that scientific development and the pace of modern life lead to social fragmentation that creates a world in which individuals can act only on their own impulses and convictions.

Another pioneer of this line of thought was the US physician George Miller Beard. Terming physical ailments such as fatigue, insomnia and depression as "nervousness," Beard offered a simple idea as to the root causes: "The modern differ from the ancient civilizations mainly in these five elements—steam power, the periodical press, the telegraph, the sciences and the mental activity of women. When civilization, plus these five factors, invades any nation, it must carry nervousness and nervous diseases along with it."[137] Medical professionals holding to these concepts believed that medicine could devise "healing" therapies to harmonize individuals with society—material conditions do not control individual lives, and there are no inherent divisions or conflicts within society or individuals, so therefore the task of medicine is to help patients reintegrate with society.[138]

Although this school begins from a standpoint very different from Freudianism, it, too, contains seeds of social control. An alienated individual, in contrast to theories derived from Freud, is rational for being alienated, but nonetheless must be adapted to the "natural" social structure. And note that one of Beard's five modern dangers was the "mental activity of women." That anachronistic idea was not left behind in the nineteenth century, evolving decades later into psychological concepts that sought to blame women for the subordinate roles that are reserved for them, or for staying in abusive or destructive relationships, thereby obscuring the social and economic roots of gender oppression. Such viewpoints continue to be disseminated widely by corporate-dominated mass culture.

These ideas developed in sometimes very different directions. One offshoot is the modern "New Age" movement, which, although well-meaning, promotes the idea that all change comes from within an individual while leaving the political, social and economic structure of capitalist society completely untouched. A much different offshoot, however, provided the underpinning for modern uses of physical and mental torture. Beard's most famous work was straightforwardly titled *The Medical and Surgical Uses of Electricity*, published in 1872. This book became such a standard that ten editions were eventually printed. Beard's co-author was Alphonse D. Rockwell, whom history better remembers as the inventor of the electric chair, which he promoted as a more "humane" method of execution than hanging. Beard, Rockwell and others were convinced that electroshock was one of the therapies that could "cure" patients of their "nervousness."

Electroshock therapy has a dark history, but perhaps none darker than the tortures inflicted by a Canadian psychiatrist in the 1950s and 1960s named Ewan Cameron. A steady stream of patients, mainly young women, were sent to Cameron by their regular doctors for treatment for anxiety or depression. Cameron, however, was interested in conducting experiments in brainwashing techniques and in erasing minds in order to rebuild new personalities—for which he received ample funding from the United States Central Intelligence Agency.[139] The CIA was interested in Cameron's work as part of its own extensive research into brainwashing and torture techniques. Cameron drugged his non-consenting patients with LSD, angel dust and other hallucinogenic drugs, kept them for weeks or months in medically induced comas, subjected them to sensory deprivation, and administered electric shocks dozens or hundreds of times at intensities far above the very lax standards of the day, all in an effort to reduce his patients to a state of infancy.[140]

Far from hiding what he was doing, Cameron regularly published his results in the leading psychiatric journals of his day. He conducted these Nazi-like experiments in a secret torture lab at McGill University in Montréal, one of Canada's leading universities, and he served as the head of the American, Canadian and World psychiatric associations. Cameron would play tape-recorded messages to his victims: "With patients shocked and drugged into an almost vegetative state, they could do nothing but listen to the messages—for sixteen to twenty hours a day for weeks; in one case, Cameron played a message continuously for 101 days," reported Naomi Klein in a lengthy discussion of these experiments in her book *The Shock Doctrine*.[141]

This "research" was useless—such techniques destroyed their victims physically and mentally, but could not put them back together—and was eventually exposed. But the corporate-dominated mass media played its usual role, mocking the CIA for experimenting with acid trips while ignoring the larger picture and the inhumanity of the project. "The CIA, for its part, actively encouraged this narrative, much preferring to be mocked as bumbling sci-fi buffoons than for having funded a torture laboratory at a respected university," Klein wrote.[142]

The fact that a leading Canadian university eagerly took part in such experiments provides a reminder that junior members of the capitalist world aren't, as their governments frequently imply, unwillingly swept along by the tidal forces of more powerful neighbors, but in fact are full participants in the dirty work required to maintain capitalism. France, for example, was more than capable of using psychiatry and torture in its ultimately failed attempt to put down Algerian resistance in the 1950s. The French psychiatric establishment presented as "scientifically proved" that Algerians are savage killers unable to suppress their impulses; when Algerians landed in hospitals they would be lectured that there are no such people as Algerians and that Algeria can only be French—treating their resistance to colonialism as a pathology to be cured.[143]

Thus, Franz Fanon, a psychologist who worked in Algeria at this time, later wrote in his classic work *The Wretched of the Earth*: "Consequently, the Algerian doctors who graduated from the Faculty of Algiers were forced to hear and learn that the Algerian is a born criminal."[144] A World Health Organization doctor termed the 1950s uprising against British rule in Kenya "the expression of an unconscious frustration complex whose recurrence could be scientifically treated by radical psychologically appropriate methods."[145] Any rebellion against oppression, no matter how draconian the tactics of the dominant power, is dismissed as insanity—the conclusion the school of individualism reaches when taken to its end.

Both the broad schools sketched above also provide an example of the appearance of free debate in capitalist society. These two schools appear to be at odds: One makes sweeping generalizations about emotionality and rationality and the other rejects such generalizations. But both dismiss the idea of social solidarity: the first rejects the idea as "irrational" and the second as "impossible."

From two directions come ideological tools to reduce citizens to mere consumers. Because consuming is a matter of individual taste, or perhaps a family matter, there is no need for people to organize—there are no common interests to rally around, nor should any such ideas be taken seriously.

An atomized society is easily dominated by powerful institutions. These institutions can vary by the type of national organization. The Soviet Union, as we saw in Chapter 5, became a society dominated by its governmental and industrial bureaucracies (collectively, the "nomenklatura"). Political force was the only way for the nomenklatura to retain power in Soviet-style countries because they did not own the means of production—they enjoyed privileges by virtue of their high positions in the sole legal party and their *management* of state property. Economic enterprises were not their possessions and could not be used to extract personal wealth that in turn is leveraged into personal control; as a consequence, the nomenklatura's privileges were minuscule compared to those of a capitalist class.

Nomenklatura dominance was institutional and because political force was the glue that enabled the nomenklatura to maintain their management of state property, that force could not be disguised. The mass media, for example, was unambiguously controlled by the sole legal party. A capitalist elite, in contrast, can wield power in a much less direct manner. A capitalist democracy does not have a single institution that exerts direct power and social control similar to a Soviet-style nomenklatura, but it nonetheless possesses dominant institutions: corporations.

This power is institutional, but here the institutions are at the service of the powerful. No single person, nor any secret group, can sit atop this system (even allowing for the fact that different personalities possess widely differing levels of desire to directly leverage money into political power) because there is a multitude of institutions. No single company or industry holds permanent sway over other companies or industries, and different companies and industries have different interests. But these differentiated interests, including those fueled by competition, are subsumed within the overall system in which they all operate. The members of the capitalist class that controls these competitive, separate corporate institutions have a decisive interlocking interest in maintaining the system that enables their domination and wealth.

Individual corporations are disposable; they are readily merged, bought, sold or broken up according to short-term needs for immediate profit by industrialists or financiers, or at the behest of speculators. It is the collective power concentrated by the corporate form that is sufficiently strong to constitute an often decisive voice—they attain immense wealth and size at the same time that their legal status as "persons" is amplified by their lack of the finite lifespan to which human beings are subject. The immense concentration of wealth, gigantic size, geographic reach and ability to outlive humans and therefore continue to accumulate indefinitely enables corporations to tower over society, yet corporations remain institutions in the service of the class that controls them.

Educational, military, religious and other institutions are "linked to the dominant economic institution, the corporation, in a kind of means-end continuum," writes the institutionalist economist William M. Dugger. "That is, the corporation uses other institutions as a means for its own ends. This is important, because it provides the first glimpse at the true source of power."[146] Dugger wrote those words in 1980, as Reaganism and Thatcherism were just beginning the process of more firmly tightening corporate hegemony—these doctrines themselves, products of Chicago School economic ideology, aggravated, rather than created, corporate power in the sense that it is experienced today. This power imbalance is most acute in the United

States, but is the model that US officials attempt to export to other countries, and serves as a model for corporate executives around the world.

Educational institutions are being reduced to job-training facilities, to the point where the main purpose even at the university level is to sort out students and prepare them for life in corporate jobs.[147] University presidents and board members are increasingly prominent business leaders who seek to make educational institutions more "business-like"; pursuit of knowledge for personal intellectual enrichment is almost an afterthought. Educational initiatives at all levels are increasingly funded directly by corporate elites. Instead of education being funded by the public through accountable institutions managed by education professionals, it is instead adapted to the needs of corporate-elite donors who seek to produce students grounded in technical skills without exposure to the types of courses that encourage creative or independent thinking.

This process is well under way in the US, where corporate funders increasingly dictate education policy; three dominant funds, each reflecting the nearly identical will of billionaire couples or families, directly place their followers in superintendent positions and condition funding elsewhere on their dictating school leaderships.[148]

Militaries in capitalist countries frequently function as enforcers of corporate prerogatives in weaker countries; militaries also underwrite corporate and university research and development, and are heavy buyers of corporate products.[149] We saw numerous examples of corporate power at work in chapters 1, 4 and 5. It is sufficient to illustrate this point by quoting the US general Smedly Butler, a highly decorated officer, who wrote the following in the 1930s: "I spent thirty three years and four months [in] the Marine Corps…During that period I spent most of my time being a high-class muscle man for Big Business, for Wall Street and for bankers. In short, I was a racketeer for capitalism."[150]

Families become part of this institutional pattern because parents are expected to instill behavior in their children so that they will conform to corporate expectations on becoming adults, and politics cannot be anything but a significant corporate transmission belt because corporations provide campaign donations and give jobs to office holders when they leave office.[151] The modern corporation also employs an army of lobbyists to influence politicians' thinking. Corporate executives additionally create a network of auxiliary institutions such as research centers and "think tanks" that can leverage lavish funding to disseminate class ideology through various channels. Churches, too, become a part of this process; political coalitions between the religious Right and big business reinforce each other. Powerful ministers are only too happy to back big business candidates in exchange for influence over social legislation, and many of these ministers use their positions of influence over their followers to enrich themselves.

The hegemony of corporate ideas, of the concept of running other institutions "like a business," leads to emulation on the part of leaders of other institutions, business leaders taking over leadership roles in other institutions, and an increased ability of corporate institutions to manipulate a capitalist society's symbols and historical heritage to suit corporate interests.[152] As in any other top-down, hierarchal institution, those who conform to the corporate mold are the ones who will someday rise to the top positions. Corporate institutions are competitors with sometimes sharply different interests (in terms of antagonisms between suppliers and buyers of raw materials and component parts; in divergence of the optimum conditions sought by different industries; and the ever-present fierce fight over the sharing of profits between industrialists and financiers) yet these conflicts and antagonisms are contained within the perpetuation of the system within which they operate. Very similar dominant values become self-perpetuating, and as this collective power grows, it will steadily be wielded in harder forms in the absence of serious countervailing pressures in the form of mass movements.

The similarity of these dominant values also reflects a class interest—capitalists fight among themselves over money, but agree their class should have as much as can be extracted. Corporations provide the means by which industrialists and financiers generate the surplus value that is confiscated from working people and converted into their fortunes. This or that company may disappear, but the web of institutions remains in place; corporate power continues as older executives inevitably retire and are replaced by younger executives in the same mold.

Corporate ownership of mass communications (these, too, are subject to larger competitors swallowing the smaller) is another factor in the spread of corporate ideology. Most large, influential broadcast stations and print publications are owned by large corporations, and a typical small-city newspaper is owned by a prominent local businessperson if it is not owned by a large corporation. Powerful corporate interests appoint the top editors and managers of their media properties—these mass media decision-makers are men and women who already see the world through the prism of dominant ideologies, and those ideologies will be reflected in the way that news stories are covered. Those ideologies are also reflected in indirect ways—pressure to increase readership or viewership easily leads to pandering to perceived (and sometimes manufactured) consumer interests such as wall-to-wall coverage of celebrity gossip and exhaustive coverage of sports teams simultaneous with the shrinking of news sections.

Dominant capitalist ideologies have as one of their purposes a goal of keeping capitalist societies atomized: Encouraging people to think of themselves as consumers serves business elites' political goals of dampening the potential of working people to organize themselves at the same time it encourages increased buying of consumer products. There is no need for any conspiracy. Ideas that there is some sort of coordination among mass media owners to project a common message should be laughed at—competitive pressures alone prevent any such collusion. It is enough that corporate-inspired ideologies pervade a society and that corporate ownership ensures that decision-making positions are filled with those who hold to some variant of prevailing ideologies or are inclined to "play it safe" by cautiously remaining within "acceptable" boundaries.

The mass media will then simply reflect these dominant ideologies, and continual repetition through multiple mass media outlets reinforces the ideologies, making them more pervasive until the emergence of a significant countervailing pressure. The very competitive nature of mass media ownership helps dominant ideologies prevail—if so many different outlets report the same news item in a nearly identical way, that "spin" can easily gain wide acceptance. Or if stories are reported differently by competing media outlets, but with the same dominant set of presumptions underlying them, those dominant presumptions, products of ideologies widely propagated by elite institutions, similarly serve as ideological reinforcement.

The persistence with which stories are reported is another reinforcement—stories that serve, or can be manipulated, to uphold dominant ideologies can be covered for long periods of time with small developments creating opportunities to create fresh reports at the same time that stories that are ideologically inconvenient are reported briefly, often without context, then quickly dropped.

One well-documented example will provide an illustration—coverage by elite media of Jerzy Popieluszko, a pro-Solidarity priest in Poland murdered in 1984 by Polish secret policemen in contrast to coverage of priests and other church personnel murdered in US-backed Latin American dictatorships. The study of four US media outlets that then often set the tone for the press—the most influential newspaper, the two main news magazines and the most authoritative television news broadcaster—found 140 articles/broadcasts on Popieluszko and 11 articles/broadcasts on 23 victims in Guatemala during a period that overlapped with Popieluszko's murder; the newspaper ran ten front-page articles on Popieluszko, none on the others.[153]

The articles on Popieluszko routinely featured graphic descriptions of the details of his murder and consistently tied his murder to Polish communist authorities despite the fact that the murderers were swiftly arrested and found guilty in a fully open trial.[154] By contrast, only four of the 23 Guatemalan victims had their names mentioned in any news account, little detail was offered for any of these murders, no remark was made concerning the fact that no arrests were made in any of these cases, nor was US material support of the Guatemalan government that was behind the murders once mentioned.[155]

Nothing in the prevailing situation precludes energetic debate in capitalist mass media within the parameters set by prevailing ideological interpretations. Similar to the two sociological schools that both provided a basis to discourage social solidarity, ideas that directly challenge corporate orthodoxy can be excluded at the same time that a debate among two or more "acceptable" ideas rages. To provide an example, at the end of the 1990s a strong debate played out in the mass media outlets of the United States concerning the Vietnam War.

This debate had all the appearances of a serious dissection of a bloody, deeply divisive blot on US history. But although the debate was heated and lively, it was only between two "acceptable" viewpoints—an honorable effort that tragically failed or a well-intentioned but flawed effort that should not have been undertaken if the US was not going to be "serious" about fighting. Left out were the widely held views that the war should never have been fought because it was a war to extend US hegemony or that the US simply had no business fighting in someone else's civil war.

Further, the first "acceptable" viewpoint implied, and the second explicitly stated, that the US didn't really fight hard to win the war, ignoring the actual intensive level of the US war effort in which most of North Vietnam's larger cities were reduced to rubble, much of the farming land was destroyed and 3 million Vietnamese were killed. Thus there was all the appearance of a free and open media at the same time that the media obscured the facts.

In countries in which the media is controlled by the government, it is easy for people to disregard what they read or hear because it is all coming from the same source, even when there is some play for different opinions. A system in which the mass media is believed to be independent is far more effective at suffusing a society with an ideology. Such a system is not the result of some sort of conspiracy or a conscious plan; it is simply a natural outgrowth of corporate institutions growing so powerful at the expense of all other institutions.

## Conceptualizations of the financial barriers to democracy under capitalism

Institutional dominance can push an ideology to extremes; indeed, without popular pressure in the form of mass movements strong enough to push back, an ideology serving the powerful will be pushed to extremes. It is a common mistake, even among people who are strongly critical of capitalism, to believe that Chicago School or neoliberal economics is the product of a cabal or represents some sort of "mutant" capitalism. Consider the history of capitalism: Force and dominance were its handmaidens from the beginning.

A series of ideologies has justified domination. Chicago School economics is simply a continuation of a long line of such ideologies—and it is the inevitable product of a system in which a dominant class seeks to leverage its power into yet more power, dominance and money. And because corporate institutions' ideologies can be, and are, propagated through other institutions, ideologies celebrating the rule of capitalists and financiers are promoted through a variety of outlets, in particular through schools and the mass media.

Most of this history required the support of the nation-state, and an increasingly confident bourgeoisie's needs for lowering barriers to trade did not play a small role in the formation of larger European countries. Capitalism is now outgrowing the nation-state, and this development is expressed in the forms of international "free trade" agreements that ban regulation and sustained ideological attacks on government (except for military spending). From this corporate desire to be free of any social constraints arises the ideology that proclaims private enterprise is always superior to government: Governments should sell off any business in which they are involved and privatize essential government services traditionally in the public domain because, whatever it is, private enterprise will do it better and more cheaply. Eventually, it is not enough for government to be run like a business—business should take over as many government functions as possible. This is repeated so often that it has become a mantra unthinkingly repeated and seemingly unquestioned across institutions.

One factor behind this development is the unquestioned belief that nothing could possibly be wrong with capitalist theory and therefore any economic problem is always the result of government interference (the convenient Chicago School device discussed earlier), a mantra that must lead to demands for the destruction of government. This ideology also flows from the need for continual expansion—if growth in existing business is difficult, then one solution is to move into new product lines. If government has previously been performing basic functions (building and running prisons, administering social-benefit payments or managing infrastructure for the supply of water or electricity) then these functions represent expansion opportunities, if a government can be moved to sell them. If the terms of the sale can be manipulated to the buyer's advantage so much the better.

What empirical data is there to support this ideology of mass privatization? In the absence of conclusive data, a common response is to repeat that "government is the problem" in a louder voice. Yet the engines of the global economy during the past two decades, the Internet and World Wide Web, are creations of the US Department of Defense and the European governmental consortium CERN, respectively. More broadly, the results of an exhaustive study of state-owned enterprises do not conform to ideological constructs. The study, by social scientist Andong Zhu, examined the economies of more than 40 nations over four decades (1960s to 1990s), using three sets of data, adding and subtracting a series of measurable variables and applying methodologies to filter out outliers to measure the performance of state-owned enterprises.

The study found that there was a net flow of income from state-owned enterprises to governments—they turned a profit and provided more in the form of taxes, dividends and interest than was given to them in government investment.[156] The flow of money was particularly strong in Latin America and the Caribbean, and increased there in the 1990s from the 1980s.[157] The study also found that the higher the percentage of state-owned enterprises, the greater was the equality in personal income—an unsurprising result deriving from the fact that jobs at state companies typically are more secure and offer higher pay than average private-sector jobs, particularly in developing countries.[158] These results are all the more eye-opening because state-owned enterprises tend to be in the most capital-intensive industries, such as public utilities, mining and transportation—private companies in these industries for the five decades ending in 2000 in the United States consumed fixed capital at rates several times higher than other industries while producing profits considerably lower.[159]

A separate study, carried out by economic historian Angus Maddison, calculates world economic growth at 2.9 percent per year for the period of 1950 to 1973, but only 1.3 percent for 1973 to 1998.[160] The earlier period was a time of widespread state-owned enterprises, while the latter is a time of widespread privatizations. A single statistic cannot be used to draw definitive conclusions, but it is interesting that the "golden age" of privatization and the spread of unrestrained capitalism does not seem to have acted as a stimulant. Many Western European countries dramatically raised standards of living following World War II by nationalizing key industries, which could be managed in part for public benefit rather than solely for private profit.[161]

The high cost of private profit is often hidden, but that cost, often in the form of public subsidies, is nonetheless high. In Chapter 4, we saw how Sandinista policies in Nicaragua steadily led to more subsidies for the country's rich, which benefited the recipients but hurt other Nicaraguans. An ongoing example from the United States provides a dramatic example of the high cost of private profit.

Health care costs in the United States are extraordinarily high. For the sake of the fairest possible comparison, US health care costs will be compared to the average of the three largest economies within the European Union (France, Germany and the United Kingdom) and to Canada, which has more similarities to the US than other countries. Each of those four comparison countries has a health care system run, or tightly regulated, by its government. In this head-to-head comparison, health spending per capita in the US was double those four countries from 1990 to 2010, despite the US having a nearly equal number of physicians per capita and only two-thirds of available acute beds and of hospital admissions per capita.[162]

High administrative costs (i.e. inefficiency and excessive

corporate profits) on the part of for-profit health maintenance organizations (HMOs) are some of the reason for the disparity. HMOs take 19 percent of revenue for overhead, as opposed to 3 percent in the US government's Medicare program and 1 percent in Canadian Medicare.[163] Despite the massive transfer of money to private insurance companies by employers and employees, on a per-capita basis government health care spending in the US is higher than total health care spending in Canada.[164] US health care costs that are double those of its closest peer countries amounted to spending an extra $1.15 trillion per year from 2001 to 2010[165] at the same time that 22,000 people died and 700,000 went bankrupt per year as a result of inadequate, or no, health insurance.[166] Those costs are part of the price of capitalism.

Another cost is the financial industry. The economic collapse that began cascading around the world in 2008 is merely the latest installment. Financial bubbles followed by crashes have long been a part of capitalism. "Tulip mania" consumed the Dutch in the 1630s, speculation fueled by the first futures contracts; uncontrolled speculation in the 1710s in the English South Sea Company and the French Company of the Indies led to the collapse of stock in both, a bubble in which short selling was born; an 1830s bubble in US real estate burst when banks stopped making payments; and an 1870s bubble inflated by speculation in railroads and construction in North America and Europe burst when the Vienna stock market crashed, followed by waves of bank failures, to note some of the more well-known examples.

Bubbles occur when financial speculation becomes more profitable than manufacturing products. The amount of money that flows upward to the rich becomes larger than they can use for personal luxury consumption or investment in their businesses; these torrents of money are diverted into increasingly risky pure speculation. Too much money comes to chase too few assets, rapidly bidding up prices until there is no possible revenue stream that can sustain the price of assets bought at inflated levels. Not altogether different from those Warner Brothers cartoons in which the character walks off a cliff, takes several steps suspended in air before looking down, sees there is nothing but air below and then falls, at some point speculators look down and notice they have no support, mass panic commences and prices collapse.

An economic collapse on the scale of what occurred in 2008 is a culmination of a long sequence of events, and this one has roots in the early 1970s, when neoliberal policies began to be adopted. Keynesianism, the belief that capitalism is unstable and requires government intervention in the economy when private enterprise is unable to spend enough to lift it out of a slump, had been in the ascendancy among economists since the 1930s. Sustained organized unrest during that decade caused governments such as the Roosevelt administration to fear the possibility of revolution and, in response, massively increase social spending to dampen that unrest. The unprecedented government spending required to win World War II pulled the West out of the Great Depression, and the United States government continued spending to rebuild Europe and Japan through the Marshall Plan, successfully expanding markets for US products.

The Keynesian compromise was not necessarily what capitalists would have wanted; it was a pragmatic decision—profits could be maintained through expansion of markets and social peace bought. This equilibrium, however, could only be temporary because the new financial center of capitalism, the US, possessed a towering economic dominance following World War II that could not last. When markets can't be expanded at a rate sufficiently robust to maintain or increase profit margins, capitalists cease tolerating paying increased wages.

Ironically, just at the time when the conservative Richard Nixon declared "We are all Keynesians now" is when the tide turned against that school of economic thought. The rebound of Western Europe and Japan eroded US manufacturing dominance, squeezing corporate profits and intensifying competition, and US manufacturers responded by moving production overseas. A steady loss of well-paying jobs became a hammer held above the heads of working people—industrialists found it easier to squeeze their employees.

By the early 1970s, the Nixon administration believed that the Bretton Woods monetary system put in place during World War II no longer sufficiently advantaged the United States despite its currency's centrality within the system cementing US economic suzerainty. Under Bretton Woods, the value of a US dollar was fixed to the price of gold, and the value of all other currencies was pegged to the dollar. Any government could exchange the dollars it held in reserve for US Treasury Department gold on demand. Rising world supplies of dollars and domestic inflation depressed the value of the dollar, causing the Treasury price of gold to be artificially low and thereby making the exchange of dollars for gold at the fixed price an excellent deal for other governments.[167] The Nixon administration refused to adjust the value of the dollar,[168] instead in 1971 pulling the dollar from the gold standard by refusing to continue to exchange foreign-held dollars for gold on demand. Currencies would now float on markets against each other, their values set by speculators rather than by governments, making all but the strongest countries highly vulnerable to financial pressure.

The world's oil-producing states dramatically raised oil prices in 1973. The Nixon administration eliminated US capital controls a year later, encouraged oil producers to park their new glut of dollars in US banks and adopted policies to encourage the banks to lend those deposited dollars to the South.[169] Restrictions limiting cross-border movements of capital were opposed by multinational corporations that had moved production overseas, by speculators in the new currency-exchange markets that blossomed with the breakdown of Bretton Woods and by neoliberal ideologues, creating decisive momentum within the

US for the elimination of capital controls.[170] Private banks quickly became the center of international finance in place of central banks, leading to international dominance of the US and British financial systems and US financial institutions.[171]

Margaret Thatcher in Britain and Ronald Reagan in the US ascended to office determined to tighten this domination, a project that would require both deregulation and lower standards of living for working people. It is no accident that the first move of the Thatcher administration, upon taking office in 1979, was to eliminate British capital controls (further stimulating financial speculation) and later maneuvering to break the miners' union (striking a decisive blow against working people's ability to defend themselves). Similarly, when Reagan took office at the start of 1981, he deregulated US banking and broke the air traffic controllers' national strike. (The ability of Thatcher and Reagan to break such strikes was strongly augmented by the lack of solidarity from workers in other industries; their reward for their silence would be to come under attack themselves, further eroding living standards.)

Although Thatcherites provided ideological ballast for Reaganites, it would be the far larger US, and Reagan administration policy, that would be decisive. The Reagan administration severely tightened monetary policy to squeeze out inflation; gave huge tax cuts to the rich, thereby providing a correspondingly large boost to the financial industry (because the windfalls of the rich would inevitably be put to use in speculation); and pursued a policy of a highly valued dollar.[172] The extraordinarily high interest rates offered by US banks attracted foreign capital, financing the Reagan administration's deficit spending and military buildup; in turn the US applied pressure on other countries to loosen their capital controls to enable this flow of funds into the US. At the same time, oil was paid for in dollars internationally; a combination of high oil prices and a highly valued dollar triggered the debt crisis of the 1980s.[173] Latin

American payments to service debt increased from less than a third of the value of the region's exports in 1977 to almost two-thirds in 1982,[174] a graphic illustration of the grip of finance capital.

That grip strengthened to the point that the Clinton administration further deregulated financial markets, seemingly on the demand of a large US bank that acquired an insurance company in defiance of then existing law, while a few small countries (such as Iceland) based their entire economies on financial speculation. Decades of Reaganite neoliberalism in the US reached its culmination in 2008's freefall, taking down the global economy with it.

Mid-twentieth-century Keynesianism depended on an industrial base and market expansion. A repeat of history isn't possible because the industrial base of the advanced capitalist countries has been hollowed out, transferred to low-wage developing countries, and there is almost no place remaining to which to expand. Moreover, capitalists who are saved by Keynesian spending programs amass enough power to later impose their preferred neoliberal policies. A vicious circle arises: Persistent unemployment and depressed wages in developed countries and inadequate ability to consume on the part of underpaid workers in developing countries leads to continuing under-consumption, creating pressure for still lower wages by capitalists who can't sell what they produce and seek to cut costs further because there is no incentive for them to invest in new production.

With no apparent way out of ongoing stagnation, the governments of the world's advanced capitalist countries have had no answer other than to prop up the financialization that led to the collapse. But another reason is that the financial industry has become so powerful; post-collapse government spending has mostly gone to bail out financiers rather than for investment.

Financial companies, having extracted immense sums of bailout money, have leveraged their power to become even bigger through consolidation, thereby enabling them to divert more capital from productive use. But even during the "boom" portion of business cycles financiers are destructive to an economy by rewarding manufacturers for mass layoffs, moving production to low-wage developing countries with few or no effective labor laws, and setting up subsidiaries overseas and using creative accounting to shift profits offshore to avoid paying taxes. Financiers provide rewards for such behavior in the form of rising stock prices, and those stock prices in turn provide top executives a rationale to give themselves stratospheric pay packages because they "enhanced shareholder value."

A combination of intensified ideological campaigns that demand traditional pension plans be eliminated in favor of individual stock market speculation, and a persistent ideology that insists that stock markets always go up, forces many people into stock markets, where they will be at the mercy of self-dealing special interests who are uncontrollable. (Until at least the 1950s, almost all pension money was invested in government bonds.[175])

Underlying this ideology is that industrialists want out of paying pensions and financiers want larger pools of money with which to play. This process creates the illusion that everybody's interest is tied to the stock market, even when their company's stock has risen in price precisely because they have just lost their jobs. These illusions can be pushed to the point where employees are said to be in charge of their company. In reality, the dynamics of capital accumulation continue unperturbed even when formal "ownership" is handed over to so-called "employee stock-ownership plans."

An excellent example of the hollowness of capitalist "ownership society" ideology—of finance capital's "efficiency" in extracting money and of how financiers and industrialists work together to enrich themselves at the expense of working people—is provided by the Tribune Company. One of the largest media conglomerates in the United States, the company was bought by a real estate tycoon in December 2007 for more than $8 billion, but the tycoon did so with only $315 million of his own money. The purchase was financed by using the company's employee stock-ownership plan to buy all of Tribune's stock. But that did not mean the supposed new "owners" actually controlled anything.

"That made the employees the titular owners of the company, but they had no say in the matter and have no control over its management," a *New York Times* report said. "They were promised the possibility of gaining access to their shares and cashing them in several years in the future, but in a bankruptcy, share values are often wiped out."[176] The company's debt was tripled to finance this scheme, causing it to file for bankruptcy within a year. Holders of common stock—in this case, the stock plan—are wiped out in a bankruptcy because they are, legally, the owners of the company. To pay off the debt resulting from the sale to the tycoon, Tribune's management cut back on its pension contributions.[177]

Who benefited from this deal? The tycoon structured the deal so that he would be in line with the company's creditors for repayment, despite the fact that he used other people's money to buy the company. Two major investment banks were paid $72 million for "advising" Tribune's board of directors, which voted to sell the company to the tycoon and authorized the raid on the employee stock plan. The same two investment banks were among those sharing another $47 million in fees for lending the employee stock-ownership plan money that the tycoon used to finance the purchase. A third investment bank was paid $10 million for issuing an "opinion" that the deal was "fair." Finally, the Tribune chief executive was paid $41 million to give his approval of the sale,[178] after which he left the company.

In the first two years of the tycoon's control, thousands of employees were laid off[179] and the bankruptcy announcement was delivered with a statement to employees that "all ongoing severance payments...have been discontinued."[180] Tribune's management then decided it should pay its 700 top managers $66 million in "retention" bonuses, $9.3 million of which would go to a mere 23 executives—these bonuses would consume one-sixth of the company's operating cash flow.[181]

It is very difficult to imagine these would have been the results if the employees actually owned this company.

The financial industry acts as both a whip and a parasite in relation to productive capital (producers and merchants of tangible goods and services). The financial industry is a "whip" because its institutions (stock, bond and currency-exchange markets and the firms that trade these and other instruments on those markets) bid up or drive down prices, and do so strictly according to their own interests. More profits make traders happy, and prices rise. Lesser profits, or merely news about a development that potentially could reduce profits, result in prices being driven down.

These gyrations in prices are what large enterprises are judged on ultimately, and a management that fails to maximize profits in the short term and deliver higher stock prices in the longer term is in danger of being pushed out, not because diffuse shareholders possess that leverage individually, but because the financial industry as a whole, through the markets it controls, can sell off enough stock to make the price nosedive, leaving the company vulnerable to an unfriendly takeover by a speculator seeking to profit from the reduced value of the company. A speculator who gains control in such a situation will change the management, or simply sell off the company in pieces when that seems more profitable.

Moreover, companies with stock traded on exchanges are legally required to maximize profits for shareholders, above all other considerations. A company that fails to make a deal, or decides against selling itself to another company, is subject to being sued in courts because angry speculators will sell their stock, causing the price to decline and then complain that the company's management failed to maximize "shareholder value."

The financial industry is also a "parasite" because its ownership of stocks, bonds and other instruments entitles it to skim off massive amounts of money as its share of the profits. People in the financial industry don't make tangible products; they trade, buy and sell stocks, bonds and other securities, continually inventing new instruments to profit off virtually every aspect of commercial activity. The flow of money to the financial industry, unless tightly governed by regulation, will steadily increase until the bursting of a speculative bubble. This parasitic flow of money can become dangerous to the point of bringing down the entire capitalist world's economy, as happened in 1929 and again in 2008.

We need not simply see this as the work of bad people, however much we may morally condemn such destructive greed. The personal quality of those engaged in the financial industry is beside the point—this conflict and behavior is built into the system. Rather than believing that if only there were fewer greedy people working on trading desks there would be less instability, it is much more useful to see greed and instability in a systematic way. The capitalist system, and in particular its most distorting sector, finance capital, are designed to reward greed. The most greedy are those who will be attracted to the work.

In the financial industry, there is potentially more reward than in any other industry. That is so because there aren't physical limits such as those faced by manufacturers and merchants. "In a boom, there is every chance that the betting will get out of hand," admits a report in the flagship journal of British finance capital, *The Economist*, analyzing the financial collapse that began in 2008. "Expansion in most businesses is held in check by the need to build assembly lines, rent retail space or hire workers. All that takes time and money. By contrast, financial contracts can be written almost instantaneously and without limit."[182] Simply hope the bet pays off.

The esoteric derivatives that are often too complex to be understood by more than a handful of financiers are the products of mathematical formulae. These models purport to enable prediction of prices.[183] Massive piling into volatile markets on the basis of formulae is not altogether different from the general neoclassical idea that an entire economy can be studied through mathematical models. The financial industry's share of US corporate profits increased from 10 percent in the early 1980s to 40 percent in 2007[184]—a tangible byproduct derived from finance capital gaining the upper hand in its perpetual tug-of-war with industrialists and representing a phenomenal drain of money taken from all parts of the economy. Money that is diverted from investment to speculation and ultimately the product of surplus value extracted from employees.

Stock markets, although much smaller than bond markets, are much more familiar to the general public and therefore are used to promote the idea of the "magic" of markets. Stock markets always go up, "experts" blandly assure us, although they seem unable to explain why, perhaps not a surprise because "experts" also are unable to explain the origin of profits. The nearest to an explanation of why stock markets rise is market players believe they will rise. (The primary reason for why market players believe stock prices will rise at a given time is because they believe other market players believe stock prices will rise.) But sometimes market players believe stock markets will fall, and they do, sometimes very sharply.

Perhaps it is the notion that stock market prices can be counted on to rise that is not necessarily correct. Stock market prices do rise and a long-term player can profit, but only by timing bubbles correctly. This does require patience—stock-market bubbles in the United States, for example, peak about every 35 years. When stock prices are adjusted for inflation, they don't seem so magical—on this basis, the benchmark Dow Jones Industrial Average was below its 1929 peak as late as 1991.[185]

Magic aside, stock markets are supposed to exist to distribute investment capital to where it is needed and to enable corporations to raise money for investment or other purposes. In real life, neither is really true. A corporation with stock traded on an exchange can use that status to issue new shares, raising money without the burden of dealing with lenders and paying them interest. But large corporations can raise money in a variety of ways, including selling shares directly to private investors, and don't need a stock market to do so. Nor do they necessarily wish to float new stock—doing so is disliked by investors because profits are diluted by being spread among more shares. Instead, it is more common for large companies to buy back shares of their stock (at a premium to the trading price), which means less sharing of distributed profits.

From 1981 to 1997, non-financial corporations in the United States bought back $813 billion more in stock through buyback programs and corporate takeovers than they issued.[186] That is money that was diverted from investment, employee compensation or community development, and constitutes still more money slipped into financiers' pockets.

Takeovers and mergers, although often done under competitive pressures to grow, also constitute an effective method of further extracting surplus value. Big Four accounting firm KPMG conducted a study of 700 takeovers in the late 1990s and found that, in 86 percent of them, the buyer either received no value from the acquisition or actually lost value.[187] But financial industry companies (and the corporate law firms that service them) receive fantastically high fees for such deals. Investment banks collectively earn tens of billions of dollars per year for providing "advice" to companies engaged in mergers and acquisitions, and often top executives at the buying corporation are granted huge "retention bonuses" to remain in their posts. That money has to be extracted from somewhere.

And what of distributing investment capital to where it is needed? That is saying, in so many words, that stock markets make finance more efficient—that capital will be put to use in the industries or companies in which a high profit is seen as a good bet because a company is filling a need with a product but lacks sufficient capital to take full advantage, or that the company already has a history of delivering profits. At bottom, buying stock is a gamble on the future profits of the company in which stock is bought. An investor is betting that profits will not only rise, but rise at a faster rate than in the past. The author of the book in your hands at one time worked on a financial news wire service, and one day was surprised when the stock price of a well-known technology company fell despite announcing it had earned a profit of $800 million for the previous three months, a higher profit than the same quarter in the previous year. On closer examination, the company was punished by speculators because the rate of the increase of the profit did not increase—this gigantic profit was lower than what stock market "analysts" had predicted.

That result illustrates that most of the action on stock exchanges is simply speculation, and as computers become more sophisticated, the speculation drives higher trading volumes and becomes more remote from the actual business of the company in which stock is bought. "Day trading," where speculators buy and sell stock within minutes to earn profits on price fluctuations became common in the 1990s, but in the following decade the big Wall Street firms showed their muscle while bringing speculation to an unprecedented level.

These firms created sophisticated computer programs that buy and sell stocks in literally milliseconds. The programs issue thousands of buy orders that are canceled in minuscule fractions of a second in order to manipulate prices to the benefit of the computer owner, taking money from other speculators. These price differences are only pennies, but are done on such an enormous scale that the profits skimmed in this fashion are estimated to be as high as $21 billion in one year—only a "handful" of these high-speed computer traders account for a majority of all stock-exchange trades.[188] "Efficient" such computerized trading may be, but for the benefit of speculators, not for investment.

Speculation tends to reinforce itself—during the 1990s stock-market bubble, traders repeatedly said the dramatic price rises could not last, but as long as the consensus view was that the long bull market would continue they were not going to step off the ride. When the bubble did burst, new forms of speculation kept the party going for several more years. Credit was the lubricant for the later round, both inflating a real estate bubble and enabling consumer spending to continue in the face of declining wages, until the speculation became unsustainable. With no more bubbles to inflate, governments representing the world's four largest economies alone committed $16.3 trillion in 2008 and 2009 on bailouts of the financiers who brought down the global economy and, to a far smaller extent, for economic stimulus.[189]

Bailouts are frequent events. One notorious example is the 1998 collapse of the Long-Term Capital Management hedge fund. This fund had $5 billion in assets but was allowed to borrow $125 billion, and those borrowings were in turn leveraged into derivatives contracts valued at $1.25 trillion.[190] The fund could do this because, thanks to the cachet that accrued to it by virtue of the prominent financiers and economists running it, it could borrow 100 percent of the value of a collateral and use the borrowed money to buy assets that were used as collateral for more borrowing.[191] The fund was gambling using mathematical formulae to bet on price changes in government bonds.

When the Russian financial collapse hit in 1998 (the debt crisis discussed in Chapter 5), the ensuing widespread market panic caused bond prices to move in the opposite direction that the fund was betting. The value of the fund's assets dropped sharply—it could not possibly pay off its bets nor meet demands by its lenders for it to put up more collateral. But liquidating the fund would have caused a cascade of losses in several countries, to the extent that, it was feared, the entire global financial system might collapse.[192]

The Federal Reserve of the United States engineered a rescue of the hedge fund that narrowly avoided a full-scale panic. The Keynesian economist Paul Krugman later wrote that "It is important to realize that even now Fed[eral Reserve] officials are not quite sure how they pulled this rescue off," perhaps not surprising since Krugman also reported, "At one meeting I attended, participants asked a Federal Reserve official what could be done to resolve it. 'Pray,' he replied."[193] This was not long after banking systems had to be bailed out in the US and in several European countries; the Spanish government spent 17 percent of a year's gross domestic product to bail out its banks.[194]

If this system "works," why does it have to be repeatedly bailed out and continually subsidized with such massive amounts of money?

## Conceptualizations of the nationalist barriers to democracy under capitalism

One contradiction of these bailouts is that they are organized on a national basis although the markets are international and the crises inevitably cross borders. The crisis that began in 2008 initially was responded to with some efforts at harmonization, but by late 2010, currency wars and other forms of every-country-for-itself behavior characterized national responses. This pattern is a reminder of the power of nationalism, which in its modern form developed with capitalism, and continues to be a force that provides a defensive line of fortification when leaders seek to distract populations from crises.

Nationalism is a concept that has mystical roots deep in the ancient past—the Old Testament contains stories of the apocryphal founder of the world's monotheistic religions, Abraham, being told he would be the progenitor of nations. Pre-capitalist societies, with rare exceptions, were organized around monarchal dynasties that sat on thrones through divine will; there was not, nor could there have been, nationalism in the modern sense because people were subjects of monarchs or ecclesiastical rule, not citizens of a state.

A fixed hierarchy, with a dynastic monarchy at the apex, kept everybody in their place in feudal systems, whereas capitalism has an internally competitive bourgeois class with no center and thus requires a state machinery to function properly.[195] The feudal peasant, who likely spent his or her life within a small area, had little need for a state and might not have spoken the same language as the peasant in the next principality, but the merchant and then the industrialist needed a state that provided protection from bandits, and laws that benefited commerce.[196]

A breakdown in the idea of monarchs ruling from divine will who are owed absolute loyalty, and the end of privileged access to "truth" contained in languages available only to elites, the latter concomitant with the development of unifying standard "print languages" through books and periodicals published in vernacular languages, helped create the conditions that allowed modern nationalism to arise.[197] Feudal European empires often didn't bother to suppress local languages; the numerically tiny elites across these societies tended to write and communicate with one another in Latin, and feudal monarchies cemented their ties through intermarriage. Rising capitalists, however, cemented their relations through commerce and literacy—they required a common language that everyone spoke.[198] By the late eighteenth century, a process of codifying a single dominant dialect as a national language was under way in several European nations, and with this process came standardization in military training and in other aspects of life.[199] The process of codifying languages and the nationalist feelings that began to be stirred accelerated in the first half of the nineteenth century.[200]

Nationalism was a concept that could be copied and directly imposed from above, as in the case of Japan after the Meiji Restoration of 1868. Seeking to catch up to the West fast, Japan's new rulers, within five years of taking power, ordered universal literacy among adult males and army conscription; the incomprehensibility of local dialects was swiftly overcome because the nation already had a unified writing system.[201]

Liberalism and nationalism thus became twin forces—nineteenth-century monarchies gradually adopted nationalism as the concept of a larger community of speakers of a common language who possess a common cultural heritage took popular root. Liberal concepts of freedom of trade, autonomy of markets and liberty of individuals, as well as promotion of "productive" industrialists in contrast to "unproductive" aristocrats, dovetailed with nationalism. Larger states needed to be created to facilitate commerce and to project military power in the service of that commerce.

The aristocracy, a dominant class in feudal societies, was not going to give up its privileged positions without a struggle, and promoted nationalism for its own purposes; by the late nineteenth century, nationalism had become a tool of the Right. As such, nationalism could be harnessed in the service of imperialism—mythologies of national superiority were invented to justify conquests physical and economic. That in turn sparked nationalism in colonized peoples who built liberation movements around their awakening national consciousness.

Nonetheless, militaristic tendencies within nationalism remained essential for the expansion of capitalism. In earlier times, the seat of a small republic such as Venice could be the leading financial center on the strength of its trading networks. Once capitalism took hold, however, the financial center was successively located within a larger federation that possessed both a strong navy and a significant fleet of merchant ships (Amsterdam); then within a sizeable and unified country with a large enough population to maintain a powerful navy and a physical presence throughout an empire (London); and finally within a continent-spanning country that can project its economic and multidimensional military power around the world (New York).

Present-day European capitalists desire the ability to challenge the United States for economic supremacy, but cannot do so without the combined clout of a united continent. This wish underlies the anti-democratic push to steadily tighten the European Union (EU), including mandatory national budget benchmarks that require cutting social safety nets and policies that are designed to break down solidarity among wage earners and different regions by imposing harsher competition through imposed austerity.

These rules are designed by central bankers to benefit European big business and financiers. As an example, during the economic crisis that began in 2008, harsh austerity was imposed on a series of EU countries to ensure that bond traders, in the first place large banks, would be guaranteed maximum profits. Europe's capitalists and central bankers are no less shy about adopting neoclassical ideology than their counterparts elsewhere, but are reliant on a supranational project to override national governments that must contend with popular resistance.

"To account for [ongoing economic] stagnation, the two non-democratic institutions which govern the Eurozone, the Brussels Commission and the [European Central Bank], have a very simple explanation which they repeat with the obsession of a litany: it's all the fault of the labour market," is the summation of economists Michel Aglietta and Laurent Berrebi.

The selfishness of wage-earners hanging on to their acquired advantages and rejecting "flexibility" is the root of all evils…To adjust to globalization is to annul the social progress which was the engine of economic development and Europe's contribution to the advance of civilization after the Second World War. In short, [structural adjustment] is to abandon social solidarity in order to espouse the inegalitarian society of the U.S.[202]

The European Union, in its current capitalist form, is a logical step for business leaders who desire greater commercial power on a global basis: It creates a "free trade" zone complete with suppression of social accountability while giving muscle to a currency that has the potential of challenging the US dollar as the world's pre-eminent currency. The weakness of the supranational form is that it collides head-on with nationalism, which acts as a disorganizing force within the EU, whereas in countries like the US and China nationalism is a potent unifying force. Nationalism provides a crucial element in the support for the militarization that is necessary to maintain the force on which global capitalism ultimately relies.

Nationalism is additionally a particularly useful social glue in the age of consumerism because it provides another method of atomizing society at the same time it provides a unifying ethos. National leaders incessantly tell everyone they are free to make their own choices thanks to the glory of their country at the same time that nationalism binds all these ostensibly independent individuals together under specific approved ideas, and the most fervent believers of those approved ideas are not often slow in denouncing those who refuse to conform.

Corporate ideologies are tightly wrapped in the flag so as to be presented as "patriotic," and public resisters to these ideologies are depicted as preventing consenting citizens from expressing themselves and impermissibly infecting them with alien ideas. Nationalist versions of "solidarity" depict independence in thought as blocking social cohesion: You are a free individual who can make any free choice you want, as long as that choice conforms to a narrow set of approved ideas.

"Freedom" is the ability to consume the mass-marketed corporate products of your choice; "individuality" is accessorizing those consumer products. "Consumers" have only individual interests—nationalism in its more virulent forms promotes hatred against people who are different, raising barriers against organic social solidarity while providing an outlet for those individual consumers to feel a part of something larger than themselves.

So far, this chapter has mostly discussed conditions in the advanced capitalist countries that collectively comprise the North. What of the South? Here mythologies of the universality of wealth collide head-on with the reality of ever-expanding urban slums and grinding rural poverty. Countries in the capitalist orbit across Latin America, Asia and Africa failed to gain ground on the advanced capitalist countries in the decades following World War II because of both the hierarchal world capitalist system and the hierarchal social systems within these countries.

Individuals cannot all be wealthy (in fact only a minuscule percentage can) because wealth derives from exploitation of others; similarly, there is only so much room at the top in the competition of states. The wealth of advanced capitalist countries is built on exploitation of other countries and it is a physical impossibility for all countries to exploit others simultaneously for similar gains.[203]

Corporations based in advanced capitalist countries that operate in the South are interested either in the cheapest possible extraction of natural resources or in setting up the lowest-wage factories. Local capitalists in the countries of the South are encouraged to produce for export at low cost, incentivizing them to keep wages low; competitive pressures to remain a low-cost supplier and the ability of Northern capital to shift production to locations with still lower wages keep these countries in poverty relative to the North and keep local working people mired in poverty beneath a minuscule rich capitalist elite that benefits from the arrangements. This poverty induces political leaders in these countries to continually attempt to gain a more secure foothold in the world capitalist system, but their countries' poverty and the powerful pressures that the North can apply force them to do so on unfavorable terms.[204]

These unfavorable terms lead to the establishment of factories with particularly harsh conditions known as sweatshops. Often owned locally but producing for a large corporation based in the North on a contract basis, it is not unknown for apparel products to be sold for 100 or more times what the laborer was paid to assemble the product. Forcing open countries of the South to a flood of imports from the North devastated Southern economies; one frequent occurrence was that local farmers could not compete with the low prices of subsidized food imports from the North.

Forced off the land and unable to sustain themselves otherwise, farmers have to either migrate to the North under dangerous conditions, risking imprisonment if caught, or sell their labor power to a local capitalist and endure sweatshop conditions. In essence, this is a modern version of the English enclosure movement, only this time, because capitalism is well established, it is seemingly autonomous "market forces" doing the same job that naked force did before capitalism established itself. The wages paid to these new conscripts to factory work are not sufficient for more than the barest existence, so poverty becomes concentrated as the cities chaotically expand into sprawling slums, and countries lose their ability to feed themselves because so many farmers have left the land or farmland is used for export crops.

The multinational lending institutions controlled by the powerful countries of the North use their capital to enforce draconian conditions, refusing to lend money without agreements to shred social safety nets and privatize state enterprises, which reduces employment and cuts wages. The corporations that contract out to the local factories can keep wages at starvation levels by threats to move to another country that will offer still lower wages, augmented by the unemployment produced by the dictated austerity measures.

Thus, much of the world is at the mercy of the advanced capitalist countries, trapped in a race to the bottom.

Starting in the 1970s, a desire of Northern capitalists to escape paying living wages in their own countries led to a shift of production to the South, and the increasing desirability of financial speculation led to a credit boom in the South, with the result that too much production led to a collapse of prices and an inability to pay back the loans.[205] The South has been trapped in a cycle of deep debt ever since, requiring more austerity to be imposed upon local populations in order to service the debt. The debt crisis is particularly acute in Latin America.

Latin American debt, however, is merely the newest form of exploitation. The era of direct colonialism, beginning with Spain's massive extraction of gold and silver, was replaced by one-sided trading relationships following the region's formal independence in the early nineteenth century. George Canning, an imperialist "free trader" who was the British foreign secretary, wrote in 1824: "The deed is done, the nail is driven, Spanish America is free; and if we do not mismanage our affairs sadly, she is English."[206] Canning was no idle boaster. At the same time, the French foreign minister lamented, "In the hour of emancipation the Spanish colonies turned into some sort of British colonies."[207] And lest we think this was simply European hubris, here is what the Argentine finance minister had to say: "We are not in a position to take measures against foreign trade, particularly British, because we are bound to that nation by large debts and would expose ourselves to a rupture which would cause much harm."[208]

What had happened? Argentina, to provide an example, flung its ports wide open to trade under British influence, flooding itself with a deluge of European goods sufficient to strangle nascent local production; when Argentina later attempted to escape dependency by imposing trade barriers in order to build up its own industry, British and French warships forced the country open again.[209] The United States general Ulysses S. Grant, following his election as president after defeating the secessionist Confederacy in the US Civil War, had not failed to notice that Britain was a recent convert to open trade:

For centuries England has relied on protection, has carried it to extremes, and has obtained satisfactory results from it. There is no doubt that it is to this system that it owes its present strength. After two centuries, England has found it convenient to adopt free trade because it thinks that protection can no longer offer it anything. Very well then, gentlemen, my knowledge of our country leads me to believe that within two hundred years, when America has gotten out of protection all that it can offer, it too will adopt free trade.[210]

The fate of Latin America has not appreciably changed; only the methodologies are different.

Africa has followed a different pattern because it was subjected to direct colonial rule longer than the world's other regions. Africa was also subject to a particularly brutal exploitation for centuries, from the slave trade to the twentieth century's starvation wages, stealing of land and intense exploitation of natural resources. The extent of the damage done to African societies by the slave trade is impossible to quantify. It takes no imagination to realize that the continual forced removal of able-bodied men and women, the continual raiding and low-level warfare in the wide areas subject to slave-trade kidnappers, the continual social instability wrought by these conditions, the disruption of trading patterns and the incentive to make easy profits by participating in kidnapping rather than in productive economic activity can only destroy the possibility of development.

The exact number of Africans kidnapped and forcibly transported across the Atlantic will never be known, but scholars' estimates tend to range from about 10 million to 12 million.[211] The human toll, however, is still higher because, simultaneous with those who were successfully kidnapped, millions more were killed or maimed, and thus not shipped across the Atlantic. This level of inhumanity cannot be accomplished without an accompanying ideology. Walter Rodney, in his outstanding contribution to understanding lagging development in the South, *How Europe Underdeveloped Africa*, pointed out that although racism and other hatreds, including anti-Semitism, long existed across Europe, racism was an integral part of capitalism because it was necessary to rationalize the exploitation of African labor that was crucial to their accumulations of wealth.

"Occasionally, it is mistakenly held that Europeans enslaved Africans for racist reasons," Rodney wrote.

European planters and miners enslaved Africans for *economic* reasons, so that their labor power could be exploited. Indeed, it would have been impossible to open up the New World and to use it as a constant generator of wealth, had it not been for African labor. There were no other alternatives: the American (Indian) population was virtually wiped out and Europe's population was too small for settlement overseas at that time.[212]

It should not be necessary to point out the hypocrisies into which this exploitation would later develop, such as the United States declaring itself to be the freest society on Earth while enshrining enslavement in its constitution and revolutionary French leaders who swore to establish "liberty, equality, fraternity" mercilessly putting down slave rebellions in the Caribbean.

The US maintained slavery until the mid-nineteenth century, enabling the plantation aristocracy to accumulate enormous wealth on the backs of its slaves, then allowed servile relations such as sharecropping, and systematic state-backed violence and terrorism, to maintain African-Americans' subjugation for another century. The wealth of the plantation owners and the desperate poverty of newly freed slaves were both transmitted to their respective descendants, locked in through terrorism. When the civil rights movement forced a dismantling of Southern apartheid, US elites countered by saying, in effect: "Look! We're all equal now! If you are not rich it's your own fault." Is this not preposterous? This delusion is another product of capitalist ideology.

When slavery began to end in the nineteenth century, new forms of exploitation were devised. Now Europeans would directly exploit the resources and land of Africa. Colonial powers confiscated huge areas of arable land, then sold it at nominal prices to the well-connected; in Kenya, for example, the British declared the fertile highlands "crown lands" and sold blocks of land as large as 350,000 acres.[213] These massive land confiscations not only enabled the creation of massively profitable plantations, but created the conditions that forced newly landless Africans to become low-wage agricultural workers and to pay taxes to the colonial power.[214]

Laws were passed forbidding Africans from growing cash crops in plantation regions, a system of compulsion summed up by a British colonel who became a settler in Kenya: "We have stolen his land. Now we must steal his limbs. Compulsory labor is the corollary of our occupation of the country."[215] In other parts of colonial Africa, where land remained in African hands, colonial governments slapped money taxes on cattle, land, houses and the people themselves; subsistence farmers don't have money to pay money taxes so farmers were forced to grow cash crops, for which they were paid very little.[216]

The alternative to farming was to go to work in the mines. Wages were set at starvation level; at best Africans earned one-sixth of what a worker from Europe or North America would earn even when working for the same company. Often the disparity was much wider—a Scottish or German coal miner earned in an hour almost what a Nigerian coal miner was paid for a six-day week.[217] European and North American mining and trading companies made fantastic profits (sometimes as high as 90 percent) and raw materials could be exploited at similar levels (a US rubber company, from 1940 to 1965, took 160 million dollars' worth of rubber out of Liberia while the Liberian government received 8 million dollars).[218]

Not only did this corporate plunder represent accumulation of wealth that was taken out of Africa, it also provided the raw-materials basis without which the industrial and military might of Europe and North America would not have been possible.

Still another method of extracting wealth was through forced labor—French, British, Belgian and Portuguese colonial governments required Africans to perform unpaid labor on railroads and other infrastructure projects. The French were particularly vicious in their use of forced labor (each year throughout the 1920s, 10,000 new people were put to work on a single railroad and at least 25 percent of the railroad's forced laborers died from starvation or disease) and the Portuguese shipped Africans from their colonies to South Africa for work in mines at starvation wages.[219] The railroads thus built did not benefit Africans when independence came in the mid-twentieth century because they were laid down to bring raw materials to a port and had no relationship to the trading or geographical patterns of the new countries or their neighbors.

An enormous amount of wealth has been removed from Africa, and transferred to the advanced capitalist countries. The same process, if at a somewhat less frenetic pace, has gone on around much of the world. This wealth has primarily gone to the capitalists, but everybody in the advanced capitalist countries materially benefits to some degree by virtue of living in one of those countries. The living standards of the North are bought in part at the expense of those in the South, and that, too, is an often hidden equation of capitalism.

Those living standards are also dependent on high rates of energy consumption, and if the South successfully emulates the consumerism of the North, energy consumption can only continue to rise. But the faster energy is consumed, the faster it must be extracted and the closer the world comes to depleting the supplies. That day is already approaching, and this issue goes well beyond oil and gas.

Oil, gas and coal account for 84 percent of energy consumption in the advanced capitalist countries, and nuclear power accounts for most of the rest.[220] But the supply of oil will last only another 40 to 80 years. Coal not only is environmentally unsound but will not last as long as its supporters claim. If world economic growth is estimated at 2 percent per year and coal consumption is assumed to grow by 4 percent a year to offset declining oil and gas availability, then the world's coal supply will last only 70 years.[221]

Nuclear energy is dangerous in that radioactive waste cannot be disposed of safely, accidents release dangerous levels of radiation and its inefficiency is illustrated by the large government subsidies required by operators of nuclear plants. But even without those problems, an increase in the use of nuclear energy to compensate for dwindling oil, gas and coal (and assuming energy demands continue to grow by 2 percent per year) would mean that the world's supply of uranium would run out before the end of the twenty-first century.[222] Finally, some of the world's metals may also reach depletion before the end of this century.

Without alternative, efficient, renewable sources of energy to replace fossil and nuclear fuels, not only would there be no more growth, the world's economy would have to shrink. This would be another crisis point for capitalism—how could a system based on growth continue without the ability to grow? How far could capitalists push when more would have to be extracted from their workforces just to maintain existing profit levels? Thus there would be an extra dimension to the ecological crisis and the general economic crisis that would ensue if humanity allows itself to run out of energy.

"Capitalism, through its pursuit of endless accumulation and growth, has fundamentally transformed the relationship between human beings and nature," according to Minqi Li, an economist who studies the limits to economic growth.

> The human activities of material production and consumption have expanded to the point that the very existence of human civilization is at stake. There cannot be a more acute expression of the conflict between the "productive forces" and the "existing relations of production," and the conflict can only be resolved by rejecting the existing socio-economic system (assuming humanity will survive the coming crisis).[223]

Apocalyptic? Hyperbolic? Perhaps. But the continued use of non-renewable energy without the invention of renewable, efficient energy sources will lead to this scenario, and would do so before the end of the twenty-first century. Li has worked out the catastrophic economic consequences if the energy to run a modern technological economy is exhausted without replacement. Modern agriculture's efficiency is based on high energy inputs; if this energy becomes unavailable, the world will need far more than the current number of farmers and agricultural workers, drawing them from the industrial and service parts of the economy. A drastic increase in the percentage of humanity who must work in agriculture in order for the planet to be able to feed itself would mean a correspondingly drastic decline in the size of the economy, and a "very serious food crisis" would become inevitable as grain production already is growing at a slower rate than the world's population,[224] Li wrote.

Additionally, there are limits to the pollution the planet can endure, the cascading effects of global warming, and increasing strains on the world's supply of potable water. These factors, too, represent physical limits on growth, and therefore on the capitalist system. Fortunately, a strong environmental movement has come into being, and dedicated environments continue to bring these issues into the public eye in the face of capitalists' scorn. Without democratic spaces to raise these issues, humanity would risk a final calamity. Li's doomsday scenario of catastrophic economic collapse is not the world's inevitable fate (and won't become a reality if there are breakthroughs in renewable energy), but nonetheless all the environmental concerns would remain just as acute and the physical barriers to capitalist expansion would still loom as an insoluble contradiction.

Democratic spaces within the advanced capitalist countries do provide spaces to discuss and potentially enact solutions to the coming crises. But all democratic spaces have been won through struggle and are not guaranteed; the years immediately following the 2001 terrorist attacks in New York and Washington will not be the final attempts at reining in inconvenient freedoms, and considerable freedom might have been lost without a concerted global movement that pushed back against wars in Iraq and Afghanistan, and against the wars on civil liberties in protestors' own countries.

Yet there remains the contradiction that capitalism and full democracy remain incompatible. Early capitalists and their publicists, as we saw earlier, themselves believed political democracy was an outright impediment. The idea that capitalism and democracy go together is a recent construct. One reason for democratic openings is the nature of the system itself. Because capitalism is an impersonal system, it does not require that members of the dominant capitalist class actually hold political posts, although frequently they do. It is enough that the political superstructure that is a byproduct of the dominant ideologies of the capitalist class's institutions, corporations, remains in place.

The modern state itself is a creation of the rise of capitalism and the need of industrialists and financiers for a structure to provide protection for investments and to settle disputes among themselves. These features are wrapped tightly in nationalism, with continual references to a given nation's mythologies, to bind working people tighter to the system. Capitalism also requires a literate, educated population, in contrast to earlier systems, and a literate, educated populace is more inclined and able to agitate for its interests.

There is more communication (this, too, is a necessity for the increased commerce of capitalism) and if the people of one nation wrest a gain from their rulers, people in other nations will know about it, and will struggle to get it for themselves as well. Further, in the early days of capitalism, its development was seldom in a straight line; sometimes there could be an incremental expansion of the voting franchise because one bloc of capitalists believed the new voters would vote for their party.

Once the vote is made available to more citizens, pressure builds from below to further extend the vote; moreover, the creation of a modern working class brings together masses of people, enabling the creation of mass movements that can organize struggles for more democratic rights. Social media has proven to be a powerful tool for democracy activists, although by itself it can't substitute for real-world organizing and a physical presence at key locations.

Capitalists intended to establish democracy only for themselves, but the spaces and contradictions contained within the political systems created to stabilize the functioning of capitalism (including institutions to adjudicate conflicts among the capitalists and mechanisms for selecting political leadership in the absence of an absolute monarchy or the continued ascendancy of a static landed aristocracy) enabled their workers to wrest some of that democracy for themselves. None of that came easy—untold lives were snuffed out and untold blood was shed, and even in cases when a struggle has been bloodless, many advances required decades of dedicated activism to accomplish. The process is called "struggle" for a reason.

"Democracy developed neither out of the positive tendencies of capitalism, nor as a historical accident, but out of the contradictions of capitalism," wrote Göran Therborn in summing up an interesting essay on the development of voting rights across the world. "Bourgeois democracy has been viable at all only because of the elasticity and expansive capacity of capitalism, which were grossly underestimated by classical liberals and Marxists alike."[225]

Not endlessly expansive, however. Hard-won political rights are not only circumscribed by the immense power concentrated in the hands of corporate institutions and the class that controls those institutions, but those rights end at the entrance to the place of work. If one class of people has the ability to bend the political process to benefit itself; arrogates to itself an unlimited right to accumulate at the expense of everybody else and at the expense of future generations; has the right to dictate in the workplaces, controlling employees' lives; and can call on the state to enforce all these privileges with force, if necessary, then how much freedom do the rest of us really have? If one developer has the right to chop down a forest to build a shopping center that the community does not need or the right to build high-rise luxury towers that force out others who already lived there because one individual can earn a profit, and the community has no recourse, is this state of affairs truly democratic?

If a capitalist decides it would be profitable to move a factory to a low-wage country and thousands are put out of work as a result, is it not capital that actually possesses freedom? If enterprises were collectively run and/or under community control, would people vote to send their jobs to a low-wage haven thousands of miles away?

If the political system is so dominated by corporate power (the concentrated power of a numerically tiny class) that a politician at the national level who might genuinely wish to give working people a better break can't because that corporate power is decisive, or that a politician at the local level who might want to make the local factory owner do a little more for the community or simply pay a fair amount of taxes can't because to push the idea would lead to the factory owner closing the factory and sending many townspeople to the unemployment office, then can this system be said to be democratic?

Men and women have the vote, and have constitutionally guaranteed rights—lives were sacrificed to gain these rights. But if there is such a concentration of power that most elementary decisions are taken by a small number of people, either big capitalists or politicians acting on their behalf or under their influence, then the rights enshrined in a constitution are mere shells. Democracy is formal, and cannot be more than formal without democracy extending to all spheres of life. That is impossible under capitalism because concentrated economic power is leveraged into power over the political, cultural, social and educational life of a nation, and that power, as wielded by capital, will be tightened at home and expanded abroad due to the impetus to expand. Capitalism is an impersonal system, and the competition that drives it inevitably leads to this dynamic, regardless of which personality is where.

If the preceding pages have touched on a large number of topics, it is because capitalism is a totalizing system—a system that absorbs virtually every aspect of human endeavor with a similarly wide scope of ideology. A totalizing system has to be understood as such, and can only be combatted through understanding the complexities and connections of the many parts that only appear to be random and disconnected.

## Notes toward a philosophy of political democracy

It is not enough to be against something; it is necessary to be for something. If post-capitalist society is to be more democratic, to extend the long trend of human history toward more freedom so that freedom in the fullest sense is finally extended to all human beings, it is necessary to conceptualize such a society. It is necessary to create new institutions reflecting democratic values. And because there is no freedom without economic democracy, it is necessary to create new political and economic institutions, with links among them all.

Political democracy comes in various permutations, but ultimately in two distinct forms: direct democracy and representative democracy. Direct democracy, where everybody has an equal voice and an equal vote, is ideal whenever possible. But some sort of representative system is unavoidable at the level of a nation-state or large national subdivision—it is simply impractical for millions, or hundreds of millions, to vote on everything. It might seem odd to be discussing parliaments or congresses, classic structures of modern capitalist states, in terms of future post-capitalist societies. Inevitably, some bricks of the past will be used to build the future—it is not possible to build a society devoid of all traces of the past. And while we shouldn't overly romanticize representative political institutions, neither should we automatically reject them. Rather, such institutions can be re-imagined and adapted for future possibilities.

World War I-era councils (or "soviets" in Russia) were seen by participants as more democratic than parliaments because seat holders were not elected to fixed terms. They could be recalled at any time, therefore quickly reflecting changes in opinion among the represented. Such an ability was critical during 1917 in Russia as party loyalties shifted rapidly. These bodies had limitations that would be more glaring today, such as a lack of representation for the unemployed, retirees and parents who stay at home with children. Crucially, these councils should not be seen as "direct" democracy—these were representative bodies, albeit much more responsive than legislatures with fixed terms.

New forms will be needed to make representative political institutions much more representative and answerable, although post-capitalist breaking of the power of capital will do much to make these bodies less agents of the powerful. Regardless, as much decision-making as practical should be devolved to local bodies of whatever form. What else can be done to make legislatures truly representative of those who elect the members?

One step should be a multiparty system, which increases voters' choices and makes electees more accountable because there would be more competition, and therefore it is easier for a disappointed voter to vote differently in the next election. But a multiparty system cannot simply be conjured; such a system can only flourish in particular parliamentary setups.

Less-than-multiparty systems are less democratic than multiparty systems. One-party systems are the least democratic, and the stability of one-party systems is illusory. All one-party systems stagnate, then degenerate, dragging down society. It does not matter where on the political spectrum the party is located; it can even move significantly along the political spectrum, but that merely slows the party's decay.

The one-party system is also a contradiction because, although it holds that there is only one permissible ideology or proper organization of society, it does not follow that opposing ideas disappear. Opposing ideas that are banned as a consequence of the banning of political parties and organizations that espouse those opposing ideas are carried into the ruling party by those who enter the party to continue their careers or to be able to remain politically active. The ruling party has to increase political repression in its own ranks because that is the only way its dominant ideology can remain supreme. The ruling party gradually ceases to stand for anything political, other than a simplified version of its original ideology that becomes calcified, and instead becomes for much of its membership simply a means to further careers. The Soviet Union, as was demonstrated in chapters 2 and 5, was an excellent example of this process.

Some one-party countries are less tied to a single ideology, and can change policies in significant ways, but the same process of degeneration is inevitable. Mexico provides an excellent example of a ruling party of this type—the Institutional Revolutionary Party, or PRI in its Spanish initials, ruled as a Left-of-Center party with progressive policies in the 1930s under Lorenzo Cardenas, but in later decades became a conservative force.

One-party systems inevitably become highly corrupt—such a party attracts opportunists and careerists. The party itself, through its control over its national institutions, is perfectly placed to advantage itself and its officials in numerous ways. The single party becomes a vehicle for self-promotion, extracting privileges, luxuries and high salaries, and its members have significant incentive to keep the party in power to maintain their status. Party officials become conservative and fearful of change—change might threaten their privileges and power, and opening up the political system surely would. The single party becomes a vast organization for patronage, and when the party is removed from power, it has lost its raison d'être.

That is why such parties, upon losing power, disintegrate rapidly. Only rarely does the single party remain an organized force seriously contesting for power when a more open political system is introduced. Mexico's PRI is one of these exceptions, but it for a time declined to the status of the third strongest of three main parties and survived in part by tacitly aligning with Mexico's other party of the Right, the National Action Party.

Modified one-party systems provide some limited scope for the give and take of political ideas, but most of the same problems of a true one-party system exist and its stability is, in the long term, no less illusory. A dominant party that almost always holds power and is, during the decades of its rule, virtually unmovable from government offices and parliament, blocks new ideas—its ultimately futile attempts to maintain the status quo also allow crises to build. Japan provides an excellent example of a modified one-party system. The Liberal Democratic Party's half-century grip on the Japanese political system loosened in 2009, but its vast patronage had allowed it to maintain its long government majority. The Liberal Democrats persistently overspent on unneeded infrastructure projects across Japan, an unsustainable way to prop up an economy while at the same time preventing the country from tackling its problems at a fundamental level.

Two-party systems (and two-bloc systems) are stable. They offer more scope for debate and enough opportunity for new policies and ideas to provide the illusion that a full democracy exists with a full range of ideas. This is particularly illusory in a capitalist democracy, as capitalists, through the concentrated power amassed in their corporations and the ability of those capitalists to suffuse their ideologies into other institutions, restrict the scope of debate within boundaries acceptable to them—ideas that question their dominance are far outside those boundaries. Still, there is much more scope for the contesting of ideas and for serious acknowledgment of problems and devising solutions than in a one-party system. Individual political figures can be voted out of office, unlike in a one-party system, and although changing personalities does not in itself change the system in any way, it does provide a safety valve.

This safety valve also gives the appearance of a free choice, and the resulting appearance of democracy serves well in stabilizing the system—a bad leader can be voted out of office. But those choices are inevitably constrained. The two parties are necessarily unwieldy coalitions; they must be because they will have to contain room for people and ideas across long portions of the political spectrum. A faction of one of these two parties might gain the upper hand at one time, especially if it is linked with an ideology promoted by an energetic bloc of capitalists, but in this instance the party will become too narrow and rigid. The other major party will inevitably benefit and eventually the factionalized party will have to loosen the grip of its dominant faction and revert to becoming a coalition if it intends to compete successfully in the future. This natural elasticity provides an additional stability to a two-party system.

If such a system exists where representative bodies are elected on the basis of winner-take-all single-seat districts, then the two-party system has considerable cement to fix it in place. Only two parties can be viable in such a system—if one large party of the coalition type described above exists, then only a second such party can realistically compete. Moreover, the two dominant parties, due to their virtual monopoly on political office, can rig election rules to benefit themselves and make it difficult for other parties to gain access to the ballot.

In the United States, this is precisely what happens, and the US is the outstanding example of the two-party system. Both parties compete fiercely for corporate money—elections there are too expensive to contest seriously without it—and corporate influence over social institutions takes care of the rest. Real choice is blocked, the power of capitalists is secured through political means, the illusion of competition is maintained and there is enough room to allow safety valves to work when needed. All this makes for a remarkably stable system: One US government has fallen in 220 years.

A two-bloc system works in similar ways, although such blocs are more truly coalitions because parties still run under their own names with their own programs. This system provides more scope to push a government into a socially preferred direction. But choice is still limited, even though the two-bloc system exists in a parliamentary system rather than a US-style winner-take-all single-seat congressional system. The choice is limited because there are only two candidates for prime minister, one for each bloc. The Italy of the 1990s and 2000s is an excellent example of this system. Like the two-party system, it tends to stress personalities more than platforms, eroding serious discussion of issues and turning elections more into referenda on individuals.

Multiple-party systems offer more choices and because such systems frequently lead to coalition governments of two or more parties, they also facilitate compromise—one governing party, or one faction of one party, cannot run roughshod over society and impose its ideological goals on an entire country. A multi-party system also allows for a sharper delineation among parties, more scope for new or different ideas, and a greater chance for more people to believe that they can be represented. It also enables more women to earn seats because parties have to compete harder for votes, making it more untenable to put forth unrepresentative slates. A more dynamic political system is more amenable to change and more responsive.

Political parties don't exist in a vacuum. They can exist only in a political system, the two basic types of which are single-seat district bodies and proportional-representation parliamentary bodies. What sort of party system a given country has is more dependent on what kind of representative body it has than on any other factor.

A representative body based on districts, each with one representative, is a closed system. With two entrenched parties contesting for a single seat, there is no room for a third party to emerge. Campaigns for elections to these bodies can be conducted on larger national issues or on the basis of an important local issue, but the tendency is for these elections to become contests between personalities. If the personality representing the other party is objectionable, or the other party is objectionable, then voting is reduced to the "lesser of two evils." Voting for a party or an individual becomes a sterile exercise in ensuring the other side doesn't win. From the point of view of the candidates and parties, the safest strategy is one of peeling away voters from the only other viable candidate, thereby encouraging platforms to be close to that of the other viable candidate, promoting a tendency to lessen differences between the two dominant parties.

With little to distinguish the two parties, the importance of personality becomes more important, further blurring political ideas, and yet third choices are excluded because of the factors that continue to compel a vote for one of the two major-party candidates. In turn, such a system sends people to representative bodies on the basis of their personalities, encouraging those personalities to grandstand and act in an egocentric manner once they are seated. These personalities are dependent on corporate money to get into and remain in office, and the parties they are linked to are equally dependent—the views of those with the most money are going to be heard more than other views. And if the district boundaries can be redrawn any which way periodically, the two parties can work together (since they control all political institutions) so that both have "safe" seats. Elections cease to be competitive, and if you live in a district in which voters who consistently favor the other party are the majority, you are out of luck.

The two parties compete fiercely to win elections—they represent different groupings within the capitalist class who have a great deal of money at stake. This is a closed competition, however: They act as a cartel to keep corporate money rolling in and other parties out. These are the underlying reasons for the stability of a two-party system—replacing it with a multiple-party system would require fundamentally changing political structures.

More democratic is a parliamentary system, which in almost all cases comes with some form of proportional representation. The two notable exceptions are Canada and the United Kingdom, which have parliamentary forms of governments (the leader of the largest party becomes prime minister and ministers are parliament seat holders) but no proportional representation. Canadian and British members of parliament are elected solely from single-seat districts but because remaining in government is dependent on maintaining a majority of parliamentary votes, representatives in this system have more incentive to vote with their party and less to grandstand as individual personalities. Canada and Britain both have strong regional parties that represent ethnic minorities (Québec, Scotland, Wales) but usually produce single-party governments. This system retains some of the drawbacks of a single-seat congressional system, with the additional weakness that governments in both countries often take office with less than a majority of the vote.

One common parliamentary system is a combination of some seats representing districts and some seats being elected on a proportional basis from a list either on a national basis or from large political subdivisions. This allows voters to vote for a specific candidate and for a party at the same time. There is more scope for smaller parties here, and this type of system generally features several viable parties, depending on what threshold is set for the proportional-representation seats.

There can be two dominant parties in this system (Germany is an example) but the major parties often must govern with a smaller party in a coalition or even in a clumsy coalition with each other (thus, Germany's tendency to produce periodic "grand coalition" governments). Parties in a coalition government will run on separate platforms and maintain separate identities—the next coalition might feature a different lineup.

Some countries fill all parliamentary seats on the basis of proportional representation. Each party supplies a list of candidates equal to the number of available seats; the top 20 names on the list from a party that wins 20 seats gain entry. This is a system that allows minorities to be represented—if a party wins 20 percent of the vote, it earns 20 percent of the seats. If the cutoff limit is set too high (as is the case in Turkey, where 10 percent is needed), then smaller parties find it difficult to win seats and voters are incentivized to vote for a major party. Thus even in this system it is possible for only two or three parties to win all seats and a party that wins less than 50 percent of the vote can nonetheless earn a majority of seats because the seats are proportioned among only the two or three parties whose vote totals are above the cutoff.

A low cutoff better represents the spectrum of opinion in a country and allows more parties to be seated. Governments of coalitions are the likely result of such a system, which encourages negotiation and compromise. A party needs to earn 5 percent of the vote in many of these systems, but cutoffs are set as low as 2 percent.

Such a system in itself doesn't guarantee full participation by everybody; a national, ethnic or religious majority, even if that majority routinely elects several parties into parliament, can exclude a minority, as happens in, for example, Israel. The most open legislative system must be augmented by a constitution with enforceable guarantees for all.

Still another variant on parliamentary representation are multiple-seat districts in which districts are drawn large. Voters cast ballots for as many candidates as there are seats—a minority group in a district should be able to elect at least one member of their choice to a seat. This is a system that also has room for multiple parties, and with several viable parties in the running, votes are likely to be distributed in a way that no single party can win all seats in a given district. Ireland uses such a system. One way to ensure that multiple parties will be seated might be to limit the number of candidates any party can run to a number lower than the total number of seats—more than one party is then guaranteed to win representation.

All the systems above are based on the traditional concept of one vote for one seat. But there is no need to limit ourselves to tradition. There are voting systems that enable the casting of multiple votes. One of these is "cumulative voting." This is a system in which each voter casts as many votes as there are seats on a legislative body, which is seated on an at-large basis (all seats are voted on at the same time by all voters). The key here is that a voter can vote for as many candidates, or cast all her votes for a single candidate, as she wishes. If the voter has five votes, he can cast all five votes for a preferred candidate, or split them among as many as five candidates if he so wishes.

This is a system that enables a minority to earn representation if that minority—racial, ethnic, political or on some other basis—votes cohesively. Cumulative-voting proponents argue that this method encourages the creation of coalitions, encourages attention to issues because community groups can organize around issues and elect candidates that represent those interests, and encourages high turnouts. "Because [cumulative voting], unlike the districting strategy, depends on high voter turnout, the incumbents will not be able to rely on low turnout to ensure their re-election. Instead, incumbents will find it necessary to mobilize voter interest and participation in an election, a task that will require incumbents to develop substantive programs and proposals," a proponent of this system, law professor Lani Guinier, wrote.[226] This is a complicated system, and probably appropriate only on the local level. A few US cities do use this system.

Another alternative voting system is instant runoff. Here, voters cast a ballot containing candidates for several seats by voting for as many candidates as they wish, ranking each candidate. This can also work for single-seat districts or executive offices. In the latter case, first votes are tabulated and if there is a candidate who earns a majority of votes, the winner is seated. If not, the candidate with the fewest first votes is eliminated, and the second votes on ballots that voted for the eliminated candidate are now added to the first votes on the other ballots. If there is still not a winner, there are more rounds, each time with the lowest remaining vote-getter eliminated, until a candidate has a majority. This system works the same way for multiple-seat elections.

The advantage of this system is that it encourages voters to cast ballots for the candidate they truly support, as their first choice, without the need to vote only for the "lesser evil." A voter could still choose the "lesser evil" as the second choice to block the worst choice from winning. It also ensures that there is some level of majority support for the winning candidate rather than a simple plurality. Australia uses such a system, but with an added unnecessary, undemocratic requirement mandating that all candidates be ranked (otherwise the ballot is voided). Instant runoff can only be democratic with full freedom of choice.

Then there is the matter of how people are represented. Traditional voting is based on geography, but in the case of single districts that can be gerrymandered or that cobble disparate areas simply because they are in proximity to one another, is this truly the best way? During the revolutionary outbreaks of 1917 and the end of World War I, workers', soldiers', sailors' and farmers' councils were created. As noted earlier, these councils had limitations, and did not prove to be lasting organs, but were intended to, and briefly did, function as genuine grassroots assemblies. At times, councils had enough popular support to temporarily constitute an alternative government. These were based, as the names imply, on representation at the workplace; that is, councils represented people as workers.

These sorts of bodies, however, are probably best seen as historical experiences. Today, more frequent career changes mean fewer people identify with the trade at which they work, and not all workers are employed at a specific site—how would freelancers and temporary workers be represented? What about the unemployed? How would retirees be represented? And what revolutionaries then didn't think about but we today could not avoid is the question of stay-at-home parents. Many more women than men fall into this category: How would they be represented in such a system?

Councils do seem to be natural spontaneous creations during uprisings—during the 2011 rebellions that broke out across the Arab world, "revolutionary committees" began carrying out tasks of local government in Tunisia and similar bodies took over management of enterprises in Egypt. But although such committees are positive developments, they aren't substitutes for permanent bodies.

During the first years of Sandinista-era Nicaragua, as we saw in Chapter 4, mass groups, such as those representing women and community organizations, were given seats in the national assembly, although that setup was later discontinued. As we saw in Chapter 3, Czechoslovak activists attempting to work out a new political system during Prague Spring in 1968 had considered the idea of a parliament that would include representation in multiple ways—geography, cultural institutions, professions and others. One possible setup for parliament under consideration there would have created "ancillary" chambers—an industrial chamber elected from factories and trade enterprises; an agricultural chamber elected from collective and state farms; and a social services chamber elected from educational, health, cultural and similar institutions—that would have been granted special powers on legislation concerning their areas of expertise.[227] (Some of the same issues that arise with councils could be repeated here, however.)

There is no reason why geography has to be the sole determinate of representation. That it is at all is a feudal remnant—single-seat districts trace their ancestry to the concept that English lords and their vassals were tied to the land and the lord was represented in Parliament as part of the lord's duties to the king; the Parliament was originally an assembly of the estates of the clergy, lords and the commons.[228]

There can be no one system that fits all societies. But a system of proportional representation with the cutoff set to a very low percentage (perhaps 2 percent) seems like at least a reasonable basis on which to build. People could be represented in multiple ways, with part of a parliamentary body based on proportional representation and other parts elected in other ways that a given society judges to be appropriate. That any representative system truly reflects the diversity of a society in all possible ways is the important thing, and that what can be accomplished at local levels or through direct democracy is decided there.

### Notes toward a philosophy of economic democracy

Inseparable from a vigorous and real political democracy is economic democracy. Economic democracy is impossible without production being oriented toward human, community and social need rather than private accumulation of capital.

In an economic democracy, everybody who contributes to production earns a share of the proceeds—in wages and whatever other form is appropriate—and everybody is entitled to have a say in what is produced, how it is produced and how it is distributed, and to ensure that these collective decisions are made in the context of the broader community and in quantities sufficient to meet needs, and that pricing and other decisions are not made outside the community or without input from suppliers, distributors and buyers. Nobody is entitled to take disproportionately large shares off the top because they are in a power position. Every person who reaches retirement age is entitled to a pension that can be lived on in dignity. Disabled people who are unable to work are treated with dignity and supported with state assistance; disabled people who are able to work can do so. Quality health care, food, shelter and education are human rights. Artistic expression and all other human endeavors are encouraged, and—because nobody has to work excessive hours except those who freely volunteer for the extra pay—everybody has sufficient time and rest to pursue their interests and hobbies.

In such a world, there would not be extreme wealth and the power that wealth concentrates; political opinion-making would not be dominated by a numerically tiny but powerful class perpetrating its rule. Without extreme wealth, there would be no widespread poverty; large groups of people would not have their living standard driven as low as possible to support the accumulation of a few.

In such a post-capitalist, classless society, there would be no going back. Why would anyone (except the most asocial and greedy) want to go back to a system of extreme inequality? If humanity is to continue its uneven, circular and zigzag-prone advancement toward expanding freedom, then eventually freedom has to be extended to all humans. Freedom and democracy are not gifts handed down from above, and never have been. They are goals that are won through struggle and determination, through a synthesis of theory and practice.

Humanity must continue to work to produce what is needed to sustain life and to make life interesting. Nature will not provide for free, and no technology will ever conjure it for free or without work. To put it another way: In a future fully free and democratic world, we'll still have to get up in the morning and go to work. Just not for so many hours, and for the greater good (and for ourselves) instead of to make an executive or a speculator rich.

Freedom in the workplace emancipates us, a good thing in itself because we'll still be spending time there. But freedom in the workplace opens up freedom in other spheres, creating an egalitarian society that allows everybody the potential to reach their full human potential. Society as a whole benefits because everybody is entitled to contribute, and the more who do so, the more likely it is that the right solution to a problem will be found. Someone who would not have been able to make a social or artistic contribution will be able to do so, enriching society. That does not mean that all ideas are equal, or good, or that all ideas are entitled to equal time. It does mean that ideas intended to better society or to advance the greater social good can receive a hearing, rather than the privileged so permeating society with an ideology that benefits themselves that other ideas are dismissed at the start.

There is a price to be paid for this democracy, and it is the same price that is always paid for an expansion of democracy: More responsibility.

A responsible member of an economic enterprise, whatever its business, will participate in whatever bodies it sets up to manage itself, or participate in elections to management and oversight bodies if that is how a large enterprise chooses to manage itself, or to participate in the enterprise's mass meetings. In the Mondragon collectives based in Spain's Basque Country, responsible participation is taken so seriously that members are fined if they miss a general assembly for a second time.[229]

In the modern capitalist enterprise, most of us complain about people in management, who so often have no experience in the lower levels and don't really understand the nuts and bolts of how the business works. Top managers collect salaries tens or hundreds or thousands of times larger than yours while making decisions that make no sense and without consulting the employees who actually do the work and who could provide insight if only they were asked. Most of us have been in at least one job like this; for many of us it might even be the norm.

Why wouldn't we want to take some responsibility for these types of decisions? Line workers could develop into managers, or perhaps different people would rotate in management positions for set periods, enabling many people to gain administrative experience. Management could be promoted from within; it seems reasonable that internal promotion would be the norm for enterprises that have continuity in management positions, and would be the only route to management in those that choose to rotate such positions. Regardless, workforces would retain the right to remove managers who deviate from carrying out decisions made by the collective. (Just as managers today are answerable to owners and boards of directors.) Different enterprises would surely develop different cultures.

With no more rigid hierarchy, no more capitalist class, a business enterprise can be run on a democratic basis, without internal exploitation of any of its staff. Yet this is not the whole story: In what sort of economic system would such enterprises operate?

The market forces of capitalism inevitably result in the cut-throat competition and inequalities that are so familiar. If collective enterprises, no matter how democratically they are run internally, compete with each other in unfettered markets, market forces would require the collectives to become more "efficient"—they would have to ruthlessly reduce costs (including their own wages) and aggressively expand the market for their products.[230] Failure to do so would mean not surviving in competition with the enterprises who do adapt themselves to market conditions. The accumulation of capital becomes paramount under unfettered market forces and because all materials and finished products would remain commodities subject to price volatility in this scenario, the cooperative workers' labor power would also become a commodity—in essence, they would "become their own capitalists."[231]

Cooperation and self-management within an enterprise—without owners, executives or speculators grabbing the profits for themselves—would mean that material gains would be distributed fairly among the workforce, certainly a far better result and itself a harbinger of a much more rational societal distribution of income. Although the hypothetical example of cooperatives competing fiercely against one another would be an odd hybrid because it would be based simultaneously on cooperation and competition, the distortions of capitalism would nonetheless be reproduced, albeit less severely.

Uncontrolled competition would lead to large disparities of income and power. An aggressive collectively run enterprise theoretically could gain control of the market for a particular product in high demand, resulting in the enterprise wresting for itself a commanding position. Perhaps several aggressive enterprises would do this, and we would once again find ourselves in a society with a power imbalance—not nearly the towering imbalance of present-day capitalism, but nonetheless the goal of creating a fully democratic society with no permanent sources of power would have been thwarted. In this hypothetical society, there would still be a market that operated on a capitalist basis and therefore capital would tip the balance of power to those who accumulated it.

There would be countervailing pressures against the foregoing scenario arising because business enterprises would not be independent of society or islands unto themselves free to act in any way they wish without concern for harm done to others, but would be embedded in their communities. Practical experience in Argentina, where cooperatives have existed in a variety of industries since 2001, has provided a demonstration.

Solidarity and community instincts have not disappeared under the stress of competition from the capitalism surrounding Argentine cooperatives. A high level of idealism was necessary to initiate the process and in turn the experience has raised consciousness to new levels. Although more prevalent than elsewhere, the Argentine movement of worker recovery of factories is not large, encompassing about 250 enterprises with more than 13,000 workers after an upsurge in new occupations in 2009.

A brief survey of Latin America at the conclusion of Chapter 4 noted that Néstor Kirchner, upon taking office as president early in 2002, suspended Argentina's foreign debt payments before agreeing to pay only 30 percent of the crippling debt, an unusual example of a country standing up to the capitalist world's multinational financial institutions. But Kirchner and his wife and successor as president, Cristina Fernández, did almost nothing internally to disturb the workings of capitalism—Argentina's worker-run factories contended with hostility from domestic political authorities and from corporate power inside and outside the country.

Most of the cooperatives formed in the worker-run factories began with similar stories: owners failing to pay employees, owners stripping the enterprises of assets, owners shutting down plants with no notice, and police using force to expel workers who had occupied plants for the purpose of getting some of the back pay owed to them after production was halted. The cooperatives were formed when workers maintaining their occupations realized that their factory owner did not intend to restart production, and decided to restart production themselves. The employees doing so first had to overcome their own doubts about themselves—pervasive capitalist ideology continually seeks to inculcate the idea that regular working people are incapable of managing a business—but were able to draw on the experience of those who went first and created national organizations to represent the cooperatives and enable coordination among them.

"Since the restoration of democracy [after the 1976–83 military dictatorship], all the laws that have been passed are against workers' rights," said Eduardo Murúa, the president of the national coordinating body National Movement of Reclaimed Companies.

The laws, enacted first by the dictatorship and then by the formal democracy, served to consolidate a global economic model organized according to the [existing capitalist] international division of labor. The changes to the bankruptcy law, for example, had left us without the possibility of severance pay. The reformed law also requires the judge to liquidate a bankrupt company's assets in 120 days. The only way to reclaim the company is to occupy it and show, first the judge, and then the political class, that we're not going to leave the factory…Certainly, if there weren't so many doubts and fears among the entire working class, there would be many more reclaimed factories. Because of these uncertainties, this process only works in places where there is some level of organization and capable leadership.[232]

The largest of these reclaimed factories is the Zanón factory producing ceramic tiles, which is now known as FaSinPat, a contraction of the Spanish-language words meaning "Factory Without a Boss." The process started when the old owner, Luis Zanón, stopped paying his employees, who went on strike in response. Zanón received loans from the provincial government to pay back-wages, but pocketed the money instead.[233] Finally, the employees went back in, occupied the silent factory, sought and received community support, and decided to restart production themselves in March 2002.[234]

Despite legal obstacles and police harassment, the collective works. In the first four years of worker self-management, the number of employees increased from 300 to 470, wages and factory output increased, and without the speedups and insensitivity to safety imposed by bosses, accident rates were reduced 90 percent.[235] New workers are not hired hands, but become part of the collective. The collective allies itself with the struggle of local Indigenous peoples, who have donated clay from their lands to the factory.[236] The collective also donates tiles to community centers and hospitals and, in return, the nurses' union donates the services of a nurse during each shift.[237]

The path of the FaSinPat collective was not an easy one. The workers had to physically defend their occupation, with community assistance, more than once and they had to wait eight years before the provincial government passed a law granting the collective legal control of the factory in August 2009.

The government also paid off part of the debt incurred by Luis Zanón—much of it owed to the World Bank, which gave a loan of $20 million to Zanón for the construction of the plant, a loan he never paid back.[238] Zanón's creditors had pushed for the eviction of the collective and foreclosure of the plant during the months leading up to the legislative vote.[239]

The cooperatives operate in a myriad of Argentine industries, including "white collar" businesses. One example is a specialty newspaper covering economic and judicial issues in Córdoba province. The newspaper, *Comercio y Justicia*, was sold by its long-time family owners to a conglomerate during the 1990s wave of massive corporate consolidation of Argentine media. The new corporate owners hired managers at enormous salaries, stopped paying employee salaries and staged a fake robbery that emptied the office of most of its equipment.[240] The workers brought in their own computers so the newspaper could continue to publish, then went on strike when the new owners failed to pay them for five months.[241] Finally, the workers went back in to restart the newspaper themselves, making it a going concern after a great struggle. In contrast to other media outlets cutting staff and quality, the *Comercio y Justicia* collective maintained the size of its staff and its quality, more than doubling circulation in its first year.[242]

In almost all of the Argentine cooperatives everybody earns the same amount, and none hires outside managers. The cooperatives are governed by assemblies of the entire workforce with their decisions carried out by managers who are elected from their own ranks and who serve limited, specified terms. One of the *Comercio y Justicia* collective members said of the new way of working: "Inside, we have a setup that goes against the logic of capitalism. A humanized work régime, a production arrangement decided by workers themselves. In relationships outside the institution, we can't detach ourselves from the economy's logic, but we give ourselves the luxury of doing work for free and doing what we decide as workers. On the inside the revolution has already happened. And looking externally, our biggest contribution is demonstrating that workers can efficiently run an enterprise."[243]

Without bosses taking exorbitant amounts of money out of the enterprise and amassing debt, it is easier for such enterprises to remain in business. But not all the Argentines who recovered their abandoned companies initially wanted to form cooperatives—there were those who wished for nationalization. There was no interest on the part of the federal or provincial governments to take over factories, so those workforces that initially sought nationalization had no choice but to adopt the cooperative form.

Proponents of nationalization argued that cooperatives would be at the mercy of an intact capitalist system and that the cooperatives would eventually be forced to pay the old owner for the recovered factory, an expense they would be unable to meet. Proponents of cooperatives argued that direct worker takeovers would be faster and more practical—the jobs would be saved faster this way, the aim of the takeovers.

Although many successfully bought their factories from the old owners at discounted prices thanks to strong community support and their perseverance through long legal battles and repeated attempts at physical expulsion, the cooperatives remain small islands in a vast sea of capitalism. They are merely tolerated by an Argentine establishment loath to appear too openly to challenge continuing community support, and they represent an example that capitalists everywhere wish to stamp out.

These cooperatives must survive in an economic environment that operates on a very different basis than they do and are at the mercy of the powerful forces unleashed by that environment, including boom/bust economic cycles. For the cooperative model to flourish, the economy will ultimately have to be dominated by cooperative, rather than capitalist, enterprises.

In any country in which a model of worker cooperation or self-management (in which enterprises are run collectively and with an eye on benefiting the community) is the predominant model, there would need to be regulations to augment good will. Constitutional guarantees would be necessary as well. Some industries are simply much larger than others. In a complex, industrialized society, some enterprises are going to be much larger than others. Minimizing the problems that would derive from size imbalances would be a constant concern.

Furthermore, if enterprises are run on a cooperative basis, then it is only logical that relations among enterprises should also be run on a cooperative basis. An alternative to capitalist markets would have to be devised—such an alternative would have to be based on local input with all interested parties involved. Such an alternative would have to be able to determine demand, ensure sufficient supply, allow for fair pricing throughout the supply chain, and be flexible enough to enable changes in the conditions of any factor, or multiple factors, to be accounted for in a reasonably timely and appropriate fashion.

Central planning in a hierarchal command structure with little or no local input proved to not be a long-term viable alternative system. What of tight regulation? That is not a solution, either. Regulators, similar to central planners, can never possess sufficient knowledge to adequately perform their job and local enterprises can use their special knowledge to give themselves an advantage rather than share that knowledge with regulators.[244]

Responsibility, then, would have to be tied to overall society. Negotiations among suppliers and buyers to determine prices, to determine distribution and a host of other issues would be necessary. Such negotiations are already common in certain industries; for example in the chemical industry, where companies negotiate commodity prices on a monthly or quarterly basis. Those are competitive negotiations in which the dominant position oscillates between buyer and supplier, resulting in dramatic price changes.

In a cooperative economy, negotiations would be done in a far more cooperative manner, with a wider group participating in the discussions. In this model, prices of raw materials, component parts, semi-finished goods, finished goods, consumer products and producer products such as machinery would be negotiated up and down the supply chain, leading to a rationalization of prices—markups to create artificially high profits or pricing below cost to undercut competitors would be unsustainable in a system where prices are negotiated and pricing information is widely available.

These would have to be fair negotiations—prices throughout the supply chain would have to be set with an eye on rational economics. Industry facilitators to assist negotiations and/or a government arbitration board to make decisions when parties are unable to agree to terms might be necessary. Community input would also be desirable, in the industries in which a given community is directly involved and for retail prices of consumer goods. It may be desirable to include these community interests in pricing negotiations directly. As more people take on more responsibility, more will gain the experience of fair negotiations, enabling more to peer over the shoulders of those involved in these decisions. In turn, more experience means more people within the community who can shoulder responsibility.

Although regulation, as noted above, is not in itself a solution, that is not a suggestion that regulation should be done away with. One method of using regulation to ensure socially positive economic activity might be a system of certification. Enterprises would be responsible for investment, production and financial decisions, but might be required to demonstrate full compliance with a range of standards on issues such as equal opportunity, workers' rights, health and safety, environmental protection and consumer protection.[245] Enterprises could be required to be certified on all relevant issues before conducting business,[246] and perhaps be re-certified at specified intervals.

The allusion to "workers' rights" in the preceding paragraph might seem a bit odd. These are enterprises under workers' control already, so what rights are contemplated? That is a more specific question than can reasonably be answered in all situations ahead of time, but in large enterprises workers might still need protections codified in the laws covering the governance of enterprises. In the Czechoslovakia of Prague Spring, as we saw in Chapter 3, this issue was directly confronted. There, the enterprises were under state ownership, and no change was contemplated to that status—enterprises were to be managed directly by their employees on behalf of the country and its people. Activists had begun to set up (until the Soviet occupation stopped it) a system of workers' councils as the instruments through which enterprises would be directed by all the employees.

Although these have a similar name, they should not be confused with the councils and soviets set up in 1917 and 1918 across Europe; these councils were enterprise-management bodies, not alternative government bodies. The Czechoslovak workers' councils were designed to give the entire workforce of an enterprise a say in management and would also send representatives to national conventions that would coordinate production at the national level. These councils were to exist simultaneously with trade unions, which would represent the same workers as employees. The activists, mostly trade unionists and grassroots Communist Party members who worked in these factories, believed that separate organizations were necessary to represent workers properly in both their roles because there are potential conflicts between being a member of an organization and an individual worker.

In a country where capitalism has been transcended, and a new system of social control and democracy is being established, employees in those large enterprises that are to be formally owned by the state will have the same dual role of managing the enterprise collectively at the same time they remain workers. It is not impossible that biases or favoritism could slowly arise in such enterprises; a union would provide another source of protection that could defend a worker as an individual when necessary. Trade union membership, then, would remain a social value to be respected.

Workers in enterprises that are collectively owned, since they would be owners and not simply managers, might find less ambiguity between their two roles, as long as strategic decisions are made collectively. Still, it may be that there remains a place for trade unions even in these types of enterprises, or it could be that unionization is simply a social value and all members of the enterprise join or form a union for reasons of social solidarity or to provide another check against any centralizing tendencies emerging within the enterprise or within government.

A system of democratic control and social accountability would require open information. Records and accounts of all enterprises and major production units of enterprises would have to be made available to all other parties to negotiations in order for the fairest deals to be reached and to prevent attempts to unfairly benefit at the expense of suppliers or customers.[247] Social-justice organizations—such as those upholding civil rights, consumer rights or the environment—should also have a role, perhaps in enterprise negotiations when appropriate, but more likely in helping to set social goals, in monitoring compliance with standards and possibly being the bodies that issue certifications to enterprises that achieve the standards.[248]

Some amount of planning and coordination would be necessary as part of the process of determining raw materials needs and ensuring that those needs are met. Any planning committee would have to be democratically controlled and have wide social representation to oversee production and to assist in the determination of investment needs.[249]

Investment would need to go to where it is needed, a determination made with as many inputs as possible, but because of its importance banking is one area that would have to be in state hands and not in collectives. Financial speculation must be definitively ended, with banking reduced to a public utility. Enterprises seeking loans to finance expansions or other projects will have to prove their case, but should have access to investment funds if a body of decision-makers, which like all other bodies would be as inclusive as possible, agrees that the project is socially useful or necessary.

Government infrastructure projects should be subject to the same parameters as enterprises, with the added proviso that the people in the affected area have the right to make their voices heard in meaningful ways on local political bodies and on any other appropriate public boards. No private developer wielding power through vast accumulations of money will be able to destroy forests or neighborhoods to build a project designed for the developer to reap profits while the community is degraded. Development would be controlled through democratic processes at local levels, and regional or national infrastructure projects should require input from local bodies representing all affected areas.

Capitalist ideology holds that the single-person management that goes with private ownership produces the most efficient system, and soon after the October Revolution communist leadership agreed that single-person management is best. But in contrast to these "givens," is it not true that a content workforce able to have control over its working life will produce better than a workforce that is alienated by a lack of control? Studies consistently conclude that measures of workers' control increase satisfaction in work, productivity and solidarity.[250] But workers' control threatens the domination of elites.

An unprecedented level of democracy would be possible in a cooperative economy because the power of capital would be broken. Social constraints ensuring responsibility to the larger community would be required to prevent the accumulation of capital that translates into power, although such tendencies would be countered by a system that rewards cooperation rather than greed. The society that has been sketched out in these very broad strokes is a society with no classes. Working people—the overwhelming majority of society—have taken control. The (ex-)capitalists are just as free to go to work as everybody else. When the power of capital is abolished, capitalists are converted into ordinary people. Surely some, those with expertise and an ability to work well with others, would be among those cooperative members elected into administrative positions; regardless, they would have to become regular cooperative workers, contributing to the production of a quality product or service and having their say equal to all others who do the work.

These are not steps that capitalists would willingly take. There is no sugar-coating this issue: The capitalists will have to be expropriated. Because of the power they possess, including the power to call the state's monopoly of violence to their aid, only a very large majority working in concert could accomplish such an expropriation. Tactics to accomplish such an enormous, revolutionary task can be worked out only in carrying out the task. Needless to say, the less bloody the process, the better—but the level of bloodshed and violence will be dictated by the capitalists and the state that acts on their behalf. It would be marvelous to simply hold a vote and declare victory, but the capitalists would not respond by saying, "Okay, you won the election. Here are the keys to the factory."[251]

The larger the majority and the more determination shown by that majority, the quicker and less violent the "expropriation of the expropriators." There have in history been "velvet revolutions," but in those cases the rulers decided to hand over power peacefully. It is the level of violence perpetrated by those asked to relinquish power, not the peaceful intentions of those seeking a better life, that determines the violence level of a revolution.

There are no magic theories as to how this might be accomplished, although one factor is certain: A significant portion of the military branches will have to be won over to the side of working people, from whose ranks enlisted personnel come. This would provide a defensive insurance for the majority and take the means of violence away from the state. This was a critical factor in the Russian revolutions of 1917—soldiers and sailors overwhelmingly joined on the side of the people, decisively countering the police, who remained as a bloc in their accustomed role as street-level repressors of working people. No longer able to wield violence at will against the citizenry, the police melted away, removing one of the state's crucial agents of repression. Without military or police support, the Provisional Government disintegrated.

Occupations would be a necessary tactic—occupations of factories helped build the union movement in the 1930s in the United States and occupations of shuttered factories with the aim of restarting production succeeded in Argentina in the 2000s. Occupations would give employees a physical presence and the ability to control production, but would also make it more difficult for the capitalist owners to destroy complexes in fits of rage. Capitalists would seek to destroy as much productive capacity as they could in revenge for their loss of control—much organization would be necessary to prevent such nihilistic excesses.

The process of expropriation is a process of assuming responsibility for production. Once again, the price for more democracy is more responsibility. It would be necessary to write new constitutions codifying the new society's changes, locking advances and rights into formal law while preventing centralization of power. Nonetheless, without the assumption of responsibility and participation, democracy will inevitably erode.

### Cooperating for the future or competing for the end

The overall, long trend of human history has been toward greater freedom. That trend has been repeatedly interrupted by reversals. Some of the reversals have lasted a long time, but those turning points are qualitatively different from the turning point humanity will soon be approaching.

The breakdown of the Roman Empire led to such an extended period of backwardness that history remembers it as the "Dark Ages." But those Dark Ages were confined to Europe; other areas of the world continued to progress. Europe came to be among the more backward places on Earth. There would have been no reason in the first half of the previous millennium to predict that it would be Europe that would come to dominate the world.

The system Europeans eventually imposed on the rest of the world, even if more recently imposed and enforced from North America, operates across the entire globe—a future "dark age" wouldn't be confined to a single continent. Nor could we be confident it would be a reversible decline because, unlike today, a thousand years ago humanity did not possess the ability to destroy the world or even inflict much damage to it. A future "dark age" would be catastrophic, whether in the form of ecological collapse or a collapse of living standards, or both, against a backdrop of a world depleted of its natural resources.

Europe was able to rise from its Dark Ages because natural resources were plentiful and other peoples continued to invent and progress; it remained for human ingenuity to begin to convert untapped natural resources into usable forms and for the sciences of Asians, Arabs, Africans and others to gradually spread. A world shorn of natural resources, struggling to cope with environmental catastrophe, might be unable to recover and thus suffer permanent decline. This is in contradiction to the long trend of progress, but, again, there are no guarantees for the future.

That dramatic scenario sounds unreal in our present age of

plenty. By no means can such a bleak future be said to be a certainty. But continuing on the same course as we are today is not sustainable. The incentives and momentum of capitalism are forcing humanity to continue down its destructive path. Resource extraction, for example, is inherently polluting but can't be shut without chaos. The only way to reduce greenhouse-gas emissions would be to enforce a drastic contraction of production in the industrialized countries, and that is impossible in capitalism because the affected industries would be committing suicide to agree to this and nobody would promise jobs to those displaced. This could only be carried out through a socialization of industry and a redeployment of labor to sectors that need to be developed for social good.[252]

Consumerism and over-consumption are not "cultural" or the result of personal characteristics—they are a natural consequence of capitalism and built into the system. Because the North's economies are highly dependent on consumer spending, this must be continually stimulated. Problems like global warming and other aspects of the world environmental crisis can only be solved on a global level through democratic control of the economy, not by individual consumer choices or by national governments.[253]

Just one country, the United States, comprises 4 percent of the world's population but uses 25 percent of its resources. How can it be physically possible for the rest of the world to match the US rate of consumption? The only way out of this dead end is to create a sustainable economy that provides for all humanity. That goal is impossible under the present world system.

Capitalism seems to be accepted—or seen as inevitable—by a decisive majority in the leading capitalist countries. But think of the widespread acceptance of slavery 200 years ago. Adam Hochschild, writing about the abolition of slavery in Britain, summed up the odds facing the 12 anti-slavery activists who met in a London bookstore in this fashion: "If you had proposed, in the London of early 1787, to [abolish slavery], nine out of ten people would have laughed you off as a crackpot. The tenth might have admitted that slavery was unpleasant but said to end it would wreck the British empire's economy."[254] And this in a country where perhaps 10 percent of men, and no women, could vote.

Nonetheless, in the face of such overwhelming acceptance of slavery, a massive social movement helped bring an end to Britain's slave trade in 20 years, and the abolition of slavery throughout the British Empire in 50 years. A series of Caribbean slave revolts, culminating in a massive uprising by slaves in Jamaica, helped convince British parliamentarians to cease dragging their feet and vote to abolish slavery.[255] Social change happens when the struggle for it is conducted on multiple fronts.

"Official" history is written not only by the victors in a war, but by those who possess the upper hand in social relations and wish to freeze those relations in place. Reclaiming history is reclaiming the knowledge of struggle. Learning the history of struggle is vital—if we don't understand where we have been, we can't make sense of where we are today and will have a nearly hopeless task to make tomorrow better.

The women's liberation movement provides an example. The modern movement in the United States can be said to have coalesced in 1968, and by the mid-1970s the movement's radical roots were already being erased and the movement had begun to stall. Feminist theorist Kathie Sarachild, in her essay "The Power of History," documented this process as it happened. Radical groups such as Redstockings launched a movement that made significant progress toward codifying equality for women in the US constitution through a proposed Equal Rights Amendment and featured tens of thousands of women marching in individual demonstrations, before moderate groups swooped in seeking to make the movement "effective," render it "safe" and "presentable," and to claim credit for what the radical originators accomplished.[256]

The corporate mass media anointed "moderate" representatives as the official spokeswomen for the movement, who were only too happy to assist the corporate media in writing out of history the radicals who had pushed the movement forward. The moderates, with no groups visibly remaining to their Left, became the targets for the inevitable Right-wing backlash, under which they retreated into a defensive posture because, by erasing the pioneers and the pioneers' knowledge from history, they did not possess the theoretical tools necessary to withstand backlash attacks nor could they have done so effectively because they had always intended to be "safe" and "presentable." The moderate spokeswomen benefited from a personal-career standpoint, but the movement received no credit at all from these attempts to "look good" in its opponents' eyes, and hadn't regained its momentum three decades later.

"How can women's history ever get written if women systematically 'forget' or obliterate the origin of the conceptions that change their lives—whether out of fear of remembering and thus taking a real political stand for the movement or in order to appropriate them as their own for career purposes," Sarachild wrote. "The origins of the most influential ideas are blurred or suppressed the fastest by those who see them as a competitive threat. These are not the kinds of careers feminism is trying to win for women, and, in any case, they will be exceedingly short-lived and will die as soon as they kill the movement off first."[257]

The history of anti-capitalist movements has been buried quite effectively by their opponents—the capitalist class and the vast apparatus that the class uses to further its agenda. These movements may appear as radical to many people, and they are in the context of today's pervasive capitalist orthodoxy. But those anti-slavery activists—and those slaves who rebelled—also were radical. The civil rights activists who risked their lives to break apartheid systems in South Africa and the United States South (and the women demanding equality in a movement that grew directly out of the civil rights movements) were radical. Are they today?

At the beginning of this chapter, six factors were offered as part of the answer as to why capitalism has not been transcended. There are additional factors, the summation of which is that people in the advanced capitalist countries have yet to be ready to make a revolution. Working people in the advanced capitalist countries have not been willing to risk what they have achieved. Yet social movements of the Left, and those movements' ability to be a strong counterweight to capitalist orthodoxy, have lifted their standards of living. The withering of those movements results in a vacuum filled by that orthodoxy and its fake-populist proxies of the Right, taking any real change out of public discourse.

The class interest of industrialists and financiers is presented as all of society's interest. "Freedom" is equated with individualism, but as a specific form of individualism that is shorn of responsibility. More wealth for the rich (regardless of the specific ideologies used to promote that goal, including demands for ever lower taxes) is advertised as good for everybody despite the shredding of social safety nets that accompanies the concentration of wealth. Those who have the most—obtained at the expense of those with far less—have no responsibility to the society that enabled them to amass such wealth. Imposing harsher working conditions is another aspect of this individualistic "freedom," but freedom for who? "Freedom" for industrialists and financiers is freedom to rule over, control and exploit others; "justice" is the unfettered ability to enjoy this freedom, a justice reflected in legal structures. Working people are "free" to compete in a race to the bottom set up by capitalists. This is the freedom loftily extolled by capitalist media.

When the means of collective defense have been sufficiently eroded, material standards of living are bought at higher personal prices—longer working hours, greater workloads, ever present insecurity from the fear of being sent to the unemployment line and fear for the future because of the lack of a secure pension. That material standard can be taken away at any moment, and for many is taken away in an era of outsourcing, corporate globalization and attacks on unions and solidarity. Even the consumer goodies constantly dangled in front of us are a source of anxiety—commodities must be designed to lead to further consumption rather than satisfy desire so as to prop up the economy, and the fact that wages are insufficient to buy what is produced leads to reliance on credit.

This is a treadmill with no way off other than to get rid of the entire system.

A better world must include *all* people. There must be a space for everyone's fight against oppression: It should no longer be acceptable to tell some people they have to wait until other battles are won. Support must be given to all struggles against oppression. If an injury to one is an injury to all, then everybody becomes free together, not separately, as part of a united struggle. Ending capitalist relations provides the necessary conditions for the end of oppression, but the actual end of oppressions is not automatic, as history has shown; therefore support for those fighting racial, gender, sexual-orientation, national, religious or other oppressions must be part of the broadest possible movement for social and economic justice. All these oppressions, along with the destruction of nature through industrialized agriculture and reduction of animals to machines existing solely for profit maximization, cannot be solved in isolation because each is intertwined with the class basis of modern capitalism.

Some oppressions, in particular sexism, long predate the advent of capitalism, and the exploitation of human divisions has long persisted because all hierarchal systems require force and repression. The above social ills are necessary for the machinery of the capitalist state to continue to function. Dividing people into antagonistic groups keeps people from uniting, nor can the exploitation of labor be maintained without extra pressure on non-privileged groups. Inequality and stratification require oppression; therefore racial, gender, sexual-orientation, national, religious and similar disparities can't be eliminated without the elimination of systems that depend on those disparities.

A century ago, Rosa Luxemburg encapsulated the choice facing humanity in the starkest possible terms: socialism or barbarism. Humanity collectively came perilously close to a collective descent into barbarism during the twentieth century, finally defeating capitalism's most morbid manifestation, fascism, at the staggering cost of tens of millions of lives and material devastation across Europe and Asia. Having peered over the edge of the cliff but pulling back, having edged toward the new cliff of nuclear war before again pulling back, humanity did not permanently lose its capacity for civilization in the twentieth century. But there are limits.

We can wait for capitalism to implode, bringing everything down with it and condemning ourselves to a struggle to survive catastrophic disaster. The alternative is to begin today to bring into being a world with enough for everyone, with no hierarchy of privileged and downtrodden, a world where we aren't buying our standard of living at the expense of our descendants or other people forced into roles of subordination. We need not put a specific name to the choice. Let us say: A better world or barbarism. Cooperating for the future or competing for the end.

Someday, we will have to confront that choice. Today, or tomorrow.

## Notes to Chapter 6

1 Lloyd Spencer and Andrzej Krauze, *Hegel for Beginners* [Icon Books], excerpted on the Marxist Archives website, www.marxists.org

2 Friedrich Engels, *Ludwig Feuerbach* (1888), excerpted in

Howard Selsam and Harry Martel (eds), *Reader in Marxist Philosophy: From the Writings of Marx, Engels, and Lenin*, pages 99–100 [International Publishers, 1987]

3 Tom Bottomore (ed.), *A Dictionary of Marxist Thought*, pages 198–9, 385 [Harvard University Press, 1983]

4 John Keracher, *Frederick Engels*, page 8 [Charles H. Kerr & Co., 1946]

5 Engels, *Ludwig Feuerbach*, excerpted in Selsam & Martel (eds), *Reader in Marxist Philosophy*, page 97

6 Karl Marx, *Capital*, Volume 1, preface to the second edition (1873), excerpted in Selsam & Martel (eds), *Reader in Marxist Philosophy*, page 99

7 Bottomore (ed.), *A Dictionary of Marxist Thought*, page 206

8 Grigorii Plekhanov, *The Development of the Monist View of History*, page 241 [International Publishers, 1972]

9 Silvia Federici, *Caliban and the Witch: Women, the Body and Primitive Accumulation*, pages 33–4, 61–2 [Autonomedia, 2004]; Chris Harman, *A People's History of the World*, pages 150–3 [Bookmarks Publications, 1999]

10 Federici, *Caliban and the Witch*, pages 33–6

11 ibid, pages 38–41

12 Harman, *A People's History of the World*, pages 154–5

13 Bottomore (ed.), *A Dictionary of Marxist Thought*, page 167

14 ibid, page 170

15 Stephen R. Epstein, *Rodney Hilton, Marxism, and the Transition from Feudalism to Capitalism*, London School of Economics paper, September 2006, pages 10–11

16 Michael Postan, "The Feudal Economy," *New Left Review*, May–June 1977, page 73

17 ibid, page 74

18 Marx, "Expropriation of the Agricultural Population from the Land," excerpted in *Pre-Capitalist Socio-Economic Formations*, page 149 [Progress Publishers, 1979]

19 ibid

20 ibid, pages 152–3

21 Michael Perelman, *The Invention of Capitalism: Classical Political Economy and the Secret History of Primitive Accumulation*, page 14 [Duke University Press, 2000]

22 ibid

23 Attributed to William Harrison, *Description of England*, an influential social study written later in the sixteenth century

24 Andy Wood, *The 1549 Rebellion and the Making of Early England*, pages 1–18 [Cambridge University Press, 2007]

25 Herbert Gintis, "The Nature of Labor Exchange and the Theory of Capitalist Production," anthologized in Randy Albelda, Christopher Gunn and William Waller (eds), *Alternatives to Economic Orthodoxy*, page 72 [M.E. Sharpe, 1987]

26 David Dickson, *The Politics of Alternative Technology*, pages 72–5 [Universe Books, 1975]

27 ibid, pages 79–83

28 ibid, pages 77–8

29 David McNally, *Against the Market: Political Economy, Market Socialism and the Marxist Critique*, pages 17–21 [Verso, 1993]

30 Eric Williams, *From Columbus to Castro: The History of the Caribbean*, pages 30–3 [Vintage, 1984]

31 Eduardo Galeano, *Open Veins of Latin America: Five Centuries of the Pillage of a Continent*, page 13 [Monthly Review Press, 1997]

32 John C. Mohawk, *Utopian Legacies: A History of Conquest and Oppression in the Western World*, pages 101, 105 [Clear Light Publishers, 2000]; Williams, *From Columbus to Castro*, pages 70–1

33 Galeano, *Open Veins of Latin America*, page 23

34 Mohawk, *Utopian Legacies*, pages 134–5

35 Galeano, *Open Veins of Latin America*, pages 23–7

36 Williams, *From Columbus to Castro*, pages 146–7

37 ibid, pages 147–8

38 Robin Blackburn, *The Making of New World Slavery: From the Baroque to the Modern 1492–1800*, pages 532–43 [Verso, 1998]
39 ibid, pages 543–4
40 Galeano, *Open Veins of Latin America*, page 82
41 Harman, A *People's History of the World*, page 256
42 Federici, *Caliban and the Witch*, page 104
43 Blackburn, *The Making of New World Slavery*, pages 34–6
44 ibid, pages 39–41
45 ibid, page 79
46 Ehud R. Toledano, *Slavery and Abolition in the Ottoman Middle East*, pages 4–7, 137–8, 157 [University of Washington Press, 1998]
47 Howard Zinn, *A People's History of the United States: 1492–present*, pages 37–8, 42–6 [HarperCollins, 1995]; Edmund Sears Morgan, *American Slavery, American Freedom: The Ordeal of Colonial Virginia*, page 327 [W.W. Norton & Co., 1975]
48 Ann Jones, *Women Who Kill*, page 43 [Feminist Press at City University of New York, 2009]
49 ibid, pages 43–4
50 Morgan, *American Slavery, American Freedom*, pages 327–8
51 Blackburn, *The Making of New World Slavery*, pages 250–2, 256–8; Harman, *A People's History of the World*, pages 251–2; Zinn, *A People's History of the United States*, page 31
52 Harman, *A People's History of the World*, pages 252–4
53 Zinn, *A People's History of the United States*, pages 53–8
54 Federici, *Caliban and the Witch*, pages 76–82, 86–7
55 ibid, pages 86–97
56 Antonella Picchio, *Social Reproduction: The Political Economy of the Labour Market*, pages 11, 95–8 [Cambridge University Press, 1992]
57 Maria Mies, *Patriarchy and Accumulation on a World Scale: Women in the International Division of Labour*, page 88 [Zed Books, 1988]

58 Barbara Ehrenreich and Deirdre English, *Witches and Nurses: A History of Women Healers* (second edition), pages 40–2 [Feminist Press at City University of New York, 2010]

59 Picchio, *Social Reproduction*, page 11

60 Ehrenreich & English, *Witches and Nurses*, pages 33–8; Mies, *Patriarchy and Accumulation*, pages 83–6

61 Mies, *Patriarchy and Accumulation*, pages 84–7

62 ibid, page 87

63 Federici, *Caliban and the Witch*, pages 171–3

64 Anne Llewellyn Barstow, *Witchcraze: A New History of the European Witch Hunts*, pages 22–3 [HarperCollins, 1995]

65 Epstein, Rodney Hilton, *Marxism, and the Transition*, page 21

66 ibid, pages 22–3

67 ibid, pages 25–6

68 Georg Lukács, *History and Class Consciousness*, "What Is Orthodox Marxism?" section, posted on the Marxist Archives website (emphasis in original) (originally written in 1923)

69 Engels, *Anti-Dühring*, preface to second edition, posted on the Marxist Archives website

70 Bottomore (ed.), *A Dictionary of Marxist Thought*, page 326; Engels, *Anti-Dühring*, excerpted in Selsam & Martel (eds), *Reader in Marxist Philosophy*, pages 32–5, 112–14

71 Bottomore (ed.), *A Dictionary of Marxist Thought*, page 525

72 Michael Löwy, "Stalinist Ideology and Science," anthologized in Tariq Ali (ed.), *The Stalinist Legacy: Its Import on 20th-century Politics*, page 169 [Penguin, 1984]

73 Marx, "The Secret of Primitive Accumulation," excerpted in *Pre-Capitalist Socio-Economic Formations*, pages 143–4

74 Engels, *Anti-Dühring*, excerpted in Selsam & Martel (eds), *Reader in Marxist Philosophy*, pages 133–7, 219–23

75 Albert Fried (ed.), *Communism in America: A History in Documents*, pages 410–11 [Columbia University Press, 1997], excerpting Dorothy Healey, *Dorothy Healey Remembers*

(emphasis in original)

76 McNally, *Against the Market*, page 44

77 *Women's Own*, interview published 31 October 1987

78 Robert Kuttner, "The Poverty of Economics," anthologized in Albelda, et al., *Alternatives to Economic Orthodoxy*, pages 18–19

79 ibid, page 19

80 ibid

81 ibid, page 25

82 Naomi Klein, *The Shock Doctrine: The Rise of Disaster Capitalism*, page 50 [Metropolitan Books, 2007]

83 ibid, page 4

84 Milton Friedman, "The Promise of Vouchers," *The Wall Street Journal*, 5 December 2005

85 Edward Nell, "Economics: The Revival of Political Economy," anthologized in Albelda, et al., *Alternatives to Economic Orthodoxy*, page 91

86 Gintis, "The Nature of Labor Exchange," page 71

87 Doug Henwood, *Wall Street*, page 180 [Verso, 1998], quoting Harry Markowitz, speech printed in *The Wall Street Journal*

88 Adam Smith, *The Theory of Moral Sentiments*, Part IV, chapter 1, posted on the Marxist Archives website (originally written in 1759)

89 Marx, *Capital*, Volume 3, pages 392–416 [Vintage Books, 1981]

90 John G. Gurley, "Marx and the Critique of Capitalism," anthologized in Albelda, et al., *Alternatives to Economic Orthodoxy*, pages 274–6; Antonio Negri, *Marx Beyond Marx: Lessons from the Grundrisse*, pages 74–6 [Autonomedia, 1991]

91 Gurley, "Marx and the Critique of Capitalism," page 276

92 ibid

93 Bottomore (ed.), *A Dictionary of Marxist Thought*, pages 265–6

94 Marx, *Capital*, Volume 3, page 118

95 ibid, pages 117–40

96 Ibn Khaldûn, *The Muqaddimah: An Introduction to History*, page 298 [Princeton University Press, 1967] (translated from the Arabic by Franz Rosenthal; edited and abridged by N.J. Dawood) (originally written in 1377)

97 John Locke, *The Second Treatise of Government*, pages 16–27 [Liberal Arts Press, 1952] (originally written in 1690)

98 Andrea Micocci, *The Metaphysics of Capitalism*, page 231 [Lexington Books, 2009]

99 ibid, page 232

100 Perelman, *The Invention of Capitalism*, page 194

101 Herbert Applebaum, *The Concept of Work: Ancient, Medieval, and Modern*, page 395 [State University of New York Press, 1992]

102 Smith, *An Inquiry into the Nature and Causes of the Wealth of Nations*, book I, chapters 1–3, posted on the Marxist Archives website (originally written in 1776)

103 ibid, book II, chapters 1–2

104 Marx, *Theories of Surplus-Value*, chapter 3 ("Adam Smith"), posted on the Marxist Archives website (originally written in 1863)

105 ibid

106 McNally, *Against the Market*, pages 43, 50–61

107 Perelman, *The Invention of Capitalism*, page 184

108 James Steuart, *An Inquiry into the Principles of Political Economy*, book II, chapter XIV ("Security, Ease and Happiness, No Inseparable Concomitants of Trade and Industry"), posted on the Marxist Archives website (originally written in 1767)

109 E. Ray Canterbery, *A Brief History of Economics: Artful Approaches to the Dismal Science*, page 53 [World Scientific Publishing, 2001]

110 ibid, pages 54–5

111 Gintis, "The Nature of Labor Exchange," pages 68–9; Nell, "Economics: The Revival of Political Economy," pages 89–90

112 Nell, "Economics: The Revival of Political Economy," page 90

113 Adam Przeworski, Michael E. Alvarez, José Antonio Cheibub and Fernando Limongi, *Democracy and Development: Political Institutions and Well-Being in the World, 1950–1990*, page 210 [Cambridge University Press, 2000]

114 Amy L. Chua, "Markets, Democracy, and Ethnicity," anthologized in Sunder Ramaswamy and Jeffrey W. Cason (eds), *Development and Democracy: New Perspectives on an Old Debate*, page 147 [University Press of New England, 2003]

115 ibid; Przeworski, et al., *Democracy and Development*, page 210

116 Göran Therborn, "The Rule of Capitalism and the Rise of Democracy," *New Left Review*, May–June 1977, page 30

117 Rosa Luxemburg, "The Accumulation of Capital—An Anti-Critique," anthologized in Paul Le Blanc (ed.), *Rosa Luxemburg: Reflections and Writings*, pages 179–84 [Humanity Books, 1999]

118 ibid, pages 185–90

119 ibid, pages 191–2

120 Gurley, "Marx and the Critique of Capitalism," pages 292–3

121 Marc Tool, "Value and Its Corollaries," anthologized in Albelda, et al., *Alternatives to Economic Orthodoxy*, page 235

122 ibid

123 Morton G. Wenger, "Lukács, Class Consciousness, and Rationality," anthologized in Norman Fischer, N. Georgopoulous and Louis Patsouras (eds), *Continuity and Change in Marxism*, pages 87–8 [Humanities Press, 1982]

124 ibid, page 89

125 ibid

126 Erich Fromm, *Escape from Freedom*, page 33 [Avon Books, 1969]

127 Janice Peck, *The Age of Oprah: Cultural Icon for the Neoliberal Era*, pages 20–1, 24 [Paradigm Publishers, 2008]

128 Edward L. Bernays, *Propaganda*, page 9 [Horace Liveright,

New York, 1928]

129 Stuart Ewen, *PR!: A Social History of Spin,* chapter 1 ("Visiting Edward Bernays") [Basic Books, 1996], excerpted online at home.bway.net/drstu

130 Adam Curtis, *Century of the Self,* British Broadcasting Company documentary, part 1 ("Happiness Machines")

131 ibid

132 ibid

133 ibid

134 Peck, *The Age of Oprah: Cultural Icon for the Neoliberal Era,* pages 30–1

135 Wenger, "Lukács, Class Consciousness, and Rationality," pages 90–1

136 ibid, page 91

137 Peck, *The Age of Oprah: Cultural Icon for the Neoliberal Era,* pages 30–1, quoting George Beard, *American Nervousness: Its Causes and Consequences,* page 96 [G.P. Putnam's Sons, 1881]

138 ibid, pages 23–5

139 Klein, *The Shock Doctrine,* pages 28–37; Alexander Cockburn and Jeffrey St Clair, *Whiteout: The CIA, Drugs and the Press,* pages 201–4 [Verso, 1999]

140 ibid

141 Klein, *The Shock Doctrine,* page 32, citing Harvey M. Weinstein, *Psychiatry and the CIA,* page 120 [American Psychiatric Press, 1990]

142 ibid, page 38

143 Frantz Fanon, *The Wretched of the Earth,* pages 210–28 [Grove Press, 2004]

144 ibid, page 223

145 ibid, page 227

146 William M. Dugger, "Power: An Institutional Framework of Analysis," anthologized in Albelda, et al., *Alternatives to Economic Orthodoxy,* page 254

147 ibid, pages 254–5

148 Joanne Barker, "Got Dough?: How Billionaires Rule Our Schools," *Dissent*, Winter 2011
149 Dugger, "Power: An Institutional Framework of Analysis," page 255
150 J. Arthur McFall, "Personality" column, *Military History*, February 2003, page 20
151 Dugger, "Power: An Institutional Framework of Analysis," pages 255–6
152 ibid, pages 257–8
153 Edward S. Herman and Noam Chomsky, *Manufacturing Consent: The Political Economy of the Mass Media*, pages 40–1 [Pantheon Books, 1988] (analyzing *The New York Times, Time, Newsweek* and CBS News)
154 ibid, pages 37–45
155 ibid, pages 38–42, 71–9
156 Andong Zhu, "Public Enterprises in Mixed Economies: Their Impact on Social Equality," pages 17–18, 30, paper posted on International Development Economics Associates website, www.networkideas.org
157 ibid, pages 18, 30, 32
158 ibid, pages 9–10, 23–4
159 ibid, pages 13–14, 28
160 Angus Maddison, *The World Economy: A Millennial Perspective* (OECD Development Centre, 2001)
161 Marcus Mulholland, "The Dynamic Dinosaurs," posted on the 21st Century Socialism website, 21stcenturysocial ism.com
162 Organisation for Economic Cooperation and Development figures, collected in Gerard F. Anderson, Uwe E. Reinhardt, Peter S. Hussey and Varduhi Petrosyan, "It's The Prices Stupid: Why the United States Is So Different from Other Countries," pages 89–91, 95, 97, *Health Affairs*, May–June 2003
163 Steffie Woolhandler and David U. Himmelstein, "The High

Costs of For-profit Care," *Journal of the Canadian Medical Association*, 8 June 2004, page 1814

164 ibid, page 1815

165 Per capita differential of $3846 (calculated from Organisation for Economic Cooperation and Development data) multiplied by 300 million, a round figure approximating the total US population

166 T.R. Reid, "No Country for Sick Men," *Newsweek*, 21 September 2009, pages 43–4

167 Henwood, *Wall Street*, pages 43–4

168 Michael Loriaux, *Capital Ungoverned: Liberalizing Finance in Interventionist States*, pages 219–22 [Cornell University Press, 1997]

169 Peter Gowan, *The Global Gamble: Washington's Faustian Bid for World Dominance*, pages 19–22 [Verso, 1999]

170 Eric Helleiner, *States and the Reemergence of Global Finance: From Bretton Woods to the 1990s*, pages 112–21 [Cornell University Press, 1994]

171 Gowan, *The Global Gamble*, page 26

172 ibid, page 40

173 Loriaux, *Capital Ungoverned*, page 222

174 Giovanni Arrighi, *The Long Twentieth Century: Money, Power, and the Origins of Our Times*, page 323 [Verso, 2002]

175 Blackburn, *Age Shock: How Finance Is Failing Us*, page 157 [Verso, 2006]

176 Richard Pérez-Peña, "Crippled by Debt, Tribune Co. Seeks Bankruptcy Protection," *New York Times*, 9 December 2008, page B3

177 Emily Thornton, "Tribune Bankruptcy Snares Employees," *BusinessWeek*, 8 December 2009

178 Andrew Ross Sorkin, "Workers Pay for Debacle at Tribune," *New York Times*, 9 December 2008, page B3

179 David Carr, "Of Layoffs, Bankruptcy and Bonuses," *New York Times*, 5 October 2009, page B1

180 Pérez-Peña, "Crippled by Debt," quoting a note on an internal Tribune Co. website

181 Carr, "Of Layoffs, Bankruptcy and Bonuses"

182 "Wild-animal Spirits: Why Is Finance So Unstable?," *The Economist* special report on the future of finance, 29 January 2009, page 6

183 "In Plato's Cave: Mathematical Models Are a Powerful Way of Predicting Financial Markets. But They Are Fallible," *The Economist* special report, pages 10–11

184 "Fixing Finance: The World Now Has a Chance to Make Finance Work Better. It Should Tread Carefully," *The Economist* special report, page 20

185 Pete Dolack, "Collecting Social Security at 100," *Z Magazine*, November 2005, page 12

186 Henwood, *Wall Street*, page 3

187 Blackburn, *Age Shock*, page 161

188 Charles Duhigg, "Stock Traders Find Speed Pays, in Milliseconds," *New York Times*, 24 July 2009, page A1

189 United States $11 trillion (CNN Money website, money.cnn.com); European Union $4 trillion (*BusinessWeek*, 10 April 2009); Japan $750 billion (*New York Times*, 9 December 2009; Reuters, 19 April 2009; *China Today*, 31 October 2008); China $600 billion (Xinhua, 27 October 2009). Non-US figures translated into US dollars at exchange rate prevailing at time of announcement. Not all money committed will necessary be spent

190 "Case study: LTCM—Long-Term Capital Management," Sungard Ambit ERisk website, www.erisk.com

191 David Shirreff, "Lessons from the Collapse of Hedge Fund Long-Term Capital Management," International Financial Risk Institute website, riskinstitute.ch

192 "Case Study"; Shirreff, "Lessons from the Collapse"

193 Paul Krugman, *The Return of Depression Economics*, pages 134–5 [W.W. Norton, 1999]

194 Henwood, *Wall Street*, page 235
195 Therborn, "The Rule of Capitalism and the Rise of Democracy," page 30
196 Anton Pannekoek, *Workers' Councils*, page 115 [AK Press, 2003]
197 Benedict Anderson, *Imagined Communities: Reflections on the Origin and Spread of Nationalism*, pages 12–21, 36, 43–5, 71–5 [Verso, 2006]
198 ibid, pages 76–8
199 Manuel De Landa, *A Thousand Years of Nonlinear History*, pages 227–31 [Swerve, 2000]
200 Anderson, *Imagined Communities*, pages 71–5
201 ibid, pages 94–7
202 John Grahl, "Measuring World Disorders," *New Left Review*, November–December 2009, page 138, reviewing Michel Aglietta and Laurent Berrebi, *Désordres dans le capitalisme mondial* [Odile Jacob, 2007] (reviewer's translation)
203 Giovanni Arrighi, "World Income Inequalities and the Future of Socialism," *New Left Review*, September–October 1991, pages 58–9
204 ibid, page 59
205 ibid, page 61
206 Galeano, *Open Veins of Latin America*, page 173
207 ibid, page 197
208 ibid, page 200
209 ibid, pages 174–5, 183–6
210 ibid, pages 200–1
211 Philip Curtin, *The Atlantic Slave Trade: A Census*, page 268 [University of Wisconsin Press, 1969]; Hugh Thomas, *The Slave Trade: The Story of the Atlantic Slave Trade 1440–1870*, page 862 [Simon & Schuster, 1997]; Paul E. Lovejoy, *Transformations in Slavery: A History of Slavery in Africa* (second edition), pages 47, 62, 142 [Cambridge University Press, 2000]; Marcus Rediker, *The Slave Ship: A Human*

*History*, page 347 [Penguin, 2007]; "The Trans-Atlantic Slave Trade: A Database on CD-ROM" [Cambridge University Press]

212 Walter Rodney, *How Europe Underdeveloped Africa*, page 88 (emphasis in original) [Howard University Press, 1982]

213 ibid, page 154

214 ibid, page 165

215 ibid

216 ibid

217 ibid, page 150

218 ibid, pages 150–56, 192

219 ibid, pages 166–7

220 Minqi Li, "Capitalism with Zero Profit Rate? Limits to Growth and the Law of the Tendency for the Rate of Profit to Fall," University of Utah Department of Economics working paper number 2007-05, page 4

221 ibid, page 5

222 ibid, page 7

223 ibid, page 33

224 ibid, pages 24, 25

225 Therborn, "The Rule of Capitalism and the Rise of Democracy," page 35

226 Lani Guinier, *The Tyranny of the Majority: Fundamental Fairness in Representative Democracy*, page 99 [The Free Press, 1995]

227 "Documents from the Fourteenth (Extraordinary) Congress of the Communist Party of Czechoslovakia," Vladimir Fišera, *Workers' Councils in Czechoslovakia: Documents and Essays 1968–69*, page 34 [St Martin's Press, 1978]

228 Guinier, *The Tyranny of the Majority*, pages 127–8, 270

229 Carl Davidson, Committees of Correspondence for Democracy and Socialism, talk at Left Forum, New York City, 20 March 2011

230 McNally, *Against the Market*, pages 179–84; Bertell Ollman,

"Market Mystification in Capitalist and Market Socialist Societies," *Socialism and Democracy*, Fall 1997, pages 21–31

231 McNally, *Against the Market*, page 181; Ollman, "Market Mystification," page 24

232 Lavaca Collective, *Sin Patrón*, pages 214–15 [Haymarket, 2007]

233 ibid, page 55

234 ibid, pages 56–9

235 Peter Elliot, "Zanon Workers in Argentina Still Waiting for Security," posted 27 June 2006, on the Upside Down World website, upsidedownworld.org

236 Ginger S. Gentile, "Argentine Lessons," posted 8 March 2004, on the ZNet website, www.zmag.org

237 ibid

238 Marie Trigona, "Argentine Factory Wins Legal Battle: FaSinPat Zanon Belongs to the People," posted 14 August 2009, on the Upside Down World website

239 Trigona, "Argentine Factory in the Hands of the Workers: FaSinPat a Step Closer to Permanent Worker Control," posted 27 May 2009, on the Upside Down World website

240 Lavaca Collective, *Sin Patrón*, pages 195–6

241 ibid, page 197

242 ibid, pages 200, 205–6

243 ibid, page 208

244 Pat Devine, "Self-Governing Socialism," anthologized in William K. Tabb (ed.), *The Future of Socialism: Perspectives from the Left*, page 194 [Monthly Review Press, 1990]

245 Diane Elson, "Socializing Markets, Not Market Socialism," *The Socialist Register*, 2000, page 80

246 ibid

247 Devine, "Self-Governing Socialism," pages 200–1

248 Elson, "Socializing Markets, Not Market Socialism," page 81

249 ibid, page 82

250 Gintis, "The Nature of Labor Exchange," pages 84
251 Thanks to Rona Smith, New York Workers Against Fascism, for this witty phrase
252 Richard Smith, "Green Capitalism: The God that Failed," *Real-World Economics Review*, March 2011, page 117
253 ibid, pages 141–2
254 Adam Hochschild, "Against All Odds," Mother Jones online version, at www.motherjones.com, excerpting Hochschild, *Bury the Chains: Prophets and Rebels in the Fight to Free an Empire's Slaves* [Houghton Mifflin Harcourt, 2005]
255 Daniel Lazare, "Intolerable Cruelty," *The Nation*, online at www.thenation.com, 27 January 2005
256 Kathie Sarachild, "The Power of History," anthologized in Redstockings, *Feminist Revolution*, pages 20–3 [Random House, 1978]
257 ibid, page 15

# Index

Contemporary culture has eliminated both the concept of the public and the figure of the intellectual. Former public spaces – both physical and cultural – are now either derelict or colonized by advertising. A cretinous anti-intellectualism presides, cheerled by expensively educated hacks in the pay of multinational corporations who reassure their bored readers that there is no need to rouse themselves from their interpassive stupor. The informal censorship internalized and propagated by the cultural workers of late capitalism generates a banal conformity that the propaganda chiefs of Stalinism could only ever have dreamt of imposing. Zer0 Books knows that another kind of discourse – intellectual without being academic, popular without being populist – is not only possible: it is already flourishing, in the regions beyond the striplit malls of so-called mass media and the neurotically bureaucratic halls of the academy. Zer0 is committed to the idea of publishing as a making public of the intellectual. It is convinced that in the unthinking, blandly consensual culture in which we live, critical and engaged theoretical reflection is more important than ever before.